D1859690

JOURNAL OF A TOUR

THROUGH PART OF THE

SNOWY RANGE

OF

THE HIMALA MOUNTAINS,

AND TO THE SOURCES OF THE

RIVERS JUMNA AND GANGES.

JAMES BAILLIE FRASER, ESQ.

GYAN

Published by

Gyan Publishing House
5, Ansari Road
Daryaganj, New Delhi-110002
Phone: 011-47034999, 9811692060
E-mail: books@gyanbooks.com

Distribution Network
gyanbooks.com
India, USA, Canada, UK, Australia, France

© Publisher
All rights reserved. No part of this work may be reproduced, stored, adapted, or transmitted in any form or by any means, electronic, mechanical, photocopying, micro-filming, recording or otherwise, or translated in any language, without the prior written permission of the copyright owner and the publisher.

ISBN : 978-81-212-9741-7 (PB)
First Published, 1820

2nd Impression 2023

Printed at: Gyan Press, Delhi.

The book is sold subject to the condition that it shall not, by way of trade or otherwise, be lent, resold, hired out, or otherwise circulated without the prior publisher's written consent.

JOURNAL OF A TOUR THROUGH PART OF THE SNOWY RANGE
Author: JAMES BAILLIE FRASER

JOURNAL OF A TOUR

THROUGH PART OF THE

SNOWY RANGE

JOURNAL OF A TOUR

THROUGH PART OF

THE HIMĀLĀ MOUNTAINS,

&c.

JOURNAL OF A TOUR

THROUGH PART OF THE

SNOWY RANGE

OF

THE HIMALA MOUNTAINS,

AND TO THE SOURCES OF THE

RIVERS JUMNA AND GANGES.

BY JAMES BAILLIE FRASER, ESQ.

1820.

PREFACE.

THE JOURNAL and the OBSERVATIONS contained in the following pages are, with very sincere diffidence, submitted to the public. The author has been induced to venture on this measure, chiefly by a desire to add his mite to the general stock of geographical knowledge; the more so, as any information respecting a tract of country so very little known, promised to be somewhat interesting, however imperfectly conveyed: and it seemed desirable to exhibit a picture of its inhabitants, as they appeared before an intercourse with Europeans had in any degree changed them, or even before they had mixed much with the inhabitants of the plains. It were disingenuous and unavailing to deny, that he was also influenced by a secret feeling of satisfaction, at being recognized as the first European, who had penetrated to several of the scenes described, as well as by that universal and powerful tendency of our nature to gratify its vanity by relating the strange, the uncommon, or dangerous enterprises in which we have been engaged.

The author did not yield to these motives without consideration, or without soliciting advice; nor was there, indeed, any want of strong arguments in his own mind against the measure. Of these, certainly, the chief arose from the consciousness of a fatal deficiency of information in every branch of physics, which deprived him entirely of the power of adding to science in those branches; which are now so interesting, as geology, mineralogy, botany, &c. Being, unhappily, ignorant of these sciences, he could only give a plain statement of the phænomena and facts that presented themselves to his observation;—a poor compensation, perhaps, to the public for so material a desideratum. The journey also was very suddenly projected; and, being connected with a military movement, little or no preparation could be made for taking advantage of the opportunities likely to be afforded to his party, beyond what a very poorly supplied camp could afford. It is remarkable that the author and his escort were even without a thermometer or barometer. Guided by circumstances, they proceeded further and further, from one step to another, far beyond the points he had at first hoped to reach; yet was his time so limited, that he could not investigate so closely, or pay so satisfactory an attention to objects that attracted his observation, as in other circumstances he gladly would have done. He was by no means insensible of his own want of talent, and of the inability under which he laboured to arrange, and duly to condense the mass of matter he had collected, and which had from the first been circumscribed by an imperfect knowledge of the language of the country.

These considerations all had their weight, and it may be the opinion of many, that it were better if they had wholly stifled the idea of thus appearing before the public (as was very nearly the case), and that the author had confined the communication of his notes to the circle of friends for whom they were at first intended. But, again, he thought that some advantages had fallen to his share, which could not perhaps be united in the person of others, who for some time could come after him. The author and his party enjoyed a perfect and unrestrained freedom, together with full access to every place and person, private and public, as conquerors and as benefactors. They proceeded through the land with perfect facility of seeing and observing, and of making every inquiry into its moral and political state, while his own want of skill in the language was compensated by the company of those who were perfect masters of it. He also enjoyed the means of procuring a tolerably accurate survey of the country, and of amassing materials for a map, in the general accuracy of which, as far as relates to its greater lines, and a considerable portion of its detail, he places great confidence.

Thus, though the country may now be visited with little risk or difficulty, and though gentlemen of science have been appointed to survey it from the Sardah to the Sutlej, who will have opportunities, at least as good as those enjoyed by the author, to make their observations, together with far greater ability to take advantage of them, and talent to describe their result, still the physical difficulties of the country are so great, and the obstacles to making such results available to the public are so numerous, that a very long time will, in all probability, elapse before any description of it can appear, and till then, even so unsatisfactory an attempt as the present may be received with indulgence.

Having resolved on publication, the author was only desirous of relating with simplicity what he had seen and heard, and of describing facts, and the impression they made on him at the moment, with truth and correctness: he is deeply sensible of the defects of his work, but he still believes that any man can describe what he has seen and heard, better than he who writes from the accounts of another, and that the errors into which he may fall are more tolerable, than the affectation which too often pervades those works, which are compiled by the professed makers of books.

In the prosecution of his task he met with many obstacles, which forced him to abandon his first intention of attempting a better arranged and a more extensive work, and obliged him to send it forth in the form under which it now appears. The precious hours immediately on his return from the hills, when the impressions of what he had seen were most vivid, and when he was near the points of reference in case of need, were wasted by sickness and distress; and even the correction and preparation which the work has undergone, with the extraction of the little information it conveys, from a cumbrous mass of materials, has been performed during moments snatched from the hurry of business, and under the languor of disease. He has neither enjoyed the advantage of literary assistance, nor much facility of reference to the few authorities that may be found on subjects where doubt existed: but, under all these disadvantages, he judged it best no longer to delay the publication of his work, as the interest lately created by circumstances would have subsided, and curiosity would have ceased till again strongly called into action.

The drawings have been completed under the same disadvantages, from sketches taken on the spot; the only merit they can claim is, that they describe the face of the country with as much fidelity as want of skill would permit. The author enjoyed the advice of an eminent artist of this country during the time he was engaged in many of the later ones.

Such as the performance is, it is now submitted to the public, without hope of acquiring from it credit or fame; but the author will be gratified and proud if the effort at all succeed in satisfying or in awakening curiosity, and inducing those who are better qualified than himself, to explore the field on which he has barely gazed from a distance.

CONTENTS.

PART I.

HISTORICAL SKETCHES OF NEPĀL—ORIGIN, PROGRESS, AND TERMINATION OF THE WAR WITH THAT GOVERNMENT.

CHAPTER I.

ORIGIN OF THE WAR.

CHAPTER II.

PROGRESS OF THE WAR.

CHAPTER III.

CHAPTER IV.

THE WAR CLOSES.

PART II.

JOURNEY FROM DEHLI TO JYTOCK.

CHAPTER V.

CHAPTER VI.

CHAPTER VII.

PART III.

JOURNEY WITH THE POLITICAL AGENT FOR THE ARMY OF GENERAL MARTINDALE.

CHAPTER VIII.

CHAPTER IX.

CHAPTER X.

CHAPTER XI.

CHAPTER XII.

PART IV.

JOURNEY WITH THE POLITICAL AGENT, CONTINUED.

CHAPTER XIII.

CHAPTER XIV.

CHAPTER XV.

CHAPTER XVI.

PART V.

JOURNEY WITH THE POLITICAL AGENT, CONTINUED.

CHAPTER XVII.

CHAPTER XX.

PART VII.

JOURNEY WITH THE POLITICAL AGENT.

CHAPTER XXI.

CHAPTER XXII.

CHAPTER XXIII.

PART VIII.

JOURNEY TO JUMNOTREE.

CHAPTER XXIV.

CHAPTER XXV.

CHAPTER XXVI.

PART IX.

JOURNEY TO GANGOTREE.

CHAPTER XXVII.

CHAPTER XXVIII.

CHAPTER XXIX.

AT GANGOTREE.

CHAPTER XXX.

APPENDIX.

PART I.

HISTORICAL SKETCHES OF NEPĀL,

AND OF

THE GHOORKA CONQUEST:

WITH

A CONCISE VIEW OF THE RISE, PROGRESS, AND TERMINATION, OF OUR WAR WITH THAT GOVERNMENT.

JOURNAL.

CHAPTER I.

IN the end of 1814 it was deemed expedient by the British government to declare war against that of Nepāl.

This power, emboldened by a long course of success and conquest, had commenced a deliberate system of encroachment on the British boundaries, and a course of insult towards its lower ministers, which, at length, it became absolutely necessary to repel.

That belt of low, wooded, and marshy, but rich land, known by the name of the Turrāee, or Turreeānā, which, lying at the foot of the hills, stretches along from the Burrampooter to Rohilcund, chiefly belongs to the countries under British government, or to those which are under its protection. This was the scene of their violence, and the object of their ambition. Our police was attacked and abused; the zemindars were plundered, and even murdered; and the petty chiefs, dependent on our protection and authority, if they did not agree to the terms of these oppressors, were insulted, and driven from their homes and properties.

After much negotiation, many moderate representations of these wrongs and grievances, with strong remonstrances, and earnest appeals to the justice and humanity of the ruling powers of Nepāl for redress, to which no satisfactory answer was returned, or explanation ever given, and after many assurances of a sincere desire for continuing that friendly understanding which had hitherto subsisted between the two powers, but which gave rise to nothing but empty compliments and political delay, a manifesto was published, which appears in the appendix, and will best show the causes of the war, and the views of the British government.

The conduct of this war, with its consequences, offered to us sources of information regarding Nepāl and the countries contained in the mountainous belt that confines Hindostan, of which heretofore there was but little known; and as it was in consequence of this war that opportunity was obtained to make the journeys related in the following pages, it seems not irrelevant to premise a short notice of the principal events that occurred in a campaign so novel and so arduous as that which gave the first great blow to the Ghoorkha power, and led to a final peace.

An account of Nepāl Proper will be found in Colonel Kirkpatrick's Narrative of his Embassy to the Court of Catmandhû, the capital of that country, in 1793; and many particulars regarding its present history and power will also be learnt there.

A few of the most interesting and best authenticated facts only need be given here.

The whole mountainous district has ever been divided into numerous petty states, each governed by an hereditary sovereign, under various titles, according to the territory he possessed. On the whole, there seems at least a strong resemblance to be traceable between the state of this country and that condition of things which existed in the highlands of Scotland during the height of the feodal system, where each possessor of a landed estate exercised the functions of a sovereign, and made wars and incursions on his neighbours, as a restless spirit of ambition or avarice impelled him.

There was, therefore, frequent change and continual warfare, which weakened each, and made the whole more ripe for receiving one sovereign, when chance or the course of things should raise up in the land a man of superior ability or talents. Indeed, the chief political dissimilarity between this country and those in which the feodal system obtained seems to have been in this—that there did not exist even a nominal sovereign in this mountainous district to whom these independent barons acknowledged a feodal subjection.

Prithenarrain Sah, a considerable number of years ago, possessed the small state of Ghoorkha, situated considerably to the northward of Nepāl. His subjects were peculiarly warlike and active; and he himself was of a very ambitious turn of mind. Raising a small army, he fell upon the neighbouring petty state of Noarcote; and, after a considerable lapse of time, possessed himself of it.

He then turned his views to the valley of Nepāl. This valley, small as it is, lying within a circumference of forty miles, then contained three separate and independent states; the chiefs of which, as may be supposed, were not amicably disposed to each other: these were, Jey Purgass, rajah of Catmandhû; Runjeet Mull, of Bhat-Gung; and Chunum Purgass, of Pātun: and they were at this time in a state of open war with one another.

Taking advantage of this, Prit-he-narrain Sah entered the country, and subdued the whole, after a long and a severe struggle; during which time strange and fearful cruelties are said to have been committed on the inhabitants by his order.

Having thus established his power in the most fertile valley of the hills, he became more rapacious than ever. The next victim was the state of Muckwanpoore; and he extended his conquests eastward to the Jeesta: when, having thus raised a kingdom and a name, he died, leaving his dominions to his son, Singa Purtab. He only reigned one year and a half, during which time he added nothing to the Nepālese dominions; and his son, Rung Bahadur, succeeded him on the throne.

Under this prince, who was of a very determined character, verging on cruelty, the work of conquest went rapidly on. First fell Lungoon and Kashka, two small states to the southward; Tunoon, Noacote, the second; Purbut, Preesing, Suttoon, Isnea, successively; then, turning further to the westward, Muscōte, Dhurcote, Irga, Ghootima, Jumla, Rugun, Dharma, Jeharee, Prietāna, Dhanee, Jasercote, Cheelee, Golām, Achām, Dhyleck, Dhooloo, and Dhotee, followed.

This last is a large state, divided from Kumaoon by the Kaleenuddee, and stretching through the hills nearly to the plains. Then Kanchee fell, and Palpai; which drew with it also Bhooturel and Sulean. By this time the whole mountainous district, from the Jeesta to the Gograh, was in the hands of the Nepālese. But, not content with this, they conceived the conquest of the states to the westward, and hoped to gain possession of even the rich and beautiful valley of Cashmeer.

Kumaoon soon yielded; but Gurhwhāl resisted their efforts for twelve years, chiefly from the delay that the capture of one fort occasioned to them. All the country, from the confines of Gurhwhāl to the Sutlej, fell an easy prey; when once established at Sreenuggur, they crossed that river to pursue their fortune, and laid siege to the strong fort of Kangrah, in the state of that name: but there their good fortune deserted them; and the inhabitants, assisted by the Sikhs, to whom they are tributary, resisted all the efforts of the invaders; and they lost more men in that long-protracted siege than in the conquests of half the country besides.

Rung Behauder, meantime, had been deposed by a strong faction, headed by the ranee, who placed her son on the throne; and the ex-rajah fled to the protection of the English at Benares. Here he did not long remain; for, having intimation that certain occurrences favourable to him had taken place at Catmandhû, he claimed and received the arrears of a pension that was allowed him, through the British government, by his own; and taking nothing with him, in a light litter, but gold and silver, he set off for his capital. His money procured him plenty of bearers; and he had reached the vicinity of Catmandhû before they had there heard of his having quitted Benares.

An uncle of the young rajah advanced to meet him with what troops were at hand; but they were taken by surprise: and, when their old master stood before them, the peculiar veneration that attaches to the person of a sovereign and a brahmin, most strongly in Nepāl, awed them into submission. "What!" said he, descending from his litter, and standing before them, "do you mean to resist, and stand in arms against your rightful sovereign?" They threw down their arms. "Seize," said he, "on that man," pointing to the leader. He was seized, and beheaded on the spot; and the rightful rajah marched into his capital with the very troops meant to oppose him.

Unfortunately for himself and for the country, his cruel disposition vented itself in various proscriptions and executions; and on one occasion he dropped a paper, in which were written down the names of many who were doomed to die. This paper was picked up by his younger brother, Sir Behauder, who read his own name among the proscribed. This was too much. Although his brother, his sovereign, and a brahmin, he stabbed him.

Great confusion followed; much blood was shed: the assassin himself fell in his turn, by the hand of Bulram Sah; and at length the present rajah, son to Rung Behauder, named Girban Joodebeer Bheem-Sah, was placed upon the throne. He, however, has little influence; for the real power has been usurped by a family, at the head of which is Ummr Sing Thappah: his son, Bheem Sing Thappah, is the minister, and has the whole power: but it is said that his family do not perfectly agree among themselves; and that, for this reason, Ummr Sing Thappah has demanded and obtained the distant and extensive command he at present holds.

The constitution of society, and gradations of cast, seem, like the nature of their religion, to be essentially the same in Nepāl as they are in the other parts of Hindoostan; but there are many subdivisions and shades of difference, created, as it were, by an union of the influences of cast and family, which give rise to appellations and distinctions unknown in other Hindoo states, and of which it is not easy to procure any satisfactory explanation: such are the terms Thappah, Chowtrah, &c.

Regarding the first of these, after many inquiries, which produced only contradictory explanations, I was at last forced to rest contented in ignorance as to its origin and meaning. It is now an hereditary rank; but of whatever political importance it may be, all genuine rajepoots consider it as beneath them: they will not eat with a Thappah. It has probably originated, as is said by some, in the intermarriage of a rajepoot with a woman of inferior cast.

Five shades of cast are mentioned as arising from different connexions of brahmins and rajepoots with women of inferior rank—Puntha, Panee, Bohra, Urjāl, Khanāl. Thus, should a brahmin have a child by a dancing-woman, it is called a Panee, and ranks lower than the father. It is said that a rajepoot will eat with an Urjāl, a Khanāl, a Puntha, or a Panee, but with no other.

The term Chowtra is applied to the brother and nephews of a rajah; and to no other: it descends no lower.

Such are a few of the materials which I picked up in conversation with the Ghoorkha officers. I cannot vouch for their correctness, although I do not think they are materially wrong, as none of those with whom I conversed had any interest in deceiving. The sketch of the conquest of Nepāl comes from the same source; and though their national vanity may have induced a degree of exaggeration, we have a check upon it, for we know the state of the Nepāl conquests, and that the whole of the hills were subdued under the power of Nepāl, from the Jeesta to the Sutlej, at the time the British declared war against that state; and I have avoided giving the dates attached to the conquest, as in them there may perhaps be some errors. The following notes regarding the population and military force of Nepāl are from the same authority, and are given with little dependance on their accuracy.

The population, indeed, attributed to the valley of Nepāl itself, so far exceeds any thing we know in the most populous parts of the world, that it is evident there must be some gross miscalculation in it; and although Colonel Kirkpatrick seems to have been furnished with information leading to conclusions nearly similar, he also is evidently staggered by the prodigious swarm of men which the mode of calculation made use of would give.

That so rich and so lovely a valley should attract a vast population is quite natural; but the numbers said to be contained therein, nay, still to subsist in the three chief towns, Catmandhû, Bhatgung, and Patun, set probability altogether at defiance.

Population is reckoned by houses: to each house there are allowed, on an average, from ten to twelve souls, and in many there are even more; for several generations, and the families of relations, live under one roof, very thickly lodged.

Taking this as their rate of reckoning, they assign to Patun, which is the largest of the three, 24,000 houses, to Bhatgung 22,000, and to Catmandhû 18,000; in all, to these three places, a population of 640,000 souls at least. There are, besides, many large villages scattered around; Kirteepoor, containing 12,000 houses; Theamee, Buneba, Pharping, Punonlee, Dhulkill, Chappagang, all from 6 to 7,000 houses; and over and above these are reckoned between twenty and thirty smaller, from 1 to 4,000 houses each, all of which are within the circuit of the valley of Nepāl.

The outrageous fallacy, and indeed impossibility, of this, must be sufficiently glaring; yet it will serve to prove that the valley must be, in truth, extremely populous: and the idea which my informant had of the great comparative difference that exists between the population of this valley and that of the neighbouring hill states may be gathered from a list of some of these states, with the number of houses which they or their chief towns contain.

It was quite impossible to obtain any idea of the revenues of the country, or of the mode in which they are levied on different classes: I could not, on this point, even obtain the same sort of loose information that they gave me regarding the population. Near the capital, it was said, that some large houses, containing twenty souls, contributed one rupee and a half annually, which diminished with the numbers to one and eight annas, and lessened as the distance from the capital increased. When there was a large contribution of men for the army, the tax on the houses was much diminished.

Nepāl is, and must be, a very poor state. Its mountain population can hardly feed themselves: and the large numbers that are found in the valley and its environs are chiefly supplied with food from those districts of the Turrace that are still under the control of the Nepālese government; and from this fruitful tract was the chief part of the revenue drawn. Without this country the Nepālese could never have risen to the greatness which they had attained; but they knew not when to stop: the value of the country attracted their cupidity, and brought on the war that was to destroy them.

From the extent of their population, it will be inferred that the military establishment of this people is extensive: and so in fact it is, considering the means possessed by the state to arm and to maintain a large force.

The whole male population capable of bearing arms are understood to be liable to military service in times of danger and necessity. They are not, however, all regularly trained to arms. But there are numbers of regular troops, formed into different corps, which are dispersed throughout the country, always leaving a large disposable force near the capital. This standing force my information has stated to amount to from 30 to 35,000 men; besides the forces beyond the Kaleenuddee, under Hustee Dhul, Bum Sah, and Ummr Sing Thappah.

These men are regularly officered, somewhat after the manner of Europeans; and they affect much the European exercise, dress, and arms. Even the denomination of rank given to the officers is English; and, besides fougedars, soubahdars, jemadars, amildars, &c. we find colonels and captains commanding their corps. The corps often take the name of the person who raised them; and, as a specimen of their military nomenclature, and of the regime of their troops, I have given in the appendix a list of the Nepāl forces and corps, taken from some of the Ghoorkha officers, as it existed some twelve or fifteen years ago. It is not by any means offered as a correct list, in numbers or in detail, of the Nepālese military establishment.

It is said that these men are paid about eight rupees per month, when on actual duty, and six only whilst not on duty, and that these sums are regularly paid. Of the better classes, I believe this to be true; and certainly the officers were often paid an annual sum by an assignment on land. I give in the appendix a pay-list of a company, actually given in by its commanding officer, when called on to furnish it, that his pay in the British service might be regulated by it. But no doubt there were differences observed between the best and most favourite corps and those not so efficient; and there is room to believe that the regular battalions were regularly paid, under all circumstances, when this was practicable.

The regular army of Nepāl has been for so long a time accustomed to active service, to a series of constant warfare and victory, that the men have become really veteran soldiers, under the advantages of necessary control, and a certain degree of discipline; and, from their continual success, they have attained a sense of their own value—a fearlessness of danger, and a contempt of any foe opposed to them. They have much of the true and high spirit of a soldier—that setting of life at nought, in comparison with the performance of duty, and that high sense of honour, which forms his most attractive ornament, and raises his character to the highest. The anecdotes of their conduct, and of the expression of their feelings, in the sequel, will exemplify this.

They are also cheerful, patient of fatigue, industrious at any labour to which they are put, very tractable and quiet, and, from what has fallen under my own observation and knowledge, not, I think, wanton or cruel. This, however, is a somewhat dubious part of their character: in various situations they have behaved in different ways; and have given reason to presume, that their natural disposition, whatever it may be, is swayed by situation and circumstance: even as a nation their character seems various and unsettled. The individuals must exhibit a greater variety still.

The Ghoorkhas, and the people of the neighbouring states, have, in appearance, a great resemblance to the Malay or Chinese physiognomy; and the Nepālese Proper I believe to partake much of this similitude. But the features and expression of the people in the various parts of the hills are very different; though very often referrible to the Tartar or Chinese, and but little to the countenance of the Hindoo of the plains.

Their soldiers are stout, thick, well built men, in general; very active and strong for their size. They understand the use of the " tulwār," or sabre, and prefer close fighting, giving an onset with a loud shout: each man wears, besides his sword, a crooked, long, heavy knife, called "cookree," which may be used in war, but is also of the greatest use in all common operations, when a knife or a hatchet is needed. The soldiers carry matchlocks or musquets: the latter have been partly obtained in traffick with the English, and are partly of their own manufacture, in various parts of the country.

Their officers, besides the sword, and shield, and cookree, carry bows and arrows, which they use very dexterously; and the sword sometimes is of a peculiar shape, the edge having a curve inwards, like a reaping hook, but far more straight, and very heavy, particularly at the point end, where it is very broad, and ends abruptly square. This instrument is called a "korah," or a " bughalee," and is formidable rather in appearance than in reality, as a blow once given and missed, with so heavy a weapon, could not easily be recovered; besides which, its shape is awkward, and could never act with effect against a regularly shaped sword.

Jenjaels, a long sort of matchlock, were in use; and they possessed a few small guns; but these were confined to the walls of their forts, and they never carried them to attack in the field.

Such was the nation, and such the troops, to which the British force was now to be opposed. They were of a far more formidable description than those of the plains, who fled from our arms in former campaigns; and the nature of the country was so new, that the whole complexion of the war wore an aspect quite different from any that we had been before engaged in.

The province of Cumaoon was under the government of Bum Sah and Hustee Dhull Chowtra; and all beyond the Ram Gunga was under the sway of Ummr Sing Thappah, who, indeed, was the chief commander of all the troops that had crossed the Kalee or Gograh river, to push the Ghoorkha conquests through Gurwhal to the Sutlej. His son, Runjore Sing Thappah, held the chief command under him at Nahn; and various inferior officers were scattered up and down the country, in fortresses and strong holds, to retain it in subjection.

Ummr Sing himself remained at the extremity of his conquests; and having been unable to gain any permanent footing beyond the Sutlej, occupied the line of posts around Irkee and Belaspoor, where were situated the strongly fortified places of Ramgurh and Malown.

CHAPTER II.

About the beginning of October, 1814, our troops began to move towards the different depôts; and the army was soon after formed into four divisions, one at Benares, one at Meeruth, one at Dinapore, and one at Loodheanah.

The first division, at Dinapore, being the largest, was commanded by Major-General Marley, and was intended to seize the pass at Muckwanpore, the key, as it was alleged, of Nepāl, and to push forward to Catmandhû, the capital: thus at once carrying the war into the heart of the enemy's country. This force consisted of 6,000 men.

The second division, at Benares, under command of Major-General Wood, having subsequently removed to Gorrukpore, was meant to enter the hills by the Bhootnuill pass, and, turning to the eastward, to penetrate the hilly districts, towards Catmandhû, and co-operate with the first division, while its success would have divided the enemy's country and force into two parts, cutting off all the troops in Kumaoon and Gurwhal from communication with, or succour from, the capital. Its force was computed at from 2 to 3,000 men.

The third division was formed at Meeruth, under Major-General Gillespie, consisting of 3,000 men; and it was purposed to march directly to the Deyrah Dhoon; and, having reduced the forts in that fertile valley, to move, as might be deemed most expedient, to the eastward, to recover Sreenugger from the troops of Ummr Sing Thappah; or to the westward, to gain the post of Nahn, the chief town of Sirmore, where Runjore Sing Thappah held the government for his father, Ummr Sing; and so sweep on towards the Sutlej, in order to cut off that chief from the rest, and thus to reduce him to terms.

The fourth, or north-western division, at Loodheanah, was smaller than the others, consisting, at first, of somewhat less than 3,000 men: it assembled under Brigadier-General Ochterlony, and was destined to advance against the strong and extensive cluster of posts held by Ummr Sing

Thappah and the troops under his immediate orders at and surrounding Irkee, a considerable town of Kuhloor, and to co-operate with the force under Major-General Gillespie, moving downwards among the hills, when these positions should be forced, surrounding Ummr Sing, and driving him upon that army.

Such was the disposition of a British force, which, with its reinforcements, was far larger than had perhaps ever been collected, in so high a state of discipline and of equipment, at one presidency, at the commencement of a struggle, which, however the minds of men might be prepared for its severity, was, from physical obstacles, rendered even more arduous than was expected, and in which we were opposed, particularly in the commencement, with an obstinacy and cool determination quite new in India.

The third division, under Major-General Gillespie, made the first movement, and commenced active operations with little delay.

The general not having joined, the troops moved under the command of Lieutenant-Colonel Mawby, of his majesty's 53d regiment of foot, from Serhampore, whereto they had been previously ordered from Meeruth; and on the 22d of October cleared the Timlee pass, through the first range of hills into the Dhoon, and took up a position at Deyrah, the chief town in the valley, about five miles distant from the fort of Kalunga, or Nālāpānee.

This fort is situated on an insulated hill, about 5 or 600 feet high, covered with jungle, and in most places very steep. The table-land on the top may be about three quarters of a mile in length; and on the southern and highest extremity of this hill was Kalunga built. It was an irregular fortification, following the form of the ground, and at this time was imperfect, the wall not having been fully raised; but they were busily engaged in heightening and strengthening it.

It was commanded by Bhulbudder Sing, nephew of Ummr Sing; and he had with him 3 or 400 men, chiefly of the regular troops of Nepāl. A letter was sent to this chief, summoning him to surrender the fort. The manner in which he received this summons was characteristic of the people, and gave a foretaste of the steady coolness with which they defended the place. The note was delivered to him at midnight; and he tore it, observing, that it was not customary to receive or answer letters at such unseasonable hours; but sent his salaam to the English sirdar, assuring him that he would soon pay him a visit in his camp.

On the next day Colonel Mawby reconnoitred the place; and, having carried up two six-pounders and two howitzers on elephants, made an attempt to take the fort by assault: however, after firing a few rounds, this was declared impracticable, and the party retreated.

General Gillespie joined, and took the command of the army. The place was again reconnoitred, and dispositions were immediately made for the assault: parties were employed in preparing fascines and gabions for the erection of batteries; and two twelve-pounders, four five-and-a-half-inch howitzers, and four six-pounders, were carried up the hill on elephants. The table-land was taken possession of without any resistance on the part of the enemy; and batteries for the above-mentioned guns were ready to open on the fort on the morning of the 31st of October, at 600 yards distance.

The storming party was formed into four columns, and a reserve.

The first, under Colonel Carpenter, consisted of 611 officers and men.

The second, under Captain Fast, of 363 officers and men.

The third, under Major Kelly, of 541 officers and men.

The fourth, under Captain Campbell, of 283 officers and men.

The reserve, under Major Ludlow, of 939 officers and men.

These were so disposed as to ascend, at a given signal (the firing of a gun), from different points, and thus distract the attention of the enemy from attending too much to any one point.

The enemy had, on his side, taken what precautions his situation afforded him the means of: the wall of the fort had been raised, though it was not then quite finished, so as to render it difficult, if not impossible, to gain the top without ladders, even in the lowest part. Every point where the fort was approachable, or thought weak, was covered by stockades, formed of stones and stakes stuck in the ground; a species of fortification in which the Ghoorkhas are very highly skilled. Guns were placed where they could do most execution; and at a wicket left open, but cross-barred, so as to render entrance exceedingly difficult, and which flanked a great part of the wall, a gun was placed, to enfilade the approach with showers of grape.

The batteries kept up a warm and well-directed fire upon the fort; but the execution was not equal to expectation; and this, perhaps, uniting with the eagerness of a sanguine temper, induced General Gillespie to give the signal for the assault some hours sooner than was intended; and which, probably from being unexpected, was not heard by either Major Kelly, Captain Campbell, or Captain Fast.

The column under Colonel Carpenter, and the reserve under Major Ludlow, then moved forward to the assault at nine o'clock, and carried the stockades surrounding the fort, putting to death, or driving in, the few of the enemy who occupied them: they pushed on to the walls, under a very heavy fire from the garrison, and suffering severely in officers and men: the few that reached them called out for ladders, which were not at first to be had. Lieutenant Ellis, of the pioneers, was shot, applying the first ladder himself, at the head of the first division; and many were killed and wounded with him. The obstacles were found too great to overcome; so that, after a long exposure, and a dreadful loss, the brave troops were compelled to fall back, under shelter of a village in the rear.

The general, seeing this, and being determined to surmount all difficulties, moved on from the batteries with three fresh companies of the 53d regiment, and reached a spot within thirty yards of the wicket; where, as he was cheering the men, waving his hat in one hand, and his sword in the other, he received a shot through the heart, and fell dead on the spot. His aide-de-camp, O'Hara, was killed beside him, and many other officers were wounded.

All the efforts of the officers were now insufficient to produce in the troops that enthusiastic courage which alone can triumph over such resistance; and Colonel Carpenter, on whom the command devolved after the death of General Gillespie, directed our force to retreat.

Both columns suffered much from the gun before spoken of, as placed in the wicket: when the reserve advanced, and got within the line it defended, the first discharge brought down the whole front line, killing seven, and wounding eleven. Several persons penetrated to this very wicket, but, unsupported, could produce no effect. A very heavy fire was kept up from the walls by the garrison, and showers of arrows and of stones were discharged at the assailants; and many severe wounds were received from stones, which they threw very dexterously: the women were seen occupied in throwing them, and undauntedly exposing their persons.

Our loss was severe: besides the lamented general, four officers were killed, and fifteen wounded; some of whom subsequently died. Twenty-seven non-commissioned officers and men were killed, and 213 wounded. According to the official returns, the heaviest part of the loss fell on a party of the 8th light dragoons, consisting of 100 men dismounted; fifty of whom were attached to each attacking column. General Gillespie placed much confidence in these men; and they well deserved it. Out of their number four were killed, and fifty wounded; and there was not one among them who would not have stayed by his commander to the last, although certain death were in his view.

Such were the results of the unfortunate affair of Kalunga, the first enterprise of the war. The army retreated; and its commander, considering the place too strong for another assault, abandoned the table-land on the hill of Kalunga, and re-occupied his first position at Deyrah, determined to wait the arrival of a battering train from Dehli, with other reinforcements.

The north-western, or fourth division of the army, under Brigadier-General Ochterlony, moved towards the hills about the end of October, and.reached the village of Plassea on the 31st.

On the 1st of November the army took up a position before Natagurh, a strong hill fort. On the next day batteries were erected, and the place breached; when the garrison, which did not exceed 100 men, surrendered both this position and that of Taragurh.

From thence the army moved towards Ramgurh, a fort, or rather a strong stockaded position, upon a mountainous ridge, said to be 5 or 6000 feet high, which was well garrisoned, and which it was necessary to reduce before proceeding to attack the positions near Malown. It was necessary, for the reduction of this strong hold, to bring battering cannon against it; and to drag them up the lofty and trackless mountains was a work of much time and labour. A road was, however, immediately commenced, which took a long time to complete.

Meantime several stockaded outposts were attacked and taken; and reconnoitring parties frequently proceeded from our advanced positions towards the posts of the enemy, who did not always permit them quietly to accomplish their inquiries.

Lieutenant Lawtie, on one of these occasions, having left the batteries, with an escort of forty men, to reconnoitre, was cut off from rejoining the camp by a large party of Ghoorkhas: he bravely cut his way through these, and took up a position in a gurhee, or small fort, where he meant to have remained till reinforcements came from camp to his rescue.

Several small parties joined him; and they would have defended themselves easily, notwithstanding the reinforcements which the enemy poured in, but their ammunition being expended, and the men, it is said, not being able to turn the wooden part of their cartridge-boxes, so as to procure the spare ammunition below, a cessation of firing took place, of which the Ghoorkhas availed themselves to rush in and close with the party, who then were overpowered; and Lieutenant Williams, who commanded the reinforcements, with about fifty men, was killed. Lieutenant Lawtie, with the remainder, escaped with great difficulty.

On the evening of the 27th, after reinforcements had arrived with the heavy guns, a detachment, under Lieutenant-Colonel Thomson, was sent to make a movement in rear of the enemy's position, which was done with effect; and, having occupied the heights, they were attacked by the Ghoorkhas in force, on the morning of the 29th, and repulsed them with much loss. Upwards of fifty dead were left in front of our position. The wounded were carried away with them.

Ummr Sing himself was on these heights, and took up a strongly fortified post in front of our troops; but our movement was of service, tending to lengthen our line of communication, and threatening to cut off that of the enemy with Irkee and Malown. They were forced to abandon several of their stockades, of which one, called by them the great stockade, was of formidable strength.

Several movements now took place, which it would be too tedious to describe and detail, and which ended by the troops under Colonel Arnold taking possession of all the strong holds formerly occupied by Ummr Sing, except that of Ramgurh itself; that chief having left them, with nearly all his force, to watch General Ochterlony, who had moved towards Belaspoor: two or three hundred men only were left at Ramgurh, and a battalion was left to mask these; whilst the army pushed on under the general, and took up a commanding position close to Malown and its fortified ridges, where Ummr Sing now concentrated his force.

This strong hold consists of a line of fortified posts, upon a very lofty and difficult ridge, which projects into the river Sutlej, between two small rivers, the Gumbah and the Gumrorah, the latter being to the northward, and both flowing westward. The neck between these two rivers is very strongly stockaded.

Colonel Arnold was detached to cross the Gumbah, and take up a position at or near Belaspoor, which he accomplished, after a very fatiguing journey, during the 31st of January, 1st and 2d of February; Lieutenant Ross, with 2000 irregular troops, having occupied a post some time before, also near the town.

The weather now became exceedingly severe, rain and snow falling for many days, whilst neither officers nor men were provided with the means of shielding themselves from the ill effects of such inclement weather.

The Belaspoor, or Kuhloor Rajah, left his capital, on the approach of the British army, with most of his people, and thus deprived us of great part of the supplies it was expected to yield.

This rajah had been an humble ally or dependant of Ummr Sing, who had drawn from Belaspoor and its vicinity much of the supplies by which his troops were supported.

There was, however, no reason to believe that this alliance was agreeable to the rajah, but rather that he would come willingly over to the British party, could he but find a sufficient excuse, in case of future need, for this defection; and accordingly, some days after our troops had possession of the points they occupied round the town, the people began to return, and the bazaars were well supplied.

Whilst the positions of Ummr Sing were thus watched, a party was detached to reduce Ramgurh; the siege of which was conducted by Captain Webb of the artillery, and Lieutenant Lawtie of the engineers. The party took up a position about 700 yards from the fort, on the 12th of February, very little molested by the enemy; who, indeed, offered no resistance till the men were secured on their ground, when they attacked the post, and were repulsed with some loss.

During the 13th and 14th the road was continued from the camp to the batteries; and on the 15th an eighteen-pounder was dragged up by

D 2

dint of great labour, which immediately opened on the fort, with considerable effect; and by the evening of the 16th, not only its three guns were silenced, but its face laid in ruins.

The garrison, consisting of 100 men, made terms for themselves, and for another small fort named Joojooree, with 160 men; who were allowed to march out with the honours of war and their guns, and to proceed to Malown, if they chose it.

They did proceed thither, and instead of receiving the due praise for their gallant defence, the chief men were seized, and had their noses cut off, by command of Ummr Sing, as a punishment for giving up the forts but with their lives; while the rest were driven off without their pay, and stripped of every thing they possessed: A singular instance of impolitic and ruffian-like cruelty, under the semblance of rigid discipline, at a time when a sound judgment would have pointed out mild and encouraging measures, to men who had already served the sinking cause with fidelity, and only yielded to imperious necessity.

Such was the situation of affairs on the 1st of March, when preparations had been already commenced for reducing Malown, and its dependent positions.

During this time, the first and grand division of the army, and which was under General Marley, commenced the crossing of the Ganges, on the 23d November, and proceeded in a direction towards Bettiah.

On the 24th, a party under Major Bradshaw, who was in advance, encamped at Goorasun, on the borders of the Terrace, surprised a post of the enemy, named Burburwah, garrisoned, it is said, by 400 men under Purserām Thappa, a sirdar of excellent character. They lost this valuable officer, killed with several other sirdars, and 150 men killed and prisoners. The loss on our side was trifling. Captain Hay, of the Chumparum light infantry, also occupied a fort called Baragurhee, which post he continued to hold.

Little activity of service prevailed in this quarter for more than a month. In the latter end of December, the chief position of the army was at Loatun; to the left and westward, Captain Sibley, with 300 infantry and fifty irregular horse, lay at Pursa, a village opposite to one of the passes, and twenty miles from the main army. Captain Hay was at Baragurhee on the right, two miles off: somewhat further on, in the same direction, there was a small post of two companies; still further, lay Captain Blakeney with the left wing of the 2d battalion 22d regiment; and on the extreme right, Captain Roughsege, with 600 men of the Ramgurh battalion, was encamped on the banks of the river Rattoo.

Captain Sibley had expressed a suspicion, that the enemy meant to attack him in force; and in consequence, Major Greenstreet was detached to his aid on the 31st of December, with four companies. On the morning of the 1st of January, he met wounded stragglers coming in, who informed him that the party had been attacked and destroyed. He, therefore, not considering his force adequate to cope with that which had beaten Captain Sibley, returned into camp. Captain Sibley had been attacked on the night of the 31st, by a large body of the enemy; the number, variously stated, said even to amount to 4000; but probably this is an exaggeration:—they attacked in three columns, got the possession of his magazine, and soon destroyed and dispersed the greater part of the detachment. The troops, whilst they had ammunition, fought well; but when this failed, they were soon broken. Lieutenant Matheson, who commanded a gun which the detachment had with them, stood till all the Europeans were killed or wounded around him; and even then served the gun himself, repressing the enemy severely by discharges of grape. At last, being entirely alone, he was forced to abandon his gun; and this most meritorious officer fortunately escaped unhurt. Captain Sibley was killed early in the action: the loss was very great: those who did escape, effected it chiefly by swimming a small nullah which flanked the camp.

At the very same time, the post on the right, occupied by Captain Blakeney, was attacked also in force; and, in a similar way, defeated with great loss. Captain Blakeney and Captain Duncan were killed, as well as about seventy men, and nearly as many were wounded.

This simultaneous attack on the two opposite points of the army shows a degree of combination not very common in native tactics. The secrecy with which the enterprise was executed, renders it matter of further surprise, and, although the consequences were mournful to us, of admiration.

The army, immediately after these affairs, moved the camp from Loatun towards Bettiah, to protect, it was said, the battering train.

The movement, however, was retrograde; and however necessary, was, under existing circumstances, of disadvantage to the cause.

After this period, nothing of consequence was undertaken for several months: the camp was frequently shifted in front of the great Saul Forest that skirts the hills; which was said to be filled with parties of the enemy. The depot was at Bettiah, and various minor movements were made in this neighbourhood, with no effect on the ultimate success of the campaign.

The force, stated to be opposed to us, was variously computed, but none attributed to the enemy less than 25,000 men; a force which is quite incredible, and which subsequent information has, it is believed, shown to be merely ideal.

On the 10th of February, General Marley left the camp, and was succeeded in command by Major-General George Wood.

On the 20th a smart and brilliant, though inconsiderable affair, occurred. Lieutenant Pickersgill, in charge of the guide and intelligence department, having left the camp at Brinjaree Pokree, to reconnoitre with a small escort, discovered a party of the enemy, about 300 in number, at about eight miles from camp; after exchanging a few shots, he retired, and sent for reinforcements, and was soon joined by a party of Gardiner's irregular horse, with many officers mounted; the picquets and ten companies, with four six pounders, were ordered by Colonel Dick (then in command) to follow.

In the mean time, Lieutenant Pickersgill had occupied the embankment of a tank, a short way from the enemy's post; and here he was found by the cavalry. When they came up, the enemy made an attack, moving up a small ravine to the tank, and then charging in good style: our party retired to the other side of the tank; while the horse filed to the right and left, as the enemy reached the top of the bank.

On seeing the infantry coming up, they halted, and brandishing their weapons, began to retire: and no sooner had they commenced their retreat, than the party of officers (about twenty in number) charged them sword in hand, followed by the cavalry on each flank: a total route ensued; and they fled, cut up by the horsemen, who pursued them; killing Bhowanee Dutt Thappa, their commander, and great numbers of men.

They formed in a village, but were again broken there; and lost, in continuing their retreat, a great many men: more than 100 bodies were counted, and upwards of fifty made prisoners. Our loss was trifling, consisting chiefly in wounded in the cavalry. Ensign Patton, who was closely engaged, received two wounds. The other gallant actors in this affair fortunately escaped unhurt.

This result not only evinces much gallantry on the part of our troops engaged, but shows that the Ghoorkhas, used to hill-fighting, are not by any means so formidable on the plain; and that they cannot at all resist cavalry: it was new, and therefore terrible to them. It is said, that here they used poisoned arrows.

Major-General Wood joined the army on the 22d, and on the morning of the 3d marched to Pursa with a strong force, and battering train of two eighteen pounders, two six pounders, and two 8½ inch howitzers, with 200 rounds of ammunition for each piece, and approached the great forest by rapid marches; turning to the eastward, reached Janickpore, a post strongly stockaded, but which the enemy evacuated on the approach of the army. Having left there Colonel O'Halloran, with five companies of sepoys, the force returned again towards Brinjaree Pokree, the original camp.

Janickpore is a place of much sanctity, where are temples to Janick and Ram, described as very curious: their base is a regular square, which decreases as the walls rise, and is at top covered with a dome, from which a spire arises.

One of the great temples is covered with a plate of metal resembling gold, of great value: it is a building of four stories, from the corner of each of which are suspended seventy-two bells: it is a very great resort of pilgrims.

Close to the village containing these temples, the Ghoorkhas had erected a small fort, provided with a dry ditch, but of little strength. They had, however, commenced a stockade that would have been highly formidable, had it been completed: it was a square of 115 yards each way; the height on the outside was twenty feet. Bastions were erected at the corners, and at each of the entrances in the centre of the sides; in the centre of the stockade was a tank, which occupied a large portion of its area. It had every appearance of having been constructed in a hurry, as green and insufficient wood was used, instead of the bamboo, which usually is preferred; and no attempt had been yet made to excavate a ditch.

No movement of ultimate importance took place after this period, although there were several petty affairs of outposts, and small detachments, some of which reflected great credit on the troops, and on their commanding officers.

On the 7th, General Wood marched to Ramnuggur—while Colonel Dick remained in command at Brinjaree Pokree; and Colonel Gregory, with the reserve of the army, remained at Janickpore. Thus things remained till the season arrived when it became necessary to withdraw the troops from the unhealthy districts they occupied, and to permit them to return to cantonments.

The operations of the 2d division of the army, under Major-General S. Wood, were not more fortunate or important than those of the grand division just related.

The army began to move from Goruckpore on the 13th of December, 1814, towards the Bhootwull pass; and, as it was said that the enemy were moving down the pass in force, a detachment sent in advance was to repel any incursions they might be inclined to make. On the 24th, 25th, and 26th, the army was encamped at Temooa, not more than twenty to twenty-five miles distant from Bhootwull; from thence the army slowly approached the pass, the foot of which they reached on the 31st. No enemy was seen—no annoyance offered.

Preparations were commenced on the 1st of January for ascending the hills, and carrying the strong post of Jeetgurh: the guns were taken to pieces, that they might be carried on elephants; and provisions were laid in for seven days. On the 3d the army, amounting to full 2,000 men in high order, leaving the camp, which had been fortified, guarded by but a few companies, moved towards the pass: a body of 500 was detached, under Major Comyn, to take the enemy in rear; whilst the main body continued their route through the forest.

The information of the enemy's movements and positions, on this occasion, seems to have been wonderfully defective. The troops had been led to expect a stockade, in a plain of considerable extent, free of jungle; whereas, whilst they were advancing without a suspicion of attack, and had reached a small break in the jungle, on the side of a hill, they were saluted by a shower of balls from amongst the trees, fired by unseen foes; and thus a number of our troops were killed and wounded, without the power of defending themselves, or annoying their adversaries.

At length they showed themselves, and were forced back by the British bayonet; but, much loss having been sustained, and some confusion having taken place, and the cooleys and bearers having thrown away the spare ammunition, it was resolved to retire.

Major Comyn had in fact taken the enemy in the rear, and would probably have succeeded in turning the fortune of the day, and in destroying much of the opposing force, but when the main body retreated, it was considered too hazardous to attempt any thing; and they joined the rest of the army, which fell back to camp.

Our loss was severe, and many officers were wounded; of whom Lieutenant Morrison, of the Engineers, afterwards died. Lieutenant Poyntz, of his Majesty's 17th foot, though shot through the lungs, subsequently recovered. The loss of the enemy was not ascertained.

After this attempt, nothing took place during the rest of the month. A battering train was ordered from Gorruckpoor, and the army moved to Bansee, where it encamped: no movement or enterprise of any consequence appears to have taken place till the 15th of April; when the battering train having reached the army, another attempt was made on Bhootwull.

On the 15th of April, the army encamped within a short distance of the town, and commenced preparations for attacking the stockade that protected it. On the 17th the batteries were opened, and the eighteen-pounders played with much effect upon the defences; which, with well-directed Shrapnell-shells, was supposed to have caused great loss to the enemy.

An attempt was made, after battering some time, to cross the river (that flows past the town) with some of the light companies, with a view of taking possession of it, from the opposite side; but it was discovered that this party was too much exposed to the fire of a body of Ghoorkhas behind a wall, and that the water was too deep to permit them to succeed in their enterprise. After wading up to the waist, and having a few men and one officer wounded, they retreated, and returned to camp.

Soon after, we find them in camp at Temooah, and there was no further movement on the part of this army during the campaign. They returned towards Gurruckpoor, about the middle of May, and went into cantonments.

CHAPTER III.

We must now return to the *third* division of the army, which, after the repulse before Kalunga on the 31st of October, lay inactive till the arrival of the battering train from Delhi, which did not take place till the 24th of November; and on the 25th active operations were renewed.

By one o'clock of the 27th, the batteries, which had been erected within 300 yards of the wall, had effected a large and fully practicable breach; and although a warm fire had been kept up by the besieged, we had hardly sustained any loss.

Shells also had been thrown with great effect; and although the enemy had attempted a sally on the 27th, they were driven back with loss, by showers of grape. The commander, Colonel Manly, satisfied that the breach was practicable, ordered a storm.

The storming party was composed of all the grenadiers of the detachment, with the light company and one battalion company of the 53d, led by Major Ingleby, of that regiment. They advanced to the breach, and stood for two hours exposed to a tremendous fire from the garrison, which destroyed many officers and men: but, after every exertion on the part of their officers, and the fall of many, in leading and endeavouring to push them forward in spite of the obstacles that were opposed to them, without any success, it was deemed expedient to order a retreat, and the whole returned to the batteries.

It does not belong to a short notice of this sort, to comment on the unfortunate result of this storm, or to seek for the causes of its failure. The enemy certainly opposed a most gallant and desperate defence, to an assault which they could have no hope of ultimately and effectually repelling; and this, after a most severe slaughter had been caused within their own walls, by the powerful means employed on our side for their destruction: they showed themselves in the breach, freely exposing their persons, though continually mowed down by our shot; and showered down on the assailants every weapon they could use — balls, arrows, and stones.

Our soldiers advanced towards the breach with perfect self-possession and coolness: a few got to the crest, and fell there; the rest remained at a short distance, firing at the garrison, and exposed to a very destructive fire in return. No one turned to fly; but none went onwards: they stood to be slaughtered. Their officers exposed themselves most gallantly and unreservedly. Lieutenant Harrington, of his Majesty's 53d, was killed on the breach, cheering and encouraging the men to follow: Lieutenant Luxford, of the horse artillery, having brought up a gun to the breach, to destroy the defences of the enemy within, and drive them from their quarters, received a shot through his body, of which he died; and besides these, there were many officers wounded. By the official returns, there were three officers killed, eight wounded; 38 men killed, 440 wounded and missing:—an awful number, where the opponents did not equal these alone.

The fire from the batteries recommenced the next day, and shells were again thrown, the effect of which was so dreadful, from the unprotected state of the garrison, and from the demolished state of the defences, that the few and faint survivors, not exceeding 70 in number, abandoned the place on the night of the 30th; and fighting their way through the chain of posts placed to intercept them, escaped with the loss of a few men; pursued by Major Ludlow, with a party.

At three o'clock that morning, Major Kelly entered, and took possession of the fort; and there indeed the desperate courage and bloody resistance they had opposed to means so overwhelming were mournfully and horribly apparent. The whole area of the fort was a slaughter-house, strewed with the bodies of the dead and the wounded, and the dissevered limbs of those who had been torn to pieces by the bursting of the shells; those who yet lived piteously calling out for water, of which they had not tasted for days.

The stench from the place was dreadful; many of the bodies of those that had been early killed had been insufficiently interred: and our officers found in the ruins the remains and the clothes of several thus incompletely covered, starting into view. One chief was thus found out, who had fallen in the first attempt, and had received this wretched semisepulture.

The bodies of several women, killed by shot or shells, were discovered;

and even children mangled, and yet alive, by the same ruthless engines. One woman, who had lost her leg, was found, and sent to the hospital, where she recovered; a young child was picked up, who had been shot by a musket-ball through both his thighs, and who also perfectly recovered; and there was also a fine boy of only three or four years old, whose father, a Soubahdār, had been killed, and who was left in the fort when it was evacuated; he was unhurt, and was taken care of. Upwards of 90 dead bodies were burnt by our native troops; and about an equal number of wounded were sent to the hospital, and carefully treated: several prisoners also were taken.

The determined resolution of the small party which held this small post for more than a month, against so comparatively large a force, must surely wring admiration from every voice, especially when the horrors of the latter portion of this time are considered; the dismal spectacle of their slaughtered comrades, the sufferings of their women and children thus immured with themselves, and the hopelessness of relief, which destroyed any other motive for the obstinate defence they made, than that resulting from a high sense of duty, supported by unsubdued courage. This, and a generous spirit of courtesy towards their enemy, certainly marked the character of the garrison of Kalunga, during the period of its siege.

Whatever the nature of the Ghoorkhas may have been found in other quarters, there was here no cruelty to wounded or to prisoners; no poisoned arrows were used; no wells or waters were poisoned; no rancorous spirit of revenge seemed to animate them: they fought us in fair conflict, like men; and, in the intervals of actual combat, showed us a liberal courtesy worthy of a more enlightened people.

So far from insulting the bodies of the dead and wounded, they permitted them to lie untouched, till carried away; and none were stripped, as is too universally the case. The confidence they exhibited in the British officers was certainly flattering: they solicited and obtained surgical aid; and on one occasion this gave rise to a singular and interesting scene:—While the batteries were playing, a man was perceived on the breach, advancing and waving his hand. The guns ceased firing for a while, and the man came into the batteries: he proved to be a Ghoorkha, whose lower jaw had been shattered by a cannon shot, and who came thus frankly to solicit assistance from his enemy.

It is unnecessary to add, that it was instantly afforded. He recovered; and, when discharged from the hospital, signified his desire to return to his corps to combat us again: exhibiting thus, through the whole, a strong sense of the value of generosity and courtesy in warfare, and also of his duty to his country,—separating completely in his own mind private and national feelings from each other,—and his frank confidence in the individuals of our nation, from the duty he owed his own, to fight against us collectively.

The remainder of the garrison of Kalunga, with their commander, Bhulbudder Sing, to the number of about seventy, retired to a hill some miles off, where they were joined by 300 men, who had lingered in the neighbourhood for some days, endeavouring to throw themselves into the fort.

Major Ludlow, with the force under his command, amounting to about 400 men, moved, on the afternoon of the 1st of December, to attack and dislodge them: he came up with them, after a very fatiguing march, about one in the morning of the 2d, on very difficult ground, on the hill where they had encamped for the night. They were on the alert; and their centinel challenged our men, who rushed forward, and fell on them, and dispersed them, with much loss. They fled, pursued by our troops, to the summit of the hill, where it was found necessary to desist, and collect our men.

The enemy's loss was great, but could not well be estimated: upwards of fifty bodies were seen; and many must have been wounded. Our loss consisted of but two officers, and about fifteen men wounded.

Colonel Carpenter, who had been detached to Calsee, sent Captain Fast with a party to occupy some positions above that town, which was effected without loss. And on the 4th of December the strong position of Barāt, situated on a mountain nearly 6000 feet high above the place, was abandoned by the enemy, and occupied by Colonel Carpenter.

The army broke up from their camp in the Dhoon on the 5th; and, re-entering the plains by the Timbee pass, marched towards Nahn. They arrived at the pass of Moginund on the 19th, seven miles from Nahn: on which day also Major-General Martindale joined and took command of the army. And on the 24th, Major Ludlow, with two battalions, pushed up the hill, and occupied that town, which had been evacuated by the Ghoorkhas; and was followed by the whole army on the 25th, save a few companies left to protect the park of artillery in the pass below.

The enemy retired to Jytock; which fort, with the town of Nahn, and all the places here mentioned, will be found described in the succeeding pages.

The pioneers had already been employed in making a road for the battering guns, which, it was evident, would be necessary for reducing the fort of Jytock; but the time likely to be occupied in this tedious operation was so great, that it was determined to make an attempt, while the impression of our approach was freshest, to take the place by surprise, or at least to occupy some advantageous position in its vicinity.

For this purpose two columns of troops moved from Nahn: one under Major Richards, of about 500 men, set out early on the evening of the 26th, making a long detour to get round the hill on which the fort was situated, and to occupy a point near the fort, known afterwards by the name of Peacock Hill.

The other, of about 600 men, under Major Ludlow, left camp towards the morning of the 27th, and was directed to cross the dell intervening between Nahn and Jytock, and push up the hill, to occupy a point in the ridge that joins Jytock with the spot where the British camp afterwards was placed, known by the name of Blackhill.

This latter column, after a fatiguing march over rocky and jungly ground, and the latter part of it a painfully steep ascent, at length reached the crest of the ridge; but many of the troops had been left far behind; and unfortunately, instead of halting to collect and breathe, those who had arrived hurried forward to dislodge a picquet of twenty men, which were posted at this point, and which fled to the stockades: our men pushed onwards, and took a post somewhat further along the ridge, driving in the Ghoorkhas who occupied it.

Had they halted here, the end desired would have been obtained; but, flushed with success that had been so easy, the few headmost troops, in spite of the exertions of the officers to restrain them, still ran on to occupy a farther and stronger stockade, known afterwards during the siege as the second stockade, and the line followed in long disjointed succession: the consequence was, as might be expected, that the enemy, alarmed by the first firing, had sent strong reinforcements towards the point attacked; and, by the time that the second stockade was endangered, these had nearly reached it.

Jespaw Qārce, the officer in command, saw the disordered state of our troops, and how few of them were together. He sallied out from the flanks of the stockade, with no great number of men, sword in hand; bore down the foremost troops, who were running up the hill; put the rest to flight, and pursued them along the ridge which they had won before. Reinforced by fresh troops, the enemy followed up the charge; and our men, out of breath and panic-struck, could not be brought to rally.

Major Ludlow and the other officers did all that was possible to make a stand: three times, at rather favourable points of ground, was it attempted to rally the troops; but as often, the Ghoorkhas coming up, they broke and fled: and at last, at the point where the crest had first been gained, our men dispersed down the hill on both sides, the Ghoorkhas following, and cutting them to pieces.

They regained the camp dispirited and fatigued, but carrying with them their wounded officers. Lieutenant Mant of the 53d was killed, whilst strenuously endeavouring to rally the troops. He had been wounded early in the action; but still pressed forwards, till he was shot through the body: sensible that he was dying, he nobly declined the anxious offers of a sepoy to stay by him; insisted on his saving himself; and took off his sash and sword, and charged him to give them, with his affectionate remembrance, to a friend.

Lieutenant Sayer, having been severely wounded in the commencement of the affair, was making his way to shelter, when a party of the enemy came up, and cut him down: Major Ludlow, with a few men, rescued him, and brought him to camp. Lieutenant Donnelly received a shot in the foot.

The detachment under Major Richards, after a most fatiguing march of sixteen miles, reached the intended point, at a later hour of the day, without opposition. Guns had been sent on elephants along with them, but could not keep up with the column, from the difficulties of the path;

and the bearers and coolies, who carried the spare ammunition, were cut off by a party of the enemy, so that the detachment was reduced to what they had in pouch.

The whole Ghoorkha force, having repulsed the other column, came down and attacked Major Richards, soon after he had taken up his position; and although they made very numerous and gallant charges, coming up to the very muzzles of the guns, they were always repelled with loss. But the ammunition was fast expending; and, with the view of saving it, our troops met the enemy in their assaults with stones: and thus a constant conflict was kept up from one P. M. till seven P. M. with great loss to the enemy, and but little on our side.

At this period a hircarrah arrived from General Martindale, with orders for Major Richards to make the best retreat he could, as the other detachment had been defeated, and the enemy's whole force was now opposed to his. Many such messages had been sent, but none had arrived till this period; and Major Richards, who had little doubt of being able to maintain his position, till reinforced from camp, still kept his ground, till a more peremptory order came for the retreat, when the word was given to commence a retrograde movement.

The Ghoorkhas were at this moment swarming round the hill. The night was darkening around. The men were weary with their long march and a six hours combat, and were exhausted by a want of water, which there had been no means of procuring for several hours. A retreat could not have been attempted under more unfavourable circumstances. The moment that the enemy saw our troops quitting the hill, they rushed in on all sides, cutting down the loiterers. The ground was so steep and broken, that it was impossible long to preserve order. Whilst descending a steep defile, the Ghoorkhas, knowing the ground, attacked a party in advance, and thus caught our people in a double fire: then on all sides they broke in with their swords, cutting down the most unprotected.

Lieutenant Thackeray, of the 26th native infantry, with the light company of the regiment, covered the retreat as well as it could be done, under the confounding circumstances of the darkness and of the ground, till he and Ensign Wilson were killed, with many men; and the rest were reduced to the necessity of shifting for themselves, in like manner as those they had been covering. The detachment, shattered down and worn out, reached camp on the morning of the 28th. Many were missing, who lost their way in the confusion and darkness. Several officers were killed; others were sheltered in the houses of the natives, kindly treated, and conducted into camp within a few days.

Our loss was severe; but it was not ascertained for several days, being lessened greatly by the return of stragglers: at length it was reduced to four officers killed, five wounded, seventy-nine non-commissioned officers and privates killed, and 281 wounded and missing: of the missing, a soubahdar and forty men were returned into camp by Runjore Sing, who commanded in Jytock, having been kindly treated, and the wounded having their option to remain and be taken care of, or to go along with their comrades. The only stipulation was, their taking an oath not to fight against the fort again.

It does not belong, as I have formerly said, to a mere detail of dates, as this chiefly is, to comment on the conduct of detachments, or of the officers commanding them; but as these unfortunate affairs have been somewhat more particularly noticed, it may be pardoned if the tribute of a few words be paid to the gallantry of the officers and troops employed on them. The commanders did all that soldiers and officers could do under the peculiar circumstances of the case.

The fatal effects of an unfortunate panic, induced by the brave but unwarrantable over-eagerness of the troops, checked in their exhausted state by a fresh and gallant enemy, master of all the intricacies of a most difficult ground, are strikingly pointed out in the failure of the first column.

Nor can there be a finer example of the decided advantage which steadiness and cool intrepidity gives to troops than the masterly way in which Major Richards maintained his post, assailed as he was by numbers so superior, and under so many discouraging circumstances.

There can be no doubt that this gallant officer, with his brave troops, would have maintained his post till reinforcements should arrive, had it been deemed expedient to put this to the trial.

The loss sustained was the more distressing, from its occurring at so late a period, after such gallant and successful opposition.

The conduct of Lieutenant Thackeray was peculiarly noble: but every officer exerted himself to the utmost; and those who fell bore with them the admiration and deep regret of their survivors.

After this unfortunate business, the army intrenched itself at Nahn; and the road for the eighteen-pounders was expedited as much as possible. No enterprise of moment took place for a considerable time.

Buhlbudder Sing, after the evacuation of Kalunga, and his affair with Major Ludlow, had thrown himself into Jountgurh, a strong place on the eastern bank of the Jumna, where he was joined by a few stragglers, that increased his actual force to about 400 men.

An attempt was made by Major Baldock, with the detachment at Calsee and Birät (about 600 regular and 400 irregular troops), to dislodge him, which failed, from some misinformation regarding the numbers opposed; and Buhlbudder afterwards retired from Jount (leaving there sixty men) across the Jumna; and crossing the country, entered Jytock about the middle of February.

On the 2d of February, Major Kelly, with a battalion of the 7th native infantry, marched and took possession of Nownie, a hill on the range of which Jytock forms the extremity, about two miles distant from it: this was accomplished, after a fatiguing march, without opposition.

On the 5th, Major Ludlow was sent to support and relieve this detachment with the 1st battalion of the 6th native infantry. The weather was exceedingly bad: much snow fell, succeeded by heavy rain, which disabled the men, who were ill provided with means of shelter; and several bearers and camp followers perished.

Several reinforcements having arrived in camp, a further force was sent to join Major Ludlow, who occupied a post in advance, called Blackhill; from whence to Jytock there is a continuous but much depressed ridge.

The light guns and mortars were now sent up on elephants, and established on a point about 1000 yards distant from the first stockade; but as these guns produced no effect of any consequence, it was determined to continue the road from Nahn, where the heavy guns had already arrived, and bring them on to this point, to batter down their formidable stockades: so that another month elapsed of nearly total inaction.

Every occurrence, from the period when the guns were carried up till the termination of hostilities in this quarter, will be related hereafter. We may now turn to a refreshing contemplation of the more successful operations of the fourth division.

CHAPTER IV.

Cautiously, deliberately, but securely, General Ochterlony pursued his course of operations: the end of which was to reduce Malown, and force Ummr Sing either to capitulate, or to retreat on the country to the eastward, where he would find hostile armies to oppose his progress, and finally destroy him.

Various movements were made, tending to circumscribe the enemy at the posts occupied by Colonel Arnold, Lieutenant Ross, and General Ochterlony; and it was deemed necessary, in view to the desired end, to gain possession of the strong holds of Taragurh, and Chumbee. A road was commenced for bringing the eighteen-pounders from Ramgurh; and, by great exertion, the batteries were completed on the 10th. Two breaches were effected by the evening of the 11th; but the garrison, of about 250 men, not choosing to stand an assault, retreated during the night.

The next day measures were taken to convey the guns to batter Chumbee; and Lieutenant Lawtie occupied a strong position commanding that place. On the 15th the light guns opened; and, by the next morning, the heavy guns were laid in battery, when the garrison, to the number of sixty, surrendered prisoners of war. Lieutenant Lawtie conducted both these sieges in a manner that reflected the highest credit on himself, and without any loss. Taragurh was found to be the strongest place the enemy possessed.

On the 13th, Colonel Arnold's detachment moved to Ruttungurh, a small stone fort belonging to the Belaspoor rajah, very strong naturally, and facing the western aspect of Malown (the position of Ummr Sing), distant about 2000 yards.

General Ochterlony occupied a position to the north; between these points Lieutenant Dunbar held a post with a strong body of irregulars; and on the east a stockade cut off communication with Irkee.

The force occupied hitherto in the siege of Taragurh and Chumbee, when these places fell, closed into the end of the Malown ridge, to attack Soorajegurh; and on the 1st of April, the 2d battalion 1st native infantry, having marched the evening before with their guns and baggage, reached a strong position to the eastward of the place, within 800 yards of its walls. The enemy, deceived by various skilful manœuvres to conceal the true intent, opposed no resistance: and though a few shot were fired from a battery between the fort and our position, our six-pounders very soon silenced them.

It remained then to bring from Chumbee the battering-guns, to act against Soorajegurh: this is a strong fort on the Malown ridge, to the eastward; and its capture was necessary to the fate of the chief place, which must infallibly follow the fall of Soorajegurh.

In the mean time, the General, aware of the length of time that must necessarily elapse in the common course of operations, before the ultimate fall of Malown could be expected, and observing the practicability of further straitening his positions, projected a grand attack on several points, which, if successful, would cut off one portion of the enemy's troops from the main body, and at once enable operations to be carried on against Malown itself. On the ridge between Malown and Soorajegurh, which were the extreme positions of the enemy, there are several intervening peaks, two of which, Ryla and Deorthul, the General determined, if possible, to gain possession of; and for this purpose five columns were formed; three of which were to advance to Ryla, and two upon Deorthul.

The first, under Major Innes, was to move from the General's camp; it consisted of a grenadier battalion and two six-pounders: the second, under Captain Hamilton, after being joined by a detachment under Lieutenant Ledlie, consisted of 200 rank and file, two companies of the 19th native infantry, and a body of irregulars, and two six-pounders.

A large body of irregulars, including a corps of Ghoorkha deserters, in all about 900, with two companies of the 19th native infantry, moved, on the night of the 14th, from Patta, accompanied by Lieutenant Lawtie, of the engineers, and gained and established itself on the heights of Ryla.

The chief column for the attack on Deorthul was placed under the command of Lieutenant-Colonel Thompson; it consisted of a battalion and four companies of native infantry, a company of pioneers, under Lieutenant Armstrong, 300 irregulars, and two six-pounders. Major

Lawrie advanced from a village called Kallee, with 700 rank and file native infantry, to support Colonel Thompson.

Two formidable attacks were also to be made against the position of Malown itself: one to move from Kallee, under Captain Bowyer, of 200 Sepoys and 500 chosen irregulars; and one from Ruttungurh, of a similar force, under Captain Strowers, of the 19th. These two parties were to form a junction in the enemy's cantonment, if possible, and to take up any position near Malown, where they thought they could maintain themselves; but the chief object to be gained by these columns was to distract the enemy's attention from the true points of attack.

Such were the dispositions for this spirited enterprise. The columns moved by signal. Colonel Thompson's party reached the height of Deorthul without opposition; but, anxious to push forward to a more commanding height, they proceeded along the ridge that led to it, so narrow that in most parts not more than two men could go abreast.

On approaching the desired point, a body of Ghoorkhas, who had been lying in ambush, started up, and fell sword in hand, with a shout, on our foremost men, who fell back, and there was a temporary confusion, which terminated in their retreat to the first point they had occupied. At this time, Major Lawrie also arrived, and immediately forming, they jointly drove away the Ghoorkhas, and established themselves on the height first attained; where, during the whole day, and part of the night, they worked hard to entrench themselves. Meanwhile the columns for the attack of Rylah occupied that valuable position, without assistance: it proved a strong, though a limited post, and even spared a reinforcement to that of Colonel Thompson.

The column commanded by Captain Strowers advanced in gallant style up the hill towards the enemy's cantonments: there the enemy met them, rushing down sword in hand, while a cross-fire was poured in upon them from the jungle on each side. Our men had not loaded, that they might be induced to depend on the bayonet; and had they been loaded, the troops that fired upon the flanks were concealed from their view.

Their gallant commander, anxious to show an example to his men, sprang forwards, and even outstripped his four orderlies, who were expert swordsmen, and attended him closely.

A Ghoorkha sirdar met him first, whom he killed with his sword: the body falling on him, from the steepness of the ground, staggered him; and several others, rushing on him before he could recover himself, stabbed and shot him dead.

At the same time Lieutenant Spellesby, severely wounded in the knee, was carried to the rear: and then the troops, discouraged by the fall of their first and second in command, and a considerable loss from a very galling fire, wavered, fell back, and retreated to the bottom of the hill, covered by the fire of the guns of Ruttungurh. Here they rallied, and drove the enemy back; but no further attempt was made on the same point: they were moved to support a body of irregulars in another quarter, the soubahdar of the 19th native infantry, who commanded them, having fallen, behaving most nobly, and cheering his men to storm a stockade on the opposite ridge.

Whilst this passed on the west face, Captain Bowyer advanced on the northern face of the hill, and succeeded in obtaining possession of a fine position, and maintained it from seven A. M. till noon; but hearing of the failure of the other column, he found it necessary to retire; which he did in a very masterly manner, retreating from height to height, pouring in heavy and destructive vollies, which thinned the ranks of the enemy who advanced to annoy him.

Although these columns were not successful in occupying any strong position, they answered in some degree the end proposed; for they diverted the attention of the enemy, and prevented a large proportion of his best troops from opposing the real attacks.

Such were the operations of the 14th and 15th of April: during the night of the 15th, the enemy made two attacks upon Colonel Thompson's position; and their best officer, Buchtee Thappa, who was in command at Soorajeegurh, left that post to visit Ummr Sing, at Malown; from thence he took the largest portion of the troops there encamped, with full directions from Ummr Sing to use his own discretion with them.

He silently posted them in ambuscade, under the cover of night; and in the morning a most furious attack was made, sword in hand, upon the detachment. The Ghoorkhas came up to the very muzzles of our guns, and were mowed down by the grape that was showered on them. Ummr Sing was on a height, encouraging his men to the assault; and Buchtee Thappa moved with them to every fresh attack.

At last this noble old officer fell; and the Ghoorkhas, then retreating in confusion, left our party in quiet possession. Their loss was very great: it has been stated at 700, which perhaps was one-third of the attacking force; but their greatest loss was in the person of their lamented chief, Buchtee Thappa. This man was seventy years of age, but preserved the fire of youth, and much of its vigour: his character as a soldier was the highest; and his mild manners and his virtues not only procured him the adoration of his own troops, but the love and respect of all who knew him. He was the strength and dependence of the army; and in losing him they lost all hope and resolution.

His body was soon recognized by our Ghoorkha deserters, and brought into the stockade; and General Ochterlony, when he heard of it, sent rich shawls to wrap it in; and a notice to the enemy, that it should be delivered to them with all respect.

A mournful deputation was sent to receive it, who, when they saw the body, burst into tears and lamentations. They were shocked, too, under the impression that he had been mangled: but he had fallen by a match-lock ball in the breast; and when our irregulars sallied out on the enemy, when retreating, his body had received some additional wounds by the sword, which they believed had been given to finish his life, knowing who he was. But in the tide of battle, when heated by revenge, or even animated with ardour, few such troops as composed our irregulars would reflect, and restrain their uplifted arm.

The Ghoorkhas, on better thoughts, were sensible of this; and also to the attention and respect paid to his remains: but they loudly bemoaned him, exclaiming that now, indeed, the blade of their sword was broken.

Our own loss was inconsiderable, considering the importance of our acquisitions and success: Captain Strowers killed; Lieutenant Bagot, of the pioneers, died of his wounds; and there were four officers wounded. In all, sixty-eight men killed, and two hundred and eighty-nine wounded, according to the official report; but not including the loss of irregulars.

Few officers have ever fallen more regretted than Captain Strowers, whose gallantry was eminently conspicuous.

Our post at Deonthul was commanded from the position which, on the 15th, had been unsuccessfully attempted; and the men suffered much by a fire from thence. Most of the artillerymen who then accompanied the detachment were killed and wounded at the guns; when Lieutenant Hutchinson, of the engineers, and Lieutenant Armstrong, of the pioneers, stept forward to the post of danger, and continued serving the one gun, whilst it was required, and secured it when the affair was over. The other gun was equally well worked by Lieutenant Cartwright, of the artillery, with one unwounded man; and Lieutenant Lawtie was particularly conspicuous for his activity, and for his application of science.

The General expressed, in the warmest terms, his sincere admiration at the conduct of these officers, and of the army in general.

Such was the brilliant and indeed decisive affair of the heights of Soorajegurh or Deonthul, and which led speedily to the conclusion of so difficult and harassing a campaign; and forcibly pointed out the happy effects of steady cool judgment, in perceiving the moment for action, and of gallant promptness in carrying through a plan formed on such grounds.

That night, the enemy seeing their communication with Malown cut off, evacuated all their positions, Soorajegurh included, between that post and Colonel Thompson's position, and were attacked on their retreat by the indefatigable Lieutenant Lawtie, with a corps of irregulars; and Colonel Thompson, on the next day, took up an advanced position, called Nerayen Kotha, in the vicinity of Malown.

The death of Buchtee Thappa produced stronger effects than were at first contemplated, even by those who were best acquainted with the influence he possessed over the minds of the troops under Ummr Sing. The unbending severity of this Chief, the hardships that seemed to accumulate the more as they were the more cheerfully endured, and the total hopelessness of their situation, had produced a considerable desertion from the Ghoorkha army, even prior to the last success; but now it could not be controlled by all the cruel precautions taken by Ummr Sing; who, not content with placing centinels, with orders to shoot such as might be found leaving the camp without a pass, actually struck off the heads of several upon bare suspicion.

After many partial desertions, nearly the whole of his troops left the fort, and came into the British camp: their Chiefs had remonstrated with him on the folly of holding out against inevitable fate, but he turned a deaf ear to them.

Even when they entreated him to agree to the alternative of fighting or of ceasing the contest at once, rather than suffer them to perish in detail, he was silent. Indeed, all judgment seems to have forsaken him. The troops, both officers and privates, left him, with only 250 men, in the position of Malown, and came over to the British camp as prisoners of war, and entreating to be taken into British pay. Still, however, all proper steps were taken to produce the surrender of this obstinate Chief, and to compel it, if necessary.

Negotiations went on for several days, attended by preparations; and it was not till some days after the guns had been placed in battery (for the General, from humane motives, would not permit them to be opened on the fort), that on the 15th of May, he signed the capitulation for giving up his last and formidable strong hold; and agreed to cause to be evacuated, and delivered into the hands of the British, every garrisoned place that yet remained to the Ghoorkhas, between the rivers Sutlej and Calee or Sardah.

By this time much unhealthiness began to appear, both among the troops and the officers; and it was well that this final success rendered it possible to allow them to descend from the dreary hills, among which they had so long sojourned; where comforts were always rare, and necessaries often far from abundant. The officers in general recovered; but the happy issue of the campaign was clouded by the death of one individual, whose exertions had greatly contributed to it; whose energy and zeal were the soul of every enterprise in which he engaged; whose skill and judgment, at a glance, perceived the measures, and the moment to employ them; and whose activity rendered him of the first utility, not only in his own department, but in the various duties which arose in this new and uncommon warfare.

In all the general orders of this division, the name of Lieutenant Lawtie is most honourably mentioned; and in those which precede the army's leaving the hills, the General most feelingly notices his death, and pays a worthy and affecting tribute to his memory. He was, indeed, sincerely lamented by all who knew him; and rarely does it happen that the loss of an officer of his inferior rank excites so much interest and sorrow.

Thus, then, was terminated a campaign, whose beginning was so inauspicious, in a country so impracticable, and hitherto deemed impenetrable, except to the inhabitants of the hills; the greater part too was achieved by our native troops alone, for there were no European troops with General Ochterlony, excepting a few artillerymen; and thus was the prosperous and presumptuous power of Nepāl shorn at once of half its beams.

Intimately connected with this happy result, and in date preceding the successes just related, the operations in Kumaoon, carried on by the detachment under the command of Colonel Nicholls, struck the first decisive blow towards bringing the campaign to a conclusion. The measures adopted by this commander were marked with judgment, promptitude, and spirit.

In the end of February, Lieutenant-Colonel Gardiner, of the irregular horse, entered the province of Kumaoon, from Rohilcund, by the Kashepoor pass; and taking possession of several small forts belonging to the enemy, without opposition, fixed himself at last in a strong position.

Captain Hearsay, also, who acted under his command, entering at another point, seized two or three similar forts with equal ease; whilst a great disposition to rise in our favour prevailed among the inhabitants, who, before the middle of March, evinced it by assisting the irregulars in several affairs of small consequence; in one of which, however, Captain Hearsay's men being attacked on the western bank of the Gogra river, repulsed the enemy with a loss, as was supposed, of upwards of 200 men, killed and wounded; themselves suffering in a far less degree.

This success, however, did not long attend our irregular force. On the 2d of April, Hustee-dhull-Chowtra having crossed the river Sardah or Gogra, at Kusmote Ghāt, Captain Hearsay, who was observing him at the strong fortress of Chumpaweet, with the largest part of his forces, attacked him impetuously; but his men were unable to cope with the veteran Ghoorkhas that composed the troops of Hustee-dhull. They broke and fled, leaving the best part of their number on the field, and their commander, Hearsay, who had bravely led them on, wounded and prisoner in the hands of the enemy.

This unhappy event brought on another disaster. Mr. Martindale, adjutant of Captain Hearsay's irregular corps, who was stationed at Kutool-Gurh, on the banks of the Sardah, with 300 men, was attacked by a very superior force of the enemy on the evening of the 3d: his men, dispirited at the defeat of the larger portion of their corps, sought for safety in flight; and Mr. Martindale with difficulty escaped.

Meantime, the regular force destined to act against the enemy in Kumaoon had assembled at Moradabad, in Rohilcund, under Colonel Nicholls, and commenced their march toward that province on the 30th of March. On the 2d of April, head-quarters were at Deeklee; on the 4th, at Futtaseth; and on the 6th, they encamped at Choumoon-ke-debee, a lofty ridge about fifteen coss distant from Almorah, after a continued ascent of three hours.

On the 9th, Colonel Nicholls having pushed forward, with three companies of the 1st battalion 4th native infantry, joined Lieutenant-Colonel Gardiner's camp, posted before Almorah, on a hill named Katāar-Mull; the rest of the detachment followed quickly, as the impediments arising from the nature of the country, and the necessary incumbrances of baggage, guns, stores, &c. would permit.

On the 12th, a feu de joye from the works of the enemy announced the arrival of Hustee-dhull-Chowtra in Almorah.

This Chief, after the defeat of the parties under Captain Hearsay and Adjutant Martindale, remained for a considerable time levying contributions on the districts around Chumpaweet, which had amicably received and assisted our troops; but our posts on the Sardah river being destroyed, there was nothing to prevent his marching straight to Almorah.

About the 20th, Hustee-dhull made a movement with a considerable body of their regular infantry to Gunnanath, a mountain pass north of Colonel Nicholls's position.

To counteract the effects of this manœuvre, as soon as it was discovered, Major Patton was detached on the evening of the 22d, with ten companies of native infantry, a ghole of irregulars, one six-pounder, one 4½ inch mortar, and the necessary ammunition, &c. with directions to follow Hustee-dhull, and, if possible, to attack him before he could intrench himself; or, if already intrenching, to occupy the nearest good position between him and Almorah, so as, if possible, to cut off his communication, and to prevent his completing his intrenchments, by plying him with shells.

The elephants that carried the six-pounder moving so slowly, as greatly to retard the march, the gun was sent back to camp.

On the evening of the 23d, Major Patton's detachment came up with the enemy, under Hustee-dhull, and attacking them, after a sharp action and pursuit, drove them over several hills, and completely defeated and dispersed them.

The Chief, Hustee-dhull-Chowtra, was mortally wounded through the temple, and soon after died in the retreat; and another, Sirdar Jeyrookah, was shot through the body, and died in a short time. The loss of the enemy was, on the whole, very great: a portion of their force found its way back to Almorah, but many never reached that place.

In Hustee-dhull-Chowtra they lost a most valuable, active, and enterprising officer, and a man whose character was particularly amiable. He was uncle to the reigning Prince of Nepāl, and his talents and virtues were worthy of this high descent. With the sentiments of respect and admiration that a brave man ever entertains for a noble and worthy enemy, Colonel Nicholls, in his official despatch, pays a most handsome and feeling tribute to his memory.

Our loss in this brilliant affair was comparatively trifling, consisting of two sepoys killed, one European officer, two havildars, and twenty-three men wounded. It is almost superfluous to add, that the greatest gallantry was displayed by all the troops engaged, who vied with each other in pushing forward, and in striving to close with the enemy.

Immediately on this success, Colonel Nicholls, with perfect judgment and great promptitude, took advantage of the depression and consternation of the enemy, and attacked his positions. At one o'clock he advanced against his principal stockade on the north end of the Sillolee ridge, with two battalions, intending to establish a mortar battery within 5 or 600 yards of that work; but finding the troops in high spirits, and observing the enemy to be proportionally disheartened, he ordered two stone breast-works to be stormed; which was instantly most gallantly and most successfully executed by the 1st battalion of the fourth, led by Captain Faithfull.

The irregular infantry, under the command of and led by Lieutenant.

Colonel Gardiner, advanced on a ridge parallel to the line of the regular march; and animated by the sight of their success, diverged to the right, when near the summit, and easily possessed themselves of the remaining stockades on the Sillolee ridge.

In the mean time fifty men of the fourth took possession of a small breast-work to the left. The 1st battalion of the fourth, after these gallant efforts, was halted until the remaining battalion (of flank companies) should advance.

Captain Leys then came up, and directed them to advance on the retreating enemy; and finding five roads, they pursued them by each, till they possessed themselves of one stockade leading to Kulmuttea, a small stone fortification, and the Rajah's palace; thus dividing the enemy's force, and cutting off their retreat to Kulmuttea.

Lieutenant Wight and Captain Faithfull led their men into the embrasure of the breast-work; in which desperate service the former was dangerously wounded, and Captain Faithfull cut down the man who wounded him. Lieutenant Purvis, who was also wounded, led the advance in a style that called forth the marked applause of the commander; which was also warmly bestowed on Lieutenant Field, of the fourth. Our loss was at this time estimated at about forty men killed and wounded.

At about eleven P. M. on the 25th, the most northern post, occupied by Lieutenant Costty, was attacked and carried by the enemy, with an overpowering force; but it remained in their possession for a very short time: Lieutenant Brown and Lieutenant Wingfield, of the flank battalion, with 100 men, were detached to support the party that had been overpowered: these were assisted by Lieutenant-Colonel Gardiner, who happened to be near, and led a ghole of his irregulars to the spot; and these officers, by a gallant exertion, soon recovered this most valuable position, which was charged three several times by the enemy; but they each time repelled him with great loss, and the post finally remained in our hands. The loss on both sides during this conflict was very considerable; for the enemy came on with very great determination, and were heroically and successfully resisted.

During this time, the garrison of Almorah, hearing the sharp firing on the hills, made a sortie, and furiously attacked our advanced position, coming up to the very wall, which, though six feet high, they attempted to mount; and one or two succeeded, but fell dead within it. These assaults and skirmishings were kept up during the whole night, occasioning considerable loss; among others, Lieutenant Taply received a mortal wound.

The small mortars had, with considerable exertion on the part of the officers of artillery, Lieutenants Bell and Wilson, been laid in battery, and opened at six in the evening; the larger ones at midnight.

On the morning of the 26th, the advanced post was pushed forwards to within seventy yards of the fort of Almorah: several eight-inch shells had fallen in the forts, which soon reduced the garrison to keep under cover; and at nine in the morning a flag of truce was sent to Colonel Nicholls, from the commander, Bumsah, requesting a suspension of arms, with a view to a termination of hostilities in the province.

This was agreed to by Colonel Nicholls, and the Honourable Edward Gardiner (political agent with the army); and on the 27th of April a convention was signed and executed by Bumsah, and the other surviving sirdars, on the part of the Nepāl government, by which all the country to the west of the Gogra, Sardah, or Caleenuddee, as far as Guriohal, with the fort of Almorah, and all other strong holds in the province of Kumaoon, were evacuated by the enemy; they retaining eleven guns, with a portion of military stores; and to be supplied with provision, and escorted across the river Sardah.

This rapid and brilliant train of success could not be achieved without considerable loss. That which our army had to lament was small, however, compared with the importance of the result. One hundred and thirty of our regular troops were killed and wounded, including one officer killed, and two wounded; of the irregulars there was only a total of eighty returned.

Such is a summary of the events that produced the evacuation of Kumaoon, cut off the hopes that Ummr Sing might have had of receiving succours from the eastward, and thus certainly tended greatly to forward the fortunate conclusion of the campaign to the north-west; which finally annexed to the British possessions a province that connects their territories with those of the Chinese empire, through the Himālāyan mountains.

PART II.

PRELIMINARY OBSERVATIONS

ON THE

HIMĀLĀ MOUNTAINS.

JOURNEY FROM DEHLI TO NAHN—SIEGE OF JYTOCK,

AND NOTES THERE.

CHAPTER V.

PREVIOUSLY to commencing the narrative of a journey through a country so little known as that now under consideration, a few general observations relative to its nature and situation may not be found useless.

That chain of mountains, of which the great Himālā range forms the central ridge, and which, stretching from the Indus on the north-west, to the Burrampooter on the south-east, divides the plains of Hindostan and the Punjab from the wilds of Tartary, has been but partially traversed by Europeans; and although the little information that has hitherto been published respecting it is confused and inaccurate, it is nevertheless a very interesting tract.

It is so to the geographer and statesman; as, besides its containing the sources of so many of the majestic rivers that fertilise and enrich Hindostan and other Asiatic regions, and the being inhabited by nations and tribes of a singular character and very warlike disposition, who have for ages defied the arms of the most powerful Asiatic monarchs, it serves as a magnificent and most efficient boundary between two empires of such extent as China, and that which once owned the sway of the house of Timor, but now chiefly the milder rule of the British government.

The portion of this region which was visited by the writer of the following narrative, is that lying between the rivers Sutlej and Alacknunda; the former bounding it to the north-west and north, the latter to the south-east and east, whilst it overlooks the plains of Hindostan to the south and south-west; and on the north-east it partly includes, and is partly bounded by, the mountains of Himālā.

This tract of country, considerable in extent, is divided into a variety of large and small states, governed by chiefs more or less dependent, in proportion as they are powerful.

Of these, though far from being equal in population and resources, five may be considered as of the first rank, viz. Gurwhāl, Bischur, Surmore, Hundoor, and Kukloor; and these occupy by far the largest portion of the tract in question, whilst the remainder is divided into a great number of petty states, all of which are recognized under the general appellation of the Baruh Thakoorace, or twelve lordships.

Twelve states, however, are more properly implied by this designation, viz.

Keoounthul.	Koonear.	Mechloque.	Coteegooroo.
Baghut.	Bhuggee.	Cotee.	Theog.
Coothar.	Dhamina.	Kearee.	Bughāt.

The general extent, value, and position of several of these chieftainships will appear as they occur in the narrative; but as some of them do not come within its scope, a recapitulation of the whole, with an account of the revenue they afforded to the Ghoorkha government, and some few further particulars, will be found in the appendix.

The other petty states are eighteen in number:

Joobul.	Kurangooloo.	Saree.
Bulsum.	Ootrock.	Rutes.
Comharsein.	Mornee.	Cotee Mundhanee.
Kuncounthee.	Bija.	Ghoud.
Dilter.	Sangree.	Bhuroulee.
Raeen.	Dodur coar.	Seelee.

Of these some are of considerable size and importance, particularly Joobul. All of them acknowledged a degree of dependence on some of the large states, which varied according to the inclination and power of the superior to enforce its sway, and to the political condition of that state, and of the neighbouring countries.

A season of peace gave no hope to the tributary of eluding payment for the protection he received; but he was generally ready to avail himself of tempestuous times to change his master, as his interest or his fancy might lead him.

Although the greater states do not in general take rivers for their boundaries, yet as these serve well for outlines in geographical delineation, it may be well to enumerate the principal streams that occur in this tract, and to state the general direction of their course.

Those which principally claim attention from their magnitude, are,

The Alacknunda.	The Touse.	The Jumna.
Bhagiruttee.	Girree.	Pabur.
Caligunga.	Billung.	Sutlej.

Since the tour of Webb and Raper, it is well known that the river Alacknunda takes its rise in a snowy mountain, close to the celebrated Hindoo Temple of Buddrinaath. It flows in a direction nearly south-west to Rooderprāg, where it forms a junction with the Caligunga.

The Caligunga rising at Kedarnauth, another celebrated temple in the Kedār snowy mountain, runs to Rooderprāg nearly south-south-west.

From this point the Alacknunda holds a more westerly course to Deoprāg, where it is joined by the Bhagiruttee; and from hence the united streams receive the name of the Gunga or Ganges.

The source of the Bhagiruttee will be minutely described in the following narrative; all that need now be observed is, that its course for several miles from its source is nearly from east to west; a few miles below Barahāt it flows to the south-west; further up, and from a point about forty miles above Deoprāg, it keeps a course to the south-south-eastward.

The little river Bitting joins the Bhagiruttee just below Uthoor.

The source of the Jumna will also be found described in the following pages: it holds a general south-west course from fifteen to forty miles distant from the Bhagiruttee, till the point where that river diverges to the eastward as far as Calsee, where it is joined by the Touse. A little lower down the Girree falls into it at Raj Ghat, and soon after it issues a more considerable stream from the hills near Padshaw Bāgh.

The Touse has its rise in a very lofty peak, far to the northward among the snowy mountains, and for a considerable space flows in a west-south-westerly direction, till it is joined by the Pabur.

The united streams then taking a southerly course, join the Jumna as before mentioned, about thirty-five miles below Calsee.

The Girree is a stream of less note; its source will also be noticed: it joins the Jumna, as has been said, at Raj Ghat, after a run of some length from the north-westward.

Besides these considerable streams, there are multitudes of mountain-streams and torrents of greater or smaller size, which, rising in the various hills, hold their course to these great drains, and swell the Ganges, the Jumna, or the Sutlej.

Among the states of the first order, Gurwhāl is the most important in every respect; its boundaries extend far beyond the limits of the country now visited.

Beyond the Alacknunda it is bounded by the river Ramgunga, which divides it from the province of Kumaoon; while to the north and east it penetrates the snowy mountains, meeting the Chinese territories in an undefined line.

To the southward it is bounded by the plains, and on the west by the Jumna, which, as far as the village of Lack-ha-mundul, divides it from Sirmore, to the northward of which it meets Bischur, between the rivers Touse and Pabur.

Sirmore, though not second in extent, is perhaps the next of the primary states in value and political consideration.

Its vicinity to the plains gives it an importance, denied to those more difficult of access in the heart of the mountains.

On the south-east it bounds, as has been observed, with Gurwhāl, having the Jumna for the line of demarcation.

To the north also Gurwhāl partly meets it; and the secondary state of Joobul, with various others of the petty states, form an irregular amphitheatre, circumscribing it from north to west, while on the south-west and south it is comprehended by the districts of the petty Sikh chieftains, in the plains between the Sutlej and Jumna.

Bischur, though far larger in extent, is much poorer in proportion than Sirmore, and lies retired within the mountains to the north of that state and all the lesser states, by which on the south it is chiefly bounded.

The river Sutlej divides it from the territories of the Rajah of Cooloo on the north-west, nearly as high as Serān; a little below which place it crosses the river, and still bounding with Cooloo, passes with that state through the snowy range; and like Gurwhāl, which accompanies it on the east, meets beyond them the Chinese territories in an undefined line.

Hundoor and Kuploor are contained in the space which is bounded by the Sutlej, the plains, and the small states; but of these I have no certain information.

A glance on the map, which accompanies these pages, will, with what has been said (it is hoped), give a pretty distinct idea of the country in question.

All this region, like the whole of the countries contained in the long range of mountains, is wild, rugged, and difficult of access, consisting of a mass of hills irregularly connected, or diverging in ranges of various heights from a huge elevated centre, but preserving no regularity of direction or of form. Their tops are sometimes clothed with forests of old and venerable wood; sometimes they are rocky, and green or brown; and it will be afterwards observed that the general aspect, to the south and south-east, is always less wooded and less broken (though still very rough), than that to the north and north-west, which is almost uniformly precipitous, formed of sharp crags covered with deep pine forests.

The ravines that divide these hills are deep and very sudden in their descent, often ending in dark chasms that are sometimes wooded, but they as often exhibit faces of bare rock of several hundred feet high, frowning at each other, with little more space between them than has been worn by the violence of the torrents; these taking their way from the mountain brows, where they have been collected from clouds, and rain, and melting snow, thunder down, and form these furrows in their sides.

There are no spreading valleys, no rich meadow lands on the banks of rivers, no gentle undulation of ground on which the eye can rest with pleasure; all is steep and difficult; toilsome rise and sudden fall. Such a country offers little encouragement to the industry of the husbandman; and, accordingly, cultivation, which is limited in proportion to the extent of surface, is laboriously and sparingly scattered among the woods and rocks.

As the country recedes from the plains it increases in difficulty and elevation, till at the foot of the snowy mountains it assumes a savage wildness; and among them, save in the passes or the beds of rivers, becomes totally impracticable and impervious.

The rivers and their beds too, it will be seen, gradually change their character as we approach nearer to their source, from the rapid and turbulent stream flowing through a deep and a rugged channel, but affording a comparatively easy road along its banks, to a furious torrent dashing from one huge block of stone to another, along which the traveller proceeds at first with difficulty, which increases to hazard of life, climbing over rocks, and picking his dangerous way across the face of precipices, till at length his career is stopped by masses of mighty ruin, that baffle all human attempts to invade them.

It is unnecessary to offer any further preliminary observations. The nature of this country, and the changes that occur in its appearance, will be described in the following pages; and it is hoped that the observations which occur throughout the narrative may, in some degree, serve to introduce to more general acquaintance a new and in some respects curious people, together with something of their character, disposition, and manners. If the attempt has success, all further observation here would be superfluous, as the object in these preliminary notices is only to give the reader a very general idea of a country, with which he may become subsequently better acquainted.

JOURNEY FROM DEHLI TO NAHN.

Circumstances, foreign to the present subject, led me to the camp of the army under General Martindale, whilst it lay before the fort of Jytock, near Nahn, in the province of Sirmore; and thus most unexpectedly arose the opportunity which I enjoyed of visiting this new country.

Leaving Dehlee on the 9th of March, 1815, by dawk, I reached Kurnāl, a town seventy-six miles to the northward of that capital; and forming the most remote military position we had hitherto held in that direction. Having laid horses at equal distances on the road from thence to the foot of the hills, I left Kurnāl on the 12th, and set off for Nahn.

For ten miles the road lay through what is called the *assigned territory*, being that portion of the Soubah-daree of Dehlee which was appointed for the maintenance of the king, but it has since been resumed, and in its stead a regular monthly allowance has been substituted for the royal expenses.

This country was principally covered with low Dhāk jungle, having a desolate and barren aspect; but, on approaching Indree, a tolerably large and walled town, the land was well cultivated.

Here we entered the territories of the petty Sikh Chieftains, who hold the country between the rivers Jumna and Sutlej, under the protection and partial control of the British government; which, however, confines its interference (as I believe) to suppressing the turbulent spirit, that impels them incessantly to wage a petty warfare among themselves.

But, with all the attention that can be paid to this end, these restless tribes are ever quarrelling; and constant appeals to arms, and frequent bloodshed, are the consequence.

Their manners, too, are as rude and inhospitable as their natures: proud and insolent, they are ever prompt to insult strangers who pass through their country; and they do not spare individuals of the nation that protects them, and which can punish as well as reward.

I cannot, however, appeal to experience in speaking on this subject; for I passed on wholly unmolested, as unmolesting; although it may be, that the presence of a few horsemen of Skinner's corps, who were with me, induced a degree of respect, that might not have been paid had I been wholly unattended.

The country continued fertile, though sandy: during this day's journey, which was thirty-six miles, we passed through the seemingly thriving town of Rodōre, a fortified place; and in the forenoon reached a small village called Topra, where the tents were pitched.

At almost every village, several lofty round towers, much resembling glasshouse furnaces, attracted observation; which I discovered, on inquiry, were intended for places of security, during the sudden and violent attacks to which all villages and towns were formerly subject, from the turbulence of the people; and it is said that these safety-keeps are still neither unnecessary, nor occasionally unemployed.

In the calm of the evening, when the dust, set in motion during the day, had somewhat subsided, the hills to the north were visible; and one peak, lofty and covered with snow, was very conspicuous. The next morning they were by far more distinct; indeed they seemed close at hand, rising rugged and wild, to appearance in three ridges.

The country continued to be rich, fertile, and populous: we passed several good villages to Seidoura, a considerable town, most of the houses of which are built of brick; and there are many of those round towers which were taken notice of in the march of the day before, as well as a fort of some strength.

The people, as we passed rapidly, contented themselves with staring stupidly at us; but they looked surly and silent, offering no civility, and as if they were well inclined to be insolent and troublesome if they dared.

From Seidoura to the hills, a distance called twelve coss, and which may be about seventeen or eighteen miles, the road lies through a country very similar to that of the former march; sandy, but well cultivated; and which stretches on a perfect level, without the least undulation, to the very foot of the hills, that rise from it, as rocks from the sea, sudden and rugged, the boundary quite as sharply marked as between land and water.

We entered these hills by a watercourse nearly dry, which divides the low ridge next the plain (that rising to a height of from 5 to 700 feet, runs from Hurdwar, all the way to this point) from the rough and more lofty range behind, on which Nahn is situated. This was called by the British officers "the pass of Moginund," from a village of that name on one of the near ridges. Here the army lay encamped for a few days.

The road soon crosses the watercourse, and ascends the opposite hill by a various and winding route, crossing several rough chasms for some miles, when it again descends into another watercourse.

Here the park of artillery, attached to the force before Jytock, was formed. It may be five miles from the plains, and just at the foot of that hill on which Nahn is situated.

The path from hence to that town gives the traveller the first true foretaste of the country he is beginning to traverse; it is entirely a steep and very rugged ascent, of so narrow and winding a nature, that I thought it prudent to quit my horse, and rather trust to my own feet than to those of an animal, in places where a slip would have been fatal; and the width was not such as to give space to recover lost footing.

Up this path, however, it was common for officers to ride; and elephants, camels, and bullocks, loaded with stores of provision and ammunition, found their way to the encampment at Nahn.

Many of the carcasses of the camel and buffalo on the way-side attracted the birds of prey; they perished in a country so uncongenial to them; but the elephant slowly and securely carried up his load, mounting the high hills, and making good his footing where even men had difficulty.

The heavy guns went by another road, scraped on the face of the rock, far more perpendicular, and in appearance more difficult, but where fewer turnings gave the power of an even pull; and they were thus dragged up by main force.

At length we reached Nahn, perched like a bird's nest on the brow of a rock, and widely overlooking the lower hills and the plains, till they blended with the sky in the distance. The view, indeed, to one accustomed to the sober, though rich monotony of the level plains of Hindostan, is quite bewitching, and almost confounding.

Facing these lovely plains on the south, from which you are divided by the singular range of low hills before spoken of, the Kearda Dhoon, or valley, extends on the left to the south-east, deeply wooded but spotted with cultivation. Beyond it, the Deyhra Dhoon is traced, till it melts into distance; to the northward of these arise the hills that retreat in wild confusion, and form an amphitheatre around to the south-west, where they bound, and are bounded by, the plains.

Turning to the north, this vast range of hills is seen, with the peak and fort of Jytock rising from and terminating a rugged range; on part of which the tents of our army were seen, speckling the brown hills; and beyond, snowy peaks bounded the landscape. Casting the eye nearer home, the scene was not less warlike: when we reached the end of the town where lay that part of the British army which occupied the position of Nahn, the irregular ground was taken advantage of, whenever it yielded space for a tent, and all the verge of the hill was spotted with them.

Sepoys and European soldiers thronged the pathways; in some places parading, recruits exercising, arms cleaning; in others, groups of officers walking, or looking with glasses at the operations going on upon the opposite ridge.

Here a brigade of guns, and the heavy cannon destined to batter the enemy's stockades; further on, a bazar well filled with provisions, and crowded with soldiery purchasing their homely fare; camp followers of all sorts, regular and irregular troops, highlanders and lowlanders, natives and Europeans, crowded the place, and formed a moving and animated picture, from the contemplation of which it required some effort to withdraw, though sufficiently fatigued by a march of near forty miles, and much requiring the necessary refreshments prepared for us at the tent of a friend.

Nahn is a small town, but the buildings are of stone, cemented generally with lime; they are remarkably small, and all have flat roofs. The effect of the whole at first is singular, giving a strange idea of diminutiveness, like the abridgment of a town; perhaps this is necessarily produced by an unconscious comparison with the vast proportions of the surrounding objects.

It is built on the crest of a hill, which is so uneven that the whole forms a collection of petty ascents and descents. There is one principal street, that, like the others, which are very confined and short, consists of many small flights of steps, into which they have been built and cut, to the great convenience of the men, but by no means so of the cattle, horses particularly, which animal indeed seems never to have been intended for use in these regions.

There are few buildings worthy of notice in Nahn: the rajah's palace has a tolerably neat but not very remarkable appearance; and there are no temples of much consequence or of any splendour to visit; it has, however, for several years been in a state of decay, since the conquest of the Ghoorkhas ruined all the country.

The hill on which it is situated is part of the north-western boundary of the Kearda valley; and from this circumstance, when seen from the plains, it appears to be on a second range of hills, which indeed is so far the case, as the low hills that form the south-western boundary of the Kearda intervene between it and the plains; but, as will afterwards appear, there is no general division into separate or parallel ridges to be detected in the arrangement of the hills in this country.

The height of that point on which the town is placed has been ascertained by a series of calculations, which I have reason to think may be depended on, to be 1950 feet above the level of the plains.

CHAPTER VI.

Jytock, the fort to which Qazee Runjore-Sing-Thappa retreated when he evacuated Nahn, and which was now besieged by the British army, is situated on the lofty end of a ridge, distant from Nahn in a direct line between two and three miles; and between it and that town there runs a deep ravine, which occasions the road to wind so much that the distance in travelling is nearly doubled.

The ridge extends, first, to the westward by a low neck to Blackhill, the position of our chief camp; from thence in the same direction, and nearly a mile distant, lies the elevated peak called Nownie, where there was a British advanced post. At that point the ridge takes a turn to the northward, and is lost in that which forms the southern bank of the Jelall river, and from which in fact it springs.

Jytock has by the same course of observation been found to be 3600 feet above the level of the plains; and Nownie is not inferior to it in height.

The face of the country around Nahn and Jytock is peculiarly rugged. The hills all the way to the Girree river assume a crumbly and rocky sharpness, rising into narrow sharp ridges and high peaks, that give a striking character to the whole tract. This seems to arise from the nature of their component parts. They are formed apparently of a hard stone, very apt to crack and break in sharp irregular ridges, which on exposure to the air easily bursts in small fragments, and then falls into dust; it consists, I think, of clay and sand, and is generally of a dusky brown colour, or of a brownish grey.

This rock is covered with a thin crust of soil, which varies much in thickness, and is probably formed, in great measure, of the decomposed stone.

The exposure of this rock from the breaking of the crust which is washed down by the heavy rains of summer, and which itself soon feels the effects of the vicissitudes of the seasons, forms these sharp ridges (scarcely affording room for footing), which are so wild and singular.

The ravines that separate these hills have a not less savage character; they exhibit great variety of rock and precipice, but not on so grand a scale as where the rock is of a less mouldering nature. The soil that covers the mountains is rich, and produces vegetation of much luxuriance and variety, plenty of wood, impenetrable, or thinner so as to admit of pasturing under them.

Here we first observed, in confirmation of a general observation already made, that the northern exposure of the hills is the most wooded and rough, whilst the southern is smoother and bare. This, however, does not apply so perfectly to the first low hills that rise from the plain; their crests point in some measure to the north-west, but are smooth toward the north-east, and covered with wood; and viewed from the ridge at Blackhill, they have a strong resemblance to a wave of the sea that has rolled by, pointing its breaking crest in its onward direction to the south-west, but here and there curling half backward to the north-west.

These low hills are all formed of a sandstone, quite different from those on which Nahn and Jytock are placed; and the same description will apply to them, I believe, all the way from Hurdwar to their termination at the pass of Moginund.

The general line of the mountains is nearly north-west and south-east. A small abrupt ridge rising from 500 to 750 feet in height, and extending from three to six miles in breadth, runs next to the plains from Hurdwar half-way to the Sutlej. This consists of sandstone, indurated clay, and beds of rounded pebbles and gravel.

The next range of hills runs from 1500 to 5000 feet in height, with sharp narrow crests, and consists of a very decomposable greyish brown indurated clay, containing siliceous matter.

Just beyond this range rises a mountain of limestone, about 7000 feet high. A large perennial stream marked the division between this range and a mass of mountains, consisting almost entirely of varieties of schist, with much mica, and veins with quartz.

Connected with these were observed a coarse sandstone, and a conglomerate of sand, mica, and gravel, cemented by a white spar easily frangible.

As the snowy mountains were approached, rocks of white quartz were observed, and of a hard semi-transparent stone of many colours, red, yellow, and greenish.

On reaching the heart of the snowy mountains, the distant peaks appeared to be stratified, and to dip to the north-east at an angle of about forty-five degrees: for several thousand feet below their tops all vegetation ceases, and no living thing is seen.

The returning route was for a considerable way along the bed of the river Pabur, which rises among the depths of the Himālā: in this bed blocks of a peculiar kind of rock were found. The neighbouring rocks were schist and limestone.

Another opportunity presented itself of viewing the summit of the Himālā from Jumnotree, which rises in two grand peaks, covered on the south and south-east by perpetual snow, but showing a precipitous rocky face towards the north-west.

The river Jumna was here traced to its source in a number of small rills flowing from the snow, and collected in a pool at the bottom of a deep slope. Nearly every sort of rock observed throughout the tour was found here, particularly the rock before referred to as occurring in the bed of the Pabur; and white quartz in veins intersected the general stratification.

From these veins a stream of hot water trickles, impregnated with calcareous matter, which it deposits on the surface of the rocks over which it runs.

There are no glaciers in any part of the snowy mountains, but a perpetual frost appears to rest on their summits.

After descending into the bed of the Bhagiruttee, that river was also traced nearly to its source. The glen through which it runs is deeper and darker, and the precipices on either side far more lofty, than those forming the bed of the Jumna. The rock in the neighbourhood of its source is granitic, and containing black tourmaline.

To return to the country around Jytock and Nahn.

Much cultivation, wherever the ground admits of being worked, speckles the sloping sides of these wooded mountains. It is entirely effected by cutting those parts most adapted to the operation into a succession of terraces, rising above one another exactly like a flight of steps, having a flat level surface, and a perpendicular face, in a manner that will hereafter be more particularly alluded to; and on the surface of these the corn grows. A large proportion of the mountain sides is thus seen carved into stripes, and exhibiting a very singular appearance.

Even where corn does not grow, the marks of former culture are evident; and the stranger's eye, next to the sharp ridginess of the hills, is attracted by the curious effect which this gives to their sides.

Villages, either inhabited or in ruins, abound all over them; and, could it be supposed that all these had ever been at the same time occupied, it would give a strong impression of former populousness, and present desolation: but the truth is, that as one place became exhausted, or as inclination prompted, or as various accidents might determine them, the people quitted one village, which fell into decay, and established themselves in another, which was new and flourishing.

True it is, that much devastation was made, and many districts were depopulated by the severity of the conquerors; but not to the degree that might be presumed from appearances.

The villages are sometimes large, but oftener very mean.

The houses are flat roofed, built of stone, with wooden beams supporting a terrace of stone and wood. Some are of two stories, but in general they consist of one. They are very rudely constructed; frequently the side of the hill serves for one of the walls, whence beams, that are fastened in it, project, and are supported by the external wall or front.

The doors are uncommonly small, so that a man must enter by the head and shoulders, and drag the rest of his body after him. But with all this rudeness, I have been astonished to see the neatness within doors; the floor is smooth, well swept, and clean; and the fire-place in the middle is well contrived, although the smoke must annoy those who are not accustomed to its effects. A few shelves are seen placed around, and in some instances a little furniture of coarse construction may be found.

The cows, their chief wealth, have always a respectable share of the house, comfortable and dry; although they do not give them a much larger opening through which to make their entrance and exit than they allow themselves; and I have sometimes admired the animals insinuating themselves through so narrow an aperture.

These villages are often very pleasantly situated, and almost always adorned with a few lemon or walnut trees, or, where they will grow, with mango trees, that throw a grateful shade over the houses, and terraces of stone built at their roots, yield a comfortable seat to the inhabitants under their branches.

But these ornaments form a contrast with the discomfort displayed in other particulars; labouring under the disadvantage of ground so very uneven, that paths cannot be made of easy access; and the presence of incumbrances and nuisances, that might be removed if they took the pains.

After the singularity of the appearance of the houses, the beauty of the situation, and the few trees are admired, the rest of the scene, if it do not excite disgust, at least does not interest.

The vegetable productions of these hills differ almost wholly from those of the plains, as may indeed be supposed; even the low range that bounds them to the south is distinguished by the pine-trees, that spring among the forest-trees met with in low situations; as we ascend other strangers in the vegetable kingdom attract the eye of the traveller, and I much regret that I cannot give a list of these. My own want of botanical knowledge was not compensated by the presence of any better instructed friend. I could only admire the beauty and variety so strikingly visible, without being able to ascertain with accuracy the place these subjects would occupy in a scientific arrangement.

At the time we were before Jytock, the season was not so favourable to luxuriance of vegetation as afterwards during the rains. The grass was long and rank, but brown and burnt up; but among it we took notice of many old friends peeping from beneath: among others, more than one species of the raspberry-bush and bramble, the strawberry, but of a very worthless sort, trefoil or clover, many ferns, bushes of thorns and plums, wild peach trees, a sort of crab-pear, and apple, and dog roses. A quantity of different sorts of euphorbium covers the lower parts of the hills, and much of the oleander adorns the watercourses. The pine-trees grow to a great height and very respectable girth; they branch but little till near the top, and then become bushy; the leaves are long spikes, from twenty to forty growing in a tuft, from small foot-stalks: they yield a considerable quantity of turpentine, and in their appearance approach a medium between the Norway and the stone pine.

Saul, Sisoo, and Toon, and a great variety of other trees, with a few of a peculiar sort of oak, are found in the forests that cover these hills.

Of animals, there are found in the two valleys of Deyrah and Kearda much the same species as inhabit the plains; and, perhaps, these may also extend a little farther into the more accessible parts of the hills.

Elephants are found and caught occasionally; and a portion of the price of those thus taken form a source of revenue to the state.

Tigers abound, as well as leopards. Deer of various sorts are very numerous. Wild hogs are not rare. Buffaloes are also, I believe, to be seen; and the proportion of smaller animals, as jackals, foxes, hares, and monkeys, is equal to that met with in the other parts of the upper provinces, which are full of jungle, and are little cultivated.

The feathered race also is similar in quantity and description. Of game, there are partridges, black and gray, and also of that species peculiar to hilly districts, and known by the name of chuccore, (which it obtains from its cry); jungle fowl, and more than one species of pheasant. Quails, snipe, and aquatic fowl, sufficiently abundant.

As we entered the hills several of those that inhabit the warmer plains disappeared, and other kinds were found, which will be afterwards described in a general remark on the animals of the hills.

Many sorts, however, as the deer, wild hogs, jackals, monkeys, a few leopards or tigers, with partridges, chuccores, and jungle fowl, are found in almost every direction, even to the remotest regions on the skirts of the Snowy Mountains.

Of domestic animals, the cow has precedency; the horse is confined to the skirts of the hills; goats and sheep are found every where; dogs accompany, and are reared by their masters: there are few or no wild or Paria dogs. In so poor a country, where the inhabitants themselves have difficulty in subsisting, food cannot suffice to encourage a breed of animals of this nature, which are so commonly found all over the East, where victuals are plenty, and the rejected offals support them amply.

The inhabitants of the country surrounding the capital, and the districts in its vicinity, are not calculated to excite much interest either from character or appearance. Generally speaking, they are contemptible in size, mean in aspect, cringing in address; their intellect appears degraded, and their ignorance almost brutal.

Those of a rank which has afforded them the means of acquiring a very circumscribed knowledge of the world, and with it some ease of manner in their behaviour, still create disgust by the servile humility which they display to those whom they deem their superiors in power.

The higher class of peasantry (here denominated zemindars) with a still greater absence of all polish, are marked by the same contemptible weakness and meanness, the same disposition to falsehood and deceit, so strongly apparent in the higher orders; and the lower class of labourers seem depressed in mental qualification nearly to a level with the beasts of the field.

Their stature is almost universally diminutive. When an individual of larger body and greater height is met with, it is as we see persons of Herculean mould in other parts of the world, forming an exception to the general rule.

They are, however, remarkably stout, and compactly made; their limbs, particularly their legs and thighs, are uncommonly muscular in proportion to their size, and their general strength, especially in carrying burthens, is very great. Their early habits will account for this: accustomed from their youth to climb these steep hills, their muscles strengthen and enlarge, and the bracing cold of their climate confirms the effect of this *education*. Comparing their strength in this way with that of the inhabitants of the plains, far their superiors in size, it is really surprising. The common load for a man in these parts is thirty seer, or about sixty pounds weight; and this, with the addition probably of several pounds of coarse flour for his own consumption, besides his clothes, &c. he will carry with sufficient ease along the roughest roads, up the steepest ascents, and down the most dangerous declivities. Those who possess superior strength will carry far more; all will, thus loaded, continue a march from twelve to fifteen miles a day up and down these rugged mountains.

The colour of these people, like that of their neighbours in the plains, is found of every shade, from dark brown or black to a tawny yellow, and in a few instances they approach to white.

Whatever the original colour may be, those exposed to severe labour and the effects of the sun speedily become dark.

Their hair is black, and they commonly wear it long at the sides and back of the head, hanging down about the ears, where it is cut round; the crown is often shaven bare; they all wear mustachios, and their own black beard, which they seem to consider a great ornament, and cherish with much care.

The general cast of their countenance is Hindoo, but they seldom possess the softness and even intelligence that may be considered a marked characteristic of the Hindoo physiognomy. Their eyes are sunk deep into the head, commonly of a black, but often of gray and other colours. The nose is prominent, sharp, and inclined to aquiline; the forehead high and round, the cheekbones high, the chin long, and the whole visage long and spare, much drawn into wrinkles at the corners of the eyes and brows, from great exposure to the sun; in short, the countenance exhibits an habitual grin.

The dress of this people is very simple: that of the middling class consists of the common jacket of cotton, ending in skirts, which are shorter than usual, more full and puckered up into folds than the Hindoo "ungurca" (a sort of gown or long skirted coat that forms the common Hindoo dress in the upper provinces), tied round the waist, and reaching to the knee, something like the Scotch highland philibeg; under these are worn a pair of cotton trowsers; around the shoulders they wrap a piece of cotton cloth in a manner resembling the Scotch plaid, which when the sun is hot they throw also over the head, but the usual covering for the head is only a dirty skullcap of cotton, beneath which their wild locks and hard features look forth in savage guise. Such is their warm weather clothing. When it is colder they exchange their cotton trowsers for a pair of thick coarse woollen drawers, and wrap a blanket round them, with which when it rains they also envelope the head.

The poorer sort, who can hardly procure such costly raiment, content themselves with a coarse blanket, and a small cloth round the middle. Many of these I have seen so wild and ragged, that they seemed scarcely human. The superior classes of nobles and chiefs dress much in the common fashion of Hindostan, but affect the Sikh turban, which being wrapt snugly round the head in many folds, towers in a round point to a great height in front.

Arms are not common; it formed a part of the Ghoorka policy to disarm the natives of the states they subdued, and few were admitted to the privilege of carrying any weapon.

When the country was raised, it was necessary to furnish with arms the soldiers who presented themselves for service. The people now supplied themselves as they could with swords, knives, matchlocks, bows and arrows, or Ghoorka cookrees, but they were deficient both in arms and in the knowledge of their use; those, however, who could procure them, always wore a sword, a shield, and a small axe (called daugrah), or a cookree.

The women are in general more prepossessing in appearance than the men; their stature is better in proportion, and their features far more delicate and regular, with much of the pleasing Hindoo softness in youth. They are commonly fair, varying in colour from a mild yellow to a slight shade of brown; but labour and exposure to the sun and storm soon destroy all delicacy of feature, colour, and all vestiges of beauty, leaving while yet young in years a wrinkled sallow visage.

The strong habitual jealousy so prevalent over the east does not seem to have power here. That plan of seclusion so universally practised by Asiatics, which shuts the women from the eyes of all but one, is here not adopted. The females appear abroad as unreservedly as the men; and far from flying at the sight of strangers, they will remain and converse, showing no other feeling than the occasional shyness natural to all uneducated women introduced to the presence of persons they never saw before. On several occasions, when we had approached the place they were in, I have seen them continue occupying themselves with their household concerns, and even give the breast to their children as if none were by.

That this state of freedom proceeds from enlightened motives, no one judging by analogy with their other habits can suppose. As eastern female seclusion is the effect of gloomy and tyrannical jealousy, and the wantonness of luxury and power; so, when these latter are not present to operate, and poverty checks the madness of passion, the inconvenience of such a custom will prevent its adoption, and the common course of nature will not be counteracted.

Females are valuable as labourers, and thus escape imprisonment. The natives do not possess that keenly sensitive and unoccupied mind which usually becomes a prey to jealousy.

They are too gross, too little accustomed to mental exercise; and the small portion of forethought they have is too completely occupied in providing for the subsistence of the day, and the absolute necessaries of life, to admit of a feeling so refined as jealousy.

So far are they indeed from any such tincture, that chastity, it is to be feared, is a virtue little known, and less valued; and this will seem the less strange when their customs regarding marriage come to be known, and particularly one of a most singular and revolting nature, which in fact establishes to a certain degree among them a sort of community of wives.

It is usual for a family of four or five brothers to marry and possess the same woman at the same time, who thus becomes the wife in common to all: of this usage a full account will be given hereafter; but the general ideas regarding female virtue may be inferred from the admission of a practice so disgusting.

The dress of the females is quite the same as that of the Hindoos in the plains: a short wrapper, or coortee, covers the shoulders and breast; a petticoat is tied around the waist, and a do-putta, or long piece of cloth, is wrapt around the head, shoulders, and bosom, like a shawl, in various and elegant shapes. These habiliments are fabricated of cotton, plain, coloured, or striped, and are manufactured in, and procured from, the low country. Ornaments are here as much affected as usual among the softer sex, and they procure all sorts to the extent of their ability.

The women of the poorer class wear any kind of dress they can get, and claim no description of peculiar costume. Indeed among them, at times, are seen creatures of extraordinary appearance, to the full as wild and savage as the men; and we have frequently, while strolling past or through a village, come upon a being of the female gender, whose appearance made it difficult to class her with any known genus of animal.

The religion these people profess is Hindooism; but their practice is chiefly confined to the superstitious belief in, and adoration of, an endless number of imaginary powers (which never had a place in any faith till they received one from these ignorant beings), and in the partial observances of cast, and other common Hindoo prejudices.

The common and established Hindoo deities are acknowledged and held sacred, and there are temples to their worship; but the powers, good and evil, with which the superstitious imagination of the " Paharia," or mountaineer (from " pahār," a hill), has peopled every hill, every grove, and every dell, are far more commonly the object of his fervent and fearful devotion.

In short, the religion, wild as it is among its most enlightened professors in the plains, is perverted and metamorphosed in the hills to a degree of such superior confusion, that it quite defies all order or comprehension.

The Paharia pays his adoration to the cow, protects it, and uses it well. He will not sell one except to a Hindoo, and refused many of the British officers who offered him gold for these holy animals merely for the sake of their milk. But he works it hard, as all his countrymen do, using it in the laborious departments of agriculture, as plowing, treading out the grain, &c.

The same detail of casts is found as in the plains. There is no scarcity of brahmins, who here, as in other places, take excellent care of themselves.

Almost every one calls himself a Rājpoot, save those who honestly confess to inquirers that they are *coolies*, that is, of the lowest class; " *chumars*," or persons who strip the skins from carcasses, and who are also shoemakers.

In short, the detail of the people in the country under consideration, as far as we saw it in the vicinity of Nahn, was very similar to what may be met with among other petty Hindoo states where Mahomedanism has not obtained a firm footing.

The origin of these people no doubt forms a curious subject of inquiry. Were they a race that from a very ancient period inhabited the hills, and perhaps sent their superabundance to people the plains, and fill up the country in the vicinity of their mountains? if so, whence did they originate? from what direction did they come? or, are the present degraded inhabitants of the mountains only the refuse of the plains which were first peopled? These are questions, however interesting, on which so few lights can in all probability be obtained, that they are likely to rest in obscurity for ever.

The fact of their religion and language being similar to those in use among their neighbours of the plains does not appear to bear any weight on either side, for these may be of comparatively late adoption; and there are no records, and very little tradition, to light us to the transactions even of the latest period of their history. Beyond the memory of man (and in perhaps some instances of a few generations back) there is little in this part of the country to guide us.

In the records of the states of Gurhwal and Kumaoon, indeed, there are notices of dates, old in comparison with the known events of other places, but very recent when referred to as illustrating the remote history of an aboriginal people.

It is natural that, on this side the Snowy Mountain's barrier, the features, language, religion, and manners of the inhabitants should partially assimilate to those of the most powerful neighbours with whom intercourse is held; but this intercourse has not been so great as to carry such a similarity to any very considerable extent, and there does not seem to be the least trace near the plains of any other language or features than those described, which are undoubtedly Hindoo.

That the scene of the great drama of Hindoo mythology, the theme of the holy books of the Shasters, should be laid in these mountains, argues nothing. If indeed the Brahminical religion was at a very distant era introduced into Hindostan, by a race who subdued by their arms, or gained power by their wisdom, they might well at a period that now defies research, and mocks at tradition or historical notice, place their holiest temples and secrets in the difficult if not inaccessible regions of the north, where mystery added awe to the reverence which they exacted and received for their deities. Mahadeo could not be more sublimely inthroned than in the recesses of Himālā.

The most probable supposition is, surely, that the mountains by degrees received their population from the plains; that those who were weak and oppressed in times of turbulence and tumult retired to the skirts of the hills, and were succeeded and pushed on by others in a similar predicament from time to time, till at length the whole tract, uninviting as it is in appearance, was pervaded and peopled. Curiosity and desire of gain, or the wish to find more fertile pastures for their flocks, might first entice persons to explore the dangerous passages through the hills, till at last they were penetrated from each side. A partial admixture might have taken place between the Tartars on the one side and the Hindoos on the other; but the nature of the country formed too great an obstacle to its extending to any great degree. It will afterwards appear that this seems to have been the case; but I am too ill qualified in every way to attempt more than to state the subject of query; and, far from appreciating the proofs on either side the question, have neither science nor means of observation sufficient to detect and bring them into notice; I must therefore leave the field to abler explorers.

The boundaries of Sirmore, in which Nahn and Jytock are situated, have already been loosely mentioned, and a more particular idea of the country will be obtained by a glance at the map which accompanies these pages.

The state is divided into twenty-seven purgunnahs, of which a list is given in the appendix: of these the valley called the Kearda-Dhoon is the only one capable of being fully and richly cultivated, as it is a level tract running from the river Jumna westward, nearly to the foot of the hill on which Nahn is situated, and is contained between the small ridge of hills that run along the plain and the first of the loftier mountains.

Although among the remaining divisions there are tracts, which, considering local circumstances, are rich and populous; yet these are insulated and small in proportion to the vast space that is incapable of cultivation, mountainous and wild, like that already described, and which will fall under notice in the ensuing pages during the detail of my journeys.

The revenues could never have been very large, and the depopulation and ruin, that have been spread over the land by the Ghoorkha conquerors, must have reduced it very greatly. In fact, the total annual amount of land revenue which the Nepālese government drew from Sirmore never exceeded 85,000 rupees, exclusive of the petty states dependent on it, which were separately assessed. But this must have been a small portion of what the country once yielded. The Kearda-Dhoon alone, which in the hands of the Ghoorkhas never yielded above 1500 rupees per annum, is said in former times to have given from thirty to forty thousand rupees, independent of the customs on transit goods, and the usual dues of the crown on the capture of wild elephants, which amounted to one-fourth of their value.

It would not be fair, however, to presume, that the deterioration of realizable revenue over the whole of the country has kept pace with that experienced in the Kearda-Dhoon. This place, from its far greater facilities for cultivation, was susceptible of proportionate improvement or decay; the rest of the country does not offer a subject for so heavy a difference in value; and any similar diminution must have reduced its returns to almost nothing. But the actual decline of the revenues of the country is enormously and evidently great, and proved by the general appearances of desolation visible to the traveller, as well as by the result of inquiry and investigation.

With the state of their military power, and the number and efficiency of the troops that they could raise before they were subjected to the power of Nepāl, I am not much acquainted. It was not, as we understand, very formidable; consisting chiefly of temporary levies raised for occasional service, each chief of a district bringing with him his followers, and the petty tributary states yielding their quota at the command of their superior. That the number, however, of this collection must have been considerable will appear from this, that the tributary state of Joobul alone was understood to be capable of furnishing 2000 hardy soldiers, and its extent is trifling compared with that of Sirmore, not perhaps amounting to more than one-fifth of that state.

These men could not boast of much discipline, nor were they well or regularly armed. The greater number carried bows and arrows, and axes, whilst only the chosen troops wielded swords, or were supplied with matchlocks.

The states over which Sirmore claims a tributary authority are, Joobul, Ootrock, Rutes, Bulsum, Raeen, Seelee, Saree.

But it was a superiority that could not always be established, and the degree of vassalage varied with the power of enforcing it.

Other states even occasionally asserted the right to demand tribute claimed by it, and according as the power of these preponderated was the claim adjusted.

Bischur and Gurwhal, each in turn stepped forward to prefer their own right to feodal superiority, and many and bloody were the wars occasioned by the desire of establishing this disputed title, barren as it was of every thing that could repay the waste of blood it occasioned. Even the chieftain of the smaller state, when he happened to be more ambitious or independent in his principles than common; and when the protecting state was weakened, perhaps by asserting the right to control him, would rise and resist, and endeavour to establish that right, which he too thought he had to liberty, by force of arms. He was seldom successful, for sooner or later one or other of the primary states poured in its strength, and, overwhelming the puny rebel, reduced his small state to subjection again.

Soon after the conquest of Gurwhal, Sirmore also fell under the Ghoorkha tyranny. The reigning prince was a bad and a weak man; and, I believe, from a principle of revenge on some of his neighbours, whom he felt himself too weak or too fearful to attack, he gave encouragement to the common enemy to attempt the taking possession of the country: thus he lost his own crown, and the whole country fell through his treachery.

The Ghoorkas proved hard and grinding masters. The old families, who were attached to the ancient hereditary government, they banished or dispersed; and they created new officers to fill the different posts of trust, who were devoted to their service, and whose interest it was that the old dynasty should never be revived.

In many instances the chief zemindars were carried away from their farms and families as hostages for the peace of a district; and frequently such persons, when suspected of a wish to change masters, were put to death. Such severity naturally produced a great change in the national character, and particularly in the more accessible parts of the country near the plains, and around the capital, where the subjugation was more complete. All enthusiasm, all appearance of love for liberty was destroyed; the people became reckless, broken spirited, bowed to the dust, and subdued in mind as in body.

The farther north, the farther removed from the seat of government, the more did the latent symptoms of anxiety to throw off the yoke evince themselves.

The first that moved and took a decided part in the English cause were the men of Jounsar. This district, wild and rugged in an eminent degree where all is wild, possesses advantages, particularly in a military point of view, that might have been of high importance, had any attempt at a junction taken place between the forces of Ummr Sing Thappa and Runjore Sing his son.

The only practicable roads for an army traversing the interior of this country from east to west lie through this tract, and it commands the chief fords upon the Touse and Jumna. It lies between these rivers, stretching from their junction at Kalsee far to the north-east, till bounded by the district of Rewaeen in Gurwhal. Though wild and apparently a mass of very lofty mountains, it conceals in their bosoms much fine cultivation, whilst its impregnable nature may entitle it to be considered as forming the main strength of Sirmore.

The people of this district were the first to take arms in support of the British and their own cause, and to expel their conquerors. In many instances they harassed the enemy: and on the occasion of Bhulbhudder Sing's retreat from Jountgurh to Jytock, a party of them hung on his rear, and came to a partial engagement whilst passing the Touse, in which, had they been supported by the regulars, who were too far in the rear, they would have cut off the enemy's detachment.

Nearly 1000 men were inlisted into the irregular corps from this part of the country.

Those of the purgunnahs, Palwe, Puchad, Sein, Rajegurh, and Mornee, lying beyond the Touse, were the next to evince their desire of liberty. They rose against their oppressors, joining the men of Jounsar and the irregular troops which were furnished by the British, and exposed themselves to the wrath of the enemy even before the power of our arms was fully manifested to their apprehension.

They suffered in many instances from this open conduct, particularly on the retreat of Bhulbhudder Sing, who burnt and plundered several villages.

Many anxious letters did these people write for assistance, encouraging the advance of troops, which it was then not deemed advisable to send. A few of those letters, with some intercepted ones from Runjore Sing to them, threatening vengeance if they swerved from their allegiance, as being the fairest proofs of the tone of mind in which those people were, are inserted in the appendix.

Joobul next sent forth a few; but the great bulk of that state, and the remainder of Sirmore, remained in heartless inaction. The usual engines of eastern policy (perhaps a more extended sphere of operation may be allowed them) were employed, sowing dissension and discord through all the land; so that unanimity and co-operation were out of the question. Even in the well disposed districts this unhappy state of things prevailed, and palsied all attempt at operations of importance.

The behaviour of the chiefs of the country and of the relatives, nay, even the members of the royal family, when urged to exert themselves, and when troops were put in their offer to command, was highly discreditable and even pusillanimous.

The conduct of the ex-rajah had even made some districts absolutely inimical and active against any measures that favoured his restoration.

The divisions of Laddee and Kangrah on the Jumna, opposite to Kalsee, had suffered from the rajah. In consequence of their delinquency he had severely punished their faults, and the whole district resented this exercise of absolute power. The same people had met with high favour from Runjore Sing; they consequently were devoted to him, and threw every obstacle in the way of our success. None of the inhabitants of these purgunnahs came in, though repeatedly invited; and the assistance they afforded to Bhulbhudder Sing in his passage through Jounsar, and across the river Touse, was of great importance to him.

The name of the ex-rajah is Kurrum-Purgass. He is a man of violent passions, no judgment, and much cruelty. His government was generally odious to the people, and he would in all probability have lost his crown and life had not the Ghoorkha invasion thus rudely put an end to the dynasty. He has a son yet a minor, and many relations, none of whom have proved themselves worthy of being intrusted with authority.

Of the origin of the royal family of Sirmore I know nothing. Almost all the chiefs of the larger hill states are originally of low country extraction; probably soldiers of fortune, more able and politic than the mass of hill chieftains, who have had power to gain a footing, and art to maintain it when gained; and to consolidate into one powerful government a portion of the vast number of ever-changing petty states, which seem of old to have divided the hills.

Of the former history of Sirmore we could learn little; since its existence as a state, it has been continually governed by a rajah in the same way as other Hindoo states, with officers of the usual description and ranks under him; and the system of collecting its revenues has been the same, viz. by amildars stationed throughout the different districts, who received the assessment, which over the whole country was fixed at one half the produce of all land cultivated.

The seat of government was fixed at Nahn, and I do not recollect that we saw or heard of any royal residence besides in the whole country. There are several forts and strong places scattered over it besides Jytock, as Birāb, Mornee, Hurrypoor, and Chandpoor, which shall be noticed as they occur in the narrative of our journey.

CHAPTER VII.

RESUMPTION OF THE CAMPAIGN BEFORE JYTOCK SINCE 5th FEBRUARY.

The progress of the campaign in general, and the chief operations in this quarter, have been detailed in the first part.

After the fall of General Gillespie, and the unfortunate failure before Kalunga, the war advanced but slowly.

This event had a seriously unhappy operation on the minds of the people of the hill states; and there was no brilliant exploit either about the same time or soon after to raise the hopes of the desponding, to fix the wavering or timid, or produce an alteration in the feelings and conduct of those who were hostilely inclined.

The natives, too, from the time that elapsed before active measures were resumed throughout the country, conceived an idea that the conquest of the Deyhra-Dhoon was our only object, and not the entire expulsion of the Nepālese forces from the whole country; and without a certainty of our future intentions they would not come forward to assist us, or rise and take arms in the cause.

Although Kalunga too was evacuated after the second bloody assault and desperate defence, yet we might be considered to have sustained a second repulse; whilst the escape of Buhlbhudder Sing from the place, though surrounded by so large a force, and his retreat to Jountgurh, was rather looked upon as a trait of distinguished bravery and of able generalship, indicating a plan to concentrate the Ghoorka forces into one part of the country, and thus wait for the strong reinforcements that were said to be arriving from the eastward, after having maintained himself as long as was required in the place, whence our efforts had at last driven him.

About this time, however, three or four of the principal landholders, who had more faith, and probably more experience of the real power of the British arms, did come over; and the country they thus placed at our disposal was of importance, as through it lay the chief road from Sreenuggur to the westward.

They were useful in bringing in supplies, and furnishing carriage for necessaries and stores, and facilitating in various ways their passage from place to place, rather than in any actual opposition to the enemy.

Of this they were themselves aware, and many letters received from them and others, in answer to invitations to come over to us, express their readiness to assist the advance of the British troops, and their happiness at their approach, but also their inability, actively or independently, to annoy the Ghoorkhas.

It was at this period that we began seriously to feel the want of means for distressing the enemy, and for aiding our own cause by various less important enterprises, such as cutting off small bodies and foraging parties, giving safe conduct to convoys of our own, protecting the friendly districts from the enemy's vengeance, and raising the spirits of the well disposed but timid; duties which, however useful and even necessary, would have worn out and harassed regular troops in an intolerable manner, besides employing a larger number than could be spared from regular duty.

This gave rise to the measure of forming a light irregular corps, to be raised chiefly among the highlanders of these friendly districts, the old soldiers and dependents of the ex-rajah, to whom arms were distributed, and native officers attached, chiefly their countrymen.

They were found useful, and the levies grew, and formed a temporary addition to the army, easily raised and soon reducible; and the species of straggling warfare that was necessarily pursued gave considerable scope for their services, which, though not to be much relied on in cases of importance and danger, were in many instances very desirable.

Sometime afterwards a body of Mewatties was employed: people accustomed to a desultory warfare like this among their own hills, which however were not so rugged or lofty as these they were now to serve in.

As farther increase was deemed necessary, Sikhs, Highlanders, Patans, and soldiers of fortune of all nations were inlisted, till the number at length was augmented to full 7000 men.

On troops thus hastily raised, formed of so many nations, casts, and characters, little reliance could be placed; and it will appear that the consequence, as was to be expected, was frequent disappointment and disgrace.

Still they had their use; and when the time and circumstances in which they were raised is considered, the greatest allowance should and will be made. Had the success of the affairs in which they were engaged, and their behaviour in general, depended on example and command, it would not have been doubtful; for they were placed under an officer, whose personal character, for conduct and gallantry, might have inspired them with corresponding ardour and confidence; who merits the greatest praise for the incessant attention he paid to render them efficient; and who, had the materials he had to work with been more congruous and sterling, would no doubt have reaped as much honour and satisfaction as he has on various occasions, from their worthlessness, most undeservedly suffered mortification and pain.

After the evacuation of Kalunga, and the retreat of Bhulbhudder Sing, the British army, re-entering the plains, proceeded along the skirts of the hills towards Nahn, and arrived at the entrance of the pass of Moginund on the 19th of February.

The progress of the army towards the town of Nahn, the evacuation of that place by the enemy, and the occupation of it by the British troops, have already been adverted to.

Early in December, the fortress of Birāt in the Jounsār district was evacuated by the enemy; this was chiefly occasioned by the revolt of the people of that district from the Ghoorkha power, which was the first open movement of any consequence in our favour. By this event the whole of Jounsār was freed from the enemy, from Calsee to near the Snowy Mountains.

But there were still circumstances, that occasioned a distrust of our final intentions in the mind of the natives. A body of the enemy, formed by part of the fugitive garrison of Kalunga, a few men from Sreenuggur, and others from Nahn, under some officers of distinction, and perhaps joined by the garrison of Birāt, were not only allowed to establish themselves at the fort of Chumoon (which overawes a considerable district to the eastward of Jounsār between the Jumna and the Bhagiruttee), but were permitted to remain there unmolested by the British troops, although it perhaps appeared to them that the enemy might have been easily driven from that post, his place occupied, the country on this side the Bhagiruttee thus freed, and the bridge over the river so destroyed, that no troops could cross it without a delay and difficulty, that would have rendered it easy to oppose them.

This act would, in their opinion, have given proof of the sincerity of the proclamations that were issued from the British camp, of our resolution to expel the Ghoorkha power, and free the whole country.

That such were the sentiments of the people is incontestably proved by several letters, written from the head men of various districts to the natives in attendance on the British camp. Several pieces of information were communicated, and strong hints were given of what they conceived to be the best course to pursue; but it appears that their views did not coincide with those of the British commanders. A few of these letters are inserted in the appendix, that the continuity of the narrative may not be interrupted.

Whilst the army lay in the plain below Nahn, ten of the principal inhabitants of the district of Jounsăr, who were confined in that town, escaped to the protection of the British, and were immediately sent to their own homes, to further the rising of the people there.

From their account there was reason to believe that the inhabitants of Joobul, and the petty states around it, were anxious to rise and assist the British to dispossess their late conquerors; and much information was otherwise gained respecting the roads that lead from east to west, through the country between the plains and the Snowy Hills.

From its nature as thus described, it was thought by some that a strong line might have been carried across the whole hilly district, stretching from Jytock over the Choor range through Joobul, crossing the river Pabur at Raeęngurh, and leaning upon Unhoul on the river Touse. Such a line would have totally separated the Ghoorkha forces into two parts, and have cut off all communication between Ummr Sing Thappa at Malown, and Irkee and Sreenuggur; whilst having to the south-eastward the friendly and impregnable country of Jounsăr, and no want of necessaries, our forces might, if pressed on, have fallen back without difficulty, or advanced with a certainty of support from their rear. Thus they would have straitened the resources of the Ghoorkha commander to the westward, in a way that would at all events have strongly operated on his apprehensions, and on the spirit of his people, and even have reduced him to the necessity of attempting to force a retreat.

But this plan was not thought expedient, as it seems, by the authorities in command, for no movements in consonance with its spirit were undertaken.

The failure of the attempt to make a lodgement on two points near the fort of Jytock on the 27th of December was followed by a long period of cessation from active measures in this quarter. Meantime, the unsuccessful movement under Major Baldock to dislodge the enemy from Jountgurh and Chumoon, and the advance of Bhulbhudder Sing across Jounsār into Laddee and Palwa, with inferior force in the face of the detachment, operated very unfavourably on the minds of the inhabitants of the hills, for it was considered as a proof of the activity, power, and decision of the enemy; and the men of the district of Kangrah, by whose co-operation the movement was facilitated, were confirmed in their allegiance to the Ghoorkha government, by which they had always been favoured.

Even several of the chieftains of the Palwa district, who had evinced favourable sentiments towards us, went over to the enemy, and the dispositions of the men of Joobul were again rendered wavering and uncertain. Those of Poonur, however, (a district of Joobul, that will afterwards be adverted to), without thinking of consequences, massacred the troops that were stationed among them, for the purposes of collecting the revenue, and freed themselves at once from the Ghoorkha yoke.

About the middle of February, Bhulbhudder Sing entered the fort of Jytock with his detachment.

It being understood, also, that a reinforcement of troops under the command of Azumber Punt Qazee had been detached by Ummr Sing Thappa to the assistance of Runjore Sing his son, and that they were near at hand on their way to reinforce Jytock, Lieut. Young, who commanded the irregulars, was sent with a body of these troops, amounting to about 1400 men, with the view of intercepting them on their way across the Sine range.

The force consisted of various small bodies, who neither knew nor had confidence in each other, and had very little bravery to induce them to expose themselves to danger. The consequence was a total defeat of the whole detachment at Chinal-gurh (a village on the Sine mountain) by the Ghoorkha force under Azumber Punt, who triumphantly, and with very little loss, pursued his way, and entered Jytock without further molestation *.

The scene of action lay in our route, and in its own place is more particularly described.

Among the deserters from the Ghoorkha camp, who subsequently inlisted themselves into British pay, I met with one in particular who had been concerned in this affray, and his account of it was interesting. When they saw the largeness of the party that were sent against them, they had little hope of forcing their way, or indeed of escape from so superior a force.

In a council of war, which was held in the evening, an old soubahdar gave it as his advice that they should attempt to force their way sword in hand, trusting little to the musquet or matchlock, but charging with drawn swords after a volley or two. His advice was followed, and they found their account in it: for, more accustomed than the Sikhs or Mowatties to the irregular and rough ground which formed the field of battle, they kept their footing when the others lost theirs, or were out-breathed. The old soubahdar, the cause of their victory, unfortunately fell by the first fire. His son came anxiously up to see how he fared, but he covered his wound with his clothes, said it was slight, and urged his son onward with his men: he soon expired. Such men could not but conquer.

* Azumber Punt Qazee had only 400 men with him.

Our irregulars left of their number 180 dead on the spot, upwards of 100 came badly wounded into camp, and the number of missing and deserters was very great; no doubt many of the missing were killed by the enemy, or by falling over the precipices, of which the hill is almost entirely formed.

Such are the fatal effects of a total absence of discipline, and of the confidence so necessary to exist in a body of troops on service. These men collected on the exigency of the moment, in small bodies, from different casts, religions, and nations, suddenly united, ignorant of each other, of course without mutual confidence, were no sooner charged by a resolute, compact, well cemented enemy, than they yielded to the shock, and fled panic-struck. Nor was there the same motive to spirited attack or resistance in these heterogeneous irregulars, who merely served for bread, as in the Ghoorkhas, who fought for existence, and for the existence of their nation, with genuine patriotism.

The irregulars, however, were not always thus defeated. A party of 370, who were detached to a post in Sine, called Becherkabagh, were attacked and surprised by 300 chosen men of the garrison of Jytock, whom they repulsed and beat, and then charging with the sword, killed on the spot twenty-five of the number.

But the disaster of the 21st of February gave rise to a determination not to employ the irregulars in the field against the enemy, but to make use of them in minor duties, such as harassing them by consuming their supplies, preventing their foraging in small parties, holding fortified places, taking charge of escorts, and even aiding the regular troops by acting in parties on their flanks.

A detachment of the army under Major Ludlow had now occupied Blackhill, a high peak on the same range as Jytock, distant from it somewhat more than two miles; and soon after Nownie was taken possession of, forming the advanced post of the army to the westward.

A further detachment had reinforced Major Ludlow from Nahn, and ground was taken in front of Blackhill, part of the camp was formed on a lower eminence, and mortars established to annoy the enemy's advanced posts with occasional shells; but cannon of a larger size than the battalion guns had been deemed necessary to batter down the stockades erected by the enemy, and eighteen-pounders were ordered up from the park of artillery.

The conveyance that had been used for bringing up the smaller guns and mortars would not answer for these; the former, with their ammunition, had been carried up with ease and safety by those admirable animals the elephants. But it was now necessary to form a road by which the larger guns might be dragged up by main strength from the park below.

This had been done already as far as the town of Nahn, and the ground they were dragged over, the precipices they were hauled up during that operation, were enough to excite wonder; but these obstacles were not to be compared with the difficulty of the country, and the length of the way they had to encounter in the construction of a road from Nahn to Battery-hill. During the space of six weeks while this was going on the army continued at rest.

The season was advancing, and the enemy far from abating in confidence; indeed the successive fortunate enterprises of Bhulbhudder Sing and Azumber Punt had inspired them greatly with that feeling, and they assured themselves of their having power to force a retreat to the east or to the west whenever necessity should appear to dictate such a measure.

A retreat to the northward, into Joobul or Bischur, would have placed the British in an awkward predicament; for it would have been exceedingly difficult to have followed them with baggage and provisions, or even light artillery, with its ammunition; whilst the carriage of heavy guns would have almost amounted to an impossibility; yet there were no means taken to prevent the enemy from adopting such a measure.

It was, however, an object of some consequence to become acquainted with the real sentiments of the inhabitants of the more northern districts; particularly of those of Joobul: and for this purpose, during this inactive period, the gentleman who accompanied the army as political agent undertook a journey towards that quarter.

He was accompanied by about 400 or 500 irregular troops, and a young officer of engineers volunteered to accompany him.

They left the camp upon the 3d of March, and, crossing the mountains of Sine and Choor, deep at that time in snow, they reached the village of Serai, in Joobul, on the 12th.

The two chief men of the state, Dangee (the Wuzzeer) and Preemoo, joined their camp that night in secret. The satisfaction of the people at the approach of this party was very evident and universal, and it had the effect of fixing the wavering resolutions of Dangee and Preemoo.

Hatred to the enemy was a strongly apparent sentiment; and the men of Poonur purgunnah, learning the advance of a British officer and detachment, collected a few days before their arrival at Serai, and surrounded the small fort of Choupal, one of the strong holds of Joobul, garrisoned by about 100 Ghoorkhas; approaching so near that one of them was killed by a shot from its walls.

A negotiation was opened by the British party with the commander of this fort; and after some demur, and the threat being held out, that the garrison should be abandoned to the rage of the inhabitants, who thirsted for their blood; and having only a provision of water for four days, he surrendered with his party, and they were received into British pay, according to capitulation.

A force of 100 irregulars was left here in the mean time, to occupy the fort, as the detachment was now obliged to return to camp, in consequence of the resumption of active measures against Jytock.

The force to act in Joobul was then increased to 700 or 800 irregulars; and the Joobulians themselves were raised by Dangee in considerable numbers: the whole were directed to act against the petty forts of the enemy in the north, in concert with the troops of the Rajah of Cooloo, who had roused himself, and commenced operations against the invaders.

At this period, the 14th of March, I reached Nahn.

The road for the eighteen-pounders was completed, and the guns were to move up the next day. It may reasonably be doubted, if ever till this period it had been contemplated to drag guns of such heavy metal up precipices so high and so rugged, and over so many of them.

When it is considered that Blackhill is 1800 feet above the level of Nahn, exclusive of a gully several hundred feet deep, that runs between them; that the length of the gun-road is five miles; that the rocks, up and down which the road necessarily passed, were covered with thick jungle, and were in many places nearly perpendicular, in all rough and ridgy, with many deep intersecting hollows; some approximation may be made towards appreciating the difficulty of the undertaking. But, I am very sure that it cannot be truly and fully understood, except by those who have witnessed it.

To an inexperienced eye it would have appeared, that the engineers had chosen the most difficult track for the course of the road; but it soon became evident that it should be brought straight up the almost perpendicular face of the rocks, instead of winding along their sides, in order to give scope for a fair straight pull of the numerous hands that were required to move the guns, which would not have been the case had there been many turns and corners intervening. The road was little more than a space made clear of wood and loose stones, and in which the small hollows were smoothed and filled up, the bank here and there cut downwards, and the edges artificially raised: in some places it wound along the brow of a dizzy precipice; at others crowned a narrow ridge, on either side of which was a dell of great depth. Such as it was, it cost much labour, and the event showed how much credit it did to those engineers who planned it.

On the 13th the guns were moved. 200 Europeans of the 53d regiment, and a number of gun Lascars, were allotted to each.

Parties of troops were detached to different heights, to protect the working party from any attempt the enemy might make to annoy them; but they offered no molestation, save now and then firing a small gun at the moving mass, which, from the distance, could do no harm. But every one of the garrison was stationed without the fort, on the hill side, viewing the operation.

Held back from too rapid a motion by the Europeans, and directed in its course by men with levers at each side, each gun made its safe descent into the valley, and they reached the bed of the nullah at an early hour in the morning.

The ascent then began, and a most laborious one it was. Main strength was necessary to drag it up the straight roads, which, viewed at a distance, seemed perpendicular; and the men in detail, with the ropes and gun attached, appeared right up and down on its face. On the edge of steep precipices again, more caution was necessary; for then, had the huge engine swerved the least to one side, it must have tumbled down to the gulf below, whence it could never have been recovered, and probably many lives must have been lost along with it.

Several times I trembled as I saw it verge towards the edge, and the ground crumble under it: but it moved on majestically, following the mass of men that drew it: and on the morning of the 2d day (16th March) two heavy guns were placed in battery.

That day and night were passed in preparations for opening a fire from all the artillery the next day.

Accordingly, at ten o'clock on the 17th of March, two eighteen-pounders, two six-pounders, two eight and a half inch mortars, two five and a half inch mortars, two five and a half inch howitzers, all opened upon one small point.

The fort of Jytock, it has been already said, is situated on a lofty point that terminates a range of hills. From this, as from the centre of a star, three ridges radiate; one runs northward in several peaks and connecting ridges towards the river Jelall. On this ridge is Peacock-hill, the position whence Richards was obliged to retreat on the 27th of December. Another runs nearly south, and ends upon the nullah, running between

Nahn and Jytock; on this there are two or three peaks crowned with small stockades.

The third runs west, and joins it to Blackhill by a neck of land of different heights, very irregular, and in some places cut deep into hollows; on a long high part of it next the peak, on which stands the fort, but divided by a deep gap, the Ghoorkha had built three stockades, known in camp by the appellations of the first, second, and third stockades.

The first stockade was placed on the brow of a hill on this neck; at the foot of which, at this period, was established the English advanced post, about 500 yards from the stockade. It was a pretty strong structure of wood, bound at the bottom with a thick stone wall; in front, stakes were planted, and small sharp-pointed splinters of bamboo were stuck all around very thickly, which would have embarrassed assailants much in an assault.

The whole breadth of the hill was occupied by this; and on each flank extending down the slope, the enemy had dug a trench, and thrown up the earth as a breast-work to protect themselves, and fire from; and it enfiladed the approaches to our post, and penetrated into it with some effect.

The second stockade was about 250 yards in the rear of this, nearer Jytock, and calculated to command the first; and the third was at a similar distance in the rear of the second, but smaller and circular in form.

From the third stockade to the fort, after crossing a deep gap, there was a steep ascent along a ridge, and the fort was defended by two stockades that encompassed it, and the whole of the hill top, one within the other, both well built with stone and wood.

The fort itself is but a small stone building about seventy feet long by fifty, with a round tower or bastion at each corner, and it only served as a magazine for ammunition and provisions.

On another part of the same peak there was a smaller stockade, and a house inhabited by some of the sirdars of the garrison; the rest, and the men with their families, lived without the two surrounding stockades, and on various parts of the hill side facing the English camp, till driven from most of them by our shot and shells.

Such was Jytock: and our first attempts were directed against the first stockade. The mortars and small guns fired at from 5 to 600 yards

N

distance; the eighteen-pounders commenced at a distance of from 900 to 1000.

The fire was kept up during the day, but the effect was not proportioned to the expense of ammunition. The line of wall presented to the fire of the artillerist did not exceed five feet in height, and situated on the brow of a hill, every ball that struck short, in its rise went clean over: the distance was too great for precise practice. The enemy did not return a shot to this heavy fire; they had no guns that could tell against ours, and they exposed themselves so little, that the fire of shells could do them but little harm.

By the evening the centre of the stockade appeared sunk and shattered, but not to a degree sufficient in the opinion of the commanding officer to warrant an assault.

On the 19th the guns continued to batter; and though, during the night, the enemy had certainly in some measure repaired the damage done by our fire, it was by the evening of that day reduced to a state which many persons considered as incapable of resisting a spirited assault from our troops.

A working party was employed during the night to advance a pathway under cover of the hill, to a point within about 350 yards of the place, and to establish there a battery for the reception of two six-pounders, which were ready by the morning of the 19th. During this also, an irregular fire was kept up from the breaching guns and mortars, and the stockade was farther ruined.

On the morning of the 20th at daylight, one eighteen-pounder was moved forward to the post whence the mortars played, and the other was left a little in the rear; from this distance they opened with effect about nine o'clock, so that in an hour the wall of the stockade was nearly destroyed.

The movement of bringing forward the guns attracted from the enemy, who had hitherto been perfectly quiet, a sharp irregular fire of musketry and jinjals from the stockade and the trenches, and bushes on either side, which penetrated into our batteries, and enfiladed the approaches to them, so that many of our men began to drop, killed and wounded.

The Ghoorkhas showed themselves with much gallantry, exposing their persons even in the very points at which our large shot were directed, and which demolished their defences. This fire was returned on our side by parties of Sepoys and irregular troops, as well as by two companies of Europeans detached in advance, or on either flank, to act as sharpshooters, and oppose or destroy those of the enemy, who galled our men severely.

But the advantage of ground was in favour of our adversaries, and they suffered (we had reason to fear), less than we did. By evening we had upwards of thirty killed and wounded. The stockade was reduced to a heap of ruins; but no storm was ordered.

Working parties were each night sent on duty, and an advanced post was established about 100 yards from the stockade; some attempts at repairing the damage done to it had been made by the enemy during the night; but on the 21st it was again reduced to ruins. The same irregular fire of sharpshooters continued night and day with little intermission, and ever considerably to our disadvantage.

Matters remained still in the same situation on the 22d; but a few of our irregulars, sent to act as sharpshooters, took advantage of a slackness of the enemy's fire in the afternoon, and crept up the face of the hill nearly to the trench they stood in, when a smart interchange of musketry took place, and a few Sepoys, who were stationed at hand for the purpose of supplying piquets and sharpshooters, moved forward of their own accord to assist them. There is little doubt that they would have turned the enemy's flank, and before he could have been materially assisted from the fort, the trench would have been gained, and probably the stockade; but the commander of the army did not approve of their forwardness, and ordered them to be recalled; and they retreated under a smart fire from the enemy (who now increased in numbers), and regained their post with some loss.

More than one opportunity of a like sort offered to bring on a general engagement, or to assault, with every appearance of probability of success, the stockade, which was thus our stumbling-block; and those who were eager for the advance of the army, and were generally considered competent judges of the subject, felt some degree of surprise and disappointment at the loss of such occasions.

But the commander was of a different opinion, and the army lay in camp doing duty in the trenches, watching the motions of the enemy, and waiting with no slight degree of impatience for orders that might put an end to the daily and provoking casualties that occurred, without the power of annoying in their turn; and might cause a resumption of active measures against an enemy they earnestly wished to take vengeance on for the various sufferings they had occasioned them.

No alteration, however, took place for many days. The advanced posts continued an interchange of musquetry which daily destroyed our men; and towards the end of the month it was understood that all active measures were to be abandoned, and the siege turned into a blockade; intelligence that spread considerable gloom and uneasiness through the army, which could not understand why so much pains had been taken and expense incurred to batter down a place, on which, when apparently open, no attempt was even made.

On the 30th March a party of irregulars, left in a post to the northward of Jytock, across the Jelall river, on a height called Nerrain Keteeba, were surprised by a detachment from the garrison of Jytock, and driven from it with a loss of 100 killed, and sixty to seventy wounded.

This disaster was chiefly owing to the treachery and cowardice of one of the native officers, who commanded a part of the force, and who, on the assault of the enemy, left with his men the remaining part, who were chiefly asleep, to be surprised and cut in pieces. The enemy lost hardly a man.

Upon the 1st April Major Richards, with a detachment of 1000 regulars and about 700 irregulars, moved from Nahn to take a position to the eastward of Jytock.

Having been forced to take a circuitous route, he did not reach his destination till the second day, on the morning of which (the 2d April) having moved before daybreak, he was attacked in the gray of dawn by a party of the enemy, consisting of 800 of the *Goruck Pulton*, or chosen battalion, and a force of 400 swordsmen.

Although it was an ambush on the part of the enemy, yet even they seem to have been deficient in intelligence, probably from our troops having left their ground at a very early hour. They suffered some companies of light infantry to advance within a very short distance unmolested, while our officers were uncertain whether the men they saw in the imperfect morning light were not a party of the irregulars that had gone on in advance.

Thus before either party knew who the other was, or ventured on a hostile movement, they were close together.

The brunt of the affair fell entirely on the advanced companies of light infantry, and a few men of the 13th regiment native infantry. On the first few shots from the enemy they formed rapidly within less than forty yards, receiving with perfect steadiness a smart discharge of musquetry and rockets. Led on by their officers, they then charged, and drove their adversaries from height to height, pushing with vigour up the hills, and never allowing them time or opportunity to form, till they at last fled in confusion.

The loss they sustained was about thirty killed, or to forty, with a proportion of wounded, and many prisoners; in all about 150 men placed *hors de combat*.

Among those who were taken was their commander, Qazee Azumber Punt, the same who defeated the irregulars at Chinalgurgh on the 21st February, and who now fell into the hands of these same irregulars on an occasion of less seeming peril, being discovered out breathed in the pursuit, with several of his orderly men who would not desert him. He was esteemed one of their best officers.

Major Richards established himself in the post of Punjal, a peak separated from the fort by a deep ravine to the north, without any further opposition.

During this time it appeared fully that the enemy were much pressed for provisions, and most uncomfortable in their cooped up situation. Deserters every day came in, who described the garrison as starving, and as parting with every thing they had to procure scanty supplies of that food which their commanders could not or would not give them. But it is singular and admirable that these privations, extending not only to their own persons, and laying them under the necessity of stripping themselves of all their property, but associating in their sufferings their women and children, so far from producing any mutinous spirit, or murmur of disobedience, or even damping their ardour in the cause in which they were embarked, only gave a character of despair and recklessness to the steady resolution they appeared to have come to of dying at their posts.

The deserters themselves (insulated examples of the power of misery in overcoming principle) talked of themselves as wretched men, forced by famine to fly the cause they had hitherto fought for, and reported those whom they had left behind as starving. When it was asked how those could remain, and how they would defend the posts entrusted to them? they answered, "they would die in their trenches, hopeless of success, for the sake of honour, and for their debt of salt." This latter expression, as is well known, is used in the East to mark the devotion and gratitude which is due to those whose bread they have eaten; and from thence gratitude in general derives the only name it is known by in India. A man who forgets or neglects his duty to the master who feeds him, is styled "nimmuc-harām," that is, wicked to his salt, or debt of gratitude, and is considered with detestation.

Those who talked thus, indeed, bore the marks of famine in their persons; they were supported in the mean time, and in the end entertained in British pay; for the cause being once abandoned for which they had fought, whilst it fed them, these soldiers of fortune had no scruple in embracing any other, even the opposite one, and showing equal ardour in its defence. They, however, were never employed against their old friends by this detachment of the army.

On the 12th of April a detachment of the 26th regiment was sent to a point a little to the northward of Battery Hill, with a view of checking the foraging excursions of the enemy on that side; and on the night of the 16th it was advanced to a height that commanded the river Jelall, and prevented the garrison from availing themselves of the corn on its banks.

A party of the light infantry battalion occupied its ground, and intermediate stockades were placed to serve as connecting posts between the more principal ones, and occupied by irregular troops, so that the fort was nearly hemmed in on all sides.

The Ghoorkhas sometimes attacked these small posts by surprise, and drove our miserable irregulars from them for the time with considerable slaughter; but they made no attempt either to attack our regular positions, or to retreat from their own, but remained inactive, as if in stupified suspense, and perhaps anxiously awaiting the success or discomfiture of the force opposed to Ummr Sing and his army in Malown.

Foraging parties were now sent out from camp in every direction to destroy the grain now fit to reap within ten or fifteen miles round the fort; a duty cruelly severe upon the husbandman, but rendered necessary to enforce the strictness of a blockade, for hunger drove the enemy to the most daring efforts to supply himself with provisions to recruit his famished troops; and we now had a proof of the mean and mercenary nature of the wretched creatures we were attempting to free from the iron bondage of the Ghoorkha sway, and how little we could rely on their co-operation. They were detected conveying into the fort of their enemies for their sustenance the corn which they frequently purchased in our own bazar, or which, cut in the vicinity, they could have sold there for its full value; and the fear of the just punishment that awaited their detection was insufficient to check the impulses of avarice, and shut the door on this trifling supply.

From this time to the 6th of May nothing occurred worth recording.

The success of General Ochterlony against Buchtee Thappa on the heights of Deounthul, and Soorajegurh near Malown, and of Colonel Nichols in Kumaoon against Hustee Dhull Thappa and Bunsah, which ended in the capture of Almorah, were both published in camp, which clearly showed that the campaign was drawing to a successful close in these parts. But these circumstances produced no movement on the part of our commander at Blackhill, and we left the camp in the same state of inactivity in which it had for so long a time before remained.

The signature of the articles of capitulation between General Ochterlony and Ummr Sing Thappa, which put the British force in possession of Malown, and stipulated for the evacuation of all the country to the west of the Kaleenuddee, or western branch of the river Gogra by the Ghoorkha forces, cut short the indecision of the commander opposed to Runjore Sing, and put an end to his intentions of so late an assault as was understood to have been in contemplation at the end of so long and tedious a blockade, that had in truth reduced the enemy to a state that they could not have long offered resistance; for, on taking possession of Jytock when evacuated according to treaty, there was not a day's consumption of grain in the place, and it became a matter of wonder how they had subsisted so long.

Nearly 1500 muskets marched out, and with women and children, the number might reach 2500 souls, who were thus released from a state of famine; and when the steady resistance which the Ghoorkha commanders offered to our attempts, whether of force or of negotiation, are considered, coupled with the severe privations they so long suffered, and to which they had subjected their troops, and the absolute hopelessness of any relief, which must have darkened the latter part of the blockade, it cannot, I think, fail to add to the admiration so justly due to their steady gallantry, although it wants the bloody seal which was set to it at Kalunga.

It is not easy to say which may claim the highest meed of praise, the commanders, for steady determination to persevere under privations of so heavy a nature, under such hopeless circumstances, and subjecting themselves to the fury of a hungry soldiery; or their soldiers, for cheerful endurance of these privations, for steady and zealous discharge of their duty, and total freedom from any attempt at mutiny, or even from unavailing but embarrassing murmurs.

The conduct of Runjore Sing Thappa in general, and his demeanour when brought into the presence of the commander of the troops in particular, was observed as being modest but dignified, and marked with uncommon propriety; and in spite of their many atrocities, in spite of the rigour of their sway over the unhappy people they had conquered, the Ghoorkhas in general left with such of their subduers as were witness to their conduct on this occasion, a most favourable impression of regard for their cheerful good humour, their quiet and orderly behaviour, and their high sense of honour, which could not but strongly engage the good will of those who studied their character, especially when placed in contrast with the wretched creatures whose country they had so long occupied.

Jytock, and its surrounding posts, were evacuated by the enemy early in May, and a British force immediately occupied them. When in our possession it was evident how ineffectual the defences would have proved against a vigorous attack, and that the stockades would have made no opposition after a short application of the power of cannon.

PART III.

JOURNEY WITH THE POLITICAL AGENT FOR THE ARMY OF GENERAL MARTINDALE.

CHAPTER VIII.

From the 1st to the 6th May preparations were made for a journey with the political agent for the army of Major-General Martindale.

While the force under that officer was investing the fort of Jytock, and the fort and positions of Malown, occupied by Ummr Sing Thappa, were besieged by the army commanded by Major-General Ochterlony, it was deemed expedient to detach a force to the northward, which might assist the troops of those petty chiefs, who were well disposed, to destroy the scattered parties and garrisons of the enemy in the remoter and more central parts of the hills, and awe those whose dispositions were either not so friendly, or so well declared, into measures of co-operation.

The enemy's force, which occupied the country between Malown and Jytock, did not much exceed 800 or 1000 men, and it was chiefly dispersed in small garrisons, seldom exceeding 200 men, who were posted in strong holds, and posts, and forts, over the country.

At this period it had been considerably diminished from its original strength, for wherever the inhabitants of the mountains dared to show their dispositions, and thought themselves more powerful than the force which controlled them, they gave a loose to their fury, and massacred every Ghoorkha soldier they could reach.

Harassed and dispersed, and unassisted by aid from either of the principal sources, the scattered Ghoorkha forces assembled, and united under their commander, Kirtee Rana, an old and brave soldier. For some time they kept possession of a chain of posts, extending above the left bank of the Sutlej, in a line towards Irkee.

Their chief position at this time was Nowagurh, where about 800 men were concentrated. They had only one or two forts besides, strong by nature, and well provided with provisions and water, such as Racongudh and Mornee, Zetheldout.

The force under Kirtee Rana wished to make good a retreat, either to Malown or Jytock, and to prevent this was an object of considerable importance.

And it was still more to be desired that in case either Ummr Sing Thappa, or Runjore Sing Thappa, should attempt to retreat and form a junction, the roads should be occupied, and every possible advantage taken of the ground, and every obstacle thrown in the way of such a measure.

The troops of the Rajah of Cooloo were sent across the Sutlej to co-operate with those of Bischur and Joobul in the above measures, and it was judged proper that a British officer should accompany and command the troops now to be detached, who might have power to negotiate as well as to direct their efforts.

Mr. William Fraser, the political agent attending the army, had collected much information relative to the country and its chiefs, the positions of the enemy, and their resources; and had already penetrated into Joobul, as has been mentioned, and successfully negotiated with its chief, at the same time gaining over by capitulation the Ghoorkha fortress of Choupal. He therefore received the orders of government to depart on this service.

On this occasion I was fortunate enough to accompany him; and subsequent occurrences, which will be related in their places, occasioned a much longer extension of our tour than at first was contemplated.

From the 1st to the 5th May, 1815, preparations were made for the march. At this period it was not thought expedient to detach any of the regular troops from the service round Jytock; irregulars, therefore, *alone* formed the force that accompanied us, and they were rather a motley assemblage, consisting of parties from various and distant countries of the East.

A party of about 600 men was formed of Mewatties, Goujers, Sikhs, and soldiers of fortune from different parts of the plains; they were all armed with swords and matchlocks, but their various garb and dress gave them an appearance which held uniformity to scorn, and many of them were poor, old, and ragged.

To these were added between 80 and 100 Patans from Afghanistan, similarly armed with the rest, but more soldierly and imposing in their appearance; many of these with red hair, blue eyes, and clear florid complexions, generally tinging the eyelids with antimony. Their dress was better and more uniform, and every five men had a large flag upon a spear, which at least gave a gay air to the march.

Next in detail were the Ghoorkha garrison of Choupal, who had capitulated on condition of being received into the British service, and who from 100, of which number they originally consisted, had been augmented by desertions from the garrison of Jytock to nearly double.

In these was perhaps to be placed as much confidence as in any troops we had; for, like other Asiatics, they fight for pay, and whose bread they eat, his cause they will defend against country, friends, and relations.

The Ghoorkhas exhibited a more tattered appearance than the others, for they had not as yet had the means of supplying themselves with necessaries.

Every man stuck in his waist the national weapon, the *cookree;* each had likewise a sword, a weapon they can well use; and they also carried the old and almost useless muskets, which they used in the service of Nepāl, some of which were manufactured by themselves, and others were obtained, previously to the war, in trade with Calcutta: such as were totally unserviceable were exchanged for matchlocks.

There are several manufactories of muskets in the Nepāl dominions, and considering the disadvantages under which they labour, they are fabricated in a pretty sufficient manner.

The lock is the part that first becomes useless.

The want of flints too is one cause which will always render their firelocks less efficient. We used to remark that the muskets of those, in the stockades and trenches, frequently snapped and missed fire many times running.

In addition to the above assemblage, a party of about thirty men belonging to the irregular horse, under the command of Colonel James Skinner, volunteered their services to accompany this little army, on every man of whom the most implicit reliance might be placed in case of actual service.

The well known corps, to whom these horse belonged, has, ever since the campaign of Lord Lake against the Mahrattas, continued under the command of the very meritorious and brave officer who first raised them, and by whose name they are known; and the character it has always preserved, and the services it has performed, are such as to have gained to it a well merited distinction, and a fame far superior to the usual estimate of irregulars. It has lately been augmented to 3000 men, in every one of whom their commander places the most implicit confidence, for the choice is made from character, and well known usefulness.

Such was the detachment that now entered the hills, under the command, and for the objects and services, before mentioned. They were sent during the time of preparation to rendezvous at Rajgurh, an old fortress four days march from the camp at Blackhill.

Those who have witnessed the march of a detachment, and the bustle and noise, and almost confusion which seems to attend it even in the plains, where carriage is in general more plentiful and more easy, the road broad, and admitting of wheel carriages, and of many persons going abreast, may form some idea what such must be when all baggage and provision must be carried on the shoulders of men (coolies), on paths where only one person can go on the breadth, and of course considerable attention is required to preserve a footing; where the difficulty of procuring even such carriage is always great, and the more so, when not only present necessaries but future provision for a large number of men is required to accompany their march.

On the morning of the 6th of May, 1815, we took leave of the camp at Blackhill, and by eleven o'clock began our march, which from the various troops composing our force, the servants of different classes who accompanied us, the wild figures of the hill porters who carried our baggage, provisions, stores, and ammunition, and the loiterers who were always joining, was a strange and grotesque procession.

It was a fresh and delightful morning, a heavy rain on the day before having cooled and cleared the air.

The lofty succession of cliffs before us rose without end, in full contrast to the smiling plains that lay spread at their feet; a spoil richly inviting to the Tartar hordes of the north. No wonder that their courage and enterprise were sharpened to achieve it; nor is it surprising, though lamentable, that so fair a country should in all ages have been an object for conquest, a prey to invaders, and a scene of bloodshed.

Our course lay somewhat to the north-west for nearly three miles, upon a road formed by the Ghoorkhas, that runs the whole way to Irkee. It is cut in the face of the hill with some labour, and though neither broad nor smooth is better than the miserable stony paths that in general lead along the hill sides.

Diverging from this, after descending and ascending some intervening steep ridges, we reached the Jelāll river, and encamped a few hundred yards above the stream on its northern bank.

The latter part of the march was toilsome from heat, being generally in low valleys, or up steep ascents, through a country rather parched, and of little beauty. Bathing in the cool pure waters of the Jelāll towards evening proved refreshing and salutary.

The distance we travelled this day did not exceed nine miles, although frequent halts for rest, and for admitting of our servants keeping up with us, protracted it to a late hour.

The village near which our small tent was pitched was called Seekhoul, poor and miserable, but pleasantly situate.

We rose early, but could not get in marching order before seven o'clock. Our course, still northerly, lay along the steep ascent of a sweet and romantic valley, which commencing nearly at the crest of the Sine range, under the village of Chinalgurh, runs down to the Jelāll.

It is watered by a clear stream, which bounds from rock to rock, and serves to irrigate a very considerable cultivation in the middle and lower parts of the glen; for which purpose it is drawn from the main body in little rills, and distributed very simply and neatly among the small fields, spreading a bright verdure over the ground in their course.

Our walk was thus very pleasant; we were sheltered from the heat of the sun, and our path was among these little streams, whose brinks were richly covered with vegetation, almost screening them from the eye, while their sounds refreshed the ear.

The cultivation of this valley is entirely on government land, which is tilled by the zemindars, who receive only a portion of it, paying the rest to the state.

We passed near the top of the glen, under the rock on which the village of Chinalgurh is curiously perched. This was the scene of the defeat of our irregulars by Azumber Punt Qaree with a very inferior force.

Chinalgurh itself overhangs the deep chasm through which the above-mentioned stream has its rapid course among a fine grove of old trees; it is a larger village than most in the neighbourhood, and from its lofty situation commands a view over all the hills to the southward, even to the plains.

Still ascending, but slanting towards the west, the road became more rugged, and lost its beauty, leading along the curiously cut ledges and masses of limestone, of which the whole hill is formed, and which the weather has worn into the most fantastic shapes; and about nine o'clock, we reached Dēener Kēener, a large village very picturesquely situated in the gorge where we cross the ridge. Among a number of strange and romantic situations, none perhaps exceeds in these respects Chinalgurh and Dēener Kēener.

The latter, from its narrow and lofty ridge, commands a view, on either side, of as extensive a nature as a mountainous country will admit; while valleys nearly as wild as such a country can produce, stretch on the one hand to the river Girree, and on the other to the Jelāll.

Looking down the former towards the north the majestic mountain *Choor* bursts on the eye, through a vista formed by the rocky cliffs that on either side of the gorge almost close over the village, and shows its large brown bosom scarred by many deep and dark ravines, all of which pour their waters into the Girree that flows at its feet.

Nearer, the wooded and rocky sides of the valley approach on either side; their bases and its bottom are hid from view, but the darkness of the hollow showed significantly the depth of the chasm we were to descend: it is truly a grand scene.

The village itself is worthy of notice: it is larger than any we had seen, and is next to Nahn in size. Many of the houses consist of two stories, although flat roofed; and we remarked something like streets and ranges, which took the line and form of the solid ledges of marble rock they are built upon, which is quite polished by continual friction.

To the northward, just under one of those ledges, seventy or eighty feet below the village, lay a fine rich bed of wheat of twenty to thirty acres, which was at this time fully ripe.

Resting here for half an hour, we commenced our descent from the gorge down a precipitous path, which for steepness, roughness, and danger, is surpassed by few in the country. The danger is much increased indeed by the polished smoothness of its rough parts; the rock along which it leads being wholly of marble, of great hardness, and cut by the violence of the weather into the most uncouth shapes. It presents nothing yielding or tenacious to the footstep, but by the treading of years has acquired a smoothness and slipperiness that calls for the greatest attention and caution in proceeding, particularly when wearing iron-shod shoes, as we did.

The path in fact is formed of a narrow and very irregular flight of steps along the face of the rock, leaving on one side a dreary precipice of many hundred feet; and it was surprising how the heavily loaded hill-porters, each carrying a weight of not less than sixty pounds, safely and with apparent ease and unconcern descended this difficult pass.

It was matter of some regret that our time did not admit of a sketch of either of the noble views from Deener Keener or of this pass, which would have given a fine idea of our mountain descents.

Continuing to descend for a considerable way, the glen opened out, and we saw several miserable villages. At one of these, called Bahun, we witnessed a very extraordinary practice to which the inhabitants of the hills submit their young children. Several straw sheds are constructed on a bank, above which a cold clear stream is led to water their fields, and a small portion of this, probably of three fingers breadth, is brought into the shed by a hollow stick or piece of bark, and falls from this spout into a small drain, which carries it off about two feet below.

The women bring their children to these huts in the heat of the day, and having lulled them to sleep, and wrapt their bodies and feet warm in a blanket, they place them on a small bench or tray horizontally, in such a way that the water shall fall upon the crown of the head, just keeping the whole top wet with its stream.

We saw two under this operation, and several others came in while we remained, to place their children in a similar way. Males and females are equally used thus, and their sleep seemed sound and unruffled.

The mode too of lulling asleep was singular: seizing the infant with both arms, with these, aided by the knee, they gave it a violent rotatory motion, that seemed rather calculated to shake the child to pieces than to produce the soft effect of slumber.

It was, however, unerring in its effects. One of the children was intently looking at the strangers, and eyeing the dresses and arms with every symptom of strong curiosity and excitement; no signs of drowsiness could be traced, yet the vigorous operation admitted of no pause; its eyes gradually closed, and in thirty seconds it was fast asleep.

On inquiry, we were informed that this singular process for sleeping and bathing the children is universally used throughout the hills where there is the means of using it, under a notion that it is very salutary to keep the head cool, and that it increases hardihood and strength. Had I not witnessed it, I could not have believed this custom.

One or two women usually sit with the children of the rest, whilst they are employed in domestic or agricultural pursuits.

The women whom we saw had mild features, much in the style of the Hindoos of the plains; they were fair, or rather of a light yellow, without any ruddiness. They evinced no objections to be looked at, but with perfect propriety and modesty answered our questions, and continued their work. They said that they were Rajpoots.

As we continued our course, the dell which had spread out and received the waters of two similar ravines, again contracted with an additional degree of solemn grandeur, and infinitely more attractive beauty.

The wild and rugged peaks almost met each other on either side, covered with finely varied foliage; and the stream sunk into a bed just sufficient to contain it, where, occasionally seen, but always heard, it tumbled over rocks and falls concealed by thickets of roses, jasmines, barberries, willows, and many other lovely or odoriferous shrubs.

Sometimes both rocky banks approached so near, and the foliage so closed overhead, that the light of day was excluded; and then we wandered among dropping rocks, and little rills stealing down the banks covered with mosses and ferns, overshadowed by these sweet thickets, and now and then by a prodigious crag which defied vegetation, and towered high above; then it would open, and give to view a wild village perched on the ledge of a hill, and the wilder and more extravagant shapes of the cliffs, which form the north-west face of the Sine range, rising over all.

Then another vista would open and disclose the furrowed bosom of Choor, and the deep glen of the Girree.

The changes that occurred were endless, and not susceptible of adequate description: imagination cannot paint a wilder, more beautiful, or in some places more horrid glen.

We emerged from its depths, however, and mounted its sides by a rocky path; and on arriving at the top of the ridge the river Girree lay beneath us, winding through a narrow but green and wooded bed. It was now a sweet and romantic mountain stream, but in the rains, and whilst the snow on the lower hills continues to melt, it must be a savage and dangerous torrent.

It is difficult to give an idea of the size of a stream even by comparison with another; every one forms his own estimate, and very different degrees of magnitude would probably be suggested to the mind of each man who heard the comparison.

The Girree was now fordable in many places, where it spread out on a bed of gravel, and at such points might extend to thirty-five or forty yards across: the deepest part was about mid-thigh deep; above or below, it perhaps contracted to a deep rapid torrent, rushing through a space not thirty feet broad. We descended to its bank by a long wearisome path irregularly winding along the face of the hills of its glen.

The hills on the opposite side assume a character of features quite different from those we left behind; the dells and ridges do not appear so sharp, the peaks are more rounded and lumpy, and there is more swell in the ground; the whole, perhaps, as viewed from the southern bank of the Girree, is less picturesque, but on a more majestic scale.

We arrived at the banks of the Girree at about two o'clock, but after a rest of near two hours we proceeded upwards along its course for several miles; and fording it, reached our encamping ground at a village called Thour, by six o'clock.

It is situated at the upper part of a piece of ground nearly level, of from thirty to forty acres; and having a view of the course of the Girree, and being embellished with many fine large trees, and much copsewood, it may be considered a very pleasant spot.

The march of to-day, we were informed, may somewhat exceed eleven miles. I should have thought it more, but it led through scenery which would have made greater fatigue light.

Asia was almost lost in our imagination: a native of any part of the British isles might here have believed himself wandering among the lovely and romantic scenes of his own country. The delight of such association of feeling can only be understood by those, who have lingered out a long term of expatriation, and who anxiously desire the moment of reunion with their native land.

The nature of the mountains, as well as the scenery on the Sine range, is very different from that on the southern side of the river Jelāll, which has already been attempted.

The Sine range, indeed, as far as it has fallen under our inspection, forms a complete exception to the general nature of the country; it is entirely limestone, and this is worn into the strangest crevices and lumps, perfectly distinct from the sharp ridges of the Jytock hills, or the rounder loftiness of those to the north of the Girree.

The mountain itself assumes the character of its component parts, and is rough, dark, and shapeless.

It was remarkable, but distinctly obvious, that thus far the northern and north-eastern face of the hills were the most wooded, and somewhat least rugged; and that the southern and south-western exposure was always most rough, bare, and brown: this more particularly applies to the hills south of the Jelāll, though sufficiently traceable upon the Sine range.

This hill is far more lofty than any we have yet crossed; its height has been conjectured at 8000 feet; but this is exceedingly vague, and I suspect much overrated, perhaps between 6 and 7000 may not be a very erroneous measure for the highest peak.

The termination of the limestone, and the commencement of slate, which predominates to the north of the Girree, is pretty distinctly marked at this point by the bed of the river; in some places the rock on either side is composed of the latter, but it extends no considerable distance up the hill on the opposite bank.

The waters of the Girree, as well as of the Jelāll, abound in fish of several sorts, some of which are tolerably good. While resting from our march on the banks of the former, I attempted to catch some with a rod and line, but without success; none of the baits I was acquainted with, or was in possession of, attracted them, nor was an artificial fly more seducing.

The village of Thour (which hardly deserves the name) consists of one or two houses nearly entire, and a few others in ruins, but it was the first we saw in which an alteration in the style of building was observable.

Instead of being built of stones and mud, with flat earthen roofs, as those we had left behind universally were, the only good house here was constructed of loose but well-shaped stone, bound by beams of wood: and the roof raised to a pitch was covered with rough slate, far overhanging the body of the house, as well as a wooden viranda or gallery which projected from the upper story; this large roof was supported by strong beams of wood, the ends of which, and the cornices under the eaves of overhanging slate, were rudely carved and sculptured. The whole had somewhat of a Chinese air, and was interesting enough.

The chief inhabitants, two Gosseins (a sect of religious mendicants well known in India, who of course during their wandering in their religious vocations profess celibacy), came out with offerings of milk and fruit to meet us. These men had wisely quitted their wandering life and vows of celibacy, and had taken wives, and settled here as tillers of the ground.

A large number of peacocks, probably encouraged on account of their sacred character, were ranging about the fields, and these, with one partridge, were the only appearances of game, or almost indeed of animals (except a large monkey near the Girree), that we saw in the march of this day.

May 8th.—We resumed our march this morning by eight o'clock, and began to ascend, somewhat gradually, a hollow behind the village: which by degrees led us to the crest of the heights above it, and we passed several deep black clefts on our way to the top of the ridge.

On the rocks above one of them we saw some deer, at which we fired unsuccessfully from a great distance.

Nearly at the top of our ascent we refreshed ourselves by a halt under a cool dropping rock, which overhung a recess near the path, and down a cleft in which a small rill of most delicious water trickled, which, as well as the verdure around, and the opportunity of resting so comfortably, was very grateful to the thirsty and weary traveller. Several fine large spreading trees of a peculiar nature, somewhat resembling the acacia, scenting the air with myriads of fragrant blossoms, grew around.

On reaching the top of the hill we looked down upon a valley more susceptible of cultivation, and better cultivated than any spot of equal extent we had yet seen, and at least a dozen villages appeared studding it in every direction.

These have a very novel and picturesque effect from the style of their architecture. In every one there are at least two or three lofty towers, rising to the height of five and six stories, with the same overhanging roofs, but many are partly decayed, and exactly resemble the ruins of old castles frowning from their heights over the valley.

Here we observed several peach trees in full bearing, and many noble walnut trees full of young fruit. A tree was likewise pointed out to us which had abundance of unripe fruit upon it of a pleasing acid, said to be very delicious when ripe, and called Kai-phul; we never had an opportunity of judging, though even now it was grateful; the fruit somewhat resembled a mulberry, but had a stone in the centre.

A little further on we reached and halted at a village called Dhrotee for a few minutes, where our notice was attracted by the first apricot and larch trees we had seen: the former were large and spreading, and full of unripe fruit; the latter had every character of the larch which is common in Britain, but their foliage was somewhat darker. Pear trees, also, cultivated, large, and full of fruit, were found there, with large luxuriant mulberry trees, and many other fruit and odoriferous shrubs.

The large extent of corn under the eye was nearly ripe; the reapers were at work; the wild brown hill with swelling round peaks rose above us, and but for the colour of our attendants, the whole scene had so highland an air, that it was difficult to believe it to be Indian.

The name of the valley I would gladly have learnt, but it seems that none in particular attached to the whole; each village has a distinct name, and the whole forms part of a purgunnah or district, the name of which I have forgotten.

We continued our course up the glen, which is bare, and the sides of which are very steep; and passing the gorge at the top, we soon saw the troops encamped at a very short distance in a hollow near the ruined fort of Rajgurh, and we reached our station by eleven in the forenoon.

The country during the short march of this day, which does not exceed eight miles, has assumed an appearance as different from that we traversed yesterday, as it did from any that had before fallen under observation.

The hills were perhaps not less rugged than those we left behind, but they were on a far greater scale, and the roundness and largeness of their features made their roughness less perceptible; and, in fact, they had not that sharp ridgy aspect which so remarkably characterises those nearer to the plains. Wood was much less abundant. The mountains are only covered with a short grass, which appears as if it was continually pastured on by cattle; this was more strongly remarkable towards the head of the glen, where the hills precisely resembled those of the Scotch highland sheepwalks, totally bare, save of the brown dry grass, their black rocky tops rising unvaried by a single shrub even of the smallest size.

CHAPTER IX.

THE novel and singular style of the buildings here also contributed to the change in the scenery. The towers, which are so lofty and remarkable, are not the habitations of the vulgar. They are temples for the gods, and it is understood that no one absolutely resides in them; they are frequently ornamented with rude sculptures in wood.

The houses, however, are also more lofty than those we have left, consisting of two and frequently of three stories, in the upper of which the family commonly resides, and this is surrounded by a balcony of wood inclosed, which projects from six to eight feet; beyond this the roof too projects some feet, so that the body of the house below the balcony appears small and diminutive.

The lower story is always appropriated to cattle, and if there be a middle one it is most commonly occupied by lumber.

Few, however, of the villages that we observed had any strong appearance of prosperity. Half the houses were in ruins, and some were totally deserted. They partook of the misfortune of the state, and the severe rule of the Ghoorkha conquerors had been sorely felt.

To judge, however, by the difficulty with which cultivation is attended, and by the successful progress which has been made in covering the steep and lofty hills with crops, both here and in the country through which we have passed, the inhabitants must be a patient and industrious race, when it is considered that a spot of ground of any considerable extent seldom occurs where even the rude plough which they employ can be used without the previous assistance of art; that the side of the mountains must be cut and levelled to produce a field for tillage; that water must be conducted for the purposes of irrigation, frequently from a great distance; and when the insufficient means, together with the rude tools they possess to effect this, are observed, it will perhaps excite wonder that corn-tillage should have been attempted at all in a land that appears only calculated at best for grazings; and it must surely appear astonishing that the inhabitants, thinly scattered as they are, can raise as much grain as is requisite for their own support, and can spare a portion to those of other districts and countries which are not so well supplied. Their method of cultivation is so ingenious and neat that it merits a particular description.

As level ground is seldom to be met with, the least rocky faces of the hills are cut into a succession of terraces, rising above each other; which operation produces a number of strips of level ground, more or less narrow according to the steepness of the hills, and more or less regular according to its ruggedness. Great labour and care are bestowed on this operation. It is generally necessary to build a retaining wall, to support the edge of the small strip of ground, of a height corresponding with that of the bank, and much attention is paid to levelling its surface, so that water may neither rest upon it, nor, in running off, carry away any portion of its scanty soil: but this exact level is also necessary to fit it for receiving the benefit of irrigation; and every rivulet (with which indeed the hills abound) is diverted from its course at a height sufficient for their purpose (consequently often from a great distance); and led by small drains, constructed with much neatness and skill, first to the higher cultivated spots, from which it flows to the rest, or is again collected into a stream, after saturating them, and carried to another and lower range of fields.

Sometimes these streams are carried across a deep dell by means of long hollow trees, supported by high piles of stones, for the purpose of irrigating the opposite side of the valley, where water could less easily have been conveyed from above.

This irrigating system is chiefly necessary for the rice crop, which, though not put into the ground till the rains have set in, frequently requires the assistance of artificial flooding. The spring and summer crop, however, of wheat and barley scarcely less require this aid, as showers are often scanty from the time of sowing till the corn is full.

This practice of cutting the hill-faces into small fields has given to them, all over the country, a peculiar ridgy appearance, which, next to their great ruggedness and steepness, chiefly attracts a traveller's eye: it produces a strange regularity, which frequently takes from the dignity of the landscape.

It is surprising how universal this practice has been: there is no mountain side, however steep, where rock does not predominate, but shows this mark of former tillage; indeed, the traces are all that for the most part are seen, and this denotes either that the land becomes after some years unfit for tillage, and is abandoned for a new and more kindly soil, or that in former times there must have been a far larger population, and more extended cultivation, which has now been abandoned.

Both these cases may in some degree consist with fact, though I am led to think that the first is not common, as they are well acquainted with the uses of manure; and experience would soon tell them, whether a large tract of land was likely to repay their labours, without risking so much in reducing to tillage, by so costly a process, that which must afterwards be abandoned.

The latter case is too certain and too apparent. The population has diminished deplorably; every where, villages are seen in ruins, and fields run lately to decay; and, judging from present appearances as well as from general report, even corrected by allowances for exaggeration, we may safely conclude, that, before the Ghoorkha conquest, a great portion of the cultivation now waste then bore crops, and the villages now destroyed were then inhabited.

It may here be observed that a reticular appearance, somewhat resembling that of the abandoned cultivation, is observable on those hills which are bare of wood, and chiefly appropriated to pasture: this they obtain probably from the numerous paths, made by the feet of animals while grazing. The slope is too great for wandering at will over the mountain side, and they are constrained to keep the paths first suggested by the inequalities of the hill, and graze on each side as far as they can reach; thus forming little tracks that intersect each other in innumerable places, producing an appearance at a little distance as if a net were spread on the slope of the surface.

The appearance, which the mode of cultivation above described gives to a country, is very singular; and when (as was the case with much that we saw) it is flooded by irrigation, the singularity is heightened by the aspect of a hilly country partly under water. The inhabitants, indeed, appear to trust much more to this mode of supplying moisture than to the rain which falls, particularly in the vicinity of the plains; and this may account for their levelling all their fields, of whatever size they may be, even where a patch of ground is found sufficiently equal to render it practicable for the plough, and which in any other country would be subjected to that instrument: without regard to the undulation it might have, they still level it as much as possible, dividing it into larger ledges according to its fall, with parapets and dyked faces as usual.

This, however, was less the case as we advanced farther into the hills, where perhaps the rains may be less violent and more seasonable. The fields there were permitted to take their natural form and extent, following uncontrolled the rise and swell of the hill, parapets and dykes continuing to be used only where necessary to retain the soil.

The breadth and extent of the ledges or strips of lands obtained by their cutting the hill face, as has been said, varies according to the nature of the ground. Where they are carried up one of their usual slopes without the advantage of a retroceding vale or bottom, they are generally not more than twelve or fifteen feet broad, sometimes not more than half so much, and the depth of the supporting wall frequently equals the breadth.

On such narrow strips it would be impossible to make use of cattle and a plough, and therefore manual labour is employed on them in preparing the soil; but wherever there is room for a plough it is preferred. The instrument here made use of is perfectly similar to that employed in the plains of Hindostan, being equally simple and inefficient: a piece of crooked wood, one end of which is fastened to a rude yoke, which crosses the necks of two bullocks, and the other end turned downwards, is sharpened to turn the ground; while near the acute angle formed by the bending, a handle is inserted to guide and press the point into the earth.

Patience, however, (the characteristic of the Hindoo of the plains), serves also the mountaineer, instead of ampler means, to attain his end; and repeated ploughings produce an effect equal to that which a superior instrument would compass in one or two, and the soil of the hills in general favours these weak means, being free and easily worked, consisting chiefly of sand, the decomposition of sandy, micaceous, and slaty stones, mixed with a considerable proportion of decayed vegetables.

The instruments used in manual labour are equally simple and inefficient. A stick crossed at right angles, one end of which is shod with iron, resembling a miserable and broken sort of pickaxe, seems to be the principal one. But whatever their implements may be, or whether the fields are worked by the plough or by the hand, they do assuredly bring them to a high degree of tilth.

The crops of barley and wheat by this time were either cut or ripening, and some fields were prepared for and even sown with rice; but those which were ready for it exhibited a clean, equal, well-worked appearance, which could not be surpassed by an English farmer, with all his various and expensive apparatus.

Of the use of manure they are by no means unaware: traces of its application appeared in most fields; but I could not learn that they pursued a regular rotation of cropping, or continued to sow the grains they chiefly required year after year. I rather believe they do, giving an occasional fallow of some years when the land is exhausted, or renewing it with manure and fresh soil.

From what has been said it will appear that two crops are reaped within the year; but it seldom happens that the same land will suit each sort of grain, or that if it should, they employ it for both crops.

The first crop consists of wheat and barley: a few fields of a species of oats were observed. Poppy, and certain kinds of oily seeds, a sort of purslane, with curiously variegated red and green leaves, and a few poor inferior grains, filled the list.

The second crop consists chiefly of rice, but about the same time tobacco is planted, and a little cotton sown; and there are several smaller and poorer sorts of grains, both oily and farinaceous, which are grown all over the hills about the end of summer and autumn.

The wheat is sown in the lower parts of the hills as soon as the snow has left the ground, or as the cold weather will admit. Further removed to the more inclement regions of the north, where the snow lies far longer, I believe that the grain is sown in the beginning of winter, previous to the time it falls.

About the latter end of April the crops were fit to cut in the vicinity of Jytock; and on the Sine range, and in the country hitherto passed through, they were not above ten days more backward.

To the northward there is a very great difference, the corn in some places not ripening till the end of July.

The opium is gathered from the poppy nearly about the same time; it grows easily and luxuriantly, but was found in larger quantities as we advanced into the interior: it is said to be an expensive crop, requiring much manure and great attention, whilst the produce is not always very sure. It is an article of considerable traffic with the plains, whither the chief part is carried by the petty merchants who come to the hills for trade.

The purslane alluded to is a singular and beautiful plant: the centre of the leaves spreading from the stalk is of a fine crimson colour, sometimes inclining to purple, and is covered with a crimson powder; the outer part of them is green, but the stalks and young shoots are chiefly red, and the whole has a singular and brilliant appearance. The leaves, while young, are used as greens; and the grain, the produce for which they plant it, and of which there are two sorts, is used, the one made into bread, the other eaten as rice to a curry. It is small, black, and shining, like the seeds of sorrel, to which the plant bears some resemblance, growing to the height of from three to four feet.

The smaller grains are of little importance, nor can I give any particular account of them.

The rice of the hills is said to be peculiarly fine. Particular situations only will answer for this description of cultivation, and more than ordinary care is taken to bring it to perfection. All those spots of land, which lie near the banks of streams and in the bottoms of valleys, are selected, where a great command of water may securely be relied on. The whole extent of the terraces is carefully levelled, and very well worked with the plough, for which purpose they lay each under water, and plough them in this state.

The parapets are put in order, and small ledges of earth are raised on the brink to retain the water let in upon the soil long enough to saturate it, when it runs off over a flat stone to the ledge below. The water-courses are also arranged so as not to receive a quantity that would deluge the fields, and yet to yield a secure supply. When all is ready, the plants, which have been previously raised from seed, as in Bengal, are planted out by hand, as in that province, while the water lies on the land.

Irrigation is kept up from time to time as the plants require it, but water is not continually retained on the soil.

A large tract of rice, thus in ledges and under water, has a singular but pleasing appearance when observed from a height. The bright green of the plant shining through the water gives a strange transparency to the strips, which being exactly level, rise in regular succession over each other, and suggest the idea of a collection of small green mirrors thus placed in order.

The period for planting rice is during the months of May and June, in expectation of the rains which commence during the latter month, but it is protracted in the more northern districts to part of July. It usually ripens in about four months, but the time of reaping it depends much on situation and climate.

Tobacco is an article of general cultivation in the hills, and its quality is considered fine: it is exported both to the plains and to Bootan in considerable quantities. It is planted about May and June, for the benefit of the rains, and grows readily and luxuriantly, although it requires nice attention and much manure.

The herb bhang (a well-known species of hemp), also grows spontaneously in great abundance throughout this country, and is likewise cultivated and sent prepared in its various intoxicating shapes to the low country, where it meets with a ready sale.

Both men and women engage in the labours of agriculture, but their departments are generally distinct. The men exclusively guide the plough and sow the corn; the women weed the fields, break the clods, &c. Both sexes reap the corn; but this is principally an employment allotted to the women, who use a small sickle, ruder than that employed in Europe, and bind it into small sheaves, which, when the weather is fine, are left to dry on the field; but when it threatens rain they carry them to places formed of large flat slabs of slate, surrounded by a small wall, on which they likewise tread out the corn by means of cattle: here the reflected heat of the sun soon dries it, and any water that falls, quickly running off, has less effect on the sheaves than when lying on the moist fields. When freed by treading from the stalk, the grain is stored in the second story of the house, and the straw is preserved in stacks or houses for the use of the cattle, and for their own beds.

The straw, however, is seldom in sufficient abundance to serve as fodder for their cattle during the winter months, especially in the more inclement parts of the mountains, and they supply the deficiency by collecting grass from the jungles, and where that is less plentiful, the fallen leaves of trees, particularly fir-trees, which serve as a substitute for fodder and for beds. A species of fir, resembling that known in England by the name of Weymouth pine, the leaves of which are long and of some consistency, is that preferred for this purpose; but many trees besides are made use of as a winter store for the cattle, of which they take much care.

The mulberry grows luxuriantly over all the hills; and they cut its young and tender shoots annually, while full of leaves, and having dried them, stack them for fodder, which is said to be both nutritious and agreeable to the animals.

A species of oak is also made use of in this manner; and both these kinds of trees have received from this practice a strange mutilated appearance, not at first easily accounted for, nothing being left except the large limbs, which in spring and summer throw out a quantity of luxuriant young twigs, that soon gain a considerable size, and these are again cut for use.

The breed of cattle seems to be the same as the smaller sorts in the plains, but are somewhat larger and better of their kind: they all have the hump, and are chiefly black, but occasionally may be seen brindled, red, or pied. They are in general fat and handsome. The people pay them much attention, and make great use of their milk in its different preparations; but we have not as yet seen any cheese.

It was observed at the end of the last day's march, that slate commenced to be abundant; and during the whole of this day's route it predominated, being chiefly micaceous, inclining to red and dead blue. Quartz was also seen, sometimes veining the schistus; and now and then masses of a hard stone somewhat resembling whinstone, perhaps a mixture of flint with slate. Iron was very obvious in many places; several springs were impregnated with it, in colour and smell.

We observed in our march to-day a singular phenomenon in the natural history of insects—a great number of caterpillars, which appeared to be migrating from one place to another; and they were proceeding along in one line, with their heads and tails united one to another, so that the whole, consisting of some hundreds, assumed the appearance of one thin animal, many feet long. The strength of their adhesion to each other was considerable, so that it was by no means easy to separate them. Their bodies were of a gray colour, striped with black, and they had black heads and tails.

The height of the gorge we reached this day must be very great, for our whole march was nearly an uninterrupted ascent; but there were so many surrounding peaks of greater elevation, that no extent of view was to be obtained.

Rajgurh is situated not far below it, upon a projecting point like a terrace, that overlooks a large valley or basin to the northward. Above it, on each side, rise the loftier points of the ridge we had just crossed. This building is of no very great antiquity; having, it is said, been erected about eighty years ago. It belongs to the royal family of Sirmore, and has been inhabited by officers sent here to collect the revenues, who were occasionally changed at the pleasure of the Rajah. It is now totally in ruins, having been burnt by order of Runjore Sing within the last six months, on account, it is said, of the trouble it gave the officers of government, probably in their collections.

It cannot, however, be called a fort; for the position alone would disqualify it for making any long or available defence, commanded, as it is, from several heights, which are so close as to allow musquetry to be discharged from them with effect. Nor do I believe it has any pretensions to so warlike a designation, as it even wants loopholes in any number from whence to annoy an enemy.

The building consists of a square wall, including, at each corner, a tower of rather more than twenty feet square, but which projects little or nothing from the wall: within, all round, are places for the accommodation of the inhabitants, chiefly in the Hindostanee taste; and the whole includes a square court, the area of which may be from thirty to forty feet each way. This has been well paved; and in the centre is a small tank, constructed with stone and lime, well plastered, in which fresh water, conducted from the hill behind, was collected.

The space between the outside wall and the court which formed the accommodation did not exceed fifteen feet in depth; and as the walls of the towers are thick in proportion to their height, the interior of these presented no extensive area.

They may have consisted of five or six stories, raised to the height of forty feet; but their heights do not seem originally to have been equal. Balconies appear to have been erected all around, of wood, as the ends of the beams which have escaped the destruction of the fire may still be seen every where projecting.

Before this main building there was a court of inferior size, where troops were stationed, and the public officers were placed; but this is now so completely in ruins, that it is impossible to guess at its extent or shape; even the thickness of the walls it is difficult to judge of, but it appeared in some places to be from four to five feet.

The masonry work is extremely neat and good; it is built entirely of dry stone and wood; the former is met with, of a nature easily to be worked, and is well squared and rendered equal in thickness without much trouble; it is entirely slate, and, I believe, soon moulders and decays.

The stones are bound together by large beams of wood, which are built into the wall, lying along the external and internal faces, and pinned together through its substance; they extend the whole length of the side, and are firmly bound together at the corners.

The wood, I believe, is of a more lasting quality than the stone, and supports a building long after the latter would give way; consequently, when by any accident this framework is destroyed, the building instantly falls to pieces, and this is the reason of the completely ruined state in which Rajgurh appears, although so short a period has elapsed since it was burnt. I should have believed, judging from the infirm aspect of what remained, that a gradual decay of many years had succeeded the violence that first gave it to ruin.

On each of four hill-tops around it, in former days, a watch-tower was kept, to warn against surprises, which frequently occurred in those turbulent times. A similar situation would be a noble one for a house of modern times in Europe, where, happily, it is no longer necessary to combine the power of resistance and offence with the conveniences and comforts of a dwelling; for it overlooks a fine valley, varied with wood and cultivation, and a grand chain of mountains closes the view all around. The country, however, is rather too rugged and steep for comfort.

We found the various troops assembled and encamped on a green hollow near the ruins; but it was too late to muster the whole, after returning from a walk to the top of some of the nearest heights, for the purpose of making observations on the face of the country.

From the intelligence, however, that reached us this evening, we began to think that there would be no very pressing necessity for the service of these troops; for, by letters from the camp at Blackhill, we were informed that the Goorkha force under Kirtee Rana had been defeated, and the whole made prisoners. No farther particulars were given; but, considering the motley nature of the force which accompanied us, we could not but think it as well that the way should be clear for us, as, in all probability, little honour or credit was to be expected from the conduct of men, who, however brave they might be individually, had neither discipline, zeal, nor confidence in each other to give effect to their operations.

May 9th.—Although every one was in motion by daybreak, it was no easy matter to commence the march; for as the whole detachment were now present, and the roads and paths were extremely narrow, considerable arrangement was necessary in marshalling their line. The van was conducted by the Risaldar, and a party of irregular horse; who, as being the most to be trusted, had charge of the magazine and treasure. Next moved the company of Ghoorkhas, with their baggage, and women and children. Then the troops of Kumaoon, similarly attended. The Patans had moved on by a shorter, upper, but more fatiguing road. And, when all these had defiled through the pass, we moved ourselves, at half past seven, with our personal attendants. Last of all, the rear was brought up by the Mewattie troops. Such was the order of march. But it is scarcely possible to convey an idea of the novel and ludicrous strangeness of the scene.

The difference of costumes, variety of features, colour, size, arms, and language, glaringly forced itself on the view, forming a multitude of extraordinary contrasts. Then the noise and uproar; the authoritative orders of the sepoys and their officers to the miserable Paharies or hill-porters, forced to serve; their unintelligible gabble, praying to be released, partly but insufficiently drowned by the shrill wild sounds of the Ghoorkha trumpets and drums;—all this, in so wild a country, amid rocks and cliffs, produced an effect, to which it must be evident that no description could do justice.

When the march was commenced, the picturesqueness of the *coup d'œil* was increased. The red and yellow uniforms of Skinner's corps; the bearded Patans, with their blue trowsers, various mantles, and numerous standards; the short and stout figures of the Ghoorkhas, with their broad Tartar faces, ragged, but preserving a sort of order, and their line attended by many women and children of all sizes; the Kumaoon company, yet more ragged and various, composed of all the highlanders to the eastward; and the Mewatties, exhibiting among themselves as much difference of feature and dress;—all these passed file by file through a black cleft in a rock, whence they were seen in a lengthened and almost endless line, stretching along the mountain side, and winding in and out from the dark ravines among the black rocks of which it was formed; their gay colours and dresses, their arms and standards glistening, presented a fine contrast to the dark hue of the hills. On the whole, it was a display far more curious and strange than ever before fell under my observation.

Having passed through the gorge, where a deep ravine commences, we pursued our course along the side of the hill forming its northern bank, descending rapidly, by a path of some danger, narrow and overhanging precipices, and with many indentings, until the stream that rolled below formed a junction with the Peirowee-Nullah, which, rising from some of the shoulders of Choor in the valley overlooked by Raj Gurh, flows in a south-west direction to meet the Girree.

CHAPTER X.

The hill we descended was entirely formed of slaty rock. Large lumps of quartz were lying about as if by accident, but no considerable part of the hill appeared to be formed of this stone. Small quantities of a stone, which seemed to be composed of sand or flint and clay, are met with; it is of a dark brownish gray colour, and breaks into laminæ regularly like slate. In the nullah we saw large blocks of granite rounded by the torrents, which had evidently come from a great distance, probably from the bowels of Choor, whose gray and bare top is said to be composed of such masses.

Crossing the Peirowee, we ascended, and passing along the hills thinly covered with wood, and having much cultivation, we went through the little village of Kubēel, and reached Gudrotee, a village of considerable size, where we halted for a little time in a country remarkably well cultivated, and where all the labours of agriculture were going on briskly. Land was under preparation for rice; while large quantities of wheat and barley, cutting and fit to cut, with a few patches of cotton, and of a species of pulse-bearing bush, well known in the plains as *urrurr*, or pigeon-pease, covered the valley and sides of the hills.

The soil seemed light, but sharp and good; and not a spot upon the lower part of the hills, where a spade could dig, was uncovered with corn; though here and there a larger extent than usual might be observed, forming fields of larger size, and little slope or undulation.

Gudrotee is a large village, built upon a point of the hill projecting above the valley, to which the ascent is steep. This is a favourite situation, every village being thus semi-insulated, where the ground admits of it, perhaps with a view to defence against sudden attacks; if so, much of the advantage of the position is lost by always being overlooked by the main hill, which ascends behind it, and which completely commands it.

This position seldom affords the advantage of shelter from the blast, and is generally rough, uneven, and circumscribed, so that no more obvious inducement presents itself for preferring such places than an idea of greater security from plunder.

This village, though larger and more thriving than most others, had many ruins in its very centre, and had evidently declined; whilst, all around, others in view showed marks of violence and tyranny.

There were several towers here of from fifty to sixty feet high, built, as usual, all of dry stone, and framework of wood. Possibly a considerable portion of the ruins which every village exhibits may not be caused by the loss of its inhabitants, but by the old houses being deserted from the wood decaying, and the fabric consequently falling, and because they prefer building a new house of new materials, to rebuilding the old whose wood is decayed, and the stone shattered from time and its nature.

Several of the temples were ornamented with much carved work in wood. Their strange overhanging roofs were fringed with a row of small pieces of wood hanging down, resembling bobbins strung beneath the cornice, and each corner had the image of a bell in wood hanging from it. The figures of Hindoo divinities ornamented the doors and windows, forming a strange combination of Chinese and Hindoo tastes. A large beam, with notches cut into it at intervals, forms the only means of ascent to these lofty edifices, each story being furnished with its separate rude ladder.

In the vicinity of this and of the adjacent villages several groves of a fir perfectly resembling the silver fir are observed, which give much effect to the landscape.

After a halt of some time, we began to ascend the ridge of the hill immediately behind the village by a very steep path, which led to its crest. On casting the eye backwards from a point in the ascent, I counted twenty villages in the valley we had left, many of them of considerable size. They were scattered over the whole face of the hills, several of them perched on their crests.

Height of situation seems not to be considered as disadvantageous; water is abundant, and the climate moderate; they therefore are seen crowning the highest hills, and spotting their sides.

On the very top of this ascent we found cotton and pigeon-pease growing kindly.

Proceeding onwards to the north, after reaching the summit of the hill, where we halted to make some observations, we passed through two villages of remarkable neatness, in good repair, and very pleasantly situated upon the brow of a hill, which does not descend too precipitously, and surrounded by walnut, apricot, mulberry, and other trees of very rich verdure; whilst a fine grove of larches, somewhat resembling cedars, close beside it, exhaled from their leaves, or the gum they shed, a delicious perfume.

These villages are inhabited by Brahmins, a race that take that exceeding good care of themselves, which is generally observed of the priesthood in all countries where superstition holds sway.

Immediately beyond this village we reached the gorge of a descent, when a fine highland scene burst upon us, giving to view a long vista of wild hills running to the north-west, with a valley below in the same direction, half lost in storm and mist, whence a rapid descent brought us to our encamping ground.

The heights were chiefly grassy, but below, in the deep dells, forests of various sorts of fir-trees met our eyes.

Choor appeared nearly covered to the top with these trees, but that top itself, of bare rock, had nothing on it except here and there a spot of snow.

At first we passed through thickets of a bush, which somewhat resembles the Portugal laurel, but the stalks are redder, and the leaves less shining; it bears a beautiful red flower, and is, I believe, a species of the rhododendron. A little below this the path led through a forest of oak, of the same sort as that found in smaller quantities on the hills about Nahn, and above the Dhoon; its leaves are long, of a pale dead green above, and much lighter below, serrated, but not indented deeply. The acorn is very distinct, but I do not recollect having seen the species any where else.

From this wood the descent was particularly steep and unpleasant, leading through the ruined village of Dhoon to the Bugetthoo-Nullah, a fine stream, on the banks of which, at a village named Shai, we rested for the night, after a short but fatiguing march of eleven miles and a quarter. Many of the troops and porters did not come up till late.

The face of the country to-day preserved the same aspect as we observed yesterday; the hills were bold, round, and grassy, with little wood. The valleys were not more broad, but extremely well cultivated; and strong evidence of activity in conducting streams of water across hollows, and general attention to irrigation in preparing fields for the reception of rice, and in cleaning those that were already under other crops, and, in short, in every branch of hill farming, was apparent throughout.

About Gudrotee the crops were particularly fine and extensive. We saw wheat in abundance that could not be surpassed in ear or straw. The cattle were far superior to the small beasts we observed about Nahn, and larger than any of the small breeds of the plains, fat, and in good condition.

The people have exhibited little change in their appearance: the same high nose and sharp features, the same dress, too; the lower orders very miserably equipped. We thought that in one or two villages some of the women exhibited distinct traces of the Tartar physiognomy: short, stout, squat in figure, with high cheekbones, and broad faces, of a light yellow colour.

At the ruined village of Dhoon there were two who certainly bore a strong resemblance to Ghoorkhas, but all these might be accidental variations, not indicative of any actual admixture of blood. Certainly, however, the appearance of those women we have seen, and they show themselves very freely, is considerably different from that of those we saw during our first marches.

The rocks here exhibited no variety this day: slate only predominated. Iron was evident every where. The soil varied in colour and darkness from yellowish red to black gray, as the slate is more dark and more destructible.

We saw some deer to-day at a little distance, and two shots were fired at them without effect. All we could distinguish of their appearance, was, that they were of a dull grayish-brown colour, and were remarkably low behind.

The village of Shai is poor, and chiefly in ruins, but its situation is not unpleasant. The valley takes its rise in the north-western shoulder of Choor, and in the upper part it is covered with wood, while that towards the village is varied with cultivation and green slopes; and the stream, though little fringed with wood, forms an embellishment by no means trifling. Our camp occupied some fields, whence the corn had been chiefly cut along its banks.

May 10.—As there was an uncertainty of always procuring an adequate supply of provisions for the people while advancing, and no grain had as yet been brought in at this stage, it was thought proper to halt for a supply where we were; a measure probably not unpleasant to a majority of the party, who, accustomed only to travel in the plains, became fatigued by the unusual toil of the hill marches.

In fact, they are exceedingly painful at first, but after a short practice it is surprising how the muscles become accustomed to the new species of action, and the breath is lengthened, so that ascending and descending heights become matters of comparative ease and indifference.

It is remarkable, that, of all the descriptions of men along with us, the men of Skinner's corps, who have passed their life on horseback, and are probably little accustomed to march on foot even on the plains, were those of the party that least complained of fatigue, and always arrived the first upon their ground.

In the forenoon many of the zemindars and principal men of the neighbouring villages attended, partly summoned to produce grain, and partly to relate grievances and disputes of their own, which they hoped might be redressed or arranged by us, and we had thus a good opportunity of remarking on the appearance and character of the inhabitants of this district.

It is strange how loth these men were found to part with the hoards of grain which they possessed, although their own price was offered for it to them. There was hardly an instance in this part of the country of the farmers giving what was wanted for the use of the army at the first requisition, though they had it in abundance, and the money was tendered to them at the same moment. The possession of it was, in general, denied, and it never was produced until force was threatened and a search ordered; when, rather than submit to that, though not until the orders were on the point of being executed, they tardily produced their stores; some, perhaps trusting to their cunningness of concealment, braved the search, but our Ghoorkhas, well aware of their ways, never failed to find what was required.

This unwillingness may partly be traced to habitual fear, and experience of frequent plunders on similar occasions, but it should have ceased with experience; and there could be little doubt of the sincerity of our proffers of payment where the money itself was offered, and frequently given in advance. They could have had no objection to part with the grain from a fear of future want, because more money than it was worth was offered for it, which would always command what they might need from other districts. And, finally, had they reflected, they must have felt that the strong arm of power was at hand to enforce compliance with its demand, whether just or unjust.

Here we have a true and striking specimen of the falsehood and cunning policy, as well as of the shortsightedness, and the inconsistency of the Asiatic. He advances with a cringing and respectful demeanour, and to a plain direct inquiry at once replies by a downright untruth, supported by many assertions and good reasons, and seasoned with a sufficient dose of flattery and entreaty. He neglects his immediate and apparent interest for a remote and contingent advantage; and, trusting to his good fortune, and to that flattery which is so cheap, and which he thinks he can use so effectually, and to his own cunning and proficiency in deceit, so often successful, he braves and often exasperates a power that can crush him.

Such was the conduct of the hill people on this occasion, and it will probably be found of a piece with the whole tenor of that uncertain, vacillating, mean, and narrow policy, which marks and stains the Asiatic character. From such men no steady or good course of conduct can be looked for; on them no reliance can be placed. Even the tie of interest seems unsteady when viewed through so uncertain a medium.

The conduct of the hill states in this quarter, since the commencement of the war, has been entirely of this character, and their subjects have not departed from it. Their appearance was quite consistent with this; cautious self-possession was apparent in each line of their wrinkled countenances drawn up into a cringing smile; but, on the whole, they differed not much from the rest of the men of Sirmore who have fallen under our observation.

In the afternoon we reviewed our troops, which, when drawn up in their different corps, formed an assemblage of the most grotesque appearance that can be imagined; for, collected as they were in haste, there was no room for choice; each who called himself a soldier, and brought his arms, was retained at the time: thus, boys not nearly arrived at their growth were found in the ranks; old men scarcely equal to wielding their arms were also there. Several had dyed their beards and hair with indigo to hide the approaches of time, but not being able to pay that attention to their toilette on a fatiguing march which they could in camp, the difference was apparent in the grisly-gray that now, having partly lost its blue, spread over their faces and heads.

Such were the doughty heroes which we had to oppose to the veteran Ghoorkhas. However, there were also many good men, and much material; and, had there been time to establish any kind of regular discipline, a considerable portion would probably have become good soldiers.

As it was, the defeat of Kirtee Rānā, as likely to render unnecessary any trial of their steadiness, was an event not to be deplored.

Observing the stream in front of our camp to swarm with fish, I got together some rude materials for angling, and succeeded in catching a couple of dozen. They were of a species totally different from those we saw in the Jelall; long for their thickness, and of a dirty greenish-gray colour, with white bellies; their mouth was small, and placed under the head, as in the shark, forming an excrescence, which was of a stiff leathery substance.

The small ones were sweet to the taste; the larger were not so good, and extremely full of bones. A string of this species of fish was presented to us at Raj Gurh, and were the first of the sort we saw.

A few of a species resembling one of those we saw in the Jelall, with bright golden and silver scales, were also remarked; these, however, were rarely caught, and we were informed that they were extremely unwholesome; and were led to believe that this might be the fact, as one of the party having eaten of it, was rather violently attacked both in stomach and bowels.

May 11.—Want of grain detained us this day also, but as the situation is not a convenient one, it was determined the next day to commence our march for the fort of Choupal in Joobul.

A confirmation of the defeat and surrender of the enemy's force under Kirtee Rānā this day reached us; they were surrounded, it was understood, by the troops of Bischur and Joobul; and from the loose accounts that alone had been hitherto obtained, we were led to fear that treachery was employed to induce them to give themselves up.

We were also informed that the chief part of Ummr Sing's army had deserted him, and come over to the British, in consequence of his mad resistance after the fatal defeat of Buchtee Thappa, and the severity of his measures, and of their privations.

The loss of that beloved leader, too, had great share in disheartening them; and as he had alone, for a long time, been the means of retaining the troops in their fidelity to Ummr Sing, with whom they were disgusted, the moment that bond became dissolved by Buchtee's death, they fled, or came over almost in a body.

It was farther said, that Ummr Sing had offered to surrender himself and Malown, which place had been closely invested.

A heavy hailstorm, with a drizzling rain, fell this day, and made the air exceedingly cold. At the top of a hill above the valley, where we ascended to take some observations, it was so piercing as to benumb the fingers, and during the night it was felt severely in camp.

Choor had been plentifully sprinkled with snow.

May 12.—Having determined on the march, we rose early, but, as usual, could not expedite all necessary business till seven o'clock, when we commenced our route, pursuing a course up the Bughetoo glen somewhat to the south-east.

We passed several villages, which were pleasantly situated, with many fine walnut-trees around them; but these villages were in a state of decay. There was, however, a good deal of cultivation.

To our left appeared a most wild, rocky, but short glen, whence a stream joins the Bughetoo. We kept our course up the latter for nearly four miles, ascending very greatly, though very gradually, till about a mile further on.

Being high above the stream, we turned quite to our left in a north-eastern direction, and proceeded, mounting by a path along a ridge covered with larches, and very rough.

The wind was piercing cold, and short showers fell, and drifted past. Choor was for awhile enveloped in them, and when it appeared again, was covered with fresh fallen snow.

Still ascending, we entered a forest of oak, holly, rhododendron, and larch, and held a more easterly course along the lofty ridge we had reached, and high above the glen below to a pass or ghāt, where a descent commenced; here we halted a little, and then immerged into a deep hollow, proceeding like the rest from Choor, and covered with a noble forest of firs, oaks, and hollies. That fir, which was most abundant, resembles the silver fir in colour and figure, but growing generally in forests, and thickly the trunk attains an immense height, whilst the branches, circumscribed in their growth by want of room, are small and short, and bear no proportion to the stem.

Larch was almost equally plentiful, and of this another species attracted our attention this day, differing in colour and in the tufted appearance of its leaves; but the tree retained the character.

Holly was abundant, and attained a great size: its leaf perfectly resembled that of the common English holly.

Many other trees added their beauties to the foliage of the forest, for which I can give no name; and the underwood was as various.

The vegetation under these was formed of wild strawberries, buttercups, columbines, ferns, and thousands of other lovely flowers that sprang in rich confusion all around.

Through this noble forest we marched for a considerable space, till emerging on a clear height we saw the glen below: its upper parts wild and woody, while lower down it appeared bare, but spotted with cultivation.

Choor frowned hoary with snow above all, sending a fine diversity of bare peaks and woody ridges to the glen beneath.

From hence we began to descend very rapidly, and at last so precipitously that the path was a mere zigzag cut on the ridge's edge, till we gained the bed of the torrent, which rolls rapidly over blocks of various stones, the ruins of the mountain above. On a very small ledge on the banks of this our little tent was pitched.

Our march was ten miles, the first seven of which were a continual ascent, and the latter three as continued and precipitous a descent.

The face of the country during this day's march exhibited a far greater variety, and a much more interesting wildness than we had yet witnessed.

It led, indeed, over the remoter parts of the heights surrounding the great mountain Choor, and was consequently more shaggy and rugged. This mountain is a most noble and conspicuous object in every way; it is the highest peak between the Sutlej and Jumna, short of the Snowy Mountains and their immediate shoulders. Indeed there is no hill as far as the Alacnunda that nearly approaches it in height. Observations subsequent to this tour have fixed it at 10,688 feet above the plains; it is seen at a great distance from every quarter, and forms an excellent point for observation; it is, moreover, the nucleus whence all the hills around radiate as from a centre. Streams are sent from its face in every direction, which swell the Girree or Pabur rivers; and standing on a height near it (for we did not ascend it), the line of every ridge was plainly perceived diverging from, or connecting with it, as far as the sight extended.

In the sequel (where a sketch of the general face of the country is given to illustrate the map), a more particular notice will be taken of this vast and majestic mountain, whose figure well accords with its importance, and commands respect.

The nature of the forests and vegetable productions has been already noticed. A new species of oak was observed, in addition to the trees already enumerated; its leaves are very bright, and serrated, preserving a roundish oval shape. We also saw a new species of the raspberry, completely resembling that of the wild sort at home; also two different sorts of strawberry quite distinct from that which grows nearer to the plains. All these, however, were barely in blossom; some had not even advanced so far, and thus no judgment could be formed of what they might be at maturity. The variety of the trees and shrubs and smaller herbs was astonishing. At each step some new plant attracted the eye; and many of those meadow flowers which are common in Europe were hailed with great satisfaction. The ferns were very beautiful, and even the humble buttercup gave rise to a pleasing recollection; for, in wild and remote regions, the remembrance of early days and youthful pleasures recurs, even when excited by trifles, with redoubled interest.

The soil and rocks have evinced no change during the day's journey; the former only varies in colour, and in some places seemed quite black, as of a coaly nature, but no reason could be discovered for this, except that the rock was darker, of a more mouldering quality, and strongly tinctured with iron.

The rocks preserve their slaty composition and laminous texture, having a great tendency to moulder away, and being frequently mixed considerably with sand.

In the bed of the nullah, where we encamped, as well as of that which we left, there were large blocks of stone, hard, and of different sorts; some a sort of plum-pudding stone, and some, I believe, of a species of granite; but the variety was considerable, and all were rounded by violent attrition in the bed of the torrent.

Our camp was pitched at the confluence of two very wild streams, which rise in Choor, and here form the Bisharee Nullah, which falls into the Girree about ten cos from hence, at a village called Bhotōg, in the petty state of Bulsum.

The Bisharee Nullah here forms the boundary between Sirmore and Joobul. The banks are so very rocky and steep to the water's edge that there was hardly room for the people to rest upon.

The cold at night, though at the bottom of the valley, was so great that double covering was absolutely necessary.

May 13.—The morning was sharp but fine. Being desirous of obtaining a sketch of the very singular hollow we had encamped in, with the mountain and ridges of Choor, I went forward a little before the party, and crossing the Bisharee torrent, was conducted by the guide up the very face of the opposing rock, by a path which at first was supposed a wrong one from its extreme roughness and steepness, and which led us more than once into situations of considerable danger, besides being very toilsome to ascend. After much delay, and several mistakes, arising from the unintelligible jargon of the guide, which even the Ghoorkhas who accompanied me could not understand, I obtained what I wanted, but was not joined by the rest of the party for more than an hour.

CHAPTER XI.

THE troops had slowly and painfully ascended the precipice, and most fortunately only one accident had occurred, which, considering the steepness and the tortuous nature of the path (the turns of which often crossed each other, and the lower parts of which were much exposed to the fall of loose stones from above), was less than could have been expected.

A Mewattie soldier received a falling stone, and was precipitated down a good way and much bruised, but not so as to endanger his life.

The extent of this steep rocky pull is nearly a mile; beyond it the ascent continues somewhat more easy, but is still very toilsome, along the face of a green ridge, from the top of which we enjoyed a noble view of the valleys and ridges diverging from Choor.

To the north-west we descried a portion of the Snowy Mountains at a great distance, probably on the other side of the Rauvee: they appeared lofty and large, but were chiefly lost in cloud, and soon were quite hid from view. We proceeded from hence to the northward, along a ridge projecting from that we were to cross, generally ascending till we reached the main mountain; when a very rude and difficult path lay before us, leading right up the face of the hill through a shaggy and various forest, in which, on every side, rough sharp peaks appeared, and bold projecting crags, that strewed the pass and the deep valley below with their ruins.

It required the application of both hands and feet frequently to get on, and the exertion continued a long time, so that when we reached the gorge of the pass at half past twelve o'clock, the people were quite exhausted, though it was only four miles and a half from our night's station. It was certainly a very savage place, and required the limbs of mountaineers to attain it with any facility. The roughness and darkness of the wood upon the south side, and the towering and irregular variety of the craigs that frowned all around, gave a very singular character to the scene.

When we reached the highest part, the view, as might be expected, was magnificent, for the height we had reached was probably not 1500 feet below Choor itself.

Several ranges of long and lofty hills running into each other, and divided only by ravines like chasms in a rock, with every variety of form and feature, in some places covered with noble pine forests, in others studded with villages and cultivation, or bursting into bare brown rocks, lay all before us, fading in distance till half lost. Above them, here and there, in storm and cloud, a peak of the snowy range might be seen, while in front a deep forest of old pines rose from the dell below, hiding its rocky masses, or only allowing them to appear to contrast with their dark foliage.

A rich carpet was under our feet, and it was pleasant to rest us after our labours. The name of the pass, taken from that of the two peaks on either side, was that of Choghāt and Bughāt.

As usual, after a long rise a descent was to be looked for: we commenced by entering a pine forest even more deep and venerable than that of yesterday, along a good path, with a gentle declivity. Through the comfortable shade of this forest we passed for a good while, and then emerged, as yesterday, upon a steep grassy slope, down which we wound, sometimes on the ridge, and sometimes on the side; the path good but slippery. The soil seems to lie thick and rich, and the grass and other vegetation was wonderfully luxuriant and verdant.

The latter part of this descent was very steep and tortuous, again entering the forest, and it ended in the bottom of a glen exceedingly dark and romantic. The torrent had made for itself a deep and narrow dell in the rocks, clothed with the finest old pine trees and richest underwood, and rushes down its craggy bed in darkest obscurity till met by the waters of a similar glen from the left.

The chasm formed by these seems not to admit of egress, and this can only be obtained by following the united stream down its still more dangerous and rugged course, which we accordingly effected, over rocks and fallen trees all covered with the loveliest verdure. Roses, jasmines, raspberries, strawberries, ferns, and thousands of beautiful and fragrant plants, the usual undisturbed occupiers of these scenes, combined to delight us, and, with the immense pine-trees, threw a deep shade over our path, but creating a chill almost to a painful degree.

We continued in the bed of the stream, till, at the junction of a similar one from the west, six miles and a half from our last night's camp, we crossed the united waters forming the Shashallee Khola, and ascended the left face of the glen, slanting on ridges of abandoned cultivation, passing through the ruined village of Khugna, where there is a neat temple, and some particularly fine old larch-trees. We made our way along the southern face of the mountain, now forming the boundary of the valley, following the deep indentings on its brown and barren side. The opposite or northern exposure is woody, and better cultivated.

Several other half-ruined villages lay in our way, and at about six o'clock in the evening we reached the fort of Choupal, the same which, in my brother's former expedition to Joobul, capitulated to the party under his charge.

Our tents were placed on a gentle declivity near to the fort, and we were met by a set of singing women, who came to welcome us to the place. One set of these at least is maintained in every district of the hills, to contribute their professional assistance at marriages and merry-makings; and they no doubt expected to be well rewarded for the zeal of their intentions, but we were too much fatigued to entertain ourselves long with their music, and dismissed them. They were yellow, but ruddy and fresh-looking women, of the middle size. Their dress was far from rich, although they wore something resembling shawls, as doputtas; nor did their voices appear to be of any considerable excellence.

The march of this day was thirteen miles, and was by far the most fatiguing we have had; not only was the length greater, but the nature of the country travelled over was more rugged and difficult than usual.

Marches in this country consist, generally speaking, of one long ascent and a corresponding descent, and thus our progress is usually from the bottom of one valley to that of another, with perhaps a considerable progress along the face of one of its sides, and this, in fact, forms an ample journey for a day; for the height of the ridges is so great, that not only the extent of ground travelled over becomes considerable, but the nature of the country more than compensates for the shortness of the journey.

Those who have been accustomed to travel in a mountainous country, such as the Highlands of Scotland, where journeys of thirty, forty, and even fifty miles are commonly performed without any great fatigue day after day, may be inclined to smile at the poor pedestrian who confesses a moderate share of fatigue after a march of only thirteen miles; but let him inform himself of the nature of these mountains before he despises the effort, and compare the difficulties of each country, at least by description, before he passes judgment. No hill in Scotland exceeds 4200 feet of elevation, calculated from the level of the sea. The true elevation, in fact, that a traveller has to ascend, seldom exceeds from one to two thousand feet in one day, and in most cases this ascent is divided by the gradual acclivity, and several small ups and downs to a degree that detracts much from its severity. The roads, too, and even the mountain paths, are in the Highlands conducted with more knowledge and attention along those lines, which present the least labour to the traveller, and though frequently laborious, do not demand a continual straining effort.

In the hilly regions we were now traversing all was different: after passing the first range, no hill reared itself to a less height than 5 or 6000 feet; and though, no doubt, the valleys or ravines dividing them were proportionally elevated, the actual height of ascent is far greater than is usual in mountainous countries; but the great source of labour is in the excessive and universal steepness and abruptness of their sides, always rising suddenly at a great angle from the streams, that fill the chasms at their feet. When there is no extent of valley there cannot well be much level ground. Where ridge and cleft succeed each other closely, little can be looked for in the roads that lead over them but steep ascent and descent; and it is the total want of any level road that fatigues the traveller in these hills.

No time is gained to draw breath, and at the same time gently continue the road. If you wish to recruit your exhausted strength it must be done by an actual stop, and rest at some convenient spot; and the ascents are so long, and thirst so great, that the day lapses without the possibility of reaching to any great distance. The springs are fortunately numerous.

Besides the steepness and length of the pulls, an excessive roughness of the path is to be supported; and it becomes necessary to pick your steps carefully, and to take heed that a slip may not precipitate you down a chasm, perhaps of awful depth, that yawns below your path.

Every exertion of body and mind or attention fatigues, and with so much to look to, added to the toil of the way, it is no wonder if the traveller proceed slowly.

I have travelled in the Highlands of Scotland, and have made long marches there without more fatigue than is usually felt, but I must aver that a twelve or thirteen miles stage, such as that of this day, has fatigued me more than upwards of three times its distance at home. The hill people themselves never attempt the extreme journeys which the Scotch Highlander performs with ease, fifteen to twenty miles being the extent they will go even on their own business.

In fact, when after an ascent of so many miles a man arrives at the bottom of a corresponding descent, it is exceedingly painful to be forced to ascend a second time, well knowing that there is no middle course to steer between resting where he is and performing a double day's work, for he must also descend a second time in general before he can reach a fit station for the night.

This second ascent, though it was a moderate one, rendered our march to-day so wearisome, besides which (as already remarked) the way was so rough and bad that many of the troops, and some of the hill porters, did not arrive till next morning.

A considerable similarity prevails between the country we marched over to-day and that which we traversed yesterday, but as we increased our elevation, and gained the northern face of Choor and its ridges, a greater degree of rugged grandeur, and of such beauty as is met with in alpine scenes, was very remarkable. The cliffs were greater and more wild in their shapes, as if nature had found free room to sport in their formation. The pine-trees increased in size, and were the tallest, straightest, and most magnificent I ever saw, and the forests covered immense tracts. What a seeming waste of noble timber! and how uselessly do these grand trees appear to flourish and decay! The natives cannot make use of them; their consumption of timber is small, and if it were greater, they have not tools with which to avail themselves of the abundance which these endless forests afford.

It is singular, but true, that in the whole of our travels through the mountains we never met with a saw, nor, as we were told, does such an instrument exist among them. When they want a plank they cut down a tree with the axes which they always carry, and split it into one or more pieces by means of wedges; thus so rudely tearing up the wood, that they seldom obtain more than one plank from the tree, which is chosen of the size required, and cut to the length they wish to give the board before they begin to split it.

All their houses are floored with planks thus procured; and the woodwork of their balconies, with every other piece of flat timber in use, costs them this exercise of labour, and loss of time, and of material.

The species of wood, which the natives make use of, are either of the larch kinds, or that which resembles the silver fir; both sorts abound in resin, which exudes plentifully from their bark and twigs; and the wood obtained from them is very durable, remaining uninjured, though exposed to the changes of weather, as we have reason to believe, for fully a hundred years. In fact, the houses are kept together for the greatest part of the time they stand by the wood they are bound with. I think, however, that the larch species are preferred.

If it were possible to transport this valuable timber to the plains below, it would be a most important acquisition. Beams of such a length as these would form are not to be procured for building in any part of India, and it is probable that the use of such wood in shipbuilding would be very extensive. There is little doubt but some one of the various pines afforded by these mountains would answer for masts and spars as well as the spruce-fir of America, or the pine of Norway. If the larch be too heavy, there are other pines fully as light as can be needed; and indeed a species we remarked yesterday so closely resembles the spruce fir that we believed it to be the same tree; its colour, and the appearance of the young shoots and branches, were very similar to that which grows in Britain.

But it is vain to speculate on the uses to which these noble forests might be applied if they once reached Calcutta, or even the great rivers of the plains which might carry them thither, for the nature of the country is such, the want of practicability of carriage either by roads or by floating is so decided, that it is evident these trees must remain where they fall, or roll into chasms, which never can have water enough to move them. If with great labour a few of these trees, which grow lowest on the mountain's ridges, might, from advantageous position, be conveyed to the river Girree, and so by the Jumna to the plains, they must be small, and form no sample of the prodigious size of those that clothe the more inaccessible and loftier parts of these mountains' sides.

We remark now six very distinct species of pine, viz. that which is found upon the lower hills around Nahn and Jytock; two sorts of larch: that which resembles the Weymouth pine, or the silver fir, or spruce; and when there may be occasion to advert to either of these sorts I shall call them by the names of those they resemble. We also found the yew-tree in abundance in this forest: of the identity of this there was no doubt. We saw several species of oak and of holly; their varieties shaded very much into each other.

Among the shrubs, one which strongly resembled the alder was observed this day; the flowers were very fragrant. The lesser productions of this rich soil were innumerable, and the verdure of the grasses, and the flowery enamelling of the open glades in the forest, were most beautiful and surprising.

That difference of aspect, which has been before remarked, between the southern and northern faces of the ridges, was to-day particularly striking; not only the formation and structure of the hills and rocks, but the vegetable productions were quite distinct on either side. While climbing the southern face, the general colour of the country was brown and dusky; the grass was short and parched, and the hills rough and lumpy; the rocks staring through the ground as if it had been worn from their faces, blackened by the weather, and the wilder and more broken crags were only in the clefts and ravines, and on the crest of the mountain.

The lower parts were quite bare of wood, and above, the stone and Weymouth pine only of the pines, sprinkled with a few larches of small size, grew sparingly on the rocks; whilst over the higher parts, oak, holly, and alder, were thickly spread, and the brownish green of their leaves well agreed with the burnt appearance of the hills.

Upon the northern exposure, a dark rich green colour was diffused over the landscape; the sides of the glen were chiefly rock, far bolder and grander than on the other side, which, pointing its crags to the northward, was almost perpendicular to the torrents at its feet: but this rock was clothed almost entirely with these noble forests of larch, silver, and spruce firs, which shrouded from view all but the highest and steepest cliffs. All was rich and dark, and here and there a glade opened, or a hill slope extended from the base of the rock, or projected between two streams of a bright beautiful green, shining through the sombre forest. This distinctness of character is very remarkable, and, I believe, very universally obvious, between the faces of different exposures all over these hills.

That the quantity of cultivation seen during the two last marches should be far less than in the country we have quitted is not surprising, because the country is less susceptible of it; but both in the Bughetoo valley, along which we passed the first part of yesterday, and in the course of our march to-day, particularly in the latter part, great traces of ruin and of desolation were discernible; much cultivation had been abandoned, and the villages were frequently little better than a heap of ruins. From the ascent of this day, however, we saw several that were to all appearance more prosperous, and surrounded by a more extensive cultivation, situated on very high peaks, and projecting subordinate ridges from Choor and Buhroque. The wheat which we saw near Choupal was still green and very bad; the barley was full, but not ripe.

The predominating rock this day was schistus of several sorts; dark and micaceous, reddish and grey. A considerable quantity of sandstone was observed among the smaller masses near the top of our ascent fallen from above, and the crags that top the ridge, at the end of which Choupal is situated, appeared by their fallen ruins to consist of fine-grained sandstone, and hard and various schistus.

The soil presented an appearance very similar to that which we have for some days observed. On the north side of the ridge there was a very great admixture of vegetable mould.

On crossing the Bisharee Nullah we observed that the dress of the inhabitants was completely changed, and their appearance somewhat altered. Instead of the dirty cotton cap and gown of Sirmore they wore a black cap of shaggy wool, somewhat like a highland bonnet compressed; a pair of trowsers of thick dark striped woollen stuff, very loose from the waistband, where it is tied with a string to the knee, but it becomes closer to the leg below, and reaches to the heels in small wrinkles. Their chief garment is a coat of similar blanket stuff, which reaches down to the knees, gathered tight round the waist, and falling round the lower parts and thighs in many folds, somewhat like the Scotch highland philibeg. The better sort usually wear a piece of cotton, much as the Hindoos do the doputta, and frequently wrap it round the shoulders as a plaid. Their shoes are formed of a sort of close net-work, or twill of woollen thread, attached to a leathern sole.

We had little opportunity at this time to judge of any difference which might exist between these people and the Sirmore men in character and disposition; but whether it were merely from the alteration of dress, and a certain degree of superior smartness of appearance, or that there was actually a difference, we believed that they discovered more of those peculiar manners usually attributed to highlanders than the wretched beings we had left behind.

We were advancing into an unknown country where every thing was new, and we were eagerly looking for what was extraordinary, and might be inclined to see common events and characters in a point of view more suited in our imagination to the remoteness of the region: so delightful is romance; and so inherent in our nature the love of the marvellous, that it is hardly possible to visit even a well known, though foreign country, without half expecting, and hoping for, uncommon adventures. But when our path leads through a novel as well as remote scene, a strong effort is needful to repress that loftiness of view, that disorder of the mental optics, which throws a false light and untrue proportion over the objects that are most natural, and the occurrences that are most common.

May 14.—It has been observed, that, when we passed the Bisharee Nullah, we left the territories of Sirmore, and entered those of Joobul. This is a hill state of considerable extent, and is one of the principal of those of the second class, if not in amount of revenue, at least in consequence and position.

It is bounded on the south and south-east by Sirmore, on the east and north-east by Gurwhal, from which it is divided by the Pabur river; on the north, north-west, and west, by the petty states of Bulsum, Coteegooroo, and Saree, which last now forms a part of the Bischur territories.

Previously to the Ghoorkha conquest, Joobul was governed by a hereditary chief of its own, under the title of Rāna, who was, generally speaking, in a state of tolerable independence, but who nominally acknowledged himself tributary to one or other of the more powerful states of the first order. This authority was most frequently allowed to be due to the Rajahs of Sirmore, for that state was nearest at hand to compel submission and punish revolt, which was always resorted to in the day of the superior's weakness.

But, as in the stormy revolutions and continual wars, which occurred in this turbulent country, others of the principal states gained the ascendant, Joobul was obliged by force or by policy to yield to the circumstances that affected its master, and thus both Bischur and Gurwhal occasionally held temporary sway over it. That this sway was most generally in possession of Sirmore, and that in fact Joobul did acknowledge a feodatory claim on the part of that rajah, appears from this, that the young chief of Joobul did always, on the death of the former rānā, receive the honorary dress and investiture of authority from the hands of the Rajah of Sirmore.

The degree of dependence, however, does not seem to be so well defined, and was probably determined, not by any fixed limits, but by the temporary means of resistance on the one side, and the want of power on the other, to enforce its claims.

After the Ghoorkha force had reduced Sirmore to their power, all the petty states fell one after another, and probably with little or no resistance, and Joobul, as well as its superiors, became integral parts of the Nepālese territories. The reigning rānā was deposed, and had since lived at one of his houses near the banks of the Pabur, on the private charity of the inhabitants, who, poor and oppressed as they were, yet felt for their former chief. What the family of this chief may have been I know not, nor is it of much importance: probably the state rose with the founder of it, who may have been no more than an able and enterprising mountaineer; and such was, in all likelihood, the origin of many of the petty lordships.

The ex-rānā, however, appears to have been a mere cypher, who passively enjoyed the comforts of his situation, leaving his cares and the exercise of his power to servants. The man who was, in point of power and influence, the true chief of Joobul, was named Dangee; who, under the title of vuzzeer, exercised the prince's authority, collected the revenues, and directed the whole state.

It frequently happens that the storm which lays the chief low, spares those who were subservient to him in a humble sphere; so it occurred in this case. It appears that the conquerors allowed Dangee to retain his situation; probably they could not quite destroy his influence, and he was found useful in collecting the revenues for them, which he formerly levied in the name of his master; and Joobul was a tract so centrically situated, that it might be convenient to have its chief subject friendly to their cause.

However that might be, when the British army marched to Nahn, and first became acquainted with the situation of the country, Dangee was found to be the principal person to treat with, as friend or foe; and as it became an object to station a force in Joobul, and to move the natives of the hills as much as possible against the enemy, all means were adopted to procure the co-operation of this man. For a long time, with true Asiatic policy, he played a double or uncertain part, by no means at once deciding on any mode of conduct, but, as in his opinion, either party seemed to gain the advantage, shifting to that side; and always, where he could do it, acting in a manner that might be well explained to either party which should ultimately prevail.

When at length he saw that the Ghoorkhas were sorely pressed, and that the campaign would terminate favourably for the British; when he saw a small and irregular force penetrate into his country unmolested, and that the commander of one of the chief fortresses in Joobul considered his affairs so desperate as to accede to our terms, and surrender his garrison; he then, and not till then, openly declared himself, and inlisted in our pay with a body of 500 Joobulians.

Although so undecided and wavering a line of conduct must in general be disgusting, and though services subsequently offered cannot be much valued or confided in, yet some allowance may be made for this man. When it was first understood that the British had advanced to the hills, for the purpose of expelling the Ghoorkha usurpers, there was doubtless a general impression in our favour. The great name which our success and moderation in India had obtained, prepossessed the hill-states, who had indistinctly heard of it, with a belief that we were invincible. Three successive failures, however, staggered this faith; and they began to doubt whether we could make an impression on their enemies, far less free them from their yoke. The Ghoorkhas had been severe rulers, and always punished a fault with cruelty. Those who held their places by favour of the conquerors, might well ponder deeply before they incurred the deadly stain of rebellion, and openly declared against their employers. They had all to lose, little to win; for, as individuals, their situation was as good as they could expect it to be made by any change.

Of those who were thus situated, perhaps Dangee was in the most critical circumstances, and required peculiar deliberation and dexterity in taking a decided part. He was not the true chief; the people obeyed him from an influence he had acquired over them by his abilities. It was necessary for him to see that he did not lose that influence: he might not only ruin himself, if the Ghoorkhas prevailed, but might also, if they were worsted, place the state itself in an awkward predicament; for these narrow eastern politicians in general, and a person so circumscribed in opportunities of acquiring a knowledge of the British general policy as Dangee, could have no just idea of the generous and liberal principles, which usually govern British councils in their behaviour to a fallen foe, or to a friendly ally; and he might be afraid of placing the country in the hands of a new ruler, who might not be more lenient to it than the Ghoorkhas were, and possibly far less favourable to him than those whom he had tried.

The claims of Sirmore on Joobul were always irksome to the people and to their rulers, and the equality to which both were now reduced, and the freedom from any invidious tribute to that state in acknowledgment of superiority (even although at the expense of a severe tyranny under the Ghoorkhas), were perhaps more grateful, at least to the chief, if not to the mass of the people, than a state of vassalage to masters whom they hated and despised. He feared the re-establishment of the feudatory rights of Sirmore in case of the country being freed from the Ghoorkhas, and restored to its ancient rulers; or dreaded that the British power would be exercised in favour of that state, of which the chief was now our ally, whilst he himself might lose the exorbitant influence and high rank he then held in his own state. If such were his apprehensions, and such the spring of his conduct, it cannot excite surprise that he was cautious and unresolved, and that such were his feelings is proved by the terms he sought when the declaration in our favour was absolutely made.

Dangee is unquestionably possessed of considerable talents, and of a cunning which is peculiarly admired, and not unfrequently is successful in the negotiations among these petty states, where bad faith, and breach of treaty or of word, are not considered as disgraceful if they gain the desired end.

Next to Dangee, a chief named Preemoo holds the highest rank or power: him we did not see, nor in fact was he at all of nearly equal importance with the other.

Of the revenues of Joobul, or of its population, I can say but little: the only fact known is, that it produced to the Ghoorkha government a yearly sum of 24,000 rupees.

Of a state so trifling in its value it may be thought impertinent to say so much, but a great part of this hilly region is made up of such insignificant principalities; and it sometimes happens that circumstances of position, or of natural advantage of one kind or other, give to a poor country an extrinsic interest and value:—such is the case with Joobul.

Joobul is situated centrically between the difficult (and indeed to an army impracticable) country at the foot of, and stretching through the Snowy Mountains, and contained between the rivers Touse and Pabur, and those countries to the south of the range of Choor which were under command of the army investing Jytock.

The chief road from Irkee and Ummr Sing's positions to the eastward passes through the Barug T,hakooree and Joobul, and crosses the river Touse at Unhoul, the Jumna at Juddoo, and the Bhagiruttee at Barahat, and is practicable and safe throughout. From Joobul also branch various roads to different fords and bridges upon the Touse, both to the north and south of Unhoul. This river is large and rapid, and by no means fordable except at a few points, which fits it well for a line of defence; and the routes to the north of Unhoul are uncertain and dangerous, while those to the southward pass through the district of Jounsar, which at this time had openly declared in our favour.

Whatever might have been the private inclinations of their chief, the men of Joobul were from an early period friendly to our cause, and willing to rise in our favour, and only wanted the consent of their superior, and the confidence inspired by a British party, to join them in arms. This disposition was evinced in more than one instance in their behaviour, as will hereafter be mentioned. Such is the situation of Joobul; and such was the disposition of its inhabitants previous to the successes of General Ochterlony over Ummr Sing; and these circumstances pointed it out as a most desirable position to be occupied by a strong party of troops in British pay.

It was proposed that a line of defence and communication, such as has before been adverted to in the observations on the progress of the campaign, should have been formed, which would connect with the forces before Jytock, across the Choor range, and occupy the strong holds of Joobul; and having a strong post at Unhoul, and from thence meeting and partly following the course of the river Pabur to the north-west, would stretch into Bischur.

Of this line a glance at the map or a slight knowledge of the country will show the strength and utility, as well as of the importance of its central point, Joobul.

The district between the Pabur and the Touse was almost totally freed from the enemy, who had begun to confine himself to his strong holds, and the inhabitants were, it was believed, well disposed.

The district of Jounsar, in the rear to the eastward, was devoted to our interests; while the nature of the country was such, that if at all skilfully defended, it could not possibly be forced; and it offered within itself some means of supply, and a hardy race suited either to act as porters for conveying provisions, or as light troops well acquainted with every pass and ford, to facilitate easy communication or to annoy a flying foe.

Thus, a line such as now described would have completely cut off communication between the two chief Ghoorkha forces, that at Malown under Ummr Sing, and that at Jytock under Runjore Sing; and in the event of either position being forced, no junction could have been formed, or, if attempted, the retreating force would have had not only to cut their way through this strong line of positions, but to cope with the whole pursuing army; whilst the people of the country they must pass through, hostile to them, and supported in their courage by the presence of our troops, would fatally annoy and perplex them.

The supplies necessary to their subsistence would be refused them, nor could they venture to delay their marches to collect it by force.

Such a line, too, would not only straiten the enemy's resources by advancing and gradually closing in on all sides, but would, in fact, become strengthened itself by the extent of friendly country in its rear, and by its approximation to the force before Malown.

In every point of view, then, it would probably have been a prudent mode of operation to pursue, and Joobul was thus invested with more consequence than it seems naturally destined to possess.

It was occupied after the first movement of the irregulars into it, and the consequent evacution of fort Choüpal, but it was only by an irregular force, which, to the extent of 7 or 800 men, were despatched thither, and were joined by the Joobul troops under Dangee.

Circumstances, however, rendered it unnecessary to follow up the above detailed plan, if it ever was seriously in contemplation. The brilliant successes of the army under General Ochterlony were succeeded by events which brought the campaign to a more speedy and fortunate conclusion than the disasters and delays of its commencement warranted us to expect.

The fort of Choupal, close to which we were encamped, is situated on the Gudhala ridge, which is a projection from a greater one that connects Choor with a large mountain to the north called Urructa, and it forms the northern side of the valley we came down, through which runs the Shashalu Nullah.

The fort is placed on a ledge overlooking the valley, and behind it stretches a gentle acclivity, which ends in a short but steep ascent to the crest of the ridge; thus it is commanded even by musquetry from many points. It obtains all its water from a hollow or tank, which is formed on the hill-side above it, distant about a gunshot, and which may be cut off from the approach of the garrison with little trouble, so that it is by no means calculated to stand a siege in any point of view: indeed, it is probable that it was not originally intended for the purposes in which it was now employed, and that it was merely the house of a chief, who thought it sufficient if it was able to repel the desultory attack of a marauding party; for even in the rudest state of warfare it must be apparent that a garrison cannot subsist without a supply of water.

The Ghoorkhas, probably seeing the value of the situation, took hold in the first building that presented itself as sufficient for shelter, and trusted to the fear their name had inspired for preventing a serious or continued attack, and in all likelihood would at a future period have erected a more sufficient fortress on a better situation, for they usually choose such with great judgment.

The present fort is a square building of no great extent, with a tower at three of its corners, and inclosing a court of about twenty feet square. The largest tower was occupied as a temple by the divinity only, and this is ornamented with considerable neatness. A second contained the apartments of the commandant, a soubahdar.

The whole is three stories high: in the lower one cattle of all sorts were stowed: probably in time of siege, these gave room to stores of different sorts. In the second and third the garrison was lodged. A great part consists of open verandah; but the soldiers of the East are not nice with respect to their accommodations, generally stretching themselves in their rosais wherever there is room, with little care about the apartment. Still less do the Ghoorkhas or hill-men care where they lay their wearied limbs.

About the court-yard lay several large pieces of fir-trees, hollowed to hold water, which had been done by the soubahdar when preparing to resist the attack he saw approaching: they would not have held more than four or five days' consumption for the garrison, which consisted of 100 men.

Around the building they had planted a good stockade, not more than six feet from the walls, which was a formidable defence, and would have prevented such troops as were likely to oppose them from an assault; and the walls were bored into loopholes for musquetry in all directions.

The troops were all under cover; but as there was no room for them to move about in, they would have been forced to remain continually motionless in their rooms, which would of itself have been no trifling inconvenience. The stockade, when we now visited it, had since the evacuation of the post gone nearly to ruin.

The soubahdar who had commanded it was with me at the time I examined the fort, and pointed out all his projects and contrivances; "but," said he, "God willed it otherwise, and I am now your servant."

The sensations with which a brave soldier views the place he once commanded in, and which he has been forced to yield up without fighting, from the dread of famine and of certain destruction to his troops, must be painful, however blameless he deems himself, and the soubahdar showed that he felt them so.

But, as he observed, what must be done at last had better be done with a good grace at first. He had no means of resisting the overpowering force that sprang up against him, nor any hope of assistance, nor the means of subsistence till such could arrive.

He pointed out the corn he had sowed never to reap, and the improvement he meditated but could not complete, with somewhat of a bitter smile. He was a steady, determined, and zealous officer; and it is pleasing to think, that in his change of service he has been so far fortunate as to lose nothing in emolument or respect, and that while with us he met with all proper regard and attention.

It is well known that in the East no obloquy attaches to a man who changes his side, and fights against the cause he once contended for, especially if the train of original service has once been broken; and although the point of honour seems to be tenaciously kept by the Ghoorkhas, and their attachment to their country is perhaps greater than among other eastern people, it does not appear to be considered a dishonourable act, if, when forced by an enemy to surrender prisoner, an officer of theirs should enter the service of that enemy.

In this way Runjeet Sing, the Sikh chief, the deadly enemy of the Ghoorkha government, has inlisted a considerable body of the Ghoorkhas and others; and the deserters from the forts of Malown and Jytock, when forced by famine to leave their garrisons, inlisted with the armies investing these places.

There is no town in Joobul which can claim a preference over the rest to such a degree as to be considered its capital.

The house of the Rānā is in the valley of Deyrah, whither we were to bend our course; but Choupal, from its centrical situation, and the importance it asserts as being a fortress, is considered that point in the state which suggests the idea nearest to that of a capital town. Near to it are the villages of the chief people, Dangee and Preemoo, and around it there is a good deal of cultivation, and a tolerably populous country. Nevertheless, although the feelings of the people in our favour were sufficiently proved to be of the warmest nature, we found that they, as usual, hung back when called upon for grain and supplies for the party, and after various shifting excuses it was at last found necessary to have recourse to strong measures, and parties were detached to search for grain in the neighbourhood, and to bring what was found into camp.

After breakfast several of the neighbouring seanas, and most persons of any rank, came and paid their respects; among them a brother of Preemoo's, who brought with him his brother, a boy of eleven or twelve years of age, as fair, I think, as any English boy. The man himself was dark, and I thought him so fine a figure, and so fair, yet so favourable a specimen of the hill-chiefs, that I took a sketch of him and his little brother: he went only by the name of Preemoo Ka Bhaee (or Preemoo's brother), and I could obtain no other for him.

Choupal itself formed a subject for a drawing worth taking, having in its distance the venerable mountain Choor in a new point of view; and as we were unable to march this day, from the delay of procuring supplies, I had sufficient time to accomplish the undertaking.

CHAPTER XII.

As authentic intelligence had been received of the total capture of Kirtee Rānā's force, leaving not a single party of the enemy to oppose our progress, and that only the garrison of Raeengudh on the banks of the Pabur (which was now invested by our irregulars and the hill-troops), remained in all the country, the necessity for travelling with a large escort ceased, and accordingly the troops were left at Choupal, encamped under the charge of the risāldār, ready to move on any emergency; while only the Ghoorkha soubahdar with a party of his men, a few picked Patāns and Mewatties, with a few of Skinner's corps, in all not exceeding fifty men, accompanied us onwards.

May 15.—The necessary arrangements and a general review of the troops delayed our setting off till past nine o'clock.

Our route lay across a deep ravine, which we descended by a rough uninteresting road, and again slanted upwards to the top, where there was a neat rustic-looking temple in a grove of larch and fir-trees; in which, among other pieces of somewhat rude sculpture, I observed an angel's face precisely similar to the heads of the cherubim represented in our sacred prints and pictures.

The descent from this place to the village of Bhuteoura is moderate though rocky. This village was deserted at our approach, probably from a fear of our Ghoorkhas. From hence by a very precipitous descent we reached the Cotha Nullah, which is a fine copious stream, formed by the numerous small rills that arise in the Poonnur valley, whence it flows.

This valley forms a purgunnah, which is occupied by a singularly bold and savage set of people, very distinct in their character and conduct from the other inhabitants of Joobul. Although forming a part of that state, they neither acknowledge the superiority of its chief, nor pay their regular assessment without force, which has frequently been found insufficient to compel them.

After Sirmore and Joobul were subdued, it cost the Ghoorkhas much trouble and several years, before this place was reduced to a temporary subjection: and at length an overpowering force of near 6000 men was sent against them, with whom they fought a bloody battle at a place called Matteële, when at last they were broken and dispersed, and the conquerors punished their obstinacy severely, by destroying most of their villages and strong holds. They, however, afterwards revenged themselves, though in a treacherous way.

Immediately on hearing of the invasion by the British, without waiting to observe on which side success might attend, or considering the certain destruction that awaited them if their enemies prevailed, and armed chiefly with axes, bows, and arrows tipt with bone, they rose upon the parties of Ghoorkha soldiery, whom they had treacherously invited into the district on the plea of giving their tribute, and massacred every one of them. This act, more than any other, displays the character of the people; wild and untameable, savage and treacherous, but brave and impatient, and strongly imbued with a love of liberty.

Upon the advance of the first party of irregulars into Joobul these men instantly assembled, and invested the fort of Choupal so closely, that one of their number was killed by a shot from the garrison: and there is little doubt that the fear of being abandoned to the lawless rage of such savages, was a principal inducement with the commandant to capitulate.

Such a conduct forms a strong contrast to that of Dangee and his dependents, and indeed to that of almost all the inhabitants of the hills. If this savage disposition was only evinced towards, and exercised upon, their enemies, it were perhaps less revolting; but they are also terrible marauders, committing great atrocities in the neighbourhood, and robbing in every direction when they have a hope of success.

It is a singular and curious circumstance that a race or clan, so different from the poor and subdued creatures with which it is surrounded, should exist thus insulated, a solitary instance of spirit and of independence, the supposed peculiar endowments of highlanders, although degraded by such treachery and cruelty, in a country of mountains, which might well be supposed to give birth to hardihood and enterprise.

Although their district is wild and rugged, it does not appear more inaccessible than others. There are many villages to be seen of great extent, and much corn-land. They are said to be able to muster about 1000 fighting men: of this number 300 are armed with matchlocks, and they are very bold and expert in a teasing and harassing kind of bush-fighting, by which, unharmed themselves, they rapidly destroy any invading force.

They have, I believe, no regular form of government. The oldest seānās, or chiefs of villages, give their counsel, and direct the conduct and enterprises of the rest, who are willing enough to obey directions which lead to plunder; and the state of hostility, or at least of segregation, in which they continue from the rest of the country, forms a strong bond of union among themselves.

The evening before we passed, one of the Poonnur zemindars came to the village of Bhuteoura to learn if it were true that an English army had reached Choupal, led by Europeans, and if possible to ascertain their views. Upon being informed that such was the case, and being told of the force (probably exaggerated), and that it was supposed to be going on to Bischur, and had no apparent intention of molesting any one, he observed, "That the English were a great nation; that for their part they lived contented on what they had, and did not want money, therefore they would not molest them on their march."

The Cotee Nullah is bare of all wood, surrounded by brown hills, and has no beauty: it abounds in fish, and our Ghoorkhas, while we rested on its banks, gave us a specimen of their dexterity in catching them. Every man of those who were in immediate attendance, jemmadars, havildars, and sepoys, stript in a moment at the word of the old soubahdar, and plunged into the stream with great glee, and surrounding large stones, with their hands only, in twenty minutes drew out a quantity of fish.

The good humour and alertness of these people at any thing to which they are put is remarkable, and makes every service they render very pleasant, and every communication you have with them comfortable, beyond what I have observed in any other people.

The fish thus caught were of the same leather-mouthed and indifferent species which we obtained at Shai.

x 2

From hence we rounded a point which is formed by the debouche of the Nār nuddee into the Cotee, and pursued our course up the bed of the former in a north-east direction, the road winding with the stream, which is full and fine.

We passed a curious temple to Kālā, Chitra, Deota, and several small villages, crossing and re-crossing the stream, the road leading along ledges of chiefly abandoned cultivation. After a course of about three miles in the Nār nulla, we ascended its right bank, and passing through Bigroulee, a fine romantic village inhabited by Brahmins, by a rough rocky road, with several petty ascents and descents, we reached the village of Bumpta, where we were to pass the night.

The scenery or face of the country to-day had little to attract attention or merit description. The back of the Choupal, or Gudhala ridge, was somewhat wooded with Weymouth pines towards the top; but the lower parts, and the whole of the intermediate hills, the valley of Cotee and Nār, were destitute almost of a tree.

The latter valley was, at its mouth, broader than common, but by no means proportionally cultivated. Some villages were in ruins by the ravages of the Poonurrees. The whole valley had a more brown and barren look than usual; its exposure was to the southward.

It might be curious to inquire what can be the reason of so striking a difference between the northern and the southern faces of the hills; but to come to any satisfactory result would require more observation than we could apply. Can it proceed from the stronger effect of the sun's rays, or does any particular wind prevail in one direction unkindly to vegetation? There is no want of water; every small fissure or ravine had its rill running to join the Nār.

The hill-face, which we ascended to Bumpta, was chiefly composed of shapeless blocks and slabs of hard micaceous slate, and fragments irregularly scattered by the destruction of the cliffs above. This slate was flaky, tinged with iron-mould, and covered with leaden-coloured pimples, supposed to contain imbedded garnets; sometimes a mixture of sand giving a hardness of texture was seen; quartz, which is generally found attached to the hardest parts, and indications of iron, were common.

In the bed of the river and on the banks were scattered blocks of a hard gritty stone, which at first was suspected to be granite, but I now believe it to have been a different stone, to which I cannot give a name. The whole ridge has an appearance of gradual decay; the soil mouldering away, and washed by the rains, leaves the cliffs bare, and ultimately they decay and fall in ruins down the hill-face.

Bumpta was formerly a fort, and considered a place of strength in the country; it had a strong wall and towers, and is situated so as to command the vale below, but it again is commanded by the whole hill above. It was probably extensive, as the ruins are large, but it was burnt down I believe by accident, and there was at this time a house building for the residence of the Rānā of Joobul upon the old foundation.

That part which was to serve for the temple was nearly complete, and in the sculpture which adorned it we recognised many of the Hindoo divinities, particularly Gonesh, with his large belly and elephant snout. It appears that, as with the ancients, a temple and household gods are necessary appendages to the dwelling-house of every considerable person: to every one we saw was attached a lofty tower dedicated to this purpose. In the houses of the vulgar the apartment of the divinity was not so obvious; he was probably contented with a niche in the wall.

The wind last night was piercingly cold, and this morning we felt it very sharply. We began our march a little before nine, ascending the valley, still in a north-east direction. The road led at first through a fine wood of Weymouth pines, but afterwards along a bare, steep, and rather green hill-face, with gray crags above us, towering to a great height on our left hand.

About eleven o'clock we reached the crest of the ridge, which branches off from the great mountain Urructa, whence we gained an extensive view to the southward and westward. Passing onwards upon this ridge for a short way, we commenced a gradual ascent, winding round the right hand slope of the northern peak of the mountain.

This noble mountain Urructa, like Choor, is covered towards the top with deep and venerable forests, particularly on the northern face. That which we now entered into was richer and more romantic, if possible, than any forest we had yet seen; not only pines of all sorts were here of all ages, from the greenest youth to the most hoary state of decay;

hollies and oaks grown to the most enormous size, with sycamore and yew of the most varied forms; these, with thousands of other trees, united in producing an effect both new and splendid.

Gradually ascending by a good path, but interrupted occasionally by blocks of stone, we reached a spot where a spring, the coldest and the most delicious as we then thought that we had ever tasted, gushes from the mountain side, and falls over a spout which has been carefully placed to receive and direct it.

The natives of the hills are particularly attentive to distinguishing and guarding from pollution, and facilitating the use of fine springs of water, by erecting over them sheds of stone, whence they are led by a spout, so that the thirsty traveller may easily drink without muddying its source; or, as in the present instance, simply place a spout from which it may run pure.

But when we had feasted on the cold spring we found that the place had other attractions which would have fixed us there for a time. A vista was opened in the wild and awful forest, through which the whole of the hills in their various ridges, to and beyond the Sutlej, appeared, boldly swelling till they faded in the distance.

Around us the fantastic forms of the old trees, their rich masses of foliage contrasting with the gray bare crags, and the blasted pines and withered oaks, formed a foreground for a picture worthy the pencil of a Salvator. Nor would our attendants, the Ghoorkhas, the hill-men, and the Patāns, formed into groups reclined around, or loitering on the rocks and cliffs, have disgraced the composition.

Some scenes impress themselves on the memory too strongly and too strikingly ever to be effaced, and this, I think, was surely one of that sort.

Here we found a birch-tree for the first time, precisely similar to that of Scotland in all respects. The bark, leaf, twig, and buds were quite the same; the leaf was somewhat larger, but seemed to possess no fragrance; yet we had been struck at a short distance before we reached this tree with a scent exactly like that of the birch after a shower, but could then discover no such tree. Hence we were induced to conjecture that there might be two varieties, one only of which we had seen, and that the other which was fragrant had escaped our notice. As we were informed that the birch-trees were abundant farther on, we did not pluck even a bough, although ancient recollections almost tempted us to do so. We found sweetbriar in great plenty, and giving a perfume perfectly the same as that from the home plant.

The soil covering the rock was a rich black vegetable mould, and it gave a luxuriant carpet of the productions usually met with in such places, viz. all sorts of strawberries, columbines, lilies of the valley, buttercups, yellow, blue, and white cowslips, a small and very beautiful flower partaking of the auricula and cowslip, purple and blue, and a superb sort of lupine of a dark blackish purple. A species of larkspur was also found of a lovely blue, as one of our people somewhat poetically observed, "shining in the forest like a bright lamp in the dark night."

Such was the slope, but steep and interrupted with rocks and fallen trees, over which we reached the pass between the two peaks of the Urructa mountain, whence, looking to the northward, the whole stupendous range of the Himālā burst upon our view, now no longer fading into distance, but clear and well defined. Bright with snow, and rising far above all intervening obstacles, they stretched, bounding our view from far beyond the Sutlej, till our sight was interrupted, where, in all probability, the hills of Gungotri and Buddrinaath arose.

The day was clear, and only here and there a black cloud rested on the highest peaks. The scene was majestic, and if the epithet can justly be applied to any thing on earth, truly sublime.

There is that in the appearance of the Himālā range which every person who has seen them will allow to be peculiarly their own. No other mountains that I have ever seen have any resemblance to their character. Their summits shoot in the most fantastic and spiring peaks to a height that astonishes; and, when seen from an elevated situation, almost induces the belief of an ocular deception.

The very lofty and shaggy ranges which are thrown from their feet up towards that on which we stood, shrunk into petty hills in their presence; unless, however, something approaching to them in its nature has been seen, it is no easy matter to form or to give an idea of the striking mass of objects which they present, seen as we now saw them: it will be best attempted by the drawings which faintly delineate the scenery. On this occasion, however, it was difficult to obtain a clear uninterrupted sketch, because the foliage in front obtruded on the view, and after searching for some time, and trusting to the guide for showing us, as he promised, a clear spot, I was forced to content myself with a very confined and inadequate position whence to take the drawing I desired, and when it was too late I discovered a much finer and more expanded one.

Continuing along the crest and northern face of the ridge with a westerly direction, we soon began to descend along the brow and ridges of a hill covered with fine forests of spruce and silver fir, carpeted with luxuriant grass, and at times opening into rich green glades thickly covered with flowers.

The view which we enjoyed from the edge of the ridge we descended was exceedingly diversified and fine. On either hand a deep glen sloped gradually down to the river Pabur, very richly cultivated, and studded with villages and groves of trees; the heights beyond were crested by forts, and the green slope and dark firs among which we wound contrasted well with them.

On the banks of a stream in the valley of Deyrah the rānā's house was conspicuous; beyond were the wild craggy roots of the Snowy Mountains, and above them towered their peaks in calm and awful stillness, lighted up by the declining sun.

In front, a deep glen, formed by a recess in these mountains, showed the course of the river Pabur. A black rough ridge, which approached from these on the left, runs between it and the Sutlej. To the left, the valley through which the Touse runs appeared at no great distance, and beyond its eastern boundary we could trace that formed by the Jumna—a wide and interesting range of vision.

The beauty and variety of the scenes presented to us would have made distance short and labour easy, but the descent itself was far from being rough or precipitous. As we approached the village of Dhār, where our tent was pitched, the path spread out, and had more the appearance of a made road than any we had yet seen.

The village seemed to be populous and of some magnitude. A great number of its inhabitants assembled to look at the strangers. It is situate on the declivity of a hill, which runs down between the two valleys facing the north, and looking down on the glen of the Pabur.

Of the scenery and aspect of the country passed through this day, enough has been said. Crossing a lofty mountain, it could not but be rocky, wild, and desert; but the valleys on the northern side surpass in beauty, and perhaps in rich cultivation, and in the number of villages, any part of the hill country through which our route has as yet led.

It excites surprise, that such mountains should bear in their bosoms so much fertility, so many men, and their food. The valley of Deyrah, in which the Rānā resides, is particularly rich and lovely.

Of the trees and shrubs nearly all has been said that I am able to relate. Of new ones, we could this day reckon the sycamore and the birch. The former appeared to us to be perfectly similar to that of Europe, except that the leaves are less numerous, and the branches longer and more slender, giving less massiness to the look of the tree, than I think it has in Britain; but its growth in a deep dark forest, where it has little freedom of air or light, may account for this.

There was here, as in most other places in our route, a great variety of trees, shrubs, and herbs, quite unknown to us. The size of the trees was generally enormous. One measured, I think, twenty-seven or twenty-five feet in girth, which spired up quite straight to its top. It was, however, in a state of decay; and we remarked that few large trees were quite sound in the heart. The holly, or oak (for to determine of which genus some trees were was beyond the power of our eye, without botanic science to determine; so much they seemed to shade into each other), towered up straight like the pine tribe, often without many branches, spreading a few leafy boughs at a great height above.

The soil throughout was deep, rich, vegetable matter, black and very plentiful. The rock has experienced little or no change of nature or structure; still consisting of micaceous slate, always laminous, modified into many variations of appearance. Sometimes there was a larger admixture of sand, in other instances, mixtures of sandstone and quartz: but there was no stone seen that resembled granite.

Our march this day did not exceed ten miles and a half, and was, on the whole, the least fatiguing we have had, although we reached a very great height.

Below, upon the banks of the river Pabur, but not in view from the place of our encampment, is situated the fortress of Raeengudh, then occupied by a garrison of about 160 Ghoorkhas, under the command of Runsoor T,happa. Letters had been despatched to him, informing him of the state of the campaign, both at Malown and Jytock, requiring him to deliver up the fortress to the British, and offering him service if he wished it, and other advantageous terms. It was a matter of some interest, if not of deep anxiety, to get possession of this fort,—the only strong hold which the Ghoorka power held to the northward, since Kirtee Rānā's defeat; and one of our principal objects was, if possible, to get possessionof it.

At the village of Dhār, our messenger returned with an answer to our proposals. Runsoor observed, that he believed what we informed him, respecting the campaign, was very true; and that he must surrender one time or other, was likewise very apparent; but that he had provision and water for two months in the fort, and could see no good reason for giving up the fort before he was forced to do so; that he had eaten Ghoorkha salt, and should prove to them a traitor, if he complied with our terms, with the means in his hands which he actually possessed. He concluded by observing, somewhat shrewdly, that, if to them he should thus prove faithless, we could place little dependence on the fidelity of his services in any future employment.

It was, however, thought proper to make another effort, as it was inconvenient to leave this strong place in our rear; and it was intimated to Runsoor, that, if he now surrendered, he should be treated with kindness, and have protection for his property, as well as that of his garrison; but that, if he should persist in fruitless and unnecessary opposition, the whole force of Joobul, with the irregulars that then were before the place, and the troops of Bischur and Cooloo also, all at hand, should be let loose against him, and would surely reduce him; when he would fall into the hands of less merciful enemies, who would wreak their vengeance on him for the tyranny which he and his employers had exercised over the land.

It was thought that he would, on consideration, yield to the fear of falling into the hands of the barbarous troops, thus standing in array against him; and we believed that he only held out for a while, for the point of honour. No one but must admire the sentiments of fidelity expressed by this man; and ourselves, although teased by his conduct, gave him all the respect and consideration it entitled him to.—We prepared to reconnoitre the fortress on the next day.

May 17.—The Rānā of Joobul paid us a visit this morning. He came attended by a considerable concourse of his subjects. He was a thin and sickly looking young man, about twenty-five years of age; his complexion pale and yellow, his features meagre and prominent, his eyes large, protuberant, and bloodshot, the lids tinged with antimony. His dress was Hindoo, plain white, with cross-striped silk trowsers. The fashion of his turban somewhat resembled that of the Sikhs. He wore a cotton cloth, of no very considerable fineness, thrown round his shoulders and head. His presence had nothing in the least degree commanding, and his whole appearance put me much in mind of a poor Calcutta shop-keeper, or Sircar. His attendants were as little imposing as himself; those who were best dressed had only to boast of a complete hill-suit of clothes (blanket), with perhaps a cotton sheet around their shoulders. It was not, however, to be expected, that the lord of a petty state, who had for several years languished in obscure poverty, and was now hardly restored to his rights, could make a very splendid figure.

The visit did not last long. The Rānā presented as a nuzzer, a hill ram goat, and two mountain pheasants, called by the natives rutnāls, and two small bags of musk. The birds were beautiful, but died almost immediately from the heat of the sun. In return, he was presented on the part of government (in whose name the presents were received) with shawls, &c.

Little conversation passed between us. The chief appeared confused and frightened, and evinced no signs of ability. He practised the usual custom of suffering an attendant to speak for him, to whom he addressed any question or answer he wished to convey.

Little change was remarked in the natives, from the time we entered Joobul. Those who are elevated above the mere populace have perhaps a more frank and active air, and approach somewhat nearer to our ideas of a Highlander. They are commonly small and spare, but active; their features hard and high; their look is rather quick, but the character of their countenance has not undergone any material change. Their complexion still continues of the same yellowish brown; those parts which are much exposed being naturally darker than the rest.

We saw little of their women, but those who did appear were short and stout, shaggy looking creatures, in ragged garments, with good-humoured light-complexioned faces.

Soon after the Rānā took leave, we struck our tents, and set out for Raeengudh. We descended by a steep stony path into the nullah on our right hand; and, crossing it, kept along its right bank on a good road, which chiefly led along ledges of cultivation, and a path made with stones projecting from the banks. We passed through some neat villages; and, in one of them, saw a furnace for smelting iron ore, but which was not at work.

Here we were met by Dangee, wuzzeer of Joobul, with a large military attendance, and much more state than waited on his master; in truth, he is a far better looking subject for a chief, than the miserable creature who claims that distinction. He was a fine looking, large, and stout man, dressed pretty much in the Hindoostannee fashion, and wore a Sikh turban; he had come from his camp before Raeengudh, where he remained blockading that place.

Another steep descent brought us to the bed of the river Pabur, and in sight of the fortress. It is built upon a small insulated rock, which rises upon the north side of the river, to the height of from 3 to 400 feet above the bed. A plain wall of dry stone, as it appeared, encircles the whole of the top of the rock, following its figure, which takes that of an irregular oblong. The inclosure contains several buildings, which are as usual attached to the wall, leaving a space apparently unoccupied in the centre. It is inaccessible in most parts; but where it was possible even to stand, the Ghoorkhas had surrounded it with a stockade.

From a similarly insulated, but larger hill, on our own side of the river, which we ascended, and which we calculated to be about 600 yards distant from the fort, we could discern piles of fuel of great size, and corn in stacks of sheaves heaped within it. The garrison all mounted the tops of the houses to see us. There were a few hours of truce, while we waited an answer to the letter written from Dhār, so that no molestation was offered; but, indeed, little could have been given, and nothing from the hill we were upon, without artillery. I could have wished to see the effect of a six-pounder on the wall; musquetry, however, commanded the work to a certain degree from two points; one was not, I think, more than 250 yards distant, but was scarcely elevated above it; from the hill, however, to the north-west, at a point about 300 to 350 yards distant, musquetry could plunge into the place; but the marksmen were so indifferent that I do not think there was much mischief done from that distance. Here, and on a ledge a little higher up, a party of the troops of Bischur and Cooloo were posted; and, from a breastwork which they had erected, they kept up an occasional fire on the garrison.

There was a spring, under this hill, about a gunshot, or 150 yards from the fort, whence the Ghoorkhas supplied themselves with water, wishing not to exhaust what they had in tanks within doors; and as they came down for this purpose, the Bischurees fired upon them: yet as the spring was commanded by the musquetry of the fort, they did not choose to expose their persons by taking post there; or by erecting any work which would cut off this supply from the enemy.

On the south side of the river, in a hollow opposite to the fort, Dangee and his Joobulians, with the irregulars that had been sent to his support (but many of whom had deserted), lay encamped.

Close to this place, and under the small hill which we had ascended, there was an inclosure, and a temple of great sanctity, named Hāt-Gobēseree; the name of the image or deity being Gobēseree, and the place being known by that of Hāt. Under a large spreading walnut tree in this inclosure, we had our tent placed, not interfering with any spot that could be polluted by this measure. This inclosure might be from twenty to thirty yards square, paved with slate, and surrounded by a dry wall: it contains two temples of unequal size, besides a number of small shrines or pagodas from eight to ten feet high. The temples are curious, but somewhat mean, built of dry stone, painted in some parts red and brown. They have the Chinese large overhanging roof slated, and, elevated above them, a large round canopy of wood; the cornices are ornamented with a fringe of wooden bobbins; wooden bells are hung at each corner, and there is a good deal of carved work about them.

The larger, or more sacred temple, may stand on a square of twenty feet, and has a paved and raised court before it; within, there is an idol, tolerably richly dressed; we were informed that he has golden *bangles* on his arms, and much of that precious metal, as well as silver, about his person. He certainly glittered very much; but the place, as is customary in all Hindoo sanctuaries, was very dark; and we were only permitted to go as far as the door, whence we could not even tell what his figure was.

That riches should remain unrifled in a conquered country, and by such conquerors, is singular: and it proves the estimated sanctity of the place. The Ghoorkhas did not dare to rob the sanctuary.

The smaller temple has, I believe, less pretension to holiness; and we saw no one approach it while we remained there, although crowds paid their adoration at the larger. On the smaller, however, there is more carved work, but I know not whether it contains an image. The smaller shrines are, like the larger, built of dry stones, cut and shaped so as to compose the whole, which resembles the Hindoo pagodas in taste; some of them are neatly carved.

The whole side of the river, in the vicinity of this place, is studded with smaller or larger temples of the same sort. I made a sketch of the two large temples, and one of the small ones. The river Pabur, at present considerably greater than the Girree, a large, clear, and rapid stream, flows by this place; and the heat rendered bathing in its waters, this evening, a pleasant refreshment.

May 18.—This day, the two commanders of the Bischur troops, T'hiken Dās, and Buddree Dās, accompanied by Dangee, and some of the other men of rank, paid us a visit. These two men are wuzzeers of Bischur, and in fact the chief men of the state, for the rajah is a child. They headed the troops that were sent against Kirtee Rānā, and were now attempting to finish their work by reducing Raeengudh. These men presented us with parcels of the medicinal root zedoary, called here nirbisee.

Soon after, a formal refusal to surrender was received from Runsoor T,happa, and what were called active operations recommenced; and the fort was ordered to be invested. We had no cannon of any sort, nor any even of the long native guns, called *Jinjauls;* so that nothing effectual could be even attempted. There was little chance of success from an assault, had we even had troops who would have made the attempt; for we had no ladders, nor any means of forcing an entrance; but, indeed, had there been every thing that was necessary, the thing was not worth the sacrifice of lives it might have cost. We therefore determined to leave those troops whom we found there, to invest the fort, and proceed ourselves on our route to Bischur. A party of T'hiken Dās's troops now crossed the river, and stealing along the ground on all fours, occupied a ridge somewhat covered from the fire of the fort, whence they partially commanded the road to the spring of water used by the garrison, and a sort of bush fighting commenced, which, from the distance and caution employed on both sides, proved very innocent.

While conversing with T'hiken Dās upon the means for reducing the garrison, he told us, that he expected a man from his own country, who would construct a machine, by the help of which, the fort would soon be compelled to surrender. On his describing this machine, we were not a little surprised to find, that it was almost exactly similar to the catapulta of the Romans for projecting large stones. He plainly stated it to be framed of strong ropes, and large beams of wood; one of which, a large tree, was to be pulled back by the force of from one to two hundred men, and a heavy stone of from seventy to two hundred pounds, to be thrown by its reaction to a great distance, which, falling on a house or fort, would destroy it and the garrison. He said, that it had been used in that country more than once, with success; and that when one or two stones of a certain weight had been thrown, they could easily judge of the weight that would carry to the distance required; and would reach their object with certainty every time they discharged stones at it. We had no better authority for believing that this machine ever had been in use here, excepting the assurance of other natives of the same country in confirmation of his report.

It is surely very extraordinary, to find in so remote and savage a country, among a people who could scarcely have had intercourse of such a nature with enlightened nations, as to learn their arts of war, the knowledge of so very complicated an apparatus, so closely resembling one of those machines used by nations the most expert in those arts before the invention of modern artillery.

Now that the primary object of the expedition was attained, or anticipated by the enemy's evacuation of the country, and a full and active declaration by its inhabitants in our favour, it was deemed advisable to obtain as extensive an acquaintance as a cursory view could give, and as our time would allow, both of the country and of its inhabitants, further towards the interior; and generally throughout those regions now fallen, or likely to fall into the British power. With this view, we resolved on proceeding towards the west, and on passing through a portion of the collection of petty states, known by the appellation of Baruh Thakooraee, by which means a quick communication might be kept up with General Ochterlony: and thus, governed by such intelligence as might reach us from his camp, we might direct our march towards Bischur, or otherwise, as might be expedient.

We struck our tent somewhat late in the evening, and following up the course of the river Pabur, in a fine and somewhat broad bed, with good cultivation on its banks, we reached a stream which runs through the valley of Nawre Purgunnah. Here we began to ascend, and passing through several villages, we halted at Karashee about eight o'clock, after a march of about six miles.

The latter part of our walk was in darkness, and very disagreeable; for the road was stony and precipitous, and we fared sufficiently ill, as our servants did not come up till late.

Of the country, I can say nothing; in fact there is nothing to be said: it was the ridge of a hill, bare enough, dividing two valleys that carry their waters to the Pabur. The bed of the Pabur is rich, and well cultivated with rice, from being lower than most of the circumjacent country. The heat is considerable in the valley, and the vegetation forward; it has more breadth, and approaches more to the flat land commonly found around the beds of rivers, than any thing we have seen here.

We were much annoyed during the time we remained in the valley, by a species of fly, the bite of which created intolerable itching, and frequently drew much blood, often producing a sore; many of the people had their legs so swelled by these insects, that they walked with pain. The fly was small, with a yellow spotted head and shoulders, and grey speckled legs.

Upon the banks of the Nawur nullah, we first took notice of the alder-tree, exactly similar to that which grows so commonly on the sides of rivulets in Scotland: it was easily recognised by the smell and taste of the leaf, and the red stain it gives to the mouth when chewed; but the trees were larger and handsomer than those usually observed at home.

Anxious to obtain an uninterrupted view of the snowy mountains, at a time when they should be free from the clouds and the vapours of noon, I ascended the ridge that rose behind Karashee, and from its crest enjoyed a glorious sight. The sun was just rising, in a cloudless sky, vividly lighting up the glittering snowy peaks that bounded the distance, and spread their rough inferior ranges down to the highest on which I now stood. The whole glen of Pabur lay before me, dividing the mountains by a deep and tolerably broad, well cultivated valley, through which the river flows, meandering in many bright curves; every variety of brown hills and rocks, villages, cultivation, and wood, gave their attractions to the landscape, heightened by the dewy freshness of the morning A sketch, which I took here, will convey a very faint idea of what I saw; but the uncertain light of the rising sun, though it beautified the scene, increased the difficulty of portraying it, and was somewhat unfavourable to the drawing.

Along this ridge called Deohra D,har, we marched about ten o'clock; the ascent to it is very steep. Previously to our setting off, an old man, who was lord of some few villages in the neighbourhood, was introduced, and gave symptoms of observation and workings of natural curiosity, far stronger than we have as yet noted among these people.

Seeing the theodolite placed, and pointed to different places around, he eyed it wishfully and curiously for some time. He had received the usual present, but as he still seemed to wish for something, he was asked what could be done for him; after much hesitation, he whispered to one of his attendants his wish to look through that glass (pointing to it), which he deemed to have some powerful quality, as he saw it always consulted on our learning the name of a village or a hill. He was readily indulged, and the glass pointed to a village, but I imagine that he was not fully satisfied, as he could not well understand what he saw; he, however, recognised a tower which was familiar to him, and then he departed, better pleased and more thankful than for the present he received.

Anxious to see the country and obtain information, we kept the ridge, although an easier road lay below. On either side of us was a valley: that of Nawur, on the left, was particularly rich and well cultivated. This purgunnah has been lately added to the territory of Bischur by little better than usurpation, for it chiefly belonged to a small state called Saree, the family of which is now nearly extinct.

PART IV.

JOURNEY WITH THE POLITICAL AGENT FOR THE ARMY OF GENERAL MARTINDALE.

CHAPTER XIII.

The valley of Nawur is divided from Joobul by the crest of the ridge, the southern exposure of which forms the northern face of the valley of Deyrah.

Thus Bischur is here divided from Joobul by that ridge. On our right hand, to the north and north-east, the snowy mountains bounded the view the whole way, but many rich valleys and hill-faces intervene in the country yet lying between them and Deohra ridge.

A little more than four miles along this ridge, which is bare and brown throughout, brought us to a descent exceedingly precipitous, and rather rocky, at about half way down which we observed in a small village a smelting furnace at work: the apparatus and construction of this is very simple, consisting of a chimney built of clay, about four feet and a half high, by fifteen to eighteen inches diameter, placed upon a stage of stone work over a fire-place. In an opening below the stage there is a hole, through which the metal, when melted, flows; and this is stopped by clay or earth, easily removed by an iron poker. The ore, which is black, but glittering with metallic lustre like black ore of antimony, was mixed with charcoal pounded, and the chimney filled with the mixture; and as it falls and consolidates, more is added from above. The fire, once lighted, is kept fierce by means of two pair of bellows, each made of a goat's skin, fixed in some way to the stone stage, and filled through apertures closed with valves as ours are. A woman or boy sits between two of these skins, and raises and compresses them alternately with the hand. Four such skins are thus applied to each chimney.

The iron produced by this rude apparatus is said to be very fine, and, in common with all that these hills yield, is in great request, being sent for sale by the petty merchants that purchase it to Lahore, the Punjāb, and other parts of the plains, as well as to Bootān beyond the snowy range. The ore that is used is found in the neighbouring hills, and, as we were informed, issues from their sides along with certain springs of water in the state we saw it, of pretty fine glittering particles mixed with dirt, from which it is cleansed by washing. It has the appearance of being rich, but I could not learn what proportion of metal is obtained from it.

Our journey this day led us, as has been said, over a bare dry ridge. Our descent continued along a path entirely on ledges of cultivation.

We passed through several villages surrounded with large groves of apricot trees, and bearing a happy appearance of undisturbed ease. In one of them the women ran out with the wildest air of savage curiosity to gaze upon us: they were extremely hideous. We gave them some trifles; and to one more aged and ugly than the rest, who saluted us with the name of *God Almighty*, we gave a rupee, which delighted her much, although she did not seem to be quite aware of its use.

A little further on we dipped into, and crossed a fine stream, one of the branches of the Nawur Nullah, and reached our camp, somewhat raised above it, after a short march of little more than eight miles. In this march, the valleys on each side of the ridge were very richly covered with crops and villages, and great part of the hill-sides, below what may be called their crests, presented easier slopes to the husbandman; and we saw several faces and gently swelling braes cultivated without many breaks and with few ledges. Wheat, barley, and some poppy, with a little rice in the lower parts, form the mass of the crops. Rills of water are less numerous, and the soil apparently less requires them, consequently less attention is paid to levelling the fields. The soil is more sandy than heretofore, and full of glittering particles from the decomposition of the rock, which, however, differs not materially from what we had seen; consisting principally of micaceous schist, with a great proportion of mica and sand, and much of it of a red and reddish yellow tinge, and very destructible, mouldering on exposure into a soil, which mixed with vegetable mould, here very plentiful, becomes extremely fertile.

The manners, or appearance of the inhabitants, differ little from those of Joobul: there was, perhaps, an air of greater wildness in their behaviour;

and though the beings whom we saw at the smelting furnaces, and the women at the village of Garote, were very little removed from a perfectly savage state, yet their expressions were not without a shade of polish, nor was their conduct rude or forward, although marked by gaping curiosity and wonder.

The complexion of the women was a shade lighter than that of the men; I know not why, for their exposure to the sun is equal.

It is to be remarked as curious, that although the country is so well adapted for sheep, and must possess them somewhere, because the clothes of the inhabitants are entirely fabricated from their wool, yet we never saw a flock of sheep of any considerable number in any one place: they were to be procured, and we fed principally on them, but they were dear and scarce. When one of tolerable fatness and of a due age was obtained, the mutton was very good; but weariness and hunger, the constant attendants on daily toilsome marches, would have made worse food palatable.

The breed of cattle continued as before, fine fat beasts, of a size considerably larger than those of the plains. Their milk is rich and good, but I believe that they do not give it in much greater abundance than is usual in Hindostan.

We passed two forts this day: one, Coatee, in tolerable repair, on a height above the nullah; the other, Teekree, is in ruins, but in a good situation, not being commanded except from the heights, whence nothing but long battering guns could do mischief.

Upon the height above the valley to the south we saw the stockade, where Kirtee Rana was at last forced to a surrender, situated upon a lofty ridge, connecting the Urructa mountain with the Whartoo range.

May 20.—Our camp was placed in a hollow about 400 yards from a village, Batreesh. We left it at ten o'clock, and ascended in a south-west direction the Nawur valley along the banks of the Mushapaj Nullah, one of the principal branches that form the Nawur: the slope was gentle, and the broad hill-face contained by this nullah, and by another that united with it at our encampment, gradually rose, covered with cultivation and villages.

Apricot and other fruit trees abounded; and we found that they extracted an oil from the stones of the peach and apricot trees, that was commonly used by them for culinary and other domestic purposes. The stones are bruised with their shells in a rude mill, consisting simply of a block of wood fixed in the ground, and hollowed deeply like a mortar. A wooden stick, loosely filling the mortar, is turned round in it by a long beam into which it is fixed, and which is attached to one or two bullocks; and the stones appear to be ground by the uncertain and irregular attrition of this pestle in the mortar.

We were led to the inquiry by the very fragrant scent which issued from one of these rude machines, and found that this oil was one of the chief products of the apricot tree, and large quantities are made, so that it sells at the rate of ten, twelve, and even fourteen seers for a rupee. Some that we procured for examination had a delicious smell, and seemed pure and good. There can be little doubt that this oil might be applied to purposes for which more expensive articles are now in use. It certainly possesses the fragrance of oil of almonds, and it might be worth the trial whether its medical qualities are not similar.

At a village further on, I obtained a sketch of one of the women, the wife of a Seana, who, on being requested to stand still for a few minutes, very good humouredly acquiesced. I presented her with a rupee when I had taken the sketch, much to her further satisfaction. She was, however, an old woman, and consequently her picture was only interesting as it illustrated the costume.

Here, too, we saw a dog of a large and fierce species, highly valued through these countries, which is produced in the northern parts of Bischur. They tell wonderful tales of their strength and activity; and it is commonly said that, of the fiercest sorts, two will kill a tiger. As no true tigers are found in the hills, it is not probable that the trial has been made; and that, if there be any foundation for the tale, it relates to the leopard, which occasionally is seen. But I doubt, from those dogs we have seen, whether two of them would even succeed in killing a leopard of any tolerable size. The one in question was not bigger than a large pointer, rough haired, and very fierce.

The ascent continued for four miles and a half to the pass or gorge of Kut'hagur, in the range that strikes off from Noagurh, and joins with Chumbee Kedhar, forming Nawur and some other valleys, and continuing from Toombroo to Urrukta. From a peak, on one side of this gorge, the whole Noagurh and Whartoo range was visible. On this range, at the post of Nowagurh, Kirteē Rānā took up his position, when he found it was necessary to concentrate his troops. A chain of fortified redoubts and stockades crowns the various heights of the range, which, if occupied by an adequate force, would keep a communication open with Irkee, and the positions of Ummr Sing.

The fort of Noagurh is situated upon a neck of land, stretching from under a high wooded and rocky peak which commands it; but the difficulty of ascending it, and the timidity of the people, or their superstition, kept away the hill soldiers, and saved the fort from being annoyed. It is considered as the residence of a deota, or spirit, whose haunts perhaps they would not willingly profane for purposes of war and slaughter. The neck on which the fort is placed continues onwards to the westward for some distance; and two other stockades were erected as positions in advance, and are in fact stronger than the post whence the whole is named. And these were the chief quarters of the Ghoorkha force.

While the snow lay on the ground, and that which they had collected, and kept in masses in the fort and on the hill, to serve for water, remained undissolved, and while their corn lasted, they maintained themselves well enough, and were but little harassed by any enemy. But when these resources began to fail, they were obliged to go in parties to forage; and were not only not supplied by the zemindars, but beset, and several of their number killed by their arrows. Water was only to be had below the hill at a considerable distance; and parties always lay in wait to assail those who went for this necessary, while it was not possible to secure it by a post, as it was on every side commanded.

At length, as the Ghoorkhas in all quarters became more straitened, the country began to take courage, and the people to gather on all sides. Bischur sent its soldiers. The Baruh T'hakooraee contributed, and the rajah of Cooloo sent troops from across the Sutlej; and the whole, forming a large force, besieged Noagurh, annoying and cutting off the unfortunate Ghoorkhas in detail.

Kirtee Rānā saw that his situation was desperate; his provisions were exhausted, his force was melting away, and those of his troops who were men of Gurwhal, Kumaoon, and Sirmore, began to desert in numbers. He determined to retreat, but was informed by those of the country, whom he yet deemed his friends, that all the passes to the west, towards Malown, were occupied by the enemy; and it was proposed that he should endeavour first to reach Raeengudh, and from thence, if practicable, either join Runjore Sing at Jytock, or push on to Sireenuggur. But his councils were betrayed, and his guides were faithless; even of his own soldiers there were many who, to save themselves, had made a tacit league with the enemy. He began his march in the morning; but from the many embarrassments of a retreat, and the numberless impediments by their numerous families of women, and children, and baggage, they had scarcely cleared Noagurh before noon; and then, instead of being conducted by a route clear of the enemy, as their guides had promised, they found the whole heights and precipices swarming with them, and shot pouring in from all directions.

Thus harassed, they made slow progress, and lost many men. Their route led by the pass where we now were, and it was evening before they reached an eminence a few miles from hence, above the valley of Nawur, called Chumbee-Ke-Teeba, where they halted for the night, and were surrounded at once by the whole army of the hills. All the water was taken possession of, and the poor wretches passed the night in hunger and thirst; continually assaulted by swarms of savages, and busily employed in erecting a sort of breast-work, with the materials that were at hand, of bushes, earth, and stones, for repelling them in the morning.

The morning came, but afforded them no relief. Every bush and precipice was thick with highlanders, who kept up a constant fire on the breast-work, and continually pressed on, on all sides, to attack it, but were as often driven back with loss; but at length fatigue, and thirst, and hunger, were too much to be borne. The sufferings of their women and children were very severe; and where confidence did not exist universally, nothing was to be hoped for from pushing on and fighting. A surrender was resolved on to save lives, if possible. They were assured that no violence should be offered to them; but that they should be immediately carried to the presence of the British commander, by whose authority their conquerors acted.

Thus, on the evening of the day after they reached Chumbee-Ke-Teeba, faint and wearied, they surrendered on capitulation, with the wuzzeers of Bischur, stipulating for protection to person and property, and immediate conduct to the British camp. A small party, not choosing to be thus captured, separated; and with some loss cut their way to Raeengudh, and joined Runsoor Thappa.

The moment that Kirtee's troops had laid down their arms, the work of plunder began, and every one was stript of all that he had. Swords, cookrees, shields, clothes, and property, all were appropriated by the hill-men, leaving their unfortunate enemies naked and miserable. They were not taken to General Ochterlony, nor to General Martindale's camp; but intimation was given to the former of what had happened, and orders were then peremptorily given to conduct them, with what they might possess, to camp.

The number assembled in this operation against Kirtee Rānā has been stated as high as 12 to 14,000; but there is reason to believe that this is an exaggeration: yet, divesting it of all improbabilities, there will remain a very overpowering force to have contended with that chief. These were armed, however, in a very unequal and inefficient manner. The chief part had only axes, bows, and arrows, with a few tulwars, or swords; perhaps, from 3 to 4000 might have had matchlocks. To what amount desertion prevailed among the troops of Kirtee Rānā, I know not. It probably was not very extensive, as we must otherwise have subsequently found many more of the deserters than actually made their appearance. His loss at Nowagurh, and during the retreat, and at Chumbee-Ke-Teeba, amounted to above 250; and of fighting men there were taken prisoners 500; and those who escaped to Raeengurh were about 70, forming a total of above 800 men, which must, previous to his concentrating at Nowagurh, have amounted to full 1000, as several small parties were cut off in endeavouring to join him.

In passing through this gorge, tokens of the recent fight yet remained. The half dried body of one of the men who had fallen was yet lying where he had dropt on the path. It led down a very gloomy, wild, but richly wooded dell, very deep and precipitous, the bed of a torrent forming a path. The rocky pinnacles towered above us through every species of mountain foliage.

After a long descent we reached the stream of another nullah, the

Thabar, which flows to the Girree; and, following its course for some distance further, we emerged, slanting along a large broad hill with a fine easy slope, chiefly fit for corn land, and, with the rest of the country in view, richly cultivated. Many villages were scattered through it, and the scene was lively and pleasing. Through this cultivation we proceeded by a rough but made road, of which the parapet of one of the ledges of a field formed one inclosure, and reached our camp by six o'clock, crossing another small but deep water-course, on which were three or four corn-mills, one below the other in succession. We pitched near the village of Ur'healoo, but on the opposite side of the water-course; and looked down pleasantly enough on the sweet valley of the Chugount nullah that runs to the river Girree.

The face of the country in this day's march was so similar to much of what has been already described, as to require no particular remark. The north-west face of the hill we descended is strikingly more rocky and perpendicular above than usual; and the distinction between the south and the south-east exposures, and that to the north and north-west, in regard to cultivation, is very remarkable. The country, since we crossed the Urructa range, exhibits much more cultivation than farther to the south; and the valley which we reached this day certainly strengthened the observation. To the trees already enumerated, we can now add the poplar, which we met with in the dark dell by which we descended; and a few strawberries were discovered, not quite ripe, but possessing the true flavour. No difference was discerned in soil or in rock, nor did any observation suggest itself on the subject in the course of this day's march of seven miles and three quarters.

The gorge or pass of Kutagurh, and probably the range from Noagurh, forms the boundary between Bischur, and the small independent state of Kurangooloo, into which we this day entered. I have no particular information respecting this petty lordship, and it is too insignificant to afford much interest.

One of the villagers brought to us this day a lump of snow as a present. He had carried it from a cleft of the hill which we descended, and it would have been grateful to us, had we possessed the means of employing it properly. But our water was cool enough; and what would have been a luxury to many who were then burning in the plains, melted by our side disregarded.

Several soldiers of Bischur, from the fort of Bajee, at the head of this glen, came down to see the strangers; and one of them with his bow, quiver, and shield, offered, in his peculiar costume, a tempting object for a sketch, which I accordingly took.

Every man we now met was armed with bows, arrows, axes, shields, and swords. The first appear to be the chief missile weapon. The arrows are in general tipt with bone instead of iron; and they assert that bone is preferable, as making a far more dangerous wound than iron, generally breaking short off, and thus producing gangrene and death.

As I conceive that the immediate disabling an enemy is the proper object in battle, and not his subsequent fate, I should hesitate in believing this savage reason to be the true one, for the preference remarked; and surely a broad sharp iron head will do far more instant damage than a sharp spike of bone. Iron, however plentiful, costs much labour, both to procure and to fabricate; and for one arrow head a man can make of iron, he will, in the same time, form many of bone. This facility of construction is probably the true reason of preference. The shaft of the arrow is a reed, and feathers are tied on at the lower end; but the whole performance is rude and coarse. Their bows are equally so, being formed of split bamboo, which, as there is none of the large sort to be found in the hills, must be brought from the plains below, and the supply, therefore, is precarious. It cannot be doubted that wood is to be found in these forests fit for bows; and the yew, that wood so famed in British archery, suggests itself at once as a most valuable substitute for a foreign production. But it is not used; and it only adds to the innumerable inconsistencies that mark the ways of men, that the rude inhabitants of Bischur and Sirmore prefer a more expensive, and probably not a better article of foreign growth and uncertain supply, to the produce of their own hills, which every man may have for the cutting and fetching.

It may be remarked that the bow-string, instead of being formed of hemp, or of any of those substances which usually are employed for this purpose, is made of a strip of bamboo, to each end of which a loop of twine is tied, and which slips into a notch when the bow is bent. This does not proceed from any want of strong and sufficient hemp, for various sorts are used by them, of strength enough for any purpose.

May 21.—The night was cold, the wind high, and there was much thunder and lightning; but the rain fell towards the plain, and none near us. The morning was particularly hazy and dull; and at nine o'clock we left our camp, and proceeded straight up the small nullah near which we had lain, about a mile and a half to the fort of Bajee, situate on the ridge continuous from Noagurh. This was one of the Ghoorkha posts, and now was occupied by Bischur soldiers. It is a wretched place, and could only have been useful to awe the villagers in the valley, and compel their submission. A poor insufficient wall, formed of loose stones, surrounds part of the crest of a ridge extremely narrow, and this has been rudely stockaded. Within this are a few huts of miserable construction, chiefly covered with large sheets of fir-tree bark. There are cisterns, or wells, sunk in the rock, and lined with wood, fit to contain water for fifteen days for an adequate garrison of about 100 men; but the place is quite commanded by a lofty wooded height behind it, whence musquetry would penetrate into it.

The haziness of the weather prevented our enjoying any extended view. Had it been clear, we should have seen the river Sutlej flowing far below, at the bottom of the Kurangooloo nullah, which rises on the north-west face of the ridge on which Bajee is placed.

The hill of Neeno-Ke-D'har in Cooloo, across the river, was distinct enough at first, but the fog thickened, and we saw it no more. The haziness and a threatening of rain, which however did not fall, continued. We took our course along the ridge towards the forts of Kurana and Whartoo, in a direction nearly west. The road lay through forests of brown foliage, fir, oak, larch, &c. sometimes opening into glades of considerable extent, covered with flowers, and very verdant. The right hand, or northern face, was very abrupt and rocky; that to the south, smooth and sloping.

The post of Kurana is similar to that of Bajee in construction, occupying the top part of a hill crest; but it is larger, and not being commanded, is more tenable: it is, however, after all, only a collection of bark sheds, affording a wretched shelter to a garrison. There are no tanks, and water is distant.

Whartoo is the highest peak of the range, after it leaves Morāl-Ke-Kanda; and on this was placed a considerable fort. Since Kirtee Rānā's troops left these parts, it has fallen to ruins; but even when in repair, it has been, like the rest, a wretched place. Two houses, or rather their remains, are yet in existence, which crown the two ends of the crest, and were surrounded and connected by a stockade, from each side of which the hill either falls perpendicularly, or at an angle which would make it nearly impracticable to storm it, against a determined defence.

Being the loftiest peak, of course it is not commanded; but it would soon feel the want of water, its elevation increasing its distance from the sources below. It is, probably, the highest peak between the Sutlej and the Jumna, except the great mountains of Urructa and Choor, and consequently is untenable in winter from excess of cold.

It was particularly vexatious, that so thick a mist continued during the time we remained at this place, as to prevent any satisfactory view of the country, which we should so extensively have commanded had the weather been clear.

This post has been seen from Blackhill, and does itself overlook a tract extending nearly, or perhaps, quite to the plains; while the hills beyond the Sutlej, to the Beya and Rauve, can not only be seen, but the valleys of these rivers may be distinguished. We traced with ease the whole of this range from Noagurh, and its various branches, stretching on one side to the Girree, and on the other to the Sutlej,—all studded and crowned with forts and stockades. It would seem as if the Ghoorkha chiefs had intended their main stand to have been made here; and it may perhaps be wondered at, that when the possibility of retaining Malown was very doubtful, Ummr Sing did not retire to these fastnesses, where he might have maintained himself, at all events, much longer than he could hope to do at a place where our troops were so near their supplies and resources. Indeed, it is not easy to comprehend how the British army could have invested him, or have given him much annoyance in a place so remote in the mountains, without roads for the conveyance of cannon, ammunition, or provisions.

All things are possible to British troops, at least it is a maxim which it may be well to support; and which indeed our people have gone great lengths to establish; and doubtless, in the end, the enemy would have been reduced to extremity, and to surrender. But when it is considered how much distress and inconvenience and loss must have been suffered to obtain this advantage, uncheered by victory, unenlivened by the splendor of gallant deeds, the languishing and wearied troops bearing the greatest privations and inclemencies of climate and weather, while also inflicting on their enemies the like calamities, it must be matter of satisfaction, that the Ghoorkha force did not choose the fastnesses of the Nowagurh range for their final stand.

We lingered on the heights of Whartoo, in hopes that the heavy clouds which lowered around might burst, and clear the air by a fall of rain, till three o'clock, when it became necessary to move onwards, as we had hitherto only marched five miles and a half: and we then entered on the deep descent of the north-western face, which is a rock cut into sharp spines by blasts of wind and storm, but covered, wherever there is soil, with venerable forest-trees; and, till we actually got upon the narrow winding path cut in the stone, no one could believe that footing might be obtained on it. At some distance below, we took to a ridge running to the westward, so narrow, that it barely gave room for the path, not much less steep than that we had left, and covered with jungle thickly, and with forests on each side.

The haze which had deepened from the morning had now condensed over our head, and heavy black clouds came rolling from the north-west, giving us promise of all the magnificence of a mountain storm; which at length burst with peals of thunder, reverberated from cliff to cliff, gradually approaching; and heavy drops of rain. The chief part passed over, but a very severe shower of hail and rain fell, and we enjoyed a moderate portion of the grand effect usual on such occasions.

While thus situated, we received an express from General Ochterlony, acquainting us with the final surrender of Ummr Sing Thappa, and the signature and the ratification of the convention, by which he evacuated all the country from the Sutlej downwards, as far as his command extended; and which, with that agreed on by Bumsah, cleared the whole tract, from the Kaleenuddee or Gogra, up to the former river.

Thus was the campaign, which commenced so inauspiciously in this quarter, happily terminated, and they who had for sixty years continued a course of conquest and usurpation were shorn of half their honours and power.

We kept the narrow ridge till we reached a gorge, whence two valleys, one on each side, take their course, both beautiful and fertile, and refreshed by the late shower, looked more than usually attractive. At this gorge there was a stone, sacred to some hill deity, of considerable eminence.

We held our way down a ridge, which sprung gradually from the gorge, and separated two valleys, each of which ran in a northern direction to the Sutlej. Great part of our path, as usual, lay through forests, and frequently sunk a little below the eastern side of the ridge: at one time, when we had proceeded thus, shrouded in darkness for some distance, and again emerged on the steep and bare face of the hill, our attention and admiration were arrested by a prospect of great singularity and grandeur, that suddenly burst on our view. The atmosphere was cleared from the haze which had loaded it. The storm had chiefly ceased; its thunders were only heard at a distance in the south-east; but heavy masses of clouds rested on the hills around, and black volumes were rolling over head.

It was nearly evening, and night itself had almost gone down on the dark glen of the Sutlej at our feet. The sun was sinking in the west, at the opening of a wild glen, which glowed with the fierce red light which it shed from a break in the clouds, and all the dark masses above were tinged with fainter shades of the same. The hills of Cooloo opposite, tipped with fortresses, showed a rough bold outline; their western exposure was lighted up by the same fiery beam. To the east, the storm had passed away, and the sky had opened in the distance; and the snowy mountains rose above the white clouds that lay on their feet, calm and chill, and freshly strewed with snow; their highest summits just lighted up by the setting sun, not shining on them as on us, through vapour and cloud, but clear and bright to the last.

Around us was a dark forest, and on either hand a deep valley; it was a scene of so striking a nature, that I can never forget it: the effect of the stormy light of the setting sun on the wild and massy surrounding objects, opposed to the calm tranquil light of the snow on the other hand, formed an exquisite and extraordinary contrast.

The consideration of our distance from our resting-place put an end to more elevated sensations, and we continued our route; but, a little further on, we were greeted by a most ungrateful sight; our tents appeared pitched on the opposite side of the valley to our right, at a distance that would take us many hours to reach; we were tired and hungry, and this mistake of our servants was no small evil, in a country where little accommodation was to be looked for.

But as there was no means of rectifying the error, we pushed on to make the best of it, and trusted to the village at which it was intended to encamp, for the means of satisfying our hunger and resting our bodies; and all the vexation we at first felt, and all our weariness, did not prevent us from admiring the beauty of the country we were in, highly cultivated, studded with numerous villages, and finely interspersed with groves of noble trees; it contrasted well with the black barren hills on the opposite side of the Sutlej, but darkness soon obscured all, and we made good the last part of our way down a very stony path, by the forced guidance of a surly peasant, taken from one of the huts in our way, who would not stir to do us this good office, until a stick was smartly applied to his shoulders.

The whole march was fourteen miles and a half, and we reached this place by eight o'clock at night; we were met by the Rānā, and conducted to a house in which to pass the night, but it was a very dirty looking wretched place, and we preferred occupying a tent which belonged to the Rānā, and was pitched close by; it was commodious enough, and charpoys (oblong frames, resting on four feet, fitted with a sort of network of tape or twine, which serve as bedsteads and beds to the simple natives of Hindostan) and blankets were procured to sleep on; and after a supper on flour cakes and milk, we retired to no despicable bed, our weary limbs not requiring down to rest upon. Had we been fastidious, the look of our coverings would not perhaps have pleased us; but a little travelling in similar regions reconciles the traveller to greater privations, and to more disgusting objects than dirty or suspected blankets.

The scenery of this day was very splendid and grand: a description has been already attempted. There is a regular descent from the Whartoo or Noagurh ridge, the whole way to the Sutlej, with no intervening hills; although its roots are various and rugged, and rise here and there into peaks, dividing the valleys that lead down to that river.

At first the beholder is led to believe that the hills on either side the Sutlej fall more than the surrounding country; but this is a deception. The gradual rise from the bed of the Pabur along the valley of Nawur to the Noagurh ridge, and the long descent to Comharsein, take from the apparent height, by the extent of country which these include; but the hills are in truth as lofty as any others in the same tract, excepting Choor and Urructa.

The descent from Whartoo to Comharsein was more than nine miles, which indicates a gentler declivity than usual; but this is diversified by many wild features of rock and ridge, that destroy all appearance of more easy slope, and assimilate the face of the country to the rest.

The smoothness of the south-east face of the hills is in this range peculiarly remarkable; and the rough abruptness of the north-west exposure, and the pointing of the cliffs in that direction, is strikingly evident every where, even in the snowy mountains themselves.

But little change was remarked among the vegetable productions of the country. A variety of that tree, which we cannot determine as holly or as oak, but something between each, was observed: its leaf was of a round oval shape, without prickles, very bright, and of a fine brownish green. It was melancholy to remark the number of noble trees that were destroyed merely for their bark: this was pulled off to a height as great as a man could contrive to reach, from the finest of the forest, for a covering to their wretched huts, and they were left thus to die; but, in truth, they can perhaps be put to no better use, and may as well be employed in this way as any other: though, to every person who knows the value of such timber in other countries, and who sees its beauty even here, the sight of such ruin cannot but give unpleasant feelings. No variation was observed in the soil or rock during the march.

The fort of Kurana, and all of those on this range which were occupied, were garrisoned, as well as Bajee, with soldiers of Bischur and of Cooloo, who had continued to hold them since the time of the Ghoorkhas' retreat, not quite to the satisfaction of the chiefs in whose territory they lie.

These men in their appearance are like those we saw at Raeengudh; tough, hard featured, square men, although sometimes little; their countenances very different from those of the men of Sirmore, but more similar to those of the inhabitants of Joobul; changing the sharp, high, and rather delicate features of the Hindoo, for the rugged, almost haggard, lineaments of the highlander. Here and there something akin to the Tartar physiognomy appeared; but we could not pronounce that to be the predominant cast. Their dress was nearly similar to what we had seen since entering Joobul; but the cap was slightly different, having a crimson crown to it. The blankets and woollen manufactures too were finer, both in material and texture. Many of them had matchlocks, not of the best description, which, with their swords, are chiefly obtained from the Sikhs in the plains; but the most common arms were axes and bows and arrows: many of them had cookrees: several had swords and shields, that had belonged to the unfortunate followers of Kirtee Rānā, the plunder having remained with the plunderers.

CHAPTER XIV.

Comharsein is a petty state or lordship of no great size, chiefly comprised in one or two valleys, which stretch to the banks of the Sutlej, from the crest of the Whartoo range, and bounding with Kurangooloo on the east and south: its other boundaries I am not certain of. Before the Ghoorkha conquest, it owned allegiance to the rajah of Bischur, except when the rajah of Cooloo, from across the Sutlej, occasionally took violent possession.

It is governed by a Rānā, of whose family I know nothing. During the period it was held by the Ghoorkhas, it was assessed at 7500 rupees per annum, and could muster 250 fighting men, 100 of whom were armed with matchlocks: probably its ability in time of prosperity was more considerable. The Rānā was deposed as usual by the conquerors, and detained for some time in prison, on the breaking out of the war with the British; but he made his escape, and fled to the camp of General Ochterlony, with whom he had remained a month, when he returned to his country and lordship: this he found in a very exhausted condition, and of course could make no great figure at this period. He was a man of better presence than his compeer of Joobul, stout, rather short, of a dark and somewhat savage countenance, with a thick black beard. He had more the appearance of a Musulman than of a Hindoo. His habit was not of the hill fashion. He wore a dress of flowered silk, with trowsers of the same material, a silk cap, and richly embroidered shoes; and his whole figure might pass for that of a man of some rank.

The town of Comharsein is mean and poor: it does not consist of more than a dozen houses, built like the rest of the hill villages, of dry stone and wood, in the Chinese fashion. The Rānā's house is similarly built, but large, and plastered with a kind of white and shining clay; which we have occasionally before remarked, particularly in the interior of their buildings. Above, it is wholly surrounded with wooden balconies, closed in with neatly carved wooden screens, forming the zenānā. One of the ladies appeared for a moment at an open window; but there was nothing remarkable in her appearance. Her complexion was yellow, like that of a mulatto; and she had, as the other women have, a handkerchief on her head.

It is strange that Comharsein should be so poor a place; as, besides being the residence of a chief, it commands one of the chief ghāts to the Sutlej.

It was inconvenient to move till our camp joined us, which did not take place till late in the day; and then it was not possible to make a long march: we therefore determined to go down to the banks of the Sutlej, of the stream of which we could just get a glimpse, at a great distance below.

We found the descent prodigiously steep and long, very nearly three miles, the first part somewhat circuitous; but the last mile was a continued flight of irregular steps, rudely constructed from the materials afforded by the mountain. These stones are of a very hard quality, composed of quartz mixed with some other flinty material; and they have been laid with considerable art, one step being formed by the small ends of long pieces, which are deeply buried in the hill side; and the next by similar long pieces laid crosswise upon the first, so as to prevent the possibility of their moving. The fatigue of such a descent is very great, and was increased to the imagination by the view of the endless diminishing flight of steps that stretched below us; for there is little variation or turning in the whole length of this extensive staircase.

About 150 feet above the river there is a certain quantity of table land, which, as far as could be seen either way, was distributed unequally or at least irregularly, along the banks, at every winding of the stream. The soil here appeared to be good; and it is all well cultivated, chiefly with rice. The breadth of the stripe in no place exceeded 200 yards: on this it is probable that the river once ran smoothly, stopped by some impediment formerly, but which has since given way; and this soil, in all likelihood, is the accumulated washing from the mountains, thus restrained from being hurried away by the comparative gentleness of the stream; which, when once let loose by the destruction of such impediment, quickly wore its way through the yielding mass to the rocky bed it now occupies. Perhaps the productiveness of this table land may have formed one reason for the construction of the ghāt we descended; which, in point of length, steepness, and singularity of construction, is surpassed by nothing I have heard of, and is as well worth seeing as any thing I have met with in India. The river runs with a very rapid stream over ledges of rock and irregularities that divide it into pools and rapids; and the descent from the one to the other is considerable, but produces nothing more than swiftness of course. The pool which we reached might be rather more than forty yards across; the narrower stream above it somewhat less. It was with considerable exertion that any of the party could throw a stone across; but there were none among us very skilful at this exercise. The colour of the water was of a dirty light green; and this was probably caused by the sand which it carried along with it, and the colour of that over which its course chiefly lay. On taking up a portion of the water, it appeared to be quite clear, but pervaded by shining particles of great fineness. The stones we noted in the bed of the river were chiefly slaty and of quartz, and soft, sandy, and argillaceous; some curiously veined, but none were of any great hardness. The pebbles and stones of a river's bed can give no good evidence of the construction of any particular part of the mountains in which it rises, or through which it runs: they must consist of a congeries of every sort of rock by which it passes, further increased by those which subsidiary streams carry along with them from their beds.

On the banks of the river we found several huts of gold-finders, who gain a livelihood by washing the sands of the Sutlej for the gold they contain. This precious metal is found in considerable quantities on its banks; and, it is said, comes from gold mines of some consequence in Bootan, at or near the source of the river, which thus carries the finer parts along with its stream, depositing them gradually in its course. One of the men showed us the process by which he separated the gold from the sand; which was simple, depending on the superior specific weight of the gold over the substances with which it was mixed. With a broad shallow wooden platter he took up a small quantity of sand from a heap that was placed on a hand-barrow, and which probably was taken from some place known to be richer than others: this he dexterously washed, by dipping in the river the side of the board frequently, to allow the light parts to drain off, and fresh water to come on. Thus, the gold and heavier parts sunk to the bottom of the shallow hollow; and at last the gold alone remained, mixed with large and heavy particles of black sand. It was small in quantity; and he informed us that his daily earnings were not more than from two to four, or even five anas; and this small quantity he sells to the zemindars, receiving food in return. Probably he underrates his profits purposely—a common expedient with the inhabitants of India, who could not, in former times, display their riches, without the danger of having them forcibly wrested from them. I bought all the gold he had, or at least produced, amounting only to two rupees.

We all bathed in the stream: the water was cold. This, together with the great rapidity, and the danger of rocks near the surface, which might be unobserved from the colour of the water, prevented most of us from attempting the exploit of crossing it. One man only swam over, and at considerable risk of being swept away.

Some time before dark we entered on our formidable ascent; and accustomed as we were, by this time, to laborious marches, we did not accomplish this till after many halts, and at a late hour. The perpendicular height of Comharsein above the river cannot be so little (I think) as 3000 feet: there must be several thousand steps in the rude flight of stairs above described; and these, added to two miles of steep though irregular descent at first, cannot well give a less positive elevation. Some fair idea may be formed of the height of Whartoo fort, from the facts that have been now stated; though the descent (nine miles) to Comharsein be less abrupt than usual, the aggregate of twelve miles to the banks of the Sutlej must certainly determine the summit of that range to be exceedingly lofty.

Just at the top of the long flight of stairs we found an orchard of apricot trees, the fruit of which was nearly ripe, but they were still sour and bad.

Somewhat nearer our tent we passed a neat temple in the Chinese taste, with many images of Hindoo deities carved in wood.

The hills on the opposite or north bank of the Sutlej, in the Cooloo country, are barren, brown, burnt up, and rocky, unenlivened by wood or cultivation. Forts and villages crown their crests and tops, as if these were the only situations they could stand upon. On the whole, the country looked far less inviting, and considerably more rugged, than that we have hitherto traversed. The lower part of the glen, on the side we were on, was also burnt up and bare; but, in all the smaller glens above, the diversity and beauty of the wood and cultivation was remarkable: and in this respect the country keeps its consistency; the southern exposure being still bare and deformed, whilst the northern aspect is comparatively green and well wooded. The difference of climate in the hollow of the river's bed was very remarkable: the wind was quite hot; and even above, the whole of the day was oppressive. Some ice, which was brought from a neighbouring hill, rapidly dissolved away.

The river Sutlej has generally been supposed to take its rise in the Himālā range; but some late accounts, as well as the common information of the natives of the hills, tend to assign it a more remote source. We were now informed, that it comes quite through the Himālā mountains, arising from their north-eastern face; but no distinct information had been obtained at this time respecting the actual place of its origin.

I here allude to the journey of Messrs. Moorcroft and Hearsay to the Lake Mansroār, given in the twelfth volume of the Asiatic Researches, which first gave reason to believe that this river had its rise on the north-east side of the Himālā mountains; but the length of course that this indicated, prevented implicit faith being yielded to the proposition; resting, as it chiefly did, on the evidence of natives; who, it might be presumed, were not correct, or perhaps might desire to mislead strangers in their researches. Distinct and separate evidence, from other natives in a different part of the country, who could have no obvious reason for misleading, has now so far confirmed the substance of what was related to these gentlemen (as will be related below), that it seems unreasonable to retain any farther doubt on the subject; and the collateral evidence of our senses, while at Serata, goes far to prove the fact by analogy.

The contracted size of the stream, and moderate body of water contained in it, might argue against so long a course as this would presume; but, at the time we saw it, the river was evidently very low, and the appearance of its banks gave proof that the stream had lately been much greater: at this time, too, the snow, which usually melts in the lower parts of the country, and swells the stream greatly, had all dissolved; and as yet no rain had fallen to act upon that of a less yielding description: thus we could not judge of the true stream of the Sutlej, from the state in which we now beheld it. The name of this stream is properly Sutroodra, which it derives from Rooder, one of the appellations of Mahadeo; for it is a sacred stream: it is called by the natives indiscriminately Sutroodra, Soottrooz, Sootlooj, and Sutlej.

May 23.—After another interview with the Rānā, in which he was presented, in the name of Government, with an appropriate present of shawls, we left Comharsein, and ascended the mountain by the same road which had brought us thither, and had a better opportunity of observing the country as we passed along. About two miles above Comharsein, we passed the fort of Teekur, built about four years ago by Runsoor Thappa, in a good situation, but quite above the reach of water: it was now deserted, and in ruins.

On reaching the Desata's stone at Nagkanda, five miles and a half from Comharsein, we commenced a descent along the right hand side of the valley, which we had seen, when we last passed, stretching towards the Girree, upon a high road made by the Ghoorkhas, that communicates with Irkee; and following many windings and indentations in the hill side, with much variety of path, and in a direction tending chiefly to the southward, we reached the village and temple of Manjnee somewhat late in the evening: our march was nearly twelve miles and a half.

The road formed by the Ghoorkhas, though varied with much fall and rise, as well as much indented from the numerous ravines it crosses, is still good and practicable, and capable of being made easy enough: it was now passable for doolies and ponies.

We passed through many villages, and saw great extent of cultivation on this side of the ridge, as well as on that we had left. Barley, wheat, and poppy, were plentiful and fine. Of the former two, much had already been reaped: the latter was fast ripening, and a good deal appeared to have been collected from the heads of the flowers.

We had more trouble from our hill coolies on this day than we had experienced on any former occasion; although very lightly loaded, many of them refused to proceed, though urged onwards in a very decided manner; and they all appeared to be of a far more stubborn, obstinate, and untractable nature, than any people we had yet had to deal with. One of them in particular displayed this persevering obstinacy with a degree of brutal courage and self-possession very surprising indeed: we found him lying in the middle of the path, to all appearance senseless, and totally heedless of the arguments, both verbal and manual, of the sepoy who had him and his load in charge.

There was no doubt that he thus feigned illness, for his pulse and breathing were perfectly regular and good; and the people of Comharsein who were with us were perfectly aware of the trick. On one occasion, when roused by some painful application, he endeavoured to escape by rolling down the hill; but, being disappointed in this, he again lay as dead; and it was only after pretty smart discipline that he was convinced of the necessity of taking up his load and moving onwards: after which, he went quietly enough. No doubt it is highly unpleasant to be forced to carry a load in a hot day up a hill, and it is not agreeable to be under the necessity of forcing men to perform this service; but, when necessity on our part urged us, and good pay was given to lighten their burthen, it might have been hoped that this, and the evident power of enforcing our orders which we possessed, would have induced a quiet performance of one day's work; and usually this was the case; but here a dogged brutal obstinacy rendered more force necessary, and the duty more painful to both parties.

Our encampment was in a small field, from which the grain had been reaped, just by the temple of Manjnee: the village was a short way above, and is small, though neat: on one hand was a sort of fort, or house, called Coatee.

The temple was remarkably neat, quite in the Chinese style, as usual: it is sacred to the goddess Bhowannee. The whole of the interior is sculptured over in wood, with infinite labour, and probably forms a detail of the exploits of the deity: with these I am wholly unacquainted; but she seems to have been frequently engaged with monsters of very uninviting shapes. That portion of the carving, however, which neither represents the human nor animal figure, is by far the most beautiful. The whole roof, which is formed of fir wood, is richly cut into flowers and ornaments entirely in the Hindoo taste, with a sharpness and precision, yet an ease that does honour to the mountain artist; and, considering his tools and materials, it is truly wonderful. The shrine of the goddess was in the centre, and a small pair of folding doors, opening, disclosed her; but the outside apartment, containing the sculptured work, was filled with people of all sorts, apparently without any scandal or sense of impropriety to the priesthood, who inhabited the interior. There were several small pagodas, similar to those at Hat-Gobeseree, and much curious sculpture in stone; but it was wholly of a schistose and crumbling nature, which appeared to be mouldering into dust, and therefore could not be very ancient.

The scene in which this temple is placed is beautiful: there cannot be a more picturesque or various landscape, in the wild mountainous taste, than the opposite hills afford; cut into alternate rocky ridges and rich dells, as they stretch from Whartoo downwards, forming the south-eastern side of the fine valley we descended. The tints of green, yellow, and brown, as varied in the corn, wood, and rock, could not be more happily blended, or form a sweeter whole.

May 24.—The morning was cold, dull, and threatening: the night had been stormy and wild. Delay in obtaining provisions for the people detained us till eleven o'clock; when we commenced our march, by ascending the hill above the village, along terraces of cultivation, to the crest of the ridge, which we crossed, and descended a steep rugged path to the dell on the other side, through which runs Noonee Kanāl, a stream from a wild glen arising in Nok,kanda range.

The opposite range of hills to the westward was uninteresting and bare: the dell we descended was rocky above; but below, covered with a fine light pale verdure, of which the poplar tree supplied the chief part: here the dark brownish green of the holly, the oak, and the fir is not seen.

Rising steeply from this dell, we reached a low ridge that forms the boundary between the states of Comharsein and Keounthul, running from Nagkanda in a direction nearly north and south. We looked from hence on a country well cultivated on all sides. By a very irregular indented path, at times in a zig-zag direction up the hill face, and at others on ledges of cultivation and rock, we wound round the northwest end of the valley, and ascended the opposite ridges in the lowest part. Our course was about north-north-west. Hence, keeping along the eastern face of the ridge, and ascending several peaks upon it, we reached the site of two Ghoorkha forts, called Punta and Jhurra, whence the ridge obtains the name of Punta-Jhurra. The whole was at one time fortified. The forts are now in ruins, but the situation is commanding; and has only the usual disqualification of being at too great a distance from water to be objected against it. Our route was now southerly, leaving the heights, and lay chiefly along the Ghoorkha high road from Comharsein to Irkee. This is broad, and might be made fit for any purpose. We, however, soon left this for a more dangerous one, leading along ledges of rock, with dark precipices below, and affording but little room for the feet to hold by, till, turning to the westward, we saw our tent pitched among some fine fields of corn near a village; and we reached the encampment soon after seven in the evening.

Our view from the top of the ridge this day was extensive in all directions, but haze prevented its being very distinct. To the westward we saw a country perfectly similar to that which we had now for some time been acquainted with. The waters from its dell all run, as I believe, to the Sutlej; and, had the weather been favourable, we should in all probability have distinguished Malown, and the scene of operations in that quarter.

To the eastward we obtained a sight of our old acquaintance, the Girree, which has its source behind a peak that was in view, and all the waters from that side run to swell its stream.

The ridge we crossed this day, as well as that of the day before, was composed to all appearance of black and grey slate, veined with quartz. Occasional blocks of other stone may be seen, but in no such quantity as to lead to the belief, that they form any considerable proportion of the hill.

The roads for these two days, which (as already observed) were made by the Ghoorkhas, from Irkee to the strong holds in this quarter, are constructed with considerable art, and are frequently from six to eight feet broad, having the side next to the precipice built up as a support. At times, however, they narrow to a mere footpath; but the line is good, and the road might be easily made fit for purposes of warlike conveyance.

The little village of Bisnorig, near which our tents were placed, is in the small state of Theog, a lordship, forming one of those properly denominated the Barŭh T'hakooraee, or the Twelve Lordships. It was assessed by the Ghoorkhas at 3400 rupees per annum; and from the smallness of its size was, of course, always very dependent on its more powerful neighbours. I believe it very generally followed the fortunes of Keeounthal.

This state, which we passed through a portion of yesterday, is the largest, richest, and most powerful of the Barŭh T'hakooraee. It was assessed by the Ghoorkhas at 42,000 rupees. I have been able to collect little further information respecting it. It is governed by a Rānā, and the chief town, Rampoor, is situate at two days journey to the southwestward.

May 25.—A very severe storm of rain and wind came on in the early part of the night, which greatly annoyed us during its continuance. The puffs of wind that came down the dells above us were alarmingly heavy; but fortunately our tent ropes withstood them, and we escaped with no other damage than clouds of dust being blown in between the tent and the ground; even the heavy rain did not penetrate in any considerable degree. The morning was chill and clear.

This day an express from Nahn informed us, that the army before Jytock were then preparing to quit the position; and that the fort was immediately to be evacuated by the Ghoorkha forces, while Ummr Sing, after leaving Malown, was to accompany General Ochterlony to Nerraingurh in the plains, to meet his son Runjore Sing Thappa.

Preparations for the evacuation of Sireenuggur, and all the Ghoorkha posts on this side of the Calee Nuddee, were also on foot, and thus the whole campaign in this quarter closed. Under these circumstances it was uncertain what course our party might be ordered to take, or what conduct to pursue; and having thus gained a position where intelligence might speedily reach us from Nahn or Malown, we determined to await the further orders of government, or letters from either camp.

CHAPTER XV.

The situation in which we halted was by no means an interesting one in point of beauty, or surrounding country; and the leisure that was thus obtained was employed in extending the few sketches that had been made, and in making inquiries relative to the customs of the country, and manners of the people. That no great satisfaction attended these, and that little interesting matter was gleaned on the subject, was perhaps equally owing to the want of acuteness and skill in the observer, as to the rude state of society, which had little worthy of attention to display, and to the consequent barrenness of the field.

That there is a strongly marked difference between the inhabitants of Sirmore, and that part of the hilly region, bordering on the plains, which has fallen under our observation, and those of the remoter and more elevated tracts, is very obvious, and was remarked at the time we entered Joobul.

As our route from that period till now has led through a country lying in about an equal parallel with the plains, little further diversity was to be expected, nor was any observed. Any that might exist was probably from the slight shades produced by accidental circumstances, local or political, and cannot bear on the general view.

The whole people inhabiting this region are still in that semi-barbarous state, between the complete savage, and that which, in consequence of a commencing intercourse with a civilized people, is just emerging from so gross a condition; but this intercourse being yet, as it were, by reflection, transmitted through the districts that border on the plains, themselves but little civilized, only faint advances to improvement have as yet been effected. Such a state may offer curious matter of study to the moralist and philosopher: but affords a very circumscribed field for interesting description.

The character of the mountaineer corresponds with the state in which he is found. Much of his original nature remains strongly indicated; he is wild and hasty, and apt to commit excesses; he will steal and rob; and those who have the power, and can command the devotion of others become petty tyrants, and attack and plunder their neighbours. Their law, if they had their will, would only be the sword. This has been signally proved by the strong enmities which the chiefs of the petty lordships, and even the more powerful princes of the country, bear to one another, and the endless feuds which subsist between them and even between the minor families of the various principalities. The instances of individual hatred and revenge are perhaps not less notorious and well authenticated, than the universal propensity to plunder and steal. Such must always be the condition of a people, when the laws and the sovereign are too weak to punish the wicked and to support the wronged and oppressed, and when the country, difficult or impracticable, favours a lawless and violent conduct. But it is to be feared, that the mountaineer of these hills is not only violent and unruly; he is wily, cunning, and treacherous, and certainly revengeful. The conduct of the men of Poonurr to the Ghoorkha soldiers, and that of the combined troops of Bischur, Cooloo, Joobul, &c. to Kirtee Rānā, afford strong proofs of this.

We can discover in them all the uncertain, wavering, and meanly cautious features of the Asiatic character, caught perhaps in some measure by their depraved intercourse with the plains, as well as remaining in the breed by blood. In every transaction with these people this was very obvious. The conduct of the chiefs of the different districts, when invited to take a decided part with the British arms, was strikingly illustrative of it, not only when some shadow of excuse existed in the ignorance of the people for such irresolution, and even double dealing, but even in cases where no chance of eventual advantage could be discovered, did they vacillate, and change, and negotiate, on both sides, with a miserable treacherous policy.

In every dealing of inferior importance that occurred on the march, they prevaricated, trifled, and endeavoured to disappoint or deceive us. Seldom could a direct answer to any question be obtained; or all was fair promise without an idea of fulfilment, although they were aware that the means of enforcing performance were in our hands, and no obvious benefit was to be obtained by withholding what was demanded. The corn wanted for the troops and required of them, but which they either declared their inability to supply, or about which they equivocated for days, was at last, on search, found in abundance in their houses, although the price fixed upon it by their own headman had been advanced for its purchase; and this at a time when they knew that the Ghoorkha power was overthrown, and the British arms had broken their own chains: this was not only a very unamiable, but a very unaccountable trait in their character. Like most Asiatics, but exceeding them, they are severe and tyrannical masters, but cringing to a disgusting degree to those whom they know to be their superiors in power. Those who were foremost in denying to us the necessaries we wanted, were, when brought before us, by far the most servile and abject in their professions of service and devotion.

The obstinacy of these people has already been noticed among the lower orders: it was most uncomfortably exemplified in the instances where our coolies refused to take up the loads, or to proceed when ordered; and severe treatment was very frequently necessary to enforce the performance of tasks far within their power. Viewed in general, they are lazy, indolent, and remarkable for their apathy; nor does the latent violence of their passions appear until they are somewhat roused.

There seems no ground for believing that these men are at all hospitable. We had not, indeed, any personal opportunity to judge of this, as our means in general superseded all necessity of relying on them for supplies, while their customs and religion would in some measure have prohibited a strong display of it, had occasion offered; and at all times they must have granted to our force the trifling assistance which we might personally have required, under a show of goodwill, although they would in all probability have refused it, if unbacked by such power.

In so far, indeed, as we could judge from their conduct to others, there was no desire shown to render comfortable those who needed to be so; no exertion was ever made to procure the necessary refreshments: our soldiers might have starved for them.

The presents of sheep and goats that were offered to us were not to be considered as the voluntary gifts of a grateful, generous, or obliging disposition; they were the peace offerings customary in the country, the tender of an inferior who needs protection, and thus solicits it from a superior.

I do not believe that a vessel of milk was ever given from a kind motive, or without its object of reward in view. No present was ever offered without a hope, nay, a tolerably full persuasion, of a more valuable consideration being returned. The very men, who bent so low to us when present, assisted more than once to rob our servants when out of our reach.

Such are the dark unhappy traits in the present character of these highlanders. They were marked and pointed out by circumstances; but it should not be forgotten, that their natural character may have been disguised and distorted by the late violent revolutions; that the grinding tyranny of the Ghoorkha reign may in some measure have warped a better nature, and occasioned the lower, more cunning, faithless, and revengeful habits, that disgrace them. The nature of an Eastern despotic government too, must have considerably depressed whatever existed of the generous, free, enthusiastic spirit, that commonly marks the highlander.

We do not know enough of their history to enable us to judge what the national character has heretofore been; and perhaps it were more just to withhold our opinion of this people until time shall show, or tradition be gleaned, to give us information; otherwise we must form our judgments on the few facts of which we are in possession, and which may have taken their colour from circumstances that show the genius of the people in a false, or overstrained, or exaggerated light.

Several districts in these parts have given proofs of a high degree of courage; many likewise have evinced an anxiety for freedom, that proves they can prize it, and must at one time have enjoyed it.

A few showed a decided faith in British power and honour when permitted to declare themselves, which would argue a corresponding generosity in themselves.

These facts apply to particular districts, where, probably, the Ghoorkha yoke had not fallen so heavily, and where the spirit of national enthusiasm was not completely quenched. From these districts troops were drawn, who acquitted themselves to the full satisfaction of their commander, and drew from him a decided opinion of their value as soldiers, and of their behaviour as men. When praise can be fairly given, it is grateful to the feelings to bestow it, and it is but justice to point out the valuable and remarkable exceptions from general worthlessness.

The conduct of the men of Jounsār should not be passed over in silence: they were the earliest who joined the British arms, cutting off supplies from the enemy, and raising their own half armed forces to oppose him. They joined the British detachment, and, in the retreat of Bhulbhudder Sing from Kalunga, after the evacuation of that fortress, they hung on his rear, and, when passing the Jumna, actually came to a partial engagement with his troops; but being considerably ahead of Major Baldock's detachment, they could not detain him till advantage should be taken of their spirited conduct.

This district extends from the junction of the Jumna and the Touse at Kalsee, far to the north between these two rivers, till bounded by Rewaeen of Gurwhal, and would have formed a valuable point of support for our troops, had the Ghoorkha troops attempted a retreat to the eastward, which offered supplies of provision and a friendly population.

A few of the zemindars of Joobul too were highly deserving of praise: two of these at once, and almost uninvited, upon the arrival of the British troops at Jytock joined the camp, and rendered many valuable services to the cause.

Whether it be the effect of the Ghoorkha tyranny longer exercised, or that of the government, which is more despotic near the capital, and in the more pervious parts of the country, near the plains, or whether it be the effect of climate and situation, or of all these together, I cannot say; but certainly the spirit and even the appearance of the mountaineer on the borders of the low country, is far different from that of his more northern countrymen.

The farther removed from the plains, the heat, and the more accessible parts of the country, the higher does the highlander seem to rise in activity of mind and body.

There is a slovenly carelessness about the people in the vicinity of Nahn, and for some days' journey into the hills; a mean degraded look, and even a diminutive form, quite distinct from the more brisk agility and hardier forms of the men of Joobul and Bischur.

The very dress of these latter, though different in materials, is better and more respectable than that of the miserable ragged Sirmorean; the jacket of coarse woollen, covering the body amply and warmly, with its philibeg-like skirts, the stout coarse trowsers, and plaid-like wrapper and waistcloth, with the snug black bonnet, which forms the dress of all those who are not the very lowest, gives a comfortable homespun air to the persons of the former, that forcibly contrasts with the tawdry cotton rags of the latter.

It is a good highland costume; it even looks exceedingly well, and very characteristic; it is warm and lasting, and yet leaves the body much at liberty, although the woollen is perhaps somewhat heavy. Some, in walking, omit the trowsers, and wear, under the kilted part of their jacket, a piece of cotton cloth, put on as the Hindostanee d,hotee.

It has been observed that they wear axes in their belts, and when they can afford it a sword; shields are not so common, but those above the common order, when they have one, always carry it. The smaller and remoter chiefs do not vary from this national dress; they only employ cloth of a fine texture, and a few ornaments: but those who are of a higher order, or are more disposed to indulge their vanity, assume the Hindostanee costume, and always affect the sik,h turban.

Hitherto we could not say that the appearance of the women had undergone an improvement corresponding with that of the men; on the contrary, they seemed to become more coarse and unfeminine. We frequently remarked in Sirmore some who were delicate in form and feature, but to the northward they disappeared; the female countenance was generally good humoured, but the form was coarse and highly vulgar.

They wore a blanket dress like that of the men, but ending in a longer petticoat; a waistband of coarse woollen, wrapped several times around them, generally all in tatters, and a piece of cloth strangely wound round the head, as a sort of turban, were their usual costume. They wore their hair twisted up into long thick rolls, ornamented with red wool hanging down their backs; an ornament in which they appear to have greatly prided themselves; and they formed this tail or huge plait of a length to reach far below the waist, and of a thickness at least equal to their arm. Those who were not so fortunate as to possess a *chevelure* of such beautiful bulk, made up the deficiency by working in a quantity of black wool; the end of all these queues was puffed out into a sort of tassel of small plaits, and the whole was tied by a string of red wool. To unravel such a head-dress must be an endless task, and I fear it must be inferred, that the heads of these fair creatures are not in a state commendable for cleanliness.

They wear N,huts or large rings in the nose, after the common Hindostanee fashion, and ear-rings, valuable and large, according to the means of the owner. Round the ancles are huge and heavy ornaments of pewter, and on the arms large bangles of the same, or of brass; the toes and fingers are strung with rings of these metals, and round the neck, and on the breast, they wear a profusion of beads, of glass, pewter, and sometimes perhaps of silver. Such were the females of these countries.

Their customs, with respect to marriage, and the general system with regard to their women, are very extraordinary. It is usual all over the country, for the future husband to purchase his wife from her parents, and the sum thus paid varies of course with the rank of the purchaser. The customary charge to a common peasant or zemindar, is from ten to twenty rupees. The difficulty of raising this sum, and the alleged expense of maintaining women, may in part account for, if it cannot excuse, a most disgusting usage, which is universal over the country. Three or four or more brothers marry and cohabit with one woman, who is the wife of all: they are unable to raise the requisite sum individually, and thus club their shares, and buy this one common spouse.

We had heard of this very revolting custom in the course of our travels frequently, and so remarkable an inconsistency with all Hindoo manners, which it is well known are peculiarly and scrupulously delicate with regard to their females, could not but excite our curiosity and inquiry regarding the cause of its origin and continuance. Little that was satisfactory could be gathered in addition to the reasons above-mentioned, and these do not appear by any means to account for it fully.

If it be expensive to maintain the woman, the charge must lie somewhere; if a husband be not at the cost, the parents must, and burthens thus left upon a family, it may be supposed, would be gladly got rid of at all events. But I believe, that the women fully earn their own subsistence, for they are employed both in agricultural pursuits and in the more domestic labours, and thus cannot be considered as unprofitable charges. But if they were expensive, it is singular that the purchase money of a wife should keep up to a height beyond the general ability of the men to furnish.

Women are here articles of property, and it is against all experience in the mutual effects of demand and supply, that when the latter is more than sufficient, the price should keep so disproportionably high.

This reasoning, in conjunction with the facts from which it arises, would induce a suspicion, that the number of females was in reality not in proportion to that of the males; but to our inquiries on this subject they did not admit that to be the case.

What then became of those who never married? This question was never satisfactorily solved. A few men they affirmed to possess four or five wives; but the number of these polygamists they allowed to be small, confined to lords of small states, the wuzzeers and nobles of the larger, and the head men of small villages.

They allowed too, though reluctantly, that some of their female children were disposed of as slaves, but wished to deny that they sold them to strangers. There is no doubt, however, that this practice does exist, and has long existed in the hills to a very considerable extent, not merely (as they would have us suppose) a transfer of their daughters, as wives to the neighbouring inhabitants, but in regular sales to dealers, who again dispose of them in the low country. But unless the number thus disposed of was very large, it would be quite insufficient to account for the female balance that must remain in question. These, they say, remain in the house of their parents; and this assertion brings back the difficulty, how the parents are to maintain this heavy charge? And I cannot help suspecting that, notwithstanding the expense which they assert to attend the keep of a wife, she is on the whole a gaining concern, and, as a strong and useful hand in agricultural labour, is rather a source of wealth and property to her husband or husbands, than any positive loss.

After all, the true causes and reasons for this custom remain in doubt; and till further observation and more minute inquiry may throw some better light on the subject, we have only to believe one of two things; either that the number of females, from the operation of certain causes, is small in proportion to that of the males, or that extremely obstinate attachments to old customs and habits, the effects of cogent circumstances, that have operated, and may still continue to operate, restrains in this instance the usual course of nature.

Should the labour of females be of actual profit to those with whom they live, instead of a loss and charge to them, it might partially account for a proportion of females remaining unmarried in the houses of their parents; but it cannot seem a full and satisfactory reason for this great restraint and reversing of the course of nature, in keeping so large a body of the sexes separate: nor can it at all, I think, be admitted as any solution of a custom that forms so singular and so unnatural a departure from the almost universal feelings and usages of mankind.

Be these things as they may, the custom has a deplorably injurious effect upon the morals of the females in this country, particularly in point of chastity. They do not see it valued, and of course do not preserve it. From the degree of community of intercourse prevailing by custom, the men do not feel shocked at an unlimited extension of it: thus the women are entirely at the service of such as will pay for their favours, without feeling the slightest sense of shame or crime in a practice from which they are not discouraged by early education, example, or even the dread of their lords, who only require a part of the profit.

This is a degree of brutish insensibility that is hardly to be found among the most perfectly rude and debased savages of other countries; and the total absence of general morality will seem less strange when these too certain facts are known.

It is strange that, in these promiscuous and complicated connexions, disputes seldom arise; but, of a family of four or five brothers, only one or two are in general at home at the same time: some are out on service as soldiers, or with the minor chiefs; others are travelling: the elder usually remains at home. If any quarrel were to arise, a common cause would be made against the offender, and ejectment from house and board ensue.

Nor does the produce of this extraordinary union give any further rise to disputes: the first born child is the property of the elder brother, and the next in succession are supplied in turn.

It is remarkable, that a people so degraded in morals, and many of whose customs are of so revolting a nature, should in other respects evince a much higher advancement in civilization, than we discover among other nations, whose manners are more engaging, and whose moral character ranks infinitely higher. Their persons are better clad, and more decent; their approach more polite and unembarrassed; and their address is better than that of most of the inhabitants of the remote highlands of Scotland; although certainly the circumstances, under which they saw Europeans for the first time, were sufficient to have confounded them much more than any that usually occur in the most distant and uncouth parts of the latter: and their houses, in point of construction, comfort, and internal cleanliness, are beyond comparison superior to Scottish highland dwellings.

The cultivation we see here is far more extensive, and infinitely better, in proportion to the nature of the ground and their respective means; and the degree of pains bestowed on agriculture far exceeds that which is apparent in our highland straths, where the subjects to work upon are much superior, and the burthens far less: for here the half of all the produce of the soil belongs to the sovereign; and the remaining moiety must be barely sufficient for paying the expenses of farming, and maintaining the cultivator and his family.

It is, in fact, wonderful, when the face of the country is contemplated, and the sharp and rugged steeps of the hills, that remain in a state of nature, are considered, to see the great extent of land that has been brought under tillage; and to recollect, that all which now smiles under corn was once as rough and unpromising as these.

The valleys of Deyrah, of Nawur, of the Pabur, Kurangooloo, Comharsein, and every one, in fact, which we have passed through, since we crossed the range of Choor, all exhibited a rich succession of waving ridges gently rising above each other from the rivulets that watered them, and interspersed with villages, orchards, and trees.

The total ruin that at first so often occurred was now less frequently observed; and although, in most villages, there were large heaps of tottering and fallen houses, we seldom saw one quite deserted. The hand of the spoiler had reached these districts later, and had less heavily pressed on them. Industry had not received so severe a check; and in agricultural pursuits these people must be allowed to be active.

As the features of the country enlarge, and valleys occur, which afford sides of greater slope and spread to the labour of the farmer, a larger continuous extent of cultivated land may be seen; and small fields, with few or no ridges, are scattered through the space chiefly occupied by the usual smaller or larger terraces. Wheat and barley were the staple articles of produce, and were very rich and good of their kinds. Poppy and the minor seeds occasionally occurred; and apricot, mulberry, and other fruit-trees, were carefully reared.

I do not think that we saw much rice in the tract more immediately under consideration, except in the bed of the river Pabur, where the carse land was probably well suited for such produce; and there the fields were peculiarly neat, and the rows of the plant distributed in fanciful and pleasing figures, such as circles, squares, spirals, &c.

The women and the men share the labour of the field with their cattle. The women weed, plant rice, gather stones, cut the corn, attend the threshing it, by the feet of cattle, on a round paved spot, and sift it from the husk. The operation of reducing it to meal is chiefly performed by water-mills; which, by an exceedingly simple contrivance, turn two stones contrary ways. These are not large, but they answer the purpose; and, in a country where water is plentiful, and there is no want of sufficient fall, such simple machines do all the work of the country, and seem to smile at our more expensive and complicated constructions. At times, four or five of these are seen, one above another, all working at the same time, with the same stream; and the cover or shed under which they work is as rude as their machinery.

Of quadrupeds, wild or domestic, we have observed none that we did not see before. There are no horses; nor would the country admit of the use of them. Sheep are met with, but do not seem to be numerous; a circumstance not readily to be accounted for, as the clothing of the inhabitants is wholly fabricated from wool; and the country appears to be most particularly favourable for their grazing. We never saw an extensive flock together. Goats are also common, and form an usual present: they seem to be of the common mountain sort, with shaggy hair, horns rising upwards, with a little inclination backwards, from the perpendicular. They afford a plentiful supply of good milk.

I think, indeed, that no country can well be imagined more calculated for sheep-farming: all the varieties of rich and plentiful pasture, a short velvet bite, cool woods and heights for summer, and warm fruitful vales and ravines for winter, may be obtained in boundless range.

To those who have seen the nature of great part of the Scots highlands now under sheep husbandry, particularly to the northward and westward, the wildness of the country will form no objection; and, if a more luxuriant herbage be a desideratum, these Indian hills must surely have it in a superior degree.

It may be that the snow lies longer here even than it does in the western parts of Scotland; but, in all probability, a sufficient tract of the lower ground is free, or covered to so little depth, that the animals could feed easily during the deep winter months.

The snow, which falls heavy generally about the end of December, lies every where till towards the middle of March; when it rapidly melts, speedily leaving a large space clear, which is as soon covered with grass.

In Scotland, from the end of November, or, at all events, the middle of December, till the end of March, and sometimes later, the higher hills, and more remote northern and north-western districts, have little space clear of snow, and very little ground that can afford feed: and, although the quantity of snow that lies in the very best wintering valleys may not be so great as in this country, still it is believed that the difference is not such as to render it unlikely that sheep could be kept in the whole tract of hills, even from the plains to the elevated spots near the snowy hills themselves.

Not having the least acquaintance with sheep-farming myself, I may have overlooked many things that might form objections to the rearing of large flocks in these hills; but, viewing the quantity of ground necessarily waste, it appears to a mere traveller that it could not be more advantageously occupied than by these animals; and if (as is conjectured) they could be supported during the winter months, by the quantity of underwood which covers the country, as well as by the high luxuriant grass produced during the warm season, and which they could easily reach by scraping, it is certain that food might be found for vast numbers during the eight temperate and warm months, in which the soil spontaneously throws up a richer and far more universal pasture than is found in any of the sheep-walks of Britain.

To aid this luxuriance, correct its produce, or quicken its effects, they have recourse to an expedient similar to that practised in Scotland, and which, I think, cannot but injure the soil in time: they burn the long rank grass produced during the rainy weather, and with the showers of spring there arises a sweet and tender shoot, that covers all the black spots with a brilliant verdure.

It may naturally be inquired, whence do the people of the country derive all the wool which they expend in their clothing? I believe that a portion of their wool and of their manufactures comes from the remoter districts to the northward; and it is also possible, that sheep may exist in greater numbers than appeared to us as we traversed the land. The villagers always showed an unwillingness to disclose the amount and the sources of their property; and it may be presumed that their sheep, as one of those, were concealed from the view of the strangers: a conduct that might arise from a fear of betraying grounds for tax or tribute to be imposed on them, at the period of settling the country.

It is possible that one reason of the limited extent to which sheep-breeding is carried may proceed from the insulated situation these people have hitherto occupied; cut off from any considerable intercourse with those countries where a market might be looked for to receive the larger quantities of produce they might raise.

It may even be more than a question, whether, in case of a greatly extended growth of wool, a market could in any way be obtained for the superfluity they might have to dispose of. Woollens are of comparatively little use in Hindoostan: the bulk of the natives of the plains cannot afford the price in general required for good blankets; and are nearly, if not quite as well covered, by rosais, or fabrics, formed of two cloths of coarse printed cotton, with a thick layer of raw cotton quilted in between them: this is cheaper, warmer, and lighter than a blanket, although it will not last so long.

Thus a market to the southward would by no means be certain: to the northward there would be none; for the wool of Bootan exceeds that of these hills in quantity and quality; and much is imported from thence for the finer manufactures.

Whether it may be an object in future to encourage the growth of wool in these parts, and to improve the breed of sheep, with a view to foreign trade, is a question that may one day or other be worth agitating.

The animal itself is sold dear. Strangers are ever charged highly, when they are supposed to be rich: we paid from one to one a half rupee for each sheep, picking, as may be supposed, the fattest that could be found.

The external appearance of the houses of these hillmen has been already described: we entered many since that time, and observed their internal economy. The lower stories are devoted to cattle and lumber; and in the upper the family lives. The rooms are never very large, but they are remarkably snug, comfortable, and clean: they are floored with broad and well smoothed planks: the walls are plastered with mud, and frequently white-washed, and ornamented with red figures. In the centre there is always built a "choolah," or fire-place, for the purposes of warmth, as well as for dressing the food of the family: this cooking place is uniformly constructed of earth and stone, and well purified every day with a mixture of cow-dung and fine earth, which is washed over it. In this room, and around the fire-place, or in one corner, the family sleep all together on one bed of grass, or under one blanket.

Sometimes several houses are constructed so as to open into one another, or to communicate by the balconies, which always surround the upper story. These are always constructed of fir-tree planks, put together often with a skill that would not shame an European workman; and they form very convenient additional chambers and passages to the body of the building. Little furniture is found in these houses; little indeed is ever seen in a Hindoostanee house; a few vessels for cooking and for containing water, a few boxes for holding corn, with jars of various sorts, are all we ever met with. I once saw a child in a sort of cradle.

These houses are entered by a very small door, seldom more than three feet six inches to four feet high, and half that breadth; and the ascent to each story is by means of a notched stick, which, as there is generally little light, and as the lower apartment cannot be clean, from its being allotted to cattle, affords a very uncertain footing.

Windows indeed are neither numerous nor large; having no glass, they cannot shut out the cold without excluding the light, and thus, small openings, occasionally closed with a piece of board, are the substitutes.

Chimnies, to give a passage to the smoke, they do not think of, nor do they seem to care in what manner it makes its escape. Want of light and of air must in one way or other occasion dirt: although they keep their rooms neat and clean as far as the eye reaches, they cannot by any care make up for a free ventilation; nor can they exclude the swarms of vermin insects that infest these houses, and which render them seriously inconvenient and disagreeable to strangers.

The Paharee, or mountaineer, is not so incommoded; indeed the persons of both sexes are overrun with them; the coarse blanket covering they wear encourages the generation of these vile insects, and the irritation they produce on the skin seems to be agreeable to them in this cold climate: when it becomes excessive, they immerse their clothing in hot water, destroying myriads, and restoring their own rest.

The habitations of these people are always in villages; a single insulated house is never seen, or very rarely. These villages consist of from five to twenty houses, some even larger are met with. They frequently form a picturesque object at a distance, crowning some height, and hanging over some glen, or intermingled with wood on the uprising face of a hill: every one according to its size has one or more lofty towers overlooking the village; these are, as has been heretofore observed, temples; some are very large and high, and are commonly ornamented with much art, and frequently with some taste.

All the inhabitants of this region, as well as those near the plains, are Hindoos. Their features for the most part, although gradually altered by the climate, as we leave the low country, and also perhaps by country customs, and possibly by the remaining mixture of an ancient indigenous race, still retain traces that point to the chief original stock in the plains.

Their language, their religion, and the general tone of their customs and prejudices tend to confirm this. Their language for a considerable way into the hills is a corrupted dialect of true Hindostanee, in which Shanscrit and Hindoo words predominate; but the farther we penetrated to the north, the more corrupt it became, till it was so mixed with foreign tongues as to be unintelligible by a low countryman.

They worship the chief Hindoo deities, adore and protect the cow, and blindly follow and practise most of the rites of Hindooism; but they are Hindoos in a sorely degraded and truly ignorant state, mingling the wild superstitions and blind adorations of that religion with the utmost grossness of character, and a total deficiency of acquaintance with even their legendary origin; and they adhere to the chief manners and customs of Hindoos, only because they were adopted by their fathers before them; nor does there seem to be a Brahmin among them of more enlightened mind, or in any degree more intelligent than the rest.

In every village, and on each way-side, there are temples to different Hindoo divinities; some to Mahadeo, or Seeva, under innumerable names; some to Gonĕsh, others to Bhowannee, or to Calee; but there is an infinite variety of deities of their own, to whom they pay much adoration, and their temples are found on every hill, at every turn and remarkable place on the road. These are the Genii Loci, and their symbols and memorials are numerous and various; there is not a Teeba, or pinnacle of a hill, that is not topped with a heap of stones; a single pillar, or a small hut, to which the Paharee turns with mysterious solemnity, and prostrating himself, prays to the spirit of the place, and to every one of these are strange tales and curious legends attached.

Superstition of this sort seems peculiarly natural to highland countries; such are the witches, spectres, and ghosts of the Scotch highlands, and these of the Indian mountains make not less impression on their inhabitants: any person taking delight in such mysterious tales, and who could follow the jargon of this country, might here find ample gratification for his taste.

In a soil so rank with superstition, it may be inferred, that the priesthood flourish luxuriantly; and indeed they are found in abundance all over the country: not only does it abound with every religious order of Hindoo mendicant, but in every purgunnah, villages are met with inhabited entirely by Brahmins, and by Byragees, Gosseins, Sunyasses, Jogees, &c., who either subsist on the superstitious charity of the public, or who, having abjured their vow of celibacy, have married and settled in the parts they liked best, according to their means.

When a community itself is poor, those who subsist on its charity, or by its respect, cannot well become rich; even the Brahmins were not positively so; but the villages and houses inhabited by them were universally the most comfortable, and in the best situations.

I could not discover whether there were any peculiar ceremonies at their marriages, or what they might be; nor had we, in general, much opportunity for observing that they employed many on other occasions. Their ignorance probably precluded them from the knowledge of most of those belonging to the Hindoo religion, and their hard life and poverty from the practice of those with which they may be acquainted; but it is fair to believe, that those observances which may yet be among them are in the spirit of strict Hindooism.

They burn their dead, carrying them to the heights of hills, and commonly erect a pile of stones, or place a large stone on end, and plant sticks with rags on them, to mark the spot sacred to the memory of the deceased.

It is not very common for women to burn themselves with the body of their deceased husbands; but it does sometimes happen, in case of the death of persons of consequence. Thus, at the death of the late Rajah of Bischur, twenty-two persons of both sexes burnt themselves along with his body; of these, twelve were females, and three Ranees; one or two of his wuzzeers, and his first chobedar, were also among the number: even at the death of some of the hill soldiers near Nahn, their wives burnt themselves on their bodies.

When a Paharia of the middling class of zemindars is asked of what cast is he, the answer at first is, in general, a "Raajepoot;" but on more minute inquiry, he may confess that he is only a "Kunnoit." Of this term it is not easy to obtain any explanation; it is, probably, a low cast of Raajepoot, or a medium between this and the lower casts; but it is a distinction not known in the plains. Most of the hill people call themselves Raajepoŏts, when in fact they have no true title to the appellation.

It appears that the principal casts into which the hill-inhabitants are divided are Brahmins, Raajepoots, Kunnoits, and Cooleys or Chumārs. We did not find any of that minute subdivision of tribes which exists in the plains, and which, probably, is the result of a considerably advanced state of civilization on a dense and extensive population, which has continued for ages in the observance of certain customs and distinctions.

The chiefs of states, and men of rank, universally assumed the distinction of Raajepoot, and probably were of such extraction; all the rajahs were certainly of that class. The seānās of villages, and zemindars, were either Raajepoots of inferior consequence and purity, or Kunnoits: many of the latter were merely Cooleys, and a large proportion of the lower order; those, for instance, who were furnished to us, as porters for transporting baggage, were of this description, and exactly corresponded with, and were put to the same offices as the Chumārs of the plains.

The people of all casts feed not only on corn, vegetables, and milk, in its various shapes, but they eat every species of fish and flesh that they can procure, excepting that of the cow. They drink spirituous liquors when they can obtain them; and they make a species of wine or spirit, with which they intoxicate themselves very readily; it is made from various ingredients.

Brahmins, Raajepoots, &c. all eat sheep, goats, and every kind of game that they can catch, including wild hogs. We had not hitherto seen any domestic fowl or duck.

Tobacco is here in as universal use as in the plains, and when they cannot procure this for smoking, they supply its place with b,hang, and other substitutes of an intoxicating nature; and use a number of simple expedients when a *hubble-bubble*, or machine for inhaling its fumes, is not to be had; to the Cooleys on the march, this refreshment was quite indispensable. When they met with cool water, and were allowed to smoke a chillum, they got on wonderfully; but as soon as the means of quenching thirst, or of recreating their spirits by the stimulus of inhaling the intoxicating smoke failed, they flagged; and at times totally yielded to their exhaustion.

The internal regulation of their villages and small communities perfectly resembles the patriarchal form of their more important governments. In every village there is a man to whom they pay great deference, and to whom they refer all disputes; who, in short, is their chief, and who goes by the name of the Seānā: he always possesses much influence, and when any requisition is to be made from a village, the Seānā is the person to apply to. He also makes the collection of tribute for government, frequently is an officer under it, and I believe is always looked to, as in some measure answerable for the conduct of his villagers.

Contrary to the usual acceptation of the term in the low country, but perhaps more agreeably to its original meaning, the word zemindar is here applied not merely to the chief landholders, but is also used to designate the whole class of those who cultivate the soil. Every man cultivates as much ground as he can manage; half the produce should go to the state. Each individual has his own field or division of land, which he tills by his own labour and that of his family; but in those operations which require speed or assistance, he is aided by the other villagers, to whom in their turn he gives his labour when required. The cultivation belonging to one village is always as much brought together as the nature of the situation will permit, and thus it appears as if there was a community of property; and when so much depends on mutual assistance, probably a virtual community to a limited degree does occur, at all events extending to mutual defence, and general operations.

Each head of a family exercises a very arbitrary right over the members of it; but this, in common with all the nations of the East, is increased by custom and by remoteness, as higher authorities can less interfere with the exercise of the parental privilege. Even the lives of the members of his family are, with perhaps little appeal, in the hands of the head of it, and their persons are fully at his mercy. The power he possesses of disposing of their liberties is too certain and too frequently exercised, as appears proved beyond dispute; and indeed the number of slaves always brought from the hills, which are met with in native families in Hindostan, affords too strong evidence to leave a doubt that this traffic goes on to a great extent.

There is no doubt that the Ghoorkhas, during their tyranny, seized and sold the unhappy mountaineers, particularly of Gurwhal, in great numbers: of that country, in the course of twelve years, two lacs of people are said to have been thus disposed of: in consequence of the desolation spread around from the seizure of his crops for military purposes, the zemindar could seldom pay the quota of his tribute; out of a family of four or five, children they forced him to give up one as a commutation, and instances have, it is said, occurred, where every one of the children were thus in succession torn away.

The distress of the parents too, their own pressure for food, frequently occasioned voluntary sales of their offspring, and one was disposed of that the rest might have food. But although this distress might partly occasion this violation of the feelings of nature, it is to be feared that such an expedient would not have been resorted to had not previous experience pointed it out: in all probability the practice has long existed, and the parents' feelings have been rendered callous by custom.

Slaves from the hills have been long known in Hindostan. The inhabitants of Bischur, however, deny that they ever thus dispose of their children; those of Sirmore and Gurwhal confess that they sometimes do, and I fear that the former state does not, in such denial, adhere to truth.

The females of Bischur are spoken of as excelling those of the other states in beauty, and, accordingly, slaves of this nation are sought after, a temptation probably not to be resisted; and in a country surrounded by states that practise such a custom, it is not likely that it should. Indeed, from the result of some inquiries, and the manner in which some offers which we made for experiment were received, I have no doubt that all they wish is, that it should not be believed that they are guilty of what nature must tell every one is a disgraceful and cruel crime.

The prices of such slaves vary greatly, and depend on many circumstances; the age, beauty, or strength of the person to be sold; the necessity and distance from market of the seller. Far in the hills, and remote from the chief marts for such traffic, the price will have, and I believe has reference to that which is given by a zemindar for a wife; contemplating that the parent is to be totally deprived of any future intercourse with his child, as well as from the benefit of his or her labour, from twenty to fifty rupees will probably be the extent of the demand in such situations.

If distress be the reason for sale, and the seller be the offerer, not the acceptor of an offer, a very small sum indeed will often answer; I think I have heard of eight to ten rupees, but of this I am not certain: hunger and distress will force a human being to make dreadful sacrifices, but I believe that at the usual places for such purchases in the vicinity of the plains, from 50 to 150, and even 200 rupees, are commonly given for a promising slave, not quite a child, of either sex, when extraordinary beauty, or some accidental circumstance, does not fix on them any extrinsic value.

It is difficult to change the long practised customs of nations, particularly when such innovation attacks the interests of individuals, and it will be exceedingly so to prevent the purchase of slaves in Hindostan, even in those provinces which are most fully under the British authority; and it must be infinitely greater in such districts as, bordering on the hills, are at a greater distance from the vigorous operation of police, and more continually under the influence of temptation to do what they do not conceive to be a crime or violation of natural right, and the reason for prohibiting which they therefore cannot understand.

The British government has done all that it well can do to prevent the continuance of this unhappy trade, by a decided prohibition, and declaring that all slaves purchased subsequently to the date of the regulation shall be freed on an application to a magistrate; and this prohibition has been duly enforced, particularly in the upper provinces, which are most liable to the temptation, liberty having been always given to those whose cases were represented to the officiating authority; but it is still to be feared that the purchase of slaves goes on to a certain extent, although with great secrecy and caution.

The natives of Hindostan are not usually cruel masters; on the contrary, their slaves live happily, and often become so attached, as to lose all wish to quit their owners.

In former times those who were domiciled in the families of the great often rose to high rank and power, but it is at all times dangerous and revolting to trust the liberty and person of one human being to the absolute disposal of another, however generally well disposed the master may be; and too frequently, beyond a doubt, in all countries, the power is miserably and cruelly abused, and every well wisher to humanity will join in hoping, that at no distant period, the trade and the existence of slavery may here and every where have an end.

CHAPTER XVI.

We remained stationary during the 26th, 27th, and 28th, the weather varying much. Sometimes storms came down from the mountains that threatened to destroy our frail tent, and tear both it and ourselves to atoms, but its humbleness preserved it, and the gale blew over it; at others, the rain that fell cleared the sky, and opened to our view the mountain scenery, beautiful in varied tints, refreshed by moisture, and rising and retiring alternately, till lost in the mellow blue of distance near the plains.

Our situation, however, was not always one of positive comfort: we had but one tent, a small pall supported on three poles, two of which being upright, were crossed by a third; over this the tent was stretched, coming down to the ground, without walls on either side, and enclosing in all a space of about ten feet square, but in the middle of which only we could stand upright: the cloth of the tent was double, but thin, and was made to weigh exactly sixty pounds, that it might form precisely a load for one man.

In this place were both our beds of straw, covered with a cotton quilt; our table and two old chairs, with most of the baggage, we carried along with us. A tent, somewhat smaller, but similar in construction, was furnished for the shelter of an European writer, who had charge of the papers, stationery, and a variety of articles, that it was absolutely requisite to carry into a country where nothing is to be procured beyond some of the simplest provisions.

To those who have been accustomed to travel in Hindostan, and who know the comfortable, not to say splendid description of tents used on these occasions, the poorness of this equipage in comfort, and almost in necessary covering, will be very obvious; while those who have suffered the hardships of an European warfare, and have bivouacked in a Spanish campaign, and even the larger proportion of travellers whose peregrinations have not led through European countries, may consider the accommodations we possessed as most comfortable and sufficient. As it was, we were contented with them, and only when threatened by wind or rain did we ever think them insufficient.

We carried with us a small quantity of wine, tea, coffee, and sugar; but, desirous to confine our baggage to as small a compass as possible, it proved in the end inadequate to so extensive a tour: for so long a residence in the mountains, out of reach of supply, was not contemplated when we commenced it; and, in the sequel, we had cause to regret our want of precaution. These were our luxuries, and for necessaries we trusted to the produce of the country. Flour of a coarse quality was always to be had to a certain extent; and, at times, a finer sort was obtained. Rice, and a sort of pulse, usually known in the plains by the name of d'hāll, was procured, sufficient for our own consumption, and sometimes to serve out to the people.

Milk could always be had, and ghee, though often not in sufficient abundance for the wants of the whole party: mutton also, though dear, and not always fat, was procurable. In justice, however, to the sheep of the hills, I must say, that, when we did get a fat wedder, it was equal to any meat I ever tasted in any country; but rams were most frequently the only kind brought to us, and of course far inferior. Vegetables were scarce and bad; and we seldom sought for them. On the whole, our living was such as to leave no room for complaint; and the hunger of wholesome, and even violent exercise, would have made worse food delectable.

We rose usually about sunrise: but the preparations for a march generally detained us till eight o'clock; and accidental circumstances, business, and visits from the natives, frequently delayed our march till much later. After a very light breakfast of milk and thin cakes of flour, with a cup of tea while it lasted, we proceeded, never at a very rapid pace, for it was found that over exertion was far more fatiguing than a regular, long-continued, but more moderate effort; and more mischief was done to ourselves and attendants by one violent and injudicious strain up a steep hill than by a whole day's work gently taken. Our progress was further delayed by observations for the purpose of surveying, and by inquiries at the different villages respecting the country. This delay gave time for the advance to reach the place of the night's encampment, and to pitch the tent; which was always sent before us, by strong people, under a trusty guard. Provisions for the people, and ourselves if necessary, and grass for our beds, were required from the inhabitants of the village where we halted; and by six o'clock, our general period of arrival, we found all ready for our reception. Disappointments occasionally occurred; but, after a while, these were rare: it need not be doubted that our rest was sound.

This short detail of our marching routine and usual daily work and fare may seem trifling; but it may contribute to place those who are quite unacquainted with this kind of travelling more in the actual situation of the travellers, which perhaps, more than any thing, lends an interest to a narrative that cannot boast of much valuable information or amusement.

On the morning of the 28th we were roused from our tent by the information that a body of people were advancing along the ridge above our encampment; and, on inquiry, we found that they consisted of the prisoners formerly constituting the forces of Kirtee Rānā, who now were marching disarmed, and attended by a body of Bischur troops, to the army of General Ochterlony.

It was a strange sight to view their wild figures, crowning the heights above us, and stretching in a long irregular line down to a small hollow a little way beyond our camp. When they assembled at their halting place, I went to look at them; and it is difficult to conceive a more uncouth and heterogeneous assemblage than were there collected. The features and figure of the true Ghoorkha are always singular and remarkable, from his broad Chinese or Tartar-like physiognomy, the small eyes, flat nose, and meagre whiskers, as well as his stout square make and sturdy limbs. These, in every description of costume, and in all degrees of raggedness, were mingled with inhabitants of Kumaoon, Sirmore, and Gurwhal; all indicating, by a varied character of countenance, the country they came from. Women and children, loaded with the few articles they had preserved from the rapacity of their captors, were interspersed among the rest; and around, all the Bischur soldiers, in their national dress, armed with bows and arrows, shields and swords, watched, standing, over their movements. Such were the materials from which the groups were formed. But it would need a lively imagination to suggest, and a far more humorous and able pen to describe, the grotesque attitudes, and the odd uncouth individuals that composed the assembly. Many miserable objects, too, faint with weariness and hunger, wounded, and ill attended to, with women, and young children perhaps weak or ill, yet forced to carry them, because their husbands were already overloaded by necessary provisions, and what baggage they had preserved, formed a large part of the cavalcade.

When we thus saw a portion of the Ghoorkha army together, and marked them, so miserable, stript, and unarmed, we could not but ask ourselves with astonishment, were these the men who had so well defended the fort of Kalunga, who had so often foiled our regular troops, and had protracted the campaign to such a length, by their constancy and bravery? Yet among them there were many fine looking young men; and there was a cheerfulness of countenance, a modest confidence of demeanor, that could not but pleasingly attract observation.

They were prisoners; they had lost their all; and they had been in the power of a cruel and treacherous enemy; nor could they well say what they had to expect: but no murmurs of lamentation or discontent were heard; good humour and lightness of heart absolutely seemed to prevail among them, yet without noise or tumult. The hum of many voices was heard, and the noise of encamping, making their cooking places, pitching a stick to suspend a blanket from, that their wives and children might be somewhat shielded from the sun; but no disputes, no quarrels occurred: and the quietness with which all was conducted might have afforded a lesson to the more disciplined troops of other nations. Among the women we remarked several who were fair, and had good features: they were chiefly natives of Bischur and Gurhwhal, who had married Ghoorkha soldiers, and now followed their husbands' fortunes.

After breakfast, Kirtee Rānā, the captive Ghoorkha chief, paid us a visit, at our request. He was a little and a very old looking man; his cast of countenance was quite Chinese, with mustachios consisting of only a few thin hairs; his nose was sunk in the middle, and turned up at the end; he much resembled an old mulatto woman; he wore on his head a dirty cotton scull-cap, and his clothes, of white muslin, were in miserable disrepair; his figure was strikingly ungainly; but the expression of his countenance was good-humoured; and, when animated by conversation, his eye lightened up with much fire, and he became communicative and at his ease.

He is a fine, brave, and spirited old soldier: we received him kindly. He related the history of his capture, with the reasons why it took place so early, nearly in the manner above stated. He said, that the endurance of hunger and thirst, without any prospect of relief, had proved too much for the constancy of a great part of his troops; and the Gurwhal and Cumaoon men had begun to desert fast, or had entered into treacherous engagements with the enemy; and that subsequently (when on his retreat to Chumbee-Ke-Teeba) he was betrayed into a road, lined by an overpowering force of the enemy. He described the sufferings of the troops from the heat of the sun, continual exertion, and thirst, as very great, and, joined to that of the women and children, too much to bear; and, accordingly, under the idea that the attack was authorised by, and under the orders of the British, he had surrendered, to preserve life and property, not having confidence in his troops to risk a final battle.

It is singular, that, while Kirtee Rānā remained at Nowagurh, before the death of Buchtee T,happa, which occurred in the decisive affair of the 16th of April, in the attack upon the heights near Malown, the desertions were by no means frequent or numerous; and even from the army of Ummr Sing they were comparatively small in number; but, after the death of that chieftain, whom they emphatically called "the blade of their sword," the men from Kirtee Rānā's party deserted faster, and in greater numbers; while nearly the whole army of Ummr Sing left him, and threw themselves on British clemency. This proved, more strongly than any thing, the devotion and love which the people entertained for Buchtee T,happa.

Kirtee Rānā is a native of Palpai, of high rank, and, I believe, a direct descendant from the original royal family of that state. The word Rānā denotes the tribe or family he belongs to; and, I believe, it originated in distinguishing those who were related to the royal house of Palpai before its downfall and the conquest of the Ghoorkhas: at all events, it indicates a high extraction.

He says that he is seventy years of age, and has served the Nepāl rajah thirteen years in this quarter. Upon our asking him what could induce him, at such an age, to leave his native land, his answer was impressive.

"My master the rajah sent me: he says to his people, to one, Go you to Gurwhal; to another, Go you to Cashmire, or to any distant part: My lord, thy slave obeys, it is done. No one ever inquires into the reason of an order of the rajah."

In the Hindoo phraseology, the words and style were remarkable and emphatic; and the action that accompanied them was still more so. The old man's eye sparkled; and he imitated, with admirable effect, the tone of high command and that of passive reverential obedience. No finer specimen could be given of the high and blind respect with which eastern potentates are contemplated by their subjects, and which has always been remarkably observed in Nepāl.

Along with Kirtee Rānā, and with several other bhāradars or chiefs, came one who was said to be an uncle of Ummr Sing, whose name I do not recollect; an uncommonly tall fine figure, clothed in a long black gown and very warlike cap, and armed with a cookree and shield. Of him also we asked many questions concerning the war, the Nepāl empire, and their customs; and concluded by asking him, whether, according to the terms of the capitulation, he would return with Ummr Sing to Nepāl.

He answered, "No; I can no more visit my country: I must look for service elsewhere. I can never face the rajah again, for I have eaten Ghoorkha salt. I was in trust, and I have not died at my post."

"Why," said we, "should you have died uselessly, where the cause you served could not be benefited by your death, when it was quite hopeless?"

"Ah!" replied he, "we should nevertheless never have deserted our posts: to have died there had been far better. We never can return to our country." And all the soubahdars and chiefs present, shaking their heads, also said, "We never can return."

These people surely possess in a high degree, almost to excess, the true sense of a soldier's duty; and it is striking to observe the miserable appearance they often make as figures, contrasted with the exalted sentiments they utter; not in a pompous manner, as if calculated or prepared for the occasion, but simply and naturally, as the usual and ordinary feelings of their minds.

The persons, who had the charge of conducting Kirtee Rānā to the British camp, had provided him with none of the conveniences, and scarcely the necessaries, that a man of his rank, and particularly of his advanced age, might most properly lay claim to. He had walked on foot, although lame and weary, from Raeengudh. We supplied him with money, sufficient to procure for himself and his men comforts and necessaries, till they should reach the camp; and we provided for himself the means of proper carriage, and some of the attentions befitting his rank and age. He took his leave, and proceeded on his journey; and I hope he left us pleased.

The commander of the Bischur troops, a chief of that country, who came from a remote part of the snowy hills, and was ordered to convey the Ghoorkha troops to the British camp, also paid us a visit. Of him we made many inquiries relating to the more northerly and distant regions of that state, and to the passes which might lead from thence through the snowy range. He informed us that he himself had passed through them, and had reached the temple of Buddreenauth, by the Nilleemana pass; that he had followed up the course of the Sutlej, till it separated into two streams, at a point called Lēōt; but it was not easy to comprehend how the route led after this point; nor could we obtain, at this time, any list of the stages, or description of the country. From what we gathered respecting the passes, we understood that, during a space of four days' journey, there is neither habitation nor food to be met with, nor wood to dress victuals with, and that the road is exceedingly bad.

The descent on the other side, when the crest of the snowy hills is passed, he says, is far less than on this; and he added, that in two days the traveller reached the plains of Bootan, which must be very far elevated above those of Hindostan. His conversation on this part of the subject was by no means distinct: he asserted however, that he had reached and come through the passes at Buddreenauth, after having penetrated through the snowy hills by the passes in Bischur, which for a considerable way lead along the Sutlej. This river, he also avers, comes from beyond the snowy hills, by two branches that unite at Lēōt.

From this conversation, although we learnt nothing that was very distinct or conclusive, enough was gathered to make us anxious to push our inquiries farther, and, if possible, to penetrate along this line ourselves; at least, so far as to ascertain the practicability of the road and passes.

Finding that a ready and ample supply of grain was not to be obtained in the vicinity of our camp, we moved on the 29th about ten miles in a south-west direction to a station in Phagoo, a district of Keeoountheel.

May 30.—Passing by the castle of Theog, a small building in the usual taste on the top of a small peak, we were met by the lord of the place, who preferred a bitter complaint against his own son, who (as he asserted) meditated to usurp the estate, and probably to murder his father. The poor creature, who, with a revenue certainly not exceeding 3000 rupees per annum, has the title of Rānā, was in great distress. He was promised protection.

The road now wound along the eastern side of a valley, that led to the Girree, which was in sight, a small stream below: from the crest of the ridge, where we occasionally reached it, a long and extensive range of the snowy hills to the north-west appeared, broken by intervening ridges, and forming the boundary of the Punjab. A further gentle ascent brought us to the height of Deshoo-Ke-D,har, formerly a post of the Ghoorkhas, but now in ruins, whence a very extensive and interesting view was prevented by mist and haze alone. Thence we descended to our tents, along smooth grassy knolls, in time to be sheltered from a fierce and severe storm, which continued till midnight, with terrible thunder and lightning, and heavy hail and rain.

The next day, the 31st, finding our situation to be too much exposed, we moved under shelter of a fine forest of fir-trees that clothed a lofty peak, and pitched our tent in a retired and romantic glade, where, though the weather was still inclement, we only felt the cold, being undisturbed by the violence of the wind.

We had now, from the natural direction of the hills to the north-west, and our own progress towards the south, advanced so far towards the plains, that we were not much further removed from thence than when we were crossing Choor. That mountain appeared to be at no great distance, with the various glens we had crossed running down to meet the Girree. From Deshoo-Ke-D,har, the geographical lines of the country, the course of its rivers, ravines, and ridges, were very easily traced: a course, intersecting that which we had before held, and carrying us by another of the more prominent ridges of the country, promised to add considerably to the accuracy of our geographical observations.

Nothing of importance offered to detain us in the quarter we now occupied. The stronger holds of Jytock and of Malown, with all others in the hills, were placed in the British possession. The armies were moving to cantonments; and, as the accounts received from head-quarters gave us no reason to believe that any orders would be issued likely to interfere with the researches we had in contemplation, we therefore purposed to hold a course to the northward, to visit Rampore, the capital, and Serān, the second place in Bischur, and then to be guided by circumstances as to our further progress through the snowy range.

June 1.—We again marched, holding an easterly course, through a fine larch wood; and sharply descending through the village of Dutān, where there is a very neat temple to the goddess Durgāh, we reached the site of an old fort named Goorjeree, situate in the small state of Rutēs.

A very short way further down, on the banks of the Girree, are the two considerable states of Bughāt and Keeoun, which bound with Sirmore, the former stretching from Keeownthul to the plains. Rutēs is an exceeding small state, depending on, and paying tribute to, Sirmore.

From Goorjeree, a very rapid descent along the edge of a ridge, that ends in the Girree, brought us to the banks of that river, at six miles from our encampment. The stream was swoln and muddy, from the rain of the day before: we crossed it; and, on the other side, while passing by a half-ruined village just above, two children were presented to us, as those of the late Rānā of Rutēs, who was murdered not long before by some of the zemindars on the opposite side of the stream, in his own lordship, but who rose upon him, and thus put him to death. Their mother, a respectable, good-looking woman, although rather masculine, presented them, with prayers for protection. This afforded an additional proof of the wretched and disordered state of the country.

We now entered the state of Bulsum, and commenced an irregular winding ascent along the course of the Bugettroo nullah (the same on whose banks we encamped on the 13th of May, much higher up), and reached the village of Sah, after a march of somewhat more than ten miles.

The face of the country was uninteresting, consisting of brown bare hills, here and there spotted with fields, from which the corn had been cut. The lower part of the nullah is narrow and deep, and the road winds irregularly from two to three hundred yards above its stream.

No variation was remarked in the nature of the soil or rock. We observed this day a neat expedient used by the Ghoorkhas instead of a directing post, when two roads meet: coming to such a place, and puzzled as to our course, the Ghoorkha Soubahdar stepped forward, and stooping down, showed where some of the party who preceded us had placed a tuft of grass, which he had rooted up, upon one of the paths, with a stone on it, thus denoting, as he observed, that the road was "killed;" we took that which according to his ideas remained alive, and found it to be the right one.

We remarked this day a very highly aromatic species of sage, in great abundance: almost every small herb in these hills possesses some aromatic quality, or has some sort of perfume; mint, and other potherbs, we had found wild before.

Bulsum is a small but thriving state, assessed by the Ghoorkhas at 6000 rupees per annum. It consists of a ridge, and two valleys, that run down to the Girree from the range connecting Choor and Urructa, and which divide it from Poonnur of Joobul.

The village of Sâh, which belongs to it, is a poor place, but we found in it a novelty, an enclosed garden, in which, besides peaches and apricots (the latter nearly ripe), we were pleased to find many apple-trees, covered with fruit of a good size, and which, though not ripe enough to be sweet, were far superior to crabs, and proved a very grateful variety. Shaddock and lemon-trees were also cultivated here, but they had been very roughly treated by the cold, and a grape-vine crept up some wild fig-trees, with which some pains seemed to have been taken.

June 2.—The Rānā of Bulsum paid us a visit this morning. He was a good-looking man, and wore the common hill dress, except that the material was somewhat finer, and his trowsers were of striped cotton. In his cap was placed a plume of the feathers of the hill-pheasant, looped with a gold ornament, and on his arms were silver bangles. He was attended by a party of hill troops, armed with bows and arrows.

We were detained there till eleven o'clock, when we commenced our march by ascending the hill behind the village, in a direction at first northerly, and then turning to the eastward, till we reached the lofty point of Churail-ke-Teeba, whence a wide view opened to us. The face of the country hitherto had been brown and uninteresting, the corn universally cut, and a good deal of land turned up for the rice cultivation; it was well tilled, and in as good order as any land I had ever seen at home; I know not, however, whether the ground was moved to any great depth.

During our ascent, which was sharp and irregular, we saw many parties of the mountain troops, all assembling to meet their rānā to do him honour. Their figures running down the brown ridges, and topping the dark rocks, gave a fine uniformity of character to the scene, and awakened thoughts of ancient story, of feudal times, and warlike clans meeting in their own heathy mountains at the call of their chief.

We passed several villages, in one of which I obtained a tolerable sketch of a woman, who occupied a good house in the place, and gave no signs of uneasiness when I signified my wish to take her likeness.

From the height of Choorail, the whole surrounding country presented as various and diversified a prospect as generally happens from a lofty station, and we remained here a long time employed in observations. We had only hitherto proceeded four miles and a half, and from hence followed the ridge a considerable distance farther, and then descended by a rough road to the village of Butlaoque, which we did not reach till eight o'clock at night, though the whole march was not nine miles, so long did we loiter on the heights, beguiled by the extensive view.

The village of Butlaoque looks down upon a wild valley, that is separated into two parts by a point of the ridge which we crossed on the 13th of May. The country around is not inviting, although villages abound, and much land is under cultivation, but the top of the glen is romantic with rocks and wood.

We remained here during the 3d, but on the 4th resumed our march, ascending the hill behind the village, which is a continuation of the Churail ridge, and reached a high peak called Deoonnur-ke-Teeba, upon the ridge that connects the mountains of Choor and Urructa, and from either side of which proceed a number of valleys that send their waters to the Touse or to the Girree.

The day was hazy, but the view was magnificent; from this point, the road lay on the crest of the ridge, which is very narrow between each rising peak, almost due north; sometimes through fine forests, at others along sharp rocks, and varied by many rises and falls.

At one very difficult pass we found the breastwork yet standing, behind which the inhabitants of Joobul, Poonnur, and Bulsum, defended themselves from the attacks of the Ghoorkha forces and the men of Sirmore, during the struggles which that warlike district made for liberty.

The Ghoorkha forces suffered a considerable loss in attempting to gain the narrow ledges of the pass, nor could they succeed till in the night they sent a body of some hundreds round to a height which was unoccupied, and which commanded the pass. These, in the morning, opened a destructive fire on the Poonurrees, who, thus attacked in front and rear, were forced to retire with great loss.

Somewhat further we reached a gorge, whence, on the east side, we looked down on Poonnur, and on the west into the vales of Bulsum, and continued onwards, occasionally dipping and rising, till coming to a wooded craggy eminence, it appeared that we had left the direct road, and had to form one for ourselves, an experiment somewhat hazardous in so wild a country, especially as it was already five o'clock, and our tents were distant across a deep dell.

No time however was to be lost, and we penetrated into a deep forest near the head of a subordinate valley, shaggy with wood, and very rocky. The soil was deep and fine, but the descent was so rapid, and the underwood so thick, that it was sometimes not easy to avoid precipices, to the brink of which the numerous falls we got often brought us. On emerging from this forest, a heavy shower fell, and continued till we had crossed two small but deep ravines, which lay between us and our tents, pitched at the village of D'hăr, and which we reached at a late hour; our march was only nine miles and a half.

This village belongs to Bulsum, and has a south-eastern aspect opposite the woody descent by which we came, which resembles the usual north-western faces of all the peaks we have seen.

Little occurred on the march of this day worthy of note: we found well-grown acorns upon one of the trees, which we usually believed to be a holly; and we found a plant very much resembling common cabbage in taste and smell, growing wild in the hills; the flower of it also satisfied us that it belonged to that species.

June 5.—The morning was fine, but with a few sprinklings of rain. We dismissed the Rānā of Bulsum (who had hitherto attended us) with the customary presents, and we pursued our march, mounting the steep hill behind the village, in a north-easterly direction, to Kanda, a high peak about two miles and a half distant. From hence we looked down on Poonnur, Bulsum, and the small state of Cotegooroo. On our road to this place a party of men brought us a hill pheasant, or rutnāl, which had been caught by the rānā's order on our account, by the exertion of upwards of an hundred men. These birds are very beautiful in plumage and form; they will be mentioned hereafter with the other sorts of game that occur in the hills. On the rough heights of Kanda we saw some, and heard others, as they rose and fled from us, with their mellow whistle. On this peak we also saw a snake which the Ghoorkhas had killed, almost the only one we had met with in our alpine travels.

Descending from this height we continued our progress upon the unequal and rugged crest of the ridge in a northerly direction, passing through a pleasing succession of wood and glade, and among forests of surprisingly fine silver-fir trees, some of which were of wonderful girth, and in scenes surpassed by nothing, save the dells in Urructa. The splendid view of the snowy hills, a scene which can never weary, would have been here enjoyed to perfection but for the haziness of the day.

Leaving this ridge we descended through similar scenery, but much scathed with fire; we passed through some beds of wild strawberries of good flavour, and very refreshing. A steep winding path along the edge of a subordinate ridge led us by two neat villages to the bed of a stream that runs to the Girree. From hence we ascended the opposite mountain side, which was steep, barren, and ugly. The nullah is the boundary between the petty states of Bulsum and Cotegooroo, which we now entered. Casting back our eyes on the two opposite slopes of Bulsum, which we had passed, we were delighted with their beauty and the rich intermixture of cultivation, wood, and villages, they displayed. The Girree was now in sight below to our left; it had taken its turn to the hills, whence it springs, and which we were fast approaching; and on turning the corner of the ridge to our right, and in an easterly direction, we saw on its banks the house of the Rānā of Cotegooroo, curiously perched on a rock above the stream, but far below us. Beyond it was the ridge that forms the southern boundary of the Nawur valley; our tent was pitched at a village a good way above the stream, and our march was eight miles and three quarters.

On one part of the road, where the ground was moist from a shower, we saw the print of a small tiger's foot, but we could not satisfactorily ascertain whether it was that of a true tiger or only of a leopard. The natives said it was a red animal, and called it bang.

In marches so near the course of our former route, and in a country which presents a succession of scenery so nearly similar, and of which the grand features are almost always the same, much novelty of description cannot be expected; little remark, therefore, has been offered on the last few marches.

Cotegooroo is a lordship, valued at about 9000 rupees per annum, and is governed by a Rānā, who pays tribute to Bischur. The country and people are similar to those of Bulsum, Joobul, and other small states in the neighbourhood. The house or village where the Rānā resides is called Cote-kaee. Our camp was situated in a pleasant grove of mulberry and oak-trees, near a cool running stream, and we were furnished by the villagers around with plenty of fine strawberries and milk.

June 6.—In the morning the Rānā of Cotegooroo came to pay us a visit. He was a very corpulent, sickly, and ill-looking man, advanced in years, and bearing the marks of excess as well as of disease. Unable from illness and fat to move of himself, he was pulled up the hills in a sort of litter by fifty men. He complained bitterly of the depredations committed on his territories by the inhabitants of Poonnur, who, making their way over the ridge which divides them from the village of Cote-kaee, surprise and plunder it.

Both these people and the men of Bulsum are noted for such marauding expeditions, and, I believe, those of Cote-kaee are not more innocent, while they who inhabit the opposite side of the ridge in the valley of Nawur are known to be notoriously daring thieves. Even whilst we were in the neighbourhood, the chief of Bulsum, that he might lose no time, seized violently on the lands of the chief of the petty state of Bhuroulee. Nothing could be done at the time but to assure him of the protection of government in common with that which would be experienced by the whole country, and to threaten the aggressor with their vengeance.

We continued our route, winding along the south bank of the Girree by many inflexions, till we crossed its stream. A short distance above Cote-kaee, the Girree divides into two streams, one of which comes directly from a lofty hill called Toombroo-ke-Teeba, and the other, which retains the name of the river, and which we followed, proceeds in a direction towards the west, flowing from one of the lower shoulders of the mountain Urructa. The bed, where we crossed it, was formed of vast masses of stone, and the road on the opposite side wound abruptly up a craggy ridge composed of similar blocks, and continued sufficiently dangerous along ledges of rock, high above the stream: we passed several villages, and ascended rapidly during the latter part of the march, till we reached Jounee, a small place situate about 4 or 500 feet above the Girree, and very near to its source.

The valley of Cote-kaee, to the upper extremity of which we had now advanced, takes its rise in a shoulder of Urructa, which branches into two parts; one meeting the ridge that comes from Choor, in a north and south direction, forms its southern side; the other splits into several parts, and, sending one down to Cote-kaee, continues in a direction to the northward, till, being turned at Toombroo-ke-Teeba to the westward, it assumes the name of Chumbee-ke-D,har, which joins the Noagurh range, and is thus connected with Moral-ke-Kanda and the snowy mountains. The opposite, or south side of the valley, is deeply wooded, and the top is highly romantic with rocks and old pines. The Girree, a very small rivulet, but now swollen and muddy from the rain that had fallen, rises among large masses of fallen rocks and precipices, covered with dark foliage, about half a mile distant. The whole march did not exceed six miles and a half, but was comfortless from heavy rain; and the night set in with so very threatening an appearance, and the mist descended so low, that we began to fear that the rainy season had commenced.

June 7.—The morning was heavy and unpromising, but we began our march by ten o'clock, ascending the height of Sak,hnea, which, high above the valley, marks the diverging of the two ranges to Cote-kaee and to Toombroo. We followed the latter ridge, descending considerably for a mile and a half, and reached a gorge, from which, on the right hand, we looked down on the valley of Deyrah, and had an uninterrupted view nearly to Raeengudh; on the other, towards the south-west, the nullah and valley of Silleh took its rise, running down to the Girree.

Silleh is a small state of no note; and the house of its Rānā was seen from hence on the brink of the stream. At this gorge there was a remarkable stone, which the natives call Oddee, whence the pass has its name. It was about nine to ten feet high, about two feet broad, and not more than four or five inches in thickness: it appears to have been marked at some time in a serrated manner, and had deep cuts in it, but has been disfigured by the sharpening of the hill axes, for which indeed it is favourable, being a species of soft sand-stone quite differing from the rocks of the surrounding hills. The natives say that this stone was placed here by the Sikhs, to commemorate a successful invasion of these hills under Gooroo Nanuc. But there is probably some mistake in this, as Nanuc, the founder of the religious sect of the Sikhs, was no warrior; nor did they, I believe, penetrate the hills, whither they were driven by the persecutions of the Musulmauns, till long after the time of Gooroo Nanuc. Some other stories were related about this stone; but I could gather nothing sufficiently distinct to be worth repeating.

The ascent to Toombroo-ke-Teeba commenced at this gorge, and we climbed up its steep but grassy sides. The top was bare of any sort of wood, but covered with stones, and some appearances of old foundations of buildings: its western and south-western faces are strangely cut into rocky ravines, finely wooded. From hence we held a north-westerly course, winding in and out of the risings and fallings of the ridge, to the gorge by which we descend to the valley of Nawur on the right hand, and by the Jushul dell, to that of Cotekaee, on the left. We followed this last path, and arrived at the village of Jushul somewhat late, after a march of rather more than eight miles.

Our tents, which had been sent on by what they called an easier route, did not arrive for a considerable time afterwards; and we pitched in the best sheltered spot we could find, preparing for a rough night.

One of the party saw this day the process of procuring iron ore from the part of the hills that here afforded it: it issues, it seems, along with the water, from a spring or springs in the mountain side; and at these the people have placed a trough of wood, along which the water runs containing the ore: it is much mixed with dirt, and is cleaned with considerable labour, giving the water a deep muddy red tinge. Iron abounds all over these hills; but, unless when it forces itself on observation, as in these springs, the inhabitants do not seek it with any labour: probably they find, without labour, a sufficient quantity for all their uses.

June 8.—The night was stormy, and the morning very cold. The village we were in, I believe, belonged to the petty chiefs of Silleh or Knoit; both of whom came in the morning to pay their respects. They are tributary to Bischur or to Joobul, according to the political posture of the times. The latter, a smart, good-humoured man, complained, with a smile, that every one preyed on him in turn; and stated the hardships of his case with more of facetiousness than of lamentation: the other, on the contrary, was heavy and dull.

The village, to whomsoever it belonged, did not appear to be under much control; for we could scarcely procure the least quantity of grain, till forcibly searched for and taken, although the chief was present, and had issued his order to have us supplied. It was rather a neat place; and the houses were more regular, and less ruined than usual. We did not march this day, but in the evening ascended the lofty peak of Urshalon, behind the village; whence, as the rain cleared the air, we enjoyed a magnificent prospect, particularly to the northward, where the snowy mountains, half in storm, and half well defined and sharp, bounded our view from right to left. Here also we disencumbered ourselves of every superfluous article of baggage, sending back every thing that was not absolutely necessary, under a guard, to the fort of Choupal; thus lightening ourselves for a journey, of the extent of which we were not fully assured.

PART V.

JOURNEY WITH THE POLITICAL AGENT FOR THE ARMY OF GENERAL MARTINDALE CONTINUED.

CHAPTER XVII.

June 8.—In the number or description of our followers we had hitherto made no alteration or reduction; on the contrary, we had been joined at T,heog by a party of Ghoorkhas, volunteers from the army of Kirtee Rānā, stout and active men, who were well acquainted with the country, as far as any one, besides the natives themselves, could know it.

June 9.—The night was exceedingly cold; and, though the morning was fine and clear, a bitter north wind benumbed our very joints. At nine o'clock we re-ascended the height of Urshalum, whence the snowy range was again visible, in a cloudless sky of pure blue, more clearly and distinctly than we had ever seen it; and I took the opportunity of sketching an outline of it, as well as of the nature of the country, and of the intervening ridges.

From this place we advanced along the ridge of Chumbee-Ke-D,har to the lofty station called Sooraroo-Ke-Teeba, where Kirtee Rānā made his last stand, and finally surrendered. The half finished stockade, or rather breastwork, which he formed by a ditch and the few stones and bushes found on the spot during the night on which his troops maintained the position, was still in the state in which he left it. Many half devoured bodies and skeletons of the wretched Ghoorkhas yet lay on the spot where they had fallen. Several of those who had borne a share in the retreat and in the engagement were now in our company, and pointed out the different lines of defence and points of attack, and showed how the ridges were lined by the enemy, where they had rushed forward to the assault and were repulsed, where the wuzzeers of Joobul and Bischur had taken their station,—in short, the whole detail of the affair. The position is a very commanding one; and, with food and water, might have been retained against any number of undisciplined troops.

From hence we passed along the ridge, following the line of the retreat, and recognising at every step marks of the march or disasters of the day. Our course for some time was westerly, but we soon turned more to the northward, and, winding under the craggy bases of some rugged peaks, we crossed our old route just at the gorge of Kut,hagurh, whence we descended to the village of Urhealoo on our road to Comharsein. On that occasion we had descended in a westerly direction, but now we ascended towards the north-west, and kept along a narrow sharp ridge with many bad steps, till we reached the true Nowagurh range, just under one of the stockades erected by the Ghoorkhas. Farther on, a path, ascending by the side of a steep grassy declivity, led us up to the fort of Nowagurh, a place which never was large, nor could have been strong; but it is singular from its situation, being a complete peak, accessible only by scrambling up the rocks on which it rests by the side at which we entered. It is commanded by the loftiest peak of the Nowagurh range, though from a distance, and could not be tenable if it were to be attacked by persons not prevented from occupying it by superstitious motives. Hence we passed along the side of this lofty peak, the path running along a steep hill-face, covered with, and winding among, huge shapeless masses of stone that have fallen from the crags above. We reached our tents a little farther on in good time, after a march of ten miles and a quarter.

This day's march was interesting, not only because it carried us over new ground, but also as being the scene of the last struggle of Ghoorkha power in this part of the country. Places which have been signalized by acts of heroism and glory, of suffering or of crime, or which have been the scene of any remarkable occurrence, of whatsoever nature, cannot be passed over with the indifference with which we view common spots. Even the sufferings of an inconsiderable body of Ghoorkhas, who, in the pride and even wantonness of conquest, had now marched so far from their home, and the distress of their old but brave commander, must claim from those, who traverse the ground on which they endured them, the consideration and pity of a moment. Although they had no *just* business there, they were brave, and at last were subdued rather by treachery than by force; and it is not easy to conceive more distressing feelings than those of their chief during a weary and harassed retreat,—betrayed by those whom he had trusted, and compelled to a final hopeless struggle against an exasperated and savage enemy.

We observed at Chumbee-Ke-D,har a decided change in the nature of the rocks of which the mountains were composed: from that place they were entirely of sandstone, of various degrees of coarseness, but still in laminous strata. The rocks about the foot of Nowagurh were cut by the weather into the most fantastic shapes, and I have hardly seen any where a more noble and various specimen of wild scenery than was exhibited in the western exposure of this peak. The shapes and tints of the rock, the richness of the foliage, with the bold forms of the crags, were, I think, more than equal to any thing that has come under our observation. The fallen masses under Nowagurh peak show another variety; they are formed of a sort of amalgam of sand, quartz, and mica, all worked into a kind of plum-pudding stone, in some instances exceedingly hard, but sometimes crumbling into loose gravel, and forming the soil and sand on which we were walking. There is, I believe, a similar kind of rock on the tops of Choor and Urructa, but it is not by any means common, nor do I recollect to have seen it before. Prodigious blocks of this stone strew the whole hill-face below the peak, which is very steep.

Our tent was pitched at a considerable distance from any village, and we found the night very cold: from the sharpness of the air we concluded that there was much frost.

June 10.—This day we made no march. Intelligence having arrived of the convention with Ummr Sing, and a letter being received from that commander to Runsoor T,happa, commandant of the fort of Raeengudh, requiring him to deliver up the place, a party was immediately despatched with this order to receive it, and arrangements were made for conveying the men and their baggage unarmed to Choupal and Nahn, leaving with them the same proportion of arms and property as had been granted to the garrisons of Jytock and Malown. But, upon these preparations being made known to Runsoor, he refused thus to deliver up his arms and property, alleging that his garrison was included among those of Gurwhal, to whom more favourable terms had been granted; and this, upon our remonstrance, he supported by the letter of Ummr Sing, who thus, to gain a very petty end, had stooped to use an artifice at least, if it may not be deemed a fraud.

The fortress of Raeengudh had originally belonged to Bischur, or in fact was situate in the petty state of Raeen, which was always under the protection of that power; but, in the troubles that often occurred before the Ghoorkha invasion, between the states of Gurwhal and Bischur, the fortress sometimes changed masters, and thus occasionally was held by the former. I am ignorant in whose possession it was at the time that the Ghoorkhas subdued Gurwhal. In all probability it was in that of Bischur; but every person who was consulted on the business, even the people of Gurwhal itself, allowed that Raeengudh was usually considered a fortress of Bischur.

Ummr Sing could not have been ignorant of this, but voluntarily misled General Ochterlony in the statement of garrisons which he delivered; and in his letter to Runsoor T,happa, he directed him how to behave on being required to evacuate the place. The transaction shows the character of Asiatic negotiation in its true point of view. Every advantage, whether honourable or the contrary, is seized, let it be never so small; every delay, whether useful or not, is to be made; and at last an ungracious forced acquiescence crowns the eastern diplomatist with honour in the eyes of his country.

Although the Ghoorkhas, in their general dealings with us as enemies, have shown more magnanimity, as well as steadiness of European warfare, than any other eastern foe, yet they cannot altogether refrain from this miserable deceit and cunning; and Ummr Sing, perhaps, has practised it more than the rest of his countrymen. In fact, the character of this man is not admired even by them. He is cruel, revengeful, impolitic, and, though perhaps brave, is not a general.

The extent of the saving to the enemy by this trick could not have exceeded a few jinjaels, some old muskets and matchlocks, a few cookrees, and some skins of powder and maunds of shot; and this was of no value to us; but it was unpleasant to be so foolishly cheated; and, therefore, orders were sent to deliver up the fortress according to its true state, as provided for in the capitulation, or that he should be given up to the mercy of the troops of the country. The desire of ascertaining the acquiescence of Runsoor T,happa in this order detained us here this day; and accounts accordingly came of his having commenced his march for Choupal unarmed, and of the occupation of the place by a party of our irregular troops.

This morning we ascended the high peak above Nowagurh fort. When we at first proposed this, the natives of the neighbouring villages endeavoured strongly to dissuade us from the undertaking, and also our troops from occupying the fort, not only on account of the difficulty of the road, but because the summit was said to be occupied by a deity, who destroyed all intruders. When we laughed at this notion, and persisted in our intention, it was intimated that, by carrying up along with us five rams, we might propitiate this cruel divinity so as to escape untouched. To this expedient we also declined to resort; and it was with some difficulty that we procured guides to show us the path, while the rest were shocked at our obstinacy. The deity, who thus accepts a compromise of rams for human sacrifices, is named Kali; that part of the peak which she or he occupies is called Coatee. I know not whether it is the same being who delights in human blood at Saugur, and is so well known in Hindoostan: if, indeed, they are the same, it is greatly to be wished that the lady in the plains would imitate her compeer in the hills, and accept of less horrid sacrifices.

We found the ascent very difficult; there was no path, and we had to thread the thick-tangled forest, among mighty masses of rock and fallen trees, upon a slope so much steeper than usual, that it was not always easy to retain a footing, or to prevent something like giddiness, whilst the toil also was great. We were, however, repaid for all our labour by the extensive and magnificent prospect we enjoyed from the summit, which we attained, notwithstanding our want of the propitiatory offering. As there was no peak or range near us of a similar or nearly equal height, the view was not interrupted on any side; and certainly it is difficult to conceive a more strange yet varied circle of alpine scenery, than that which lay spread around us. Ridges over ridges rose in long succession to the north, to the west, and to the east, till terminated by a line of snow more craggy and fantastic than any of them. We had never till now been near them, and consequently could not so well discern their strange forms and wonderful ruggedness. The valley of the Sutlej was distinctly visible to a great distance, where its direction lay much to the eastward, and was shut up from view by the overlapping of the hills. Moral-Ke-Kanda, and the great snowy mountain whence it takes its rise, lay on our right to the eastward, forming the left bank of the river. On the opposite side, a similar huge mass was detached to serve for its other bank, and came down in subordinate rocky ridges, which were the hills of Cooloo. The glen of the Sutlej is very narrow and deep throughout. Beyond, the opening formed in the hills by the bed of the Beya was very distinct, but there is no distinct break in the snowy hills; and the natives say that this river does not pass through them, but rises in their south-western face. Although beyond this the tops of other hills were visible, and those across the Rauve were pointed out to us, they formed, to our apprehension, only a confused mass of points, of which we could make nothing. There cannot be a finer point whence to obtain an idea of the great lines of the country than this, and we made what use we could of the opportunity. We sketched the outline of this extraordinary landscape.

The top of Nowagurh peak, which the natives call Coatee, is a mass of chaotic fragments of rock, huddled together in the strangest forms; and among them grow trees, whose ancestors' ruins and their own falling foliage have formed a very rich vegetable mold, that lies in the clefts and crevices, nourishing a profusion of flowers, grasses, and other herbs. The whole peak is wooded to the top on three sides; the fourth, to the north-west, is a steep precipice, more sparingly sprinkled with trees. From the strange manner in which the lumps of rock lay piled on each other, one would be tempted to attribute the whole to some great convulsion of nature, that ruined a more lofty spire of rock, and strewed its fragments on this less elevated and broader base. Were we to have recourse to less violent and more probable agency, it might be supposed that the more destructible parts of the rock, and the soil continually forming from these, and from the lichens and other vegetables which these nourish, had been from time to time abraded by the weather, and that the harder parts had thus been left bare in masses as we saw them; while the bases and interstices cherished, in a part of that soil still remaining, and constantly accumulating as it forms, various luxuriant alpine vegetables. It is a curious spot. The rock is of the same nature as the fragments scattered below, and adverted to in the march of yesterday. On every great rocky fragment a large pile of small stones is placed; and similar collections, built into the shape of very rude temples, are scattered all around, to the honour of the deity of the place.

We descended safely, although the ground was such as might have caused serious accidents—I believe, to the no small amazement of the natives, who looked for some signal punishment of our presumption.

June 11.—This day we entered on quite new ground, and turned our faces to the northward. As the march was represented to be a long one, we began it early, and were all in motion soon after six o'clock. The morning was cold and frosty. We continued along the wooded and rocky ridge on which we had encamped, winding up a very wild road with some dangerous steps, till, by a gradual and very various ascent of three miles and a half we reached a high peak of the Soongree range, to which we were attracted by its commanding situation. The view was similar to that which was enjoyed yesterday from Nowagurh; but, being some miles further advanced, we saw more of the country, and the day was particularly favourable to us. The points above the two towns of Rampore and Serān, both on the Sutlej, were now quite distinct. The boundary across the Sutlej, between the states of Cooloo and Bischur, was pointed out, being formed in a country that appeared not worth the dividing. On the east, the lofty mountains called Jumnotree and Gangotree almost terminated the snowy range. It is not easy to say how interesting these views were. We found ourselves placed in the sight of those wild and remote spots which have hitherto been heard of more as fabled places, and indistinctly alluded to, than as having "local habitation and a name;" and as we became familiarized with the lines of the country, and could connect its parts with each other in our minds, this interest increased. Descending somewhat from this height, we held our course along the ridge for more than three miles further, through rock and forest, and sometimes on the bare hill-face, sensibly approaching the range of snow, whose dimensions enlarged at every new glimpse we obtained of them.

We passed, on the left, the fort of Moonal-gurh, erected during a war which, at some distant period, had been waged against this country by the united force of Sirmore and Gurwhal. The point we had now reached was the extremity of the Soongree-Kanda range, on which an old fort or post, called Oogoon, was once established on the same occasion as Moonal-gurh. This range is connected with Moral-Ke-Kanda by a low neck, which we now crossed in our descent. At first the declivity was moderate, but after a short way the path led down the very sharp edge of a ridge, exceedingly steep, and so completely slippery, from the fallen leaves of the fir-trees that strewed the ground, that we could hardly keep our footing. On either hand there was a deep precipice, so that a false step would have been seriously dangerous; and at length we were obliged to take off our shoes, as a security against slipping. With this precaution we succeeded in descending safely. Near the bottom the path was rocky and rugged, in addition to its slipperiness; the precipices approached on either side; a torrent ran below, and the opposite sides of the united glen rose dark above us. The dusky foliage shut out the light of day: it was a savage, gloomy, dangerous place; but when we reached the bottom, at the union of the two nullahs, the uncommon beauty of the scene amply repaid us for any risk we had incurred. The extent of this slippery and zig-zag descent is rather more than two miles; but the first part of it is easy, though narrow. One of the streams, that form the nullah we had now reached, takes its rise in Moral-Ke-Kanda, the other in Soongree-Kanda, whence we descended. They both run in rocky chasms, but the former is the wildest and most considerable. At this point the rocks nearly met overhead, and they were covered with the greatest profusion of noble foliage; among which a number of magnificent horse-chesnuts, rich in blossom, was not the least remarkable; and a quantity of white roses, jasmine, and other fragrant and lovely plants, climbed up the stems, and on all sides covered the rocks and ancient stumps of trees.

We descended this shaded stream, which, a little below this point, joins another more considerable, coming also from the western side of Moral-Ke-Kanda, and the whole runs westward to the Sutlej, under the name of the Coonoo nullah. At the point where we crossed this stream we found a mill at work, constructed for turning wood. It was simple, as all the other contrivances of these people are. An overshot stream turned a wheel, on the axle of which, at one end, several small spikes of iron served to fix any piece of wood required to be worked. As we passed, a man was fabricating a certain sort of cups, which were intended to be sent to China. These are formed from the knots and excrescences of a particular kind of tree, which are much esteemed by the Chinese; and, being thus rudely turned, are sent through the passes of these hills to the usual marts of traffic, and sell at from four to eight anas each. The tools with which the wood was cut were long pieces of steel fixed in a handle, the blade-end bent broadwise into smaller or larger semicircles, the edge of which is sharpened. This both served to hollow the cup and to smooth it, where lightly applied; in fact, it is used for the same purposes as the gouge by our turners, and is applied, resting on a frame, in nearly the same way.

At this place we met with the first palpable instance of admixture of Tartar manners and customs, as well as of countenance, and it deserves notice. Observing an old man with a brass box of curious fashion hung round his neck, and wishing to examine it, we requested him to open it, which with considerable reluctance he did, saying that it contained his god, (Thakoor). He took from it two figures: one was a Lama of brass, the common idol of the worshippers of the Grand Lama, and given by him to those who visit his shrine on pilgrimages, and which are often sold in abundance by persons who have no authority to sanctify them; the other was a small Chinese figure, painted on porcelain or clay: both were wrapped up in a piece of yellow silk. He said that he had received them both from the Grand Lama at L,hassa, whither he had many years since gone on a pilgrimage. This man was a Hindoo by professed religion, and worshipped these foreign idols after the Hindoo manner; yet he received them from the head of another faith, whom he had visited to all appearance from a religious motive, offering a curious specimen of ignorance or of toleration; perhaps a confusion not unnatural in one so far removed from the more civilized professors of his faith; and, at all events, an edifying example of moderation and respect for what he did not understand.

The toleration of the Hindoos, even in their days of power, and at their seats of most profound religion and learning, has been generally remarked; and of this toleration we have a strong evidence in their commonly known doctrine, that all faiths may reach heaven by one gate or other, only reserving to themselves the shortest road. They even have great respect for the holy places, and usages, and gods, of other religions. It is quite common to see them prostrating themselves at the splendid monuments of Moslem faith, and they will pay an equal reverence to a Christian church. How unlike the savage exterminating creed of the Mahomedans! Perhaps the meekness of the religion he professed mingled with an ignorance of its mysteries, in the person of this highlander. Avarice, however, got the better of religion, and, after some negotiation, he consented to transfer his Lama to me as a present, receiving from me in like manner a remembrance of eight rupees. He was, I believe, a native of the remote district of Kunawur, in Bischur; and, like several of those we remarked here, had strong marks of Tartar physiognomy.

From the banks of this stream we gradually ascended, in a north-westerly direction, to our encamping ground at the village of D,huloque, which overhangs the Coonoo glen, and is situate among fields of barley. Our march was eleven miles and a half.

We this day made a great stride to the northward of our former line, and towards the loftier mountains; and the features of the scenery enlarged, and became rougher and wilder in proportion. Our elevation was great. We had reached and crossed a shoulder of Moral-Ke-Kanda, the loftiest mountain in our sight, next to the snowy range themselves. This noble mountain, which has already been frequently mentioned, is very interesting on many accounts, besides its venerable appearance. It forms the ridge that divides and turns the waters of India. Taking its rise from a mass of snowy peaks that advance on the east of the Sutlej, above Rampore, it sends branches to the westward that form part of the banks of the Sutlej, and on the east, that extend to the Pabur; while the ridge we crossed this day extends in a south-westerly direction, but very irregularly, and under various names, the whole way to Irkee, and even to the plains.

The waters that arise upon the eastern and south-eastern faces of this splendid range are thus sent to the Pabur and to the Girree, and, with those of the Touse and Jumna, find their way by the Ganges to the Bay of Bengal; whilst those which flow from the western and northern exposures are carried by the Sutlej and the Indus into the Gulf of Sinde and the Arabian Sea. The mountain is worthy of its great office, massy and dark, but streaked with snow, and cut into deep and numerous ravines, wild with rock and wood. The face on which we encamped was too steep to admit of much cultivation, and we seemed to have left the more hospitable tracts behind. Fruit trees, however, were abundant, especially apricots, peaches, apples, and pears, but they were all quite green. Mulberry-trees were as usual common, and a number of horse-chesnuts appeared to be preserved, if not cultivated. On inquiry, we were informed that a species of food is prepared with much trouble from their bitter fruit, which is used by the common people. The soil and rock entirely resumed its original form; and, on the march, we observed nothing but slate and mica of various colours and kinds.

One of the zemindars from a neighbouring village brought us this day the skin of a bird with the most splendid plumage I ever beheld. The chief part of the feathers resembled those of a Guinea fowl, but had a far richer tinge, and each had a beautiful white and black eye on it. The under part of the throat, and part of the head, were furnished with stiff small feathers of a brilliant crimson. It seemed to have had gills like a cock; a crest of bright black feathers crowned its head. I believe this bird to be known in Europe by the name of the Nepāl pheasant.

June 12.—The morning was cloudy and threatened rain; but, by half-past six, when every thing was in readiness for the march, the weather became fine, though the yet heavy clouds hung upon the hills, magnifying their real majestic height by half shrouding them in the veil of uncertainty. For a considerable way our road ascended but little, though the rapid descent of the nullah below gave to it the appearance of rising greatly. Afterwards, however, an indenting irregular rise carried us up to the top of the ridge, which is called Bahilee, and proceeds directly from Moral-Ke-Kanda to the Sutlej. Half a mile further on is situate the fort of Bahilee, a square redoubt surrounded by an excellent stockade. It was built by the Ghoorkha force which occupied Mustgurh, a fortress opposite to this, on a branch of the Nowagurh range.

Bahilee is built with much neatness, and consists of one square building inclosing another. The interior served for a magazine, the outer for the residence of troops. In both places there are a great number of hollow trees for water cisterns, the place not having any spring sufficiently near to depend upon. It is a strong place against musquetry only, and was loop-holed all round; but it could not stand against a gun for a single day. From this place we saw the Sutlej far below, in a narrow rocky bed, running from the north-eastward. A large stream, called Nowgurree-Khola, runs at the foot of this ridge, which apparently has its rise at the point of junction of Moral-Ke-Kanda with the snowy hills.

At this place, the seana of a village presented us with some small raisins, which he called dak,h, and some apricot kernels and stones, which we found to have a sweet taste, and to be fully as pleasant as almonds. The raisins, he told us, were cured by himself from the common wild grape, and the apricot stones, he said, were selected from a particular tree: about one in an hundred, it seems, have sweet-kernelled stones instead of bitter: they are much valued, and kept for eating and for presents, as in this instance.

Bahilee was somewhat more than four miles from the village of our encampment, and we here entered on a descent surpassing any we had yet encountered in steepness and length, except that at Comharsein. It was altogether full three miles, and very little of it, if any, could be at an angle of less than forty-five degrees. In some places, as at Comharsein, steps were necessary; but the Ghāt did not appear by any means of so much importance, or so much frequented as that: the latter part ran on the edge, and among the rocks, of a precipice of considerable depth. When we had proceeded about two-thirds of the way down, the wind became warm, and before we reached the bottom, was very hot; while the sun, high above, struck his beams on us reflected from rock and stone, and increased the heat to an almost insufferable degree. On reaching the bottom, however, we got under the shelter of a projecting rock on the banks of the Now-gurree-Khola, which here joins the Sutlej, and, forming a clear limpid stream, just under cover from the sun, invited our exhausted people to recruit themselves by bathing. At this place there was formerly a bridge over the nullah, of the sort here called a sango. Stout beams of wood are placed upon strong foundations of masonry, with a slight angle of inclination towards the ground, and this lower end is fixed in the pier by heavy stones; over them others are laid, the exterior ends of which project over those of the lower ones; and in like manner a third tier is laid, and this is repeated on both sides of the river, till the space remaining between the highest projections is small enough to span by one row of strong beams, which are fixed firmly to these ends: the whole is strongly supported by good masonry-work, and the bridge is complete. I know not whether the fault in the present instance was in the structure of the bridge or in its situation, but it had given way twice in no very long time, and was now in ruins, while a single fir-tree was all that served to cross the stream. It comes down at times, as we were informed, with great force in a prodigious torrent, and even now was a respectable stream.

Having refreshed ourselves for some time, we continued our way to Rampore, along the bed of the Sutlej: the heat was excessive, and the wind felt as if it came from the mouth of a furnace. After a while the path left the bed, and ascended from one to two hundred feet above the stream, at times being very narrow, and on the brink of very ugly precipices: in some places also, narrow steps were cut from out of the rock by manual labour, and considerable attention was necessary to pass those which were narrow and broken.

Having pursued a path of this sort for four miles and a half, we at length beheld Rampore, the capital of Bischur.

CHAPTER XVIII.

June 12.—The approach to Rampore is wild, rugged, and unpromising, lying over and among huge amorphous masses of stone, ledges of rock, and all the usual obstacles of a mountain river's bed; nor is the first appearance of the town better than its approach leads us to expect. At the foot of a lofty and perpendicular rock, that terminates a projection of the mountain on the south-east side of the river, forming a small semicircular reach, there is a spot of ground very rugged and uneven, but affording a larger site for building than usually occurs on the banks of the Sutlej, at this distance from the hills. On this spot the town of Rampore is situated, rising in tiers of streets and houses one above another, while the river foams and dashes at its feet, and the mountains hang over it in precipices all around.

When we had clambered over the ledges of rocks and flights of steps that brought us to this site, the first thing that struck us was a great row of houses wholly in ruins, and only here and there occupied by a few Chumars, and people of the lowest cast. A little further on there is a Ghoorkha fort or redoubt, which accounted for the ruin by which it is surrounded. Passing onwards by some neat houses in good repair, occupied by Brahmins, we reached the Dewan K,hanch, or Hall of Audience. This, with the other better buildings, is situated on the highest terrace, and overlooks the greater part of the town below. It bears the marks of some degree of neatness and costliness, if not of splendor: the wood work of the interior is well carved, and all around on three sides there are pannels which contain the remains of pictures in the Chinese taste, and evidently the work of a Chinese artist. The third side, overlooking the river and town, is quite open.

Still further advancing, along a level and broad terrace, we reached the muhul, or palace of the rajah, and found that our tent was pitched under the shade of a noble peepul-tree in the enclosure before it; but we preferred taking up our abode for the evening in a small but very neat summer-house, that also had the advantage of a shady tree, and was well calculated for enjoying every breeze that blew, and overlooked the whole of the town. All, however, was insufficient to protect us from the heat of this place, so as to render us even tolerably comfortable: the rays of the sun, confined, and as it were concentrated, in the funnel-like hollow, at the bottom of which the town is placed, and reflected from the bare rocks, by which it is completely surrounded, caused as intense a heat as is experienced in the plains; even the night was insupportably close, and little refreshment was reaped from sleep.

During the first part of our march to-day there had been little variety in rock or soil; slate and a laminous sandstone prevailed: in some places there were masses of the same sort of plum-pudding stone which we had remarked at Nowagurh, but this was always in detached lumps. The rocky precipice above the Now-gurree-Khola, which terminated our descent, was chiefly composed of an exceedingly white stone, disposed in laminæ, sometimes crumbling and mouldering as if it had felt the effects of air, in others hard and firm, apparently unaffected by the weather; but we could not say whether this was limestone or quartz. Intermixed with this was a good deal of quartz and micaceous slate, with sandstone, all in strata, and in different stages of decomposition; and the great mass of the rock, particularly to the north of the Now-gurree-Khola, consisted entirely of these substances. Evidences of copper appeared, by a quantity of green stains, in more than one place.

The bed of the river, where it did not flow over the native bare rock, consisted of a multitude of different sorts of stones, rounded and reduced to gravel by the action of the torrent, and forming no ground by which we could judge of the formation of any particular part of the mountain, as they must evidently have come from great and various distances. On the side of the river, and also in its stream, there lay great blocks of a stone, chiefly white, but varying in purity to different degrees of grayness, and in substance somewhat like a sandy marble: our acquaintance with the nature of rocks did not enable us to determine whether it was a quartz or a limestone. From subsequent inquiry, however, I am inclined to think that some of these masses were quartz, and others a sort of close-grained granite. Many pieces of a sort of greenish stone, of great hardness, were also observed, which we had not seen before, except on the banks of the

Now-gurree-Khola, where the white rock has been noticed. The native original rock was uniformly slate and quartz, and the varieties of the slate in colour and consistence were more numerous than formerly. One sort, of a dark brownish purple, splintery and brittle, was new and remarkable. All the undetached masses of rock that formed the mountain lay in strata, and at a considerable angle with the horizon.

The depth to which the stream had here worn its way in the lapse of time was very evident, from observing the sides of the hills that formed the bed of the river a few hundred feet above its stream. Several strata of gravel could be traced at various elevations, and in many places the composition of the mountain at its feet and banks was nothing but a congeries of stones and gravel, all evidently rounded and worn by the action of the torrents. In other places the soil was more clayey than usual, red and white, and variously mixed with mica. The sand on the sides of the stream was of a grayish-white, with which also the water was much loaded, so as to appear quite muddy; and the stream varied in breadth from thirty or forty to one hundred yards.

Of the scenery little need be said. During the first part of the march it was brown and bare, and the long steep hill-face which we descended was not less so. The opposite side of the Now-gurree-Khola was remarkably arid and burnt up; and on either side the river, as we marched in its narrow rocky bed, not a tree or bush, and hardly a tuft of grass, relieved the eye from the scorched and craggy barrenness that on all sides oppressed it.

June 13 and 14.—We remained the two successive days at Rampore, and employed that time in making our observations on the town, and in acquiring information relative to the state of Bischur, and the general character of the country and people in the surrounding regions; and although by far the chief part of the information and of the facts that will here be related were acquired during our subsequent stay at Serān, it may be better to give the whole in as connected a way as possible in this place.

Rampore, the capital of Bischur, has far juster pretensions to the appellation of a town than any of the miserable villages through which our route has led: it was once a flourishing place, and the entrepôt for the merchandize brought by the traders of Hindostan, and for the produce of Cachemire, Ludhak, Bootan, Kashgār, Yarcund, &c. In the days of its prosperity it may have contained three or four hundred houses, and a large bazar, well filled with the commodities of these various countries. For this commerce, the passage of the river Sutlej through the hills forms a convenient channel, and the road, which is now very difficult, might be much improved without incurring any extravagant expense. There is no ghāt practicable for the conveyance of merchandize through the Himālā range between that at Buddreenāth, and this of Rampore; and doubtless it was this circumstance principally that gave to Rampore the importance it acquired, and made it to the westward, what Sireenuggur was to the eastward, a depôt and mart for the products of the abovementioned countries.

When the Sik,hs were a more predatory race, wandering and unsettled, this route to the Trans-himālāyan countries was much followed and prosecuted through the hills to Nahn, the D,hoor, and Hurdwar. Since the rise of that nation under Runjeet Sing, the roads from Ludhak, through Cooloo and Chumba, direct to Umrutsir, are in general use.

The city of Umrutsir is the chief and holy city of the Sik,h territories, although Runjeet Sing chiefly resides at Lahore, which thus virtually becomes the capital. The other, however, is the ancient scene of the commencement of the Sik,h sect, and of their glory, as well as of their persecutions and martyrdom, and is looked upon with great reverence by the nation.

Much was told us of the splendour of the late rajah and his court, and the opulence of the place in former times, till the struggle with the Ghoorkhas first impoverished and distressed the country; and soon after the death of the rajah the finishing stroke was put to the destruction of the capital by the sudden and unexpected arrival of a Ghoorkha force, from which the young rajah, with his mother and attendants, barely escaped, flying to the recesses of Kunawur, and leaving the accumulated riches of the capital a prey to the conquerors. At this time, by far the greater proportion of the houses was in ruins, and the rest very thinly inhabited. The bazar, which formerly was a tolerable street, and where the remains of good shops and large houses may still be traced, at present contains only the booths of a few poor Bunyas, miserably supplied, and every thing bespeaks wretchedness and poverty. So little encouragement is there now for the traders of the low country to bring their goods hither, that the most common luxuries, the produce of the plains, are often not to be had.

We could not procure sugar of any kind to recruit our stock, though so common and cheap in its various shapes in the neighbouring districts of Hindostan.

Rampore (for what reason, I know not) is a place of considerable sanctity. It possesses several temples for Hindoo worship, of tolerable construction, viz. one to Māhā Dēo, to Nērsing, to Gonēsh, to Hoonoomaun, and smaller ones to inferior deities. That to Nērsing has been lately erected, and is neat, though not large. To officiate at these shrines there are a sufficiency of Brahmins, and a host of byragees, gosseins, sunyasseas, and other descriptions of fuqeers and mendicants; indeed, they are the only people who seem to have escaped the desolation, and yet inhabit the place. The houses of the priesthood were neat and comfortable, and their persons and circumstances were apparently thriving.

There are two royal residences in Rampore: one appears to be far more ancient than the other, and was lately occupied by the dowager Rānee, with her family and court. It is built on a rock overhanging the river, somewhat as a strong hold; but in the interior is like most other hill-chieftains' houses, containing a square court, around the interior of which small apartments are ranged in the Hindostanee fashion, chiefly open to the court, except those intended for the women, which are closed by screens of wood, finely cut into flowers and various figures, so as partially to admit the light without exposing those who are within: in the centre of the court there is a holy pagoda. The second palace is a more modern structure, and though considerably more elegant and better built and finished than the other, it does not depart much from the usual style in the interior dispositions. It stands at the north side of an inclosure that extends about 150 yards along the highest stage or terrace of the projection, on which the town is built, and though not more than half that breadth, stretches quite to the foot of the lofty precipice that frowns over the place. The terrace itself overlooks the whole town and the river which flows around it. The building is a square, the front of which, looking to the southward, is very highly ornamented with rich carved work in wood; in the centre, above the entrance, projects a small balcony, in which the rajah sat and showed himself to the people; the other three sides are rather plain, and with their slated penthouse roofs, which do not project far above the walls, bear a great resemblance to those parts of a common English house which are least exposed to public view. There are no towers at the corners of this square, as in most other hill castles, nor much to give it a resemblance to the usual fashion of the country: from the left or east side of the front a projection runs out of three stories; the two lower are open in front, exposing the interior; the uppermost is shut in with carved wooden screens of trellis-work, and the whole front of this projection is most richly ornamented in a similar manner. This wing was chiefly appropriated to the use of the Zenānā. On the opposite side, also projecting forwards, was placed the summer-house in which we took up our quarters; and this, though small, was exceedingly neat and well ornamented. Another small building in the same line, I believe a shrine to some deity, projected to a length that corresponded with the extent of the left-hand wing. The space between those two rows of building in front of the main body of the palace is paved as a court.

Above the summer-house, and behind the palace, several venerable peepul-trees extended their shade in a very refreshing manner, and gave to the whole a truly delightful cast of cool repose and summer quietness, notwithstanding the positive heat which we could not help acknowledging.

Both these palaces are built in the same manner, viz. of dry stone bound with wooden beams, as before described when speaking of the buildings of the country, but that now under consideration is by far the best constructed which we have seen. The roof, in particular, attracted our attention from the tasteful way in which it was disposed. The slates were large, of a deep purplish blue, and placed with the utmost regularity; each cut square, and the joining covered with a long piece like an isosceles triangle with its base upwards, and the apex cut off below; rows were thus formed, and kept accurately straight. I never saw the best slating at home produce any thing like so good an effect. It was impossible to look at the carved ornaments in wood, the pillars, the screens, the cornices, or the smaller and nameless pieces that every where covered the walls in front, without being struck with admiration at the beauty of their execution. The wood used was wholly fir, of the same species; I believe it to be the larch; and we were told that the screens and most of the ornaments were imitations of those similar works in marble which beautify the palace in Dehlee. The interior, though corresponding more nearly than in the other palace with the beauty of the outside, has nothing to merit description. Suites of small closed and open apartments, all looking into the court in the centre, form the detail of all the three stories, which, like most native buildings, are low, and when not entirely open, dark. In the inclosure where the palace stands there are several small houses which were built as places to sit in, and enjoy a cool breeze when it blew, or as offices and quarters for the attendants of the royal family.

There are no other buildings in Rampore that have the least title to notice. The houses of the wuzzeers are mostly in ruins; and, as before observed, the houses of the Brahmins and religious castes alone preserve even the appearance of comfort.

A communication is here kept up across the Sutlej by means of that singular and dangerous kind of bridge (if it may be so called) which in the hills is termed a *j,hoola.* At some convenient spot, where the river is rather narrow and the rocks on either side overhang the stream, a stout beam of wood is fixed horizontally upon or behind two strong stakes, that are driven into the banks on each side of the water; and round these beams ropes are strained, extending from the one to the other across the river, and they are hauled tight, and kept in their place by a sort of windlass. The rope used in forming this bridge is generally from two to three inches in circumference, and at least nine or ten times crossed to make it secure. This collection of ropes is traversed by a block of wood hollowed into a semicircular groove large enough to slide easily along it, and around this block ropes are suspended, forming a loop, in which passengers seat themselves, clasping its upper parts with their hands to keep themselves steady; a line fixed to the wooden block at each end, and extending to each bank, serves to haul it, and the passenger attached to it, from one side of the river to the other.

The j,hoola at Rampore was somewhat formidable, for the river tumbles beneath in a very awful way; and the ropes, though they decline in the centre to the water, are elevated from thirty to forty feet above it; the span is from ninety to a hundred yards. It was amusing enough to see several of our low country attendants arming themselves with courage to venture on this novel mode of transit; and I must confess, that although it was evident that the actual danger was small, it was not without certain uncomfortable feelings that I first launched out on the machine to cross the Sutlej. We found, however, that accidents do sometimes occur; and it was scarcely twelve months since a Brahmin who had come from Cooloo, having loaded the ropes with too great a weight of his goods, and accompanied them himself, fell into the stream, was hurried away, and dashed to pieces.

Just opposite to this j,hoola the Cooloo government has established a custom-house, and there is a small hut in which a Brahmin officer resides, to collect the duties on whatever passes the river, and enters the territories of Bischur.

A great jealousy has always subsisted between these two states, and even the passage of the bridge is often a subject of dispute. One morning, wishing to pass with a view to take a sketch of the town, I found that the Cooloo men had taken away the traversing block of wood from the ropes, and consequently I could not cross the river. After a while, some active fellows on the Bischur side clambered over in a very ingenious way, supported by a crooked piece of wood tied round the body, and over the rope-bridge by a cord, and thus swinging under it, belly upwards, one of them pulled himself over by the hands and feet, and soon recovered the traversing block. When I could cross, I thought fit to take to task and highly threaten the men of Cooloo for their insolence in thus obstructing our progress; but they seemed stupid, and I found had removed the block from a confused feeling of fear at the arrival of our party, which they magnified into an army at Rampore. I believe that the appearance of our Ghoorkhas, whom they hate and fear, partly induced the measure.

The country of Cooloo stretches along the north bank of the Sutlej, all the way from below Comharsein, and indeed, I believe, from the Belaspore territories to a point a few miles beyond Rampore. The aspect of these hills, which descend abruptly from a very lofty height, and at this place almost immediately from the snowy cliffs themselves, is peculiarly dreary and barren. Here especially they exhibit little, except high craggy precipices and pointed peaks, with roughened stony faces staring through the scanty soil, and no green thing chequers the inhospitable brown and gray hue of the hill-sides.

They are cut into deep and rocky chasms, void of beauty or magnificence, except that the whole scene is on a grand scale, and hardly any sign of cultivation or inhabitants is seen, but where a fort or village, inclosed by a wall or hedge, crowns the top of a peak or ridge. About the town, on every side, precipices descend to the very river, the bed of which is studded, and the stream impeded and chafed into a succession of foaming rapids and waves by the huge fragments that have fallen from their brows. A small mountain-stream tumbles down a dark ravine that debouches in the recess corresponding with the projecting site of the town. Such is Rampore, and the scenery in which it is placed.

The Rajahship or province of Bischur was formerly confined to the valley through which the Sutlej flows, from the line where it bounds with the Chinese territories beyond the Himālā range, to a point not far from the town of Rampore. A series of subsequent encroachments and conquests has increased it to the extent it now occupies. To the southward, the valley of Nawur and district of Teekur form the extreme of its possessions, and the numerous petty states of Joobul, Cotegooroo, Bulsum, Kurangooloo, Comharsein, &c. bound it in a very irregular line. On the north-west the Sutlej confines it, till, at a point between Rampore and Serān, it crosses that river, and bounding with Cooloo in Kundrār Nullah (a deep dell that runs directly down from the snowy ridge), it assumes nearly a northerly course, and crossing the Himālā range, joins the Chinese territories, probably in a very undefined line; for, both while contiguous with Cooloo through the bare rock and snow of the highest mountains, and also in the barren tract immediately beyond them, the country is too inhospitable to form ground of much dispute. To the north and north-east, those countries under the Chinese sway continue to confine Bischur, till it is met by Gurwhal, with which province it re-crosses the snowy range in a similarly indefinite line; but in a south-westerly direction, and dividing the districts between the Pabur and Touse, the boundary falls upon the former river, which here runs to the south-eastward about eight miles below Raeengudh, leaving to Bischur the whole bed and rich valley of the Pabur. The short remaining line on the south-west from the end of that range of hills which divides the Nawur and Deyrah valleys downwards, is marked by the course of this river.

In its present state, the country of Bischur may be divided into districts, nearly as follows: first, Kunawur; secondly, that tract which, including Rampore and Serān, extends down the valley of the Sutlej, with the smaller glens and ravines that drain into it; thirdly, the valley of the Pabur, with all that lies on its left bank, and including Sambracote and the other smaller ones that debouche from the Morāl ridge and snowy hills into that river; lastly, the Nawur and Teekur valleys, with all the intervening tracts between it and the Sambracote valley, where the river takes its decided turn to the south-east.

Kunawur is that part of Bischur which embraces all the northern, north-eastern, and eastern tracts, and lies entirely in and behind the snowy hills, chiefly comprised in the glen of the Sutlej, and running through and beyond these mountains, cutting them in a line, diverging not far from east and west; the Himālā range here taking a direction from north-west and south-east to west-north-west and south-south-east, while the river runs through in a nearly similar course. On the west, all that barren tract which bounds with Cooloo, and sends its waters to the Sutlej, is included in Kunawur, as also is the whole tract between that river and the head of the Pabur, to the eastward and south-eastward, where it is met by the districts of Rewaeen in Gurwhal, called Futteh Purbut and Pauch Purbut, from which places passes lead into Kunawur.

From this description of its situation, it will be inferred, that it is inhospitable and bleak in climate, barren and unproductive in soil: in fact, it is a mass of rocks and wild chasms, which only drain the waters as they melt from the peaks that frown above them, covered with eternal snow. Nevertheless, it is inhabited, though thinly in proportion to its extent; and the greatest strength of Bischur lies in the wild passes and hardy population of Kunawur. It produces but little grain, and the inhabitants supply themselves from more fertile districts, exchanging with those of the Pabur valley and others the productions of their country, viz. salt, wool, woollen cloths, dried grapes and currants, and the seeds from the cones of a peculiar species of fir, which are sweet like almonds, and various other things, for corn of all kinds.

Salt is brought from Bootan, with which country a constant intercourse is kept up. The little corn they rear consists of barley and a sort of grain, which, from the description given, may be a kind of rye. Many sheep and cattle are reared in Kunawur, and a great deal of wool is exported, both raw and woven. In the remoter parts is found the soorajee, or yāk, of Tartary. They breed this animal in numbers, and account it their best riches next to corn. They also have a breed between the yak and the common hill cow. Ponies, called gounts, together with asses and mules, are likewise bred and kept; and all these, as well as sheep and goats, are used as beasts of burthen.

The inhabitants of Kunawur speak a language altogether different from that used on the southern side of the snowy hills; but it is also said to be distinct from that of the Bhoteas in the Chinese territory. They are strongly marked with features of the Tartar physiognomy, and all have an openness of countenance and a frankness of conduct and manner that quite distinguishes them from the race to the south-westward of the mountainous boundary. The difference in character is at least as great: they are brave, hardy, and independent; open, courteous, and hospitable; honest and sincere. Such as we met and had any intercourse with, justified this character, which is generally attributed to them. They appear to bear a great resemblance to the Scots highlanders in disposition, being fond of enterprise and travel, and also great traders. Indeed, they are almost exclusively the commercial couriers between Hindostan and Tartary, as also between Tartary and Cashmere; frequenting the routes from Leo in Ludhāk, to Lassa and Degurcha and Nepāl, on trading speculations.

From these circumstances probably they have acquired many of the valuable qualities they possess. Commerce is the foundation of civilization; they have few pursuits at home that require a constant attendance like agriculture, and the natural restlessness of the human mind has driven them to roam; an unbounded confidence is placed in them by the people of Ludhāk and Cashmere and Tartary, who find them strictly honest. They are acute and punctual, but liberal and unsuspecting. Every person is safe in Kunawur, of whatever religion or sect he may be, whether Hindoo or Lama, Mahomedan or Christian.

Long after this tour was made, a pleasing instance of the honest punctuality of these people appeared in the conduct of a Kunawur travelling merchant, one of those from whom a considerable portion of our information was gathered. He was invited to make a trading voyage into Bootan and Yarkund, and a sum of money, very considerable in his estimation, was entrusted to him, to procure some of the produce of these parts, partly with a view of verifying his relation, and partly to judge of the value of the commodities in question, and of the possibility of procuring them. The man was with difficulty induced to take charge of the money, and with still greater difficulty prevailed on to promise to deliver the articles in the plains of Hindostan, at some distance from the hills, with his own hands. But he fulfilled his promise, and in a way that proved his honesty, for he himself brought, very nearly at the time he was expected to arrive, a quantity of the things ordered, which showed he had strictly adhered to his bargain of only making a profit on the articles of intermediate traffic, while the full value of the money was restored to the lender in goods of these countries at the cost *there.* It is delightful and refreshing to record a circumstance that marks a valuable trait of character among the wretched features of depravity and savageness which must be pourtrayed, in order to give a true delineation of the people of the country under review.

Such being the character of the people and the district of Kunawur, once forming the chief part of the territory of Bischur, it is no wonder that they should be so highly trusted, and so much in power. Many of the chief families in the state, and the principal officers of government, are of Kunawur extraction; the personal attendants on the rajah are of that country, and the soldiery are chiefly raised there. Guarded by such a people, a country wild and impregnable like this might defy the power of invaders if it possessed resources in itself against famine; but, cut off from the fertile districts to the south of the Himālā, it would soon fall before its pressure. An invading force, to proceed with any probability of success, should be well furnished with provisions, and fully prepared with ample and well secured magazines. The Ghoorkhas attempted to attack Kunawur, and penetrated three days journey within the valley, but were driven back in consequence of falling short of provisions. Hence the young rajah who fled into this district on their advance from Serān, baffled his pursuers and preserved his liberty.

Although the Kunawurrees are recognised as Hindoos by descent and general profession, they most generally follow the Lama religion. No Brahmins have ever settled in this district, nor will they go there; perhaps the poverty of the country, and the privations necessarily to be suffered during a residence there, have deterred these holy men, who usually seem to prefer those places which afford them all the comforts of life. The Lama priests are scattered about the country, and the people carry about their persons small idols purchased at L,hassa, or such as are brought for sale by the Lamas.

There is a small division in Kunawur distinct from the rest, containing four or five villages, and called Scolkhur, inhabited by Bhoteas or Tartars alone; of this country and the people, as well as their manners and customs, together with a few particulars concerning the Bhoteas in general, mention will be made hereafter.

That division which forms a continuation to Kunawur, and includes the western and south-western portion of Bischur, does not claim any very particular notice. To its boundaries we have already alluded. Little of it lies beyond the Sutlej, and that little, as well as all above Serān, partakes of the character of Kunawur, as well in aspect of country, as in produce and population.

The valleys and slopes that extend from the crest of the ridge, proceeding from Morāl-ke-kanda, and end in the Sutlej, are fertile, though wild and rocky where they take their rise; all these valleys, indeed, except that of Now-gurree-ke-Khola, which is very barren, like those of Kurangooloo and Comharsein, exhibit much richness and beauty.

The inhabitants of this district vary in proportion as they leave Kunawur and the snowy hills, till those who occupy the lower portion may be considered as described in the observations made at T,heog. When we crossed the Coonoo nullah, a change in dress and appearance was remarked among the people, and it was still more distinct at Rampore and Serān.

That district which includes the Glen of the Pabur is by far the richest and most productive in the territories of Bischur: the upper part of that glen, and of those which fall into it, with the tract to the north and north-west, bordering on Kunawur, is doubtless savage and barren like it; but for a course of from fifteen to twenty miles above Raeengudh, the river runs in a comparatively level valley, which, with the hill slopes on either side, particularly on the left bank, or northern exposure, is covered with corn land and numerous villages. The Sambracote valley is also well cultivated, and produces much grain.

We had little opportunity of remarking on the inhabitants of the Pabur glen and its subordinate valleys; but they do not stand much higher in character than those of the neighbouring districts, and closely resemble those of the Nawur valley adverted to below, except that they are rather more industrious in agriculture, and being richer, are perhaps somewhat less vicious. A happy climate, a fertile soil, and a situation somewhat farther removed from temptation to plunder, may have produced this industry and shade of goodness.

The last division of Bischur consists of the Nawur and Teekur valleys, between the Deohree and Chumbee ridges, with the Seekree valley to the north of the former. This district, though not so extensive, is next in productiveness to that last described. The whole valley gently slopes to the nullah that runs through it, and is cultivated with considerable care and success. It affords iron of an excellent quality, which is exported in considerable quantities to the Punjāb and the Sikh territories to the west of the Sutlej, being very much esteemed for matchlock barrels. This valley, with the Kootlaha district, once formed the chief part of the lordship of Saree, but is now, by conquest, become an integral part of Bischur.

The inhabitants of Nawur and Teekur are notorious for infamy of character even in this country, where all are bad. They are revengeful and treacherous, deficient in all good qualities, abandoned in morals, and vicious in their habits. As a proof of the savage indifference with which they look on the life of another, and on the act of shedding human blood, it is said that mere wantonness or a joke will induce the crime of putting a fellow creature to death, merely for the satisfaction of seeing the blood flow, and of marking the last struggles of their victim: and some facts that came under our observation of a tantamount nature, give too much reason for believing the assertion to be founded in truth. Female chastity is here quite unknown; and murder, robbery, and outrage of every kind, are here regarded with indifference.

Besides the above divisions which compose the rajahship of Bischur, there are many small states which are dependent on, and, in time of need, aid it with their troops, besides paying an annual tribute for protection. Most of these have been noticed before in the course of our journey. They are as follow, viz. Dilt, on the banks of the Sutlej, in which is situate the fortress of Mustgurh; Kurangooloo, in which are the forts of Whartoo and Kurana; Coomharsein, above the left bank of the Sutlej, containing Sircote with other forts; Kuneountee; Cotegooroo, in which is Jodhpoor fort; Bhuroulee, a very pretty place; Bulsum, which has Chourna fort, where resides the T,hakoor or Rānā; Theog, a small state, the T,hakoor of which lives in the castle of Theog; and Dodur Coar, which comprises only two villages. Any account of the nature of the country in these petty states would only be a repetition of what has already been said.

The character of their inhabitants has also been chiefly noticed above. They lie, equally with those of Nawur, under the stigma of abandoned villany, and total want of good principles, and, it is believed, but too justly so. They are generally unpleasing in appearance, mean, groveling, cowardly, and cruel. It would seem as if the faint approaches they have made towards civilization had only awakened the evil passions and propensities of the mind, which yet remain quite uncontrolled by and ignorant of the restraints of religion and virtue. They do not possess the almost admirable qualities that are attributed to the wild, stern native of North America, or the mild inoffensive submission of the southern savage. They have lost whatever native virtue may have existed in the savage state, and have not acquired that which would probably result from a happy, free, and liberal intercourse with civilized beings.

It is painful to observe this disgusting state of a people, who (it is fair to presume) are yet capable of improvement, and may be raised from so degraded a condition. We may hope that the dawn of their political and moral regeneration is even now appearing. They have been rescued by British power from the tyranny under which they groaned; and the spell which, as it were, lay on their mountains is broken. Security of person and property will be guaranteed by the British Government, and with this security riches will increase; industry, of which there is no want, will flourish; and vicious habits will be checked, because they will be less profitable and more dangerous than those of order and propriety, and will by degrees become infamous and rare. It may be said, that this is mere speculation, and that such effects can neither be easily nor speedily produced; and this is true. But amelioration, though gradual, will take place, and benevolent and wise interference will ultimately be successful. These effects, indeed, are regarded, by the most intelligent of the natives themselves, as necessary consequences of the late events. They hail the success and coming of the British as a revolution in the world, as the dawn of their civil happiness. The people think that they will become good, free, and happy, as by inspiration; that it is the necessary result of the British power and government. A British officer is looked upon almost as a supernatural being. From the rajah to the peasant there was not one who did not talk thus with confidence and enthusiasm, and uniformly concluded with saying, "Now we shall live, and improve, and be raised from beasts to men." Such are the ideas, such the veneration entertained by these rude savages for the British name; and it is a proud and exulting feeling for a British subject to trace them so strongly in so remote a clime. It is no wonder if his heart swell with love for his country, and his zeal and devotion be more firmly bound to its glory.

Bischur is governed by a rajah, whose office is hereditary; and it appears, that under him the different districts have always been regulated by hereditary chiefs, who have assumed the titles of wuzzeer, and exercise each their separate authority. They assess and collect the revenue, and settle minor disputes; but the rajah has always been lord paramount, and looked up to with perfect submission. It is probable indeed, that, in the former reigns, (and certainly in the late rajah's time), the wuzzeers were by no means so powerful as they are at present in the reign of the child his son; but the troublesome times, and the infancy of the heir to the throne, have necessarily thrown into the hands of these men all the executive, and, in fact, all the real power.

It is to be regretted that the archives and records of the state, as well as of the rajah's family, were entirely destroyed by the Ghoorkhas. Thus nothing certain relative to the origin of either came under our observation, or resulted from our inquiries; but there is no doubt that the rajah is descended from an ancient and noble Raajepoot family; it is said from Chittore. Of the date of its ascending the throne, or of the commencement of the state, or of the succession, till the reign of the last rajah, we are totally ignorant, as well as of the transactions of his reign previously to the Ghoorkha invasion.

There always was an enmity between the houses of Bischur and Cooloo, which state frequently sent parties across the Sutlej to the left bank, and seized on different tracts and states tributary to Bischur, building forts for the purpose of maintaining them; and even now, though they coalesced against their common enemy the Ghoorkhas, their natural jealousy could not be suppressed, the soldiers of Cooloo unwillingly yielding to Bischur the forts taken by the combined troops from the Ghoorkhas, and garrisoned by them. It is also said that none of the families of rank on the south side of the Sutlej will intermarry with those of Cooloo. With Sirmore, likewise, there were continual feuds and disputes, till the late rajah married a daughter of that house, when a friendly understanding took place. Before the Ghoorkha invasion, a similar vexatious warfare subsisted between Gurwhal and Bischur, which was only terminated by the issue of that invasion, and the destruction of the former state.

The late rajah dying, left two Rānees; one, the daughter of the house of Sirmore, by whom he had no issue; the other was a relation of the Dhammee T,hakoor, or lord, and by her he had the present young rajah and a daughter. The Sirmore lady is said to be high-spirited and of a powerful mind; the other quiet and domestic. But neither of them have any actual power or influence in the government. The wuzzeers rule entirely, and apparently agree very well with each other.

The revenues of the state are accounted for, and probably misapplied by them; but they are popular and moderate, and possess a perfect influence and authority. The affairs of the country are said to be improving, and probably the power they possess, if exercised in the name of the young rajah, and under the eye of the British government as his protector, will be beneficial to the state. Of these wuzzeers, there are four superior, and one of lesser importance, who divide the country. A note of their charges will be found in the Appendix.

The Rānee possesses a jagheer. The rajah and his mother, as well as the Sirmore Rānee, at present reside at Serān, where they came on their return from Kunawur, after the discomfiture of the Ghoorkha forces. He is said to be eight years old, of good natural abilities, but it is to be feared that his education is much neglected, for there are no good instructors to be procured in Bischur; and the present rulers of the country may have thought it their interest to bring him up in sloth, ignorance, and dissipation. His youth, the state of the country and of the people, are certainly objects of considerable interest; and every one must hope that their connexion with the British government may be productive to them of security and future happiness.

From the nature of the country the revenues of Bischur are limited;

and far from being proportioned to its superficial extent. The mode of assessment also is indefinite, sometimes being collected in money, at others in kind.

The household expenses of the rajah are supplied by payments of revenue, made in the different articles which he requires, as sheep, goats, wool, woollen cloth, corn, oil, ghee, musk, &c. &c. It does not clearly appear from this irregular mode of collection, what the amount of the true revenue might have been. Bischur Proper paid to the Nepāl government only 80,000 rupees annually. Its dependent lordships were separately assessed; but the country was never thoroughly subdued, far less organized. Many families had fled across the Sutlej on the approach of the Ghoorkha army, and the country exhibited the greatest marks of devastation and depopulation. Hence it may be fairly inferred, that the sum collected by the conquerors bore no proportion to what the country would have been brought to yield under a mild and equitable government. Under the comparatively moderate and just rule of Kirtee Rānā, who seems to have left much to the native authorities, the country began to improve; and many families, seeing some prospect of security, had returned from across the Sutlej.

The military force of Bischur is not great, nor does it appear that any considerable standing army was ever kept up. Military service seems to have been accepted, as in other feudal and patriarchal states, in lieu of pecuniary contribution; and this, in some measure, accounts for the smallness of the nominal revenues. When a military force was required, the people were summoned by their chiefs to follow them to the field; and they brought with them the means of subsistence for a certain time.

Such a force can never be very efficient. A soldier's supply of money or provisions is exhausted, and he returns home without asking leave to supply himself, or oftener to send his brother or relation in his stead. Thus the individuals of the army are continually coming and going, and changing the duty from one to another, to the complete destruction of discipline and co-operation. However, they all act as one family. The chief regards each soldier as his son, and all are one brotherhood. He is like an elder, respected and obeyed, without being feared; he assumes no glitter or pomp of authority, and is scarcely to be distinguished by his dress from the common soldier. But the only people who can be accounted trustworthy as soldiers are the inhabitants of Kunawur, and of the northern parts; and to them the above description applies more particularly. Levies from the lower districts are far less tractable, and they are never summoned except in cases of necessity; nor will they act at a distance from home, or continue in the field even for a moderate period.

The arms used by the Kunawurees are chiefly the matchlock and the hatchet; they do not make so much use of the bow as those from the southward. Swords and shields are scarce.

It is impossible, from any information we could gather, to make even a guess at the population of Bischur, consequently no computation can be made of the fighting men it can muster. It brought lately into the field about 3000, of which about 1000 were armed with matchlocks, and the rest, who were chiefly inhabitants of the lower districts and independent states, had only bows and arrows. But, distracted and disorganised as it is, its subjects scattered, many sold to slavery, or led away to serve in hostile armies, no fair judgment can be formed of what its power might be if in a situation to call its energies into action.

Bischur can boast of but few natural productions of much value, and these have been already noticed, viz. sheep and wool, cattle and ghee, iron, and corn of various sorts. The finer grains are wheat, barley, and rice, with a multitude of smaller grains; tobacco and opium in small quantities, musk, &c.; of fruits, apples, indifferent pears, apricots and peaches, wild grapes, which they preserve for use, as well as a small currant prepared in Kunawur, whence also come the eatable seeds of a fir-cone. Turnips, onions and garlic of inferior quality, and a peculiar sort of carrot, with several other useful herbs, grow wild in the mountains.

Their agriculture is similar to that which is common throughout the hills. The wheat and barley commonly occupied the less rugged faces of the hills, as the rice does the low lands by the sides of rivers and rivulets; and where these will not readily grow, the less valuable grains will often yield a saving crop.

From the grapes they procure two sorts of strong liquor: the one they call *sihee*, which is the first juice they yield, and I believe it is fermented in the common way, and only used by the first classes, such as the wuzzeers and nobles; the other is prepared by pouring hot water on the residue of the fruit, but I know not whether it undergoes any sort of distillation. The musk is procured in small quantities from a species of deer to be noticed hereafter.

Iron has already been noticed, and is produced in various parts of the country. Lead also is generally found. It is likewise probable that copper exists in some parts of this state, and several other sources of hidden wealth may lie concealed in these rude tracts; but the industry or ingenuity of this people has never been awakened by demand or inquiry.

The chief and almost only manufacture of Bischur consists in the fabrication of woollen cloths of several sorts, and in this they excel the inhabitants of all the countries between the Sutlej and Alaknunda. The wool produced here is of a superior quality, and they import from Bootan a quantity of still better. From this they weave blankets of different sizes and fineness; woollen cloth for trowsers, chiefly black; fine webs for cummerbunds, and for throwing around their shoulders in the fashion of a Scotch plaid; a sort of well napped cloth, called by them seek-cloth, which is used for their coats and dress, and the black bonnets which they wear on their heads. The fabric of many of these cloths is remarkably good. Their blankets are of the twilled sort, close and fine; and the seek-cloth is nearly equal to our finest English blankets. It is curious to find this word seek-cloth, which is a Persian term for broad cloth of any sort, used in so remote a region. The word, I understand, is prevalent in the above sense all over the East, and it would argue that the manufacture was of recent date, probably an imitation of cloth imported with its name from the Caubul territories, as so exact a similitude in the terms used in naming two articles of the same nature in two countries, whose language have no resemblance, can scarcely be presumed to have occurred otherwise. They also manufacture a small quantity of shawl-wool, imported from Bootan, into pieces resembling the coarse shawls called D,hoossas. Sometimes they mix it with sheep's wool, thus giving it more substance but less fineness. These cloths have no great beauty, but the texture, twilled like the shawls, seems to indicate that the people with proper encouragement would in all likelihood produce an useful and perhaps a fine manufacture from this material.

At present both the woollen and shawl cloths are only made for home consumption, and a partial and casual sale in the neighbouring states. Few except the highest chiefs can afford the price of the latter, small as their value is; and the troubles of late have so much interrupted the usual course of labour, that it was with great difficulty we could procure five or six specimen pieces of the shawl wool-cloth; the price was from seven to ten rupees each on an average. Their fineness did not vary much, and they were made in two breadths sewed together, forming a piece of one and three quarters to two yards broad by four yards long.

The thread is spun by hand in the same way that cotton is spun all over Hindostan; indeed, the manufacture is very simple; the cloth, also, is wove by hand. The woof being extended upon two sticks, placed at a distance corresponding with the intended length of the web, the alternate threads are separated from each other by a succession of small pieces of smooth wood, that are alternately placed and withdrawn as the warp is passed between. A single frame formed of split bamboo is employed, through which the threads are passed to keep them separate. I believe that there is no machinery of greater complication used. Nothing more nearly approaching to a loom is used throughout the hills.

The trade of Bischur, though of late interrupted and oppressed, has always been considerably greater than its importance as a state, and its own produce or consumption, would warrant us to expect; and this, as we have seen, arises from its local position, and the peculiarly commercial turn of a portion of its subjects. The Kunawur merchants carry on a trade not only with the plains and the neighbouring Chinese provinces, but, as above remarked, they are also the chief carriers between Gar,ha, Ludhak, and Cashmere, and even push their commercial enterprises as far as La,hassa on the south-east, exchanging commodities between that place and Nepāl, and between the latter and the Chinese towns in Little Thibet, and to the northward, trading between Cashmere, Yarkund, Kashgār, Gar,ha, and the various cities and people of these quarters. We met with several people who had from their youth been engaged in these commercial enterprises, and who gave us the chief part of the information here detailed. One man in particular was very intelligent; and from his general character, the unconstrained and natural way in which he gave his relations, and their coincidence with other information on the same subject, we were inclined to attach much credit to his statements.

The direct commerce of Bischur with other hill states and with the plains is very limited, chiefly consisting of imports of sugar, cloths, small quantities of iron work, brass utensils, indigo, &c., which is returned by raw iron, blankets, opium, a little tobacco, musk, bhang, turmeric, which is much esteemed, and the articles which pass through the hills from Bootan. The exports to Bootan and Găr,ha are, corn to the nearer and barren parts, ghee from Kunawur, iron, opium, tobacco, and wooden cups for tea; and from the plains it becomes a thoroughfare for all the common articles of produce and manufacture, as sugar, sugarcandy, cloths both coarse and fine, indigo, &c. The returns are almost entirely wool, both shawl and common, of a fine quality. Salt, as much tea as they can afford, with a little fine Chinese cloth, some musk, borax, &c. are brought to exchange for low country commodities at Rampore.

Kunawur sends little to Ludhak besides ghee, but from various openings the produce of Hindostan is carried there, chiefly through Cashmere, whence also they bring shawls; and in return the Cashmerians receive tea, and shawl wool, with some China cloths.

Yarkund sends to Leo in Ludhak, silver, Russian leather, called *Bhul-R,hāl*, felt carpets, called *Numbdas*, coarse and fine China silks, tafetas, velvets, and earthen ware, sable fur, small coral beads, and seed pearls; and in return receives all manner of produce from Hindostan, keen-kabs, embroidered cloth, baftas, and other white cloths, moultan chintz, quantities of red tanned skins of sheep, goat, and kid, nerbisee or zedoary, silk manufactures of Benares, soongrees, and all sorts of spices.

The trade from the countries of the Lamas to the south-eastward and eastward with Gar,ha, as well as that between the Nepālese dominions and Thibet and China, is of a similar nature; but the articles brought from the plains are carried through different passes. Zedoary is chiefly from a district near Nepāl, and is much prized by all the inhabitants of the hills and of the plains behind them.

In all these routes the Kunawur merchants are found, and their acquaintance with these countries is intimate and extensive. At present, want of capital, as well as the difficulty of the country, cramps their speculations; but it is believed that if encouragement were given, and perhaps some moderate assistance in opening the roads through the most difficult passes, a very direct and easy intercourse might be opened between the plains on the banks of the Sutlej and the Chinese dominions on the north-east of the Himālā range, and this without passing through any intermediate independent state that could levy arbitrary imposts on the transit. At present the bulk of this traffic goes entirely through the dominions of Runjeet Sing, the Sik,h chief of Lahore, and the best roads are first through Chumbee, Jooala, Mookhee, and Hoorpore, to Umrutsir, by which horses, mules, and asses pass easily, next that through Cooloo by its capital Stanpore.

If, however, roads were made along the banks of the Sutlej to Rampore, a measure perfectly practicable, and from Rampore to Soongnam, all passage through the country of the rapacious Sikhs and their tributaries would be avoided, and the productions of Thibet, Yarkund, and all Chinese Tartary, with those from countries even more remote, would flow unrestrained into Hindostan; while government might, with the greatest ease, place what restrictions it pleased either on trade itself, or on the mere passage of individuals.

It is not easy to estimate what the value of such a trade might be, nor is it here intended to enter on so wide a field of speculation with so few leading points for guidance; but it is impossible that any one who has seen the country and considered the subject, should not be struck with the facilities given by the passage of a considerable stream, even though not navigable, for communication through this difficult range, or should be indifferent to the apparently splendid nature of the communication when effected.

The author may, however, be permitted to advert loosely to one object, viz. the shawl-wool trade, which is now monopolised by Cashmere. A new channel opening to a profitable market would not, it is believed, fail to direct a portion at least of this trade to Hindostan; while, when the skill of our weavers is known, it is not to be supposed that they would fall far short of the perfection to which the Cashmerian artisans have arrived. It is well known that this trade is by far the most profitable which that small state enjoys; indeed it is almost that alone which enriches its people, while government derive a principal share of their revenue from the duties on their sale. It seems at least well worth while to encourage the trial, to divert a share of this source of wealth into our own hands.

To our inquiries as to the possibility of procuring any quantity of shawl-wool through the pass at present, it was answered, that a few hundred maunds might be procured, but that if any large quantity was required, it would be necessary to make some reference to the Chinese authorities at Gar,ha, or the towns where it is chiefly sold. This would not appear to be a matter of much difficulty to obtain, as from certain late occurrences it is to be presumed that the officers are rather well disposed towards Europeans; and it may be believed that any offer of competition which would raise the price, if not indiscreetly pushed, would be listened to, particularly if accompanied with some profit to the authority permitting the trade; and the distance from the seat of empire makes the officers on the frontiers too independent to render it possible that any interference would take place from the court of Pekin to the prejudice of an agreement so made.

PART VI.

JOURNEY WITH THE POLITICAL AGENT FOR THE ARMY OF GENERAL MARTINDALE CONTINUED.

CHAPTER XIX.

Although the scanty information which was collected during the whole of our journey, and which forms the basis of the map that accompanies these pages, with other observations of a general nature concerning the hills, might perhaps be more properly referred to the Appendix, they are, nevertheless, inserted here, because a natural pause occurs at this place, offering an opportunity for all desultory remarks and information; and, should they prove uninteresting to any one, they may be totally passed over by the reader, both here and also in the Appendix. So minute a description as is given below of the nature of the country and materials from which the map has been projected, may be deemed tedious and uninteresting by many; but some will employ it as a touchstone by which the degree of authenticity to be attached to the map may be tried, and for this reason consider it as of importance.

The great Himālāyan snowy range is only the highly elevated crest of the mountainous tract that divides the plains of Hindostan from those of Thibet, or lesser Tartary. Far as they predominate over, and precipitously as they rear themselves above the rest, all the hills that appear in distinct ranges, when viewed from the plains, are indeed only the roots and branches of this great stem; and, however difficult to trace, the connexion can always be detected between each inferior mountain and some particular member of its great origin. At times, indeed, this connexion seems nearly broken; and a lofty peak, rearing itself, as if in rivalry, presents a very extensive ramification of lesser ridges, separating ravines which extend down to the great drains of the country, and thus becomes, as it were, the nucleus of a subordinate district; from the lofty height of which, the country between it and the principal chain seems comparatively low, though very rugged; and in this hollow generally lies some river, with its subsidiary streams, which drain a large portion of the snow that annually melts from their sides. All the regularity of ranges which deceive the eye, in viewing this mountainous belt from the distant plains, thus vanishes on entering the country; and the whole becomes a confused and chaotic assemblage of most rugged mountains, huddled into masses and peaks, and running into ridges which defy arrangement; and it is only by attentive observation that they can be traced to one or other of the mighty piles that compose the snowy range.

The horizontal depth of this mountainous tract, on that side which overlooks Hindostan, is no doubt various; but, from the difficulty of the country, a traveller performs a journey of many days before he reaches the foot of the immediate snowy cliffs. The best observations and survey do not authorize the allowance of more than an average depth of about sixty miles from the plains to the commencement of these, in that part of the country that forms the subject of this narrative. The breadth of the snowy zone itself in all probability varies still more; for huge masses advance in some places into the lower districts, and in others the crest recedes in long ravines, that are the beds of torrents, while behind they are closed by a succession of the loftier cliffs. Every account we receive of a passage through them (and this is no doubt found most commonly where the belt is narrowest) gives a detail of many days' journey through deserts of snow and rocks; and it is to be inferred, that on the north-east side they advance to and retreat from the low ground in an equally irregular manner. Indeed, some accounts would induce the belief, that long ranges, crowned with snow-clad peaks, project in various places from the great spine, and include habitable and milder districts; for, in all the routes of which we have accounts that proceed in various directions towards the Trans-Himālāyan countries, hills covered with snow are occasionally mentioned as occurring, even after the great deserts are passed and the grazing country entered. The breadth, then, of this crest of snow-clad rock itself cannot fairly be estimated at less than from seventy to eighty miles.

Of the distance to which the hilly country extends beyond the snowy crest we must judge chiefly by inference, assisted by the limited information we can obtain from the routes held through it by natives, which must always be taken with very great allowance, even where there seems to be no inducement to deceive. The only European travellers who are known to have entered on this new ground are Messrs. Moorcroft and Hearsay, who penetrated by the Nitee-Mana pass, and reached the lake of Mantullaee, Mansrowar, or Mepāng. All these sources lead us to presume a pretty extensive detail of hills beyond the loftiest belt, that by no means terminate even at Gara or Gartope, though they do not reach the height of those to the westward and southward. A branch of the Cailas range, undoubtedly a ramification of the Himālā, stretches out beyond the lake Mansrowar, a considerable way towards Gartope. Beyond this point there seem at present to exist no grounds, on which even a conjecture may be formed concerning the nature of the country. The general character of the hills on the north-east side of the Himālā, if we judge from information, seems somewhat less rugged and inhospitable than those on the south-western face. The route subsequently detailed will show that the valleys there are more even, the roads less difficult, and the hills less abrupt and rocky, than the latter exposure exhibits; and this seems to harmonize with the rule generally observed in the primary formation of this tract, that the western, north-western, and south-western exposures are uniformly the most rugged and precipitous; while those to the south-eastward and north-eastward are ever the roundest and most accessible. It seems that all the north-eastern hills are much tinged with red soil. Is there any analogy or connexion between this colour of the soil and the gold, which is found in considerable quantities in these districts, particularly in the beds of its rivers?

The great snowy belt, although its loftiest crest is broken into numberless cliffs and ravines, nevertheless presents a barrier perfectly impracticable, except in those places where hollows that become the beds of rivers have in some degree intersected it, and facilitated approach to its more remote recesses; and courageous and attentive perseverance has here and there discovered a dangerous and difficult path, by which a possibility exists of penetrating across the range. Few rivers hold their course wholly through it: indeed, in the upper part the Sutlej alone has been traced beyond this rocky barrier; and there is a path along its stream, from different parts of which roads diverge, that lead in various directions through the mountains. No reasonable doubt can now exist of the very long and extraordinary course which this river takes: the routes given below will trace it particularly nearly to its origin. Several other passes through the Himālā exist to the south-eastward; but I am unacquainted with all of them beyond Kumaoon, between which and that of the Sutlej, the passes of Joar, Darma, Nitteemana, Lamanittee, Gurooneettee, and Birjee, are found practicable for the conveyance of goods, and all cut the range in a direction little varying from west to east, which coincides with that in which the hills are divided by nature, by the ravines through which the principal drains have their course, and in which most of the great masses that jut down from the snowy crest towards the plains send their continuous ridges, showing an intimate connexion with the great primary formation of the country and the peculiarities of its chief features.

Besides these chief passes there are others of more danger and difficulty that pervade the snowy range in various directions, finding outlets to the milder countries beyond. With these, however, I am only acquainted by accounts of less minute detail, and on the authenticity of these beyond their mere existence there is little reliance to be placed. Such is the pass by the course of the river I,hannevie related below, that from Bhurassoo to the neighbouring districts of China; a path also said to exist near Kedarnauth, &c. &c. These are all so dangerous and toilsome that few but the wildest inhabitants of the most inhospitable regions choose to invade their deserts of eternal rock and snow, where no living thing is seen, and no means are to be obtained for long preserving life. To the westward of the Sutlej the passes are perhaps more frequent, certainly less difficult. The pass of Cooloo through Stanpore, by Sucklote to Gārā and Ludhak, and that through Chumbee, by Joocela, Mookhee, and Hoorpore, are among the best and most frequented. With those which may exist farther to the westward, between Chumbee and Cashmere, I am unacquainted; but it is well known that a comparatively easy and much frequented road is found from the Punjab to Cashmere, and through that valley to Ludhak, and the other states and districts of Thibet. I am unacquainted, even by information, with the actual course through the hills to Cashmere, but it doubtless leads along the river Jy,thure, which arises in the hills bounding that valley to the north-east and east.

A route is given below, leading from Ludhak to Hymap, which place is said to be four days' journey only from the capital of Cashmere, and on a road fit for horses. Hymap is on the banks of the great river Sing-kechoo, which, rising in the mountains around, and to the north of lake Mantullace, runs by Gārā through Ludhak, by its capital Leh; and changing its course more to the westward, flows round the Cashmerean mountains, probably forming, according to the best information we have, a branch of the Attock, or Indus.

Our informant did not distinctly state where the road to Cashmere quits the river, but he was clear enough in pointing out that the river ran to the north-westward of Cashmere: this seems also to be the opinion of Mr. Moorcroft, founded, no doubt, on similar information; and as we are not acquainted with any stream that penetrates through the mountains in a direction that can correspond with that taken by the Sing-kechoo, it seems nearly beyond a question that it forms a portion of the Indus. That the name given to this river by our informant should differ from that by which it was known to Messieurs Moorcroft and Hearsay, is not surprising. In different districts it would be known by different names, and, probably, even at Gārā it may be known by this name here given, though, by an easy analogy, it assumed that of the chief place by which it flows.

Cashmere appears to be the true limit of the Himālā range. Beyond the point where the mountainous chain is cut by the Attock, and, indeed, even to the south-eastward of it, according to every account I have heard, the mountains decline in altitude, and the hilly country spreads out on both sides to a less circumscribed space. To enter, however, on this tract, and to advert to the further ramifications and connexions of this great range with other chains of mountains, would be quite foreign to the limited scale of the present objects; and, where all must be speculation, would be worse than presumptuous.

It has appeared from several portions of the foregoing narration, that the whole of this great mountainous tract, as is usually the case in countries of a similar description, has been always divided into a number of larger and smaller states; the boundaries of which, and often the sovereigns, were continually changing. The short detail of the Ghoorkha power having risen on the ruins of so many petty principalities, forms a strong example of this condition of things; and the nature of the country through which our route led, as already detailed in our progress through the Baruh Thakooraee, gives a further illustration of it. It appears probable by inference that a similar state of affairs exists on the north-eastern side of the great range; and our information goes to prove this in great measure, but with this difference, that the influence of the Chinese empire, or at least that of its deputies in Thibet, who are indeed very independent in all but name, has been exerted with greater success to reduce the petty sovereigns to a more complete state of feudal dependence upon itself. They are generally tributaries to China.

The state that attracts the chief attention is undoubtedly Ludhak: its territorial extent seems to be considerable, and our information leads to the belief that it possesses a good deal of importance from its political and commercial relations with the Chinese government at Gārā, and the territories of the Lamas, and with Cashmere, as well as from its own internal resources and valuable exports. It is bounded, to the best of our information, on the west by Cashmere and its dependencies, on the south-westward and southward by Chumbee, Cooloo, and Bischur, which also circumscribes it on the south-eastward. The districts under Chinese sway, of which Gārā and Tuling form two of the chief stations, lie to the eastward and north-eastward; perhaps it is not far removed in these quarters from the country recognised as Yarkund. Many small states have, doubtless, had existence between these just mentioned; but they seem chiefly to have been absorbed into the large ones, and are now at least of no consequence: we were given to understand that Ludhak was in some degree tributary both to China and to Cashmere.

This may relate more to the terms of certain commercial treaties and political relations with these two states, than to any actual assessment which it submits to pay to them. There is no doubt, however, that these relations are most favourable to itself, for it seems to enjoy a sort of monopoly of the whole valuable trade in shawl wool, engrossing to itself at a fixed and low valuation all the wool that is collected in the Un,dēs, or wool country (as it is called by Mr. Moorcroft), which is disposed of to the manufacturers of Cashmere, from whom they receive in return the produce of Hindostan, &c.

It appears, that on one occasion this monopoly was infringed by the sale of some shawl wool to strangers, which called forth the most rigorous enactments and threats of punishment to future defaulters from the authorities of Gārā. This circumstance is taken notice of by Mr. Moorcroft, who adverts also to the monopoly and its cause, as arising from some assistance in time of mutual danger, and which called forth these immunities in favour of the Ludhak community.

Ludhak itself is, probably, chiefly a grazing country, and supplies much shawl wool, though the principal mart for this is at Gārā. The routes through its territories describe chiefly rugged mountains topped with snow, projections certainly from the Himālā range, and lower hills of reddish soil, covered with short grass, representing a country fit for sheep; but little is said of cultivation until we are brought to the valley of the Singkechoo, which seems to be the rich district of the country. This is full of cultivation and villages; here also is placed the capital of the country, Leh, or Ludhak.

This town, our accounts inform us, is situated on the north or right bank of the river, but about two cos distant from it, and is watered by a rivulet, which here empties itself into its bed. From the village of Humee to Leh, a distance, it is said, of sixteen or seventeen cos, we are told that the valley widens much, and is from two to four cos broad, very richly cultivated with wheat, barley, and oe, or rye, and thickly studded with villages; the road along the river excellent, broad, and planted on each side with chiloomah-trees: and this prosperous state continues for a considerable distance below upon the river's banks. The town itself once contained about 1000 good houses, but report states it to have fallen off, and it is now reduced to about 700. These generally consist of several stories, the lower story built by uniting two thin walls of stone filled with mud between them; the upper is entirely formed of the latter material, as is the roof, which is flat, forming a terrace: they are said to be well constructed. There are well stocked bazars, and several shops (twelve or thirteen) kept by the Cashmerian Mussulmauns, but no Hindoo bunyas, or shopkeepers: flour, ghee, grain, flesh, and all articles of consumption are sold in the market by the people from the country, who bring them to town. The palace of the rajah is at Leh; we were told that his title among the people of the country is "gealbo," which is equivalent to rajah. His name is Neena Mungreal. I believe his religion is that of the Lamas; but an universal spirit of toleration seems to prevail under his sway, for all persuasions find protection there, Hindoos, Mussulmauns, Lamas, and Chinese.

Cattle are freely slaughtered, and flesh of all sorts is publicly sold in the market. It is said that rice, ghee, and sugar, are very dear; wheat and barley are also expensive, but more common. Wheat is most preferred, of which, and rice, they encourage the importation from Bischur and Cashmere, and consume a great quantity. Barley and oe, or rye, is chiefly used, boiled into a sort of porridge.

The general nature of their commerce has been touched upon in the preceding pages. It appears singular that, in a grazing country, ghee should be a scarce and dear article; but it is so: and from this circumstance we may presume, that sheep and goats are more encouraged and reared than horned cattle: no doubt from the same reasons that have so thinned them in the Highlands of Scotland, the greater productiveness of sheep.

Three grand fairs are held in the year at Leh, viz. one in Kalick, or October; one in Phagoon, or February; and one in Bhadgoon, or August. The first of these is called the Jung Dooz, and is the least; the second, called Dummooche, is the chief one; and the third, termed Sooblās, holds a middle importance. At these fairs the concourse of Mussulmauns from Yarkund, &c. of Lamas from Lassa Degurcha, Hindoos from Imritsir and all the Punjab, and of merchants from Cashmere, and all other places, is said to be immense; and the valuable productions of these countries are all poured into Leh, which seems to be used as an entrepôt for their riches, exporting them again by the various natural channels to their ultimate markets.

Such are the few particulars we collected respecting this state. Slight and little satisfactory as they may be, they may stimulate curiosity, and awaken a desire to become better acquainted with the country to the north-east of Himālā.

To the eastward, and probably to the southward of Leh, and sixteen days' journey entirely along the course of the river Sing-kechoo and Eckung, as more fully noted in the route below, (the chief part of which lies through the Ludhak territory), is situated Gārā, or Gartope, or Ghertope, which, though insignificant in itself as a place, is nevertheless a station of considerable importance in this part of Thibet. From what we could collect, it consists but of a few huts and tents; but it is the residence of a dēba, or governor, the meeting place of a great annual fair, and the chief market of shawl and other wools, the produce of the countries around.

Many particulars respecting this place may be collected from Mr. Moorcroft's account; those which we could collect are few and vague. It seems that Gartope is situated in the valley of the river Eekung, which is here of considerable extent, though surrounded, it appears, with hills. To this place the Ludhak merchants come to purchase the wool which is brought for sale from all the country round to a great distance, for the Cashmere market: and to this place, also, do the dealers from the low country of Hindostan come to dispose of and exchange their goods. The great metah, or fair, is held annually in the month of Bhadoon, and when well attended there are seen from 12 to 15,000 people. The person who gave us a great portion of the information now detailed was at Gārā when Messrs. Moorcroft and Hearsay were there, and was sent by the dēbah to decide who and what they were; for an idea had gone abroad that they were Ghoorkhas in disguise; a people, it seems, not in favour with the dēbah. But this man having seen them, immediately knew them to be Europeans, which he accordingly reported, to the great satisfaction, as he assured us, of the dēbah, who declared the "Franks" to be good people; but threatened any Ghoorkha that might put his foot in the place with death, as they were, he said, a treacherous and dangerous people. Be this as it may, he mentioned several slight particulars that vouched for the truth of the story; and as he first volunteered the information without any hint from us, I have little doubt that he did see these gentlemen there.

The great and holy Lake of Mantullace, or Mansrowar, is about eight days' journey from Garha, according to this man's account, which nearly corresponds with that of Mr. Moorcroft. Gārā appears to be situate near the forks of the Sing-kechoo, or rather the Eekung, or chief branch of the Attock, where it collects the different streams from the mountains in the vicinity of this great lake, if not from the lake itself. The route from Gārā is probably the same which these gentlemen traversed; and Mansur, the resting-place of our informant, as the third day's stage, is, in all likelihood, the Misar where these travellers halted; and the place called by him Dumchoo, situated at the foot of the Kailas Purbut, is certainly the same as Darchar, said by them to be placed so near that lofty range of hills, the streams from which both he and they call Gangree, forming the chief supply of the lake Rawenhrudd. This place (Gangree) is held in the greatest veneration by the Tartars and Chinese. There are four temples of the Lamas at the mountain foot, with their entrances to the four cardinal points, which are held very sacred; and to journey round the Kailas mountain is reputed to be of as much efficacy as a pilgrimage to Loretto, or to Mecca, was to a Roman catholic of former days, or to a Mussulmaun of the present.

The lake of Mansrowar, or Mantullaee, we are informed, is of considerable extent. A journey round it, which is reckoned a very necessary religious exercise, occupies from six to eight days on horseback. This is probably a great exaggeration, and certainly, according to Mr. Moorcroft's opinion, is so. He estimates the lake at sixteen miles long, by eleven broad; but irregularities on the bank, causing the road to retreat from it, may lengthen the journey considerably. Our informant describes the hills around it, however, as consisting more of soil than rock, with little wood, but chiefly covered with grass, and a sort of furze called damak. He also declared that one branch of the Sutlej comes out of the lake; but Mr. Moorcroft seems to have ascertained this to be a mistake, and refers the source of this river to Rawenhrudd, a lake in the vicinity. It seems, however, scarcely possible that a lake, which receives from the Himālā so many streams, and collects so large a body of water, should have no outlet; and if this is not apparent, we must suppose that there is some subterraneous communication, possibly with Rawenhrudd itself, by which the superfluous waters are carried off.

We made particular inquiries of this man whether he was aware of any stream that ran from the neighbourhood of Mantullaee to the southward; and he informed us very distinctly that, from one of the lofty mountains to the south of Mantullaee, and which sends its north-western waters to the lake, a stream arises on the south-eastern face that flows in that direction, and is the same that subsequently passes by Lassa: it is called, he says, the Sampoo. The mountain in which it rises he called Murgiūlana, and describes the river as being a bow-shot broad, and running slowly along the plain, after leaving the hills. Lassa, he says, is ten months journey distant from Mansrowar. Thus it appears as if this lake were the great centre whence all the waters separate around the Himālā, part running to the south-eastward, and part to the north-westward; and it is certain that the Sutlej, and pretty nearly so that the chief branch of the Attock, take their rise in its vicinity. The confirmation, beyond dispute, of all this surely is an object of much geographical interest.

In collecting the imperfect hints that were to be procured respecting the country and its principal places, we more than once heard of the cities of Tuling and of Chaprung, but of their actual position I never was able to form any correct notion.

The two Bhoteas, whom (as will afterwards be seen) I met at Gungotree, gave vague and unauthentic accounts of routes to both these places. They state the distance from Gungotree to their village (Chounsah) to be a full month's journey; from Chounsah to Chaprung another month, and from thence to Gārā occupies a similar time; and that Tuling is midway between Chaprung and Gārā. From this imperfect information we can only collect, that both these places are within the space intercepted on the map, between Ludhak and Gārā, or the line of the Sing-kechoo on the north, and the chief crest of the Himālā from Cashmere to Mantullaee on the south; but it seems quite fruitless to attempt assigning any particular place to either.

Tuling is said to be a place of much importance, and the residence of a grand Lama. Chaprung is also stated to be a considerable town, the residence of a chief, or rajah, called "Cotock," situate in a plain, but surrounded by hills, and the road to it and from it to Tuling is very bad, and much of it through snow. It is situate on a river, which, if any credit can be given to these people, forms a part of the Sutlej. These are very vague and unsatisfactory particulars; but intelligent travellers were rarely met with, and none could afford us any information beyond the line of his own route.

We had little opportunity for gaining information respecting the country which occupies the space between the river Sutlej and Cashmere, the chief states of which, we heard, were Cooloo, Chumbee, Mundee, Kangrah, Sukhet, and Goolihur. The first two are of very great extent, stretching, like Bischur, through the snowy range, and bounding, in all probability, with Ludhak. The capital of Cooloo is Stanpore. To the south-west of Cooloo lies part of Kuhloor, or Belaspore, and Kangrah. Mundee lies still more to the westward, and stretches down to the plains of the Punjab. Sukhet is a small state upon the banks of the Sutlej. Chumbee lies to the north of these petty states, and is by far the most considerable of any on this side of the Himālā range beyond Gurwhal; but I know nothing of the country, except that it is wild and savage. I believe its capital town is Hoorpore. All these states are tributary, and dependant in a greater or less degree on the Sik,hs of the plains, and acknowledge obedience to Runjeet Sing.

Many petty states doubtless exist in the different districts of the country in question, but I know nothing of them. Some are alluded to in the routes given below, but this allusion is all the information I possess concerning them; and I now proceed to give a more minute description of the map that accompanies these pages, and to explain the sources from which it is chiefly compiled.

The great general outlines of the portion, more particularly the subject of this narrative, both natural and political, will easily be distinguished; and the line of our route, also very obvious, will account for the more particular detail that appears in the parts over which we passed. Our survey, though it was deficient in the precision that can only be attained by combining correct observations of the heavenly bodies with accurate trigonometrical measurement, was yet so far complete in the latter requisite, that I have reason to think many points are well fixed, at least, in their relation to one another; and on each side of these, minute observations of the position of villages, peaks, and streams have afforded materials for filling up a map upon a larger scale than this in question. I believe, indeed, that this minuteness of detail is of little general utility; but, as the face of the country is every where very much the same, I thought it well that one small district should be thus depicted, as a sample descriptive of the rest. And perhaps I was unwilling that the labour which procured these details should be entirely thrown away; a feeling which I am sensible is too apt to lead into the error of enlarging, beyond due measure, on subjects of which one feels master, without justly estimating the real interest they are calculated to excite.

From many points in our route, which frequently intersected itself, we had a fine opportunity of detecting the geographical arrangement of the country. Such were the stations on the Sine range, in the lower part of the hills near Nahn; at Habun farther removed; at Chogut and Gudhala above Choupal, in Joobul; on the ridges dividing the Nawur valley from Sambracote, on Nowagurh-Teeba; the heights of Sooraroo and Urchalum as we advanced onwards; on Puntajhurra ridge, Teckur, Mundapoor, Deonhur, and Deoonnur, as we retired from Comharsein to the southward; Deoonnur, Kanda, Sunknee, and Toombroo-Teebas, as we again resumed a northerly course, on Moondulgurh, Oogun, and Bahilee farther onwards, Shikaree Quila across the Nowgurree Khola. Our views from these points, with the connecting observations made in the country between, have enabled me to fill up a considerable portion of the space that lies between the Sutlej and Jumna with a detail which I have great reason to think chiefly accurate.

Of this tract the great mountain Choor, which rises from the banks of the river Girree to the height of 10,560 feet, forms the most prominent feature between the plains and the snowy mountains, in a geographical point of view, as being the first object that arrests the eye from below, and is seen towering over all the other mountains from every quarter. From it diverges a large radiation of hills that intersect the country variously; some being joined to the roots of the snowy mountains, and others after many intricate ramifications reaching the plains. One ridge, like a great spine, strikes off to north 25 east by Dhurma and Chogut peaks, and runs continuous, but with several inflexions, to Sunknee, and from thence to Soombro-Teeba, whence it again diverges; but the principal part, taking a north-westerly course, joins at Chumbee-Teeba, and the pass of Kuthagur, with the great range which will soon be spoken of, stretching from Moral-Ke-Kanda, and is thus connected with the snowy mountains.

From this great chine many smaller ranges break off at the different elevated points, ending on the north-west side in the Girree; and from the south-eastern face stretching towards the Pabur and Touse. Thus, to the north-westward, the ridges that compose the petty state of Colegoroo are projected from Kandee; to the southward, those which spring from Toombroo. Then Sirgool runs down by Nagun Quila; after which, advancing to the southward, we find the range of Bulsum; then a projection from Chogut; that above Shai called, I believe, Deothee; the Habun ridge, with those from Buhroge, and the southern face of Choor, on which are Rajeghur, next succeed; but our observations did not extend to the rest.

With these ranges, too, that extend from Choor to the south-eastward, by Hurrepore to the Touse, we were also little acquainted. The Hamultee nullah and valley, on which the village of Suraee is situate (a point fixed by latitude), commences in the Choor mountain; and, joined by that which is the bed of the Shahshalee, or Cheela nullah, from Chogut and its vicinity, runs by the fort of Choupal to the Touse. Somewhat to the northward of Chogut, at a peak called Koongoo, the Gudhala range stretches to the south-east. Fort Choupal is situate on this ridge, and it forms the separation between the Shashalee, or Chulee, and the Cotee nullahs, which meet a few miles further on.

From Koongroo springs another small ridge, which forms one side of the Cotee nullah, called the Bitecouree ridge; and between it and the Gudhala range runs a fine stream, called Sunt,ha,nuddee, which falls into the Cotee almost at the same point where it is joined by the Nar. This last stream arises in the bosom of Urructa, where it gives off the Chuttur-Teeba, which, running in a north-westerly direction, joins at Sunknee, the great ridge in question; thus uniting Urructa and Choor, the two principal points in this part of the country.

A subordinate ridge, on which are situated Matile and the villages of Poonnur, runs also to the southward from Chuttur, and divides the Nar from the Cotee nullah. From Urructa mountain, the Purgattoo and other ranges stretch down to the eastward and southward, ending on the Cotee and Cheela nullahs, and on the Touse. The valley of Deyzah arises from the bosom between Sunknee and Toombroo-Teebas, and runs down in an east-north-easterly direction to the Pabur at Raeengudh; and at this point the range takes its great turn to the north-westward.

On the north-eastern side of this ridge, now recognised as the Chum-bee-ke-D,har, runs the valley of Nawur, which is itself divided from the valley of Sukree and Sambracote by a ridge called the Deouhree-D,har, springing from Kuthagur-teeba pass, at which point one of the branches of the Nawur-nullah arises. To the south-westward the valleys of Silleh and Khuneountee run down to the Girree, from Tombroo and Urshalun. The range continues by Chumbee, sending down one or two inferior ramifications to Whartoo, Bagee, and Kurana; and this portion then ends on the Girree, nearly opposite to Nagun-Quila; but from Whartoo, connected by Nagkanda, it runs by Puntajhurra, Theog, Teekur, Mundapoor, and Deshoo-ke-D,har, in an uninterrupted line, but which we had no further opportunity of tracing, to Irkee and the plains. From the north-western side of this range run down the Comharsein, Kurangooloo, and other valleys: the Seeleedan, Mustgurh, and other ridges, all terminating at the Sutlej; and, further to the southward, the state of Keeounthul on its south-western face.

The immediate range of Whartoo unites a little to the north-westward of Bajee, with a neck projected from Nowagurh-Teeba, another great point on this chain, from which diverge many subordinate ones. Turning to the eastward, and then following a north-eastern direction, by Moonoolgurh and Oogun, it is almost lost at the low pass of Soongree Kanda; by which, however, it keeps up its connexion with, and is joined to, Moral-ke-Kanda, the great turning point of this district, and by it to the snowy range lying along the Sutlej. From this great mass proceed the rivers Coonoo and Nowgurree-Kholas, on the western side, with many subordinate streams that hasten towards the Sutlej; and on the eastern side its waters swell the Pabur, by various drains, of which we are wholly ignorant, above the Sambracote nullah, which rises at Soongree Kanda pass, but is swollen by many sources that originate in that mountain.

Such is a detailed sketch of this portion of the country, which may serve as a specimen of the materials from which the map has been composed. Where it is evidently much filled up with detail, it is unnecessary to continue it in this minute way; and I proceed to give a more cursory view of the remainder.

From Serān, till we reached Cotee on the Jumna, the weather being exceedingly foggy and indistinct, did not admit of very accurate or minute survey; but we occasionally obtained glimpses that gave the means of filling up this portion in some degree; and the whole is corrected by the addition of a few points fixed by a friend, which may, I believe, be much relied on for accuracy. Thus the rivers are brought into their proper places, and the great lines of the country are accurately displayed.

In laying down the course of the Jumna, from Cotee to Jumnotree, along the river, and from thence to Gungotree, and downwards along the Bhagirutee, much attention to the general course of the rivers and principal points of the country, as well as to the minutest circumstances that offered any assistance in pointing out the true positions of places, has been exercised, in order to remedy, as far as possible, the numerous disadvantages I had to contend with in surveying this route, roughly as it was done.

Every one who has attempted to lay down a route knows the inaccuracies that will arise in the use even of a good surveying compass, without the means of further correcting the angles it gives; and a succession of dark foggy days robbed me of the best opportunities I could have had to obtain extensive and distant bearings, that might, by fixing certain points, have given the relative position of others. I feel, however, tolerably confident that the general course of both rivers is laid down with considerable accuracy; and the positions of the great mountains Bunderpooch and Roodroo Himālā, as well as the places of Gungotree and Jumnotree, are nearly, if not correctly right.

On first laying the route down on paper, it appeared that the position of the village of Sookhee, and consequently the whole course of the river, lay too far to the northward; and, upon mature consideration and due examination of the whole route, the error evidently lay in the direction given to the three days' journey from Cursalee, near Jumnotree, across the snowy shoulders of Bunderpooch and Soomeroo Purbut to Sookhee. The whole of this portion of the route was performed in most unfavourable weather; and, in the places where a momentary view of surrounding objects would have been invaluable, the whole was enveloped in the deepest obscurity.

The direction, therefore, was taken from little more grounds than were afforded by constant reference to a pocket compass, which was carried almost always in the hand, with a reference to the general lines of the country, taken from the peaks that now and then appeared for a moment. In constructing the present sketch, the whole of these three days' journey has been laid down in a general course, tending more directly to the eastward than at first; and the proof of the justness of this correction is, that the whole of the positions on the Bhagiruttee fell by the operation into their proper relative places, as is somewhat strongly evinced in the direction of the village of Petara on the Bhagiruttee, near Dhurasoo, from Bongee and Marma Teebas; also the latitude of Barahat, which agrees with that of Messieurs Webb and Raper, and the distance of the positions Cocassoo, Bhalee, and Belee, near the valley of Deyhra Dhoon, from the fixed points of Deyrah, Nagel, Kalunga, &c. &c. Thus I have little doubt that this portion of the map is as nearly correct as is necessary for all common purposes, and more I could not have hoped for.

Beyond the tracts above detailed the route of this journey did not extend, and the rest of the map has been constructed from such information as could be obtained from the various sources that our situation enabled us to command, connected with such portions of the country as had been previously fixed by survey.

Those parts to the eastward of the Bhagiruttee have been laid down from the known routes of Webb and Raper, and the concentered information contained in Mr. Arrowsmith's admirable new map of India. The chief lines, however, are only given, as the object was to describe that part of the country alone on which I am entitled to speak from observation or particular information. The valley of Deyhra Dhoon is given from a variety of observations relative to different points in that place, from which, I believe, a tolerably correct general view is exhibited.

To the north-westward of Nahn, in the vicinity of the plains, as my particular information did not extend far, I was obliged to connect the few points I obtained from the scene of General Ochterlony's campaign, with the known outlines of the hills as they bound with the plains: when there was no information that could be relied on, blanks have been left, and the whole tract from the Punta Jhurra and Theog ridge to Irkee is accordingly in this situation. A large blank also occurs between the river Touse and Choor, even to the banks of the Girree: I possessed much detail of the country from report, but not being able accurately to lay down the positions described, I deemed it better to leave the whole unfilled. To the north-west of the Sutlej I have not ventured on a line, though acquainted with the states that lie in that direction, and even in some degree with their relative positions, as has been seen above: being ignorant of their absolute extent and boundaries, I believed it better to leave them entirely out. All the rest is the result of the desultory and various information above alluded to, fitted, where it could be done, to the known great lines of the country.

The routes will be found more fully detailed below: the difficulty of thus adapting routes, taken down from the verbal communications of unscientific individuals, to a map laid down by rule, must no doubt be sufficiently intelligible to every one; but those who have attempted it can alone estimate its extent.

This difficulty is further enhanced when the route to be described is over rough and unequal ground, as the distance from place to place is of course always much more uncertain in such cases than in level or easy country.

In the present instance the cōs was a most dubious measure; we found that most people exaggerated it, and that a cōs seldom equalled three quarters of a mile; in some few cases we discovered that a ten or twelve cōs journey did not amount to more than four or five English miles, or even less in toilsome or difficult country; and if one-third be taken from this, as a fair quantity to be allowed in the distance gone, for inequality of ground and divergements from the general direction, many of the apparently excessively long distances we hear of between one place and another will be greatly diminished, and dwindle into insignificant spaces. But in laying down the routes to Ludhak, Gara, and Mantullaee, from the words of Puttee Ram, I was induced to give credit for a more true appretiation of distances, as by comparing the length of his stages with spaces of which we knew the extent, he proved his understanding of the subject. It is curious to remark the inconsistencies, however, that appear, even with all his intelligence, in his routes when transferred to paper.

The route to Leh or Ludhak by the river Lee, and the lake Chumorcoul, &c. &c. I should conceive not to be very far wrong in its general direction and distance; because when following up the subsequent part, from Leh to Hymap, and from thence to Cashmere, the position it would give to the latter plain is not very erroneous. Probably, however, if the distance were somewhat shortened, and Leh laid down somewhat more to the southward, it would be nearer the truth. That it cannot be farther westward, is proved by the number of days' journey he has given from thence to Gara (confirmed nearly by Messieurs Moorcroft and Hearsay), which already do not allow to the latter place a sufficiently easterly or southerly position, according to the route of these gentlemen, the only existing authorities on the subject.

The route from Leh to Gara lies perhaps (indeed most likely) somewhat more to the south-eastward of that given in the sketch; and certainly the routes along the Sutlej, and from Suchtote on the Lee to Numroo and Garha, seem to lead farther to this conclusion. I apprehend that some confusion exists in the detail of stages in the last-mentioned routes, and that from Oopshee on the Sing-kechoo to Gara, where they approach the latter place, a stage called Nummoo is found near Gara in each; and though from other discrepancies I have been induced to lay down two places under this name, I have strong suspicions still that they relate to one and the same place, and this would cause a difference in the southerly position of Gara of nearly twenty miles.

But, in fact, the position which this place and the lake Mantullaee or Mansrowar take up, according to the routes given by Puttee Ram, differ so much from that given in Mr. Arrowsmith's new map, and which I believe to be from the information of Messieurs Moorcroft and Hearsay, as to make it evident that one at least, and both, in all probability, are very erroneous.

I am disposed to think that the latter position is as much too far to the south-east, as the former is to the north-west; that the course of the river Danlee, and the route to Gartope, incline far too much that way, and have too short a course. I conceive that the position given in the sketch cannot be wholly in the wrong, because, in the first place, if Leh or Ludhak be placed further to the south-eastward, and it be allowed that the information respecting its distance from the capital of Cashmere in any degree can be relied on, the true space would not be left between the river Sutlej and that valley, so that we must suppose the positions of Ludhak, with reference to Cashmere, to be nearly right.

Secondly, if this be so, and as our information does not induce us to believe that the distance between Leh and Gara is greater than represented in the sketch (Mr. Moorcroft's account agreeing with ours), it appears that the latter place cannot with propriety be placed further to the eastward than has there been done. I believe, indeed, that both places, and the whole course of the Sing-kechoo, have been laid down too far to the northward; and should this conjecture be right, Gara would obtain a more southerly, though scarcely a more easterly position.

As Messieurs Moorcroft and Hearsay travelled without the advantage of instruments that could be relied on, or even the means of knowing with any accuracy the distance they travelled daily, it is no severe reflection on the accuracy or intelligence of these gentlemen to presume that they may have in some degree erred in their idea of the courses they went, and that truth may lie between their account and that we received from Puttee Ram.

Routes, such as these in question, extracted with great labour from a man not accustomed to yield such information, will present numerous inconsistencies, which, at a future period, it is difficult, if not impossible, to reconcile, and that which at the time seemed perfectly plain and intelligible, becomes, upon future reference, totally useless for want of some petty connecting link, which at the time might easily have been obtained, but which afterwards is lost for ever. In the present sketch it has been attempted to reconcile these inconsistencies with the positions that are in some degree known, and no labour has been spared to accomplish the object.

I have laid down each route after passing Serān, according to the result of this exertion of my judgment, strengthened by a recollection of the general impressions I gained from various conversations on the subject.

It is very possible that these conclusions have been erroneous, and therefore I annex a detailed account of the routes in question, that such as choose to attempt the same labour with the belief of a different result, may have the means in their power to do so. And I doubt not but that those who have been in the habit of adapting information of this nature to fixed positions will be able to make valuable corrections. A great change will no doubt take place in the relative positions of places in this map when its scale is corrected, by laying it down in geographical miles, and by reducing the size of the degrees according to rule; and this change will act powerfully in reducing the apparent inconsistencies that now exist: this I have not attempted, as I deemed it better to leave this nicer and more scientific part of the task to those better qualified to do it justice.

The map as here given is projected on a scale of four common miles to an inch, a scale recommended as being more manageable than any other in reducing the work to those most generally in use. Little more remains to be said; the narrative itself affords means to judge, in great measure, of the opportunities and the nature of the materials from which this sketch has been produced; and the above remarks may serve to concentrate these into one view. I now proceed to detail the routes already so frequently alluded to.

Route given by Puttee Ram from Serān, in Bischur, to Gara, along the Course of the Sutlej, by Soongnam, Poee, &c.

STAGES OR JOURNEYS, viz.

From Serān, the first day.—Nine or ten cōs to Chounde; direction north-north-east. First three cōs are on level and tolerably good road, after which one cōs and a half of ascent, one and a half of descent, two and a half level, but bad. One cōs more of descent; half a cōs of level road brings the traveller to Chounde, which is a place about one cōs and a half above the Sutlej, where there are three or four small villages.

From Chounde, the second day.—Ten to eleven cōs to Whangtoo; direction north-north-east. One cōs and a quarter ascent leads to a large village, Trendē, which lies to the eastward above Chounde; two cōs and a half further of descent to the village of Soldung; five level cōs more to Nachar, about two cōs above the river, from which Whangtoo is only two cōs further of descent along the river bank.

The third day's journey is eight cōs to Che-gang; road very bad, course east. The road ascends for one cōs and a half, and descends again for the same space; the rest rises little from the river's bed, but is rocky, dangerous, and painful.

The fourth day.—Seven or eight cōs to Rajalo; direction from east to east-north-east. The whole way along precipices forming the banks of the Sutlej is dangerous and difficult, but without much ascent or descent. Rajalo can hardly be denominated a village; it is a place for grazing sheep, where on the river bank there are a few wretched huts.

The fifth day.—Eight cōs to Cheenee; four first cos ascend to the northward, and the rest are tolerably level, and the road passable to the eastward. Cheenee is a long village of twenty to thirty houses.

The sixth day.—Five to eight cōs to Pangee village, or to Kashung, where the villagers of Pangee keep their sheep; the first being five cōs, the second eight; course about east-north-east. The road has only one cōs of ascent and another of descent, the rest level and practicable enough. The country thus far is described as much resembling that around Serān, except that the wildness and barrenness somewhat increases, and wood diminishes much in quantity.

The seventh day.—Nine cōs to Kannum Labrung; direction east-north-east. First three cōs ascend, next three descend to Lūpēe village; a straight path then leads to Labrung, which is two cōs above the Sutlej: here are two villages together.

The eighth day.—Ten to eleven cōs to Soongnam; direction north-north-east. Five cōs general ascent and descent, and as much of general descent, lead within half a cōs of Soongnam, which is in a dell, on a nullah called Burgeoo, which, joined to another called Ropēs, falls into the Sutlej four cos down the dell. The whole road is described as better than the preceding part, and fit even for the hill ponies. The face of the country is quite sterile, the hills are bare and rocky, and the whole place is surrounded by snowy mountains; but it is nearly quite through the chief range. Cultivation is miserable; but barley, wheat, and ōē or rye, are still seen in small quantities.

The ninth day.—Eight to ten cōs to Hango; nearly north. Four cōs of ascent, four cōs descent, but moderate, and sometimes slanting over a ridge called Hungnung. Hango is in a dell with little water, and is a village of fifteen or sixteen houses; at this point the roads to Ludhak and to Gara diverge. That to Gara is as follows:

The tenth day.—Cōs to Poee or Pooee. Poee is on the right bank of the Lee river, which forms a branch of the Sutlej equal in size to itself, and falls into it at Mamptso, about half a cos below, where there is a fine wooden bridge or sango.

The eleventh day.—Eight cōs to Shipke; direction east. Crossing the Sutlej on the Mamptso sango, the road, very bad and difficult, ascends gradually to Shipke, a village of twelve to thirteen families, situate three or four cōs from and high above the Sutlej, which river, however, is in sight from it.

The twelfth day.—Eight cōs to Kuooch; direction east. The road is a series of various ascents and descents, along a steep precipitous face, very dangerous and painful. The village, which consists of about fifteen Bhotea families, is five cōs from the Sutlej, which is seen from it. The houses are described to be flat-roofed with mud. The scanty crops to consist of barley and rye, and the live stock of a few shawl goats and sheep.

The thirteenth day.—Eight cōs to Blupscha; direction east. The road is similar to that of the last stage, very bad, hilly and rugged; about a cōs above the banks of the Sutlej. Blupscha is merely a resting place for travellers, where there is a sango to cross the river.

The fourteenth day.—Nine cōs to Nooh, in the same direction. Crossing the river at Blupscha, the road ascends high above the river over dangerous and very uneven ground, but keeping its course. The Sutlej is, however, not seen from Nooh. It is a village containing fifteen Bhotea families, with plenty of shawl goats and sheep, but little or no cultivation. Here we lose trace of the river, though, I believe, the road accompanies its course for some space further. I regret that the actual spot when it leaves it is not mentioned, nor can I recollect it.

The fifteenth day.—Eight cōs to Shreerunghut; still east. The road of the same description, difficult, and continually ascending and descending. Shreerunghut is a desert resting place, without village, or any sign of habitation.

The sixteenth day.—Eight cōs to Tang; course north-east. Road similar to the last. Tang is a Bhotea village of four or five families. There is a little barley cultivated here, and sheep and goats continue.

The seventeenth day.—Nine cōs to Rugzhuk; direction north-north-east. The road now begins to improve, and the hills are less rugged, exhibiting more soil, and less stone and rock. The station consists of a few Bhotea families, around which there is a little rye cultivation. They also possess some shawl goats and sheep.

The eighteenth day.—Eight cōs to Shahung; direction east by north to east-north-east. The road is good, and lies along a valley, which is described as being from one to two cos broad, level, and with a stream running through it. It is without wood; but the hills, which are formed of soil, are covered with furze and short grass. The nearest are not high, but lofty ones appear at four to five cōs distance. There is some cultivation of barley and rye about this village, which contains four or five houses.

The nineteenth day.—Seven or eight cōs further to Shakunpoo, in a northerly direction, along the same valley to a resting place at the foot of a hill. There is no village.

The twentieth day.—Eight cōs to Nummooe; direction north. Leaving the valley, the road ascends the high hill of Lahochē for two cōs, descending as many, and then leads along a plain valley for four cōs to the village Numroo, of about four or five Bhotea tents.

From Numroo it appears that there is only one stage to Gara, of about eleven or twelve cōs, but neither the nature of the road nor its direction are distinctly laid down; for the route was first followed from Numroo to Mantullaee by Dookheeoo. It is laid down in a subsequent page.

But the more direct road from Bischur to Gara does not lead along the Sutlej bank from Hango, the ninth stage of the preceding route; it proceeds as the tenth day's journey:—Six cōs to Lee, in a northerly direction, along a left hand hill slope of a hill forming the Lee river's bank, to which, at the end of the march, the road descends for a cōs, and crosses on a good wooden bridge or sango. The village of Lee lies on the left or north bank of the river.

The eleventh day.—Six to eight cōs to Chango, in a northerly direction. The road leads along the left bank of the Lee, sometimes in its very bed, at others a bowshot above it; very rough and stony. The village, consisting of about thirty houses, is about half a cōs above the river.

This village marks the boundaries of the territories of Bischur with those of China. About half a cōs farther above, close on the opposite bank of the river, is situated the fort of Kheolk,hur, or Shealk,hur, on the Chinese confines. A wooden bridge crosses the river at this point.

The twelfth day.—Nine to ten cōs to Suk,hlote, in a northerly direction. The road at first ascends one cos, descends nearly one cos to a wooden bridge, over a nullah called Chaladockpō; after crossing which there is a second steep ascent of two cōs to Changrezung, a small piece of cultivation on the crest of a ridge, without a village; thence the road becomes very difficult indeed along the face of a right-hand precipice, where it has been made with great difficulty; it is necessary in getting horses along to assist them greatly, otherwise they could not pass. Suk,hlote is on a small level piece of land on the left bank of the river Lee, and consists of fourteen or fifteen houses. It belongs to the Chinese territories; and there the roads from Bischur to Ludhak and to Gara separate.

The thirteenth day.—Eight cōs to Soomgecool, along a valley about half a cos broad. Both sides of the stream that runs in it are cultivated with wheat and barley. Soomgecool is a village of thirty houses, possessing many shawl goats and sheep.

The fourteenth day.—Nine cōs to Doondoonche, a resting place uninhabited. The road all the way is easy; and the hills are grassy, and formed of soil, without so much rock as heretofore.

The fifteenth day.—Seven cōs to Lursa; the road similar to the last, good and easy. Lursa is a resting place at the bottom of a hill, but there is no habitation. The word Lursa signifies, indeed, a stage, or resting place; and "Lursa," and "Purle-Lursa," as stages, occur continually in making inquiry respecting routes in this country.

The sixteenth day.—Eight cōs to Purle-Lursa. The road now ascends, and crosses a lofty hill called Bootpoo, which is covered with perpetual snow; but in favourable seasons there is not much inconvenience from this in the road, which is good, and little roughened by rock. The place, like the last stage, is only a resting place.

The seventeenth day.—Seven or eight cōs to Chuckrachurn, which is a place of encampment for twelve or thirteen tents of Bhoteas. It is the residence of a Pumpo, or sort of Rānā, to whom the Bhoteas give that appellation: he is tributary to China, and the name of his small state is Choomruttee. The road during this stage is good and plain, leading among furze and short grass.

The eighteenth day.—Nine cōs to Dooderchun, which is only a resting place. The road gently ascends for six cōs on hills of soil, covered with furze and short grass; then two cōs of gentle descent brings the traveller nearly to the resting place.

The nineteenth day.—Eight to ten cōs to Koorkunchurn, a place belonging to the Choomruttee Pumpo, whose winter residence it is. It consists of fourteen or fifteen mud houses with flat roofs. The road continues the same.

The twentieth day.—Seven cōs to Nekeh; a resting place without habitation. The road, soil, and productions as before.

The twenty-first day.—Nine cōs to Teoorkung; a resting place, with occasionally four or five Bhotea tents. The road perfectly good; might even be travelled in the night.

The twenty-second day.—Ten to eleven cōs to Sheangpo, or Shahungpo, in all probability the same place mentioned in the former route as next to Numroo. The road as before.

The twenty-third day.—Eight cōs to Lahoche; a desert resting place. The road as before.

The twenty-fourth day.—Eight to ten cōs to Temchoong; another resting place. Road similar. The hills low from hence to Gara.

The twenty-fifth day.—Eight cōs probably; the distance not particularly noted. It is obvious that by this route the road falls into the former one at Shahungpo, though the stages thence to Gara are differently named; but these are often far from regular, and depend on the strength or inclination of the traveller, being generally places convenient for resting; and thus a variation might easily take place without involving the presumption that the road was intrinsically different, or the narrator inaccurate. The routes were given at different times, and the result of different journeys (of course) undertaken by the narrator.

The Route from Gara to the Lake of Mantullaee on Mansrowar is thus described:

The first day's journey.—Eight cōs from Gara to Dookheeoo; course south-east, over broken ground, along the skirts of a range of mountains to the right. There are no villages on the way; but about half-way a camp of four or six Bhotea tents, called Geeakheeoo. Many torrents are crossed on the road, running from the right-hand mountains. The country is covered with short grass and furze called Damak.

The second day.—Ten cōs to Jurgoodra, a place of a few tents on the road; course south-east. Road good, but over broken ground, with hills on each hand, but on the left they approach, on the right they recede much.

The third day.—Ten cōs to Munsur, a place of ten or twelve tents; course south-east. Country and the road similar.

The fourth day.—Eight cōs to Dokpo, where there is a nullah with a wooden bridge; the road is more even along a level valley; course south-east.

The fifth day.—Seven to eight cōs to Dokpo (2d), where another nullah runs into the river Gara, and has a wooden bridge over it. Road and course as before.

The sixth day.—Twelve cōs to Dumcheeoo (the Darchur of Moorcroft, in all probability), at the foot of the Cailas Purbut (or mountain); course south-east. The road good in the valley. Here, at the foot of the mountain, there are on a hill four temples of the Lamas, with their entrances to the four cardinal points, and held by the Chinese and Tartars in very great veneration. The Cailas mountain by them is called Gangree, and to walk around it is esteemed as great and proper a religious performance as in old christian times it was to make a pilgrimage to Loretto.

The seventh day.—Ten cōs to Mantullaee, on good plain road in a broad valley; course south-east.

The Routes to Ludhak are as follow:

Taking up the twelfth day's journey from Serān at Suk,hlote, the thirteenth is twelve cōs to Burgeo; general direction north. Crossing the Lee at Suk,hlote, on a wooden bridge opposite the village, the road passes through the village of Chooreet, consisting of from thirteen to sixteen houses, and ascends a broad ridge for two cos, after which are two cōs of level road, and one cos further ascent; from thence it descends slanting to Burgeo. This is a fort of mud, with towers and loopholes, built on a level spot on the Burgeo nullah, and garrisoned by the armed inhabitants, who are Bhoteas.

The fourteenth day.—Nine cōs to Ukte; general course west. For three cōs the road proceeds along the bed of the Burgeo nullah, crossing and recrossing it frequently; after which, leaving it on the left-hand, there is a steep ascent up a hill-face half a cōs on a level though rugged path, and then a descent of a similar space in the bed of a small rivulet, over the bank of which there is a second ascent of about a cōs, with a similar descent; at the end of which a little level ground brings the road to the bank of the Lee river again, which is here crossed by a ford. The river has now assumed the name of Pārā. A steep ascent of half a cōs, and a similar descent, leads the traveller to Ukte or Ukche, a village containing five houses. Thence two roads diverge, but both lead to the same points: one for the summer months directly over a high mountain, the other calculated for the winter season, proceeds round its base.

The fifteenth day.—Eight cōs to Seelah; direction west (the summer road). A gentle ascent for two cōs, one cōs more level; at the end of which descend very sharply for half a cōs, and cross a little rivulet, from which there is a steep and dangerous ascent of three cōs to the top of the Seel mountain, whence you descend equally into the Seela dell, where there is pasture and firewood, and water for the use of travellers, but no habitation.

The sixteenth day.—Seven or eight cōs to Sirpoogma, where the summer and winter roads meet; direction always west. Proceeding down the Seelah nullah for half a cōs the road crosses it, and ascends a left-hand hill-face, leaving the nullah to the right; where, turning the crest of the ridge, it descends very gradually a left-hand slope on good road for three cōs, which brings it again on the Pārā nullah, along the banks of which, for three cōs or three and a half, it proceeds dangerous and difficult, sometimes dipping into its stream, sometimes on the face of a precipice. Sirpoogma is merely a resting-place for travellers on the banks of the Pārā, without any habitation in the vicinity.

The seventeenth day.—Seven or eight cōs to Choonnur; direction about the same. The roads along the left bank of the Pārā are good and even; on each side of the stream there is level land cultivated with rye to the breadth of one or one and a half bow-shots. The stream is strong, and reaches to the middle, but is fordable every where. Choonnur is a village of only four or five houses, where an officer lives with the title of goba; he is a Bhotea, named Patkun. The houses are said to be constructed of unbaked bricks, with flat roofs formed of wood and earth. The wood, which is of the Chiloona tree, is brought from Burgeoo. Two roads separate from this point.

The eighteenth day.—Nine cōs to Choormurcreel; direction west. Leaving the Pārā far to the left, the road proceeds along a fine plain, without stones or rocks. The hills on both sides keep asunder at a distance of four or five cōs, forming a fine valley, in which the Pārā runs; on the right-hand of the road they are about one cōs and a half distant; on the left, a good deal farther off. When our informant passed this way in the month of June last, both ridges had snow on them. Within about two cōs of Choormurcreel there is a gentle ascent over a low earthy hill, whence descending in an equally gentle manner, you reach the resting-place. Choormurcreel itself is a large piece of water or lake, from twelve to thirteen cōs in length, and five to six in breadth. The water is brackish and bad; it is completely frozen over in winter time, but in summer the climate around it is said to be very fine. It is open, without reeds; the borders consisting of fine grass, without any swampiness or muddiness; it has both fish and water fowl in plenty. About a cōs from the resting-place is situated Korzog, a house of the Choonnur goba's.

After this stage we hear no more of the Pārā river, which was left far on the left-hand, on which side also, it seems, by inference, that the lake is left (though this is not distinctly stated). As the right-hand hills are represented as all along coming pretty close, and the only place on the lake noticed at all is on the left, the Pārā river, being fresh-water, does not probably rise in the lake, but most likely has its origin in the streams that flow from the snow-capt mountains on the left (or southern) hand; among which, probably, also the lake retreats, and from whence it draws its supplies.

The nineteenth day.—Ten cōs to Chucksung; same direction. The road is good, and proceeds over level soil among low scanty grass. Low hills are seen on both sides to the right about a cōs distant, on the left-hand from two to three distant. They are not rocky, but of red soil covered with thin grass, but there is no wood or jungle; their tops are even, without peaks or precipices. In summer the Bhoteas bring sheep, goats, and sooragoees (or yāks), to pasture: they have none of the common cattle. There are no habitations to be seen. Chucksung itself is a place of five or six Bhotea tents.

The twentieth day.—Eight cōs to Puloogonga, a resting-place, desert; course west. Two cōs of gentle ascent, and six of very gentle descent, on a right-hand slope, along a nullah with little water, which is distant from half a cōs to a cōs to the left. To the right are gently rising hills, over which horses could easily ride. Puloogonga is situated on an elevated piece of table land, where there is a small temple with many little flags.

The twenty-first day.—Eight cōs to Thoggie Chunmo; same course. Descending gently from the height of Puloogonga for about a cōs, the road is good and equal, proceeding along a valley about two cōs broad: it is sandy and grassy. On the left-hand side the hills are very lofty, but there was no snow on them in the month of June preceding that in which the route was taken down. Those on the right-hand are low, formed of very red soil, so that the scanty grass is scarcely seen. There is no wood, nor do rocks or stones prevail. Thoggee Chunmo is a spot where there are five or six Bhotea tents with their flocks, but no cultivation. There is here also a salt-water lake, two cōs long, and about a gunshot broad.

The twenty-second day.—Twelve to fourteen cōs to Lursa Thuglung; course nearly the same. The road plain and good, lies along a valley from half a cōs to a cōs broad, of good black soil. The hills on either hand are of moderate height; the soil of which they are composed, as well as the rocks, are red, and far from rugged; described as fit to be traversed in all directions by horses. There is no water to be found in all this march; but snow or ice is to be had to supply its place in a deep dell about a cōs from Lursa, which is a desert place on the hill Thuglung; Lursa signifying merely a stage or resting-place in the Bhotea language.

The twenty-third day.—Six cōs to Purlehursa, or nine to Geeah; direction to both places west. One cōs and a half of zig-zag easy ascent, with as much of descent, after which two cōs along a narrow pass, with a stream of sweet water, which runs towards Leh; then three cōs on to Geeah along the same dell. Geeah is a large village of thirty houses on the left-hand bank of the nullah: opposite is the fort of Geeah, in which in times of trouble the people place their families and valuables. The nullah here is narrow, knee deep only, but easily swollen in the rains; the valley not more than a bowshot across, bounded by pretty high hills of the usual red soil.

The twenty-fourth day.—Eight cōs to Meeroo, along the same valley, crossing and recrossing the stream to favour the road. Meeroo is a village of fifteen or sixteen houses, where there is an old fort. Both here and at Geeah once resided two petty independent chieftains, called, in the language of the country, "Chō," but they have both been reduced by the Ludhak Gealbō, or Rajah, and the country absorbed into his dominions.

The twenty-fifth day.—Eight cōs to Heemea. After proceeding three cōs along the same valley to the debouche of its stream into the Sing-kechoo, the road turns to the left (say south-west) five or six cōs to Heemea, which is at the junction of the Thuglung nullah with the Sing-kechoo. The village of Oopsehee is a little further on the left side of both. The road is good to Oopsehee. The river runs in a valley, said here however to be no more than two bowshots across, but highly cultivated with wheat, barley, and rye, watered from canals raised from the river. The hills on each side are lofty, and continue their red colour.

The twenty-sixth day.—Nine cōs to Sheh. At Heemea cross the Sing-kechoo on a wooden bridge, and proceed along the right bank of the river through rich cultivation, with thickly strown villages, and planted with chiloona-trees, which border the road: the valley gradually widens to Sheh, where it is from three to four cōs broad. Of the villages on the same side, as Heemea (the left bank), Chunga is one cōs further on, Tungna three cōs, Cooshat one cōs more. From Sheh, the capital, Leh, Leo, or Le, is but three cōs and a half distant. The royal residence is about two cōs from the river. The country around is thickly inhabited, and well cultivated.

From hence the following are a few of the stages towards Cashmere.

Peerang.—Three p,hurs, or about nine hours' journey, which, on a good road, for an unloaded man should not be less than twenty to twenty-five miles; but let it be only fifteen, as distance is generally exaggerated: along the Sing-kechoo river or valley of Leh, two cōs broad, along fine cultivation, and by many villages; direction south-west.

Busgee, a fort of Ludhak, nearly a whole day's journey along the same valley, on good and even road, say eighteen miles; direction more westerly, south-west by west. There are apricots found on this road.

Hymap.—Along the same river for fifteen cōs, or a day's journey. Road continuing the same, but in one or two places stony. The valley from one cōs to one and a half broad, all cultivation, and containing a great number of Bhotea villages. Hence the capital of Cashmere is only four days' journey distant; but our informant not having gone by this route, we could not learn any thing further. If we can believe that any degree of confidence is due to the above routes, and the calculations, the capital of Cashmere will then appear not more than from 120 to 130 miles from Ludhak: perhaps too small a distance, though this position is far nearer the truth than that hitherto assigned to it in the maps of this country.

The following are the stages of the route from Stampore, the capital of Cooloo, to Leh of Ludhak; but there are no descriptions given of the face of the country, the respective length of the stages, or the direction.

1. From Stampore to Koonour.
2. — — Lursa.
3. — — Purle Lursa, thus far in Cooloo.
4. — — Koorjour, hence Ludhak.

5. From Stampore to Runglee.
6. — — Kuckcoomb.
7. — — Lursa.
8. — — Purle Lursa.
9. — — Choormurcreel, hence as laid down in the route from Serān by Sucktote.

The route laid down from Leh to Gara is as follows. It is retraced to, and commenced at, Oopshee, the village at the junction of the Thuglung nullah with the river Sing-kechoo. The general direction is described as easterly; but we have no precise information regarding it.

From Oopshee, 1st day, 6 to 7 cōs to Shuras Sango. 2d day.
— 3d — 6 to 8 — Likehe.
— 4th — 9 — Teereedō.
— 5th — 10 — Choomatang.
— 6th — 8 — Mayhé.
— 7th — 9 to 10 — Neelima Fort (to Ludhak).
— 8th — 6 — Rongah.
— 9th — 10 — Kugzeeoong.
— 10th — 10 — Olōk.
— 11th — 7 — Donzog, thus far in Ludhak.
— 12th — 8 — Tuzhzheegong (a Chinese fort).
— 13th — 6 to 7 — Bunmongoo.
— 14th — 13 — Gungoonza.
— 15th — 8 to 10 — Numroo.
— 16th — 12 — Gara, or Gartope.

From Oopshee to Tuzhzhagong the road lies entirely along the banks of the Sing-kechoo; the valley desert and uninhabited, except by those who live at the villages laid down as stages, and one or two other intermediate ones. Heemea, a small village, lies between Likehe and Teeredo; another, Geaee, half-way between Teereedo and Gireh: Keemaming and Kissen lie between Gireh and Choomatung. There are no trees. The soil is dark, and covered with short grass. So far as Choomatung the valley is narrow, and wild, and rugged; from these to Mayhé it opens out, and continues to Tuzhzhagong the whole way about a cōs broad.

Neelimah contains from twenty to thirty houses. Two cōs beyond it lies a large village, Moon, of fifty families. Rongah is a poor village of four houses; Kugzheeong only a resting-place; Dimzog consists of only three houses. They are all inhabited by the Bhotea subjects of Ludhak.

Tuzhzhagong is a fortified village, built of stones and mud, in which two Chinese officers reside, denominated "Debahs," who regulate all public affairs, dispense justice, collect the revenue, and watch over the interests of the state. There may be twenty or thirty houses within the walls. The inhabitants are soldiers, and form the garrison; they have about forty matchlocks. The fort is built on a little plain about a quarter of a cōs from the river, and two streams meet half a cōs below it forming the Sing,ke,Choo. One, under the same name, comes from the hills in the vicinity of Mantullaee, the other also rises in the same vicinity, a little beyond Gara (where we have above already traced it), and under the name of the Eekungchoo passes by that place, and joins the Sing-kechoo at this point.

The road continues along the Eekungchoo in a valley of the same breadth, passing only a few Bhotea tents with their flocks, to Beenmongo and Gurgoonza; the first of which is only a resting-place; the latter is said to be a winter residence of the Debah of Gara, who has a considerable number of tents and servants here.

The valley remains the same in breadth and appearance from these places to Numroo, which is described as only an encampment of four or five Bhotea tents, whence, however, it widens as it approaches Gara to a breadth of four or five cōs.

It certainly does appear probable that the direction of the river and road are in reality a good deal diverted from the easterly and westerly line given them in the route, which would bring the position of Gara into a lower latitude than that given in the sketch; but if a great liberty is taken in this way we shall be constrained to diminish the distance allowed the route first given along the Sutlej to Gara; or, by lengthening the course to the eastward, also to lengthen the space between Ludhak and Gara and the course of the Sing-kechoo, and this, I apprehend, will lead into another dilemma, as it would induce us to consider Cashmere, the distance between which and Ludhak has been spoken of before, further eastward than can be consistent with truth.

Our anxiety to procure information, such as should throw a degree of light on the very obscure geography of this country, brought to our observation a great many routes leading in various directions through the remoter parts of the mountains; but all, except those above given, came before us in so imperfect a state, as to the great points of distance and direction, that they do not admit of being laid down here, far less in the sketch that accompanies these pages. Such are the routes above adverted to, along the J,hannevie to Chownsah, and from thence to Chaprung by Teeling to Gara;—the desert route from Serān, and the remote parts of Bischur, to Buddrenāt by the Neeteemana pass;—from Bhurassoo to the Chinese districts beyond the Snowy Crest;—from Gungotree to Kedār and Buddreenāth along the range of snow;—the road along the Goomtee Gunga by the Nehel mountains to the banks of the Sutlej;—that from the Bhagiruttee along the Sheangadh across the Dhumd,har ridge to Bhurassoo, and various other similar ones. It was intended to lay all these down as accurately as the nature of the information would admit, but its vagueness rendered it impossible. Few would have at all agreed with the better known lines of the country, and any guide to a true direction was in others wholly wanting.

That by the Ghoomtee Gunga over the Nehel hills must be totally through deserts of rock and snow, as the spot at which it is said to emerge on the Sutlej is as barren and inhospitable as its debouche on the Bhagiruttee.

It would have been desirable to give some description of the various passes known to occur, and to be in use as routes of commercial intercourse, through Gurwhal and Kumaoon to Bootan through the great range; but our information is not precise enough to state more than their number and general character for practicability. Dharma and Joar, the two that are situate in Kumaoon, have already been adverted to: they are a good deal used in traffic, but are less practicable than the more northerly passes in Gurwhal. Guree Nittee and Nitteemana are the two chiefly in use. They are open six months in the year; and by these much of the merchandize from Bootan is brought. Passing the vicinity of Buddreenauth, there is a path that leads directly into the Kumaoon territory, through which the merchants proceed to Kasheepoor in Rohilcund, the great mart for the hill produce. The Lama, Nittee, and Bhirgeo passes are only open for two months, and are little used. The first is said to lead from Rewaeen purgunnah; but I am ignorant of its true position, as well as of that of Bhirgeo.

CHAPTER XX.

GEOLOGICAL REMARKS, IN A CONDENSED VIEW OF THE CONTENTS OF THE NARRATIVE, RELATIVE TO THE FORMATION OF THE HILLS.

It may tend to give clearness to the subject, if we bring under one view, in a condensed shape, all that is scattered through the narrative, and collected in every way, relating to the structure of this great range, and the appearances of its formation and stratification, from the plains to the greatest depth to which we penetrated. Much valuable knowledge cannot be expected from the observations of an unscientific individual; but, given as they are, with much attention to truth, and to avoid giving as facts whatever may have in any degree been the result of supposition or surmise, it is possible that something interesting may be found, even in these communications.

It is known that the mountainous country proceeding from the roots of the great Himālā range is, for a great part of its extent to the south-east, divided from the great plain of Hindostan, through which the Ganges rolls, by a strip of country called the Terraee, or Terreeāna, which is even lower than the greatest portion of that plain, and is chiefly covered with thick forests and low swamps, and is little cultivated, comparatively speaking, for its extent; but, when subjected to tillage, is very fertile. It however lies under the imputation, very deservedly, of being very unwholesome. This strip of land, however, does not extend to the north-west further than through a portion of Rohilcund, where the healthy and cultivable parts reach to the foot of the hills; and this is the case with that part which forms the subject under attention.

The line of the mountainous tract, as it bounds with the plains, is nearly from south-east to north-west; and the low hills forming the boundary of the Deyrah-Dhoon, and the roots of the more lofty ones, rise abruptly from the sandy flat that stretches at their feet, without any undulation of ground whatever: their aspect is rocky and brown, though they are found tolerably clothed with wood; a mixture of the productions of the low country, with a few of those that affect a loftier situation. Their south-western and southern aspects are steep and broken; while that of their backs, to the north-east, exhibits an easy slope, covered with much wood in most places, but green where wood does not extend. These hills rise to a height of from 400 to 750 feet; and the range separating the Dhoon from the plains may extend from three to six miles in depth. They seem to be formed of sand-stone, more or less destructible, of indurated clay, and beds of rounded pebbles and gravel. Their aspect, viewed from a height, is singular, and much reminds one of a wave of the sea, which has rolled by, showing here and there its broken crest, half turned backwards. Beyond these first low hills others rise more lofty and majestic, and are found of various heights, from 1500 feet to 5000. They are very sharp, rough, and run into numerous ridges, divided by deep shaggy dells; and the crests of the ridges are frequently so sharp, that two persons can hardly stand abreast upon them.

Such seems their character, so far as we could judge from the different points at which we saw them, from Hurdwar up to the Sutlej; and the cause of the very sharp ridgy appearance, which marks these hills, may probably be found in the nature of the rock of which they are composed. This seems chiefly to consist of a strongly indurated clay, with a large mixture of siliceous matter, which forms a rock exceedingly hard; but, upon exposure to the air, very destructible, soon splitting into variously sized fragments, which also very soon moulder into dust. The fracture of this rock is generally in straight lines, but preserving no regularity of form: its colour varies from brown to dark grey; and it is at times probably much tinged with iron. This class of hills has no sensible disconnexion with those more remote, that rise to a still greater height: although the materials of their composition differ entirely from them, they seem to form a continuation of those beyond, which fall into them, without any break or divisions into ranges.

It has before been observed, in the remarks on the great lines of the country, that the appearance which the hills present from the plains, of being divided into many distinct ranges, rising one above another, is quite fallacious: thus the alteration which is observed in the nature of the materials that composed them, is not marked by any alteration of country, and is only accompanied with a change in the appearance of the hill, referable to the material.

An accidental coincidence, however, sometimes gives a more distinct demarcation than usual; and such is in great measure the case where we penetrated the hills at Nahn. The small river Jelāll runs there just behind this range of ridgy hills; and on the other side immediately arises a mass of hills, entirely composed of lime-stone. This vein of lime-stone certainly extends a long way nearly parallel (or perhaps cutting the hilly range in a direction more nearly east and west) with the plains: and, though the mass of hills in question, known as the Sine or Sein range, ends at the junction of the rivers Jelāll and Girree, yet we found a continuance of it, evidently connected, on the banks of the Pabur and Touse, and even across the Jumna, to the Bhagiruttee; and though we had no opportunity of determining from our own observation, we may presume that it extends up towards the Sutlej; for the Sine range can be seen, keeping the same appearance and character, for a long way to the north-westward.

Their round, lumpy, rugged character, cut into strange shapeless heaps, has been adverted to before, and owes its origin entirely to the nature of the rock, the destructible parts being worn away, and the hard marbly masses staring through the scanty soil, dark and stubborn. The height of this range, at the highest points, may be from 5 to 7000 feet.

Of this range, as well as that last spoken of, it should be remarked, that the south and south-eastern aspects were invariably brown and bare; while on the opposite exposures, to the north and north-west, they were always more green, and generally covered with more extensive and more luxuriant woods.

Crossing the range of lime-stone in a northerly direction, we descend to the bed of the river Girree: and here is also a very marked line of division, between the termination of the lime and the commencement of schistus, or slate; the former stretching down to the very brink of the river, and forming its southern bank; while the northern is entirely composed of schistus, which also approaches the river. When the Girree deflects from the lime, it here pursues and joins the Jumna; the line of demarcation ceases; and the two species of rock are mingled together, as may be remarked in the course of the narrative, in the beds of the Pabur, Touse, &c. &c.

The whole of the great and most irregular mass of mountainous country, from this line to the more immediate roots of the snowy mountains, is composed, with little variation, of different schistose rocks, pervaded with much mica, and exhibiting every variety of colour and texture, mingled with veins of quartz, but in which the latter forms but a small comparative ingredient. Various other rocks occur, but they seem rather exceptions, and very trifling ones, to the general rule. Adventitious heterogeneous substances unaccountably come there, rather than component parts, which should claim consideration in the reasonings that suggest themselves, from the nature of the country and from its formation.

Some are found in the beds of rivers, evidently brought from more remote and higher regions by the torrents of spring; others are insulated specimens, far more difficult to account for; but some may bear, and even call for, a more particular consideration, from their situation and the circumstances they are found in: such are the masses of harder stone, and probably granite, found on the tops of the high mountain Choor, and in the beds of the torrents that proceed from it.

The sand-stone, and sandy plum-pudding stone, on the heights of Urructa and Nowagurh, were evidently masses that had at all times formed constituent parts of the mountain; and their situation, and the uniform height at which they were found, seem to point them out as leading marks, in forming any theory regarding the country.

After crossing the Nowgurree Khōla, we could not but consider ourselves as among the true Himālā or snowy mountains; and, in rising among them, it was to be expected that the component parts of the hills should alter, or at least that a variety of rock should be found; and this was the case. As we increased our elevation, though schistus at first predominated, and was generally to be found, the peaks and crests of the ridges consisted of that variously coloured semi-transparent stone described on our journey to Serān from Rampore, to which I am unable to give a name: probably a chief ingredient in its composition was quartz; but it was mixed with other substances, so that the quartz had lost its tendency to show crystallisation, or to break in regular figures: it owed its various colours, perhaps in great measure, to iron in different shapes. The specimens were unfortunately lost, with many other things, during the journey.

The lofty spires and masses of the snowy range, and of their ridges, were in all probability formed of a different rock from any we had seen in quantity; and although, from subsequent observations, it was to be presumed that the principal portion was granite, still the obvious stratification that existed in some places, among others in the peaks about Serān, would, as I have been informed, militate strongly against this supposition, granite not in general assuming a stratified form. At this place the snowy peaks were not more than from two to two miles and a half horizontal distance from us. We had good glasses, and thus were enabled to make pretty accurate observations respecting them. The lines of stratification were particularly obvious on the steep perpendicular faces of many, especially those pointing to the south-west; and that distinction which was obvious throughout the whole hills, between the north-western and western exposures, and those to the south and south-eastward, was finely confirmed here, as will be more distinctly stated hereafter.

Where the rock is perpendicular the snow cannot of course lie; and even on faces not so precipitous, it slides down as the lower portions melt, thus giving to view a large portion of the more elevated cliffs. The rock then was black in colour, occasionally veined with red and yellow. It was remarkably sharp, and its fracture seemed to preserve this character: at times it spires up into slender peaks, of most fantastic forms; and even in these we could detect the stratification and direction of the strata. For some thousand feet below their top all vegetation ceased, and there did not appear to be any soil: at the foot of each cliff were spread the ruins that had fallen from it, mouldering as weather and time acted on them, strewing the mountain side (where it was not covered with snow) with various sized fragments.

At Jumnotree, as will be seen in the subsequent pages, we were still more absolutely among, and in contact with, the grand snowy mountains: for, as the Jumna has its rise in the great mountain known generally by the name of Jumnotree, and as this source is at a great height, as it were, in the bowels of the mountain, so we were enveloped in its substance, with the disadvantage of being too completely under the principal peaks, which, however, are so steep, and so much overhang the whole very steep mountain, that we could discern them overtopping us; and we were surrounded by their ruins, carried down by the avalanches that hang on their brows, till the melting of the lower snows or a mountain storm sends them down to the valleys.

Our journey up the bed of the Jumna, from near Kalsee, confirmed the truth of our observations relating to the lower mountains; and, when we reached its source, the similar nature of the rocks with these we saw, and those near Serān, the other point, when we nearly approached their summits, in great measure strengthened those we had there made.

In the following pages a detailed account is given of the nature of the rocks found at this elevated station; but it is perhaps as well to state them shortly in this general view.

Two sorts greatly predominate. The first is a hard, grey, striated stone, first observed in the bed of the river Pabur, very irregular in its fracture, composed apparently of quartz, mica, a black substance (either hornblende or schorl), with much gritty matter, all strongly cemented by a grey substance, and forming a grey striated mass. This was very abundant; and I have since understood it to be gneiss. The second kind is a pure laminated white quartz rock, from the interstices of the laminæ of which trickled the hot water which springs from the mountain side at Jumnotree. Besides these, we saw micaceous schist of all colours and varieties of consistence; red, blue, grey, white, soft, and hard, found in abundance: and there are several other sorts of stone found in the bed of the torrent, which I cannot particularise, and which are only found in small masses.

In all the masses forming the banks of the river, whether consisting of the hard striated stone, the quartz rock, or of schistus, a regular stratification is most obvious; and, whether the peaks of Jumnotree themselves consist of these substances, or of granite of a different nature, they evince also the same complete stratification.

The closest and most attentive observation of these peaks gave us reason to believe that their materials were much the same as those by which we were surrounded, or chiefly composed of gneiss, or of some sort of granite and quartz. The veins and strata of the latter were particularly distinguishable by their whiteness; and the dark colour of the general mass was broken by lines and veins of red and yellow, sometimes in strata, sometimes in irregular spots. And the tremendously deep precipices that pointed to the north-west and westward, gave us an excellent opportunity of examining the appearances which they assume. There were many rounded dark masses of rock that did not evince marks of this stratification, and are possibly lumps of granite: they were on the southern aspect of the mountain, and to this position perhaps owe their entire roundness.

Our road from Jumnotree to Gangotree, over a shoulder of Bundurpouch and Soomeroo Purbut, gave us another, and even a nearer and more intimate view of the loftiest ridges: at the Ghăt of Bamsooroo, indeed, we were once high in the region of continual snow; and certainly might consider the ruins around us as having been constituent parts of the peaks that spired above us. Our journey included about thirty miles of country, all very much elevated; but, with few exceptions, the soil and rock exhibited much of the same phænomena which the lower country had presented: in some parts there was much white and dark sandstone, together with occasional lumps of sorts not usually met with, like whin-stone, and a hard blueish-grey stone, of which I know not the name or nature.

At Bamsooroo Ghăt we found almost exactly the same sort of rocks as we had remarked in the bed of the Jumna, at the source. The gneiss, or striated, hard, grey stone, predominated greatly. There was much soft micaceous schist, veined with quartz. There were several varieties of the blueish-grey stone; and some was much harder than others.

Our observation of the more elevated faces of rock gave precisely the same result as at Jumnotree: the stratification, its direction, and dip, were the same; and red, white, yellow, and blue veins and spots on the rock were equally remarkable: that of the white was more particularly in strata; while every thing gave us the fairest reason to conclude that the peaks themselves were composed entirely and invariably of the same substances as their ruins that surrounded us. The colours that variegated their surface must have their origin in the natural colour of the stone, perhaps acted on somewhat by the vicissitudes of weather; for there is no vegetation with which to cover them, not even lichens, or mosses: this ceases at a very considerable space below. At this dreary pass there is nothing but barrenness and desolation.

While descending into the glen of the Bhagiruttee we again encountered the staple and customary rock schistus; but the banks of this river, even at the point, when we descended, evince very obviously their difference of substance from what we had been so much accustomed to. Here all appearance of stratification ceases; the rocks take irregular shapes, and spire into more lofty and fantastic pinnacles the further we advanced up the bed, and we soon found that the whole of the glen, as well as the stupendous surrounding precipices, were formed of a hard stone, generally white, pervaded with mica, and black bars and marks in various proportions, and of as various colours; in short, a true granite.

This usurped the place of all other stone, for many miles round Gangotree and below it: the country around that holy place was composed of this stone alone. It evidently is the sole component substance of the neighbouring stupendous mountains: it never affects stratification, but, in fracture and formation of every kind, exhibits nothing but amorphous and irregular masses. It shoots up into crags and spires, the sharpness and boldness of which amaze; but all seems the effect of chance, and the ruggedness of the material, and by no means arising from any particular disposition of the stone to assume such shapes; for there are many other instances of as round and bold a nature.

This being the extent of our journey into those mountains, there is no further observation to offer concerning them. Our journey down the Bhagireettee, and across the mountains inclosing the valley of Deyrah Dhoon, presented to our observation the same appearances of country and formation as our journey into the hills, and gives fair reason to conclude, that the same succession of soil and rock extends to the south-eastward, and perhaps for a long way among these hills. Schistus certainly predominates. Lime occurs only in veins, and near the termination of schistus, perhaps here and there irregularly throughout the country. The high ridges and crests of this great range are probably of granite, while quartz is every where to be found; and varieties in small quantities occur, but not in such masses as to hold any proportion to the chief staples here mentioned, and rather seem to appear as if to puzzle those who are attached to particular theories in geology. Iron and lead are very common throughout the country; copper exists in Gurwhāl, perhaps also in other parts; and it is far from improbable, that other metals might be discovered, were attention and encouragement given to the pursuit.

A few words may be said of the great lines of the country; and on the observations made on the stratification of the rocks; and on the difference between the faces of the mountains which have different aspects.

The general direction of the range of hills has been before mentioned; from the banks of the Burramputra nearly to Kumaaoon they have a course from south-south-east to north-north-west; but, beyond that point, they tend more to the westward, and run nearly from south-east to north-west. It will be seen, in adverting to the course of the rivers, that all the passages that lead through these hills, or even that penetrate far into their recesses, which are of course the beds of rivers, have a course varying from east and west to north-east and south-west. In many instances, after having passed through the loftiest portion of the ranges, they are deflected at some stubborn bluff point, to a course nearly at right angles, and issue from the hills with a direction more to the eastward than westward. It appears not unlikely, that this universal tendency of the hills to give way in a direction to the south-west and west has some reference to their formation, and is derived from the same cause that so universally points the perpendicular and sharp cliffs to the north-west, west, and even south-west.

This most remarkable phænomenon of formation, so often taken notice of, was among the first that forced itself on our observation; and it became only more distinct the further we penetrated into the mountains. It was combined with as remarkable a difference in the appearance of the exposures to the southward and northward. The former being invariably the least wooded, the least precipitous, and most brown and lumpy. No particular cause appeared for this, unless a greater exposure to sun be accounted sufficient to produce so great a difference. The south side is as plenteously watered as the north, but the vigour of the foliage is far inferior, and the trees it produces are quite different: the destructibility of the rock on the northern exposure is remarkably more rapid, and the formation of soil is plentiful, and every ravine, and even the steepest precipices, are covered with noble forests; while, on the southward, the rock is blackened with years and exposure, denuded of soil by the heavy rains, and is far from soon supplying the waste of soil occasioned by them; so that, where it is untilled, the soil becomes hard and parched, with the russet colour that marks the southern faces of the mountains. The pointing of the precipices, and direction of the peaks to the north-west and south-westward, and even to the northward, was particularly striking in all the great arms of Choor, and the ridges that spread from that mountain; in the great mountain of Urructa; in the Nowagurh and Whartoo ranges, even up to Moral-Ke-Kanda; and, finally, in all and every part of the snowy hills which fell under our observation. The whole glen of the Sutlej illustrated this beautifully, as well as the difference of colour between the southern and northern exposures; while the line of the river served to show the line of their penetrability.

At Serān, where the peaks and highest ridges were near us, we had an opportunity of viewing this effect, in some degree interrupted by the passage of a great stream, the rupture for which may be supposed to have discomposed the natural arrangement. Here were many sharp faces turned to the southward; but, though situated to the south-eastward of those of which we had the clearest view, we could distinguish many of them rearing their more threatening and important precipitous faces to the north-west and west. Our passage to the Jumna, and along its bed, showed no exception to the general rule; and as we viewed the cliffs of Bunder Pouch and its branches with the hills around, it appeared on a grander scale, and was more magnificently illustrated. In the higher parts of the Bhagirutte alone did this otherwise universal tendency seem to fail. The mountains here seemed to have a greater inclination to spire up in straight uncontrolled and perpendicular forms, as if despising the rules that confined the lesser hills, and asserting their independence. No general direction, no stratification was visible. The stubborn masses of granite seemed unsusceptible of either, and stood fixed and barren, crowned with unmelting snows in stern sublimity.

It remains only to speak of the stratification in general, which, in fact, is but a repetition of what has already been said.

It is difficult to determine with accuracy and truth the direction of strata in any large mass; and it would certainly be quite absurd to attempt to name a direction for the strata of a mountainous and an extensive country. Probably an able geologist might detect a regular stratification in the greatest part of these hilly districts. The schistose rocks certainly bore marks of it frequently, yet not distinctly enough to ascertain the dip and general direction. The limestone in like manner certainly exhibited strong symptoms of stratification, the edges of the strata often projecting from the hill-side; but no probable opinion could be formed of dip, or direction, each varying as the face of the hill changed aspect, or degree of slope.

The first distinct stratification was seen in the loftiest peaks of rock in the snowy ridge at Serān. The numerous perpendicular faces within the range of our observation of glasses, pointing in various directions, gave us an excellent opportunity of judging of the direction of the strata, and the angle they formed with the plane of the horizon; at an angle of somewhat less than 45 degrees, and from the south-west to the north-east, that is to say, their elevated end pointing to the south-west, and, however sharp and small the spire, this was still observed to hold good.

At the source of the Jumna again this was strikingly distinct in the lofty peaks around. The angle of the dip and direction were as nearly as possible the same, and this strongly marked stratified formation pervaded every rock within our view, and particularly the precipices forming the river's bank. And it was curious to observe the quartz rock, from whence the hot water trickled, always in lamina, which had a different direction to that of the strata, but through which the stratification was distinctly seen, dividing the rock and giving it a tendency to the south-west.

We again had a beautiful view of this stratified formation in the rocky faces in our immediate neighbourhood at Bamsooroo ghāt, on the way to Gungotree; but at the latter place, as has been said, all appearances of that nature cease, and do not re-appear till we reach about three days' journey down the Bhagiruttee, where stratification is again detected, chiefly in schistose rock, and may be traced in every rocky face till we reach the point a good deal further down, when the mountains become less rugged, and their structure less obvious.

ON THE HEIGHT OF THE HIMĀLĀ.

It is impossible to take leave of the Himālāyan mountains, and conclude the observations that arise in considering their various claims on curiosity, without adverting, however insufficiently, to that very interesting object of inquiry, their altitude, though my total want of scientific skill, as well as of sufficient data upon which to found an opinion, might render the omission pardonable. Indeed, under these circumstances it may appear so presumptuous to attempt any discussion of the subject, that I will only venture to notice and consider the opinions that have been entertained by others, with the ground on which they have rested; and add the few conclusions that have forced themselves on my mind from a comparison of these with my own observations. The latter will, I trust, be received with indulgence, as they are given with great diffidence, even in the power I possess to apply the principles on which others have founded their conclusions; and, proceeding from a sincere wish to promote by every means the solution of this interesting problem, they court criticism and correction.

Mr. Colebrooke, late President of the Asiatic Society, in his Memoir "On the Height of the Himālā Mountains," contained in the twelfth volume of the Asiatic Researches, gives a list of the measurements of a number of peaks in different parts of the range, estimated from data there set forth; but chiefly from the observations of Captain Webb of the Bengal establishment, who has of late been employed on a survey of the province of Kumaoon. This paper has attracted much notice, and particularly from two distinguished quarters. The celebrated and scientific traveller Mr. Humboldt has written and published a short memoir on the subject; and it has fallen under the critical observation of the Quarterly Reviewers, in their Review of the twelfth volume of the Asiatic Researches in their thirty-fourth number. Mr. Humboldt's paper rather presents to observation the general difficulties, that occur in ascertaining with precision the exact height of lofty and inaccessible mountains, than impugning the accuracy of Captain Webb's measurements; and then enters into a short comparative view of the two great American and Asiatic chains of mountains, the Andes and the Himālā.

He adds a short but comprehensive sketch of the general scheme and direction of the chief ranges of Asiatic mountains, commencing from what he considers the great central mass, or diverging point, according to the present received geography of this huge system, with a detail of the table lands which these form and include. The Quarterly Review takes a more decided part. The reviewer challenges the sufficiency and accuracy of Mr. Colebrooke's and Mr. Webb's data; suggests on various grounds strong doubts as to the truth of the conclusions they deduce; and concludes with declaring his opinion, that the Himālāyan mountains, so far from proving to be *more* lofty than the Andes, will on proper investigation be found to fall far short in height of the great American range.

I mean not to be guilty of the presumption of entering the lists against opponents so incomparably superior, unable as I must profess myself to appreciate the objections they offer to Captain Webb's calculations, which seem chiefly to rest (after the obvious chance of error, from the smallness of the angles of altitude and observation) on the probability of a very great error in the estimate of refraction, and which, if well founded, would reduce the height of the loftiest observed peaks of the range to less than 20,000 feet of altitude above the level of the sea.

Mr. Webb, however, who has ever since continued in that country pursuing his observations with fairer opportunities and better instruments, to ascertain the elevations of the mountains, having seen both Mr. Humboldt's memoir and the critique in the Quarterly Review, forwarded to the Asiatic Society a paper containing a few observations on these works, and some of his more accurate admeasurements of the snowy peaks, being a ground-work and prospectus of a more detailed and elaborate memoir, which he is now preparing for the Society, and which will appear in due time in their fourteenth volume.

In this he freely agrees with the reviewer, acknowledging the insufficiency of the data on which the heights of Jumnotree and Dhawlagirree were first calculated, and the very easy possibility of a great error creeping into the results from an erroneous assumption of the distance and amount of refraction; but he cannot, he says, give his unqualified assent to the supposition of the reviewer, "that one-third of the intercepted arc may perhaps be insufficient to allow for the refraction of a ray of light passing through every degree of heat, from 0° of Fahrenheit to 80° probably and upwards." And he suggests the probability that this refraction may be much varied by the different degrees of heat through which the ray passes, and at different seasons of the year to an observer in the plains. Captain Webb further observes, that one-eighth of the intercepted arc is the allowance he has always made for refraction, whether in calculating the height of the snowy peaks themselves, or in deducing from them the altitude of the station of observation; and that, in about twenty stations at very unequal distances from the Himālā, the heights of which have been calculated both geometrically and barometrically, he found the agreement between the results very satisfactory, while the difference that did occur between these results did not seem to increase or decrease in any ratio analogous to the distance of the station from the Himālā, which he conceives would have been the case had the allowance of one-eighth for refraction been very erroneous.

He next adverts to the limit inferred by the reviewers, as that of perpetual congelation on the Himālā, in this parallel of latitude, which is fixed at a point *below* 11,000 feet above the sea. In protesting against this limit he annexes a list of places, the heights of which are deduced from barometrical observation; and, though the particulars of the calculations are not given in his paper, it is mentioned that five good barometers were employed; consequently their claims to accuracy, under the conduct of a scientific man, have surely some force; and these reach from 10,653 to 11,682 feet above the level of Calcutta.

Near the temple of Milum, elevated 11,405 feet, there were large fields of oe, or rye, and buckwheat; and, from a station 1500 feet higher, or at an elevation of about 13,000 feet, he procured some plants of spikenard (iatamassi). On the 21st day of June, Captain Webb's camp was 11,680 feet above Calcutta. The surface was covered with very rich vegetation as high as the knee; very extensive beds of strawberries in full flower; and plenty of currant-bushes in blossom all around, in a clear spot of rich black mould soil, surrounded by a noble forest of pine, oak, and rhododendra. On the 22d of June he reached the top of Pilgoenta-Churhaee, (or ascent,) 12,642 feet above Calcutta. He was prevented from distinguishing very distant objects by a dense fog around him; but there was not the smallest patch of snow near him, and the surface, a fat black mould through which the rock peeped, was covered with strawberry plants (not yet in flower), butter-cups, dandelion, and a profusion of other flowers. The shoulders of the hill above him, about 450 feet more elevated, were covered with the same to the top; and about 500 feet below was a forest of pine, rhododendron, and birch. There was some snow seen below in deep hollows, but it dissolves in the course of the season. He was informed by the goatherds that they carried their flocks to pasture in July and August, to a ridge to the eastward, rising above Pilgoenta as far as it does above the site of his camp of the 21st of June, or at least 13,000 feet above Calcutta. But of this, Captain Webb purposed to have ocular demonstration.

These facts lead Captain Webb to infer, that the inferior limit of perpetual congelation on the Himālā mountains is *beyond* 13,500 feet, at least, above the level of Calcutta: and that the level of the table land of Tartary, immediately bordering on the Himālā, is very far elevated beyond 8000 feet, the height at which it is estimated by the reviewer.

Of this detail of facts, given thus publicly by a scientific man of character and known accuracy, who thus, in some measure, stakes his credit on them, there can be no reason, *à priori*, to doubt the correctness: and though, in applying them to the observations made in my own journey, I may not be able, either to make all the deductions which they will afford, or to shun any errors that they may involve, they will still, I think, yield some ground of inference to estimate the height to which I ascended; and consequently give some approximation to the heights of the surrounding peaks.

On the night of the 16th July we slept at Bheemkeudar, near the source of the Coonoo and Bheem streams. There is no wood near this place, even in the very bottom of the valley, and we had left even the stunted birch at a considerable distance below; but there was a profusion of flowers, ferns, thistles, &c. and luxuriant pasturage. Captain Webb's limit of wood is at least as high as 12,000 to 12,300 feet. I would, therefore, presume the site of Bheemkeudar to be considerably above that level; say 13,000 to 13,300 feet above the level of Calcutta. From thence we ascended at first rather gradually, and then very rapidly, till we left all luxuriant vegetation, and entered the region of striped and scattered and partially melting snow, (for nearly two miles of the perambulator.) From calculating the distance passed, and adverting to the elevation we had attained, I would presume that this was at least 1500 feet above Bheemkeudar, or from 14,500 to 15,000 feet above Calcutta.

We proceeded onwards, ascending very rapidly, while vegetation decreased gradually to a mere green moss, with here and there a few snow-flowers starting through it; snow fast increasing, till at length we entered on what I presume was the perennial and unmelting snow, entirely beyond the line of vegetation, where the rock was bare even of lichens: and in this we ascended, as I think, about 800 feet; for, though Bamsooroo Ghāt may not be so far above this line, we continued ascending, even after crossing that point, and I would incline to estimate this utmost extent of ascent at 2000 feet more, or nearly 17,000 feet above the level of Calcutta.

Whilst proposing to consider the point of 16,000 to 16,500 feet as that of inferior congelation, I must observe, that there was no feeling of *frost* in the air, and the snow was moist, though hard, chiefly through the influence of a thick mist, which, in fact, amounted to a very small drizzling rain, which fell around: all which would seem to indicate, that the true line of congelation had not there been attained; but we were surrounded by snow which evidently never melted. To a great depth below it extended all over the hills, very little broken, while, on the valleys from whence the Coonoo and Bheem streams issue, at full 2000 feet below, it lay covering them and the surrounding mountains, in an unbroken mass many hundred feet thick. Thus, though it may seem contradictory, the line of perpetual congelation, in fact, seems fixable at even below the point I have ventured to indicate; and, I presume, might, on these grounds, be placed somewhere between 15 and 16,000 feet above the level of Calcutta.

I am aware of the boldness of this proposition; nor can I support it against the objections that will be urged by those who deem it worthy of notice, except the plain statement of the facts above given. I know that it may be objected, that at an elevation of 17,000 feet, the air would be so rarified as to lose the power of distending the lungs; that this was the experience of those who ascended Mont Blanc and Chimboraço, and the remarkable law which the reviewer adverts to, of the incapacity of the air, beyond a certain height, to sustain clouds at all; with the further improbability, that those clouds, above the point of perpetual congelation, should descend in any other shape than that of snow; all form very strong presumptions against my conclusion: and it appears a very interesting subject of inquiry, to examine whether there may not be some operating causes in the position of these mountains, or some peculiar circumstances which affect them, that tend to raise the level of perpetual congelation on them beyond the limits of experience hitherto; and with this effect, to render the circumambient atmosphere capable of supporting vapour in the shape of water, and of inflating the lungs of animals so as to preserve life at the presumed great altitude.

The changes which the wisest are, by experience, continually forced to make in their theories of the different branches of science, and consequently in their practice; the numerous and striking exceptions that are met with, even to those rules which seem laid down on the firmest principles; the extraordinary and important discoveries that daily occur, and the total insufficiency of all human acuteness and genius to detect and follow the apparent caprices of nature, which seem to scorn the labours of the philosopher; all seem to warn him from forming hasty conclusions against the existence of apparent but extraordinary facts, merely because they do not consist with past experience. Such phenomena should rather stimulate to investigation, by the hope and prospect of new discoveries; and, while a worthy and proper caution should set him on his guard against the delusions of specious appearances and beautiful theories, he should be equally careful to dismiss scepticism and prejudice from his mind, and examine with perfect impartiality the evidence that may be brought before him.

In bringing under one view the facts and observations above detailed, I am not aware of being prejudiced in any way; I neither feel anxious to establish the height of the Himālā at the lofty level to which these mountains have hitherto laid claim, nor to depress them to a lower elevation than that of the Andes: but I do feel desirous to know the truth; and, in the spirit of this wish, have ventured to offer these hints in addition to the stock of better information which has been collected on the subject by those who are so much more fitted for the task. If they excite criticism they will answer a good end; for by such discussion error is dispelled, and truth is brought to light.

The present pursuits of Captains Webb and Hodgson give so much valuable opportunity for observation on these points, that we may hope, in no long time, for most satisfactory results from them: and the industry and acuteness of these gentlemen, however great it may naturally be, cannot fail of being stimulated to a higher degree of accuracy by the interest which the subject has created, and by the rigid criticism it elicits at this period from the public in general, and men of science in particular.

When placed on the most elevated positions, it was natural, in looking round me, to attempt an estimate of the height at which the loftiest peaks in the neighbourhood were elevated above me. The noble pyramid of Soomeroo Purbut (Purbut signifies a large mountain), and the huge back and lumpy top of the eastern summit of Bunderpooch (or Jumnotree of Webb and Colebrooke), were those of the greatest consequence which I nearly approached. The cave where we had slept was at the mouth of the snowy valley, at the bottom of the latter; and a little way to the eastward lay that which proceeds from Soomeroo Purbut, but which, by our progress to the heights on which we stood, had been brought between ourselves and Bunderpooch. The top of this mountain could not, I conceive, have been more than two miles and a half of direct distance from us, at the largest calculation. Nor was that of Soomeroo more than one mile; and I do not think that the elevation of these peaks above our station could have exceeded 4000 feet; that of Bunderpooch was certainly the greatest. Every one knows the extreme vagueness and liability to error in judging of the heights and distances of mountains merely by the eye; yet it seems impossible that these peaks could have been so much loftier than they appeared, as 7, 8, or 9000 feet above our station, instead of 4000. Yet, admitting that we had attained an elevation of 17,000 feet, a matter itself of considerable uncertainty, Jumnotree must have been nearly 9000 feet raised above us, to give the elevation which has been attributed to it by Mr. Colebrooke. The ghāt by which we descended from the heights which we had reached was even more precipitous than that of our ascent, and therefore better calculated to exhibit the gradations and zones of climate, and permit us to appreciate their relative elevations. From the point where this precipitous descent commenced (and which was considerably below that of our utmost ascent, though not below that which I presume to call the limit of perpetual congelation), to the very first appearance of stunted wood, was a distance of exactly two miles. As the descent was as rapid and precipitous as any I ever saw (and by no means very tortuous), so much so, that in looking back, the face of the hill had almost the appearance of a wall, I believe it will not be too much to assume, that the whole elevation was equal to one-third of the distance gone, or about 3500 feet. This, added to Captain Webb's limit of the woody zone, gives an elevation of about 15,800 feet.

The exposure of this descent was easterly, and the snow did not descend quite so low here as on the north-western face; but the opposite side of the Bhagiruttee, seen from the top of this ghāt, exhibited a mass of snowy mountains most imposingly grand, that irresistibly impressed the beholder with the idea of a far greater altitude than that to which the mountains he was placed among aspired. The peak of Sreekanta, in particular, reared itself far above all surrounding ones, and no doubt far surpasses Jumnotree.

In our farther progress we had no good opportunity or ground of judging of the elevation of the surrounding mountains; but since that period Captain Hodgson has fixed the height of the place whence the Bhagiruttee first issues from the snow (in the valley which lies between the fine peaks described in this narrative) at 12,194 feet above the level of the sea, by barometrical measurement: and a huge lofty peak, which he calls St. George, and which I presume to be the same which the Pundit calls "Roodroo Himālā," is estimated (I believe, by trigonometrical measurement and calculation from the above point) at 22,240 feet above the sea.

The result of all the considerations that arise out of the foregoing remarks is a belief, that the loftiest peaks of the Himālā range will be found to fall considerably short of the height attributed to them by Mr. Colebrooke, but that they will likewise be found in general to rise above the limit which the Quarterly Reviewer seems inclined to assign, and considerably beyond the height of the Andes.

There seems no doubt that the portion of this range, about the centre of its length, or from the river Bhagiruttee to the valley of Nepāl, includes the loftiest peaks, and that both to the north-westward and south-eastward the mountains decline in height.

The height of Dhawlagirree, which is the loftiest peak that has fallen under observation, is, by Mr. Colebrooke, calculated at 26,862 feet above the level of the sea; that of Jumnotree at 25,500. Captain Webb has only affixed numbers to the measurements he has lately made public (and which are referred to both by Mr. Humboldt and the Quarterly Review), which present the possibility of comparing them with the formerly calculated altitudes: but as none of these latter reach the height at first attributed to Dhawlagirree (all being included between the extremes of 18,000 and 25,600 feet), it seems probable that the more correct results indicate altitudes somewhat short of those calculated from former data.

If the foregoing observations are well founded, the altitude of Jumnotree, according to Mr. Colebrooke, must be overrated at least 4000 feet; and as Captain Hodgson has only attributed 22,240 feet of altitude to the peak of "St. George" (which it seems probable is the same hill as Roodroo Himālā, and Mahadeo Kalinga), from better data than any former calculation could have been founded on, and as this peak was I think (for I have not the means of reference to the original paper), rated above 25,000 feet; this seems also to have been overrated.

We may perhaps be permitted to infer a similar excess in the calculation of Dhawlagirree, and thus it will appear very probable that, to approximate to an accurate estimate, a general reduction must be adopted in the height now attributed to the Himālā range.

From the valuable and interesting labours of the above named gentlemen, Captain Webb and Hodgson, we may at no distant period hope for a near approximation to the truth; and till then there seems little danger of falling into a great error in believing, that the loftiest peaks of the Himālā mountains range from 18,000 to 22 or 23,000 feet above the level of the sea.

The speculative idea just hinted by Mr. Humboldt, of the possibility that loftier ridges may yet exist beyond that now recognised as the Himālāyan range, does not seem to be strengthened or supported by the information gleaned from the natives or travellers. All these assert that the ridge which we saw, and of which the peaks that reared themselves so high were the elevated points, was, in fact, the crest of the mountainous country; and that behind it the mountains declined in height. This information is borne out by the description which various travellers give of the country they have traversed behind this ridge. Though we hear of snowy hills, we do not learn that they consist of such impassable deserts as those of the Himālā: they are generally only tipped or streaked with snow, or it is represented as melting in June or July. Even the Cailās mountains, near Mansrowar lake, are not spoken of as vying in height with the Himālā, nor are those near the lake Choonur-creel represented as nearly so lofty: indeed, beyond the Sutlej, they are constantly described as of inferior height to those about Gungotree, Buddreenauth, and Kumaoon.

The information of Messieurs Moorcroft and Hearsay, and the description they give of the country through which they travelled, seems further to strengthen the opinion that the country and mountains in general decline as it tends to the north-east and east. We hear of no stupendous mountains like Jumnotree or Mahadeo-ka-Linga, Dhawlagirree or Dharbun. We are told, indeed, of snow-topt mountains of Cailās, a branch of the Himālā, but without any comment on its vastness. After all, our knowledge of the whole subject is yet in its infancy, and it will not, I think, be matter of great astonishment if future discoveries shall in a great degree alter and new model the incipient and uncertain ideas we have yet been able to acquire of the country immediately behind the Himālā range.

ON THE PEOPLE CALLED BHOTEAS.

The word Bootān, or the country of the Bhoteas, as well as the appellation Bhotea, is used in a very indefinite manner by all the inhabitants of the hills, even by those best informed; and instead of being applied to the circumscribed country which we know as Bootān, it signifies, generally, all the country lying behind the crest of the Himālā that professes the Lama faith. Not only those who are directly under the Chinese government, but those of the petty hill rajahs who exercise their own authority, either independently or as feudatories to China, are known by the sweeping term Bhoteas. The manners and customs of these people have never been accurately or even tolerably known, far less described. And in so extensive a tract of country it is reasonable to suppose that they vary materially, although the great common tie of religion must give a general tone of similarity to a considerable portion of their habits.

The following particulars are taken from persons who had frequented the country much, and were familiar with a large portion of it under every facility for observation, though, of course, without much to direct or sharpen it, further than as the natural curiosity of man directs his attention to what is new and strange to him.

The great Lama at L,hassa is the deity they adore, and the priests of their religion are termed Lamas, and are distributed in abundance about the country: they are distinguished into two classes, those who marry, and those who make a vow of celibacy. They make a study of the books that contain the principles and tenets of the Lama faith. They perform the ceremonies of marriage, and bury the dead; and, it appears, are regarded, as the priesthood is in all countries, with much reverence.

Marriages seem here, as in many other places, more contracts of convenience, and matters of mere bargain and sale, than the result of a preference founded on affection or esteem. The fathers of the parties propose and conclude the bargain. He who has a marriageable daughter to dispose of, goes and seeks for a husband of his own choice, and, having found him, agrees with his father for the match, and gives a sum of money, according to his means, to bind the contract. After a time, which seems to have no particular limit, and perhaps has reference to the age of the parties, as well as to circumstances, the father of the boy, with the bridegroom himself, and from ten to twenty friends, according to an invitation which comes from the father of the lady, proceed to her house, and stay a night, when the ceremony is performed by the Lamas. This visit never exceeds one night, on the morning after which, the bridegroom and party carrying the bride, her father, and a party of his friends, double in number of those who were entertained at his house, proceed to the house of the bridegroom, and there also remain one night only, and leave the couple to themselves. They return alone, after eight or ten days, to her father's house for a short time, and then remove entirely to her husband's house. No women accompany the bride to the house of her husband, except one as an attendant; but the women of the village are entertained as well as the men, and all the expense falls on the bridegroom, as do the expenses of feeding and travelling from one house to the other of the whole party. We could not obtain any description of the marriage ceremony itself. Marriages take place at all ages after twelve, and generally between that and twenty.

If a man lose his wife, it is expected that he will continue three years a widower; and the external sign of deep mourning is said to be turning his cap, and wearing it inside out for eight days. The corresponding sign on the part of a widow is, to take off her head-dress for the same time, but they never burn themselves with the body of their husband. Upon the decease of an individual the Lamas are called in, and they do not quit the body till it is interred. The bodies of the better sort are kept for three or four days, during which time the priests and friends are feasted in the house.

The women of the vicinity meet and utter loud lamentations, in which, however, they are not joined by the men, except by those who are really much affected. The body is not washed, but wrapped up in cloth, rich and costly in proportion to the means of the family, and is carried to the grave or to the funeral pile by the nearest relations.

The women follow with their lamentations to a certain distance, but not to the grave. Over the body the priests read or repeat some form of prayer, but we could not ascertain the nature of it, and the body is buried or burnt with a little grain and ghee. The grave is made, and the whole ceremony is as expensive as the means of the party will allow; and the Lamas, who remain to the last, are feasted, and receive presents in the same proportion.

On their return from the ceremony, grain, ghee, and salt are distributed to all the people of the village by poor men; with the rich this donation extends much farther. On the eighth day after death, the priests are again collected and receive presents; but on the third year the greatest expense is incurred in gifts and offerings. A small monument is erected either over the grave, or in any other place, to the memory of the dead, on which they make offerings of ghee, &c. and light up lamps on particular days.

The Bhoteas, like other Paharias, are very superstitious. Each hill, cave, mountain, or inaccessible place; each gloomy dangerous spot is tenanted, in their belief, by spirits and beings of supernatural orders. Every village has its particular demon, to whom they pay a respect wrung from them by fear. Spirits, ghosts, and other bugbears, are as commonly dreaded as in the most superstitious countries.

The moral character of these people must partake of the uncivilized, and, indeed, savage nature of their country and political situation; yet, in some respects, if we may trust reports, it is not exceptionable, it is even amiable. They are courteous and hospitable to strangers; liberal and honest in their dealings. The oath or promise of a Bhotea is said to be perfectly secure: they confirm them by joining hands, or by swearing on the religious book of the Lamas, or placing an image of their idols on the head. Robbery, theft, or any of the atrocious crimes, are said to be unknown among these people. The traveller and his property are quite safe while travelling through the Bhotea divisions of Bischur, and the countries inhabited by that people in general, particularly within the limits and under the jurisdiction of the Chinese empire.

Intestine discord, or serious disputes ending in murder, or the usual effects of revenge, are very rare. Quarrels and litigation are usually settled by the arbitration of men appointed by the parties, or whose character gives them a sort of claim to such a distinction, and are generally the elders and chief men of villages. When such arbitration fails of effect, or is regretted by either party, the case is referred to the prince or governor of the province or district (who have various designations in their respective countries), before whom the trial by ordeal is performed, for which several means are used. A small copper coin is thrown into a pan of boiling oil, out of which he who professes to clear his innocence or right must take it with his naked hand; or he must, unhurt, hold a red hot ball of iron in the palm of his hand; or, each party taking a goat, gives poison to the animals, and that which survives denotes the owner's innocence, or gains his cause. The wuzzeers, or ministers of the chief, settle all minor causes, and from them there is always an appeal to the superior.

Like the people of the southern hills, their notions of female delicacy and virtue are loose and disgusting. Polygamy is permitted; promiscuous intercourse is by no means disgraceful to either party; the female is not considered as less eligible on account of her frailty. The debauching of a woman is either held as nothing, or is only punishable by a small fine. She may marry her betrayer, but he is not obliged to marry her. The offspring is the property of the mother. Adultery is punished by the husband, who administers a severe beating to his offending spouse; but he seldom puts her away. Should the woman die in consequence of the beating, no punishment is inflicted on the husband. A severe beating is administered to the adulterer by order of the headman of the village, and he is moreover obliged to pay a fine to the injured party. Chastity is indeed little regarded, and very little practised. The disgusting custom of a community of wives between brothers, five or six cohabiting with one woman, obtains here, as well as among the countries we have seen in the hills.

We made inquiries to ascertain whether some of the unfortunate and distressing customs practised in Hindostan were also in use here; such as that of selling their female infants, as in Gurwhal and Bischur, or putting them to death, as among the Rajpoots; but they strongly denied these practices, and said, that no one sold his daughter, but that when indigent they received money for them in marriage. The children receive a name three or four months after their birth, which ceremony is performed by the Lamas, who receive presents on the occasion.

Women are in no degree constrained or confined, as in many parts of the East: they work hard at all the laborious duties, domestic and agricultural, but do not plough. The plough is drawn by a mixed breed of cattle, produced between the small hill cow and the Thibet bull or yak, called in the hills goorabyl. These cattle, and those of the yak breed, with ponies, mules, and asses, sheep and goats, are accounted their best riches, next to corn, and the means of procuring it. Wheat and barley are the grains most esteemed, and in the more hilly parts are very valuable, as the country is chiefly pastoral. Sheep and goats, asses, cows, yaks, and ponies, are all used in carriage.

The Bhoteas eat all manner of flesh; they kill and feed on the yak and cows, but in the district belonging to Bischur, the rajah (a Hindoo), once put a man to death for killing one of these animals, since which the practice in that part has been discontinued. Of the milk of these cattle they make much use: they make ghee, or clarified butter, and afterwards boil the residue to separate the whey from the cheese, which is pressed and kept.

Tea is much used; it is their best refreshment; and before commencing, as well as after completing a fatiguing journey, they regale on it. Although they have a kind of spirituous liquor, and several substitutes for this stimulus, tea is used in preference by all who can afford it, and to as great an extent as their means will allow. They mix it with ghee, salt, and milk, using no sugar. Salt, they say, makes it give out its flavour, and I believe they often eat leaves and all made thick together. We had some made up this way, but whether it was the original bad quality of the tea, or the other ingredients and cookery, the composition was by no means good.

The tea comes from China, made up in small square packets, sewed up in skins as hard and solid as a brick, and of course the tea (generally black), compressed into a hard solid mass, which must be broken down to pieces before it can be used.

They do not allow that they eat horse-flesh, nor even in time of famine do they readily kill mules, asses, or ponies, though no obloquy follow the eating such food; no loss of cast, or expulsion from society. They are said not to use the milk of their mares or asses.

The dress of the Bhoteas may be partly conceived from the sketch which is given of two seen at Gungotree—actual portraits. A long loose gown of woollen, loose woollen trowsers gathered together tight below the knee, and those who can afford it wear a sort of boot, and a cap on the head; the cap indeed is the national dress. They particularly affect red clothes, and their gown or dress is often seen of a faded crimson. Their houses are formed of bricks baked in the sun, with flat roofs. Pitched roofs of slate or shingles are not used; and, in fact, a considerable portion of the population live in tents, being a pastoral people, often changing abode. Those who can afford it use cooking utensils of brass and copper, but wooden and earthen platters are most common.

From the two Bhoteas mentioned above, whom I met at the village of Dhuralee, near Gungotree, I gathered a few curious particulars, which are given distinctly from those which have been better described, and more satisfactorily attested. They probably relate to different and insulated parts of the country, and may be correct so far, if not generally so.

These men were natives of a Bhotea village in the Chinese dominions, called Chounsah, in the district of Chaprung; which village they reported as being a month's journey from Gungotree, over a very difficult road, going through or over the snowy mountains, among the snowy peaks of which two days are passed. But I suspect that the distance which they travel daily is so small that the place cannot be very distant.

They assert that they continue for ten days going up the J,hanneire alone; but their journey is alluded to above. They describe their village as a very poor place; they aver that they throw their dead into the river near it. Those who can afford it partly burn the body, and then throw it in.

At Chaprung, which is described as a large populous place, a month's journey from their village, when any man of property dies it is customary to treat his corpse in a way that sounds exceedingly savage and unfeeling to our civilized ears: they take the body and bruise it to pieces, bones and all, and form it into balls, which they give to a very large sort of kites, who devour them. These birds are sacred, kept by the Lamas, and fed by them, or by people appointed for the purpose, who alone approach them: others dare not go near them, perhaps from superstitious motives, for they are held in great fear. This is a ceremony which is very productive to the priesthood; an expenditure of very large sums (many thousand rupees, said our informants), being made on the decease of any great man, and the Lamas receiving presents of very fine and expensive caps. Poorer people are sometimes buried, and at others thrown into the river.

They, as well as others, assert, that in marriage the bridegroom buys the bride at a great expense, as proportioned to his means; the father of the bride only furnishing ornaments, &c. They assure us that the Lamas do not attend marriages, nor perform any ceremony at such contracts, as even the sight of a woman is forbidden to them, far more any communion of such a nature; and they denied that any great expense was made among the Lamas at marriages.

All this is probably a mistake, perhaps resulting from misunderstanding, or bad interpretation of their language, or it must apply only to a very limited district, as that which relates to the Lama priests must evidently be false. They declare that marriages are contracted at all ages from that of childhood to manhood, but that they do not carry away their wives till they are fifteen or sixteen years of age. They speak very highly of the reverence and confidence they repose in their priests, and the solid proofs they give of such sentiments; and indeed they may well fear to offend them. Those who do not make the meet offerings of ghee, corn, &c. are punished, it is said, by a spell or enchantment thrown over them, which they call the great *Munter* (a Shanscrit word for some sort of magical spell or work); this makes the culprit quiet enough, for it is said to render him immoveable in whatever position he is caught by it, and to become, as they phrase it, like stone or earth; nor is he released until it is deemed probable that he may become more tractable, or he is left to die so.

They give the same account of the dispensation of justice as above, adding, that the *lex talionis* is in great repute, so that every man is punished in the same way in which he offended another. He that slew with a sword is put to death by the sword, and so forth. In some instances the criminal is tied to four different places by the hands and feet, and branded to death by iron and brass instruments. A thief is branded on the forehead with a red hot iron; his goods are forfeited to the state, and he is banished from the country.

PART VII.

JOURNEY WITH THE POLITICAL AGENT, CONTINUED FROM RAMPORE, IN THE STATE OF BISCHUR, TO THE RIVER JUMNA.

CHAPTER XXI.

June 15.—We left Rampore at half past six A. M. and climbed up the precipice that overhangs the town by winding paths among its ledges, till we reached the Ghoorkha post of Ood,ha, built at its top to awe the town, which it quite overlooked. From hence was a long ascent among brown and barren hills, according with the general face of the country as far as we could distinguish it, forming the glen of the Sutlej. The whole comprises a most singular collection of arid, brown, and scathed precipices, unmarked by the slightest attempt at cultivation. The snowy hills again came in view on all sides of us, opening to the east-north-east, where the Sutlej finds its passage through them.

Having ascended somewhat higher, we again came to traces of cultivation, and soon passed several villages situated in agreeable groves of fruit trees and horse chesnuts, and enjoyed some fine ripe apricots. Grape-vines covered with small fruit, but very luxuriant, climbed up the trees in great abundance. We left this more pleasing region, however, and continued our ascent up a very steep and lofty hill, which was strewed with fragments of rock of various sorts. In addition to the usual schistose and micaceous rock, we discovered blocks, which I believe to be a species of granite, gray with many black spots, and some mica interspersed among it; and we observed a considerable quantity of that stone which has so strong a resemblance to marble. Our ascent was slow and deliberate, and it was noon before we reached the summit, which is crowned by a Ghoorkha fort, well stockaded, called Shikaree-killah. The interior is fitted up in a manner somewhat more comfortable than usual for the accommodation of the garrison, which, to the amount of 100 men, was stationed here. It is lofty and commanding. We held an eastern course from hence, and from the neck of the peak on which the fort is situated, looked down on the upper part of Nowgurree Khola, which here opens out into several very savage chasms, some of them falling directly from the snow behind Moral-ke-Kanda. It is strange that in the lower part of the basin thus formed there are many fine villages and much rich cultivation, cradled, as it were, in the ruins of nature.

We now passed under the brow of lofty peaks that seem formed of that marble-like stone which has before been mentioned, but which here assumes various appearances and colours: it is semi-transparent, of a compact texture, and it varies from white to dark blueish-gray, light gray, green, and yellow. Its fracture is bright but irregular, and it is pervaded by a number of brilliant sandy particles. I have now no idea that it is calcareous, and if any that we have seen be so, it must be different from this. The abrupt broken face of the cliff, as usual, pointed to the north-west.

At this place we passed through endless tracts of the finest scarlet strawberries in full ripeness, large and finely flavoured, which proved a pleasant refreshment. A various path descending, first through rough forest scenery, and at last through fine cultivation, brought us again towards the bed of the Sutlej; but we retained a great height above its stream, and saw ourselves wholly surrounded with the magnificent masses of the snowy mountains, which gave a most impressive character of desolation to the scene.

A further winding road led us to Busāle, the situation of our encampment for the night, twelve miles and a half from Rampore. It is unnecessary to recapitulate the changes we remarked in the rock this day: as we declined from the great height we had attained, we found the old sorts re-appear. The village is situated in a sort of more level recess in the hills, very finely cultivated, and very beautiful; it forms a strong contrast to the bare brown hills that rise abruptly from the other side of the Sutlej. Nearly opposite to this spot, the Kindrār nullah comes down from the snowy peaks, forming the boundary on the north side the Sutlej, between the states of Cooloo and Bischur; beyond this point both sides of the Sutlej are included in the latter country. From hence the horizontal distance to Serān is inconsiderable, but a deep nullah forms a difficult and laborious obstacle in the road by which we were forced to go.

June 16.—We recommenced our march at ten o'clock, and passed through a wooded country on a made road for about a mile to this dell, which is narrow, and deep at the mouth, but widens above into a considerable hollow, in which there are several villages. The road continues, all the way to the bottom of the valley, rough, but artificially constructed. At the village of Muscoulee, a considerable and prosperous looking place, near the foot of the descent, we observed a very large crop of apricots gathered in, and exposed upon broad paved terraces to dry in the sun; the pulp for winter stores, the stones for oil.

There is a very precipitous descent into the bed of the stream from this place; and we found the air most oppressively hot, while the reflection of the sun from the rocks around us was overpowering. We remarked that the earthen bank, under which we were sitting, was saturated and incrusted with a species of salt, which exhibited to the taste a mixture of the saltness of borax and the cool alkaline taste of nitre: it possessed also a considerable degree of austerity, and somewhat of a corrosive nature, like white vitriol: at the time, I believed it to be a mixture of borax and alum. The specimens which I took with me were unfortunately lost. It seemed to be in considerable abundance.

We left the bed of the nullah (which is an impetuous mountain torrent, evidently supplied by snow water), and slowly and painfully ascended the opposite hill, which was extremely steep, and the heat excessive. A various ascent along ledges of rock, and sometimes through apricot groves, that refreshed us with their grateful fruit, brought us at length to the height of the ridge; and, turning sharply to the north-east, and passing through some thriving villages, we came in sight of Serān, the second place, forming the rajah's residence in Bischur. The situation was pleasant, in a fine cultivated recess among the hills, surrounded with villages; but it hardly assumes the appearance of a town, the rajah's palace forming not only the most prominent, but almost the only cluster of houses. Our tent was placed near the palace, under the shade of some trees, in a field of corn which had been reaped. Serān is deeply retired within the snowy mountains: it is considerably elevated above the immediate channel of the Sutlej, the descent to which may be from two to three miles. It thus enjoys a moderate climate, and is raised above that region of extreme barrenness, which marks the lower portion of the Sutlej glen.

The opposite, or north side, however, of the river, exhibits a most steril aspect, the whole course of the hills from the snowy crests being clearly visible. The course of the river here is not far from east and west; so that the stream runs between two ridges of these hills, and does not cut directly through them, thus causing an idea of much greater depth or breadth to be attached to the snowy crest than belongs to it, as the glen is seen for a great way penetrating the hills, which, melting into distance, come down on either side, and soon shut up the lower part from view.

As the rajah and the female part of the family were residing at the palace of Serān, we did not choose to propose visiting its interior: indeed, those houses of hill chiefs which we had seen, so ill repaid us for our trouble in examining them, that we had no wish to explore this residence. Its external appearance is rather prepossessing: it embraces a considerable square, which contains two of those lofty towers consecrated as temples to the gods, and several smaller ones, in which the rānees and young rajah reside. To the north-eastward of the palace is placed a Ghoorkha fort; a mark every where left of the degree of subjection in which the land was once held by its oppressors.

Still farther to the north-eastward a small village contains the house of T,hicken Das, one of the wuzzeers; and that of one of the others is at somewhat greater distance below. The sketch made of this place will convey a tolerably just idea, both of itself and the scene in which it is placed.

June 17.—This morning the young rajah came to pay his respects to the British authority. He is a small, ill-grown child, of between six and eight years old; his manners and countenance both marked and formed, and not at all like those of so young a person. His nose is much hooked, and he has large, full, and sparkling black eyes. He is affected by that species of glandular swelling of the neck so common among the people of the hills, known in Europe by the name of goitre. His father, we learnt, was afflicted with it; and in this boy it was certainly hereditary. He seemed much frightened, or overpowered, either by terror and confusion, or by *mauvaise honte*, and continually made salaams and prostrations to us, which seemed to have been studiously taught him, and which he had got by heart with much success. After he had been some time seated on one of our knees he appeared more at ease, and answered several questions naturally enough, displaying some intelligence and freedom; but he was kept apparently in great order, and felt much awe at those who were with him, as well as those whom he was visiting. We did all in our power to inspire him with confidence, and to make him pleased with his entertainers, presenting him with such little articles as he was likely to admire; and I think he went away far less frightened, and a good deal gratified. He was attended by a considerable suite of retainers, heads of families and landholders, who seemed very solicitous about him. A most earnest and strenuous request was made, that, while the young rajah was in our tent, no Ghoorkha might be permitted to venture near: they were afraid lest these dreaded people might throw spells on the child, and bewitch him. We respected their prejudices, and took care that no such dangerous characters should have access near the sacred person of the young rajah; who retired in about two hours to his own house, after having made his nuzzur to the British government as to a respected superior.

It was our intention (having penetrated so far into the hills) to pursue our travels up the glen of the Sutlej, and to ascertain, if possible, beyond all doubt, whence that river derives its remotest source. Our information, however, was not sufficiently precise to afford perfect certainty with regard to our future route; but it was proposed, if time should permit us, after pursuing the river Sutlej to its source, and passing (as we were aware would be the case in such a route) through the snowy mountains, to recross them to the south-eastward, at the pass of Nitteemana, near Buddreenauth. With these views, we collected all the information we could; and the result of that which relates to the geography of the country, as well as the manners of the people, has been comprised in the details already given.

After considerable preparation, however, and much inquiry, our plans were rendered abortive, by the orders of government arriving for my brother to proceed, with all convenient speed, to assume the charge of Gurwhal and its affairs; and, when all should be mature, to place the rajah on the Musnud, under the conditions and terms which the British government judged best for the comfort and safety of the country.

This was a severe disappointment; but we prepared to render it as conducible to good as we could; and contented ourselves in the belief that we should see a very long and interesting tract of country in our progress to Sreenuggur from Serān, the route lying partly along the foot of the snowy mountains, which would have entirely escaped our view, according to the former plan of our journey.

We remained here till the 24th of June, during which time we were completely prevented from any considerable excursions or observations by violent rain. We had projected the ascent of a snowy peak directly behind Serān; but, on the day intended (the 19th), the clouds fell down to the very foot of the hills, enveloping all in the most complete and impenetrable darkness. It was not like a common mist, it was really a sinking of the clouds from the rarefaction of the atmosphere, till they quite shrouded us; and all attempt at mounting the hill, or making any further observations, was quite fruitless. We turned our attention in despair from the face of the country, to examine the habits and manners of the people, and to compare these with what we had formerly remarked.

The dress and manners of the men have varied little since we entered Bischur; or, at least, any slight difference that may be traced is not of a nature to call for a description. That they are more open, more free, and more respectable and independent in their carriage, may be felt; but it is not easy to explain the causes of the impression thus given. The dress of the women has undergone more alteration: the handkerchief which used to cover the head is here discarded, and its place is occupied by a woollen cap resembling that of the men; the crown of which is sometimes crimson, sometimes plain black. The hair is not now suffered to hang down the back in a long thick tail, but this tail is carefully rolled up behind the head, and fixed there; so that the end, in its formidable tassels of red wool and hair, appears behind each ear, and is tied up with much red wool and flowers. A string of flowers is hung from the side of each bonnet, by both the sexes. Instead of a courtee, or coat, like that of the men, the women wear, besides the petticoat, a blanket that folds partly round the body, and partly comes up around the shoulders and across the breast, where it is fastened by a large copper or brass broach: in other instances, the blanket only comes over one shoulder, somewhat like the Scots plaid. On the whole, the dress is more fanciful and becoming; and there is much more use made of a striped stuff, resembling the tartan of the highlands, than I have before observed. The women are certainly improved in looks. I have seen several that might be considered as handsome and fair, with something of a good complexion: indeed, I think that both the sexes may be fairly pronounced more comely and personable to the northward than they are further south.

We had not much opportunity for observation relative to the diseases prevalent among the people of the hills. Fevers and pleurisies occasionally attack them, and those ailments more peculiar to a mountainous country, where sudden variations of temperature are common. Some of those diseases which afflict them are more obvious and apparent. Most persons, after ascending a height, and frequently without such exertions, were distressed by a severe cough, which had every symptom of being chronic, and the effect of climate and mode of life. But the most remarkable complaint was that glandular swelling of the throat, the goitre, which was extremely prevalent. It might be too much to say that every second person we saw was thus diseased; but the sufferers were certainly very numerous. No new or plausible cause was assigned, in the course of our inquiries, for this singular ailment: the attributing it to snow water does not seem at all sufficient, as many are afflicted who are scarcely placed within the reach of such an agent. The natives say that it is hereditary; and I believe there can be little doubt of the fact; for the disease may be traced in infants of very tender age, as we had, more than once, reason to observe. We understood that it was sometimes cured, when early means were taken; and these are said to consist in extirpation of the part by the knife. We saw some persons who had the scars on their throat, resulting from this mode of cure, which had in these instances been completely successful.

We several times saw people with swellings of very great size, which rendered them most uncouth and shocking objects; and, when this occurred in women, it was doubly disgusting. We did not discover any persons practising medicine, or pretending to that art; although some such must exist, as is proved by the operations performed on the neck—too nice an attempt to be made by any but those who have had at least some degree of experience or teaching.

It is probable that the knowledge of these people in medicine is confined to the application of a few simples, which every old person acquires in the course of life. Wounds and hurts of all kinds are cured in the simplest manner, assisted by the natural low habit of body of the people in general, which resembles that of all Hindostan. They recover from the severest wounds with hardly any attention, dressing them with turmeric and a few simple ingredients formed into a poultice, which promotes a gentle healing suppuration. In habits which seldom tend towards fever, it is a mockery of art to see how even loss of limbs, lopped off in the most summary way and most savage manner, are cured by this simple process, while the patient hardly seems to suffer.

There is a very sensible difference to be observed between the language spoken by these people and that which we hear in the more southern districts. The change has been obvious for some time; but our few last marches made the difference very sensible indeed: even at Rampore it was less so than here. The Hindoostannee language almost ceases to be understood; and our people could not communicate with the peasants here without an interpreter. It is not that a provincial dialect obscures the language; it seems that the people are accustomed to one, which is radically distinct from Hindee. In Kunawur, Hindoostannee is not understood at all; and, upon making inquiry concerning the tongue spoken there, we found it totally distinct: the radical words and nouns, the simple names of things, are altogether different. I suppose a modification of this language, probably the aboriginal language of the hills, is in use here; for it is as distinct from the language of the Bhoteas, on the other side of the snowy range, as from Hindee: we were unable, however, to make any satisfactory discovery on the subject; and could only rest contented in the establishment of the fact, that such a difference does really exist.

Nothing has hitherto been said of the animals that inhabit these hills; and I much regret that the notes I can give relative to this branch of natural history is necessarily scanty and unscientific.

Among the larger inhabitants of the forest are the tiger, and various kinds of wild cats of different sizes, bears, wild hogs, monkeys of many varieties, deer of many and curious species. Although the tiger has been mentioned as one of the denizens of the woods of these hills, the existence of the true tiger is at least doubtful. It has been mentioned that the foot-print of one of these animals was seen in our line of march; but there was no certainty that it did not belong to a smaller species, perhaps the leopard. The natives gave contradictory answers to our questions respecting this appearance, and to those which related generally to the existence of the tiger in the hills. They asserted its existence, and seemed to entertain a fear of it; but we never heard of any accident having happened by any such animals. In the case of the foot-print, they averred it to belong to a formidable beast which they called bāng, and that it was large and red, but not striped or spotted, which would argue the existence of some other beast of prey, though it may probably belong to some ideal creature, of which they have an indefinite dread.

That others of the feline species find shelter among the recesses of the mountains is certain; but I am not so well prepared to describe them as to assert their existence. One day, turning sharply round a cliff, we saw two animals somewhat like martens, but of more brilliant fur, and more like cats, sporting among the broken masses of the cliff; but they soon disappeared among the thick brush-wood, and we saw no more of them. Smaller cats, of a size and colour approaching the domestic cat, we met with more than once among or near villages; but I do not recollect seeing that animal ever retained in a house in a domestic state. Bears are not uncommon, and we saw them at a distance more than once among the cliffs that overhung our path. They are black or brown, and I believe do not vary from the same animal in the plains.

We never saw hogs in their wild state among the forests; but the evidences of their existence were too numerous and too palpable to admit of a doubt. The natives assured us that they frequent the forests in large numbers; and we saw large pieces of ground routed up evidently in the manner that a hog does in search of food; indeed, they must be abundant among these immense woods, which afford quantities of acorns and roots, of all others fittest for the sustenance of these animals. Once at a village we saw a very young one of this sort. He was of a reddish brown tinge, and longitudinally striped and spotted with black. His figure was somewhat finer than the common hog; the head small and pointed; and the legs fine and higher from the ground than usual; the body round, and altogether it possessed a sort of wild-game appearance, that proved at once that the animal was of a totally different description from the domestic hog.

We had no very good opportunity to ascertain the various sorts of monkeys that inhabit these extensive woods. A long tailed ape of a dark brown colour, and considerable size, was common; and we frequently saw a smaller species, the body of which is covered with a greenish-grey fur, the face bare and red, and the buttocks bare from their always sitting on them. It is one of the commonest monkeys all over India. I believe that other sorts are to found; but we might be deceived when we thought we saw them, as distance and variety in size may give a very different appearance to the same species.

Deer are numerous, and of various kinds. The most curious and worthy of attention is, perhaps, the musk-deer. It is an animal by no means common in any situation, but keeps entirely to the most inaccessible and remote heights, among rocks and forests that defy the foot of man. They cannot endure heat, and several young ones which were presented to us invariably perished, after being exposed for a few days to the warmth of a lower region. The figure of the musk-deer is somewhat singular. It attains the size of a fallow doe, or small buck, and its body and legs are completely those of a deer. The head, however, bears some resemblance to that of a hog; the eye is black and full, but not so large as that of a deer usually is; and the sharp snout and wrinkled countenance gives it a considerable resemblance to a pig's head, which is rendered more remarkable by the two tusks that project from the upper jaw, and hang, pointing downward, considerably over the lower; and their colour is dark brown. It is commonly known that the musk is contained in a liquid state in a small bag near the navel of the animal. When it is caught, this bag is taken just as it is found, and cut from the beast while yet alive. A small hollow reed is inserted into it that the musk may not suffer, as it would be apt to do, from want of air; and the whole is tied around with a sinew of the animal. In this state, when it has dried, which it does in the shape of small brown grains, it is sold together with the skin for about twice its weight in silver. It is said that the animal must be caught alive in order to obtain its musk. Should it be shot, the drug (it is affirmed) is absorbed into the body, and consequently not only lost, but the animal is rendered uneatable. The great value of the article makes the animal an object of great request. Whenever, therefore, it is understood that a musk-deer has been seen on any particular hill, the whole country is turned out, to hunt him down. This alone would tend to create scarcity of the animal; and if it is as rare in the hills to the south-eastward, and on the opposite side of the Himālā range, as it is in that portion between the Sutlej and Alacnunda, there is little danger that the market will ever be overstocked by the genuine musk.

This scarcity, however, and the high price of musk, as may readily be supposed, gives rise to many modes of adulterating it to increase the quantity. The common way is by injecting a portion of the blood of the animal into the bag of musk, while both are warm, and they then unite. Great caution is therefore necessary in making the purchases, and, indeed, none but very experienced persons can ever detect the fraud. Musk-pads are generally sent to the rajah, or chief man of a district, either as nuzzurs or at a certain valuation, as a portion of tribute. Some fall into the hands of the Bunyas, from the low country, who take this article, as well as opium, iron, and other commodities, in payment for their goods, such as cloth, sugar, and other manufactured articles, and these persons sell it at a great profit in the plains. It is highly prized as a medicine as well as a perfume. It is also smoked by the luxurious debauchees in hookahs, in which way it acts as a strong stimulant; but only men of great wealth can afford this fascinating drug. It also invariably forms a part of the offering presented from men of rank to their superiors, as a nuzzur, or to their equals, as a usual token of regard. The name by which the animal is known in the hills is *custoree*, and the drug also obtains that appellation. A common sort of deer, which we frequently saw browzing among the heights, and bounding from rock to rock, is called by the natives *gūrrl.* It attains the size of a roebuck; the colour is dark brown, the belly much lighter; the horns branch into several divisions, like that of the roebuck, are rough at the lower parts, and very sharp at the points, and they run from six inches to a foot in length. Its activity is very remarkable.

We frequently saw the horns of an animal, a mixed species of deer, that were singular in their form and appearance. They grew near each other at the base, curving very much backward, and receding from each other gradually. The exterior curved side is divided from the root to the point by raised articulations, two or three inches distant from each other; and when they are of a middling size they are at least three feet long. The animal to which they belong is described by the natives as resembling the goat in appearance as well as the deer, but more particularly the former. That it is of considerable size may be inferred from its horns; and the skins, several of which we afterwards procured, confirmed this inference. Its colour is a dark gray, approaching to brown; the hair of its skin is very thick, soft, and elastic, but by no means fine: each hair has the appearance of a spongy hollow tube. They form very comfortable and warm beds to lie on, and are used for this purpose. The animal is found only in the most remote and inaccessible parts of the mountains, ever keeping among the snow, delighting in cold; but, in the winter time, when the valleys are deeply covered with snow, it approaches the habitations of men, driven, in all probability, by want of its usual food, and even comes to the highest villages, along with herds of other animals of similar habits, but it retreats as the snow melts, and was seldom or never to be seen while we were in the hills. The name of this strange animal among the natives of the hills is "burrl."

They seem to attach to its horns somewhat of a sacred and mysterious virtue, hanging them at the doors and in the ante-chambers of their temples, and placing them by the graves of those who were accounted of peculiar sanctity in their lives: we found in a very remote and distant region a pair of these horns on the tomb of a man who had perished in the snow many years ago, in the route we were then passing. They do not, however, confine this sanctity to any one sort of horns; their temples were always adorned by many pair of various kinds, and we even saw ram's horns holding a conspicuous station in their holiest places. We remarked two other distinctly different kinds of horns belonging to animals of the deer species: one was short and very thick at the base, bending somewhat back; they are said to be the produce of a smaller sort of deer, that also lives on the verge of the snow, and comes in flocks to the very doors of the villages in severe weather: the others are small and dark, without branches, rough, but sharp pointed. Of the animal that produces these I have no account.

Dogs are found domesticated, particularly to the northward, and the breed of Bischur is noted for its size and hardihood. The finest that came under our observation bore a considerable resemblance to a mastiff, but retained a good deal of the cur. Their colour in general was black and white, with a little red occasionally; their hair is long and thick, and the tail long and bushy, curling up behind: their head is somewhat long and pointed, like the common shepherd's dog. They are often very fierce, and sometimes attain a considerable size, but are seldom so large as a full sized mastiff. These animals are furnished with a down under their long shaggy hair, which is as fine and soft as shawl wool; this comes off easily in warm weather, and is regularly shed with the hair. Every animal is similarly furnished in this cold country. We found that the natives used these dogs as sheep-dogs, in the same way as those of other countries, and also for hunting all sorts of game, even birds which they tire out in flying; and some were valued at a very high price.

Of the more curious sorts of the feathered creation there is but little variety. That which first challenges attention is, beyond all doubt, the large and beautiful bird called in the hills "rutnāll," and in the higher districts "monāl." This lovely bird is a pheasant. The cock bird attains the size of the largest dunghill fowl; its body is of an intensely dark glossy blue; the neck and breast are splendid, like that of a peacock, with varying purple, green, and gold: on the head he carries a crest of several feathers, which form a brilliant changeable plume; when flying, his back, uncovered by his wings, is white, and he spreads a large tail of ruddy brown feathers. His note is a peculiar and very mellow whistle, which generally gives intimation that he has taken his flight. The hen bird very much resembles the heath hen, or female black grouse of Scotland, but is of larger size; her gray plumage and game look makes the similarity very striking. These birds haunt the highest and coldest places; and it appeared, subsequently, that the nearer we approached the snowy and more inaccessible regions, the more numerous they became: on the whole, however, they cannot be considered as abundant. They have broods of from four or five to eight or ten young ones, but I cannot say whether they keep in pairs; I am inclined to think, however, that they do, as we seldom started a hen and her young ones without seeing a cock bird at no great distance. Their flesh, particularly that of the young ones, is exceedingly delicate and delicious.

Another bird, which seems to partake of the nature of the pheasant and the common fowl, has been slightly mentioned before, when the stuffed skin of one was presented to us at a village one day's journey from Rampore. Its brilliant red crest and throat, the beauty of its speckled feathers, each furnished with an eye of white, made it an object of inquiry where they were to be found, but we understood that they were far more rare than even the monāls; that they were very seldom seen at all, and could only be procured when their situation was accidentally discovered, by the united efforts of a great number of men, who taking advantage of its heavy flight, which is incapable of bearing it up more than three or four times, weary it, till at length they come up with and catch it: but it never was our fortune to meet with any one alive, nor indeed did we ever see but one skin of this species.

Another kind of pheasant approaches more nearly the common pheasant at home, but has not his more splendid plumage; these we seldom saw; indeed our mode of travelling in a narrow path, with many attendants preceding us, as well as following us, was little favourable to the view of game, which must have been frightened from the vicinity of the path, however usually untrodden, long before we reached their lair, by the noise of our approach.

One sort of bird was brought to us at Rampore, the cry of which we had frequently heard, and from which it obtains the name which the natives give it, viz. *crāās:* it participates in resemblance to a hen pheasant and a partridge, has brown game-like plumage, and in size equals a common fowl, but we found the flesh insipid and very bad food.

The chuccores, or the common hill partridge, which obtains its name from its cry, is common, and tolerably numerous throughout the hills. This beautiful bird has more resemblance to a quail than to a partridge; its plumage is red, gray, and black, in fine varieties; it delights in scratching among dust and dry earth, and in lying covered with it in the sun: its flesh is excellent. Black partridges are also common, and inhabit the small fields and brushwood that are scattered over the mountain sides: they are very beautiful birds; the rich black and ruddy brown feathers of the body and wings are finely contrasted with the speckled and varied neck and breast; and their flesh is particularly delicate.

The common dunghill fowls in their wild state, called in India *jungle fowls*, are found every where, but their habits of running instead of flying make it almost impossible to procure them, either by catching or shooting: they inhabit the most tangled jungles, exhibit a very various and beautiful plumage, and are delicately flavoured. We did not see many peacocks after penetrating far into the hills: they keep rather in the skirts of the highlands, but are very plentiful about Nahn and the lower parts of the Girree and the Jelāll.

These are the principal birds which fell under our observation, or of which information reached us during our excursion, and which may be considered as game.

Of birds of prey there was no scarcity; kites and hawks of all sizes and descriptions abound. I am not aware that there are any eagles. We remarked among the small birds several of those which are found in the plains; among them the minas were very numerous, and of various sorts. One old friend we recognised with some delight,—the cuckoo: its note and appearance are the same as in Europe; and the natives had bestowed on the same name as that by which it is known among ourselves.

We remarked that the country produced very few snakes. We saw only two in the course of our travels, and these did not seem to be of a venomous nature. There were lizards, toads, and frogs, as in other parts; but it did not appear that the reptile branch of natural history would experience any considerable addition from our knowledge of this country.

Of insects I cannot venture to speak: they seemed to be as numerous as elsewhere, but of the varieties I can give no account. Such are the meagre memoranda that I have been enabled to make respecting the animal creation in these regions. I much regret my having possessed no knowledge suited to render them more copious and interesting.

With much reluctance foregoing our further progress into the hills, we left Serān on the 24th of June, and turned our faces towards the south-eastward. The morning was clearer than it had been for many days, and the view down the glen of the Sutlej towards the plains, seen from a height, was enchantingly beautiful. It was evident that towards the skirts of the hills the fog which obscured our view existed in far less quantity, if at all; and the clear, sharply defined, blue hills in the distance, varied with every tint that cultivation and foliage can give, contrasted most strikingly with the stern and frowning cliffs we were perched among, half hid in cloud and storm.

In the vicinity of Serān there was a collection of singular stones near the road, which we did not remark on our way thither, reared on end as tombstones, memorials of the dead: they are rudely, but somewhat curiously carved, chiefly bearing the representations of men and women; their shape is thin and broad, like flat pillars, and they rise to various heights, some exceeding that of a man: the only account that could be obtained was, that they commemorated the deaths of various persons who anciently lived in Serān, and probably belonged to the rajah's family. It is a prevalent custom here to place stones to the memory of the deceased on the place where the body has been burnt, or sometimes on high teebas, or peaks, where frequently they stick a pole with a flag on it, and each passenger hangs a small rag, or adds a stone to the heap. Such places become not unfrequently sacred, and the dead enjoy the reputation of a deota, becoming identified or confounded with the deity of the spot.

It was remarkable that around Serān there were many persons and families, who had taken up their abode in caves under stones and projecting rocks, which served them as houses. Of these rocks a great many were scattered around the ruins of the cliffs above, under every one of which some wretched looking people resided. Thus, although there are but few houses to be seen, forming the town of Serān, the number of the inhabitants attached to the place is very considerable. It is a curious sight, either in the dusk of the evening to see the numerous glimmering fires that start up all around, though no houses appear, or in the calm of the morning to mark the multitude of smokes that spire up to the sky from these half subterraneous dwellings. It seems singular that the people should thus prefer living so precariously and uncomfortably, to building moderately substantial houses, of which the expense would not be great, and of which the comfort would in all probability be so much greater. It may, however, be accounted for, by considering the present circumstances of Serān; it is for a time the residence of a court, which, in all countries, however poor, draws a certain dependent population along with it. The rajah has only lately returned from the recesses of Kunawur, and it is probable that he may soon leave Serān to reside at the chief town of Rampore.

Thus the superabundant population now temporarily settled at Serān, will have to remove along with the magnet that attracts them; and to build houses there would be an useless expense; they therefore occupy the dwelling which nature has given them. They choose those rocks which from their shelving position yield most room below, and which on the face of a hill give least encouragement to the lodgement of water. They dig under them, and improve the hollow, and thus contentedly do hundreds live in weather that really renders a good house no despicable blessing.

We retraced the steps of our last march, till we came to Munglār nullah, where we had suffered formerly so much from heat, and crossing at the same spot, the water, now a furious torrent, we commenced a steep ascent in a direction totally different from our former route, and which carried us towards the snowy peaks connected with Moral-Ke-Kanda. Our ascent continued very sharp, during a very hot day, for near two miles; when we halted at a village named Shā, where a whimsical dispute was brought before us for adjudication. One of the Ghoorkhas now in our party had, it seems, purchased a wife from a zemindar of this village (his daughter) for the sum of fifteen rupees, but on condition that he should remain in the country with her and her relations; this was now impossible, the Ghoorkha power was annihilated, and he had no inclination to remain behind, but desired to carry his wife along with him: to this the father objected, and not only refused to allow his child to go along with her husband, but also objected to refund the money for which she was purchased. It was a delicate question to interfere in, and after all parties had been heard, it was agreed to refer the subject to the decision of the lady herself. She was about twelve years of age, and by no means handsome; she declined to proceed with the man, and so the dispute was terminated. The gentleman behaved very philosophically on the occasion, honestly confessing that he regretted the loss of the fifteen rupees, and of the clothes he had given her, more than that of the lady; but as he had had twelve months' possession of her, it was judged that he had in some sort received compensation for his expense.

CHAPTER XXII.

I TOOK the opportunity of the occurrence related in the last chapter to put many questions relative to the strange custom of the community of wives which exists in the families of brothers in this country. The information I received was uniform with that produced by my inquiries in all other quarters, and here my informants seemed to be sensible and intelligent men for the country. They unanimously admitted the universality of the custom, that it was usual always to purchase wives, and that the zemindars were too poor to be able to give from ten to twenty rupees for a woman, and therefore contributed their quota, and each enjoyed their share of the purchase. They explained the modes usually adopted to prevent quarrelsome interference, and described every thing as already detailed; but when I came to put questions relative to the disposal of the surplus of females, they could give no satisfactory answers whatever.

They denied the practice of selling their women to foreigners as slaves, but I have great reason for believing that they only disclaim this shameful custom from a sense of its evident impropriety. I began to sound the people I was talking with about purchasing a particular woman, then in company, as a means of trial; and I am satisfied, from the way in which they received my overtures, that I should have succeeded had it been my object to continue the negotiation.

We continued gently ascending through a various but thinly cultivated country, which affords little for remark, to a village named D,harin, situate on the steep slope of a hill-face, and near its crest, among a fine grove of horse chesnuts. The village overhangs a very deep and exceedingly wild dell, and faces a grand snowy mountain; but the clouds hung so low, and passed so thick, that our view was quite obstructed. I examined the village in the evening with minuteness, and entered many of the houses, the disposition of which agrees perfectly with the remarks already made regarding their interior economy. The verandah forms the chief accommodation of the house, and the middle room serves to cook and to sleep in. The masonry work of all is good and substantial. Several were plastered with shining earth, I believe with a composition of white clay and talc pulverised, and used as a wash. The roofs of all these houses consist of large slabs of slate, more or less neatly worked and laid on.

There were in this village a great number of hives of bees: these insects are much attended to all through the hills, and their honey forms a favourite article of diet, as well as of extensive and ready sale. The mode they adopt of keeping them, and of obtaining their honey without destroying the bees, merits a description. A hollow tree, or sometimes an earthen pot, is built into the wall with apertures externally, by which the bees enter and go out. There is a valve in the centre; and the internal end of the hive, which opens within the house, can be closed or opened at pleasure by various contrivances, as a door or a clay bottom. When the combs are full, and they wish to take the honey, they merely make a considerable noise at the internal extremity of the hive, which drives out the insects: they then close the valve, open the interior, and take the honey unmolested. They then close all up again; the bees return to their rifled hive, and recommence the labour of replenishing it. The honey, when fresh, is very fine. There is no want of food of the most various and luxuriant sorts, all over the hills. The bee appears to be the very same insect as those which we domesticate in Europe.

We remarked this day, both in the village Shā and here, several very large and fierce dogs, apparently very powerful; but they did not come up to our ideas of the Bischur dogs, as those animals had been described to us. The rain had favoured us through the day; but this evening it began to pour in torrents, and continued to do so all the night, and the clouds closed around us with redoubled gloom. Our great height and vicinity to the high peaks may probably account for the violence of the weather, which even surpassed what we encountered at Serān; and it was all that we could do to keep our small tent tolerably dry; but it was impossible to prevent the ground under foot being very damp and uncomfortable.

During the 25th, 26th, and 27th of June, we were confined to our tent by incessant floods of rain. All attempts at marching were vain and absurd. On the morning of the 27th we prepared for our journey, but were prevented by a recurrence of heavy rain. At an early hour the lofty snowy peak, which we had intended to ascend from Serān, appeared close above us across the ravine, covered with snow; but all was soon enveloped in cloud and darkness. We were enabled, however, in the evening, to make an excursion to the top of the ridge on which D,harin is situated, and enjoyed a strange confused view of snowy and rocky peaks, partially covered with cloud, and rising out of a sea of vapour, giving a pretty tangible idea of the desolation of a chaos.

June 28.—On this day we took advantage of a period of the morning being free from rain, and proceeded on our march by nine o'clock. We had considerable trouble in arranging the bŭrthens of the coolies: they were discontented, and not numerous; and every thing was wet and heavy, so that there was no small difficulty in procuring carriage for all our necessaries. On reaching the gorge of the hill, where our descent commenced, we looked down upon a mass of vapour that defied our eyesight to penetrate; and heavy rain again came pouring on us, till we were near the bottom of a steep hill, where we reached the village of Put,hnee. This descent is in parts rapid and dangerous. We were here presented with a ram which had four horns; a breed not uncommon in the hills: they are even seen at times with six. We also procured a pair of those large horns belonging to the bŭrll, above described.

At a short distance below the village we crossed Buree-gad,h, or nullah, and continued gently ascending along the left hand bank, by a tolerable path, among forests of various character. Passing through one or two villages, we gently descended, on rough road, till we reached the shoulder of a part of the ridge, where was once situated an old fort, called Bahilee-Moonus-Ke-Cōtiluck, made by the Sirmoreans, in one of their successful inroads on Bischur. Here began an irregular and unpleasant descent to Nowgurree-Khola, the same stream which we passed close to the Sutlej, on the way to Rampore, and which we now recrossed in its infant state, near its origin: it was swollen to an impetuous torrent by the rains; and, having torn its way through a most savage rocky chasm, swept foaming along, without the least division, into pools, over a bed cut in the white rock, which it has worn for itself.

A single fir-tree formed our bridge; and it was a formidable effort to cross this headlong torrent on so narrow and so unstable a footing. We all got over, however, without accident, and commenced a very steep irregular ascent on the opposite side, along a hill face formed of huge masses of rock that had fallen from crags above, and were fantastically heaped on one another: at times, a very steep and abrupt precipice made the path along its brink somewhat dangerous, and it was ever wearisome and exhausting. Such a winding and various road, after a march of somewhat more than nine miles, carried us to the village of Bursoule, strangely situated on a projecting rock, the chief tower occupying its very peak, and surrounded by rock and deep forests, and hills clothed with mist. This was a fatiguing day, more from the wild nature of the ground and the continual rain than from the real distance travelled: in fact, we had reached a country more remote and impracticable than had hitherto been entered on; and, after crossing a shoulder of the loftiest peaks themselves, we were now in the very centre of Moral-Ke-Kanda.

The rock during this march consisted chiefly of varieties of that hard semi-transparent stone resembling marble, white, green, brown, and yellow, once or twice adverted to before. All the loftier peaks seemed to consist of this stone. A large quantity of particularly white sand was remarked to-day, on our ascent from Nowgurree Khola, with the parent stone undecayed, and lumps of the above-mentioned stone bedded in it. At lower elevations we returned to the old micaceous schist, some of a wonderfully white, fine, and soft nature. The situation of the village was so peculiar and picturesque that I endeavoured to take a sketch of it.

June 29.—This day we left Bursoule a little after nine, descending into the dell below, and crossed the Seallee Khola, which joins the Nowgurree stream, and commenced a long ascent of four miles through a forest composed of oak, birch, horse-chesnut, walnut-trees, and many others, with a fine carpet of ferns and flowers. This led us to the top of the shoulder of a hill whence we could trace many points of our former marches, and the course of the Sutlej at a great distance. Hence a further ascent carried us up a shoulder of the highest part of Moral-Ke-Kanda. The path was not very bad, but steep, and there were many dangerous rocky steps, through a deep forest of old wood. From the top of this gorge called Seelanee Pass, a noble view would have been obtained, but deep fog and heavy clouds overhung the most interesting part of the landscape. We saw, however, in the openings of the flitting clouds, glimpses of the country we had gone through, bright and sharply distinct in all the clearness of a southern sky. The beauty of the soft though decided tints, in so pure an atmosphere, cannot be described. They belong to such scenes, and only can be fully enjoyed by the contrast of wild gloom such as was spread around us.

After waiting a considerable time for more favourable weather, we were forced to descend; and the hill, from this gorge to the village where we were to pass the night, is more precipitous than most we have seen, even to a degree of danger. We arrived at the village of Buranullee, after a fatiguing march of only seven miles, about five o'clock in the afternoon. The journey of to-day presented several plants of some novelty, some fine large yellow raspberry bushes, with ripe fruit on them, almost equalling the yellow Antwerp raspberry. The common red sort was in profusion. A very lovely shrub attracted us, with blossoms resembling the lily of the valley, disposed in bells of milk-white hue, around a red stalk. A little farther on, the true lily of the valley grew in abundance. The birch was common in all the woods, growing to a larger size than is common at home, and bearing a larger leaf; but the tree could not be mistaken; its bark, its form, even the leaves and twigs, vouched for its identity. As we came through the deeper parts of the forest, among the mosses and lichens that cover the trees in great profusion, and which were also on the ground, several varieties were remarked of that sort which bears, in the materia medica, the name of *lichen islandicus*, and is supposed to be of great virtue in pulmonary complaints.

June 30.—We resumed our march about eight o'clock, first diving deep into the dell below the village; and, after crossing it, pursuing our way on the left hand face of a hill, very much indented and irregular. Then again sinking into a deep ravine, and mounting its sides, till by a very devious track we reached a low gorge, from either side of which a ravine and stream diverged in opposite directions. This ridge is the connecting link between the mountain Moral-Ke-Kanda, and the great Nowagurh range; and the ravine to the north carries its waters to the Coonoo nullah and the Sutlej, while that which flows to the south runs through the long and fertile valley of Samtracote, swelling the stream of the Pabur. On the open, and grassy, and ferny braes, along which we came to-day, we saw a profusion of a very lovely species of blue iris, which was quite new to us. From this gorge the path descended by a sharp ridge into Samtracote valley.

The exposure being southerly, it is bare of wood, and the upper part is but little cultivated; as, however, we proceeded onwards, villages and corn-land were abundant. Two streams, divided at the higher part of the valley by a ridge, unite a short way down, and the hollow becomes deeper, though still with a considerable portion of shelving ground. At six miles and a half from our encampment, and about four from the top of the valley, we reached the old castle of Samtracote, formerly an occasional residence of the royal family, but now deserted. It stands on an insulated hill above the stream, but forms no very interesting object. We continued our route in the bed of the stream, which winds very much, and has on either side abundance of fine rice cultivation which it irrigates. We passed by and through several very thriving villages, crossing many subsidiary nullahs, one of which has forced a strange passage about twenty feet broad through solid rock, to the depth of fifty or sixty feet. The bridge is formed of two pine trees, and is rather narrow considering the nature of the gulf that yawns below.

Several of the smaller valleys leading into this valley are strangely formed, contracting like this at the mouth, and swelling out above into spacious cultivable places. Much rice seemed to have been destroyed by the unusual swelling of the torrents from the late heavy rains. The valley turns suddenly from the south and south-eastern direction it had pursued, to an easterly one, with considerable flat land in its bed, very cultivable, and much of it under rice, and joins the river Pabur a few miles further on, a short way below the village of Rōroo, where we encamped for the night, after a march of sixteen miles, but less fatiguing than many of our far shorter journies, great part being a gentle descent, and some of it on almost level ground. The village of Rōroo is tolerably large and prosperous; it is placed on a fine flat on the banks of the river Pabur, which for many miles above presents a smiling scene of fertile cultivated land. The crops about the village are various and rich: we here saw maize, and a quantity of the herb b,hang grows both wild and cultivated all around. Here we found some Mussulmaun merchants, who had come to collect the produce of the hills, such as musk, opium, b,hang, blankets, drugs, &c.

July 1.—We were in motion by seven, proceeding down the Pabur: the course of the river for some miles above the village is to the south-west; it runs through a valley nearly a mile broad in some places, and in a devious narrow channel, often branching into small streams that frequently change their course. About three miles below Rōroo it takes a sudden turn to the south-east. We continued our march along its bank: several old houses are scattered on insulated rocks by the river side, belonging to the different T,hakoors, who have, at different periods, held power here. Passing all these, we reached a level spot on the Pabur, opposite to Raeengudh, where the party encamped.

A detention of several days here was occasioned by the difficulty of procuring a sufficiency of coolies for the carriage of our baggage towards Srenuggur; in the meantime we went and examined the fort of Raeengudh, which had proved a stumbling block in the way of negotiation on our first approach to it. We found the situation and appearance only pretty formidable, and perfectly calculated to resist any storm, unassisted by cannon: but the wall was very infirm, and the interior miserably fitted up. There is but little accommodation, and the rock rises so much to a point within, that there is no space where men might be safe, except close to the walls, that sit like a crown around the rock. The supposition that the fort was commanded from various points, even by musquetry, was found correct, and, by a sharp fire of matchlocks, the garrison would soon have been killed in detail, or confined entirely to their wretched sheds. There were tanks of water cut in the rock, which held a sufficient store for twenty days or a month, and much corn and fuel were found in the place.

We received a visit from the Rānee of Saree, a small lordship now totally merged in the Bischur territory. She had but small means for travelling comfortably, and lodged in a large cave in the rock near at hand, where she was attended with sufficient respect by those who yet remained attached to her. The way she took to approach was curious; she had so much of the low country feeling as not willingly to expose her person to public view: her litter stopped at a little distance from the tent, and several sheets were held by her attendants around her, forming a screen, in the envelope of which she walked to our tent, which she entered without scruple. The approach of the walking screen, surrounded by attendants, had a curious appearance: she was a woman of about twenty-five years of age, rather good looking, but already faded; she had high features, dark eyes, and a tolerable person; her colour was yellow, with a faint ruddy tinge in her cheeks. Her dress was loose, of rather coarse muslin; her head was covered with a handkerchief wrapped round it, in the fashion of the country. She came to communicate her tale of oppression, and her fears of further distress from her neighbours, small and great. The situation of widows in this turbulent country must be wretched enough. Nothing could be done but to promise her protection, and a representation of her case to the proper authorities: and she took her leave soon after, retiring to her rock, refusing any other accommodation.

As we are now about entering the territories of Gurwhal, it may be proper to introduce here the scanty accounts which we gleaned concerning that state, its nature, and government.

The boundaries of Gurwhal have been adverted to with sufficient accuracy in the prefatory observations to this narrative. It is a country of very great extent, though of small comparative value. Many of the larger rivers of upper India, and all those which form the origin of the Ganges, have their rise in its mountains, and hold their course through its territory. It is, however, by no means easy to comprehend the divisions of Gurwhal. There seems to have been a primary division into large districts or *fougedarees*, which were subdivided again into lesser ones; and the whole country was divided into t,hats or purgunnahs, apparently without reference to the second subdivision.

Thus I was informed that there anciently were three fougedarees, viz. those of Rewaeen, of Malkee, and of Tulān, and several lesser trusts of the same sort, viz. of Jounpoor, of Bunghur, of Delgour, of Nagpoor, of Chandpoor, of Lobha, and of Rudhan.

Of the topographical situation of many of these I am ignorant: such as are established are marked on the map; several of these were subdivided, as Rewaeen, which included in itself Upper and Lower Tucknour, Futteh Purbut, and Pauch Purbut, with several other districts, each of which contained several *t,hats* or purgunnahs. I cannot pretend to detail all these, nor would the detail be of much interest: it is enough to give an idea of the irregular divisions of a country, so far from being valuable, and so impracticable.

Rewaeen contains upwards of thirty purgunnahs; within the territories of Gurwhal there would be about 120 purgunnahs, according to a note I have, but which I do not consider as correct.

Of all the possessions attached to the state of Gurwhal, the Deyrah-doon is by far the most valuable. This valley stretches from the Jumna to the Ganges; confined towards the plains by the low range of hills, which, commencing at Hurdwar, run to the north-west as far as Nahn, and on the north-east by the roots of the mountainous region that bounds all the plains. The breadth of the valley may be from eight to eleven miles, and its length about forty miles. The whole of this beautiful tract consists of level ground, here and there rising into hillocks, richly cultivated, and studded with fine villages. It is well watered: two fine streams, the Asseen and the Soone, rise near the centre, and run, one each way, to join the different larger rivers; besides which, many rivulets contribute their moisture in the rains, although, during the continued hot weather, they are chiefly dry. Those portions of the valley which are uncultivated, together with some of the small hills it contains, and the skirts of the range which separate it from the plains, are covered with forests of valuable timber, such as saul, seesoo, toom, with one species of pine, and various other woods, from which a large supply of valuable timber might be drawn, and from the vicinity of the rivers, in many parts, might be conveyed to market with little trouble.

Near the centre of the valley stands the small, but respectable town of Deyrah, containing many good houses, with a royal residence for the rajah, and some temples of considerable size, splendour, and sanctity. The whole is surrounded by mango topes, and the town itself is full of these trees. About six miles to the north-east of Deyrah is situated the hill on which the Ghoorkhas established the fort of Kalunga, the fate of which has already been related. The hill does not exceed four or five hundred feet in height, and it may extend to the length of three-quarters of a mile: the fort was situated at the eastern extremity, which is most elevated.

There are many villages all around, and a profusion of mango groves, which vary the appearance of the country in a most advantageous manner. The inhabitants of this valley, from their vicinity to the plains, and the richness of the country, have contracted an appearance of comfort unknown in more removed parts of the hills; the upper classes particularly, who in manner and dress vary but little from their neighbours in the Dōab. Towards the hills, and in the villages that are situated among their skirts, of course there is an approximation to the more uncivilized people of the hills: Brahmins and Fuqeers, and Gossains, particularly, are very numerous about Deyrah and its vicinity.

The Deyrah-Dhoon, in the reign of Purdoomun Sah, is said to have yielded to the government a revenue of a lac of rupees; but the Ghoorkhas having much ruined it, never realised more than 20,000 per annum: it was, however, beginning to recover from the severe treatment it had received, and may now rapidly increase in value. There are no other valleys in Gurwhal that can stand in competition with the Dhoon for beauty or value, although there are several strips along the banks of rivers that swell out into a fine flat, and admit of a good deal of cultivation. Such are some parts of the bed of the Bhagiruttee in its lower course at Barahāt and Dhurassoo; but of all the large and cultivated spots which here and there are found throughout the country, the valley of Rama-Serai claims the first place after the Dhoon.

This valley is situated in that part of Rewaeen which lies between the Touse and Jumna. The Rama stream, to which it affords a channel, rises in the mountain of Kedarkanta, and has a long course to join the Jumna. Nine or ten miles of this lie through a level tract of land about two miles broad, and which is very cultivatable, and was once well cultivated. This, which was emphatically called by the natives the *Happy Valley*, will again be adverted to in the succeeding pages. The rest of the country consists of a wild congeries of mountains, affording no extent of level ground; and though there are many rich cultivated glens, they are all more or less precipitous, like the country heretofore described, and, like it, the cultivation is entirely carried on upon terraces raised above each other on the sides and faces of the hills.

Sreenuggur, the chief town or capital of Gurwhal, is situated on the south bank of the Alacnunda, about twenty miles above its junction with the Bhagiruttee at Deoprague, where a strip of level ground stretches along for three or four miles, forming the valley known by the same name as the town. It was once comparatively populous and prosperous, forming, as it did, not only the residence of the court, but a considerable entrepôt for the produce of the various countries in and on either side of the snowy mountains, which exchange commodities by the Nitteemānā and other passes.

When Colonel Hardwicke visited this place in 1796 it was perhaps not in its prime, but contained (as he computed) 700 or 800 houses, and a good bazar. When Messrs. Webb and Raper in 1808 passed through it, on their way to Buddreenauth, it had sunk deeply in importance, and was, to all appearance, rapidly advancing to total decay. It had not only to contend with the common enemies of the country, oppression and tyranny, the consequence of invasion and conquest, but also with natural causes no less ruinous. An earthquake had occurred in 1803 which had done considerable injury; many houses were ruined; all were shaken; and the rajah's palace was particularly shattered; and the encroachments of the river Alacnunda yearly destroy a portion of what yet stands, threatening in time to sap the foundation of all. I had no opportunity of visiting it, but, according to accounts on which I can depend, the desolation has increased.

If we may form a judgment of the original state of the building from what remains, the palace was never very splendid, and had little of any kind to excite or gratify curiosity. The situation of the town was exceedingly hot and uncomfortable, and the wind at times, when not cooled by rain, was very parching. The houses are described as exactly similar to those of the villages in the rest of the country, excepting that some are of larger dimensions, but a perfect uniformity of architecture runs through the whole.

Deyrah was the next town of any consequence, situated, as already described, in the valley of Deyrah-Dhoon, and Barahāt on the Bhagiruttee (an account of which will be found in the course of the journey), once ranked next to Deyrah; but this and various other villages, which may claim a petty distinction among the wretched hamlets of the country, can only attract notice by comparison with them. Local and incidental circumstances occasionally exalt a petty village to temporary riches and prosperity; but, when these cease to operate, it relapses into its original nothingness, and the ruins that continue visible for awhile only tell what it once was.

As the chief scene of Hindû mythology lies in this country, and is concentered chiefly about the sources of the rivers that flow from the recesses of the snow-clad Himālā, the temples and places of interest are comparatively numerous. Although a long list of holy names, and places made sacred by acts of their gods and saints, might be produced, they evince little splendour, and little to attract the eye of any except an enthusiast or devotee. A great portion of these places, like the acts they record, and of which they were the theatre, are fabulous; and of those which do exist little appears, excepting a spot arbitrarily marked out as that which should attract the reverence of pilgrims. A few are places of interest, and some of these the succeeding pages attempt to describe.

CHAPTER XXIII.

GUNGOTREE, the source of the most sacred branch of the Ganges, ought to hold and does bear the first rank among the holy places. Here all is mythological if not holy ground. Here Mahadeo sits enthroned in clouds and mist amid rocks that defy the approach of living thing, and snows that make desolation more awful. Gods, goddesses, and saints here continually adore him at mysterious distance, and you traverse their familiar haunts. But, although Gungotree be the most sacred, it is not the most frequented shrine, access to it being far more difficult than to Buddrinauth; and consequently to this latter pilgrims flock in crowds, appalled at the remoteness and danger of the former place of worship. This may pretty fully account for the superior riches and splendour of Buddrinauth. Here are temples of considerable extent, priests and officials in abundance, who preserve an imposing exterior, and an appearance venerable from power and comparative magnificence, and consequently procure rich and ample offerings to keep up their comfortable dignity.

The following account of this great resort of Hindoo devotion is extracted from the journey of Captains Webb, Hearsay, and Raper, to the sources of the river Alacnunda, and to Buddrinauth which is situated there, given in the eleventh volume of the Asiatic Researches. The whole narrative will be found to contain much interesting matter relative to this part of the country, as also much scientific information upon the subjects of research, which led these gentlemen to perform the journey.

" The town and temple of Bhadri-Nāth are situate on the west bank of the Alacknunda, in the centre of a valley of about four miles long, and one mile in its greatest breadth. The east bank rises considerably higher than the west bank, and is on a level with the top of the temple. The position of the sanctuary is considered equi-distant from two lofty mountains, which are designated by the names of the Nār and the Náráyena

Purvatas*. The former is to the east, the latter to the west, and completely covered with snow from the summit to the base.

"The town is built on the sloping bank of the river, and contains only twenty or thirty huts for the accommodation of the Brahmins, and other attendants of the deity. In the centre is a flight of steps leading from the water's edge to the temple, which occupies the upper part of the town. The structure and appearance of this edifice are by no means answerable to the expectations that might be formed of a place of such reputed sanctity, and for the support of which large sums are annually received, independent of the land revenues appropriated for its maintenance. It is built in the form of a cone, with a small cupola, surmounted by a square shelving roof of plates of copper, over which is a golden ball and spire. The height of the building is not above forty or fifty feet; but its advantageous position on the top of the bank renders it the most conspicuous object in the valley.

"The æra of its foundation is too remote to have reached us, even by tradition; but it is considered as the work of some superior being. This specimen, however, of divine architecture was too weak to resist the shock of the earthquake, which left it in so tottering a condition that human efforts were judged expedient to preserve it from ruin; and the repairs which it has lately undergone have completely modernized its external appearance. The body of it is constructed of large flat stones, over which is a coat of fine white plaster, which adds to the neatness, but has destroyed all its outward pretensions to antiquity. Notwithstanding the summons, we were not allowed immediate access to the temple, as it was first necessary to have an interview with the Rauhil, who was to introduce us in due form into the presence of the sacred image. Instead, therefore, of ascending, we went down the steps leading to the baths. About the middle of the bank is a large cistern about twenty or thirty feet square, covered in with a sloping roof of deal planks supported on wooden posts. This is called Tapta-cund, and is a warm bath, supplied by a spring of hot water issuing from the mountain by a subterraneous passage, and conducted to the cistern through a small spout representing a dragon's or a griffin's head.

* From purbut, a mountain.

"Close to it is a cold spring, which is conveyed by another spout, by which means the water may be reduced to any degree of temperature between the two extremes. The water of the Tapta-cund is as hot as a person well can bear, and from it issues a thick smoke or steam, strongly tainted with a sulphureous smell. The side of the cistern towards the river is raised only to the height of three and a half or four feet, and over it the water flows as the supplies are received from the opposite quarter. This is the principal bath in which people of both sexes perform their ablutions under the same roof, without considering any partition necessary to preserve the appearance of decency. The water from this cund, independent of its supplying the cistern, is conducted through the huts and private houses, to which it imparts a suffocating warmth. From hence we descended to the bed of the river, where, in a small recess of the bank, is Nareda-cund, sheltered by a large rock, whose projecting angle breaks the force of the current.

"A little to the left of it is Surya-cund, another hot spring, issuing in a very small stream through a fissure in the bank. There is no basin or reservoir to receive the water, but the pilgrims catch it in their hands as it falls, and sprinkle themselves over with it. This ceremony is observed as much for comfort as from any motive of piety, for the water of the river is so cold at this season that, after performing their frigid ablutions, the bathers are glad to have recourse to the element in a more tepid state. Besides these, there are numerous other springs, which have their peculiar names and virtues, which are, no doubt, turned to good account by the Brahmins. In going the round of purification the poor pilgrim finds his purse lessen as his sins decrease; and the numerous tolls that are levied on this high road to Paradise may induce him to think that the straightest path is not the least expensive.

"As we descended the steps, the arrival of the Rauhil was announced. We met him near the Taptacund, where a cloth was spread for us, and a small carpet of flowered China silk for the pontiff. He was preceded by three or four hircarrahs and chōbdars, with the silver emblems of their office: behind him was a man bearing a chauri of peacocks' feathers; and in his suite were the chief officiating priests of the temple. He was dressed in a quilted vest of green satin, with a white shawl cummerbund. On his head he wore a red turban, and on his feet a pair of party-coloured socks.

His ears were ornamented with a couple of large golden rings, to each of which was suspended a very handsome pearl, of considerable size. His neck was decorated with a triple string of small pearls; and round his arms he wore bracelets, composed of precious stones. On most of his fingers were golden rings, studded with sparkling gems.

"After the usual salutations, a short conversation passed for about a quarter of an hour, when he signified his readiness to conduct us to the sanctuary. On our arrival at the outward portico, we were requested to take off our shoes; and, having done so, we ascended five or six steps, and passed through a small door, which brought us to the area of the temple. About twenty feet beyond was a vestibule, raised about a foot and a half from the terrace, and divided into two apartments, the inner one a little more elevated, and adjoining to the sanctuary. In the outer room two or three bells were suspended from the roof, for the use of the religious visitants, who are not permitted to go beyond it. We were not allowed to advance so far; but taking our stand immediately in front of the image, a few paces from the outer threshold, we had a perspective view of the sacred repository.

"The high priest retired to one side, as the dress he then wore was incompatible with his sacred functions.

"The principal idol, Bhadri-nāth, was placed opposite the door, at the farther extremity: above his head was a small looking-glass, which reflected the objects from the outside: in front of him were two or three lamps (which were all the light the apartment received, excepting from the door), diffusing such feeble glimmering rays, that nothing was clearly distinguished.

"He was dressed in a suit of gold and silver brocade. Below him was a table, or board, covered with the same kind of cloth; which, glittering through the gloom, might impress the beholder with the idea of splendor and magnificence; but an impartial observer might suppose it one of those deceptions of priestcraft which are so successfully practised on the Hindū.

"This artificial obscurity may have the double effect of passing off tinsel and glass for gold and precious stones; and, by exhibiting the image in a dubious light, the superstitious mind has a greater scope for its own conceptions. From the indistinct view we had of it, we should suppose it to be about three feet high, cut in black stone or marble; but the head and hands were the only parts uncovered.

" To the right of him are the images of Udd'hara, Nar, and Narayena; to the left Cuwera and Nareda, with whom we were only nominally acquainted; for to us they were veiled, as ministers of perfect darkness.

" Having satisfied our curiosity, and signified our wish to depart, a large silver salver was brought forth to receive any offering we were inclined to make. Our means were very insufficient to answer the high expectations which had undoubtedly been formed, from the marked and unprecedented distinction which had been conferred on us; but, as it was necessary to acknowledge the favour by some pecuniary token, we presented one hundred rupees at the shrine, and took our leave, without absolution or remission.

" Although we derived little gratification from the inspection of the temple, it was pleasing to find we had not offended any of their religious prejudices by our presence; for we were apprehensive some scruples or objections might have been raised, as none but Hindūs have ever visited the place.

" Our Mussulmaun servants were prohibited from approaching the spot; and a particular request was made on our arrival, that no kid or living creature might be deprived of life within the precinct of the temple; but a large stone on the opposite side of the river, at a short distance from our camp, was pointed out for the slaughter of any animals we might require for the table.

" The temple of Bhadri-nāth has more beneficed lands attached to it than any sacred Hindū establishment in this part of India. It is said to possess 700 villages in different parts of Gurwhal and Kumaoon: many of them have been conferred by the government; others have been given in pledge for loans; and some few, purchased by individuals, have been presented as religious offerings.

" All these possessions are under the jurisdiction of the high priest, who holds a paramount authority, nominally independent of the ruling power. The advantages which the government derives from this institution would make it cautious in infringing openly its rights; while the accumulation of wealth secures to the state a certain resource in times of exigence.

"The rajahs of Srenuggur were in the habit of applying to this quarter in any case of emergency; and, under the plea of borrowing a sum of money, would give up two or three villages as security for the repayment; but the produce of them was so inferior in value to the sum lent, that the loan was never repaid, and the villages continued under pledge. Thus the appearance of independence was maintained on the part of the rauhil, who was so well aware of his actual weakness, that it was more for his advantage to yield to a request than subject himself to the risk of compulsion. The selection to the office of high priest is confined to the caste of Dekhini brahmins of the Chauli or Namburi tribes. In former times the situation was a permanent one; but, since the Gurchali* conquest, the pontificate is held up for sale, and disposed of to the highest bidder.

"All the villages belonging to Bhadrinath, which we had an opportunity of seeing, were in a very flourishing condition, and the lands in a very high state of cultivation. The produce is brought hither, and disposed of to the pilgrims, who are obliged to pay dearly for the food furnished from the ecclesiastical granary. Two seers and a half of rice for the temasha, equal to about seven seers, for the rupee, was the established price of this market, and other grain in the same proportion. These exactions do not escape observation: numerous complaints are vented privately, but as the profits are supposed to be applied to the use of the divinity, it might be deemed impious to raise any open clamours; the only resource, therefore, left to the deluded pilgrim, is to pay his devotions, and take his departure as quickly as possible.

"The territorial revenue forms, probably, the least part of the riches of this establishment; for every person who pays his homage to the deity is expected to make offerings proportionate to his means. The gift is included under three heads, for each of which a separate salver is allotted. The first, which is called the "bhet," which is an offering to the idol; the second is the "bhōg," constituting his privy purse, the amount being appropriated to the expense of his wardrobe and table; the third, and last, is for the rauhil. These presents, however, are voluntary, and many persons assume the garb of poverty to avoid a contribution equal to their abilities, while others lay the whole of their property at the feet of the idol, and trust to charity for the means of returning to their homes.

* Or Goorkha.

" It is impossible to form a conjecture of the probable amount of these collections, for although every person's name, with the sum presented, be registered, the book is withheld from the inspection of profane eyes. The merchants and sahucars from the Dekhin are considered the most welcome visitors; for, if we may believe report, many of them have been known to distribute and expend lak,hs of rupees in this holy pilgrimage. In return for the oblations, each person receives what is called a presād, which consists of a little boiled rice, and in the distribution of it due regard is paid to the amount of the offering. Many of our Hindu servants complained that they had been used very scurvily, having been put off with a very scanty meal, insufficient to satisfy the cravings of appetite.

" However sparing the dispensation of his favours in this world, the deity holds forth ample rewards in the next, by the promise of an unqualified remission from the state of transmigration. As we were not entitled to the same act of grace, the high priest seemed desirous to make amends by conferring more immediate benefits, and in the evening sent to each of us a muslin turban, a gazgäee, and a small quantity of cedārpati, an odoriferous leaf taken from the garland of the idol. The former was stained in large spots of a saffron colour, with the incense placed on the head of the deity, and we were requested to wear them in honour of Bhadrinath. This is considered one of the greatest marks of distinction that can be conferred; and as a compliment was intended, we could not do less than acknowledge the favour by placing the sacred badge on our heads.

" The temple is opened every morning at daybreak, and continues exposed for the admission of pilgrims till one or two of the clock in the afternoon; the deity is then supposed to be ready for his dinner, which being prepared for him, he is shut up to take his meal and evening repose. The doors are again opened after sunset, and remain so till a late hour, when a bed is laid out for him, and he is again left to his meditations. The vessels he is served in are of gold and silver, and the expenses of his clothes and table are said to be very considerable. A large establishment of servants of every description is kept up, and during the months of pilgrimage the deity is well clothed, and fares sumptuously every day; but as soon as winter commences, the priests take their departure, leaving him to provide for his own wants until the periodical return of the holy season.

" The treasures and valuable utensils are buried in a vault under the temple. It is said that a robbery was once committed by a few mountaineers, who, taking advantage of a sudden thaw, found their way to the sanctuary, and carried off eleven maunds* of gold and silver vessels. The theft, however, was discovered, and the perpetrators were put to death. The only persons who have access to the inner apartments are the servants of the temple, and none but the rauhil is permitted to touch the image.

"The Brahmins who reside here are chiefly men from the Dekhin, who have been led hither by the prospect of acquiring a subsistence from the funds of the temple, and from the small fees or donations presented by the pilgrims. As they all arrive in a state of celibacy, colonisation is prevented by the insuperable obstacle of there being no women here of their own caste with whom they could form a lawful alliance.

"During their residence at this place they are most strictly enjoined to maintain a state of carnal purity; but on their return to Jōsēmatha they give a greater scope to their pleasures, and the above restrictions may probably be the cause of their running more eagerly into acts of profligacy, very inconsistent with the sacerdotal character.

"Our short acquaintance would have enabled us to gain very little insight into their moral conduct had not the hopes of relief induced several of them to make a confession of complaints they laboured under.

"Narāyena Raō, the present rauhil, is a man of about thirty-two or thirty-three years of age; his appointment was conferred on him by an order from Nepāl, not, we may presume, on account of exemplary conduct, for he was the first who applied for remedies to cure a certain unaccountable disorder with which he had long been troubled, and which he innocently ascribed to the rarefaction of the atmosphere; but it was sufficiently evident that the shrine of his deity was not the only one at which he had been paying his devotion.

"The number of pilgrims who have visited Bhadrinath this year is calculated at from 45 to 50,000; the greater part of these fakirs, who came from the most remote quarters of India. All these people assemble at Haridwār, and, as soon as the fair is concluded, take their departure for the holy land: the road they follow is by Dēvaprayāga† to Rudraprayāga, whence they strike off to Cēdār-Nat,h.

"This place is situated about fourteen or fifteen miles in direct distance

* A maund is about eighty pounds weight.

† Or Deoprague.

to the west-north-west of Bhadrināth: but the intermediate hills are inaccessible from snow, and the travellers are obliged to make a circuitous route of eight or nine days by the way of Jōsi-matha hither. The road to Cēdār is much obstructed, and in many places leads over beds of snow, extending for several miles. Two or three hundred people are said to have perished this year on the journey, having fallen victims to the inclemency of this climate, and the fatigues they underwent.

"By the time that the pilgrimage to Cēdār-Nat,h is completed, Bhadri-Nath is ready to receive visitors, who, having paid their devotions, return by the road of Nandprayāga and Camprayāga, which conclude the grand circle of pilgrimage.

"The ceremonies which Hindus undergo here, differ in no respect from the customs usually observed at other places of holy ablution. After washing away their impurities, the men, whose fathers are dead, and those of the female sex who are widows, submit to the operation of tonsure, which may be considered as an act of mourning and of purification, by which they are rendered perfect to appear in the presence of the deity. One day suffices for the observance of these rites, and very few people remain here above a couple of days, but endeavour to make their retreat from the hills before the commencement of the periodical rains. The great crowd had quitted it before our arrival, and the number which now came in daily did not exceed forty or fifty. By the middle of June the lowlanders will have taken their departure, leaving the place to the mountaineer inhabitants, and a few stragglers from the southward."

From the above account it will be seen that the temples of Mahadeo at Buddree-Nauth, are in truth places of great resort and much riches; and a comparison with the description of Gungotree in the subsequent pages will show how totally different the places and interests excited by them severally are. Few will venture on the perilous path to Gungotree, painful as it is, and rendered additionally painful by the many penances and previous ablutions which are necessary to purify the devotee, and render him worthy to approach this holy solemn spot, whilst the comparative smoothness of the way, and the facilities yielded to all those who can spend a little money, induces thousands to visit the rich shrine of Buddree-Nauth.

Next in importance to the latter place is the temple of Kedār-Nauth: this is situate about half way between the two first mentioned places, and probably at no great distance from either, though, from the nature of the country, it is impracticable to go from the one to the other without a long and painful détour.

The same enormous mountain, though deeply cut into divisions and pinnacles, in all probability gives birth to the rivers, whose sources are marked by the temples of Gungotree, Buddree-Nauth, and Kedār-Nauth. They arise from the same lofty region, and the savage impracticable desertness of snow and rock alone prevents the traveller from going directly from one place to the other. Thus, eleven days journeys are spun out from Gungotree to Kedār-Nauth, while seven or eight days are expended in reaching Buddree-Nauth from the latter place.

Kedār-Nauth is situated at the source of the Kalee-Gunga, a stream far smaller than either the Bhagiruttee or Alacnunda, which joins the latter at Rooder-prague. It has never been visited by an European; not on account of any physical difficulty or particular obstacle, but because the other places were more interesting, and attracted observation first; while time was not sufficiently at command to allow of a visit to this place, which, from either of the other places, would occupy twenty days, if a return were contemplated, and would create a difference of ten or twelve, if from them a direct route was made to the capital. From the best information I could collect, the temple of Kedar-Nauth is of indefinite antiquity, not lofty, but of some extent, and sacred to Mahadeo or Seeva, under the name of Kedar: there are several Dhurrum sallahs, or huts, erected for the accommodation of the pilgrims who resort to the shrine, and who are pretty numerous from year to year. There are many *counds* or wells in the river near it, which are mere pools sacred for the purpose of preparatory ablution, one of which, Gource-cound, is one day's journey from the sacred spot. Concerning its riches, or the number or quality of its priests, I have not been able to obtain any particulars.

Such are the places of eminent sanctity throughout this province; but of shrines of minor note there are multitudes: every village has its temples; every mountain, its divinity. Among these, a few that fell under our observation, as most remarkable, were Barāhāt, Lak,ha,mundal, Mungle-nauth, &c. which meet with notice and description in their places.

The early history of Gurwhāl, like that of every hill-state in its vicinity, and like the remote accounts of all countries, is indistinct, and not to be depended on: the most common tradition is, that at a distant period, the country was divided into a number of petty rajships, each governed by a separate and independent sovereign; the number is stated at twenty-two or twenty-four. One of these, the Rajah of Chandpore, had been a soldier of fortune from the plains, and had, as usual, by bold murderous actions usurped the throne. This man, it is said, was told by a fuqeer, that he should one day unite the country and reign over it, as a large and independent state. Fired by the prophecy, or more probably by his own ambition and thirst for conquest and power, he attacked his neighbours, made himself master of their countries one by one, and at last united the whole, as was predicted, under the name of Gurwhāl.

To the time of this event various dates are attributed. In the account given to Colonel Hardwicke by desire of the rajah, during his visit to Srenuggur, in 1796, the extremely remote period of 3774 years is fixed on, as that when Bohg Dhunt thus formed and established the rajship of Ghurwhāl. This, of course, can only be considered as fabulous; but others ascribe this to the Rajah Adjib Paul, who, according to the story told to Colonel Hardwicke, was the fifteenth lineal descendant from Bohg Dhunt. As this name is in every person's mouth, and highly revered by all the country, it is more probable that he may have been the founder of the dynasty as well as of Srenuggur, than that it should be referred to a more remote sovereign. From Adjib Paul, sixty-one consecutive sovereigns are given in Colonel Hardwicke's account, comprised in a period of 2874 years, which are said to have elapsed from this reign to that of Purdoomun Sah, the late and last sovereign of Gurwhāl.

It is unnecessary to observe, that in a country so rude, where records are so loosely, if at all preserved, and where the genius of the people runs so much upon fable and superstition, there is little faith to be placed in any details of history relative to so remote a period, particularly when affecting such accuracy as these do; the years of each reign being specified, not in round, but in particular and definite numbers. The very great extent of the period is sufficient to destroy every appearance of probability; and if it were not, the prodigiously lengthened reign of each sovereign, far beyond all example in any consecutive hereditary chain of kings, is sufficient to determine all that relates to the time at least to be fiction: but the natives of India in general have so confused an idea of all that relates to dates and age, that it is not wonderful to find even a very enormous error in the account of the duration of the Gurwhāl monarchy, and the reigns of its sovereigns, especially when a considerable allowance is made for the usual and natural vanity which every country displays, and of which most individuals feel, more or less, the influence, even though unconscious of its existence in themselves.

The result of our inquiries on this subject was a far less splendid series of reigns with regard to duration; but all seem to agree, that the dynasty remained hereditary in the same family from its foundation, till it was overthrown together with the country. The era of Adjib Paul, the first Rajah of Gurwhāl, according to this account, of less pretensions, was about 480 years ago; and Purdoomun Sah was the fifty-sixth hereditary sovereign of this series. The few garbled and unconnected facts that are to be collected of the history of the country under this dynasty, are too uninteresting for notice; and Gurwhāl exhibits no historical occurrence worthy of detail, till the first efforts of the Ghoorkhas for its subjection in 1791.

This enterprising race having subdued the whole detail of petty lordships between Nepāl and the Rangunga rivers (including Kumaoon, a state always connected with its neighbour Gurwhāl), first made an attempt in 1791 to reduce this also under its sway. They were repulsed, and finally failed in their object, from the detention they experienced in the siege of Lungoor, a strong fortress near the capital, and in consequence of the Chinese invasion, which it required all their efforts to repel, and which subjected them at last to great humiliation: but they seem to have frightened the Rajah Purdoomun Sah so much, that he consented to pay an annual tribute to the Nepālese government. But though a nominal peace existed, the tempers of the two nations were not such as to admit of any long continuance of this state of affairs; the conquerors burned to complete their conquest, and by no means restrained the licentiousness of their soldiers and authorities on the boundaries, who pillaged the country, and distressed the inhabitants of Gurwhāl; while little care was taken to repress insult to the court itself.

The Gurwhālees partially subdued, but yet not quite broken or patient under their degradation, roused by the encroachments of their tyrants, met their hostile approaches half-way; and a strife was soon raised, which could end only in the perfect subjugation of the one, or the complete discomfiture and disappointment of the other. In 1803 a large army was sent to invade Gurwhāl, under several able and veteran commanders, whose lives had been passed in the species of warfare which they were to commence. These chiefs were Ummr Sing T,happa, Hustee Dhull Chowtra, Bunsah, Buchtee T,happa, and many others, since well known in the late war with Nepāl. Perfectly acquainted with the country, and accustomed to such marching, they found no difficulty in making rapid progress towards the capital, little opposed by the rajah, who was an indolent man, not much calculated to command in the day of danger, or to encounter the fatigues of war with such a foe. Some ineffectual attempts were made to stop the career of the Ghoorkhas; but the troops of the country, though said to be very numerous, could make no stand before them; and a final engagement took place in the Deyrah Dhoon, in which Purdoomun Sah was killed, after maintaining the conflict for some time.

As usual, a dispersion of the whole army and considerable slaughter followed. I have heard that the number of Gurwhālee soldiers composing the army on this occasion amounted to upwards of 12,000 men. This day finished the contest, and Gurwhāl fell into the undisputed power of the Ghoorkhas, while the long continued dynasty that took rise from Adjib Paul at once came to a close. The Ghoorkhas have ruled with a rod of iron, and the country has fallen in every way into a lamentable decay. Its villages are deserted, its agriculture is ruined, and its population has decreased beyond computation. It is said that two lacs of people have been sold as slaves, while few families of consequence remained in the country; but, to avoid the severity of the tyranny, they either went into banishment, or were cut off or forcibly driven away by their tyrants.

Yet some of the individual rulers of these conquerors were mild, and not disliked. Bum Sah and Hustee Dhull, the governors of Gurwhāl, were disposed to indulgence; and in some situations the country was now again improving, and getting reconciled to their new state. Runjore Sing T,happa was also a well-disposed man, and a mild governor, and inclined to justice; but the executive officers were severe. Their manners as conquerors were rough, and they despised the people they had conquered: so that, at some distance from the seat of government, exactions went on, insults and scenes of rapine were continually acted, and the hatred of the people to their tyrants was fixed and exasperated: the country was subdued and crushed, not reconciled or accustomed to the yoke; and, though the spirit of liberty was sorely broken, and desire for revenge was checked by the danger of avowing such sentiments, a deliverance from the state of misery they groaned under was ardently, though hopelessly, wished for. In this state were the people of Gurwhāl when war broke out between the Nepālese and the British. The facility of conquest hitherto had blinded the Ghoorkha government to the danger they braved in encountering the British arms, or perhaps they knew not or believed not in their might. But the avenger of the hills was at hand; and the Ghoorkha power at this time has melted from them like a mist of the morning.

From the description already given of the country, it will be readily presumed that the revenue is extremely small; and it is not only trifling, but very irregularly and inefficiently collected. The amount stated to Colonel Hardwicke in 1796 was somewhat above five lacs of rupees, including every tax and tribute that could be collected in any way; the produce of mines, corn, washings of gold in the rivers, &c. &c.; and this was so ill collected, that all military officers, and even the meanest servants of government, were paid in orders on different zemindars. It is said, that when the great Akber had, by the vigour of his government, and the dread of his name, forced even several of the hill chiefs to do him homage, and become his tributaries, he called on the rajah of Srenuggur to bring the papers and documents relative to his revenue, and a chart or description of his country, which was promised. Accordingly, on the next day of audience, after having displayed the documents relative to his revenue, he brought to view a very lean camel, assuring the Shah that such was the best chart and description of his country: it was all sharp heights and hollows, up and down, and very poor. The emperor smiled, and bid him remove the semblance of his country, assuring him, that from one so poor he had nothing to demand.

The natural productions of Gurwhāl are very similar to those found in other hill states. The exports are nearly the same as those of Bischur, viz. wool, blankets (which, though chiefly coarse over the most of the country, are said to be manufactured of considerable fineness in the vicinity of Buddreenauth), corn, tobacco, bhang, and its preparations, opium, iron, much of the low country produce, which is brought partly by foreigners, partly by natives of the country on speculation, as cotton cloths of all sorts from Rohilcund and the Doab, sugar, indigo, &c. &c. The imports from Bootan are various: chouries, or cow-tails, musk, rock salt (also imported from Lahore), wool, saffron from Cashmere, borax, and nerbise, or zedoary. In a word, the same traffic which is carried on by the men of Kunawur in Bischur is in practice here, and often by these very Kunawurees.

Iron is abundant: copper is found, as well as lead; and there is no doubt but that the precious metals do exist in some abundance, as gold is found in the beds of all the rivers and many of the mountain streams; but it is too laborious to obtain a quantity of it in this way, sufficient to enrich the seeker. A considerable traffic was, however, carried on in this country and capital, in bullion with Bootan and the low countries: this chiefly passed through the hands of shroffs, who were agents of banking-houses in the large towns of the low country.

The character and disposition of the inhabitants of this country cannot be considered as differing very materially from those of the middle districts of the small states, and southern parts of Bischur already described: what variation does exist, probably consists in a greater degree of clownish bluntness, a rougher address, and still more unpolished state of nature, which appears to mark them from their neighbours. They are fully as much addicted to robbery and pillage, with every atrocious violation of social order, so prevalent in the hills; in fact, even the shade of difference which suggests itself, may be resolved into that which accident and circumstances may have created between nations originally of the same disposition and natural tendencies. In particular parts of the country however, these shades become more strongly marked, to such a degree indeed, that one is tempted to believe the radical stock and principles must have been different. Such is that which is found between the inhabitants of the northern, and bordering districts of Bischur and Gurwhal, and which will be taken notice of in its place; and possibly several other discrepancies may exist, that have not come under our observation.

The manners and customs of the Gurwhālees are very similar to those of their neighbours of the same religion, under the same sort of government, and inhabiting a country, the face of which varies but little. The Highlanders, as far as our observation extended, and probably far beyond our range, form but one great nation, subdivided into several principalities, and under different individual dominions indeed, but uniting in the leading features of character, manners, and customs. Very considerable deviation may be found from this general rule; but it is in general correct, as far as regards those who inhabit the southern face of the great belt of hills.

I can add little more to these meagre particulars regarding Gurwhāl; the remainder of these pages describes a journey through part of it, which however relates more to the primary objects of penetrating to the sources of the two large rivers, and describing their beds, and the country through which they flow, than to the general nature of the land, its history, or its inhabitants.

Fertile as some spots may be, and rich as are some of their productions, magnificent as is their scenery, and splendid the covering of forest thrown over these hills, they seem doomed to uselessness and barrenness. Their inhabitants are almost savages, and the remoteness of the deserts in which they live repels all efforts at improvement; and a total change in the nature of things seems necessary, before the country can become valuable, and pervious, or the people civilised and good.

After a delay of three days, during which some decision and severity were rendered necessary to procure a sufficiency of conveyance for the baggage, we left our encampment opposite Raeengudh on the 5th of July, and took our course down the right bank of the Pabur, just below Kātgobesery, the curious temple before spoken of.

The banks of the river, which above were considerably asunder, now closed in, confining its stream in a deep rough gully, between two lofty abrupt mountains. All cultivation ceased, except a few minute specks of rice, the bright green of which shone on the brown circumjacent rock.

There is no wood on the mountains, which are rough and uninteresting. About the margin of the stream, wherever there is a spot of soil, a few alder-trees rise luxuriantly, and in one or two places the river runs through a lofty deep grove of them; but it is uniformly a tumbling torrent.

Our route lay on the right hand face of the hill, dipping and rising as we crossed the frequent nullahs, which, swollen by the rain, were often troublesome. Our path was interrupted by huge blocks of stone, which had the appearance of having undergone the action of a torrent, they were so rounded by attrition. Those which were found at all heights were composed of quartz and mica, rough grey lumps, and darker matter, forming a very hard compound, and of a strange irregularly striated texture, the fracture partaking of this stubborn, compact, irregular nature. There was much limestone rock, of a grey and white, frequently veined, and affecting a laminous form ; the fracture fine and compact, the exposed surface becoming white by the effect of air: the strata of this rock always dipped more or less, but so irregularly, that we could not determine the direction. Micaceous schist was also abundant, and good blue slate of a tolerable texture, with plenty of quartz.

We reached our place of encampment towards evening, in a patch of abandoned cultivation, on the banks of a small nullah. During the whole day we hardly passed a village, or any symptom of habitation—it was a wild and deserted course.

An unfortunate accident occurred this day. A party of Ghoorkha sepoys had been despatched in advance with a view to put in order for the passage of the people, a j,hoola, or bridge of ropes, by which we were to cross the river Touse in the course of the next day's march. The ropes were found defective; but, having made them fit for use, as we supposed, the party began to cross to the opposite side. Several had crossed, but one poor fellow, a havildār, who was accompanied by his wife, wished to carry her over along with himself. It does not appear clearly how he had fixed her; but he accompanied her in the loop, which is the means of suspending the passenger. The hawling rope broke, and he, desirous to release her from this perilous situation, resolved to cut himself free from the loop; and, dropping into the water, swim with the end of the rope ashore. He did so, but in his fall got entangled in his blanket, or in the rope, and was hurried away by the stream, and drowned; probably dashed to pieces on the rocks of the rapids a little way below, for we saw him no more. We met the woman returning in great distress to the party. The man was regretted as a willing active fellow and good soldier.

July 6.—After a rainy night we began our march at seven o'clock in a gloomy morning, along the course of the Pabur, the bed of which continues the same, being narrow, rocky, rapid, and winding, joined by numerous torrents tumbling over broken beds filled with foliage. The rocks are similar to those seen yesterday. They break much into large square masses, often of a reddish colour when exposed to the air; but the fresh fracture is grey and white, exhibiting a true limestone.

About seven miles from the place of encampment the river Touse unites its stream with that of the Pabur. It appears very little, if at all, to exceed in size the latter stream; and greatly resembles it in the nature of its bed, as far as we could judge from the short reach we saw. The hills are chiefly bare and rocky, but a great deal of alder grows about the streams, and some fine pine trees on the hills looking to the north-west. The accompanying sketch will give some faint idea of the scene, which was rather interesting.

From hence a sharp ascent was necessary to pass some lofty precipitous cliffs; and a severe descent along the brow of the hill, on which, above the bank, a road has been scraped out from the hard rock, brought us to the bottom of the ghāt, where the j,hoola, or rope bridge, is fixed over the stream. On this bridge between 2 and 300 men, with their baggage, &c. were to cross a wild roaring torrent, from twenty-six to thirty yards wide, on which only one individual could be passed at a time, in a loop suspended from a piece of wood hollowed into a semicircle, and embracing a twist of six ropes of dubious sufficiency, fixed to a large piece of wood secured by large stones, and passed over a forked branch stuck in the ground on the one side, and on the other going over limestone rocks worn smooth, and also fixed to a beam. Although we arrived at noon, and several had then passed, yet small progress had been made in the business before night; and during the whole night the troops were hauling the ropes backward and forward, and the morning came long before the transit was completed.

The rock and soil did not vary from that which we had observed yesterday. In several places where the white and blue veined limestone rock jutted out into the river, it exhibited a remarkable and beautiful appearance. The action of the water, and the stones it rolls along with it, have cut it into a multitude of grotesque and beautiful shapes, which, together with the lamina and veins of the rock, produce a collection of forms not unlike the fretwork of Gothic architecture; and it is wonderful to see the smoothness, approaching almost to a polish, which these stones have attained. One of the most singular specimens of this effect is seen in the rock to which the j,hoola bridge is attached, which is much exposed to the violence of the water, and bears marks of having felt it at a great height, above the point it can now possibly rise to. Our encampment was just on the left bank of the united rivers, now recognized as the Touse, above the j,hoola, nine miles from our camp of yesterday, and two from the junction of the Touse and Pabur.

July 7.—Previously to our marching this morning, one of the Coolies was brought in dangerously ill of an inflammatory affection of the breast, probably true pleurisy, or peripneumony. He consented to be bled, and it was wonderful how immediately he felt relieved. We understood that such illnesses were very frequent among them, and often ended fatally; indeed, we could not discover any mode of treatment to have been adopted by which cure was to be accomplished. Affections of the breast are but too common among the hills, and coughs are very prevalent; indeed, you seldom see a native climb to the top of the hill without being affected with a violent fit of it. The sudden changes of climate to which these people are liable, even in passing from a valley to the top of a hill, with the frequent checks of perspiration excited by violent exercise, and chilled by a sudden cold blast after reaching the heights, are enough of themselves to account for this disposition to irritable lungs without much deeper inquiry. Fevers are also said to prevail at times, and to be very destructive, but I could never discover any means they proposed as a remedy for them. I believe them to be acquainted with the use of some simple herbs, but through ignorance they most frequently attribute virtues to them which they do not possess, and therefore fail in their object.

We commenced our march at nine o'clock, keeping for some time along the course of the river, by a rough devious ascending path, till, reaching a subsidiary stream, the road struck off into the glen which it forms, and, crossing it a little way further up, ascends a steep opposing hill. The range ends on the river in a remarkable peak, which is marked as a melon with deep indentures, vertically cutting its bulged conical shape. From hence the path hung above the river which, turning the hill, met us by a larger course. It was frequently cut in the face of steeps and precipices that were sufficiently dangerous; and one unfortunate Coolie proved them to be not only so in appearance: for, going along in a narrow part, he missed a step and fell headlong over, tumbling and sliding a good way down the bank, which was fortunately here not very rocky, but chiefly composed of loose earth. He was, however, rendered senseless by the shock he had received; but upon strict examination no injury appeared, except a cut on the back of the head near the crown, of about one inch and a half in length, deep and clear, on probing which it appeared to slant downward, and went quite to the bone, cutting the periosteum, but no fracture could be ascertained, and no limb was broken. A few superficial bruises were also detected. It is curious to see how much these creatutes will bear, slight as their frames generally are compared with those of an European. Had one of the latter received this fall, I feel convinced that he would have broken his neck; and at all events that the blow on his head would have fractured his skull. Probably exposure to sun and weather hardens and thickens both scalp and skull, so as to bear more heat and injury than those whose heads are habitually defended. We left him with assistance to carry him home, and his companions seemed to have no dread whatever of his not recovering speedily.

A deep descent brought us to a dell and a fine stream by twelve o'clock in a burning noon, and we refreshed ourselves in the waters before we proceeded. The stones in the bed of the nullah, which were exposed to the action of the stream, we remarked to be deeply encrusted with a rough calcareous coat, evidently deposited by the water, which must be very strongly impregnated to have so remarkable an effect. The evidences of lime are indeed obvious in a peculiar degree all around. From this place we had a corresponding, but longer and more fatiguing, ascent, during which the heat was exceedingly violent till we crossed a depressed part of the ridge, where were several ruinous villages. Our toils did not stop here, for, after a deep indent round the head of a valley, we had to encounter another steep pull, which was very severe on the fatigued people, particularly the coolies, the women and children; and when we reached the top we had still a weary rugged path of nearly two miles before us, before we reached our place of encampment, so that we could hardly enjoy one of the loveliest and most striking effects of sun-set, with distant hills shining in mellow light, that I ever saw.

Our place of encampment was named Doongree, and the distance marched little more than twelve miles; but the continued labour of these successive ascents and descents made it one of our most fatiguing day's journeys. We had very great difficulty in bringing on our baggage and coolies; the latter were totally knocked up; and though Sepoys were stationed by every one, we could not prevent several from throwing their loads suddenly down, and running into the thick jungle that skirted the path.

Limestone prevailed every where to-day, particularly the marble-like veined blue and white stone, remarked before. We also recognised some of the semi-transparent stone met with first above Serān, several sorts of sandstone, and much of a dark brownish purple rock, with many spots scattered through it, which certainly contain iron.

It was very curious to see in many places all these stones mingled in one huge mass, as if they had been melted down together, suggesting the likeness of marbled paper; much calcareous matter was found binding this mixture, and settling on it in masses closely resembling hard mortar, as it is detached from old buildings, full of small stones and gravel bedded in its substance: these masses were perfectly amorphous, and, with the mortar-like substance of rock attached to them, it seemed as if, when the whole had melted, the harder parts had settled downwards, and that this, like dross, had remained floating at the top.

July 8.—We left our village encampment, which, situated on a projecting rock, is surrounded by cliffs on all sides, and a little before eight o'clock resumed our march over the rough and sloping ledges of a limestone rock that project from the hill side, and peculiarly roughen this dell. The path was sufficiently dangerous, and the country through which it passes bore a great resemblance to that which we had traversed yesterday; the only difference lying in the size and ruggedness of the ravines and mountains we cross. We had descended a succession of very steep declivities, and commenced our ascent up the opposite mountain, while, as we recruited our exhausted strength by resting under the shade of some fine larch-trees, we were alarmed by the appearance of a man coming up covered with blood, and evidently wounded.

He was a Ghoorkha traveller, who, with five or six Sepoys, had been sent in advance to secure provisions and coolies; and he informed us, that having rested with his party at a village some distance off, the zemindars of this and the neighbouring villages attacked him in the morning when about to proceed, and, as he declared, killed five men, and wounded him, while he hardly escaped, fighting his way for a considerable distance. Upon more minute inquiry we found that he had encountered on his march a man of this village, who induced him to lodge with him, and to whom he imprudently discovered that he possessed, and had with him, effects to the value of 500 rupees; he had with him also his wife and infant daughter, whom he carried in his arms. His treacherous host laid an ambush for him in the morning, into which he fell, and was attacked; his wife, who carried part of his property, was seized and carried off, and he asserted that his daughter was killed in his arms; that he long fought with a sword that he had, but being wounded, he was forced to a retreat.

We afterwards discovered that there was much exaggeration in the account he gave: for most, if not all, the men whom he had declared to have been killed returned to their duty, having effected their retreat from the zemindars. Even the fate of his daughter was not clear. It is certain, however, that the people were attacked by the zemindars of the village, and that he lost his wife, daughter, and property, and received several wounds; but his courageous conduct was probably all a story invented to cover the disgrace of his retreat. It is true that the people had most carelessly left the camp unarmed, except with one or two swords: the villagers had bows and arrows, and axes. This outrage will serve to convey a very striking picture of the lawless state in which the people live. Strangers, passing through the country, are enticed into an ambush under the faith of hospitality, robbed and murdered; and these the servants of the power, which subdued their enemies and delivered them, were insulted, attacked, and plundered, even while they were aware that the means of punishment were at hand, and that though they might escape into the jungles till the storm blew over, their village, with the innocent part of its inhabitants, would in all probability suffer in the punishment of the outrage. This, however, was neither in our contemplation, nor, without much delay, in our power. We passed the place at a distance, and merely wrote an account of the transaction to the commissioner for the affairs of Sirmore, in which this district (Jounsār) is situated.

Our ascent, long and painful, carried us across a lofty gorge, whence a winding path along the ridge of a very noble mountain, and a deep wild descent, brought our journey to a close at the village of Mindrāl, after thirteen miles and a half of very fatiguing marching.

These two marches have lain through the district of Jounsār, which we acknowledge well to deserve the character for wildness which it has acquired. The mountains are peculiarly rugged and precipitous: there is much cliff and rock, little and laborious cultivation, and few villages. The whole rock is limestone, which lends its rough, lumpy, and irregular character to the mountains. In all probability this great vein of lime is continuous with that of the Sine range just beyond Jytock, and which, in that case, runs pretty nearly east and west, cutting the hills slantingly. We saw little or no slate to-day, but it must exist in the vicinity, for the villages were partly roofed with it.

On a height between two ravines we found many lumps of iron ore, in a shape precisely resembling the scoriæ or dross from a smelting furnace, in large drops perfectly metallic. We were informed not only that no furnace was ever in the vicinity, but that such scoriæ were found commonly on the neighbouring Teebas of much greater size, frequently weighing many pounds. I am not sufficiently acquainted with the history of the metals to know whether iron is commonly found in this state, but it seems to point a curious subject of inquiry to the mineralogist and the geologist.

July 9.—Our march, which we commenced at about eight in the morning, much resembled that of yesterday. We yesterday left the Touse a good way to our left, crossing the high ridges that terminate upon it. After a succession of ascents and descents of various importance in a space of twelve miles and a half, we reached the ridge of a lofty d,har, and saw the river Jumna winding far below us like a silver line in the deep dark hollow of its bed. The sun was just setting, but we had three heavy toilsome miles (including another hill) to traverse before we reached Cot,hā, the village assigned for our night's rest. The latter part of our journey was not accomplished until long after dark.

PART VIII.

JOURNEY TO JUMNOTREE.

CHAPTER XXIV.

July 9.—While thus on the banks of the Jumna, and so near the spot whence it derives its source, and so near also to the several remote and holy places of Hindoo pilgrimage, I was exceedingly anxious to visit these remarkable spots, and trace to their source the rivers that form the celebrated Ganges; places to which no European had ever penetrated, and of which so many fables have been related.

For some days previously I had been reflecting on the possibility of realising this idea, and now determined to profit by an opportunity so excellent, and which never could again occur to me, viz. to separate from my brother, in whose march I had so long participated, and with his assistance to pursue my course upward along the Jumna, and to cross over from its source to that of the Bhagiruttee, and thence, if time permitted, to make my way to Kedărnauth and Buddreenauth, and return by the way of Sreenuggur, where I should rejoin my brother.

There was, in truth, not much real difficulty to be contemplated in the undertaking: our ignorance of the country, and its wildness, and poverty in population, as well as in means of subsistence, with the doubtful capability of the necessary servants to perform the journey under the prospect of much privation and exposure, were chiefly the obvious obstacles, and these were provided for as far as possible by procuring the best guides; —one or two old servants of the late rajah, well known among the people of the country, and who could rely on procuring whatever it really afforded for our party, and by taking only the strongest and most willing servants, many of whom were desirous of providing for the safety of their souls by so pious a journey. Little time could be given to preparation; a very small parcel of necessary clothing, with the needful articles of food, and the means of preparing it,—a small stock of wine, &c. formed my baggage: but it was necessary to carry three or four days provision for the party in case of accident, and with the necessary escort it was increased to a considerable number. Our company was nearly as follows, viz.

A Ghoorkha jemmadar, with twelve Ghoorkha petty officers, and sepoys; a Mewattee jemmadar, with a like number of men; four servants styled chuprassies; the necessary people for procuring and preparing provisions, and for carrying personal baggage; coolies sufficient to carry the provisions and necessaries for the people, with the heavy baggage, and these never were fewer than twenty-four, and often more.

We were also accompanied by Kishen Sing, a favourite servant of the late rajah, who was his chief chobedar when he was killed, and who himself bore marks of suffering, for he had received three severe wounds, one of which had nearly cut his head in two, and the parts having been ill joined, it gave to his face a most singular expression, for the visible scar reached across his nose from the left cheek to behind his right ear, which, with his nose, had been divided. From this man we expected much intelligence and many facilities in traversing, as well as inspecting the country. He was accompanied by two Gosseins, who were bound to the holy places under our protection. All these people swelled the number of coolies and attendants, with their servants and baggage, so that our total number was not less than sixty, which may well be deemed cumbrous and large with which to undertake a rough journey of discovery; but when the customs of the country are considered, the comforts that are absolutely necessary, and perhaps as much as all, the policy which urged that the first European who penetrated these untrodden regions should not be meanly attended, the number will be acknowledged, as it really was, quite as small as was consistent with prudence and propriety.

It was desirable to collect as much knowledge of the country as possible during the route: I therefore determined to keep an itinerary, and to survey as we proceeded with as much accuracy as my own want of skill and the deficiency of instruments would permit, for these only consisted of a surveying compass on a tripod, a small pocket compass, and a perambulator. I had neither a thermometer nor barometer; not having foreseen such journeys, no such provision had been made.

Thus equipped we left Cot,ha on the morning of July 10, and took the road towards Jumnotree, which winds along, following the deep indentings of the ravines and valleys that furrow the mountains, and pour their streams into the Jumna, which winds far below. At times it is varied by sharp ascents and descents, but on the whole keeps on a general level till we reach Chumree-ke-ghāt, on our way to which we passed through several villages, but the cultivation is neither extensive nor promising.

From this station, as from one or two in the course of this route, an extensive view would have been obtained, including Birat, Budrāge, and several of the hills above the Deyrah Dhoon, as well as the extensive ranges on which Jountgurh is situated, with a general view of the course of the Jumna, from the snowy mountains to Calsee; but this was prevented by a thick fog, which enveloped the tops of the mountains, and only now and then discovered a peak glimmering through mist.

From hence we entered on a very deep descent into the bed of a nullah, a small but rapid stream, called Goot,har-Ke-Gadh. The valley or hollow, of which this stream is the drain, is somewhat curiously formed: it contains the Bundur Khut, or division; and there is in it a good deal of detached cultivation—wheat and barley, rice, cotton, and a grain called cheena, resembling bird-seed. The rice is neatly cultivated here, as in other parts of the hills, in well levelled ledges, the water being led over each by small courses, taken from some stream, at a distance sufficient to allow of the necessary fall. This ravine or khola is very deep, and the hills lofty and rugged, rising suddenly to their height. The descent from Chumree-ke-ghāt is very severe and painful, irregular and zigzag: it passed through the village of Cot,hal, which had been ruined by the Ghoorkhas, and crossed the nullah, the banks of which are wild and wooded; and thus we arrived at the village of Lak,ha Mundul. This village is situated almost upon the banks of the river. It is claimed by Sirmore and Gurwhāl. It cultivates the land of each state, and pays an assessment to both. It is apparently wholly appropriated to the maintenance of several temples and their priests; and there are some fine rich pieces of land, both on the banks of the Jumna and of a nullah a little farther on, set aside for this holy purpose; for which the village pays half tribute to each state. There is a neat temple to Seewa, and to the five brothers, called the Pundos,an, viz. Joodisthul, Bheem Sing, Arjun, Saha Deo, Nircolo; one to Bhysram and to Purseram; an old ruined place of worship to Mahadeo, under the name of Kedār; and some curiously carved stones, representing the Hindoo deities. Two figures in stone, representing Arjun and Bheem Sing, are remarkably well executed;

but their faces have been mutilated, it is said, by the Rohillas, in an old incursion. There is also a curious stone, representing in relief a number of the Hindoo divinities; Gonesh, Doorgah, Bhowanee, &c. which are very readily distinguishable. There is also at this place a narrow passage leading under ground through the rock to the river side, used (it is said) by the people of the country in time of danger, when pressed by their enemies.

Opposite to this village, Birnee-Ke-Gadh, a large ravine proceeding from the lofty peak Bougee-Ke-Teeba, debouches into the Jumna. In this ravine there is a curiously situated house, on a small teeba rising from the nullah belonging to a zemindar of some consequence, called Bhoob Sing. Our route now lay along some table land, just on the river bank. Passing Bundergurree, a ruined fort situate on a teeba 200 feet high above the road, we descend to Neekrāll-Ke-Gadh. This is said to be the boundary here between Sirmore and Gurwhāl; but there seems to be a tract of *debateable land* around Lak,ha Mundul, which contains some spots of level cultivation far richer than that we have generally met with in the hills. The stream in this nullah is very considerable, and is said to take its rise in T,hirar-Ke-Teeba, two days' journey from hence: its immediate banks are steep, rocky, and woody; and much alder grows on the edges of the water.

From hence a sharp ascent up a bare rocky hill, high above the Jumna, soon brought us to Bunkoulee, a large and apparently populous village, where we halted for the night. Our quarters were in the outer chamber of a building, which is a temple sacred to M,hassoo, (I believe another name for Seeva), who is worshipped with almost exclusive devotion. As we approach the sacred places, and the wild snowy peaks, the peculiar seat and residence of his divinity, he is found under many names and forms, but is still Mahadeo. The temple is neat, in the same style as those we have met with through the hills, with Chinese overhanging roofs, and carved wood-work, and it has brass-covered doors. The village has the appearance of having been once more considerable: the chief zemindar, or seana, as he is called, upon being questioned with regard to its population, averred that it had but twenty-eight houses, and might contain about 100 inhabitants; but his answers were hesitating, obscure, and prevaricating; and I suspect that he feared our questions might be preparatory to some imposition or tax, which prevented the truth from being told.

I should have supposed the village to contain full 250 inhabitants. It does not exactly belong to any purgunnah, but is in some measure attached to Rewaeen.

July 11.—At seven o'clock we left this village, and proceeded still along the left hand face of the hill above the Jumna, following the deep indentings and long rounds of the valleys and ravines, with various irregular ascents and descents, till, by a very rough and clambering path, we reached a point in Ganganee-Ke-Dhār, called Ganganee-Ke-Ghāt, from which a very extensive and noble view is obtained, though it was at this time partially obscured by mist. Hence we gained the first distinct view of Bunderpouch, the mountain, in a part of which is Jumnotree, the birthplace of the Jumna. This mountain exhibits two grand peaks, both very white with snow, and of great magnitude and height. This station is high above the river, but the horizontal distance from it is short; it commands a good view both upwards and downwards: below this the bed of the river is narrow, deep, and rocky, except where the few green spots at Lak,hamundul relieve the eye. Above it runs in a far richer country; much table land and cultivation are on its banks, with several villages: the hills shelve down easily to the level spots, covered with variety of forest scenery and cultivation. Further up they frown and close, and are of darker hue; beyond, and above all, Jumnotree towers above the clouds, which slightly chequered all the landscape with their shade.

From thence we pursued a wild and rocky path, tangled with thick jungle, and probably not much frequented, often following small indentings in the face of the hill. On arriving at the gorge of the next ridge, I was informed by Kishen Sing that there was a valley of considerable magnitude which stretched on our left hand, from the Jumna to the westward; and in hopes of seeing a thing so new in these rugged hills, we left the road to endeavour to get a glimpse of it: on arriving, however, at the top of a hill, whence we expected it might appear, we saw nothing but the lower part of a ravine, entirely of the same nature as the rest of the country. It is called Garee-Ke-Gadh, but above has the name of Rama Serai, and I obtained only the following particulars descriptive of the place.

The old and ruined fortress called Sircote is situate on a high Teeba of the same name, that projects at the end of the lofty range of Kedar-Ke-Kanta, which stretches down from one shoulder of Bunderpouch. Two or three cōs further up in this mountain, the stream Rama has its source at a spot called Sheallee, and is joined by several others from the sides of this as well as from Sircote, and from the range forming the other side of the valley (which is, I believe, called Renai-Ke-Dhān, and appears to have a course from about north-east 70 to 80), either from Bunderpouch, or from some of the Dhārs it gives off. The end of this range was in view, and shuts out from our sight the whole of the valley. Just at the point of this range Rama Serai commences, and runs up to Sircote for a distance of from five to seven cōs, probably about nine miles, in a direction, which, judging from that of the mountains, and of the position of the points we see, may be from north-east 40 to 50. The breadth varies from one and a half to two and a half miles, and is level throughout.

Formerly this valley, which occupies one t,hat or division, was well cultivated, and contained many populous villages, but now, like the rest of Gurwhāl, it has fallen much into decay, and four half ruined hamlets alone remain: viz. Goondiat, Biral, Keemola, and Kulān. The two former are near the head of the plain. The whole t,hat forms a part of the purgunnah, or district of Rewaeen, and had been given by Purdoomun Sah, the late rajah, to his brother Prithum Sah, who lived for six or seven years in several parts of it, his chief residence being at Goondiat. The rajah himself frequently came here with his brothers to hawk in the valley: they rode upon gounts or B,hotea ponies, and killed many partridges, which are here very abundant.

From the foot of Sircote proceeds another nullah or valley, the name of which is Guddoo Gad,h, the waters of which, after a course of about six miles, join the Touse, about the same distance above Unhowl. This is also said to be a fine, level, and formerly well cultivated valley, from a quarter of a mile to one mile in breadth, but far inferior in all respects to Rama Serai, which appeared confessedly the largest and finest valley in the whole raj, excepting the D,hoon, and to have been considered as a place of delightful retirement for the court in the days of their greatness.

Between Kedar-Ke-Kanta and the Touse, there is one more range of hills, called Barkēel, but probably Kedar-Ke-Kanta is the highest ridge, or turning point, between the Jumna and the Touse. Regaining the road, and passing the ruined village of T,hullee, we descended a steep, rough, and rocky path, very irregular and tortuous, to the bed of the nullah, here called Saree-Garee-Ke-Gad,h. The mouth is uncommonly narrow; the water seems to have worn its way down by force, between opposing rocks, which have yielded more slowly than the soil of the hills behind; and this may in some measure account for the singularly different nature of this valley from those universally met with in these hills. The stream is a fine and copious one. The rock here, as well as that we have to-day descended, is principally limestone; in the upper part very hard, and mixed with sandstone. That in the neighbourhood of the village of Bunkhoulee, and during this day's ascent, is also limestone under different shapes: among others, we saw the same remarkable concretion, resembling masses of old mortar mixed with gravel, adverted to before. Common and micaceous slate are also met with, and a very soft white silvery earth, which feels soapy between the fingers. The top of Gunganee-Ke-Dhār exhibits a singular appearance, totally denuded of soil; the rock is cut into strange shapes and fissures, by the action of the weather; it appears a curious compound of sand and lime, and where there is little of the latter to bind and harden the former, rain and storm have worn it away.

The road from hence lies along the river side, sometimes rising a little above its banks, to round the small nullas and irregularities which frequently occur: the heat in the descent to the nullah was excessive, and continued great along the river banks. We now reached Moungrālgurh, an old house which stands on a nearly insulated rock, from 150 to 200 feet high, boldly projecting into the river, and was lately occupied by Dhumunchund, Omeid Sing, and Dowlut Sing, the rotillas* of the rajah of Gurwhāl.

This residence was entirely appropriated to these connexions of the royal family: it appears to have been of considerable extent, but constructed as all the houses of the small T,hakoors which we have noticed in our tour; but now it is in ruins, having been burned three years ago by some discontented zemindars. Just above this place the remains of a sango, or wooden bridge, which kept up communication with the village near Moungrālgurh, are yet visible.

Hence the road lies along the river bank, about 160 feet above its stream, passing many subsidiary nullahs which swell the river from either

* The term *rotilla*, as far as I can understand, is applied to a son of the rajah, born of a slave woman.

side, that take their rise from the noble mountains in view, till about fourteen miles from our morning station, we reached a large stream, Bunāl-Ke-Gadh, which has its source in Surootāle-Ke-Teeba, seven or eight miles hence. In the lower part of this valley there is a considerable extent of flat land under rice, well watered and cultivated. At the time we passed it the zemindars, their women and children, were busily employed in ploughing and planting it. They were numerous, and were peculiarly wild and savage in their appearance, both men and women laughing like ideots as we passed. We were met by singers and dancers with instruments, who were employed in cheering the labours of the field. The people here are remarkably fond of the uncouth noise they make, and doummers, singers, &c. are found in every village. There is, it is said, much rice cultivation along the whole of this valley, which forms the Bunāl t,hat.

From the mouth of this valley there is a sharp ascent, up a hill, which is the tail of Dhooloo D,har: a little further on, on the banks of a very small nullah, along the brow of the hill, is situated the village of Dukheat, where we lodged for the night. This village is very neat, and of considerable size; from it we had a fine view of the valley, which appears well cultivated, although there is not much level land; on the opposite side are several villages and single houses. This evening the clouds were very low and heavy, and much rain fell. I took up my quarters in a rather poor house in the village, but was well supplied with necessaries for myself and the people: several Ghoorkha soldiers joined us here, and solicited service.

It was usual, during the time when that people were in power, to station parties in the different districts, for the purpose of collecting the revenue, and, in progress of time, many of them took daughters of the zemindars in marriage; not always with the good will of the latter, but the connexion formed a tie between the conquerors and the conquered, which, though far weaker, from the savage and treacherous nature of the people, and the circumstances of violence under which it was formed, than a similar one in most other countries would have been, was still sufficient, during its existence, to guarantee the life, and prevent the murder of the son-in-law. When the power of the Ghoorkhas was broken, and their troops taken prisoners or scattered, those in the remoter districts, who were thus connected, chose to domesticate with their wives and families rather than run the hazard of retreating through a country of hostile savages, ripe for revenge upon tyrannical, but now fallen masters. Others too, in like manner, although not enjoying the security resulting from any such tie, chose rather to trust to the protection of some zemindars whom they had known, and had possibly once obliged, and by whom they believed that their lives would not be attacked, than risk their safety in a more dangerous flight, although the loss of property in both cases was nearly certain. Thus individuals of this wretched people were found in the hills in every district, and almost every one was stripped of his property, even till they were in want of clothes to cover them from the weather. Many were more deplorably situated. Some, wounded and neglected, were found languishing unassisted, and wanting even necessaries. Others had fled to the jungles, to escape the massacre to which their comrades had fallen victims, and for a long time subsisted on the roots and fruits found in thick forests.

Even the marriage tie did not always insure good treatment; and not unfrequently, when the terror of consequences ceased, the zemindars reclaimed their daughters, and forced them to leave their husbands, although the stipulated prices had been paid for them. Several curious cases were referred to us for decision, in which, of course, nothing could be done, except to leave it to the ladies' uninfluenced decision; and where the contract was broken, it generally appeared that the loss of the twelve or sixteen rupees paid for the wife was the most grievous part of the injury. The money they never would restore, arguing that the contract had partly been made by force on the side of the Ghoorkha. Many, however, of the women left their families and country, and voluntarily followed the party with their Ghoorkha lords, and appeared to be not only fully equal to the march, but were of the greatest use to their husbands, sharing their burthens, occasionally carrying their children, and always cooking their dinners when arrived at night on our ground.

The people in question at this village excused themselves from attending the party to Gungotree, as was offered them, on the plea of having neither clothes nor arms, nor means to procure either; probably they were not anxious to encounter so long and fatiguing a journey: I therefore gave them a note to my brother, and desired that a few Sepoys in the service of Goving Bhisht, the fougedhar of Rewaeen, should be sent as a protection, and see them safe to Srenuggur. This gentleman joined us this morning, to accompany or conduct us through his district. He is a man of high caste and considerable consequence, and has had the entire administration of the extensive purgunnah of Rewaeen; in fact, he has been of late like an independent prince under the Ghoorkha Raj, for in so distant and impracticable a situation he could not well be called to an account either by the rajah or his conquerors, and he had kept on good terms with the Ghoorkhas, owing, as I understand, much of his consequence to them. He has several residences, but generally lives at one on the banks of the Bhagiruttee. He is a tall good looking man, fair, and far superior in appearance to the people of the hills, and they here seem to pay very great respect and devotion to him.

July 12.—This morning proved fine, and we left the village at about half-past six, accompanied by Bhisht and some of his attendants, ascending higher upon the end of Dhooloo-Ke-Dhār, which proceeds from Kedar-Ke-Kantā. The opposite side of the river is desolate and uncultivated, although the ruins of several villages were perceptible. The Patrain nullah opposite has a good deal of fine level land, but all is abandoned and waste. We crossed the hill, and reached the banks of Budyeargadh, which we crossed at Shellee-Ke-Sango. Just below the mouth of this nullah there is a sango thrown across the river, and immediately opposite to it, in a rock at the foot of the hill on the other side the Jumna, there is a spring of water of considerable size, respecting the origin of which a curious tale is told. It is asserted in the country that this is the water of the Bhagiruttee, which flows through the extent of hill and rock between the two rivers (about one day's journey), and that this subterraneous passage was formed on the following occasion.

There yet exists in the neighbourhood a place of worship dedicated to M,ha Deo, in which a Brahmin of great sanctity anciently ministered: he used to go every day to perform his ablutions in the Bhagiruttee, though so far distant, till great age rendered him no longer able to take this severe diurnal exercise, when he prayed that some means might be afforded him to continue it. His prayer was heard, and he was directed to drop his handkerchief in the Bhagiruttee, and whenever that should appear on the Jumna bank, there to wash, with confidence of its being the waters of the holy stream. The Brahmin is gone, but the waters remain flowing, and retain their sanctity in the eyes of the country people, who confidently believe that they are the effect of a miracle,—a miracle ingeniously and successfully framed to continue to laziness or inability the odour of sanctity derived from penance, without the pains of it.

Shellee-Ke-Sango is thrown across Budyear-Ke-Gadh, and is rather a fearful one, consisting merely of two pieces of wood laid together upon the points of two projecting rocks, below which the stream, which has worn its way deep between them, foams with great violence; and as the pieces are laid on an ascent, and are somewhat slippery, it is a matter of some difficulty to pass it when unaccustomed to such bridges. The stream is full and rapid: it has its rise in a large hill called Buchooncha. From the sango a steep but not long ascent leads to the village of Naguan, in the T,hat of the same name. In this village Goving Sing has a residence. There are five villages still inhabited in the Nugwan T,hat, viz. Palee, Shalwa, Coorsela, T,hau, and P,hooldar, besides many now in ruins.

From this village our road lay up a steep ascent to the northward. The first part was along a steep grassy, but stony hill-face, afterwards through a thin fir-wood. From a point in the ascent I got a bearing of Bunderpouch west peak, north-east 54° 30′, and put down the names of the different peaks and kholas on the opposite side; but the more distant points downwards, as well as the loftiest upwards, were buried in clouds. Hence to the village of Shalwa there is an easy sloping ascent through a country which is perfectly susceptible of cultivation, and indeed bears the traces of former tillage: at present it is very much neglected, small fields in bad order being scattered through the rank weeds and jungle. Passing through this place, the ascent continues moderate along tolerably cultivated land to the heights above Chount,hull, which is a singular hollow, surrounded by peaks of rich verdure, and formerly cultivated, though now only covered with fine grass, and a profusion of flowers. Strawberries were scattered about here and there under the shade of the trees, bordering a little rivulet close by. The road, now descending, winds along the left-hand back of a valley, which debouches into the Jumna, to the very bottom of a very steep ascent up a shoulder of Toorul-Ke-Dhar, the top of which we reached after a tiresome march.

From this point a fall of water from the snow near the bottom of the Bunderpouch mountain is very plainly seen, and Bhisht informed us that it was the true Jumnotree. It did not appear at any great distance, though it was said to be three days' journey. The road now led along the face of the hill, inclining upwards through a wood of various sorts of trees, oaks, firs, &c. to the ghāt where the descent begins. The path is tolerably good, though narrow and high above the river, at times with tremendous precipices below. A little below the point where this dhār meets the river the hills approach on each side, and the bed becomes narrow, dark, and very precipitous; at times forming one perpendicular and rugged wall from the height of the peaks to the water, which foams through its confined channel.

The scenery on the whole has very much changed its character: instead of the villages and extensive faces of cultivation, and sharp and steep, yet practicable hills, we now saw nothing but the brown rocks staring through the dark pine and oak woods, which hang shaggy around their brows, and clothe their feet, as well as the deeper and less stony glens, which are numerous and romantic. The tops of these hills are spotted with green or brown, as the bright verdure of the rainy season springs from the scanty soil, or is denied to the barren rock, and clouds and darkness hang over all. Having reached the top of the ascent, we looked down upon a very deep and dark glen, called Palia Gadh, which is the outlet to the waters of one of the most terrific and gloomy valleys I have ever seen. The lofty peak Buchooncha stretches forth a rugged ridge called Tolpoorra to the southward, which becomes continuous with Toonul, the lower part of which we crossed. This ridge forms a side and part of the back of the valley or hollow of Cot,ha, the chief ravine of which, however, commences at the top of the bosom of Buchooncha; this is joined by smaller but equally rugged clefts from the back, which all unite their waters below, and roll a great and rapid torrent to the Jumna.

But it would not be easy to convey by any description a just idea of the peculiarly rugged and gloomy wildness of this glen: it looks like the ruins of nature, and appears, as it is said to be, completely impracticable and impenetrable. Little is to be seen except dark rock; wood only fringes the lower parts and the waters' edge: perhaps the spots and streaks of snow, contrasting with the general blackness of the scene, heighten the appearance of desolation. No living thing is seen; no motion but that of the waters; no sound but their roar. Such a spot is suited to engender superstition, and here it is accordingly found in full growth. Many wild traditions are preserved, and many extravagant stories related of it.

On one of these ravines there are places of worship, not built by men, but natural piles of stones, which have the appearance of small temples. These are said to be the residence of the dewtas, or spirits, who here haunt and inveigle human beings away to their wild abodes. It is said that they have a particular predilection for beauty in both sexes, and remorselessly seize on any whom imprudence or accident may have placed within their power, and whose spirits become like theirs after they are deprived of their corporeal frame. Many instances were given of these ravishments: on one occasion a young man, who had wandered near their haunts, being carried in a trance to the valley, heard the voice of his own father, who some years before had been thus spirited away, and who now recognised his son. It appears that paternal affection was stronger than the spell that bound him, and instead of rejoicing in the acquisition of a new prey, he recollected the forlorn state of his family deprived of their only support: he begged and obtained the freedom of his son, who was dismissed under the injunction of strict silence and secrecy. He however forgot his vow, and was immediately deprived of speech, and, as a self-punishment, he cut out his tongue with his own hand. This man was said to be yet living, and I desired that he should be brought to me, but he never came, and they afterwards informed me that he had very lately died. More than one person is said to have approached the spot, or the precincts of these spirits, and those who have returned have generally agreed in the expression of their feelings, and have uttered some prophecy. They fall, as they say, into a swoon, and between sleeping and waking hear a conversation, or are sensible of certain impressions as if a conversation were passing, which generally relates to some future event. Indeed, the prophetic faculty is one of the chiefly remarkable attributes of these spirits, and of this place.

The officiating Brahmins sometimes venture farther than the vulgar, and are favoured by communications of future import. It is said that they prophesied the misfortunes and death of Purdoomun Sah, the loss of his kingdom, and his life at Deyrah Dhoon, and the commencement of the Ghoorkha Raj. They also foretold, as is asserted, the termination of that tyranny the very month that the final issue would take place, and the commencement of the English power over the country. Upon my smiling at this, and remarking on the easiness of converting into a prophecy what had already happened, both Bhisht and Kishen Sing assured me of the fact with great earnestness, and the former averred that he had told Ummr Sing of the prophecy, but that he had defied it. I inquired whether there had been any late oracles, and, after some hesitation, and with much reluctance, I was informed that it had been predicted within the last three weeks, that there would, in the course of the next twelve months, be wars in Hindostan, of so bloody a nature, that the nullahs would run red: but between what powers, or who was to be the conqueror, they would not, or could not say.

The awe, however, which the natives feel for this place is great and remarkable. The moment that Bhisht and Kishen Sing came in sight of the place, they commenced prostrations, and the forms of worship, with many prayers of much apparent fervency, to the spirits of the glen. They assert that no man ever ascended the valley to any considerable height, and that natural as well as supernatural obstacles are too great to be overcome; that of the few who have attempted it, none ever returned, or ever enjoyed his reason again: and I believe that the former of these obstacles may be nearly paramount, for a survey with the glass showed the difficulty to be at least very great; and, certainly, ascending the hill to the top would be altogether impossible. Had I had time, however, I would have attempted it, and I am confident, that though none of the hill people would have ventured, several of my Ghoorkhas, and two of the Hindoo chuprassies, would have followed me.

We began our descent, which is truly wild and even dangerous: the path rocky and rough, slippery from wet and from the fallen leaves, winds down sometimes on the face, sometimes on the sharp projection of the hill, with a deep precipice at times on one hand, and a high rocky wall on the other; sometimes sinking into a deep nullah amongst dark woods of oak, pine, larch, sycamore, horse-chesnut, and a thousand smaller trees and shrubs, carpeted with ferns, strawberries, and a countless, nameless variety of flowers beneath them.

At other times the track stretched along a bare rocky face with no more break than what had been worn during ages by the feet of cattle, and by the few passengers who reach these wild abodes, and where a false step would be fatal. This descent continued the whole way most precipitous, till we reached the nullah, which is here a pretty copious stream, though evidently very much beholden to the snow and rain for its increase, and we passed it upon two sticks thrown across from one stone to another. From hence by a short steep ascent we gained a piece of land more level than any we had seen to-day, but yet of no great extent, on which is situated the village of Palia, our resting-place for the night. This day's journey led us into a country very far different in character from any that we have before traversed. I recollect nothing that approaches to it except a glen, proceeding from the snowy hill above Moral-Ke-Kanda, seen from the village of Dharin, where we were detained two days' journey from Serăn.

As before observed concerning the hills on the banks of the Jumna, the mountains here have lost all vestiges of cultivation, as well as of animal life. They are far more rude and impracticable. The rocks tower more suddenly to their height. There is less wood and fewer ledges and clefts where cultivation could be performed.

The glen above described is by far the most gloomy savage scene we have yet met with. I regret that the weather did not permit a sketch of it to be attempted. Beyond this we could see nothing in the course of the river but rocky banks. The opposite side is particularly precipitous; yet along its face a road is carried, which is frequented as much as this, and leads to the villages still further up. By the time we had reached the village, the clouds which had lowered around and sunk down on the hills, began to burst with loud thunder and heavy rain. The noise was fearfully reverberated among the hills; and during the night more than once the sound was heard of fragments from the brows of the mountains, crashing down to the depths below with a terrific din. Our quarters were good. I slept in a temple neat, clean, and secure from the weather.

The village of Palia is of considerable size, consisting of about fifteen or twenty houses, but neither so neat nor so thriving as Duckheat, our last night's stage. Around it there are several acres of cultivation in broader ledges than usual; however, the whole is of no great extent, and it is quite insulated. I observed here many of the people to be particularly fair complexioned, several as much so as the fairest of the Moguls met with in Hindostan, and they were fine looking men. It already began to be evident that Bhisht, who accompanied us as guide and provider, would be rather a clog than an assistance to us. He appeared to be quite exhausted with the march, and arrived at the ground two hours after we were housed.

CHAPTER XXV.

FROM PALIA GAHD TO JUMNOTREE.

July 13.—We left Palia with a promising day, after a rainy night. We have certainly penetrated into the very heart of the region of superstition, the seat of Indian mythology. While waiting for the despatch of the baggage I was listening to the numberless tales which were related of the valley we were leaving, when Kishen Sing pointed out the brow of a precipice, where, he says, on a former occasion some extraordinary appearances were observed. It was whilst on an expedition with Prithum Sah, the brother of the late rajah. They were leaving this village in the morning, when, in sight of the whole train of attendants, columns of smoke or mist of various colours, green, red, and blue, rose from a cleft in the hill, and proceeded to the course of a small stream, which takes its rise in the same hill; and, returning again, vanished. They possessed no shape or distinct form; but, as he expressed it, were like the shades of men without corporeal substance. The general character of the spot might assist imagination to a very great degree in giving to airy nothings "a local habitation and a name."

Our road commenced by leading down almost to the debouche of the Palia Gadh for nearly a mile and a half, chiefly along small ledges of cultivation upon a steep slope, with many indentations on the hill side: there, crossing a gorge in the point running down to the Jumna, it continued along its banks from 2 to 300 yards above the stream. From hence the path is very rough, rocky, and dangerous, winding along, ascending and descending across the faces of steep precipices and down deep ravines; at times also leading along banks of loose earth and stones where the face of the mountain has fallen, and rendering the footing exceedingly uncertain and difficult. The brows of the mountains on either side now approached very close, and their sides, in precipices of many hundred, and in some parts thousand feet deep, form at once the banks and bed of the river.

Along these steeps, however, the road is led, and they are occasionally traversed by hunters in pursuit of the musk and other deer, pheasants, and jungle fowl. Here we beheld several fine and lofty cascades, which owe their origin to the rain, that now daily fell in the mountains, but which in the dry months have no existence. One in particular falls from the high peak of Pinjera, and is lost in a fearfully deep hollow. It cannot be less than 300 feet high; but the stream of water is not sufficiently large to produce a very grand effect, contrasted as it is with the gigantic features of the surrounding scenery. The foliage of this remote tract assumes a character suited to the general tone of the country. It is dark, luxuriant, and heavy; yet still we saw among the dusky firs and thickets of oak the white rose rising in rich clusters to the tops of the old trees, and the jasmines creeping lower, but at times almost overarching the path; while under foot the strawberry, ferns, and yellow, blue, and white blossoms of innumerable flowers furnish a sweet and remarkable contrast, on which the eye, weary with a continual stretch to the crags above, reposes with pleasure.

This various yet dangerous path continued for a considerable way, and ended in a very steep descent to Usuree Gadh, which is a considerable stream, at present swollen by the rain, and has its rise in a peak that springs from Buchoonchoo. At the mouth of this stream there is a peninsulated rock of some height, on which is an old fort called Usuree Gurh. The rock is connected with the mountains overhanging the river by a low cultivated piece of land. The appearance and situation of this rock and old fort is singularly romantic and fine. It is washed on three parts of its circuit by the Jumna, with a wild rapid current on one side, at the very foot of the rock; and in the bed of the river there are several small springs of hot water which we went to see. Some of these sources, we observed, appeared to rise with considerable force, giving a stream of four or five fingers in thickness from the surface of the earth, quite close to the solid rock, and much came trickling down from between the laminæ of the rock of which the hill is formed. These are in large white flakes, and consist, I believe, entirely of quartz. They form an angle of about sixty or seventy degrees with the plane of the horizon. The water is beautifully clear; it is more than blood-warm, and is strongly impregnated with acid; it has much of the smell common to sulphureous springs, and is evidently impregnated with this substance, and probably with iron; for the rocks around were tinged and incrusted with a red matter resembling iron rust, mixed with clay or lime: the acid may be sulphuric or sulphureous.

Quite close to the warm springs, and in their stream, a cold one bubbles up; but the mixture is so immediate, that it is impossible to say whether the acid, which it also contains, is communicated from the warm water or not. It had, however, both an acid taste and smell, like the other; and around its source, upon the rock, there was a collection of scum, formed of green slime and the red concretion before mentioned, which occurred in the united streams till they joined the river. From the manner in which this water issues from the rock, it would seem that its source was in the body of the hill above; but there is no other appearance whatever to lead to any probable conjecture respecting the formation of it. There are many such springs of warm water in the course of the Jumna.

From the bed of the river we ascended to the road we had left by a rough path through jungle; and for a short way it leads along a fine green bank: after which we again descended to the bed of the river, by a zig-zag stony path, leading to a temporary bridge formed of a few sticks laid across two rocks, with brushwood and small stones upon them, called Terkeēla-ka-Sango. The river is here diminished to a small but rapid mountain torrent. The span of this bridge is not more than from fifteen to seventeen feet: the stream foams about six feet below it, and is so violent, that no chance of escape would remain to any one who might unfortunately fall into it. From this bridge the road leads through jungle and high grass, and is apparently little frequented, till we pass through the village of Terkeela, small and poor. Hence a long, various, and rather laborious ascent, among jungle, and along ledges of abandoned cultivation, led us to the village of Coopera, which has been a large and populous place; but now, like most others, is in total decay.

There is a temple to Vischnû, under the name of Nag-Rajah; and we found the villagers preparing to perform the annual ceremony of carrying the image, with songs and dances, to be bathed near Jumnotree.

The hills forming the banks of the river above Usuree Gurh, separate from each other somewhat more than below; but, though the landscape thus gains a little in openness, it loses nothing of its savage wildness. The river seems to have had a hard struggle through opposing rocks, and the course is accordingly more irregular and winding; and the glen in which it flows is more wildly divided. Solid rocks, forming stubborn barriers at the ends of the ranges that meet the river, turn its stream in every direction, till it passes Usuree Gurh, whence it flows nearly straight for a considerable way. Here is very little cultivation; and the opposite, or west side, has none: the whole tract, indeed, from Palia upwards, except the few fields at Usuree Gurh, is perfectly barren; and between this river and the Touse,—perhaps thirty cōs,—the whole country consists of impracticable ravines and precipices, high and wild ranges of snow, and rock totally unsusceptible of any sort of improvement or cultivation, and hardly to be penetrated even by travellers. On the banks of the Touse, however, even almost to its source, there are several villages, and a good deal of corn land.

The distance between the Jumna and Bhagiruttee here is said not to exceed one day's journey; but from Cursalee, the nearest village to Jumnotree, we were told that the country across, from the one river to the other, is very difficult, and the road much longer, being three days' journey through a country in which there are no inhabitants, nor can any supplies be procured. This I suspected to be exaggerated, as our guides seemed quite afraid of the difficulties of the hills, and delighted in alarming and in throwing obstacles in our way. Pursuing our route by a moderate descent, along ridges of land once cultivated, we reached the bed of the Chunghawl-Ke-Gadh, the banks of which are dangerous on either side: it has hollowed out a course through solid rock, which, by a succession of falls, joins the river below.

The path here is very dangerous, leading over one narrow ledge of a rock so overhung by another, that one is obliged to creep on hands and knees to pass it: below is a fearful precipice. How the loaded coolies passed it safely I can hardly comprehend. Some time since a Ghoorkha woman, travelling with a detachment, fell over, and was dashed to pieces.

A very circuitous descent, leading us back a long way, at last brought us to the village of Consale, chiefly in ruins. The road proceeds along abandoned land and jungle to the bottom of a steep ascent, from the top of which we saw yesterday's descent, which did not appear at half the distance we actually came. Immediately opposite this spot are the remains of a village most wildly situated upon the brow of a precipice, overhanging the Jumna, at least one thousand feet high: there is a curious winding path along its face to the river side. I believe it was, and is, almost entirely a nest of thieves. A very bad irregular path, passing several small streams, and all the way in wood, led us to the village of Rānā, where we were to pass the night.

This, as well as yesterday's, was a short day's journey; but I was assured that there is no village between this place and Cursalee, our next stage, which was stated to be eight cōs distant. The whole day had been cloudy as usual, and the heights were enveloped in mist; but, as we approached the village, a heavy shower fell, and the evening cleared, showing the magnificent mountain and snowy peaks of Bunderpouch, free from any intervening cloud, their bold outline being strongly defined on the deep blue sky behind.

I took advantage of this moment to make a hurried sketch of these peaks and the range that shuts up the glen. But here I discovered an unfortunate omission, of a very disappointing nature; the whole stock of paper I had laid out for taking sketches of any interesting scene on the road had been left behind by a servant's neglect, and little was left except the common paper of the country, which was nearly useless for my purpose.

From this point we plainly saw the water running down from the different masses of snow, that fill the ravines below the region that is totally covered with it. The valley ends here apparently in an immense basin, the whole of which yields its waters to the Jumna. From the great mountain proceed very high and rugged ridges, which stretch down along the river (themselves broken into inferior ones), and shut out all communication with the other larger valleys. While the fog kept off, the whole was full in our view, and the connexion of every peak and ridge clear and apparent; but darkness soon overwhelmed the landscape, the clouds descended, and all was shrouded in gray mist.

July 14.—This morning all was clear, and not a cloud rested on the surrounding mountains: the view was even more perfect and grand than on the preceding evening; for the sun rose in a cloudless sky, gradually lighting up the high peaks with a most vivid crimson and gold, till all the landscape glowed.

We did not leave the village till seven o'clock. It is a poor and dirty place; but my quarters were in a temple, and good and clean. For a short space our road lay along the very easy slope of a hill, whence we descended gradually, passing through the ruined village of Paria, to the confluence of two nullahs, the Doocun-Ke-Gad,h, and the *Birain*, or Bheem-Ke-Gad,h. The road was in some places steep, difficult, and bad; and the immediate descent to the beds extremely precipitous. Doocun-Ke-Gad,h is the least considerable in course and size, and takes its rise in Ooncha-Ke-D,har. Bheem-Ke-Gad,h is little inferior to the Jumna in size, and comes from one of the ranges springing from Soomeroo-Purbut, called Bheem-Ke-D,har, which we shall pass on our way to the Bhagiruttee. We crossed it here by a temporary bridge.

We now entered on a very steep ascent, to the top of a hill that intervened between us and Bunderpouch, whence a very fine view of the range was obtained. The first part of this is a steep slanting path, on a grassy slope; after which it leads among huge fragments of rock and old and noble forest trees, which form a complete shade, but shut out all view. At length we arrived at an open space, covered with a thick carpet of flowers and strawberries, whence the desired range of vision was fully possessed. We enjoyed it, however, but for a moment; for clouds, as usual, soon concealed all from our sight.

This was a delicious spot; and we remained here a long while: we had not the shadow of trees, nor did we want them. The cold wind, which blew gently off the snow, rendered the sun, which shone bright, rather a comfort than an annoyance.

From this station we had a far nobler and more satisfactory view of Bunderpouch than we had hitherto enjoyed, or would probably have again. It is a prodigious mountain; though, from our close vicinity, and comparatively low situation, we could not conceive its full height. Two lofty and massy peaks rise high above the rest, deep in snow, from which all the other inferior ridges seem to have their origin. These peaks are connected by a sharp neck, considerably lower than themselves.

The south and south-east exposure is the least steep, and bears a great depth of pure unbroken snow. Little or no rock is seen, except a few points at the ridge of the connecting neck, where it is too sharp and steep for snow to lie; and there it appears of a red colour. Here and there lofty precipices are seen in the snow itself, where the lower parts have melted, and masses have given way and slidden down to the ravines below, leaving a face several hundred feet high, that shows the depth of snow which has accumulated for ages.

The formation of the valley through which we have journeyed, and the size and the direction of the ridges, as they spring from this great centre, are here finely traced. From a point to our right, as we looked to the mountain, a ridge strikes off to the southward and westward, which ends in a small nullah at a short distance in our front: this D,har is called Kylaroo. To the west of this, and nearly north-east of us, another large mass runs down, called Doomun-Kundee, forming between itself and Kylaroo a basin, whence runs the Oonta Gunga. Further to the westward, a considerable way to our left, a range, consisting of many high and irregular masses, taking its rise from Damaeen, a continuation of Bunderpouch, forms the western side of the valley; and, between this range and Doomun-Kundee, the Jumna is formed from many sources in the snow. The Oonta Gunga and Jumna unite at the point of a level piece of land, lying at the foot of Doomun-Kundee, which thus, in fact, subdivides the valley into those, giving birth to these two rivers, which are nearly equal in size.

The name of Bunderpouch properly applies only to the highest peaks of this mountain: all the subordinate peaks and ridges have their own peculiar names. Jumnotree has reference only to the sacred spot, where worship is paid to the goddess, and ablution is performed. There are said to be four peaks which form the top of Bunderpouch, only two of which are seen from hence; and in the cavity or hollow contained between them tradition places a lake or tank, of very peculiar sanctity. No one has ever seen this pool, for no one has ever even attempted to ascend any of these prodigious peaks. Besides the physical difficulties, there is one to be encountered far more conclusive than any other, that could be opposed to the superstitious and blindly obedient Hindoo. The goddess has especially prohibited any mortal from passing that spot appointed for her worship. A fuqeer once lost his way in attempting to reach Jumnotree, and was ascending the mountain, till he reached the snow, where he heard a voice inquiring what he wanted; and, on his answering, a mass of snow detached itself from the side of the hill, and the voice desired him to worship where this snow stopped; that Jumna was not to be too closely approached or intruded on in her recesses; that he should publish this, and return no more, under penalty of death. Indeed, I suspect this prohibition to be unnecessary, to prevent an ascent to or near the top of any of these snowy peaks: even the extreme steepness, the rugged nature of the rock, where it is bare, and the hard slippery smoothness of the snow, are, independent of the immense height and consequent fatigue to be borne, sufficient obstacles to such an attempt. The existence of such a lake, therefore, rests entirely on tradition, and probably on some obscure legend from the Shasters; for it would appear that all these mountains, with their various cliffs and valleys, are frequently referred to as the scenes of mythological story; and to one of these the mountain owes its name.

Bunderpouch signifies "monkey's tail." It is said that Hoonooman, after his conquest of Lunka, or Ceylon, in shape of a monkey, when he had set that island on fire by means of a quantity of combustible matter tied to his tail, being afraid of the flame reaching himself, was about to dip it in the sea (Sumunder) to extinguish it; but the sea remonstrated with him, on account of the probable consequences to the numerous inhabitants of its waters: whereupon Hoonooman plunged his burning tail in this lake, which ever since has retained the name. Another account relates, that Hoonooman laid his tail on the shore, while Sumunder laved water on it, and so extinguished it. There seems to be some confusion between Sumunder and the lake on the mountain top, for which no distinct name is given; but there is none with regard to the name of the mountain, which is universal in the country. The zemindars aver, that every year, in the month P,hagun, a single monkey comes from the plains, by way of Hurdooar, and ascends the highest peak of this mountain, where he remains twelve months, and returns to give room to another; but his entertainment must be very indifferent and inhospitable, as may be inferred from the nature of the place; for he returns in very bad plight, being not only reduced almost to a skeleton, but having lost his hair and great part of his skin.

On our right, to the eastward of Kylaroo, the mountain stretches out into many ridges, which spread as they leave it, giving their waters to the different streams that supply the Jumna, but chiefly to the Oontagunga and Bheem-Ke-Gad,h. From this station, however, we could have no farther prospect in this direction. We promised ourselves much delight and useful information from a view of the country, should the weather prove clear, on crossing these high ranges. To the left, or westward, we could only see that the ridge runs continuously from the western peak of Bunderpouch, at a far inferior height, yet in many high singular peaks, and tending more to the northward; while, from each height, ridges varying in height run down to the southward and south-westward. Of the northern and north-eastern sides we did not, and indeed could not, hope to see any thing; but as the highest peak rises on that side, we may presume that very lofty ranges stretch out in these directions, and this corresponds with the accounts of the people of the country.

Leaving this station, we descended gently along a lovely, wooded, and flowery path, for some distance, through varied ground; and, after several irregularities, reached a small water-course from Soonapery-*Ke-D,*har. There is some cultivation here, partly of a grain called *papera,* and partly of wheat in a very backward state; but there is much more land that has been tilled formerly, but which has now returned to its original state. Here also we saw larger flocks of sheep than we had before seen; but their wool, like that of all other sheep in these parts, is extremely coarse.

Passing through the site of an old village, where we observed a few of the finest walnut-trees I ever saw, and turning the corner of a projecting hill by a trifling descent, we reached a bridge over the Oonta Gunga, which we here crossed. There is a deep fall under the bridge, which roars as we pass, and adds to the terror of crossing an old and nearly rotten frame of wood, at a great height above the water, and, as usual, joining two projecting rocks, but rather better constructed than most we have met with. From hence the village is scarcely two furlongs distant.

Cursalee, the highest village in this glen, is situate on the banks of the Oonta Gunga, from 100 to 200 feet above its stream, and only a short way from the end of that plain before spoken of, as forming the point between the Jumna and Oonta Gunga. This is of considerably greater extent than any single piece of land I have seen, probably 200 acres, and is well cultivated: there were once several villages on it, but now we only saw the remains of two, besides Cursalee. This village is large, tolerably neat, and probably populous; but at present it is full of the inhabitants of all the neighbouring villages, who have brought the images of their gods to bathe. The Seana, with the Pundit, and Brahmins of Jumnotree, attended by a great number of both sexes, came out to meet us. The Pundit, a mean and dirty looking fellow, clad like the rest in coarse blankets, came forward, and insisted on marking my forehead with the sacred yellow; a ceremony which I submitted to with a good grace as to a high compliment, and which was eagerly sought for by the Hindoo attendants, who, as well as the Seana, and most of the villagers, received this blessing after me. We then proceeded to our quarters, which were very tolerable, clean and dry. As for coolness of situation, it is not here much required.

The annual ceremony of carrying the images of their gods to wash in the sacred stream of the Jumna is (it appears) one of much solemnity among the inhabitants of the neighbourhood; and the concourse of people here assembled has been busily engaged, and continues to be fully occupied in doing honour to it. They dance to the sound of strange music, and intoxicate themselves with a sort of vile spirit, brewed here from grain and particular roots, sometimes, it is said, sharpened by pepper. The dance is most grotesque and savage: a multitude of men taking hands, sometimes in a circle, sometimes in line, beating time with their feet, bend with one accord, first nearly to the earth with their faces, then backwards, and then sidewise, with various wild contortions. These, and their uncouth dress of black and gray blankets, give a peculiar air of brutal ferocity to the assemblage. The men dance all day, and in the evening they are joined by the women, who mix indiscriminately with them, and keep up dancing and intoxication till the night is far advanced. They continue this frantic kind of worship for several days; and, in truth, it is much in unison with their general manners and habits,—savage and inconsistent. At a place so sacred, the residence of so many holy Brahmins, and the resort of so many pious pilgrims, we might expect to find a strict attention to the forms of religion, and a scrupulous observance of the privations and austerities enjoined by it. So far, however, is this from the truth, that much is met with, shocking even to those Hindoos who are least bigoted.

All classes and castes of people, Brahmins not even excepted, eat every sort of meat except beef, and, I believe, fowls, and drink spirituous liquors even to excess. Fowls are found in plenty in this and the neighbouring villages, and they were even offered as presents to me by the zemindars, which could not have been the case had they been held in abhorrence. I was also surprised at their indifference to what might have appeared, and certainly would in the low country have been deemed a pollution of their temples. Themselves pointed out the outer room of a place of worship for the use of the kitchen, and saw with perfect composure a Mussulmaun servant kill in it the fowls they had provided, and dress them for dinner. I know not whether the place was in general use for worship; it was old and in bad repair; but even to a ruined temple the Hindoo of the plains would probably have paid more respect than to suffer it to be converted to such an use.

The dress of the people is in fact the same which prevails through the whole country, since we left the lower parts of Sirmore. It consisted of a jacket or dress of blanket, tied round the waist like the common Hindoo ungurca, and open down the right breast. Tight in the body and arms, but formed with short skirts all round, very ample, and gathered in folds like the philibeg of the Scotch highlanders. Around their waist they wear a cummerbund, either of woollen stuff, or of rope formed of goat's hair, neatly plaited. They wear drawers or trowsers very loose to the calf of the leg, but tighter and falling in numerous creases below it to the heel. A piece of blanket stuff, somewhat lighter than the rest, is worn round the shoulders like the Scotch plaid, as rain or sun may require to keep the body dry, or to protect the head from heat. On their head they wear a black cap of hair and wool, fitted to the shape, and ending in a small point. The wool from which they manufacture these cloths is of extreme coarseness, very far inferior to that seen in Bischur, or any other part of the hills to the westward, which sometimes was woven into blankets of considerable beauty and fineness.

There are only two colours in use, viz. a dark brown and a dirty gray. The former is most affected by the men of superior rank or means. Not an instance of cotton cloth was seen, and the dress of the women in no respect varied from that of the men, except that sometimes their heads were covered with a blue or checked handkerchief; and they wore beads of glass or pewter in as great profusion as they could obtain, and bangles of the same metal, of great size, round their arms and ancles.

The personal appearance of these people is much the same as that of the Bischurees about Rampore and Serān. They have stout well-built figures; their complexions are frequently very fair, though much sunburnt; their eyes often blue; their hair and beards curled, and of a light or red colour. They seem admirably calculated to form a body of soldiers fit to act in this hilly region. Occasionally traces may be observed of the Tartar features: the small eye, high cheek bone, and meagre mustachios; but they were not sufficiently prevalent to authorise the supposition of any considerable intercourse or intermixture. The language is Hindostannee, and though still bad, is rather better and more intelligible than that we heard in Bischur. The cold is here very considerable the whole year round; even now it was extremely sharp, morning and evening, and in the winter it must be excessively severe. Worsted stockings and double blankets were necessary for comfort during the night.

On making inquiry as to the distance from hence to Jumnotree, and the possibility of passing the night there, I found it called six cōs by one route of very bad and rough road, in the bed of the river, and a considerably greater distance by another, which leads over a high ascent, sometimes travelled when the river is too high to pass and repass, as is necessary in going in its channel too frequently. There is no place, as we were informed, at Jumnotree where we could pass the night; not even a cave under which shelter might be sought against the weather. I had some suspicion, however, that the difficulties of the road were exaggerated, and that the latter part of my information was incorrect; accordingly, I determined to set out the next morning early, and arranged matters so, that if there was a possibility of remaining the night and day at the place, we should do so, carrying the necessary food and covering with us; and leaving all the baggage at the village, under care of the Mussulmaun soldiers, whom it would not have been proper to carry to the sacred spot.

July 15.—The morning was extremely cold; the heights were clear and beautiful, but clouds hung low all around: we were too much under the lower precipices of the mountain to see the highest parts, but the snowy peaks to the right and left of Doomuncundee rose very conspicuous and close. We left the village for Jumnotree at six o'clock, the wind blowing sharp and raw from the hills, down the glen of the river, like a cold winter's morning at home. All the Hindoos and Ghoorkhas of the party went on this pious errand; and the Jumnotree Pundit, with four or five Brahmins, led the way. Passing through the cultivation, the path is practicable enough for a mile and a half along the bed of the river, which we crossed on a stick; it is not large, but very rapid: there is a very bad and dangerous step here, and the way becomes difficult and painful. The path ceased, and we proceeded entirely along the bed of the stream, crossing and recrossing it, as the rocks on either side jutted into the river, and alternately opposed our progress; even the crossing is exceedingly hazardous, for it was necessary to wade through the stream, which is very violent and cold to a most painful degree, up to mid thigh, and sometimes deeper; and as those places where it is practicable to ford it are generally on the verge of falls of a considerable height, where a false step would be certain destruction, not only considerable strength, but a steady head are necessary to the safety of the passenger. The course of the river here is a mere chasm, cut in the rock, and worn by the action of the waters and of winter storms. The sides, which are chiefly solid rocks, approach each other almost as close at the top as at their base; and the foliage on either brow mingles together. Above, the mountain is continued craggy and bare, the dark glen hardly showing itself at any distance.

Our path along the base of these wild precipices was thickly set with very dangerous steps, and always difficult and laborious; sometimes leading us along the face of a precipice above the deep pools, where there was little hold for hand or foot, where it was necessary to spring from a very uncertain footing to a distant bank, while a failure in the leap, or in the support, would have plunged us in the rapid stream. At others we clambered up banks of loose fragments of gigantic size, fallen from the cliffs above. At length we reached a pass, where there was no possibility of continuing in the bed of the stream, and ascended through a thick and devious jungle of forest trees, and dwarf bamboo, mingled with various creepers and small shrubs, which rendered our progress painful and slow, for we had to creep on our hands and knees, clinging to the roots of trees, and the stalks of bamboos, placed there by former passengers, and thus force ourselves up, along the sloping crest of a steep crag, to a point, on which is placed a small shrine to Bhyramjee.

This spot is said to be half-way from the village, and Bhyramjee is understood to be the *avant courier* of Jumna, and the announcer of all those who come to worship her: he is a subordinate divinity, who seems to act somewhat in the capacity of a chobedar to the goddess. His temple is only constructed of a few loose stones, and is not three feet high; there is no image, but it contained a great number of pieces of iron with one, two, or more points, some plain, some twisted: a small brass canopy hung from the centre, together with a little brass lamp, and a small bell of the same metal, which is rung during worship. Here the officiating Brahmin said a long prayer, with some fervency, ringing the bell, and offering flowers, which were also presented by all the attendants worshipping; thus propitiating the deity towards the strangers. The place is curiously chosen, extremely wild and gloomy, on the point of a rock overhanging the stream, which roars below: it is surrounded by higher and more craggy precipices, covered with dark and thick jungle, and here and there the snow is seen through an opening far above. The descent from hence is more dangerous than even the ascent: it leads along the brink of the rock, and where there is no footing naturally, sticks are laid along upon the roots of trees, or upon pins driven into the crevices of the rock, on which it is necessary to pass for several yards; the stones are all loose, and the ground very uncertain and soft. Descending thus, we again reached the bed of the river, and the path continued to increase in difficulty and danger, the water being more confined, the descent more rapid, the current stronger, and the falls more frequent and more grand. Again we crossed and recrossed the stream, the coldness of which (it having immediately left the snow) was so intense, as almost to benumb the joints; each time we plunged in we felt as if cut to the bone. At length we reached the spot which had been pointed out to us from below, as Jumnotree; but this was not the sacred source: here, however, there is a junction of three streams, and the place is more open than the channel below.

From the bed of the torrent the mountain rises at once to its height, apparently without any very extensive irregularities; and the steepness of the declivity at this point may in some degree be estimated, when it is understood that here, though at the foot of this upper region of the mountain, the very peaks are seen towering above us, as ready to overwhelm the gazer with the snow from their summits: and, in fact, the avalanches from above fall into the channel of the river. There was then, at this spot, a prodigious mass of snow, which carrying down along with it a mighty ruin of rocks, wood, and soil, had blocked up the course of the river. From beneath this mass, one stream flows; just above it, is that called the At,h Pysar Gunga, equal in size to the branch which retains the name of the Jumna, and which, rushing down the mountain side, in a broken cataract, from the snow that gives it birth, joins the sacred stream. Turning to the left, and following up the channel, still ascending fast over a succession of rocks, stones, and precipices, in a short distance we reached Jumnotree.

CHAPTER XXVI.

FROM JUMNOTREE TO CHAIAH-KE-KANTA.

The spot which obtains the name of Jumnotree is, in fact, very little below the place where the various small streams formed on the mountain brow, by the melting of many masses of snow, unite in one, and fall into a basin below. To this basin, however, there is no access, for immediately above this spot, the rocks again close over the stream, and, though not so lofty as those below, they interpose a complete bar to further progress in the bed of the torrent: a mass of snow too had fallen from above at the farther extremity of this pass, under which the river runs. Between the two banks, the view is closed by the breast of the mountain, which is of vivid green from perpetual moisture, and is furrowed by time and the torrents into numberless ravines; and down these ravines are seen trickling the numerous sources of this branch of the Jumna. Above this green bank, rugged, bare, and dark, rocky cliffs arise, and the deep calm beds and cliffs of snow, towering above all, finish the picture. Noble rocks of varied hues and forms, crowned with luxuriant dark foliage, and the stream foaming from rock to rock, forms a foreground not unworthy of it.

At the place where it is customary to perform ablution, the rock on the north-east side of the river is very steep. This seems to be of the same nature as that which has been noticed at Usureegurh, apparently quartzose, and chiefly white, but exhibiting different shades and colours. The structure also is laminous, and from between these laminæ run several small streams of warm water, forming, together, a considerable quantity. There are several other sources, and one in particular, from which springs a column of very considerable size, is situate in the bed of the river between two large stones, and over it falls a stream of the river water. This water is much hotter than that already noticed: the hand cannot bear to be kept a moment in it, and it emits much vapour. I could not detect the least acidity by the taste, nor any sulphureous or other smell in the water; it was exceedingly pure, transparent, and tasteless. A great quantity of red crust, apparently deposited by the water, which seemed to be formed of an iron oxide, and some gritty earth, covered all the stones around and under the stream. This, on exposure to the air, hardened into a perfect but very porous stone, whilst below the water it was frequently mixed with a slimy substance of a very peculiar character, of a dull yellowish colour, somewhat like isinglass, certainly a production of the water, as well as the above crust, for it covered the stones over which the stream ran, and was very abundant.

The violence and inequality of the stream frequently changes the bed of the river. Formerly it lay on the side opposite to this rock, and the numerous sources of this warm water were then very perceptible, many of them springing from the rock and gravel to some height in the air; but several of these are now lost in the present course of the stream. These warm springs are of great sanctity, and the spot for bathing is at that point before mentioned, where one of a considerable size rises in a pool of the cold river water, and renders it milk warm. This jet is both heard and seen, as it plays far under the surface of the pool. These springs have all particular names, such as Goureecound, Tubutcound, &c.; and, as usual, a superstitious tale is related concerning their origin. Thus it is said that the spirits of the *Kikees*, or twelve holy men who followed Maha Deo from Lunka (after the usurpation of the tyrant Rawen), to Himālā, inhabit this rock, and continually worship him. But why this operation should produce springs of hot water in this place is not so clear. Here, however, all the people bathed, while the Pundit said prayers, and received his dues; and here also I bathed, was prayed over, and submitted to be marked by the sacred mud of the hot springs in the forehead like the rest, and of course was obliged to make my present to the priest for his ministry.

I complied with the custom of approaching the spot with bare feet. The whole of the people had put off their shoes a long way below. We looked around in vain for a situation where to pass the night under cover; and, as the weather was too cold to keep the people exposed to it, with the imminent appearance of rain, I agreed, though unwillingly, to return.

I would gladly have attempted an ascent beyond the point which the Brahmins assured me had never been passed, and this did not appear very difficult. A circuit would have been necessary, and much toilsome climbing, but I am confident that it would have been comparatively easy to gain the top of the green bank opposite on the breast of the mountain. Beyond this, difficulty would doubtless have much increased; and I believe it might have been impossible to reach the height of the snow for the reasons before given. This, however, was vain speculation: by the time we had all bathed, and I had taken a very rough sketch of the place, the day was so far advanced that it was necessary to descend.

It is an object of considerable interest, particularly to those who delight in geological researches and theories, to ascertain the nature of the substances that compose the various ridges and regions, and particularly the summits of very lofty mountains. I once more regretted exceedingly my want of scientific acquaintance with this branch, as well as most others, of physics, which has denied me the pleasure of rendering any certain useful information on subjects of this nature, to those who may not have the same opportunities for making such researches as fell to my lot.

While, however, I was at this height, and as it were in the centre of this wonderful range of mountains, I did attend to the appearance of the rocks and minerals which we saw on our route, and occasionally took specimens when uncertain as to their nature. Towards its source the stream diminishes in force, from the want of the tributary waters which gradually swell it below, or, as in the present case, it splits into a great number of inconsiderable rills, neither of which, if even they did descend from the mountain top, have force to carry with them portions of its substance. It appears clearly that beds of rivers can only give a just idea of that part of the mountain through which their course is rapid and destructive. The high parts must yield to other and very powerful agents, before their ruins descend to our reach. Frost and the fall of avalanches may now and then produce this effect; but on peaks which, formed of solid rock, have been covered from the beginning of time with a depth of snow that never melts, and which in all probability are little exposed to the vicissitudes of heat and cold, of moisture, frost, and thaw, even these agents can work but feebly; because, in all probability, an uniform cold above the freezing point prevails in so elevated a region. All moisture is frozen, no rain falls, no partial thaws take place, or there would be glaciers, a phenomenon that did not present itself to our view during our whole journey. The true materials of these mountain peaks, therefore, although they may be conjectured from below, can only be established when they shall have been ascended ; till then we must rest contented with observation and analogy.

Almost every sort of stone and rock, which we have seen in our course through the hills, is recognised in the bed and on the banks of the upper part of the Jumna, and of these there are two in particular that predominate.

That met with in the course and on the banks of the Pabur, in large rounded masses, is particularly plentiful. It consists of much mica, quartz, and coarse sand or grit, with a great deal of a hard black substance, either hornblende or schorl. The mass is of various but generally of great hardness, and I then believed it to be a species of real granite. This has since been pronounced (from the specimens I collected), by a friend skilled in these matters, to be that modification of granite called gneiss.

The other sort is that white laminated rock from which the hot springs trickle, and which has been called quartz. It sometimes breaks regularly, affecting squared forms. At times its regularity is only perceptible in one way ; it breaks in irregular flat pieces, varying in density as well as in colour. The fracture is at times most perfectly like that of quartz, semi-transparent and shining ; at times more like marble, more white, close, and less crystalized ; yet still I think it is the same species of stone. It is met with of red, green, and yellow tinges, but is always in laminæ.

Soft micaceous schistus is also abundant, of all colours and various degrees of hardness, grey, red, whitish, and blueish, and is always plentifully veined with quartz. This stone is by far the most abundant all over the hills. We observed no limestone here, unless some specimens of that white stone described above, as resembling marble, be of a calcareous nature, which I think not improbable ; but I had no means of ascertaining this point, not having any acid test with me.

The continual disposition of the abrupt and craggy faces of the hills to point to the north-west and north (which has frequently been noticed in the preceding pages), became exceedingly distinct as we more nearly approached the high rocky peaks of the snowy range. It was also obvious that the structure of the rocks was stratified, sometimes consisting of different stones ; at others, apparently of the same sort, merely showing this tendency in their formation and fracture. These strata were always at an angle with the horizon, differing materially in its elevation, but generally dipping to the horizon at an angle of about 45 degrees, and most frequently pointing in a line from north-east to south-west. This formation was peculiarly evident in the rocks forming the banks of this part of the Jumna. Such was the angle and direction, and the stratification was evident and remarkable, whether the rock was quartz, granite, or schistus.

The higher parts of the hill presented the same appearances both in formation and colour. A pretty attentive examination with a good glass gave reason to believe that they consisted of much the same sorts of rock, viz. granite and quartz. The chief objection to the supposition that these are granite is the predominating appearance of stratification that exists. Many huge black masses, however, did not exhibit this formation; but they were lower and less perfectly seen, and had their south-eastern sides turned to us, which, as before observed, are far more rounded and less precipitous. On some of those higher faces, which had a western and south-western exposure turned to our view, the veins of different coloured stone were strongly marked, sometimes in straight lines, and sometimes much deflected. Those high cliffs which were uncovered with snow were always equally denuded of soil and vegetation. The line where this last ceases is indeed sufficiently and distinctly drawn, and probably is nearly the same as that which marks the want of soil. Above this, as far as the glass could determine, all seems bare rugged rocks and sharp peaks, cut into fantastic shapes, and in their interstices, and at their feet only, the ruins of themselves lay, scattered in small fragments.

The snow lies in some places to the south-east, smooth, hard, unbroken, and glitteringly white; in other places it is cut into deep ravines, or fallen into precipices of great height, and here and there much discoloured, as with dust. Towards the skirts it descends in long wreaths and streaks, filling up the nullahs far below the great mass above. It would be pleasing to speak of the vegetable productions, but here I am equally unable, as in geological inquiries, to afford satisfaction. Those trees and shrubs which are met with through the whole range of this hilly tract were also seen here; and there were several additions, which (could they be botanically described) might be interesting. Among the pines we found that which resembles the silver fir, and spruce fir, as well as one which I believe is the true Weymouth pine. Two sorts of larch, the birch, a species of sycamore, oaks of more than one sort, with a very great profusion of trees and plants, cover the rocks and hills to the extent of the woody region. The strawberry, both the scarlet and alpine sorts, large of their kind, with raspberry and blackberry bushes, were in abundance; and here, for the first time growing wild, I recognized the black currant. In the leaf, stem, fruit (not ripe,) as well as in the smell and taste, I could not be mistaken. We also met with a species of rhubard, different from that of our gardens at home. Instead of the large and very deeply indented leaf of the latter sort, that which we found was large and rounded; but the tender shoots of the plant resembled those of the European sort in appearance and taste, and were presented to me by some Brahmins as pleasant food. The roots had the precise colour, smell, and taste of rhubarb. I could not find, however, that they were used medicinally by the natives; but the Ghoorkhas employed them as a poultice, applied to bruises or hurts.

Just at the height of the day's journey the Pundit pulled and presented to me a small plant which he called mahé, and told me it was sacred. It grew on the rocks, and not in soil, and had a very peculiar and pleasant smell. It was very small, not exceeding two or three inches in height, and consisted of a small bunch of leaves resembling fennel. Our return was rendered much more difficult and dangerous by an increase which had taken place in the size of the stream since we had ascended.

The Pundit took this opportunity, like a true Asiatic, to pay a compliment; and said that it took place as a proof of the favour of Jumna, who thus acknowledged her satisfaction with her new votaries. He observed also that, at the moment of bathing, the hot spring, which was scanty, had gushed out with uncommon abundance; a sign of very peculiar favour. Be this as it may, it was a most inconvenient mode of signifying it, for every time we crossed the stream now, it was at the imminent hazard of our lives. One Ghoorkha was actually carried down, but fortunately dragged out just on the verge of a considerable fall, with the loss of his tulwar, which went as a sacrifice to Jumna. The only Mussulmaun of the party, who had inadvertently been allowed to come (a khidmatgar), lost his clothes, and nearly his life, in crossing the stream,—a circumstance which did not pass unnoticed by the Hindoos. At length, however, we all arrived safe, though weary, at the village by evening.

Sudden fluctuations in the size of the river are very common, without any immediate apparent cause; and they are to be sought both in the changes of the atmosphere, which take place very rapidly in these hills, and have a speedy effect on the lower parts of the snow, and consequently on the many sources of the river, and also in the partial falls of rain which occasion a quick but momentary rise. Even when the waters are low, the dangers of the way are considerable.

I am confident that, by the road we took, it would be impossible to reach the place if the river were at all higher than we found it. Though trifling in detail, the obstacles are numerous and serious in practice; and it was the first day's march we had made where I really thought the danger and difficulty considerable. One woman, however, the wife of a Ghoorkha jemadar, the only one who accompanied us even the whole way without shrinking, instead of being a hinderance to her husband she was really a support and comfort to him. Her notions of piety led her to visit these holy places, and her constancy and constitution enabled her to persevere, though the roads were severe and the way long. She never complained, never fell behind, was always in good humour; and, when we came to our ground, she prepared her husband's food, and attended him as a servant. Let it be added that he was kind and good to her in return. She was, I believe, a native of Bischur.

On our arrival at the village, I made inquiry respecting the road from thence to Gungotree. It appears that there are two: by the one it would be necessary to return back three days march on the road we came, and then, crossing the country between the Jumna and Ganges, where it is narrow, we should reach Bārāhāt on the banks of the Bhagiruttee. This would of itself require four days, and from thence to Gungotree is a journey of six more; but the road is somewhat easier than the other, and provisions and people to carry them and our baggage are found in plenty. The other road, it was said, leads over a high country partly in snow, and (as it was alleged at first) for four days we should not meet with a village or a human being. The whole way is desert and wearisome. But, on further inquiry, we learnt that the road is tolerably good, and sufficiently well marked; and Goving Bhisht says, that many years ago he went the whole desert road in three days. But both he and the zemindars here earnestly dissuaded me from attempting it. They assured me that, during the chief part of two days' march, in crossing a high hill with much snow, there appears to be a poison in the air, which so affects the travellers, particularly those carrying loads, that they become senseless, lie down, and are perfectly incapable of motion. They cannot account for this phenomenon, but believe it to proceed from the powerful perfume of myriads of flowers in the small valleys and on the hill sides; but they do not seem quite satisfied with this solution of the difficulty themselves. I inquired whether the flowers were always in bloom, and whether this poison was felt all the time the road is open: they answered, that it was most felt in the months (I think) of May and June, and did not know how it might be now. They talked wildly of a serăr or wind from the mountains, pregnant with this mysterious poison, and concluded by again most earnestly dissuading me from going.

On weighing and reflecting on all the circumstances that had passed, and were now laid before me, I determined to attempt this dangerous route. My object was to save time; and I should thus save at least fourteen days: besides, I had particularly observed how prone these people, particularly Goving Bhisht and Kishen Sing, were to exaggerate difficulties and the length of the road, and to throw obstacles in the way. I believed that we should compass in two days what they averred to be the work of four; and I own that I laughed at the idea of a poisoned atmosphere. I was also particularly anxious to ascend some of the high peaks, hoping to obtain from thence some very interesting bearings, and to be able to determine more precisely the nature of the rocks. Accordingly, a sufficiency of provisions for four days for the party and for the people to carry it was made ready, and the march ordered for the morrow.

It is a singular fact, that the better classes of the natives in the hills were found unable to vie with our low country attendants in the power of supporting fatigue and a continued march in this difficult country. Goving Bhisht and Kishen Sing, with several of their people, had begun to show symptoms of being quite exhausted, while our own servants, and the sepoys from the plains, did not complain materially. The Ghoorkhas had been too much used to the work to render it matter of surprise that they held out; but I believe that the Europeans, myself, and my brother, were by far the freshest, and continued much the longest capable of supporting fatigue. Bhisht himself was by far the least able of the party, and he here quitted us: he had lagged terribly behind, and seemed very unequal to the marches we were making; and he complained of a pain in his knee, from some old hurt. Accordingly, thinking him rather a clog than an assistance to our progress, and believing Kishen Sing to be equally efficient in procuring supplies and in describing the country as Bhisht, I signified to him that there was no further need of his attendance, at which I believe he greatly rejoiced.

July 16.—The night was cold, the morning sharp but clear, and all was ready at six o'clock. Our route lay across the Oonta Gunga (which is here a good deal less than the Jumna), a few furlongs above the bridge; and we then ascended the hill, which forms its left hand bank, at first through grain (papera), and thick forest-wood and jungle: the ascent was various, frequently steep; and the trees were much the same as usual.

Here we saw many rutnāls, or peacock pheasants, but had no opportunity of shooting any. On the way up I got a few bearings; but, on reaching an elevated spot, whence a noble prospect was expected, a cloud enveloped all. This ascent, for two miles and three quarters, carried us very high; and from hence an extensive and useful view would have been gained, but all was so dark, that there was no hope of seeing any thing.

We had now reached the region where wood ceases, and only small stinted bushes thinly spot the ground. Birch was very prevalent in the forest: it differs a little from the common British species; the leaf is larger, though of the same shape; and it is not so fragrant as the beautiful ornament of our woods.

This spot is called Sunapulee. From hence we continued an ascent up a steep hill-face, covered with short grass and small mountain flowers, and stunted birches; and which bore altogether a strong similarity to some of the Scotch Highland hills: and here, indeed, I first discovered their own characteristic plant, the true heath, or heather. And no one who acknowledges that lively feeling of attachment to his country, so peculiarly called into life by the association of ideas, by the sight of a flower, of a scene, however rude, that he has seen in the days of his youth, but will sympathise in the joy with which I hailed this much loved and long looked for remembrancer of the "land of brown heath and shaggy wood." I plucked it, and placed it in my hat, with a delight that I believe much amused my attendants. It is not exactly of the same species as that most common in the Scotch Highlands: its small leaves cover the stem in regular rows, pointing so as to give it a four-square appearance, and its bell is delicate and white; but at some distance it looks very similar, excepting that it has not the blooming purple glow which gives our mountains their rich colour. I have seen it, however, among other species, but not so abundant. Here, too, those beautiful birds, the peacock pheasants, were seen and heard in greater numbers the higher we rose, and might have been taken for grouse in our own heather.

The ascent from Sunapulee is steep and irregular, and leads us over a number of very high peaks, on the brink of a most awful precipice; the full depth of which we could not discover, from the fog which now enveloped all the landscape. The ridge is called Dig-D,har, and seems exceedingly craggy and wild: it is the continuation of a ridge from Bunderpouch. The road below the crest is various; and, though the path is well traced and clear, it is sufficiently tiresome and difficult. It was peculiarly mortifying that the thickest fog which we had experienced continued obstinately this day to shroud every object from our view, so that the route was rather uncertain.

Reaching Goormoo-Ke-Ghāt, we descended into the Coormi-Ke-Gad,h, or nullah, by a painful and remarkably steep and rough path. This stream runs from hence to join the Bheem-Ke-Gad,h, about a mile to the south-westward. The ascent from it was equally severe, along a loose stony bank, through some scraggy jungle. There is little wood in the whole ravine, and none above the junction of the Malla-Ke-Gad,h. From hence we looked across the Bheem-Ke-Gad,h, mentioned on our way from Rana to Cursalee. Here all the hills seem abrupt to the south, and point their strata in directions from south-west 20° to south-east 20°, at an angle with the horizon nearly the same as that mentioned before, about forty-five degrees.

In the first part of this day's route the predominating stone was the old micaceous schistus, soft and reddish: as we ascended, it changed to white and black sand-stone; but there was a very various mixture, in description and hardness, some being very hard, and some very soft. We also passed much snow in the clefts and gullies, and in situations on the hill where least exposed to sun and wind. From the last ascent the road was unequal, irregular, and bad, with much indenting, and a varying level, for about a mile, and then descended rapidly amongst wood, chiefly very scraggy birch, and along a deep ferny slope, to the bank of the Bheem-

Ke-Gad,h. This stream is here larger than the Jumna at Cursalee; but it had every appearance of being temporarily swollen by a fall of rain, that was heavy in the mountains, and of which we had a good deal on the march: it was very muddy, and extremely rapid.

The hills forming the opposite side of the valley present their northern face to us: their feet are covered with straggling wood: above, they are green and brown, as if they had much heather. There is a great deal of snow upon them not far off; and large scars of black and white rock streak their breasts, where the snow or the torrents have brought down the soil. They are much more rounded than ordinary; and their appearance strongly reminded one of the loftier Grampian mountains in the north of Scotland. Wherever a peak was seen which presented a more southern or south-western aspect, it pointed its rough head sharply to the south. The opposite or northern hills, of which the southern aspect is exposed to us, are as wild, fantastic, and rocky, as can well be conceived. The skirts, sloping to the river, are scantily fringed with stunted wood; from thence steep slopes rise, green with a thick carpet of most beautiful thistles and ferns, and adorned with a profusion of flowers of every hue. Their summits rise in sharp rocky cliffs, frowning over and strewing both these slopes and the glen below with their ruins.

As we continued our route along the side of the stream, we reached a spot where two rocks jut into the river on each side, and between which it has cut its way, and boils along a very confined passage. Above this lay a prodigious mass of snow, filling up the bed of the river, which runs under it for more than a furlong: it seems to have accumulated either from avalanches sliding down the steep mountain side, or from drifting into this hollow, whence it cannot well be carried by the current, owing to the narrowness of the channel at the above-mentioned rocks. The mass must be of great thickness and solidity, for large rocks have fallen from above upon it, without making any impression on it: it is strong enough to bear twenty elephants. Much of this must melt, as the river runs under it. Above this place the fall of the river is considerably more rapid, but the valley spreads out considerably.

The bases of the hills have a more easy slope, and the body of the valley may be full half a mile broad; above, they are wild and rocky as ever, and the snow lay all around in the hollows and ravines, but the rest is a lovely green. At this place, indeed, the snow lies for nine months continually, consequently no cultivation can be attempted, but the verdure is sudden and rich, and affords grazing for many sheep in the absence of the snow. Our encamping ground for the night was not far from hence, at the top of the glen: it was a cave under a large stone, called Bheem-Ke-Udar; in a dry night it is sufficiently comfortable, but rain would readily beat in. In this cavern, and under a few other large stones around it, there was some shelter, though scanty, for our company, to the number of sixty or more, who were thus forced to accommodate themselves: it is a little more than ten miles from Cursalee. The evening was raw and very cold, but, for one quarter of an hour, the fog, which had lain heavily around all day, cleared, as it were to give us a view of our situation: it was, in truth, a strangely wild one. We were at the top of the valley of Bheem-Ke-Gad,h, and in the very bosom of the snow. The hills which form the valley on either side are continuous from the range of the snowy hills, which, close to us in front, bound our view with an impassable line. On the left the ridge joins with one that comes direct from the south-western peak of Bunderpouch, which was, however, hid from us. But the sharp ridge that connects it with the north-eastern, or highest peak, was visible, and that noble mass formed the back ground of the valley to our left. In front, a ridge falls from the south-eastern shoulder, dividing the valley into two parts, as Dumunkundee does at Cursalee. To our right the south-eastern half retreats, and has for a back ground the Soomeroo Purbut, with its sharp snowy cliffs, hardly inferior to Bunderpouch itself. Both these valleys are vast beds of snow, and we could not be more than a mile and half from the very centre of them. Bunderpouch exhibited one prodigious snowy mass, without a black speck, and, in the bosom below, it lay in vast chaotic masses, cut into ravines and precipices by the rain and the thaws, of a wild and fearful depth, not to be described. When I hazarded a conjecture to the hill people of their being 300 feet in depth, they smiled and said, that 500 cubits would not fathom them: but only wild surmise can here be offered, for what mortal can reach them? They are desolate, cheerless, and unapproachable. Through the left valley, from the bosom of this side of Bunderpouch, runs down Coonāl-Ke-Gad,h, and from the other, proceeding from the foot of Soomeroo Purbut, and from various sources in the hills about it, flows the true Bheem-Ke-Gad,h, and they meet just about this cave.

The night was very cold, and the coverings for the people being very scanty, they suffered much. Wood is not to be had within some miles, and it was a severe task on weary people to fetch it, so that many rather eat their flour raw, than take the trouble to get wood to dress it. Fortunately there was little or no rain: the clouds dispersed during the early part of the night, and showed the magnificent mountains by the light of the moon. There is something peculiarly awful and solemn in the sight of these huge masses and depths of snow by faint moonlight; a total lifelessness is shed over their calm chill features, and the cold that emanates from them feels as it would freeze the soul itself: they resemble, indeed, the death of nature.

The journey of this day was the first that was wholly desert; we met not with the slightest sign of man; not a house or hut appeared; not the smallest trace of cultivation: it was desolate throughout, but the hills were particularly verdant, and the pasture wonderfully rich. Not only a great variety of grasses covered the ground, but a profusion of the loveliest flowers, every where bursting through the green carpet, gave the richest effect to the slopes and banks we traversed: the beauty of the thistles and ferns was particularly conspicuous; cowslips and polyanthuses of yellow, blue, and purple, were in great abundance; indeed, the variety and richness of the colours and their mixtures is hardly to be believed. I have mentioned the heather. We also found the real juniper common at home; both the leaf (or prickles) and berry were similar.

We experienced much trouble to-day from our coolies, who were, probably, many of them the same that we saw so much intoxicated, and busily engaged in dancing for the two previous days: they were with difficulty urged on, and sat down after very short turns of work, although the loads had been lightened and proportioned to the severity of the march. They told us that they were affected by the Serān, or poison in the air, from the flowers above noticed; and though I believe that their situation may in some degree be referred to drunkenness and excess, and something may be allowed for laziness, still their general behaviour and appearance indicated a good deal further that could not be accounted for.

When they arrived, they laid down their loads, panting and sick; some went to sleep at once, and few thought of preparing victuals till obliged to do so. We were told that the march of the morrow would be much more fatiguing, and that the people would be far sooner exhausted than this day: and it would have been a very serious evil, had I apprehended it to be fully true, as it was difficult to say how we were at all to get on. In truth, the first part of our road seen from hence, leading over a snowy shoulder of a very rugged part of Soomeroo, called Bumsooroo-Ke-D,har, promised a good deal of labour; but as my wish was to obtain the most extensive views of the country, I was pleased with the elevation which this road promised us, provided our observation should not be obstructed by clouds or mist.

July 17.—The morning was cold and foggy, with little hope of a fine or clear day: the people had passed the night rather better than was to have been expected; three or four only complained. However, we were all in motion by a little after daylight, and proceeded upwards by Coonal-Ke-Gad,h, which we crossed very near its debouche from the bosom of snow below Bunderpouch, upon a mass of ice or snow under which the water runs. From hence we turned to the eastward along the foot of the D,har, mentioned as dividing the nullahs or valleys of Coonāl and Bheem, and which comes down from one of the peaks of Soomeroo: it is called Coonāl-Bheem-Ke-D,har, and from its root a point runs out at which the two nullahs join. We crossed several small rivulets, running from beneath large masses of snow, over which our road lay, and which join Bheem-Ke-Gad,h, and then commenced a very steep ascent along the course of that stream, which here has some considerable falls, after passing under much snow.

We now met with new and curious flowers at every step, which I shall notice at the end of the day's route, and continued a very painful ascent up the ridge of a rock, which runs down from a point in Bumsooroo-Ke-D,har, so steep and slippery, that the people had much difficulty in making their way from height to height.

The ground here was bare, and the grass stunted, but still there was plenty of flowers: on all sides we were surrounded with snow: a little further on vegetation diminished still more, hardly any thing being to be observed when the ground was bare of snow but a scanty green slime, and brown moss, similar to that which is found on barren, damp, moory grounds.

There is a sort of basin here in the mountain, formed of snow, and the ruins of the peaks around heaped on each other, but scarcely any soil.

It was excedingly cold, and only by the toil of climbing did we preserve any sufficient warmth. Many of the coolies, and several of the Mewattee and Ghoorkha sepoys and chuprassies now lagged, and were hardly able to proceed, and every one complained of the bīs, or poisoned wind. I now suspected that the supposed poison was nothing more than the effect of the rarefaction of the atmosphere, from our great elevation, which made it unfit for the full purposes of respiration: it failed to distend the lungs, and I was led to suspect this from my own sensations. I felt more than usual efforts necessary to continue our course, and could hardly command strength to climb the steeps. I experienced in breathing considerable oppression, as if there was a want of air. We certainly could not have supported this very long.

We passed a small pool of water, held very sacred, called Matree-Ke-Tāl, from which the chief source of the Bheem-Ke-Gad,h issues: it is in a low part of this basin filled with ice, surrounded with snow, as was almost every place where snow can lie. A further ascent led us to another basin or hollow, near the top of the D,har, also filled with snow, and which we passed, as well as a steep snowy ascent, covering wild masses of rock, rather dangerous and uncertain. This ascent, the extent of which was not more than three furlongs, was the most painful piece of road we travelled; it was slippery and steep, and we were powerless. At its top, however, we reached Bumsooroo-Ke-Ghāt, and took a long rest; but all was dark, and no valuable bearings were obtained, nor any view to the extent of even a mile.

If the line can be drawn with any degree of exactness, the bottom of this ascent appears to be the extreme height to which vegetation extends. At the top there is not even the dull moss, or lichen, seen below. The stones are bare and unchanged, except by the air, and no sign of life appears, except a few monāl, or pheasants; and even these, as fearing the sacred solitude of the scene, flew together in packs, or small companies. The cold was excessive; it was painful to remain any time inactive. As soon as any of those who complained of the oppression at the breast lay down, they dropped asleep, and it was not thought proper to permit this propensity to be indulged. Eating a few mouthfuls afforded slight relief, but nothing materially alleviated it; nor was any one free from the general symptoms of debility. As this was probably the highest point we should reach, I took particular notice of the rocks which composed the mountains, fragments of which formed the ridge we stood upon. They were chiefly the same as those met with in the bed of the Jumna. The hard gritstone, already mentioned as probably being granite (gneiss), and first met with in the Pabur, was observed in greatest abundance. Micaceous schist, much veined with quartz, and a species of moderately hard blueish stone, much pervaded with shining particles, common in rivulets in Scotland, and with several less remarkable sorts, lay in varying quantities all around. I think I also saw the common whinstone, but in very small quantities.

During the short opportunities afforded me by the partial openings of the fogs, I took particular notice of the nearest and highest cliffs in view, and, as far as the glass could be trusted, they consist of the same species of rock as those found in our route just described: their colour, shape, and fracture, are the same, white, red, reddish, yellow, black, and blue, sometimes running in strata, sometimes in shapeless masses; but the primary formation of the hills is always stratified. The angle of elevation and direction of these strata is ever the same.

The ridge in which Bumsooroo-Ke-Ghāt is situated is sharp and narrow at its top; it is continuous with Bumsooroo-Ke-Kanda, which in several peaks sweeps down to the southward from Soomeroo-Purbut, and thus is connected with Bunderpouch. Beyond the pass to the southward it rises into several high peaks, and is lost in Bakree-Ke-D,har and Pundarasso, &c.

The western side we ascended, and it has been described. The eastern side looks into a similar basin, from whose snowy bosom Bumsooroo-Ke-Gad,h flows to the Bhagiruttee. After descending a short way, the road winds along the back of the valley, which is formed by this neck or pass, and a d,har, which leaves it some hundred yards to the northward, and divides Bumsooroo-Ke-Gad,h from Sathkeăr-Cote-Ke-Gad,h. It is curious that on this eastern side there is much more soil, though not more vegetation; and even where the snow has left the ground bare it is, comparatively with the other side, smooth and soft, although, from the inclined nature of the slope, the snow in melting must yearly carry down with it, as it melts, much of the earth which covers the stones. Much snow and loose stones made the path slippery and dangerous.

On reaching nearly to the point of the above-mentioned D,har, a steep snowy descent led us into Phina-Ke-Khola, one of a number of small streams, which, running from Kear-Cote-Ke-Kanda, forms the Gad,h of that name, and which joins the Bhagiruttee by another name after uniting with Bumsooroo-Ke-Gad,h. The aspect of the hill at this part is singularly different from that of any part which we have before passed: it is more level on the whole, yet wrought into hollows and inequalities containing small pools of water, and thinly covered with a light black earth resembling decayed peat-moss. Vegetation scarcely reappeared, and there was nothing but fungi and mosses of the same sorts as before described. Still the day was dismal and wet, and the mist obstinate. From this point we experienced a succession of ascents and descents, with excessive curvings and indentings in the mountain side, following D,hars of different names, with their dividing ravines, along a path most difficult and toilsome from snow and loose stones, and severely tormented by the difficulty of breathing, till we reached Chaiah-Ke-Kanta.

PART IX.

JOURNEY TO GANGOTREE.

CHAPTER XXVII.

Chaiah-Ke-Kanta is the ghāt at which the descent commences, and is, I believe, little inferior in height to any point in this day's journey. It presents nothing remarkable, except that the zemindars of the country have instituted (as they say) a custom, that every one who passes this ghāt safely for the first time shall pay a sum of money to those of his company, who have travelled the road before. They stated it to have originated in a collection for the tomb of some being, whether man or dewta, who either died or resided here; for it frequently happens that they cannot explain whether the object of their fear or adoration be a god, or only a saint, as in the present instance; and as I believed the whole tale to be a fabrication to extort money, I gave none. The place, however, was plentifully studded with small pyramids of stones, which had been raised by those who complied with the custom. It is said that the plains of Hindostan may be discerned from this place on a clear day; but even a thicker fog enveloped us at this point, as if to baffle and disappoint all hope of fixing the situation of the spot on which we stood. A rapid and dangerous descent begins here: a careless step would be serious.

Just at the bottom of the rocky crest of the D,har the mist for a moment cleared, and showed us a wonderful and wild maze of lofty, sharp, and snowy peaks in all directions around; but before a single bearing could be taken all was dark again. An irregular and very steep descent carried us to the source of Chin-po-Ke-Gad,h, which at this point is formed by many sources from the melting snow. We continued rapidly descending along the course and bed of this torrent, till, at a spot called Lama Th,alhun, it is joined by another and far larger nullah, called Rindee-Gad,h. This is a lovely spot. Only a few furlongs above we had re-entered the region of wood, and the banks of the river were thinly fringed with birch. Here all was verdant and exceedingly pleasant, and, for the wild and rougher alpine scenes we have left, luxuriant woods of that beautiful tree, with the darker foliage of the more distant pines, and the lively green of the rich grass, meet the weary eye, which reposes on them with delight.

Rindee Gad,h has its rise in Doondiān-Ke-Bamue, an immense snowy peak to the north-west: it is a large rapid stream, and impassable without a bridge. We crossed it, however, a little below the junction with Chinpō nullah, upon a prodigious mass of ice or snow, which has probably been formed here for ages, and now fills up the bed of the torrent for a great space. From hence we followed the nullah, keeping above its bed for somewhat more than a mile, to a spot which, thick in forests, is marked by some very noble fir and sycamore trees, under which our guides proposed that we should pass the night. The next village was said to be from three to four cōs off, and half that distance a severe ascent; therefore, as it was five o'clock in the evening when we arrived, and as the coolies were exceedingly wearied by the very laborious ascent of the morning in so high a region, I thought it more prudent to accede to their proposal than risk the loss of baggage, or the illness of the people, by an overmarch. A small cave fell to my share; but most of the people were obliged to trust to the shelter of the trees and the goodness of the weather through the night.

Thus the formidable journey, from which our guides had so much dissuaded us, proves to consist of not more than twenty-seven miles, or eighteen cōs, though reckoned by Bhisht at forty cōs, viz. one day's journey of ten miles and a half, one of eleven and a quarter, and five miles to the village; and we could with great ease have performed it in two days, but for the following reasons: There are few situations where the requisites of shelter and fuel are to be met with so as to answer for a halting-place, Bheem-Ke-Udār being almost the only one, and even there fuel is not easily procured; and the steepest and most painful ascent commences near Bheem-Ke-Udār, while between that ascent and this place there is not a spot where these necessaries for a night could be obtained. Thus travellers must remain there the first night, as the two days' journeys are far too laborious to be performed in one; and the severity of the second fully makes up for the ease and shortness of the first, both by the steepness and difficulty of the country, the badness of the road, and, above all, by the artificial fatigue brought on by that oppression of the chest which we all felt so much.

I had no idea that height of situation could have so severely affected the strength and chest, and yet it must have been this alone, for severe as was the ascent, and bad as the road was, we had met with fully as bad days' journeys before; and though the people asserted that the air was poisoned by the scent of flowers, and though there really was a profusion of them through the whole of the first part of the march, yet the principal part of them had no smell, nor could I perceive any thing in the air except a cold and somewhat raw wind. Besides which, the chief distress was experienced after we reached the lofty gorge of Bamsooroo, which was beyond the region of vegetation, and consequently could not be easily affected by the perfume of flowers. After reaching that place no one was proof against this influence. It was ludicrous to see those who had laughed at others yielding, some to lassitude, and others to sickness, yet endeavouring to conceal it from the rest. I believe I held out longer than any one; yet after passing this gorge every few paces of ascent seemed an insuperable labour, and even in passing along the most level places my knees trembled under me, and at times even sickness at stomach was experienced. The symptoms it produced were various: some were affected with violent headache; others had severe pains in the chest, with oppression; others sickness at the stomach and vomiting; many were overcome with heaviness, and fell asleep even while walking along. But what proved the fact that all this was the effect of our great elevation, was, that as we lowered our situation, and reached the region of vegetation and wood, all these violent symptoms and pains gradually lessened and vanished. The appearance of the higher cliffs, however, both snowy and rocky, and the sensations of this day, proved most satisfactorily that it would be a very arduous undertaking, if not an impracticable one, to ascend even nearly to the tops of these loftiest hills. We could not have been within several thousand feet of even those peaks of snow which were tolerably near us.

The natives consider it as an impracticable undertaking, and it is hardly credible that in many ages there should not have been one man born, of sufficient curiosity to make the attempt, if it were not so. It is true, that when the question is put, why this has not been done, they add to the assertion of its impossibility the question, "to what good could it tend? for there is nothing to be had for man or beast." Still I think that if the enterprise were not at least highly dangerous, some one among a nation must have achieved it long before this. A failure in the person of an enterprising man would no doubt induce others less curious to rest satisfied with common reports on the subject. I shall never cease to regret that I had no barometer with me to obtain some idea of the height of this pass, and that the weather prevented any view or bearings being taken to fix the spot with accuracy. The nature of the stones and formation of the hills have been noticed. In the descent along Chinpo-Gad,h traces of lime were observed, and we passed a large rock, whence is taken the chief part of the best blue slate used in this neighbourhood.

The vegetable productions of this day's march are very various, and many of them new, and differing from those formerly met with. Two flowers particularly attracted attention. One was called goo-gool, and grew somewhat like the common flat thistle, with leaves radiating from a centre like a sun, in which centre grew a flower, on a level with the flat leaves, and much resembling the blossom of a pine-apple. This plant is held in much religious veneration. The other was a very curious one: a stalk covered with large and long leaves, somewhat like those of a primrose, ended in a cup like that of a tulip, but which appeared merely the continuation of these leaves closing, and forming the petals of a very noble flower, in the centre of which the stamina and pistil were seen. The leaves which compose this flower have a green tinge at their insertion like those on the stalk, but the middle and higher parts are black and yellow, as is the centre of the cup, but more vivid. It is called by the hill people *birmah counla,* because, as the guide informed us, it was like the rajah among the other flowers; the "sequitur," of which I in vain searched for, particularly as I could get no translation of the component parts of this name. It has since been suggested to me that the name is *brimah counla,* the latter part of which (*counla*) means the flower of the lotus plant, from which Brimah was produced at the commencement of the creation, according to Hindoo mythology, and therefore of course a flower held in high esteem, which caused its being likened to a rajah among the flowers.

Various, rich, and lovely were the myriads of large and smaller blossoms which decked these wild scenes, and I much regret my inability to give their names and botanical descriptions. Many varieties of the primrose and polyanthus, many orchides, and others resembling our common meadow flowers, grew in profusion. The only other plant, however, that I shall notice, is one which was found on the very extreme verge of vegetation alone: like the goo-gool it was low, but not quite flat, perhaps about four inches high, somewhat resembling a thistle just blossoming; but the leaves did not lie on the ground; they shrouded the blossom, which was enveloped in a thick covering like the web of a spider, which, spangled with dew, had a most singular appearance. The root was small, but firmly fixed in the ground: it displayed no colour but a brownish green. I could not obtain any name for this very curious mountain production. It seems to delight only in the close vicinity to the snow. During this day's march no living thing was seen except the monāls, which flocked together, and which I suspected to be of a species somewhat different from that which is met with lower down. They sat on the gray stones like ptarmigans on the loftiest hills at home, and in the short brown moss and grass looked exactly like grouse. I shot only one young one, which was a little larger, but precisely like a young moorfowl or blackgame, but could not succeed in killing any of the older birds.

July 18.—We were again fortunate in a fine dry night, nor was the cold so intense as during the preceding night, but in the morning the mist still hung on the mountain tops; we, however, distinguished the gorge at Chaiah-Ke-Kanta, at a prodigious elevation above us. Our descent had been very great and rapid.

I find that the green hills beneath Chaiah-Ke-Kanta were once the scene of a great battle between the rebellious zemindars of the remote parts of Rewaeen, and the rajah's troops, who had been sent into the hills to the number of 2000 to bring the district into order, and punish the robberies which were carried on to a great extent among the inhabitants. The rajah's troops were encountered at this pass by the zemindars as thieves, who united together on this foreign interference, and who killed the greater part of them.

Leaving our sweet grove, where pine-trees, sycamore, horse-chesnuts, and oaks, formed a noble shade, and sufficient shelter for the traveller in the dry season, we descended to the bed of the nullah; and kept along its banks by a very rough intricate path, perplexed by thorny underwood, sharp rocks, and small ravines, to the junction of Soonēē-Gad,h a rapid torrent, about the same size as the Rindee-Gad,h, which we crossed by a wooden bridge, and commenced ascending the hill on the left of the united streams by a steep circuitous path, till we reached the pass of Kandee in Kandee-Ke-D,har. From various points in the ascent we got glimpses of some of the hills around, and particularly of the Chaiah-Ke-Kanta, its pass, and its course towards Bunderpouch. During these two last marches, our route has led entirely across ranges thrown off from Bunderpouch, and its different shoulders, of which the principal are the Soonapulee and Dig D,hars; that of Bamsooroo, and Bakree-Kear-Kotee-Kanta, between which and Chaiah-Ke-Kanta several smaller ranges intervene.

Bhurteecoonta divides the Rindee and Soonee Gad,hs, and Kandee on which we now stood, proceeding from Sunghaunce-Ke-Dhār, and probably from some shoulder of Doondian-Ke-Bamur. It completes the detail of ridges which may fairly be said to spring from this mountain, and end on the Bhagiruttee. Its ramifications and connexions northwards and to the westward, I could not ascertain. All the ranges just mentioned are divided by ravines, which send their waters to the Bhagiruttee at different points between the villages of Sookhee and Goosalee; but in the numerous inferior d,hars and mountains into which they branch to the southward of this line, many and large streams arise, which swell the Bhagiruttee in its course to the plains. From this point the first momentary glimpse of the Bhagiruttee was obtained, running far below in a narrow rocky bed: but here, as every where else, the thick fog effectually prevented any interesting or useful observations.

The prodigiously lofty and sharp peak of Tree-Kanta alone was distinguishable for a moment, and gave a noble earnest of what the view might be were the day to clear. It is said to equal, in height and sanctity, both Bunderpouch and that mountain from which the Ganges springs. After remaining near two hours here, despairing of any view, we left this lofty spot; and by a very steep, rough, and irregular descent, reached the village of Sookhee, which is situated near the foot of a hollow that runs down from Kandee-Ke-D,har, and near a mile from the Bhagiruttee high above its bank. We passed through some straggling cultivation, but the country had much the appearance of neglect and depopulation; and the village is chiefly in ruins. There are around it some fine old walnut-trees and apricots, which indicate that more attention was paid to cultivation in former days.

The river from hence looked nearly as large as the Sutlej when we first saw it at Rampore; but the banks are wilder than any thing we had yet seen. It seemed as if the steep and shaggy roughness of part of the Jumna's banks could hardly be exceeded; but the chasm in which the Bhagiruttee rolls is on a far larger scale, and the savage majesty of its mountainous precipices keeps pace with their increase in size. Bare rock is far more predominant; and wood, every where thinly scattered, still more scantily sprinkles the sharp pinnacles which form but one precipice from their peak to their base. Such is the appearance of the bed of the river, viewed downwards from Sookhee (the direction a little to the west of south), till shut in by the closing mountains.

Leaving the village by a well beaten but stony path, which soon ended in a smart ascent, and descending a hill face embarrassed by jungle, we obtained a view of an opening in the bed of the river of a singular nature for full two miles. It meanders through a flat shingly space, which may vary in breadth from one to four, and even six furlongs. On the west, or right bank of the river (on which we then were), just above this shingly level, three villages are situated on a slope less inclined than the surrounding hills, on which there are many fields of wheat, and fruit-trees of different sorts. On the left, or opposite bank, the precipices descend quite to the bed of the river, which is contracted at the lower end of the shingly plain by the hill we descended, which meets the opposite precipices; and at this point a slight wooden bridge is thrown across, on which we passed it: and in truth it is a rather dangerous business, for the whole fabric from its length and form shakes much, yet there is no rail nor parapet to prevent accidents. The rapidity of the stream beneath is very apt to turn the head giddy, and a slip would be fatal.

The river may here be from forty to fifty yards broad, and certainly does not appear less than the Sutlej. Its rapidity both below and above the bridge is very great; and even while running through the sandy plain above, it flows with much violence. From the bridge we continued along the bed of the river for nearly two miles, now and then rising above it to avoid turns and precipices, and clambering along the rock by roots of trees and artificial ladders formed of stones and branches. We passed Shean-gad,h, which rises in Drum D,har, a very lofty and wild range to the north of Bunderpouch; and along which there is a very alarming road leading to remote parts of Rewaeen, which will be adverted to at the end of the day's route. Indeed, the hill itself appears to be an object of fearful superstition to the inhabitants of this district.

The road now mounted the bank of the river, very difficult and irregular, with several bad steps, which are only made passable by artificial ladders. The course is nearly east. We observed many noble pine trees of various sorts; but the aspect of the country was exceedingly wild. Many snowy ranges and peaks appeared for a moment, and it was plain that we were at no great distance below the region of snow; but so confined by the high hills around us that the occasional sight of one or two of the nearest points was all that was offered to our view. Two large streams join the river a little way beyond this, the Ghoomtee Gunga, and the Hersila Gunga. The first bears a very large body of water along a most craggy and tremendous cleft on the right bank. The Urselee, or Hersila, just above, is smaller, but equally wild; and there is only a high but narrow rock between the debouches of the two rivers, which, leaving the rocky banks, run foaming for a short way along the side of the Bhagiruttee, in a small slip of wooded land, before uniting with it. The Ghoomtee Gunga is said to take its rise in the south-east side of one of the snowy hills, called Nēhēl, which forms part of the boundary between Rewaeen and Bischur; and runs probably in a direction from south-west and north-east to east and west, on the north of Bunderpouch and its range. It is stated to be eight days' journey hence, in a north-west direction, chiefly through snow, and the whole road is very impracticable. The Bischur men, who go to Gungotree and the neighbourhood, either from religious or predatory motives, sometimes make use of this road when the season admits of it.

To the west of the Ghoomtee a range, called Deo-Goōsār, runs between it and the Shean Gad,h. From Bheetee-Ke-D,har (snowy hill), between the Ghoomtree and the Hersila, a range arises, called Poodoonga, which ends in the sharp rock above-mentioned, called Cookdormai. This last river rises in the Gurērō range, which comes down in a point called Nageen, to the Bhagiruttee, and forms its north-east bank. The break made in the right bank of the river by the rocky beds of these two streams, is most wild and remarkable. The bed of the river, which at Shean Gad,h had contracted to its usual rocky channel, here again opened out; and it flows for some distance through another shingly plain full of the ruins of the mountains around, which have yielded their soil and their productions to the violence of storms, of torrents, and the havoc of thaws and frosts.

Fir-trees of immense size, and large fragments of others, are seen half buried in sand and gravel; and huge masses of earth and rock lay in wild confusion at the mountain feet. The river rolls its uncertain but rapid course through all, changing probably after every season, as its channels may have been filled up or interrupted. Just beyond this there was formerly a considerable village, called Cutcharoo, in which a Rānā resided, who held sway over all T,hucnour; but some quarrel arose with the Bhoteas, under the Chinese dominion, part of which is at a very short distance from hence; and these people came and destroyed the village, deposed the Rānā, and demolished a temple which was in considerable repute, dedicated to the god Rait.

The Pundit of Gungotree, who was the relator, could not say when this happened; but as it is traditional, and as this species of information does not appear of long continuance among these people, it may probably refer to no very distant period. The ruins of the mût, or temple, are still to be seen. From this spot to the village of Duralee is short, and we reached it by five o'clock. This village, the highest in the bed of the Bhagiruttee, is situate just above the confluence of the Keeree nullah with the river, and is stated to be twelve cōs from Gungotree. It was formerly populous and comparatively rich. Its revenue was seventy-five rupees annually; and twenty-two of this sum were appropriated to the holy purpose of supporting the shrine and worship of Gungotree.

In the Ghoorkha raj, forty-five were thus bestowed; but according to the Pundit's account, who related these particulars, it now produces little or no thing. On the other side of the river, just opposite, is situate the village of Mookubba, formerly populous; and of its revenue (also about seventy-five rupees per annum), one half went to the religious establishment of Gungotree; the other half was allotted to the catching and training of hawks for the rajah's amusement. At present, the Pundit and his family, consisting of about fifteen people, are the only inhabitants. The village of Cutchoora also, till lately, produced seventy-five rupees, which went to the crown; but now it is desert, and this total desertion, or partial deterioration, is almost universal in the country. A village, called Suparga, which formerly existed at some distance below, was presented to the establishment by rajah Man-sing when he came to bathe at the sacred spot. Now the zemindars have deserted it. It is, I fear, too certain that this defalcation in cultivation, inhabitants, and general prosperity, may be chiefly referred to the iron rule of the Ghoorkha conquerors.

The village of Duralee was never very large, and was probably chiefly supported by the pilgrims, who resorted to it on their way to Gungotree. When we reached it there were no male inhabitants to be found, except a few old Brahmins and decrepid men, who, with the women and children, remained in the houses. To our inquiry, whither the young men had gone, we were answered, "that they had gone either to buy corn or to steal sheep," with an indifference and readiness, that proved most clearly that no idea of turpitude or impropriety was attached to an act of so common occurrence. It is indeed lamentable to know the extent to which this lawless species of enterprise has reached: we every where heard complaints, or boasts, or threats, or details of occurrences, all relating to pillage, robbery, or murder; and this is perhaps the more to be deplored than wondered at, when the very remote situation, and wild inaccessible nature of the country, and the semi-barbarous untameable manners of its inhabitants, are considered.

From the description given of the nature and appearance of the banks of the Jumna, it may be conceived that nothing wilder or more impracticable could well present itself to the traveller's view than the scenes there witnessed; and I confess that this was my own idea. Nevertheless, it is certain that the character of the mountains that form the banks of the Bhagiruttee, in the quarter we have passed to-day, is not only different from that of any yet seen, but marked by features unspeakably more lofty, rugged, and inaccessible. There is even less of beauty, and more of horror; more to inspire dread, less to captivate. The variety of character to be met with in these mountains, particularly after reaching their more remote and difficult regions, is remarkable; and to a person who has only travelled in the lower parts, and seen the better cultivated and more inhabited tracts of the country, scarcely credible. Perhaps a more complete and better marked example of this cannot be produced in any purely mountainous country, certainly not in that under consideration, than is exhibited in the features we see, marking the beds of the Sutlej, the Pabur, the Jumna, and the Bhagiruttee.

The mountains which form the valley of the Sutlej, particularly on the north-west side, are brown, barren, steep, and rocky; but they have these characters without the grandeur produced by lofty precipices or fringing wood. The nullahs that furrow them are dark uninteresting chasms, and their breasts in general are unenlivened by cultivation; and, though their heights are thickly crowned with forts, there are no neat villages surrounded with trees, on which the eye may turn and rest from the dark desert around. Such are the Cooloo hills, which met our view from below Comharsein, even to beyond Serān. And on the Bischur side, though there may be somewhat more cultivation above, and wood yields its verdure here and there to embellish the valleys, still the lower parts of the hills, for a descent of full three miles, to the narrow, rocky, and arid bed of the river, exhibit little except black rock peeping irregularly through brown burnt grass.

The smiling vale of the Pabur offers a delightful contrast to the black chasm through which the Sutlej rolls. We cannot speak of this river very near its source; but, from a long way beyond the village of Pooroo, which is seven miles above Raeengudh, it flows meandering through a valley of moderate breadth, in which pasture and crops are checkered with its different streams; and on the banks and roots of the hills, rich cultivation, villages, and wood, form a lovely picture, which extends up the stream as far as the eye can distinguish, and till brown hills, topped with snow and rocks, close the prospect.

If any success has attended the perhaps too detailed descriptions of the banks and bed of the Jumna, the reader will already have formed an idea of them: though rocky, precipitous, and wild, they are woody, green, and varied with some sloping faces, which are rich with cultivation and verdure. Here and there the river runs through a level though narrow bottom, and many well cultivated and beautiful valleys lead into it: even at its source, though a wilder collection of requisites for a romantic and imposing landscape, as rock, wood, precipice, and snow, could not well be drawn together, they did not form so truly desert and stern a scene as is exhibited in the bed of the Bhagiruttee.

I have said that these mountains are more lofty and bare; in fact, we had now penetrated farther into their higher and more inclement regions; and the Bhagiruttee, a far larger river than the Jumna, has worn a deeper bed, even in the stubborn materials of their bowels.

It is not easy to describe the change of scene effected by this change of situation: not only is luxuriant foliage more rare, all rich and lively greens giving way to the dark brown of the fir, which spots the face of the rock, but even that rock is evidently more continually acted on by the severity of the storms. Instead of being covered with rich and varied hues, the effect of lichens and the smaller herbage, that usually clothe and variegate even a precipice, the rocks here are white, gray, red, or brown, the colour of their fracture, as if a constant violence was crumbling them to pieces. Their sharp and splintered pinnacles spire up above the general mass: their middle region and feet are scantily sprinkled with the sombre unvarying fir-tree; while the higher parts, retiring from the view, present little more than brown rock, except where a lofty mass of snow overtops them, and calls to our recollection how nearly and completely we are surrounded by it. No green smiling valleys yield their waters to the river: the white and foul torrents which swell its stream pour their troubled tribute through chasms cleft in the solid rock, or are seen tumbling down its face, from the snow that gives them birth.

The whole scene casts a damp on the mind: an indefinite idea of desert solitude and helplessness steals over it: we are, as it were, shut out from the world, and feel our nothingness. Like the scenes they are placed among, the inhabitants of this village are wild in their appearance, and uncouth in their manners; but there is no essential difference between them and those with whom we have heretofore met. I met, indeed, with one or two who were peculiarly intelligent; but their language forms a considerable obstacle to taking advantage of their acuteness: it was still Hindoostannee, but so disguised by accent and dialect, and altered by new terminations and expletives, that it was difficult to understand the simplest sentences without an interpreter, or frequent repetitions. The Pundit was not only an intelligent man, but gave his information in the most intelligible language. Their dress is the same as that of the peasantry at Cursalee, black and gray blankets of coarse wool.

Just at the entrance to this village I found a true gooseberry-bush, a plant I had long looked for without success: it was to all appearance wild and neglected; but there was fruit nearly ripe on it, small and sour; and there could not be a shadow of doubt concerning the plant. Thus almost all the European garden-fruits had now been recognised in these hills.

Being comfortably settled for the night, in the outer room of a temple, I proceeded to make several inquiries respecting the roads that diverge from this point towards Buddree-Nauth, Kedar-Nauth, &c., and which pervade the snowy range in many directions towards Bischur; and also respecting the passes that lead quite through them to the Chinese territories, which were said to commence at no great distance hence; and having heard that two Bhoteas, inhabitants of a village within the Chinese dominions, were in the neighbourhood, I directed that they might be brought, for the purpose of questioning them on points that I thought might throw some little light on the geographical disposition of the country, and the manners and dispositions of the people. The information which I obtained at this time, and in this manner, forms part of that which has suggested the small geographical sketches that have been attempted; which must, in great measure, be rude and unsatisfactory, as my informants were inaccurate and indistinct. There are, in truth, no roads from this spot which lead through any practicable, or indeed to any inhabitable country, in the first instance, except that by which we came. But there are, as before mentioned, several paths used by travellers in the summer months for shortness, or by thieves on excursions to plunder neighbouring districts of their sheep and cattle. Of this nature is one which leads by Shean Gad,h and Dhum D,har to Bhurasso, one of the remotest t,hats or divisions of Rewaeen. Of this road I obtained the following account, which may serve as a good general specimen of the tracks that pervade the more inclement and inaccessible parts of the snowy mountains.

It is wholly desert, very dangerous and dismal, and at all seasons lies chiefly through the snow. Proceeding up the ravine of Shean Gad,h, by an ascent steep and rough, a more level path is gained; which leads to the usual resting-place, a cave: the whole distance only about four cōs, and the latter part entirely through snow. The second day's journey is about the same distance. This, like the first, is in a direct northerly direction, having Punderpouch to the south-west on the left hand; and during the whole day nothing is seen but immense masses of snow, with rock here and there appearing through it, in high bare peaks. The oppression of the chest, and difficulty of breathing, during this day's journey, is said to be excessive; and the place of rest is also a cave in the snow. The third day's journey carries the traveller quite across the Dhum D,har at the point where the river Touse arises from its west side; and, following its course downwards for about a cōs, he reaches Thangoon Saloo, a cave on its banks. The latter part of the descent is north-west. From this place a day's journey carries him, in a south-west direction, along the Touse to Ooslah, a village in Bhurassoo. About one cōs below Ooslah the village of Gunga is situated in a south direction; and three cōs below, to the south-east, is Dhatmere. Another person made the journey in three days, reaching Thangoon Saloo on the second, and Ooslah the third day.

The direction of this very extensive and lofty range is certainly nearly north and south; and it is most probable, from the accounts of these people, that the Touse river rises far north on its western face, and thus has a course from far to the northward of the Jumna: in this they all agree, and in the danger and difficulty of the route.

Some strange tales are related respecting this fearful range. It is said that a number of zemindars were travelling by this road to purchase salt, while it was deep in snow, and the foremost suddenly exclaimed that his eyes were sore; whereupon the eyes of the whole were affected, and they became for that day blind. This accident was, as usual, attributed to the agency of evil spirits, of the nature of those at Cot,ha; but probably, divested of the marvellous sympathetic affection, might be explained by the effect that a bright sun, shining on pure white snow, would naturally have on the eyes.

As no wood is found on this road, those who travel by it, and in general along the higher and more inclement regions of the hills, are under the necessity of carrying blankets to defend them from the severity of the cold, while they lie in holes in the snow, or under stones, and eat food raw, or previously dressed. This is probably no very uncommon attendant on travelling; for there is a road from Bischur, and particularly the remoter provinces of that state, to Buddree-Nauth and Kedar-Nauth, very little of which can possibly pass near the habitations of men; and this is frequented both for purposes of devotion, and of traffic in salt, wool, &c.

It is related that, about thirty-five years ago, a band of four or five hundred men from Bhurassoo, and the remote parts of Gurwhāl, made an incursion through the hills into the Chinese country, with a view to plunder the cattle. I could obtain but few particulars, either relating to their route, or to the length of time they were absent; but they did effect their purpose, and brought back a good many sheep. This, if true, itself proves that there are passes, besides those which are well known and frequented, through these hills, which lead into the Chinese territories, and that, though difficult, it is yet practicable to bring even small animals by these routes.

There is an acknowledged, though small portion of that territory which approaches very near to this place, not more distant, it is said, than one day's journey; but it is a mere desert, an uninhabitable mass of rock, no village being within many days' march. The road to Kedār and Buddree-Nauth, I find, is similar to that which we had travelled from Jumnotree to this place, and parts are represented as equally bad and dangerous with that across D,hum D,har. It is likewise stated that this desert road extends for the space of eight or ten days' journey, even by forced marches. I could obtain no correct information of the route beyond the first two or three days' journey, and these are described as very laborious.

The nature of these accounts called for instant decision relative to our future progress, both as to going to Buddreenauth at all, and with regard to the route to be taken. If there were no shelter better than caves or hollows, and the cold were as great as we experienced on our desert route thus far, if wood were not procurable to dress our victuals, and if it were found necessary to carry the provisions requisite for eight days with us, it was too much to be feared that it would be necessary to give up the proposed plan of visiting Buddreenauth by this high route. The people were so utterly exhausted by our late unintermitted marches, and even two nights' exposure, that it did not seem likely that many of them could reach the end of our desert march. And the difficulty of procuring carriers is so great, that it would be hardly possible to find enough for the provisions, far less to carry any number of sick. The route by the lower road by Cut,hoor was unfortunately equally out of the question; for the time at command was now fast drawing to a close, and we were imperiously called on to reach Srenuggur. We therefore agreed to set off the next morning for Gungotree, which is reckoned at full twelve cōs from the village, and is a long day's journey; but there is no intermediate stage or resting-place.

CHAPTER XXVIII.

July 19.—A MISTY morning succeeded a night in which drizzling rain had fallen. There were several points to be arranged before we could set off. In the first place, it was agreed to leave all the Mussulmauns of the party at the village. The Pundit next represented, that it was not customary to permit any armed person to approach the sacred shrine, nor even to pass beyond the village, and that all persons here put off their shoes, and performed this stage with naked feet.

As by the general voice it was allowed that marauding and plundering were common occurrences in this neighbourhood, I did not deem it proper or safe to go wholly unarmed; but I agreed that only five men should be permitted thus accoutred to attend us, and that I should myself carry my gun. But all these weapons of war were to be put aside before we got within sight of the holy spot, and deposited in a cave near it, under a guard. I also pledged myself that no use should be made of these instruments, nor any life sacrificed for the purpose of food, either by myself, or by any of my people, after leaving the village, until we returned; moreover, that I would not even carry meat of any sort, dead or alive, along with me, but eat only rice and bread. As to the putting off my shoes, they did not even propose it to me, and it could not have been done; but I volunteered to put them off, when entering into the precincts of the temple and holier places, which pleased them greatly. All the Hindoos, including the Ghoorkhas, went from the village barefoot.

It was seven o'clock before all these matters were adjusted, and we were fairly in route. The road, for rather more than two cōs, lies generally through a wood of large firs, a little above the river bed: the path is good, but there are some very bad steps. We then ascended the projection of a rock, which closes up the view, by a curiously constructed rude set of steps, formed of beams of wood and stones, stuck into the fissures of the rock. From this point the river had run to the village, chiefly in a shingly bed of unequal breadth. But here the rocks close over its stream, and confine it as in a trough: the chasm is very deep, dark, and narrow, and from hence we held a more devious path, over enormous fragments fallen from above, broken pieces of fallen trees, all interlaced together by tangled jungle, to a retired spot beneath some spreading trees, where a cool spring, and the pleasantness of the place, generally induces pilgrims to halt.

The river runs below this at a depth of more than one hundred yards, closely confined between two winding walls of solid rock, in which it has hollowed itself a bed, only sufficient to contain it, hardly broader above than it is below, where it tumbles over a succession of falls for a considerable way. Beyond this the road is difficult, and frequently dangerous, passing along the face of scars, in the beds of torrents, across rocks, and over fragments of trees and rocks, and ending in a very ugly and perilous descent, about six cōs from the village, which leads to Bhyram Ghauttee.

This is a very singular and terrible place. The course of the river has continued foaming through its narrow rocky bed, and the hills approach their heads, as though they would meet at a prodigious height above. At this point the Bhagiruttee is divided into two branches: that which preserves the name descends from the eastward, and the other, of a size fully equal, called the J,hannevie, joins it from the north-east. Both these rivers run in chasms, the depth, narrowness, and rugged wildness of which it is impossible to describe: between them is thrust a lofty crag, like a wedge, equal in height and savage aspect to those that on either side tower above the torrents. The extreme precipitousness of all these, and the roughness of their faces, with wood which grows near the river side, obstructs the view, and prevents the eye from comprehending the whole at a glance; but still the distant black cliffs, topped with lofty peaks of snow, are discerned, shutting up the view in either of the three ravines, when the clouds for a moment permit them to appear.

Just at the bottom of the deep and dangerous descent, and immediately above the junction of these two torrents, an old and crazy wooden bridge is thrown across the Bhagiruttee, from one rock to the other, many feet above the stream: and it is not till we reach this point that the extraordinary nature of the place, and particularly of the bed of the river, is fully comprehended; and there we see the stream in a state of dirty foam, twisting violently, and with mighty noise, through the curiously hollowed trough of solid granite, cutting it into the strangest shapes, and leaping in fearful waves over every obstacle. From hence the gigantic features of the mountains may frequently be seen, overhanging the deep black glen; their brown splintered crags hardly differing in colour from the blasted pines which start from their fissures and crevices, or even from the dark foliage of those which yet live.

It is wonderful how much the character of these trees harmonizes with the place, sometimes bare of leaves or limbs, shooting up like an arrow from their roots; at others sending a fantastic bough athwart the dell, or stretching forth their gray and dry arms like gigantic skeletons. But no description can give just ideas of this spot, or reach its sublime extravagancies. The attempt even is a mockery.

The bed of the J,hannevie is at least equally savage and picturesque; but I had not equal opportunities of acquaintance with it: the perpendicularity of its rocky sides, and their height above the water, is, perhaps, even greater than those of the Bhagiruttee. This river is said to have its origin in a very lofty mountain, called Ree-Kee-Soor-Stan, situated in the territories of China, and which is fifteen days' journey from hence, in a direction nearly that of its apparent course from hence, viz. north-east. I should incline to think it had a course more from the eastward. Just at the end of the bridge there is an overhanging rock, under which worship is performed to Bhyram, and a black stone partly painted red is the image of the god; and here prayers and worship alone were not performed, but every one was obliged to bathe and eat bread baked by the Brahmins, as preparatory to the great and effectual ablutions at the holier Gungotree. This occupied a considerable time, as the party was numerous; in the meantime I took a very imperfect sketch of the scene, after which I bathed myself at the proper place (which is the junction of the two streams), while the Brahmin prayed over me. Among the ceremonies performed, he made me hold a tuft of grass while he prayed, which at the conclusion he directed me to throw into the eddy occasioned by the meeting of the two waters. The spot where we bathe is a mere point of shingle, just under the rock which divides the two streams. It is necessary to be somewhat cautious in proceeding into the water, as it is exceedingly deep close to the shore; and about two yards towards the middle the stream becomes so rapid as to leave no chance of recovering a movement that should carry one into it.

It is extremely cold, as may be imagined, the whole being fresh snow water. Near the bridge there is a spring tinctured with iron.

From hence we ascended the rock, at the foot of which the bridge is situated, by a path more curious, dangerous, and difficult, than any we had yet passed. As the rock is too steep and perpendicular to afford a natural path, the chief part is artifically constructed, in the manner before mentioned, of large beams of wood, driven into the fissures, on which other beams and large stones are placed, thus forming a hanging flight of steps over the fearful gulf below: and as this sometimes has suffered from age and weather, while the facilities for attaching it to the rock are rather scanty, or altogether wanting, it is frequently so far from being sufficient, that it strikes dread into any one not much accustomed to this mode of ascent. Sometimes it is even required to make a leap to reach the next sure footing, with the precipice yawning below; and, at others, with merely the support afforded by a slight projecting ledge, and the help of a bamboo hung from some root above, to cling to the rock, and make a hazardous passage.

By this unpleasant path we reached a step, or level spot on the first stage of the mountain, where, in a thick grove of fir-trees, is placed a small temple to Bhyram, a plain white building, built by order of Ummr Sing T,happa, who gave a sum of money to repair the road, and erect places of worship here, and at Gungotree. Having paid our respects to Bhyramjee, we proceeded along the side of the hill on the right bank (north) of the river, gradually ascending by a path equally difficult and dangerous as the first part of our ascent, but more fearful, as the precipice to the river, which rolls below us, increases in height, and exceedingly toilsome from the nature of the ground over which it passes, and which consists wholly of sharp fragments from the cliffs above, with fallen trunks and broken branches of trees. Three cōs of such road brought us opposite to a considerable stream, which tumbles down a deep ravine called Mianee-ke-Gad,h, and through which opening is seen the snowy range of Mianee, with the extensive bosom of snow that feeds the stream.

From a point just below this, we had a view of the most singular and lofty peak Roodroo Himālā Bah,in, a prodigious spire of bare rock, the top of which is enveloped in snow, the loftiest insulated peak I ever saw. Just opposite to Mianee-Ke-Gad,h, we obtained bearings of the river, both upwards and downwards, and first came in view of the site of Gungotree, the direction of which, as well as of the source of the river, as pointed out by the Pundit, was nearly east, and that to Bhyramghattee somewhat to the north-west.

The path increases in difficulty from the very irregular nature of the ground, as well as the steepness of the hill face across which it leads, ascending and descending as the small, though deep, watercourses furrow the mountain side, in loose soil, formed of the small fragments fallen from above, and which slip down, threatening to carry the traveller to the gulf below. The shapeless blocks of rock now more completely obstructed the way, and for hundreds of yards, at times, the passenger must clamber over these masses, heaped as they are one upon another, in monstrous confusion, and so uncertain and unsteady that, huge though they are, they shake and move even under the burthen of a man's weight. So painful indeed is this track, that it might be conceived as meant to serve as a penance to the unfortunate pilgrims with bare feet, thus to prepare and render them more worthy for the special and conclusive act of piety they have in view, as the object of their journey to these extreme wilds.

One cōs from Gungotree, and two cōs from Mianee-ke-Gadh, we reached a spot called Patangnee, which is noted as the place where the Pandooan, or five brothers, Bheemsing, Arjun, Joodishteer, Sahadeo, and Nakeel, remained for twelve years, worshipping Mahadeo, after his retreat to Himālā from Lunka. After that period they left this place, and ascended Soorga-rouinee, a peak of the sacred hill, whence the Ganges flows: there four of the brothers died, and their immortal parts ascended to heaven; but the fifth, Joodishteer, without tasting the bitterness of death, or quitting his earthly tenement, was assumed, body and spirit, into the heavenly mansions. The spot which bears the name of Gungotree is concealed by the roughness of the ground, and the masses of fallen rock, so as not to be seen till the traveller comes close upon it.

A gunshot below Gungotree, the Kedār Gunga, a rapid and considerable stream, debouches into the Bhagiruttee, at a place called Goureecounda; and this is a holy place, where a second ablution is usually performed before Gungotree can be approached. I could not learn the reason of this sanctity, but I believe there is an allusion in the name to some mythological story. The same name was given to one of the hot springs at Jumnotree. There is no holy place of purification by bathing which has not a cound or well of this name.

The hills which form between them the bed of the river, and which are exceedingly precipitous and close the whole way from Bhyramghattee, here recede a little, and without losing any thing of their savage grandeur, admit somewhat of a less confined view, and more of the light of day. Below Goureecounda, the river falls over a rock of considerable height in its bed, and continues tumbling over a succession of petty cascades or rapids nearly the whole way to Mianee-ke-Gad,h. Above the debouche of the Kedār Gunga, the bed widens into a small shingly space, in which the river rapidly rolls, obviously changing its course as the floods direct it. Just at the gorge of this space a bridge has been thrown across, which is formed of two parts, the interior ends of the beams resting on a large rock in the centre; and just above the bridge, in a bay formed by a reach of the river in this shingly space, fifteen feet above the stream, is situated the small temple, or mût, dedicated to the goddess Gunga, or Bhagiruttee.

In former times no temple made with hands was provided for the worship of the deity, but within these few years, the piety of Ummr Sing T,happa, the chief of the Ghoorkha conquerors, appropriated a sum of money of about four or five hundred rupees for the erection of the small building which is now placed there; and it by no means clearly appears whether he has in truth done an act pleasing or disgusting to the goddess: on this subject the Pundit's answers were by no means explicit.

Jumna prefers simple worship at the foot of her own and natural shrine, and has forbidden the erection of temples to her honour; and probably were it not for the comforts which have accrued to the holy Brahmins of Gungotree, from the warm and dry tenement built for their accommodation, their attachment to ancient customs would have induced them to declare that the original mode of worship was here also most acceptable. It is remarkable, if there be not some superstitious reason for the non-erection of temples, that among the number of donations presented to this establishment by the many pious persons who have visited it either themselves or by proxy, in the lapse of so many centuries, there should never have been any thing of the sort, nor any provision for a building. Whereas at Kedernauth and Buddreenauth, places not in themselves so holy as this, there are places of worship. It is, therefore, fair to suppose that the want of them here is not from neglect, but in consequence of some superstitious prohibition. The temple is situated precisely on the sacred stone on which Bhagiruttee used to worship Mahadeo, and is a small building of a square shape for about twelve feet high, and rounding in, in the usual form of pagodas, to the top. It is quite plain, painted white, with red mouldings, and surmounted with the usual melon-shaped ornaments of these buildings. From the eastern face of the square, which is turned nearly to the sacred source, there is a small projection covered with a stone roof, in which is the entrance facing the east, and just opposite to this there is a small pagoda-shaped temple to Bhyramjee. The whole is surrounded by a wall built of unhewn stone and lime, and the space this contains is paved with flat stones. In this space too there is a comfortable but small house for the residence of the Brahmins who come to officiate. Without the enclosure there are two or three sheds constructed of wood, called *dhurm salluhs*, built for the accommodation of pilgrims who resort here; and there are many caves around formed by overhanging stones, which yield a shelter to those who cannot find accommodation in the sheds.

The scene in which this holy place is situated is worthy of the mysterious sanctity attributed to it, and the reverence with which it is regarded. We have not here the confined gloominess of Bhyram Gattee: the actual dread which cannot but be inspired by the precipices, and torrents, and perils of the place, here gives way to a sensation of awe, imposing but not embarrassing, that might be compared to the dark and dangerous pass to the centre of the ruins of a former world; for, most truly, there is little here that recals the recollection of that which we seem to have quitted. The bare and peaked cliffs which shoot to the skies, yield not in ruggedness or elevation to any we have seen; their ruins lie in wild chaotic masses at their feet, and scantier wood imperfectly relieves their nakedness; even the dark pine more rarely roots itself in the deep chasms which time has worn. Thus on all sides is the prospect closed, except in front to the eastward; where, from behind a mass of bare spires, four huge, lofty, snowy peaks arise; these are the peaks of Roodroo-Himālā. There could be no finer finishing, no grander close to such a scene.

We approach it through a labyrinth of enormous shapeless masses of granite, which during ages have fallen from the cliffs above that frown over the very temple, and in all probability will some day themselves descend in ruins and crush it. Around the inclosure, and among these masses, for some distance up the mountain, a few fine old pine-trees throw a dark shade, and form a magnificent foreground; while the river runs impetuously in its shingly bed, and the stifled but fearful sound of the stones which it rolls along with it, crushing together, mixes with the roar of its waters.

It is easy to write of rocks and wilds, of torrents and precipices; it is easy to tell of the awe such scenes inspire: this style and these descriptions are common and hackneyed. But it is not so simple, to many surely not very possible, to convey an adequate idea of the stern and rugged majesty of some scenes; to paint their lonely desertness, or describe the undefinable sensation of reverence and dread that steals over the mind while contemplating the deathlike ghastly calm that is shed over them; and when at such a moment we remember our homes, our friends, our firesides, and all social intercourse with our fellows, and feel our present solitude, and far distance from all these dear ties, how vain is it to strive at description! Surely such a scene is Gungotree. Nor is it, independent of the nature of the surrounding scenery, a spot which lightly calls forth powerful feelings. We were now in the centre of the stupendous Himālā, the loftiest and perhaps most rugged range of mountains in the world. We were at the acknowledged source of that noble river, equally an object of veneration and a source of fertility, plenty, and opulence to Hindostan; and we had now reached the holiest shrine of Hindoo worship which these holy hills contain. These are surely striking considerations, combining with the solemn grandeur of the place, to move the feelings strongly.

The fortuitous circumstance of being the first European that ever penetrated to this spot was no matter of boast, for no great danger had been braved, no extraordinary fatigues undergone: the road is now open to any other who chooses to attempt it, but it was a matter of satisfaction to myself. The first object of inquiry that naturally occurs to the traveller, after casting a glance over the general landscape, is the source of the river. Here, as at Jumnotree, you are told that no mortal has gone, or can go further towards its extreme origin than this spot; and the difficulty is indeed very apparent. I made a trial to gain a point about two furlongs beyond the temple, both for the purpose of observing the course of the river and of seeing Gungotree in another point of view. But having with considerable difficulty made my way over the unsteady fragments for some hundred yards, at the risk of being precipitated into the stream, I was forced to turn back. The precipices beyond descend more abruptly to the water's edge, and in all probability it would be nearly impossible to make one's way along their face. Crossing the stream to take advantage of easier places on either side to pass along is out of the question; it is too large and too rapid, and climbing the mountain side higher up is equally so, for the crags increase in ruggedness and steepness till they end in snow. Thus, though in a particular water-course or chasm it may be possible to ascend for a short way, yet no end except that of a somewhat more extensive view of what we already know could be thus attained. It may be that some enterprising persons remaining at this spot for several days or weeks might explore a path, or form one, towards the source, for time and patient perseverance with courage may do much, but I am convinced it will be found extremely difficult; and probably the Paharies, whose assistance would be necessary to strangers, will be with difficulty persuaded to overcome the religious prejudice which has hitherto kept them below.

In the want of time I experienced an effectual obstacle to exploring difficult or remote situations, and I was obliged to rest satisfied with the conclusion formed on the Pundit's report, strengthened by observation as far as it went, and by reason and analogy where observation failed.

The source is not more than five miles horizontal distance from the temple, and in a direction south-east, 85° nearly; and beyond this place it is in all probability chiefly supplied by the melting of the great bosom of snow which terminates the valley, and which lies between the peaks of the great mountain above mentioned.

This mountain, which is considered to be the loftiest and greatest of the snowy range in this quarter, and probably yields to none in the whole Himālāya, obtains the name of Roodroo Himālā, and is held to be the throne or residence of Mahadeo himself. It is also indiscriminately called Pāuch Purbut, from its five peaks; and Soomeroo Purbut, which is not to be confounded with the mountain so called near Bunderpouch; and sometimes the general appellation of Kylās is given, which literally signifies any snowy hill, but is applied to this mountain by way of pre-eminence.

It has five principal peaks, called Roodroo Himālā, Burrumpooree, Bissenpooree, Oodgurree Kanta, and Soorga Rounee. These form a sort of semi-circular hollow of very considerable extent, filled with eternal snow, from the gradual dissolution of the lower parts of which the principal part of the stream is generated: probably there may be smaller hollows beyond the point to the right above Gungotree, which also supply a portion.

This is the Pundit's whole account, and I believe it to be the true one, for the following among other reasons: in the first place, our ascent from the village of Sookhee, which itself is high among the hills, has been very great, and from Dhuralee rapid, so much so as to leave no doubt that we had now attained a height far above the level of the countries beyond the snowy hills.

Indeed our perpendicular distance from the snowy region was very inconsiderable; and were it not for the increased heat of this spot from the reflexion and confinement of the sun's rays among so much rock, which creates a great degree of it, the snow would most certainly lie continually even at this place. The cold here at night is consequently great. When on the banks of the Sutlej, and to a considerable extent within the range of snow, we were a long day's journey, had the ascent been direct, or probably equal to twelve miles of regular gradual ascent, from the commencing line of the region of snow, and yet the heat in the river's bed was intolerable, nay, at Serān, near three miles above its bed, it was far from cold. The Sutlej certainly comes through the snowy hills; and it must be allowed that the difference of altitude, which these circumstances indicate, proves that the Bhagiruttee cannot do so, its course even at this point being so very elevated. If it does not come through the Himālā, its source cannot be far from hence. The snowy peaks have no very great breadth; they generally consist of one very lofty ridge cut into many and very irregular peaks, which project several equally irregular ridges on either side towards the north and south. These inferior ridges are never equal in height to the parent peak, but nevertheless at times shoot up enormous masses, whence in their turn diverge other ranges that either themselves or in their branches reach the plain.

The breadth of the mountainous region may probably occupy a space of from sixty to eighty miles at most. The grounds for supposing this to be the extreme breadth are, not only our own observation, but the information we received from different and intelligent persons relative to routes through the passes: and it appears that we have now at least penetrated the larger portion of this extent. Thus reasoning from probabilities, observation, and information, Roodroo Himālā is at least removed to the centre of the snowy range, and it is fair to suppose that the land, mountainous and lofty as it is, rather falls than rises to the north and north-east of this mountain. This the Pundit also asserts, as well as the zemindars, who have been accustomed to view it from lofty situations on either side of the glen of the Bhagiruttee. No one seemed to have any doubt of the fact of the river having its rise in the above-mentioned hollow of snow; and some went so far as to assert that, when climbing in search of stray sheep, they had seen the river and its glen ending thus, and marked the deep precipitous ravine, through which it breaks down into its bed; and further declare, that no considerable stream appeared to join it from any other quarter.

The Pundit also mentioned a road by which the Bischur men travelled to the country about Kedar for salt, which runs behind this among other mountains passing no stream that runs in this direction; and that the Bhoteas and others, by the accounts they had given of the country directly behind this hill, had very completely confirmed this point, which also is written in the shasters. To all this may be added, that the stream of the Bhagiruttee, though large and rapid, is not perhaps greater than may be accounted for by the large mass of snow that supplies it, and that there are few streams of any magnitude to join it above the J,hannevie; the Shewrie Gadh, the Mianee Gadh, the Bouge Gadh, and the Kedar Gunga, being the only ones from the south-east; while on the north-west side it does not receive a single stream larger than a mere rill. All which renders it probable that few, if any nullahs from above unite with the main stream; and that it really is formed by a collection of the numerous torrents that run from the melted snow, uniting in a deep ravine formed by their violence.

It has been observed, that the appearance of the bed of the river and hills closing our view, confirmed the information we received. About two furlongs beyond Gungotree, a point on the left from the northward shuts out the immediate view of the stream. Somewhat less than a mile of horizontal distance further on, another point from the southward stretches down behind the former, and hides a larger and higher portion of the bed and banks. Beyond this the course seems nearly straight for a considerable distance from the southward of east; and a rough and craggy ridge that shoots into very sharp peaks forms the north-eastern bank, and ends in a point round which the river appears again to turn, and which stretches down from Soorgarounee.

Soorgarounee is the nearest peak of the five, and forms the western point of the great snowy hollow. Roodroo Himālā is the eastern, and forms the other point; but from that point a huge snowy shoulder runs down, that, as far as we could observe, gives off or ends in the mountains that surround us, and form a great unbroken, though unequal snowy ridge, bounding and confining the glen of the Bhagiruttee. The other three peaks form different points in the back of the immense hollow, and altogether compose one of the most magnificent and venerable mountains, perhaps, that the world can produce. The preceding explanation and discussion may seem tedious and excessive; but when the object is to throw every possible light on even the remotest and least important part of the course of this noble river, this may be pardoned.

The old popular idea that the Ganges issued from a rock, like a cow's mouth (Gae Mouk,h), did not fail to occur to me. This idea is extremely prevalent, and it is difficult to account in a satisfactory manner for its universality, for it is *not* authorized by the shasters; and the numbers of pilgrims and devotees who have reached the place of Gungotree (it might be presumed) would have served to give sufficient publicity to the true state of the case. By one Persian author (of the life of Timour), in his records of that prince, when he relates his visit to the spot where the Ganges issues from the hills, called by him Durreh Cowpela (evidently Hurdwar), it is stated that, fifteen cōs above it, there is a mass of rock, or stone, in the form of a cow, from which the river issues. On which account the infidels regard the place with the most enthusiastic veneration; and esteem a journey to it in the same light as the faithful do a journey to Mecca. Thus, even after so near an advance to its source, the popular error subsisted in these days, and we have far later evidence that it did so.

Father Tieffenthaller, who describes the route (in a very erroneous way, indeed), towards the source of the river, takes notice of this cow's mouth; and it seems to have gained ground by time, instead of the truth having appeared. It does not seem at all a point of religious or superstitious imposition, as the Pundit of Gungotree would not then have treated it as he did. In all probability it must be referred to that love of the marvellous said to be so inherent in travellers; and which, like a sort of freemason craft, none of the fraternity choose to disturb by undeceiving the public, and disclosing the frauds of each other.

When I made inquiry concerning the origin of this story the Pundit laughed; and observed that most of the pilgrims, who came from the plains, put the same question as to its source in several shapes. One asking whether it did not take its rise from the leaves of a sacred birch, (Bouge-Ke-Putta); others, from its roots; and others, if it did not really and visibly come down from heaven. He gravely assured me, however, that no such thing happened, but that the river really came from the spot above-mentioned: and he then gave the account which has been inserted, adding that this was in truth the account given in the shasters; and that he believed it not only for that reason, but (pointing out the landscape to me, and showing the five peaks) because, as might be seen, it was supported by appearances, and from the situation of those things we saw around us it could not possibly be otherwise.

It may be remarked that the Moonshee sent towards this place by Messrs. Webb and Raper alludes to, and, indeed, describes this rock. The relation of his journey affords a singular mixture of marks of truth and authenticity with falsehood and error, creating a complete indecision in my mind whether he really reached Gungotree or not. So far as these people of this place, Pundit, Brahmins, zemindars, were questioned merely about their own district, and the places contiguous, their answers were distinct and ready, and had every appearance of correctness and truth to the best of their apprehension. But where any attempt was made to carry them further abroad, or to collect any thing of the geography of the country beyond this great range, they failed altogether, either at once saying that they knew nothing about the matter, or giving improbable and contradictory accounts. Some of them averred that there was a plain and well-cultivated country at no greater distance than twelve cōs (horizontal) from the other side of Roodroo Himālā, though it be impossible from the nature of the country to reach it, except by a very circuitous route; but whether they alluded to the great plains of Tartary, or some intervening valley, I could not ascertain. If such plain does exist, it cannot be near the level country on the north-east side of the Himālā, as the routes we have obtained from more creditable authority speak of a far greater extent of hills, stretching even further to the south than Kumaoon.

They, however, assert that it may be seen from the top of some of the high peaks in the neighbourhood; an assertion which I must believe to be false, as I think there cannot be any means of ascending a peak high enough to give such a view from hence.

CHAPTER XXIX.

It may be amusing to relate the fabulous origin of this mountain, of the range, and of the two rivers as given by the Brahmin. Whether it be the same as is assigned in the shasters I have not the means of ascertaining. It was, however, attributed to them.

The common tale of the usurpation of the empire of Lunka, by Rawen the son of Maha Deo, who rebelled against his father, is well known; as also are the adventures of Ram and Lutchmun, driven from their father Maha Deo's presence, by the trick of one of his wives; the history of this pair, and of Sita the wife of Rām; their meeting with the Hoonoomaun in the Amrita gardens in Lunka; the rape of Sita by Rawen, tyrant and usurper of Lunka; the conquest of that place, and recovery of Sita, with the union of the three brothers in favour with their god and father, Maha Deo. When Maha Deo retired from Lunka, disgusted at the rebellion of his son Rawen, and, as it is said, forced by him to fly, he formed Kylās, or the Himālā range, for his retreat; and Soomeroo Purbut, or Roodroo Himālā with its five peaks, rugged and inaccessible as it is, for his own dwelling, that none should find him out. Both Bhagiruttee and Alacknunda are there said to have sprung from the head of Maha Deo. Twelve holy Brahmins, denominated the twelve Reekhee, left Lunka in search of Maha Deo, and penetrated to Bhyramghattee, where the J,hannevie meets the Bhagiruttee, but could not find him. Eleven of them in despair went to Cashmere, but the twelfth, named Jum-Reekhee, remained at Bhyramghattee, sitting on a huge rock in the course of the stream of the Bhagiruttee, which, instead of flowing on as usual, was absorbed into the belly of the Reekhee and lost, while the J,hannevie flowed on. The goddess of the stream (Bhagiruttee) herself was at Gungotree worshiping Maha Deo, and making her prostrations on the stone on which now the temple is founded. When she felt that the course of the stream was stopped, she went in wrath to Bhyramghattee, clove the Jum Reekhee in two, and gave a free passage to the river. One half of the Reekhee she flung to the westward, and it became the mountain of Bunderpouch. From his thigh sprung the Jumna, and from his skull arose the hot springs mentioned when treating of Jumnotree. Thus far the extravagancies of the shasters; and still they show the large rock which the Reekhee sat upon, and which was divided in two by the same fatal cut. It is a very large block of granite, which appears to have fallen from the cliff, above the point of union between the two rivers, and is curiously split in two.

From the time that we entered the bed of the river at Sookhee, one species of stone chiefly predominated: it was hard, white, pervaded more or less with black spots, streaks, and stars, and frequently with mica. The structure is remarkable; and, though the colour and the different proportions of the component parts vary, still it is the same stone. I was almost convinced that this was a true granite; and subsequent inquiries have established the fact. It closely resembles that sort of stone first met with in the bed of the Pabur, though generally white, some almost purely so. Other specimens are more spotted with jet-like particles; others with long black bars, irregularly crossing each other; some with mica, in a gray bed; some with dark black or blue veins; some slightly red; some yellowish; and other specimens gray. In the bed of the river, from Sookhee to Dhuralee, it was found in large, rounded, and irregular masses; but, from that village to Gungotree, the whole mass of the mountain seemed to be composed of it; and the bed of the river consists of the same.

From hence to a mile or two below Bhyram-Ghattee, the river has forced its way through a solid bed of this rock, hollowing out an irregular trough, not broader than is sufficient for its waters to rush through, in a succession of falls and rapids. These waters are loaded with a quantity of white shining sand, which doubtless is produced by the attrition of the stones rolled along this channel, and their gradual but constant action on the rocks through which it passes. The fragments and masses of rock which lay piled on the mountain side, and over which our path from below Bhyram-Ghattee lay, were uniformly of the sort of stone above described; and the nearer peaks, from their base to their top, as far as it was possible to judge, were formed of the same material; and, by comparison between these and the most lofty, there can be little doubt that they are the same.

Even the summit of Soorgarounee, a bare rock, is evidently of similar composition. The fracture of this rock is perfectly irregular; and there is no appearance of strata or lamina in any of the mountains near Gungotree. Their tops certainly spire up in very sharp and lofty peaks; but the rock appears accidentally to have taken these shapes, and not to affect any peculiar one. Below Duralee, schistus, I think, was common; and just above the village, there is a large shelving rock, which is laminated, and, I think, is either schistus or sand-stone: part of the village, indeed, is built on it. On the night we arrived our fatigue was sufficient to prevent much further exertion; and a bed under the roof of one of the dhurrum sallahs, or pilgrim's sheds, was very acceptable.

July 20.—The night was cold, and the morning misty. In hopes, however, of a better day or hour, I took a rough sketch of the foreground of the landscape before us.

During the forenoon I questioned the Brahmins respecting the points above adverted to, and towards evening bathed in the holy spot where the goddess used to stand. The water, just freed from the ice, was piercing cold; and it required no small effort of piety to stay long enough in it for the Brahmin to say the necessary prayers over the pilgrim, which are much in the same form as at Bhyram-Ghattee: I held also a small tuft of grass in the hand, which, on the prayer ceasing, is thrown into the stream. Afterwards, with bare feet, we entered the temple, where worship was performed, a little bell ringing all the time. The necessary presents were then made, and all parties fully satisfied.

The outside of the temple has already been described. Within there are three images: one, I think, is that of Kāli: and the elevated stone shelf on which they were placed was wet and soiled with the offerings made: there was a peculiar smell, but I know not whence it proceeded. The place, as is usual, was lighted by a small lamp: no daylight had admittance. Just below the temple, on the river side, grew three poplar-trees and a few small larches: above there are the remains of a fine old silver fir-tree, which overshadows some of the caves and sheds. The whole people also bathed, and contributed something to the priesthood; and it was a matter of serious importance, as well as of great joy to every one, that we had thus happily reached a place of such supereminent sanctity:

such, indeed, that the act of bathing here is supposed to cleanse from every sin heretofore committed, and the difficulty of which is so great, that few, except professional devotees, ever attempt reaching the holy place.

It is customary that those who have lost their father and mother, or either of these, shall be shaved at this spot; and it was curious to observe the whimsical changes produced by the operation, which numbers underwent. It appears also, that one chief ordinance was the going frequently round the holy temple; and we particularly observed that those who were noted as the greatest rogues were most forward in this pious exercise: one man in particular, who had been a notorious thief, was unwearied in his perseverance.

Immediately after bathing the day cleared up, and I obtained a noble view of the five peaks of Roodroo Himālā, and the surrounding rocks, and I took advantage of it to sketch them on paper. The clearing of the mountain, which remained without a cloud for nearly an hour, was considered, or at least pronounced to be a very special sign of favour from the mighty deity there enthroned, as it was a very uncommon circumstance at this time of the year, and happened just after the pious act of bathing. Indeed, it was asserted, that favour was eminently shown during the whole act of our approach; first, in that we crossed safely the great hill from Jumnotree to the Bhagiruttee, with cool, moderate weather, without which, it was said, we must have perished; then, in our safe arrival in these wild lone regions, where none but the pious venture, or could penetrate; and, lastly, in showing to us, unveiled, the sacred cliffs, at a season when they are usually covered deep in clouds.

Well, indeed, do they say, that Seeva has formed these recesses which he inhabits, inaccessible to all but those whom true devotion leads to his shrine. That man must have been indeed strongly impelled by devotion, ambition, or curiosity, who first explored the way to Gungotree. It were unavailing to inquire, and perhaps of little use, if known, to which of these motives we owe the enterprise; but patience, perseverance, and courage, must have been strongly united with it to lead him safely and successfully through those awful cliffs, that would bar the way to most men. Another omen of favour pointed out was, the increase of the river after bathing, as at Jumnotree; and it is singular enough, that during the time we remained here, I remarked several increases and decreases of the water, without any obvious causes; but these may fairly be referred to the effects of sudden changes of temperature occurring frequently among the hills, and acting on the body of the snow that feeds the river. All these things, however, gave room for fresh showers of compliments, and served as a theme for flattering the British, who were now lords of the ascendant, and to whose rule they promised permanence and prosperity.

It would have been very desirable to have remained here for some time longer, as perseverance and opportunity might, no doubt, have enabled us to procure some additional information, or confirmed that of which we were in possession; but my days were numbered, and the time for which we had prepared had now elapsed: another day or two could have yielded little that was interesting to us; our provisions also were exhausted, and I prepared to return on the morrow.

I have mentioned two Bhoteas who had come to a spot near Dhuralee, and for whom I sent to make some inquiries of them respecting their routes towards the Chinese dominions, and to this place. They came, but they were not men from whom much could be expected: they were inhabitants of a miserable village, and had never travelled much. What they knew, however, they communicated in a way that showed they did not want acuteness. They spoke a broken Hindostannee acquired in their intercourse with the Paharias, but their own language was perfectly distinct in every respect. They were short stout men, who wore their hair very thick and bushy, ending in a long plaited tail after the manner of the Chinese. Their clothes consisted of a gown or wrapper of coarse brown woollen stuff, with something like drawers of the same sort, very loose above the knee, but bound tight around the calves of the legs and ancles. Their dress and whole appearance differed exceedingly from that of the Paharias. Their features were entirely of the Tartarian cast: high cheek bones, flat noses, and small eyes, the corners of which turned upwards. They said that they were from the village of Chounsah, a poor place consisting of a few houses, in the purgunnah or district of Chaprung, the chief officer or soubahdar (as they called him), of which is named Catok. They represented this to be about one month's journey from hence at the rate of nine to twelve cōs per day; but they evidently have no definite notion of a cōs. I do not believe that their day's journey exceeds five or six miles, as they travel over a very difficult country, proceeding slowly and only a short way in each day. They represent the road as exceedingly bad, lying for ten days' journey along the bed of the J,hannevie, tracing it to its source, which lies in a lofty snowy hill, called Sanctian, (different, as will be observed, from the account given by the Pundit, who called this hill Reekeesoorstan): probably both are wrong, and the river has its rise in all probability in a part of the same hill that gives birth to the Ganges or Bhagiruttee. Its course is said to be very winding, but flowing chiefly from the eastward. Another river has its rise in Sankliaw peak, which runs to Bischur, and debouches into the Sutlej, at a place called Hobbe. Chaprung, they say, is a large town in a plain, where there is not a vestige of any sort of wood, being only covered with short grass. The distance from their village to Chaprung they describe as a month's journey to the northward; one day's journey of which lies through snow, and about six through hills, all very bad and rugged; the rest through a level plain, or at least very little over rising ground.

A confusion, or perfect non-comprehension of distance is evident in all they say: and, among other obvious proofs of it, it may be observed, that they place their own village in the same purgunnah as Chaprung, which indicates an extent (according to their scale, a month's journey, at ten cōs each day; say 300 miles) that is quite absurd. To Garah from Chaprung is also a month's journey to the northward, through a perfect plain, without wood, covered with small grass; and there are plenty of shawl goats and sheep, both at Chaprung and Garah.

On inquiry being made of them, whether they knew any thing of the river Sutlej, or crossed it, or heard of it on their way to Garah, they distinctly stated, that they do cross the Sutlej between their village and Chaprung by a sango; that there it is large, and goes, in their language, by the name of Lang-gin-T,hang; but that they are quite aware that it is the same river that flows through Bischur under the name of Sutudra or Sutlej. I paid particular attention to their manner of relating this, and did not allow a word to be said that could lead them to guess what answer was expected. I therefore feel pretty confident, that they tell, at least, what they believe. They could not say distinctly where its source was. On the road from Chaprung to Garah they pass through the city of Tuling, described as a large place, where a great lama presides. The country where their village is situated is very mountainous and snowy. The only grains they know are barley and papera, and these are scarce. They aver, that Sirce-Kanta peak is perceptible from their village; but I do not think they understood the question that led to this, nor stated their answer distinctly. In the notes on the Bhoteas, before given, I have already detailed the result of our inquiries regarding their manners and customs, and need not repeat them here.

July 21.—The morning was clear and fine; and the snowy peaks of Soomeroo Purbut shone forth in full glory. In our route from this place to the village, having only retraced our former steps, no subject offers for fresh observations. The gooseberry was found in abundance every where; and a few trees of cedar were pointed out by the Brahmins as of great sanctity, under the name of d'hoop: our pious Hindoos all carried pieces of its wood along with them. It appears, that from the time we entered Gurwhal on the Jumna's banks at Lak,ha,mandhul, our route has lain through the district of Rewaeen, until we crossed the pass of Chaiah-ke-Kanta, where we entered that of Upper Tucknoor, which was occasionally attached to that of Rewaeen, and formed a different ãmil.

July 22.—About noon we left the village of Dhuralee, and measured our steps back to Sookhee: the weather was rainy and comfortless; and we obtained very bad quarters at night, both for myself and the people.

July 23.—The morning was exceedingly foggy, with drizzling rain, which had fallen almost all night long. The state of the atmosphere, both on the evening before and this morning, disappointed me of any bearings or observations of much utility. I endeavoured, however, to remedy this as far as possible, at least with regard to the course of the river, by keeping a small compass in my hand, and referring to it every moment.

The pass at Kandee, of which I was particularly desirous to gain a view, was seen but very insufficiently. We left Sookhee at seven o'clock, and descended to the river by a stony and steep, but beaten path, through ridged cultivation, and crossed it by a bridge suspended on two large rocks: it is very rapid, and here enters between banks more confined than those opposite to and above the village.

From hence, the road wound along the face of the eastern or left bank, rough, stony, and difficult, forcing us to climb up faces of rock, holding by roots of trees, through jungle loaded with wet, and most uncomfortable. Somewhat lower down we passed the debouche of Rindee Gad,h, and continued a similar path, very irregularly, ascending and descending into the beds of rapid and dangerous nullahs, that swell the river. The rocks here resume their stratiform appearance, pointing as before to the southward, and their structure has changed. A little further on we crossed the river again on Loārnād-Ke-Sango. It here widens much, running with violent rapidity between the banks, which approach very close, and are exceedingly precipitous and rugged. The road, which at first led us clambering up and down precipices with much toil, here wound along the foot of one of the banks. Just below this bridge, the bed of the river rapidly descends for more than half a mile, in which space, though no absolute fall of great magnitude occurs, yet the whole forms a steep declivity, over which water tumbles with a noise like loud and continued thunder, in a mass of discoloured foam. Here and there a piece of the solid rock, which forms the channel of this long rapid, resists the headlong stream which is thrown upwards to a great height, and plunges over it in a terrible cataract. The effect is in truth very grand, but stunning and appalling; for the body of water is great, and the roar of it, with the frequent crash of immense stones striking, in their descent with the torrent, is truly terrific. Just at the end of this rapid, we again crossed the river to the left bank by Dubranee-Ke-Sango, which is very long and narrow, and vibrates so much as to render it not a little dangerous, having no sort of support for the traveller in case of a trip, whilst under it the water pours with fearful violence.

From Loārnād-Ke-Sango the road is painful and difficult, crossing over the high piled ruins of the cliffs above, and much tangled with jungle and thorns, rising and falling frequently and irregularly; and it continues thus till we reach Dangalo-Ke-Sango, on which we crossed the Bhagiruttee for a fourth time this day. Just above it the Kunoulee Khola, which in a former page is called Gedār Gad,h, gives its waters to the Bhagiruttee, and is in fact the same into which Sathkear-Cote and the Bunsooroo-Ke-Gad,h flow. A little below the bridge, and in a small nullah not far above the bed of the river, is situated the village of Bunghelee. On the left bank of the river, a little beyond Bunghelee, there is a small village called Ooree; and from thence begins the T,hat, or district of Cuthoor, which extends down the river. From Dubranee-Ke-Sango to this place, the river runs in a succession of rapids, such as above described, at times offering to the view scenery of the most picturesque nature, and perhaps little, if at all, inferior to regular cascades. Two miles more of exceeding bad road carried us to a nullah called Coormee-Ke-Gad,h, the bed of which we ascended to get round a high rock that projects into the river's course. It is said that, at the debouche of a small nullah near Bunghalee, and Janganee-Ke-Gad,h, the zemindars of the country commit their dead to the river. Our ascent along the banks of the Coornee-Ke-Gad,h was exceedingly toilsome, and in some places dangerous. Its length was a mile and a half, after which the road wound in and out along the bosoms and sides of various inferior ridges, continuing very bad and unpleasant, at times along ledges of rock on the brink of deep precipices, and rendered more disagreeable by a continual and cold fall of rain.

After crossing this stream, which was effected with much difficulty, we found that another ascent and descent were to be encountered; after which another sharp ascent brought us to the village of Teeār, our resting-place for the night.

The journey of this day was, I think, the most painful we had yet encountered. The road was exceedingly bad throughout; and the ascents which came on towards the latter part of the day were doubly distressing. The weather was peculiarly unfavourable, the whole jungle was wet, and the rain incessant. Several of the people had now sore feet from falls or bruises, owing to the irregularity and difficulty of the road; and this not only retarded us, but perhaps made the way appear more tiresome than it otherwise might have done.

Kishen Sing, our guide, became at this place so entirely exhausted, that it became necessary to bring him forward in a litter. No other person, however, lost their strength so much as to require this assistance, although several were nearly disabled by bad sores on the legs. One man only was quite exhausted by illness, and we were forced to leave him at Cursalee, under care of Govind Bhisht. One other man, who had charge of the perambulator, was disgusted by the increased fatigue it gave to the march, and ran away from us.

The face of the country had altered considerably, though it was still exceeding rough and steep. There is more wood to cover the naked rock, and the banks gradually open out, and the higher parts of the mountains recede considerably. The perambulator, which accompanied us the whole way through the hills, became so crazy and broken at the village of Dhuralee that no farther use could be made of it. This was a considerable loss to us; and from this circumstance the length of this day's march could only be judged of, by computing the distance from point to point as we came along. It could not be less, however, than fifteen miles.

It was mentioned that the men of the village of Dhuralee were all absent when we lodged there. It was ascertained, indeed, that the object of their journey was plunder; and to-day we found that they had actually succeeded in driving away 4 or 500 sheep and goats from the district of Cat,hoor, a little lower down.

Just after crossing Dangalo-Sango we overtook a large party of men, to the amount probably of 100, armed with axes, bows, and arrows, who it appeared had come from a village called Ryht,hal, thus accoutred to way-lay and rob the booty from the thieves. Their information, however, was too late, and the plunder was safely carried off. When questioned on the subject, they told their errand without the least hesitation, nor affected to conceal their intentions. When I told them that such misdeeds would draw on them the vengeance of government, and that probably twenty or thirty of them would be hung, they coolly answered, "that it was well, and must be as the sircar (ruling power) pleased."

The fact is that the police of Rewaeen and Thucknour, and, indeed, throughout the whole remote countries at the foot of, and through the Himālā, is wretchedly defective, or it should rather perhaps be said that none exists. The zemindars of one village or valley set out to plunder another, with as much coolness and system as did those of either border in Scotland or England, to drive their neighbours' cattle in less civilized days. They prefer in general the carrying their predatory expeditions to some distance from home, but it is merely to throw thereby more difficulties in the way of retaliation. Any sense of wrong or disgrace seems wholly out of the question. They even appear to consider any obstacle thrown in the way of their thieving habits as unjust and tyrannical. Their reasoning on the subject is primitive and simple, although not quite consonant to the acknowledged laws of meum and tuum, in those countries which boast of equitable and learned regulations on the subject.

"When we have no meat, nor means to procure it, what are we to do?" say they; "Are we to starve? No! we prefer taking from those of our neighbours who have plenty."

The difficulty of regulating men who have imbibed such notions of property, and are in general so totally void of all moral principle, is obvious; but when the nature of the country they inhabit is considered; the impossibility of promoting civil order by any other than military aid; its imperviousness to any troops but such as may unite the qualities of zeal, activity, hardiness, and discipline; the extreme difficulty of supplying troops of any description with necessaries; the wild, remote, and almost impenetrable fastnessess to which these thieves can retire, together with the numberless minor obstacles thus thrown in the way of the executive power in carrying into effect its regulations and decrees; this state of anarchy will not appear extraordinary: and it will be evident that the vigour and decision of the British government alone can be effectual to reduce these turbulent and enterprising robbers to any tolerable order.

This tendency to rapine and enterprise seems almost universal among, and natural to highlanders, arising, no doubt, from the same causes that render it impossible for a weak government to restrain it; as, distance from the centre of law, and justice, and government, and imperviousness of country, which hinders the enforcement of the decrees of justice, or even the claims that arise on it, from coming to the notice of its officers. It seems but too probable, therefore, that, in the common course of native administration, these mountainous districts will ever remain in the lawless state of almost uncontrolled savage freedom in which we found them; and the family feuds, and strife of petty chiefs for temporary authority, will continue to render them scenes of puny, but wasting warfare.

If these free, untamed, and roving principles were found united with the usual highland virtues, it would be well; but it is melancholy to observe that, of the warmth of heart, of that generous and open hospitality, of that keen sense of honour, rigid fidelity to trust, and steady romantic friendship which adorn the rough character of the European highlander, which in some measure redeem his ruder and more lawless acts, and force admiration to mingle with our censure, no traces are here to be met with. The mean, cringing, and crafty nature of the Asiatic has blended with the hardy impetuous courage of the highlander, and, like poison, blasted all the good that belonged to the character. In the course of our tour through these hilly regions, much of treachery, of theft, of usurpation, of low despicable knavery, of falsehood, nay even of murder, came to our ears; but not one honourable, not one generous or hospitable act. The excitement of all the better feelings to virtue is unknown; and fear is the only effectual instrument to compel them to honesty, even in their simplest dealings.

July 24.—Our lodgings last night were comfortless, and little was to be had to render them more tolerable. All the inhabitants were absent on the plundering expedition. Neither the people nor myself could procure dry lodging, and it rained all night. The morning was cloudy, but some of the snowy peaks still appeared at no considerable distance on the opposite side of the river, with nullahs and ravines proceeding from their deep bosoms streaked with snow. Two large Kholas join the Bhagiruttee opposite this village, Coola-Gad,h and Deenee-Gad,h. The courses of each are pretty clear from hence.

There are several petty villages opposite Teear. Itself is small and poor. The houses in the vicinity are chiefly thatched with grass, slate is probably scarce; and wood is only used to cover the temples.

We left the village at half-past seven. A few furlongs onwards our view down the river opened greatly, and several villages, with a good deal of cultivation appeared, instead of the unvarying desert of rock and snow that had for so long lain around us. A various and irregular road, passing Shewār-Ke-Gad,h, and through the village of Cousin, a small wretched place, carried us to Patu, a village, situate on a projecting point of land high above the river, on which, and in the valley below, there is a good deal of cultivation.

A similar path brought us to Ruithul. This village is large, and seems more thriving than usual; and from hence the chief part of the robbers we met with yesterday issued. We passed through Noturna, a poor small village, and Doar, not much larger; and along several ridged fields of cultivation, half a mile further on, through the village of Goossalee, which is tolerably neat, and may contain from fifteen to twenty houses, thatched, like all those we saw this day, except the temples, and one or two houses which are covered with wood; but the strong peculiar look of Chinese architecture which generally marked the houses higher up in the hills, was now wearing much away; they more resembled Hindostannee common huts.

This village, and in fact all the country from Teear downwards, lies in the district of lower Tucknour. The small village of Incolla is not distant more than a mile horizontally, but by the road, which is stony and bad, we had full two miles to traverse, passing over three small nullahs. This wretched place was for our night's resting: the accommodations certainly got worse as we approached the lower country; the houses were more dirty, close, and full of vermin. The mountains in this day's march have lost still more of their rough and savage appearance. They slope occasionally more towards their bases, and are frequently wooded to a considerable height. Cultivation is more common, villages more frequent, and the predominating colours of green and yellow give a far more cheerful look to a country that can, however, only appear less wild by contrast.

July 25.—The night was rainy, and morning cold, wet, and comfortless. We found that our guide of yesterday had, either by a mistake of his own, or that of our attendant Kishen Sing, taken a wrong road, which proved considerably more toilsome and painful than the proper one, which leads on the opposite side of the river; and in the course of it we were likely to meet with serious obstacles from the rise of one or two large nullahs, the temporary bridges of which had been carried away by the floods. Directions were given to erect others for our passage, but the indolence and natural slowness of these people, in the common business of life, are so great, that we could place but little reliance on their exertions, and we set off without any certainty of reaching Barahăt that night.

A great and remarkable difference exists, I think, between the inhabitants of the remote parts of Bischur, and those of the neighbouring district, Rewaeen of Gurwhal, in manner and disposition, in degree of civilization, and particularly in the superiority of their manufactures and agriculture. The extent of our observation hardly perhaps justified so general an application of this remark; but whenever we had an opportunity of judging, certainly we were strongly led to it. The people of all ranks in Bischur evinced a degree of acuteness, of reasoning, of curiosity, and of a certain degree of politeness, which was peculiarly unlike the gaping stupid wonder, and coarseness of behaviour, that marked the inhabitants of Upper Thucknour, and the remote parts of Rewaeen. The former, though certainly they must have seen among us many things which were quite new and astonishing to them, made pertinent remarks, and asked sensible questions, that denoted some reflection, intelligence, and reasoning. The others remained lost in stupid and uninquiring wonder. One day I shot a rutnāl with some quickness, the moment she hopped from the hole in which she had laid her eggs. The man who was with me was so struck with it, that he came and prostrated himself at my feet. He had seen matchlocks, and probably death caused by them, and nothing but the quickness of the act could have been really novel to him, yet he had not recollection or sense enough to understand the cause of his astonishment.

The manufactures of Bischur are still more remarkably superior to those of Rewaeen and of Thucknour, both in materials and workmanship; the great fineness, close texture, and beauty of the blankets and woollen stuffs of the former, have already been subject of remark, but those of Rewaeen are coarse, unsightly, and bad. The wool of the former is of a fineness equal to some of our best English wool, while the produce of the latter districts appears to partake of the character of hair, and the thread spun from it is bristly and stubborn, and calculated rather to produce a coarse hair cloth than any comfortable warm woollen fabric: the reason of this difference is even less explicable than that of others that will be mentioned; and, it is to be feared, has its rise only in natural indolence and sloth. The superior state of agriculture is notorious in all the districts of Bischur we have traversed, and cannot entirely, though it may in some measure, be referred to the more untoward and impracticable nature of the country in these under discussion. The houses in the former countries are also far more calculated for comfort in general than those of Upper Rewaeen, though this difference is more perceptible internally than externally.

The circumstances in which these two districts are placed, though they appear to assimilate pretty much, perhaps really differ in a few points; and as it is possible that the difference of character above remarked may at least in some measure be referred to this dissimilitude, it is but fair to state them. The Ghoorkhas have ruled in Gurwhāl for nearly twelve years, previously to which, a severe contest had been kept up, which drained the country of men and money. They appear, in their subsequent conduct to this unfortunate province, to have borne in mind the trouble it cost them to win it, and acted as if determined to revenge it. Its old families were destroyed; all those persons of rank and importance who were taken were murdered or banished, its villages burnt and desolated, and great numbers of its inhabitants sold as slaves. The remaining part were oppressed by heavy taxes, and many voluntary banishments and emigrations took place to avoid a tyranny they could not withstand. Thus, throughout great part of Gurwhāl, the traveller sees only the ruins of villages, and the traces of former cultivation, now abandoned: the inhabitants that remain are, in all probability, the lowest and most ignorant; and it may fairly be presumed, have sunk lower in exertion and mind from the oppression they have groaned under.

The Ghoorkhas have only succeeded in subjecting the province of Bischur within the last three or four years, and even then its subjection was far less complete than that of Gurwhāl; the conquerors have had less time, less opportunity, and probably saw that they dared less to destroy the country and villages, or murder or disperse the inhabitants. Into the remoter districts they scarcely penetrated; and though certainly we trace through the whole of Bischur the marks of Ghoorkha violence, and the proofs of their temporary power, in forts and strong holds, still the former are far less obvious than in Gurwhāl. It may be inferred from this, that the ancient spirit of liberty and resistance is less subdued, the mental energies are less depressed in this scene of recent and somewhat milder conquest, than in that of long established tyranny.

It appears also that Bischur, even in the remotest parts, has kept up a greater and more commercial intercourse than its neighbouring province. The course of the river Sutlej, passing through its wildest districts, and communicating with the plains of Bootān on the one hand, and those of the Punjab on the other, give facilities for trade not possessed in the north-western parts of Gurwhāl. Many persons reach the plains of Hindostān from Bischur, and many merchants from these parts frequent it in turn, whilst, except a pilgrim to Gungotree or Jumnotree, none ever go or come to the countries in which these are situated. Those districts of Gurwhāl which lie more in the track of the roads from Hurdwar and Sreenuggur, to Buddreenauth and its passes into Bootān, possess these advantages perhaps in a greater degree than Bischur: but whether they have profited by them I cannot from observation say. It will, however, be allowed, that commercial intercourse generally does tend to polish the savage, and gradually lead him to adopt some of the customs and manners of the countries with which he trades.

CHAPTER XXX.

We left Incolla at nine o'clock, having been detained by very heavy rain, and after proceeding a short distance along the face of the hill, we descended for upwards of a mile to the bed of the river, by a very steep, rough, and slippery path, which there winds along its bank, following the inflexions of the stream, to a nullah called Selcour-ke-Gad,h. Hence our road ran for a considerable distance along rice cultivation, and partly upon some flat table land, which is here found a little elevated above the river bed, in its various reaches.

We passed Jum-ka-gurh, an old house or fort, built on a projecting rock on the opposite side of the river, which formerly was a place of considerable sanctity, where religious people performed one of the many customary ablutions, as preparatory purifications in the way to Gungotree. Just below it the Jum-ke-Gad,h empties itself to the river: somewhat further on we passed the small poor village of Innoo, where were some of the largest peaches I ever saw, either in India or at home. The path still leads along the river bank, occasionally on rice grounds; at times through thick tangled, but small jungle, to Goaree-ke-Gad,h, about two miles from Innoo, which we crossed with some difficulty, being deep and rapid, and went on to Reene-ke-Gad,h, a large and headlong torrent, much swelled by the rains.

This k,hola, which we reckon to be about nine miles from Incolla, is that over which the zemindars had been sent to throw a bridge; but we were detained a full hour till it was ready, and a most frail fabric it was when finished, consisting of two small round sticks, extending from the one bank to a large rock in the middle; and from thence to the other side, three still smaller tied together, formed the whole machine, on which a wild mountain stream was to be crossed by fifty or sixty persons, many of them heavily laden.

By care, however, we succeeded, though it bent and shook till nearly touching the stream, with the exception of one unfortunate cooley, who missed his step from the reaction of the timber, and fell into the furious water. In a moment he was carried away to the junction of the nullah with the river, about 150 yards below, where his head appeared for an instant, and his load floating beside him; but the foaming current of the Bhagiruttee, here tumbling over large rocks with a mighty roar, seized him, and hurried him along with its tremendous torrent.

The difficulty of travelling in these countries during the rains is very considerable, from the frequent occurrence of these rapid streams: they come down, as in all mountainous tracts, with very little warning, and what was fordable for a man in the morning may, by noon, be too rapid and fierce even for an elephant: even the smaller ones are very dangerous from the precipitous nature of their bed, and consequent force, as it requires both strength and skill to stem a rapid stream, though, perhaps, not more than mid thigh deep, and to preserve your footing while making a step. The unfortunate cooley who suffered on this occasion was loaded with the property of our Ghoorkha jemmadār and his wife, and one or two of the soldiers: they did not affect much distress for the death of a creature, whom, perhaps, they considered as no better than a beast of burthen, but they lamented sorely the loss of their property; and the lady in particular loudly expressed her grief. All her clothes and little trinkets, the saving of several years, were thus taken from her; and though it would doubtless have been more amiable had she been thus affected for the wretched end of the being who innocently caused her loss, still we could not refuse our sympathy to the surviving sufferers. Some of the relations of the poor drowned cooley were in company, and more deeply lamented him. I understood that he was a very useful member of a family,—an additional source of sorrow for the accident. One of his brothers was summoned when we reached our night's quarters, to whom I made a tender of some money to alleviate the distress of his family, being the only means I had of mitigating it. I am ashamed to say how little was given; our funds did not allow of more; and I am still more ashamed, for the credit of human nature, to say how speedily the man's face cleared up at the sight of the pittance he received. I fear he would have given another brother or son for such another compensation. Means too were found, subsequently, to restore the tranquillity of the poor Ghoorkha lady, and make her forget the loss of her apparel and jewels. These people were so good-humoured, quiet, and cheerfully alert, that it was a real pleasure to yield them assistance, and evince to them our sense of their merits; and the woman in question had created much interest by the patient and cheerful perseverance with which she accompanied the party through its most painful marches: never was she a burthen or hinderance, on the contrary, a most useful assistant to her husband and his people.

From this place, by a winding irregular road, we reached the top of the valley, or reach of the river, in which Barahāt is situated. At the upper extremity, on this (west) side of the river, we passed the temple of Lack,ha,-Joorroo, sacred to Seeva, and another to Doorgah. Somewhat farther on, upon the opposite bank, is placed the village of Mandhoul; and a very short way below it, that of Irlōtē. Barahāt lies somewhat below this last, and is situated on the north-west side of the river, at the foot of a high hill, and on a narrow piece of level land, which commences with the valley at Lack,ha,-Joorroo. It is a most wretched place, consisting of not more than five or six poor houses, surrounded with filth, and almost buried in a jungle of nettles, thorns, and every rank weed, the produce of dunghills.

The people looked as miserable and poor as the place. It may be supposed that little comfort was to be obtained in it: neither provisions nor quarters of any tolerable quality could be had; nor till after much delay and loss of time, which, to people who had travelled from morning till night, amid incessant rain, was sufficiently comfortless. Such did we find Barahāt, which had been boasted of as the end of our toils, and our haven of rest, and a place of plenty; but our informant had not seen it for eighteen years.

Tradition, for it may almost be said to amount to that, says, that Barahāt was a place of note and of wealth, containing a bazar of fifty or sixty shops,—a large one for the hills; and situated in the midst of a fine, rich and well cultivated country, abounding in corn, in flocks, and their produce. It was also a place of much sanctity; and this is all that remains of its former state; but even its holy places are in a state of sad dilapidation, though they yet abound in Fuqeers and Brahmins.

One place, Duthateree, is sacred to Seeva; Purseram has a temple; Moorlee-Manōor is either a temple, or the name of a divinity to which it is sacred; and Sook-ke-Mundur contains the famous *trisool* or trident.

There are likewise many holy spots for ablution, Soorj-Cound, Burrum-Cound, Viseshur-Naūt; all formerly frequented by pilgrims on their way to Gungotree. It seems that worship there was more acceptable in proportion as the pilgrims purified themselves by frequent ablutions at the sacred stages on the way upwards. Still, however, these places are frequented; but their former high prosperity is gone: indeed, the difficulties thrown in the way of pilgrims during the Goorkha-Raj, and the deterioration of the roads, have rendered Gungotree a place of far less resort than formerly. There were several fields and pieces of land formerly attached to the temple of Purserām, for the purpose of feeding the pilgrims during their stay here; but they have been taken from it, or are now waste.

July 26.—After a most uncomfortable night, and after procuring the means of carriage with difficulty, we proceeded on our journey, and I went to look at the temples and places of interest belonging to Barahāt; but there was little worthy of record besides the trident, which is a curious specimen of the taste of ancient times: its threefold composition, the elegance of its shape, and the unknown characters which occupy much of its shaft, point it out as a singular object of admiration and interesting speculation; for by what means it came there must, I suspect, remain a very undecided point. This pillar has been so minutely described by Messrs. Webb and Raper, that it is perfectly unnecessary to offer any additional description in this place. While surveying it, and taking a sketch of its general appearance, the Brahmins mentioned to me the names of Captain Hearsay and Mr. Webb; adding, that they were the only European gentlemen who had ever penetrated so far; and relating several other circumstances, such as their sending a man on to Gungotree, who was stopped by the snow: and they moreover mentioned, that Captain Hearsay took impressions of the characters on the pillar with blackened paper; which satisfied me, that no more remained necessary for me to do. He said that they staid here four or five days.

At a place on the river side called Ootervannee, where ablutions are performed, not far from hence, there lives a very old and holy Fuqeer. His years are said to be upwards of one hundred; and he is a fine looking, but withered old gentleman. He sits on a sort of elevated stage, with a cake of holy ashes before him, with which he marks the foreheads of those who come to pay their respects to him; and he talks with considerable energy. He paid several compliments to the strength, power, and wisdom of the British government, with some prophecy that it would endure very long, and contrasting it with that of the Ghoorkha sway, in a manner of course rather flattering. Just opposite to the dwelling-place of the old Fuqeer there is an old fort, or rather the ruins of one, called Urrassoo, and below it the Baragudh debouches into the river.

At the turn of the river below Barahāt there is a j,hoola, or hanging bridge of ropes, over which leads the direct road to Sreenuggur. This spot is the bottom of that reach of the river in which Barahāt is situated. Below it, another and longer, as well as broader valley stretches for three or four miles; both, however, are so much connected that they may be considered as a continuation of one another. From this bridge we wound along gently, ascending by a watercourse carried for purposes of agriculture, from Barettee-Ke-Gad,h, which we soon dipt into and crossed, arising from it to Barettee, a village about two miles from Barahāt. The village enjoys a fine prospect over the valley; but over it, as well as over the rich cultivation and villages it surveys, the hand of destruction has passed and left little but ruins.

Just above Barahāt, the Bhagiruttee begins to assume somewhat more the character of a great river, spreading out into a wider channel, yet still retaining much of the impetuosity of the mountain torrent; and it sweeps in numerous windings through this fine valley, which is from three to four furlongs broad, consisting chiefly of table land, probably the bed it once ran in, and is here and there finally swelled into rises. All is cultivable, and has evidently been once under the plough, and in various places the remains of villages evince thicker population. All now appears waste, but green and lonely.

The scenery within the course of our last two marches has undergone a farther alteration. The height and ruggedness of the hills have considerably decreased; and, though steep and worn into ravines according to the general character of the country, they present smoother faces, covered chiefly with firs of the stone and Weymouth pine sort, instead of those found in higher situations, such as the silver fir and larch, and they are every where beautifully green.

Two or three miles from Barettee, we crossed the Ruthore-Ke-Gad,h, another torrent swollen by the rain, by a temporary bridge, the preparation of which detained us considerably. Somewhat further on, scrambling along the river side, we reached a similar but smaller stream, named Singolo-Ke-Gad,h, which we forded with great difficulty as it was deep and strong.

It is hardly to be conceived how hazardous and painful it is to ford these petty streams. The strength of their waters, which, from their very irregular bottoms, are frequently very deep, is rendered still more formidable by the slipperiness of the large rounded stones over which they run, which makes it exceedingly difficult to keep the feet; whilst, if a person were to stumble, he would be hurried over a succession of petty falls without the possibility of receiving any assistance, and bruised to death. This nullah is just at the end of the above-mentioned long reach of the river. Opposite to it, on a piece of table land, upon the point round which the river runs, is situate the village of Ut,hāl, with a little cultivation. Here the rocks close again for a short space, occasioning some difficult steps along the banks of the river before entering on another reach of one or two miles in length. Half-way down this reach the village of Doonda is seen on a rock hanging over the river, and about seven miles distant from Barahăt. At present both these places are in the district of Rewaeen; but the opposite side of the river belongs to the purgunnah of D,hurannee.

The river here flows onwards in a generally uniform course, till it is joined by the D,huranee-Ke-Gad,h, a large stream, when it again enters between high rocks, and assumes a more southerly direction. At the foot of this reach, on the left bank, and in the D,huranee valley, there is much rich rice cultivation. That nullah a little above is divided into two by a lofty wooded hill, and in both branches there are many villages.

At the village of Dhoonda we left the river, and ascended the hill behind it, first by an easy gradual path along ledges of cultivation, and, turning the edge of a hill, proceeded along the right hand indent to a small nullah; after crossing which there was a very sharp ascent to the top of a pretty lofty hill. Two more similar ascents and descents brought us to the village of Petārā, our home for the night. During this day's march the heat became extremely oppressive. Yesterday it was allayed by the continual rains; but, during the steep ascents of this day, the sun shone forth with considerable force, and several of the people, exhausted by more than a month's incessant marching, were quite disabled. The ascents, too, occurring at the end of the day were more toilsome than usual. The character of road, of scenery, and of country, for the latter few miles, and all that we saw around us from the heights, reminded us strongly of that in the neighbourhood of Nahn and Jytock. The foliage both of trees and shrubs, and the appearance of the hills, bore a strong similarity to those places. The village of Pelārā is not much superior to those through which we have lately passed. It is poor and dirty; but, bad as were the accommodations, weariness made them welcome. Our march this day was reckoned at about twelve miles; but heat, bad road, and wet, amply accounted for fatigue, in spite of the shortness of the distance.

July 27.—The night as usual was bad, but the morning was lovely. Not a cloud was to be seen, except here and there a low mass hovering over the distance, or a milk-white fleecy vapour reposing on the beautiful green of the hills, and serving richly to contrast with the mellow tints of the wood and cultivation that spotted their sides. It is impossible to tell the delight which such a scene, in such a morning, affords to the eye, weary with rocky deserts and foaming torrents. For some weeks we had only risen to behold heavy mists half concealing black barren rocks, thinly covered with dark wood, and rapid destructive streams tumbling down gloomy ravines, while heavy and unceasing rain added to the cheerlessness of the prospect.

Here at last we saw the cheering face of heaven; hills of a lovely green, wooded to the top and divided by valleys, studded with villages and rich with cultivation. There are few, I believe, who would not feel the enlivening effects of such a change, and acknowledge the kindly glow of satisfaction that it sheds over the mind. Surely in these moments we must confess that, however the grand and remote scenes of savage nature may delight and astonish for a season, they are not fit for the residence of man. The most ambitious must at times descend from the lofty but solitary and barren tracks of his greatness, to solace himself with the lowlier but kindlier charities of life. Deserts and solitude may be endured for a time, but sooner or later we feel the want of, and languish for, the intercourse and conversation of our fellow creatures, for the sweet interchange of human affections, for the comforts and elegancies of polished life, and return to them with enhanced eagerness and zest.

The situation of the village is lofty, and the view from it extensive and beautiful, particularly down the course of the Bhagiruttee; and we recognized from hence many points, which in another direction formed objects of observation, when beginning our progress up the Jumna.

The lofty peaks of Bougee and Marma-Ke-Danda arose in the north-west. Below, the Gudoul-Ke-Gad,h flows through a fine valley, and joins the Bhagiruttee at Dhurassoo. From thence the river runs in a long and comparatively broad valley, sprinkled thickly with numerous villages, and richly cultivated.

Beyond, the eye stretches to the hills above Uthoor, and even those near Srenuggur are discernible. To the southward and westward, hills of considerable height arise, two or three distinct ranges of which intervene between us and the Deyrah Dhoon. Over the first of these lay the journey of the day, for, in consequence of information that reached us here, we were reluctantly induced to give up the idea of proceeding to Srenuggur, and from thence perhaps eventually to Buddreenauth, my brother being obliged to return to the low country. It was, therefore, determined to cross the hills from Pelārā, and meet him in the vale of Deyrah.

The road from the village to Dhurassoo is all a descent. This place was formerly of some religious consequence, but it is now wholly ruinous. It is situated on a rock at the junction of the Gudoul-Ke-Gad,h with the Bhagiruttee. Just at the bridge by which we crossed this nullah, there is a temple to Bhyramgooroo, where a Jogee man and woman reside for the benefit of the pious pilgrims, who are expected to contribute to their support.

Rising from the bed of the Gudhoul-Ke-Gad,h, and proceeding a mile onwards, we reached the village of Burethee, situated on a rising ground at the upper end of the valley seen from Pelārā. A little way from this place there is an establishment of Jogees, and a temple to Mungulnauth, where there are some uncommonly fine mango-trees, but the fruit was hardly ripe. There were several villages now on either side the river, as Neree, Poleara, Cheenalee: those on the east side are in the purgunnah of Joul; that of Oudepore commences on this (west) side at Gudhoul-Ke-Gad,h,

From Burethee our road lay through this fine valley, level and easy. The river keeps chiefly on the eastern side, winding with no large sweeps along the foot of the hills to the debouche of Nugoon-Ke-Gad,h, a pretty copious stream, arising in Marma-Ke-Danda, which we here crossed. At this point the ends of two opposite d,hars come down towards the stream, and intercept the range of the valley, which, however, continues, though less level and fertile, till shut out from view by various intervening points.

Here we left the river entirely, and commenced ascending Jan-da-gan-ke-D,har, under every disadvantage. The weather was excessively hot, the sun shone bright, and our road lay up the sunny side of the hill, at one o'clock in the day, without a breath of wind stirring; consequently, though the road was not very bad, and the ascent various, it was exceedingly painful. On the face of this hill we found many trees of the cassia lignea, or tēz puttah, the flavour of which was very good and powerful; it is the same as that which forms an article of trade from Nepāl, and the lower parts of the hills, and is mentioned by Colonel Kirkpatrick: it was perfectly wild, and in considerable quantity. We continued our ascent, chiefly through wood, occasionally along a bare hill side, and sometimes along rice cultivation, on ledges near little water-courses, passing several miserable villages, but frequently very steep and painful, till we reached Coiassoo-gorge, in the d,har of that name, which is continuous to the eastward, with Marma-Ke-Danda, being full four miles and a half from the place where we left the river, and at least ten and a half or eleven from Pelārā.

The whole road was irregular and wearisome, and this gorge is a very elevated spot: the wood towards the top, besides the common fir, consists chiefly of the long-leaved oak, and a species of bhododendron. We had from hence an extensive view, but the day had become rather misty, and intercepted the points of most interest: not a peak of the snowy hills was visible; they were all deep and dark in clouds. Of a point called Seeam-Ke-Teeba, on the opposite side of the river, the following strange tale is related. It is the haunt of a deity, who is by no means fond of company, and is so much feared, that none will ascend it. A man, it is said, while gathering the dwarf bamboo, found himself close to the dreaded spot, and espied a large feast set out, and many persons busily employed in nautching and amusing themselves. He was interrogated as to his intentions and wants, and having told what brought him there, he was asked to partake of the feast, and having eaten some rice he was desired to retire, and by no means ever to relate what he had seen: that if he kept silent, such food would always be at his command, were he to live a thousand years; but, on the contrary, if he should be indiscreet, he should die. Having reached his village, the fool told what he had seen, and dropped down dead.

The range, of which this is the highest point, stretches along the Bhagiruttee from Dhurassoo, for several miles, giving rise to many nullahs, and sending many roots to the banks of the river. From this point we commenced a steep descent by a very irregular path; at first, through deep red slippery soil on the banks, and in the bed of a stream, that rises in this gorge. We passed through Mucrora, a miserable village, ruined, and half buried in nettles and weeds. And after a further fatiguing descent, we arrived at the village of B,haloo, which is very small, but somewhat better, where we remained for the night. There is nothing worthy of observation respecting this place; it is, I believe, one of seven villages, forming the Bhaloo T,hat in the district of Jounpoor.

July 28.—We left B,haloo at twenty minutes past seven, and kept a course descending rapidly in the bed of the B,hul Gad,h. Opposite the mouth of this nullah, but at a considerable distance, we saw Sowa-khollake-Teeba, which is just above the D,hoon. The path crossing and recrossing the stream, which was very large from heavy rain, was extremely toilsome and unpleasant. A little below, it is joined by the Singulo Gad,h, a wild glen, in which are three villages, named Khulloee, Agindo, and Singulo: and at about two miles from the village of B,haloo, the whole takes a turn to the west, and is soon joined by Jumlee-Gad,h, which runs in a westerly direction from Dhunoulee-ke-D,har: the point between these two streams which we crossed is projected from Mukrele-Ke-Danda.

We had now entered the purgunnah of Dus Iola, and descending a little, crossed the Jumlee Gad,h, and began immediately to ascend, passing through the two little dirty villages of Dangolo and Bahime. This place we computed to be three miles from B,haloo.

The hills here are green, and rather bare of wood. The houses had now totally lost their Chinese appearance, and were chiefly thatched, degenerating into common Hindostannee huts. The dress of the people, both men and women, which had begun to change even at Barahāt, from the blanket occasionally to the cotton cloth, is here universally of the latter material, sometimes of coloured and checked stuff; and the cotton skull-cap becomes again in general use. From hence we experienced a steep, hot, various ascent, from the top of which we had an extensive view, and traced the whole of the valley we had crossed from Dhunoolee nearly to the Jumna, where its waters are emptied at a village called Gurh. The stream and valley change their names frequently in their course, being first called Jumlee-Gad,h, then Agloar-Ke-Gad,h, then I believe Pali-Gad,h.

To the northward of this valley, and forming, in fact, its northern boundary, the range of Marma-Ke-Danda is spread, stretching from Jountgurh, in the west, and taking in Coiassoo to the east, and losing itself in the mountains that form the Sooree, or Dhunoulee ridges. From this long ridge many subordinate ones stretch down, including between them valleys and streams, that find a general outlet to the Jumna through Agloar-Ke-Gad,h; of these, Bul-Gad,h from Coiassoo, Pali-Gad,h, joined by Moungla-Gad,h from Marma, and Chumoan-Gad,h from Kearee, are the chief. From this station we kept along the face of the hill for about a mile, when, turning sharp to our left, across the ridge, we came, by a short, but rough descent, upon the village of Bĕlee.

This is a small, poor place; but as there is no other resting-place between it and the village of Nagel in the D,hoon, a distance said to be twelve miles, we were forced to remain there for the night. The march of this day little exceeded seven miles.

July 29.—We were assured that this day's march would be a long and fatiguing one; for which reason orders were given for retiring early, and beginning our march betimes: it was, however, six o'clock before we were on our route. It was a lovely, fresh, dewy morning, the sky clear, the weather cool, calm, and reviving; perhaps the hope of reaching a comparatively civilized country, and of experiencing the charm of seeing the face of a countryman, gave an additional brilliancy to the morning. The road wound along the left-hand side of the hill, on a rocky path, formed entirely of limestone, to the head of a valley or hollow, formed by the junction of the eastern extremity of Sawa-Khola-Ke-Teeba, with the Lickneana range, which strikes to the north-westward. This place is called Mugra. It is a dark, gloomy, wooded ravine; and there is a perennial spring, of remarkable coldness, well known to travellers.

From hence a sharp ascent carried us to a point in the crest of the Sowakhola ridge, and all the beautiful D,hoon, and the still more lovely and smiling plains of Hindostan, burst full upon our view. Scarcely a cloud obscured them; only in the hollow at our feet they floated sparingly, and we enjoyed undisturbed the enchanting scene. The full beauty of this sight, and the delight it gave to us, can only be comprehended by those who have travelled over mountains as immense and rugged as those of Bischur and Gurwhāl for four or five months, partly alone, marching continually, with few comforts, and in unfavourable weather. Such may recollect how cheering to the sight would be, under such circumstances, the dwellings of civilized man, and how sweet the voices of friends to the ear. From hence we obtained a short and last glimpse of the snowy hills and of the peak of Bunderpouch; Hurdwar was also seen, with several points which we could not well distinguish.

Our road led us along the crest of this high range from height to height, but when we reached the highest, whence we expected the most perfect and useful view, a heavy cloud enveloped us in darkness, and when it passed away we found that all below us was shrouded from our sight: still, however, the landscape towards the mountains was grand and interesting, for the clouds, being scarcely yet in motion, partially concealed the hills and valleys, and small masses rested on each mountain head; here and there a point of snow, too small to be distinctly recognized, reared itself above them, and high over all a calm blue sky, streaked with a few flaky clouds of most delicate tints, shed a soft repose over the whole that harmonized well with the scene. Still passing along the crest among thinly scattered oaks and stone-pines, we began to descend by a subordinate ridge that stretches into the valley below.

The descent was very rapid, long, and winding, to the banks of a small nullah, which we crossed, and then again ascended, but gently and slanting along the right-hand face of the hill tending westward.

It began to rain most heavily, and continued to pour pretty constantly all the day: only at one point did we get a peep of the valley, and then the town and gardens of Deyhra were seen with much rich cultivation around it. Fatal Kalunga was just at our feet; one red line marked where its wall had been, now perfectly destroyed. Many wooded eminences spot and vary the valley in every quarter. The latter part of the descent is precipitous and rocky. From the foot of the hill we passed along the bed of several small nullahs created by the heavy rain, and through the thin jungle that covers the rising grounds at the foot of the hills, till we reached Nagel, a small village not far in the plain.

From hence a level path conducted us to Deyhra, among cultivation and mango topes, leaving Kalunga on the left. I regretted that I had not time to visit this place, but neither the weather nor my time permitted; it has, however, been sufficiently described, and is indeed too well known, as well as the town of Deyhra, to need further description. In fact, having only passed through it, once in arriving, and once in leaving it, I could give no interesting account of it.

Nagel is about six full miles from Deyhra, and the whole country was inundated in consequence of the heavy rains. The distance of Nagel from Bēlee I cannot so well guess, but believe it to be at least seven or eight miles, making a stage of twelve or thirteen miles.

The next morning we left the D,hoon, which was chiefly under water, through the Teeree pass, and reached Saharunpore on the night of the 30th of July.

APPENDIX.

APPENDIX.

No. I.

Proclamation by the British Government against Nepāl.

(Referred to in page 3.)

THE British Government having been compelled to take up arms against the Nepālese, His Excellency the Right Honourable the Governor-General has judged it proper to make known to the powers in alliance and friendship with the Honourable Company the origin and progress of the transactions which have terminated in this crisis, in the full conviction that the exposition will establish beyond dispute the extraordinary moderation and forbearance of the British Government, and the injustice, violence, and aggression of the state of Nepāl.

The course of the Ghoorka conquests having approximated their frontier to that of the Honourable Company, and of its ally, the Nawaub-Vizier, and the protected Sikh chieftains, throughout an extent of country stretching from the eastern border of Morung to the banks of the Sutlej, it was scarcely to be expected that differences should not occasionally arise between the inhabitants of the contiguous districts belonging to the two states, and even among the local public officers of each government; but a just and firm line of conduct on the part of the two governments, combined with a sincere disposition to maintain uninterrupted the relations of amity, and to respect the rights of each other, could not have failed to arrest the progress of those unhappy disputes which have terminated in war. While the conduct of the British Government has been uniformly regulated, in its relations with the Nepālese, by the most scrupulous adherence to the principles of justice and moderation, there is scarcely a single district within the British frontier, throughout the whole of the extensive line above described, in which the Ghoorkas have not usurped and appropriated lands forming the ascertained dominions of the Honourable Company.

Questions originating in the usurpations of the Nepālese have arisen in Purnea, Tirhoot, Sarun, Goruckpore, and Bareilly, as well as in the protected territory between the Sutlej and the Jumna; and each case might be appealed to, in proof of the moderation and forbearance of the British Government, and the aggressive and insolent spirit of the Nepālese. It will be enough, however, to advert, in detail, to two instances only; namely, those which have occurred at Sarun and in Goruckpore, which more particularly demonstrate the systematic design of the Nepālese to encroach on the acknowledged possessions of the Honourable Company; and have, in fact, been the proximate causes of the war.

In the former district they have, at different times, established their authority over portions of the territory of Betteah; but the British Government, abiding by those principles of moderation and forbearance so conspicuous in all its transactions with the Nepālese, contented itself, for a considerable period, with remonstrances and representations; trusting that the justice of its cause would become apparent to the Nepālese Government, and produce its proper effects on the mind of the Rajah and his ministers. The repeated complaints of its subjects, and the occurrence of a new instance of encroachment in the Tuppah of Nunnoar, forming a portion of Betteah, which led to an affray, in which Subah Luchingir, an officer of the Nepālese Government, was slain, at last induced the British Government to depute one of its civil officers to the spot, where he was met by deputies from the state of Nepāl; in concert with whom proceedings were held, and evidence taken, for the purpose of ascertaining the claims of the parties. The result left no doubt of the right of the British Government, and of the unjust and violent procedure of the Nepālese.

A more striking proof of the spirit of rapacity and unjust aggression by which the Nepālese were actuated cannot be adduced, than the fact, that after having agreed to the investigation referred to above, and after the actual deputation of officers by each Government, the Nepālese suddenly seized an additional tract of country belonging to the Company, at a very short distance from the scene of their former aggressions.

This violent and unjust procedure would have warranted an immediate demand for restitution, or even the actual re-occupation of the lands by force; and it may now be a subject of regret to the British Government, that this course was not pursued. Far, however, from resenting or punishing this daring outrage as it deserved, the British Government resolved to persevere in the amicable course which it had pursued in other cases, and permitted Mr. Young, the gentleman deputed to meet the Nepālese commissioners, to extend his inquiries to the lands newly seized, as above stated, as well as to those which formed the original object of his deputation.

The pretext by which the Nepālese attempted to justify their occupation of the lands in Nunnone, which consisted of no less than twenty-two villages, was, that they were included in the Tuppah of Rotehut, forming a division of Purgunnah Sunnoun; which Tuppah was restored to the Nepālese, in the year 1783, with the rest of the Terraice of Muckwanpore, which had been conquered by the British arms under Major Kinloch. The utter groundlessness of this pretext was proved by the evidence taken by Mr. Young; which clearly established, that the disputed lands were situated in the Tuppah of Nunnone, a portion of Purgunnah Simruwun, which had been reserved by the Company at the time of the restitution of Rotehut, and the remainder of Muckwanpore. But, had it been otherwise, the tacit acquiescence, by the Nepālese, in our possession of those lands for a period of thirty years, would have amounted to a dereliction of their claim, however well-founded it might originally have been. The abrupt and violent manner in which the Nepālese have invariably possessed themselves of these portions of the Honourable Company's territory to which they have at any time pretended a right, will not allow the supposition that they would have refrained, during so long a period, from doing themselves justice in the present case, if they had felt conscious of the solidity of the claim. It is evident, from the whole tenor of their proceedings, that they acted on that premeditated system of gradual encroachment, which, owing to the unexampled forbearance and moderation of the British Government, they had already found to be successful; and that the assertion of the twenty-two villages having been included in the Tuppah of Rotehut was merely brought forward to give colour to the unwarrantable act which they had committed, when it became necessary to assign a reason for their conduct.

The Nepālese have attempted to fix on the subjects of the Honourable Company the guilt of the murder of Suba Luchingir; and have stated, as matter of complaint against the British Government, that the Rajah of Betteah and his followers have not been punished for that act; and they have endeavoured to found on this charge a justification of their own subsequent proceeding. It has been ascertained, however, by incontestable evidence, that Luchingir had, previously to the occurrence of the affray in which he died, possessed himself of some villages in Betteah, and was preparing to extend his encroachments.

Whatever degree of culpability, therefore, may attach to the subjects of the Honourable Company for forcibly opposing his proceedings, their offence was towards their own Government alone; and the Nepālese could not, with any colour of justice, demand the punishment of those persons for an act produced solely by the misconduct of their own officers, or charge the British Government with a culpable omission of what would have been, under different circumstances, due to a state professedly on friendly terms with it; still less can they found on this transaction any justification of their own conduct in other instances.

As the final resolution of the British Government, with respect to the usurped lands in Betteah, was, in part, influenced by the conduct of the Nepālese relative to the disputed territory of Bootwul and Sheoraj in Goruckpore, it will be proper to advert to the circumstances of that transaction in this place.

It is notorious, and has also been proved by reference to authentic records, and by the unimpeached testimony of living witnesses, that the whole of Bootwul, to the very foot of the hills, with the exception of the town of Bootwul alone, was held by the Rajahs of Palpah from the Nawaub Vizier, for a considerable period antecedent to the treaty of cession 1801, and that it was transferred to the Company by the terms of that treaty, being specifically included in the schedule thereunto annexed. It is no less matter of notoriety, that the district of Bhootwul actually came into the possession of the British Government by virtue of the cession, and that a settlement was made by the collector of Goruckpore with the agent of the late Rajah of Palpah, at that time a prisoner at Catmandhoo, for an annual rent of thirty-two thousand rupees, without the semblance of an objection on the part of the Rajah of Nepāl.

So it remained until the year 1804, when the Nepālese commenced that system of gradual encroachment below the hills, which terminated in their occupation of nearly the whole district of Bhootwul. The Tuppah of Sheorag was occupied by the Nepālese antecedently to the cession; but it is no less certain, that it was a part of the territory of the Vizier, and, together with the rest of the lowlands skirting the hills in the district of Goruckpore, included in the cession.

The Nepālese pretended to found their claim to Bhootwul and Sheoraj, and to the other portions of the lands below the hills, on the circumstance of their having formed the terraiee, or lowlands, of the hill-countries of Palpah, Goolmee, Pintaneh, Kamchee, &c., which the Nepālese have conquered. Admitting that the lowlands were possessed by the chiefs of the neighbouring hill-principalities, the admission does not affect the question, since it is perfectly ascertained, that for a considerable period before the Ghoorka conquest, they formed a part of the dominions of Oude; and the conquest, therefore, of the independent hill-principalities cannot give to the conquering power any just claim to other lands, which, though in the occupation of the same chiefs, were held on dependent tenures from other states.

To show the little confidence that the Nepālese had in their claim of sovereignty over these lands, it is sufficient to observe, that soon after their usurpation of them, they actually made an offer to hold Bhootwul, in farm, from the British Government, on the same terms as the Rajah of Palpah; a proposition to which this government did not think proper to accede.

The system of gradual, and, at times, almost imperceptible encroachment, pursued by the Nepālese, was calculated to deceive the British Government with respect to their ultimate views; and, combined with the just and moderate course of proceedings which the British Government has pursued in all its intercourse with the Nepālese, prevented it from resorting to those means which would at once have repressed the outrages of the Nepālese, and re-established its own authority in the usurped lands. The remonstrances and discussions which followed the first usurpation of the Nepālese in this quarter continued, with frequent interruption, for a period of some years; during which the Nepālese continued to avail themselves of every favourable occasion of extending their encroachment. At length a proposition was made by the rajah of Nepāl, that commissioners should be appointed to meet on the spot and investigate and decide the respective claims of the parties, under the express condition, that whatever might be the issue of the inquiry, both governments would abide by it.

Notwithstanding its perfect conviction of the justice of its own claims, the British Government did not hesitate to submit to the delay and expense necessarily attending the proposed investigation, confiding in the ultimate, though tardy, admission of its rights by the Nepālese, and anxious to afford an unequivocal proof of the moderation of its conduct, and the justice of its cause. The proposition of the rajah of Nepāl was accordingly acceded to; and Major Bradshaw was directed to proceed to Bhootwul and enter on the investigation in concert with commissioners to be appointed by the Nepālese Government.

The commissioners of the two governments met; and, after much delay and procrastination on the part of the Nepālese agents, the proceedings were brought to a close, and the right of the British Government to the whole of the lowlands confirmed by the most irrefragable proofs, both oral and documentary.

The Nepālese commissioners, unable to resist the force of this evidence, and clearly restrained from admitting the right of the British Government, by the orders of their court, pretended that they were not authorised to come to a decision, and referred the case to the rajah's government for orders.

The advanced period of the season when the commissioners closed their proceedings rendered it impracticable to take any steps founded on them till the ensuing year. The immediate procedure of the British Government was therefore confined to a communication to the rajah, stating, in general terms, the conclusion necessarily resulting from the proceedings of the commissioners, and requiring the rajah to give up the lands according to the condition on which the investigation was acceded to, on the grounds of the conclusive proof of its right, established by those proceedings. To this just and fair demand, the rajah of Nepāl replied, by repeating all those arguments, in favour of his own claim, which had been entirely overthrown by the evidence adduced to the commissioners, and refused to restore the lands. In this state the affair necessarily remained until the ensuing season, 1813-14.

In the meanwhile Major Bradshaw proceeded, as soon as the state of the country admitted of his marching, to the frontier of Betteah, where he was met by commissioners from Nepāl, empowered to adjust, in concert with him, the depending claims in that quarter; no practical measures having yet resulted from the inquiry conducted by Mr. Young. Major Bradshaw, soon after his arrival, renewed a demand which had been made by the British Government, but not enforced at the time, for the restoration of the twenty-two villages of Nunnone, previously to any examination of the question of right. This demand was acceded to by the Nepālese, and the villages re-occupied by the officers of the Honourable Company, subject to the ultimate disposal of them according to the issue of the intended inquiry.

The refusal of the Nepālese government to abide by the result of an inquiry sought by itself, in the case of the encroachment in Goruckpore, notwithstanding the full and complete establishment of the rights of the British government to the disputed lands in that quarter, now led the Governor-General to pause before he consented to incur the loss, inconvenience, and anxiety, attendant on a new investigation of the claims of the respective governments to the usurped lands in Sarun. On duly reflecting on all that had passed, on the actual proof of the claim of the British government, established by Mr. Young's inquiry, conducted in concert with Nepālese commissioners, an inquiry which embraced the testimony on oath of all those persons who could be supposed to possess the best local knowledge, and which had moreover this advantage over every subsequent investigation, that it was held at a period so much nearer the time of the transaction; and on the presumptive proof of our right, arising out of the fact, acknowledged by the Nepālese themselves, of our uninterrupted possession during thirty years; the mind of the Governor-General, in council, was perfectly satisfied that a further investigation *de novo* would be an unprofitable waste of time, and that the utmost that the Nepālese government could in fairness expect, was, that the commissioners of both governments should meet for the purpose of discussing the question on the basis of the investigation actually closed, and of supplying any defects which might be discovered in that investigation by further inquiry on the spot.

When this result of the deliberations of the Governor-General in council was notified to the Nepālese commissioners by Major Bradshaw, with an offer to meet them for the purpose stated, and to produce documents which he had obtained, confirming the correctness of the conclusions drawn from the evidence already taken, the commissioners declared, that they would not meet him, nor hold any communication with him; and, revoking the conditional transfer of the usurped lands, demanded that Major Bradshaw should instantly leave the frontier. They immediately afterwards returned to Nepāl.

This insulting and unprovoked declaration could be referred to no other cause than a previous determination not to fulfil the obligations of justice towards the British government, and left to it no course, but to do itself that right which was refused by the government of Nepāl. Acting on this principle, the Governor-General addressed a letter to the rajah of Nepāl, reviewing the conduct of his commissioners, and claiming the full renunciation of the disputed lands; adding, that if it were not made within a given time, the portions of those lands still in the hands of the Nepālese would be re-occupied, and the twenty-two villages which had been conditionally transferred to the British government declared to be finally re-annexed to the dominions of the Honourable Company.

This demand not having been complied with, the resumption of the lands was carried into effect, and the authority of the British government re-established throughout the tract in dispute. While these occurrences were passing in Sarun, the British government perceiving from the tenor of the whole conduct of the state of Nepāl, and from the answer to its demand for the restitution of Bootwul and Sheoraj, that no intention existed on the part of the rajah to restore these lands, was compelled to prepare to take possession of them by force, if that necessity should arise. Previously, however, to ordering the troops to advance into the disputed territory, the Governor-General in council made one more effort to induce the rajah to restore them, by renewing the demand founded on the result of the investigation, and declared at the same time, that if the orders of surrender were not received within a limited time (which was specified), the British troops would proceed to occupy the lands. The specified period having expired, without the adoption of any measure on the part of the Nepālese government towards a compliance with the just requisition of the British government, the troops were ordered to march, and the Nepālese forces, and the public officers of that government, retiring on the advance of the British troops, the civil officers of the Honourable Company were enabled to establish their authority in the disputed lands.

The commencement of the rainy season shortly rendered it necessary to withdraw the regular troops, in order that they might not be exposed to the periodical fevers which reign throughout the tract in that part of the year.

The defence of the recovered lands was of course unavoidably entrusted to the police establishments. The apparent acquiescence, however, of the Nepālese in what had taken place left no room for apprehension; especially as no real violence had been used in obliging the Nepālese to retire from the district. On the morning of the 29th of May last the principal police station in Bootwull was attacked by a large body of the Nepālese troops, headed by an officer of that government named Munraj Foujdar, and driven out of Bhootwul with the loss of eighteen men killed and six wounded. Among the former was the Darogah, or principal police officer, who was murdered in cold blood, with circumstances of peculiar barbarity, in the presence of Munraj Foujdar, after surrendering himself a prisoner. Another police jannah was subsequently attacked by the Nepālese troops, and driven out with the loss of several persons killed and wounded. In consequence of the impracticability of supporting the police jannahs, by sending troops into the country at that unhealthy season, it became necessary to withdraw them, and the Nepālese were thus enabled to re-occupy the whole of the disputed territory, which they have since retained. The British government had not ceased to hope that an amicable adjustment of its differences with the state of Nepāl might still be accomplished, when the perpetration of this sanguinary and atrocious outrage, by which the state of Nepāl at once placed itself in the condition of a public enemy of the British government, put an end to the possibility of any accommodation, except on the basis of unqualified submission and atonement. Still the Governor-General would not proceed to actual hostilities without giving to the rajah of Nepāl one other opening for avoiding so serious an issue. Therefore his excellency wrote to the rajah to apprise him of what must be the consequence of the insolent outrage which had taken place, unless the government of Nepāl should exonerate itself from the act by disavowal and punishment of the perpetrators. This letter received an answer wholly evasive, and even implying menace.

The requisite submission and atonement having thus been withheld, the British government had no choice left but an appeal to arms, in order to avenge its innocent subjects, and vindicate its insulted dignity and honour. The unfavourable season of the year alone prevented it from having instant recourse to the measures necessary for chastising the insolence, violence, and barbarity of the Nepālese, whose whole conduct, not only in the particular cases above detailed, but in every part of their proceedings towards the British for a series of years, has been marked by an entire disregard of the principles of honour, justice, and good faith, aggravated by the most flagrant insolence, presumption, and audacity; and has manifested the existence of a long determined resolution on the part of the court of Catmandhū to reject all the just demands of the British government, and to refer the decision of the questions depending between the two states to the issue of a war.

Ever since the murder of the police officers in Bootwul, and during the unavoidable interval of inaction which followed, the Nepālese, with a baseness and barbarity peculiar to themselves, have endeavoured to destroy the troops and the subjects of the Company on the frontier of Sarun, by poisoning the water of the wells and tanks in a tract of considerable extent. The fortunate discovery of this attempt baffled the infamous design, and placed incontrovertible proof of it in the hands of the British government.

The impediment to military operations arising from the season of the year is now removed, and the British government is prepared, by the active and vigorous employment of its resources, to compel the state of Nepāl to make that atonement which it is so justly intitled to demand. The British government has long borne the conduct of the Nepālese with unexampled patience; opposing to their violence, insolence, and rapacity, a course of procedure uniformly just and moderate. But forbearance and moderation must have their limits, and the British government having been compelled to take up arms in defence of its rights, its interests, and its honour, will never lay them down, until its enemy shall be forced to make ample submission and atonement for his outrageous conduct, to indemnify it for the expense of the war, and to afford full security for the future maintenance of those relations which he has so shamefully violated.

If the misguided councils of the state of Nepāl shall lead it obstinately to persist in rejecting these just demands, it will itself be responsible for the consequences. The British government has studiously endeavoured, by every effort of conciliation, to avert the extremity of war; but it can have no apprehension of the result, and it relies with confidence on the justice of its cause, and on the skill, discipline, and valour of its armies, for a speedy, honourable, and decisive termination of the contest in which it is engaged.

By command of his Excellency the Governor-General,

(Signed), T. ADAM, secretary to government.

Lucknow, November 1, 1814.

No. II.

On the Population of Nepāl.

(Illustrative of the statement in page 8.)

Wild as they are, it may be amusing, and perhaps satisfactory, to see the ideas which the natives of the country entertain of its power and population.

The following note is taken down exactly, as the account from three Ghoorkha officers; it is only given as a curious specimen of their ideas, and by no means as an authority which is to be depended upon, in estimating the true population of the valley.

	Houses		Houses		Houses
Catmandhû	18,000	Boagang	200	Kurreeseedee	1,000
Patun	24,000	Jandugang	2,000	Bisung	5,000
Bhadgun	22,000	Bondha	1,000	Changoo	1,000
Kirteepoor	12,000	Bhymal	1,000	Loombhoo	1,000
T,heanee	7,000	Boodhanelcuntha	1,000	Dhumunloolee	1,000
Buneba	7,000	Mala Tirta	700	Phancole	6,000
Phurping	6,000	Theechoo	700	Deopatna	4,000
Pinoulee	6,000	Sanga	1,000	Mulchugang	700
Dhulkill	7,000	Sankhoo	4,000	Lamboodanda	6,000
Bookmutter	400	Tokha	1,000	Chowcole	100
Dhachock	3,000	Chappagang	7,000	Papeegang	1,000
Goorkhan	2,000			Bullumbo	700
			19,600	Malagang	6,000
	114,400			Doluchat	700
	19,600				
	35,200				34,200
				Simbhoo	1,000
					35,200

In all 169,200 houses, which, at an average of twelve souls, which they insist is not too much for each house, would give the absurdly incredible sum of 2,020,400 souls for the population of Nepāl Proper.

It is unnecessary to comment on this statement; nevertheless I have reason to believe that those from whom it was received did not intentionally deceive farther than national vanity always occasions to a certain extent. The following statement, from the same sources, gives a very different account of the states and countries in the vicinity.

	Houses	
The state of Noacote has	8,000	in a large town.
Goorkha	12,000	with several large villages.
Lumjoon	8,000	
	28,000	

	Houses	
Brought forward	28,000	
Kaskee -	8,000	has several considerable villages.
Tunhoon -	8,000	
Beenug -	6,000	
Gheering -	700	
Noacote 2d -	6,000	
Gulcote -	4,000	
Sutoung -	8,000	
Bheercote -	12,000	said to be a fine raj, and produces several mines of metals.
Dhurcote -	6,000	
Purbut -	12,000	
Dhon -	2,000	
Isma -	2,000	
Musncote -	4,000	
Gurhoong -	6,000	
Dhurcote 2d -	4,000	
Pintana -	14,000	a large raj, stretching from the plains to the Snowy Mountains.
Goolima -	8,000	
Pyngoo -	4,000	
Acham -	6,000	
Canchee -	6,000	
Pheetee -	7,000	
Dang -	12,000	said to be a large state, and which possesses a large valley resembling the D,hoon.
Tulecan -	12,000	
Mallatta -	2,000	
Bhingree -	1,000	
Choongree -	400	
Bhoogum -	4,000	
Mushecote -	4,000	
Darma Jakree -	12,000	
Jasircote -	12,000	
Joomla -	22,000	This is a large country, which stretching behind the three or four last-mentioned states, bounds with the Chinese empire.
Palpai -	14,000	This is a large state, and has a large town.
Dhooloo -	——	
Dunglick -	6,000	
Channa -	8,000	
Goorba cole -	2,000	
D,hotee -	32,000	a very considerable state, which stretches from the plains quite through the hills.

In all 305,100 houses, containing at the same average 3,661,200 souls existing in the countries between the boundaries of Kumaoon on the north-west, and the state of Nepāl, which would itself, I suspect, be very far beyond the truth, although the extent be very great. But though in the above memoranda there are many states and districts mentioned that we know of, the whole is so far from being clear, that it was very difficult, in many instances, to comprehend whether the number given was intended to include the whole population of a state, or only of its chief town; if for the latter, they are evidently as much exaggerated as those relating to the valley: but I believe, in general, they referred to that of the whole country in question.

There is perhaps little satisfaction to be received from the perusal of such wild and vague speculations, and it may be wrong to insert them at all; but when all false impressions are guarded against by a fair confession of their wildness, they may serve at least to give some relief to curiosity where nothing more authentic, at least of a public nature, as yet exists.

No. III.

On the Military Force of Nepāl.

(Referred to in page 10.)

It is said that when the country was turned out *en masse*, on occasion of the Chinese invasion, there were seven lacs (700,000) of men in arms. This estimate is taken from the same vague popular sources of information which furnished the preceding memorandum relative to the population; and it is equally absurd and incredible. They say that each house can turn out on an average five persons fit to bear arms, more than a third of the whole population—a manifest absurdity, and a mode of calculation that would give much more than 700,000, unless, indeed, it was meant that this was the produce of the valley alone. The effect of this overwhelming force, however, seems not to have been proportioned to its bulk, as we gather from the severe terms to which they acceded with the Chinese, and the evident terror in which the country was at their advance, disastrous as it was to the invaders.

The following is a list of the army of Nepāl, as it existed about fifteen years ago; and it may, probably, be more to be depended on than the vague accounts of population, and the levy en masse.

A standing camp at Caleejung in the Nepāl valley, near Catmandhû, is said to consist always of about 18,000 men. It was then formed of the following corps.

Corps	Men
Calee Bux pultoon, or battalion	6,000
Suboorj, or green	4,000
Sreenath	4,000
And the Goruck pultoon, or Goorkha battalion	4,000
which has several times, since the relater's time, been raised and renewed. (There is also another).	
Sreenuhur company	2,000
Debee Bux ditto	1,000
Sreejung ditto	1,000
Sulz (stationed at Palpay) ditto	4,000
Birjabanee ditto	500
Calee Dull ditto	500
Suttur murdun ditto	500
Jung Behadoor ditto	200
Mja Seereenat,h ditto	500
Runajung ditto	500
Tripoora Dull ditto	100
Singanath ditto	200
Buruk ditto	300
	33,800
Brought forward	33,800
Burujnat company	100
Ram Dull ditto	240
Tara Dull ditto	200
Lew Dull ditto	100
Mai Bux ditto	100
Bhum Dull ditto	100
Caleejung ditto	100
Debee Dhul ditto	100
Bara Dull ditto	100
Siree Dull ditto	100
Bughotee Dull ditto	100
Gorukh ditto	100
Nyagoruk ditto	100
Myeesereemekin ditto	100
Doorga Bux ditto	240
Byhroom ditto	200
Reepoomurdun ditto	100
Runbheem ditto	100
Buttook Dull ditto	100
Jubber Jung ditto	100
	36,280

Brought forward	36,280
Joalla Dull company - -	100
Runa bum (Acham) ditto - -	200
Rumsa Dull ditto - -	240
Cuttukjeet (Kaskee) ditto -	100
Dullamindur ditto - -	100
Urjoor Bān ditto - -	100
Hoonceman Dull ditto -	100
Buna Dull ditto - - -	100
	37,320

Brought forward	37,320
Urree Durn company - -	240
Sulz ditto - - -	240
9 Pālpai ditto - - -	900
Remajung ditto - -	100
Nina Bux ditto - - -	100
Poorana Goruk ditto - -	400
7 Dhotee ditto - -	700
	40,000

All these were said to have been well armed with English musquets, in good order, and with swords.

The Soubahdars and Jemmadars carried bows and arrows, and spears; and they are said to have been regularly paid. The excellent effective state of their arms is certainly greatly exaggerated.

No. IV.

Muster Roll.

(Referred to in page 10.)

Of a company of Ghoorkhas, under command of Soorbeer Gheertee Soubahdar, in charge of the fort of Choupal (surrendered to the irregular force sent into Joobul), and entertained in British pay.

1 Soubahdar - -	700 rupees per annum.
4 Jemmadars - -	820
1 Adjutant - -	125
1 Major - -	125
1 Colun, or quarter-master	135
2 Colours - -	135
8 Havildars - -	560
8 Umildars, or naiks -	520
85 Soldiers - -	4,250
6 Ammunition -	240
2 Trumpeters -	90
1 Drummer - -	50
2 Kettle-drums -	90
2 Marfee - -	80
1 Fifer - -	35
1 Smith	
1 Shoemaker	
	7,955

No. V.

Intercepted Letters of Ghoorka Officers,

(Illustrative of the history of the recent war with Nepāl, p. 3—48.)

1. *Translation of a Letter from Runjore T,happa, Jespow T,happa, Lutchben T,happa, Ryrab Sing Khwas, and Bursore T,happa, to the Rajah of Nepāl.*

The following letter was intercepted at the place of Kangrah, between Calsee and Jytock, together with many others; and will serve in some degree to characterise the people, whose production it is. There is a strange mixture of truth contained in it, with much exaggeration, and a sort of imposing tone of moderation and coolness, affecting to treat the success it records as a matter of course, and not as a signal instance of good fortune. It is translated almost literally.

" Here it is well. On the day of the full moon, of the month Mangsur, the 15th of the month, of the week Somewar, by the road of the village Chumtron, at the hillock near the enclosure for catching hyenas, Budul T,happa, jemmadar, with 25 men, was posted, being the way which leads from Nahn to the temple of the goddess Jumpta; at the temple Suchtee T,happa with 25 men was stationed. Bhudroo T,happa, jemmadar, and 25 men, were placed on picquet on the road leading from Nahn to Jytock, a little underneath the village Kheetan-kegoon, which lies below the post at the enclosure for catching tigers. At the second hour after nightfall until the sixth hour, by the Rynka road, which strikes off from the road leading from Nahn to Kansur, the enemy moved; when having returned to the fort from a review of the outposts, a firing was heard in the dell. The jemmadar sent Purtab Gooroong and Kihen Sing Rawut to report: and they arriving about midnight, were stating the advance of the enemy, whose firing was heard in the hollow of the Jumpta road. The jemmadar returned the fire. Fifty-seven loads of ammunition, one pētee, and a horse were captured. A soldier arrived about the third watch of the night, for people to bring away the captured property. I immediately sent Rumtrumkai Soubahdar, with his company, to the Jortee hillock, below Jytock; and Bahadoor Rana, jemmadar of the Goruck battalion, with 25 men and porters to bring off the captured property, which they did. In the mean time, a firing was heard at the post of Sachtee T,happa, and I despatched the Hoonoomandhoj and Shamdull companies, under Runjeet Khudkha, soubahdar, and Umroop Ghurtee, soubahdar, to the stockade of the Jumpta goddess temple. The firing commenced again there, and the post was reinforced by the Burrick Kushadull and Saidooljung companies, under Qazee Jespaw T,happa. The Qazee continued in the stockade.

" The companies advanced out of the stockade, having unfurled their colours: 300 Europeans drove them back. Jespaw T,happa, and about 15 or 20 men, remained in the stockade, and all the rest fled on the high land from Jumpta to Jytock. I immediately ordered out the Runtrun and Debubuksh companies, under Runsoor T,happa, Bhyrubsing, and soubahdar Runbun Kaskee, and a soubahdar of the Goruk battalion, to their support; and they advanced: the

Europeans had pushed on and laid hold of the posts of the stockade in which Jespaw Jazee was defending himself with about twenty men. Runsoor T,happa, Runbum Kaskee, and the Goruk battalion, Soubahdar, gave their fire, and drew their swords; Quaree Jespaw also advanced, sword in hand, out of the stockade, and received the enemy's fire. We beat them back to the Jumpta temple, where they stood in a scattered, confused body; they kept up a retreating fire in subdivisions, and we followed the pursuit, the enemy fighting and retreating. We surrounded them on all sides, killed a great many, and drove them completely back; majors, captains, lieutenants, soubahdars, and men altogether, to the number of a battalion, were killed by musquetry or by the sword; drums, musquets, swords, and all manner of arms, were captured. The contest continued from three o'clock in the morning till ten. Our soldiers having dispersed the enemy, returned, and collected under the Jumpta temple.

On the east side of the fort, the Jooladull and Leitchbun Sakee companies were on duty; the Jooladull company had advanced a party of twenty-five men upon the Peacock hill; a battalion of Europeans, and another of native infantry, advanced by the Rynka hill against the Peacock hill. The advanced part of the Jooladull company was driven in, and retreated upon the fort stockades. The hill which the enemy possessed themselves of was almost as high as the fort. The road was even, and the top rather a plain. The enemy showed a post on three sides, and continued prepared for action. I recalled the division from Jumpta, which had defeated the enemy in the morning. They had not time to eat, wash, or refresh themselves, but were hastily given to drink. The Sheamadul and Hoonooman Dhooj company were left in the Jumpta temple stockade; the Nyna Buksh and Bhubso Khuwas companies were posted on the hill below Jytock, towards Nahn. The whole of the Goruck battalion, and the remaining companies, advanced against the Peacock hill, within a stone's throw of the enemy, and commenced the action about mid-day.

The artillery fired upon the enemy from Jytock hill and the hill upon which the Lutchbun-Sah company were encamped: three men were killed by the fire. Two hours after nightfall our force drove off the enemy; a close fire of musquetry was exchanged three successive times; and afterwards side-arms were used: until ten at night the conflict continued. The enemy being surrounded, 300 captains, lieutenants, and Europeans, and 200 natives, were killed; a soubahdar, jemmadar, and forty soldiers taken prisoners. Many stand of arms and other plunder was taken.

The field of battle was plain, and the enemy fought bravely, with their breasts a rampart. The musquetry crossed in conflict, and the fire of the opposing combatants mixed; we have lost soubahdars and officers both killed and wounded. The city of Nahn would have been destroyed by artillery, and our force was small, and not able to defend it; it was therefore judged expedient to retire upon Jytock. My father and the superior officers directed this measure. Nahn was left empty, and the British army took possession of it. In the battle of Jumpta, Buhadoor Rana was the first man who drew his sword, and distinguished himself; he is a jemmadar in the Goruck battalion to the eastward: in the action of the Peacock hill, Deechurd Kheeoas of the same was the foremost in valour.

2. From Ummr Sing and his sons, Ram Doss and Urjeen T,happa, to the Rajah of Nepāl; dated Rajgurh, 2nd March, 1815.

The following very energetic, original, and excellent letter was intercepted in the course of our progress in Almorah; together with many others, both in original and duplicate. It may well be considered a very valuable and interesting document; showing the policy of the Nepāl government and of its chiefs with regard the British Government; and exhibiting a strong characteristic picture of our enemy and chief opponent, Ummr Sing T,happah. The gallantry, patriotism, and nobleness of his sentiments cannot be too much admired; while the acuteness of his reasoning, though not founded on the liberal policy which actuates British councils, and which no Asiatic understands, is also worthy of attention. I deem myself fortunate in the liberal permission I have obtained from Government, to add this interesting document to these notes.

A copy of your letter of the 23d December, addressed to Runjoor Sing, under the red seal, was sent by the latter to me, who have received it with every token of respect. It was to the following purport:

"The capture of Nalpanee (Kalunga) has been communicated to me from Gurwhāl and Kemaoon, as also the intelligence of the enemy having assembled his force and marched to Nahn. He now occupies the whole country from Bareh Pursah to Subtree Mahontee. My army also is secretly posted in various places in the jungles of the mountains. An army, under a general, has arrived in Goruckpore from Palpa; and another detachment has reached the borders of Bijypoor. I have further heard, that a general officer has set out from Calcutta to create more disturbance. For the sake of a few trifling objects, some intermediate agents have destroyed the mutual harmony, and war is waging far and wide. All this you know. You ought to send an embassy to conciliate the English, otherwise the cause is lost. The enemy, after making immense preparations, have begun the war; and, unless great concessions are made, they will not listen to terms. To restore the relations of amity by concession is good and proper; for this purpose it is fit, in the first place, to cede to the enemy the departments of Bootwul, Palpeh, and Seuraj, already settled by the commissioners, and the disputed tracts towards Bareh. If this be insufficient to re-establish harmony, we ought to abandon the whole of the Terraei, the Dhoon, and the lowlands; and if the English are still dissatisfied on account of not obtaining possession of a portion of the mountains, you are hereby authorized to give up, along with the Dhoon, the country as far as the Sutlej. Do whatever may be practicable to restore the relations of peace and amity, and be assured of my approbation and assent. If these means be unsuccessful, it will be very difficult to preserve the integrity of my dominions from Khunka Trishta to the Sutlej. If the enemy once obtain a footing in the centre of our territory, both extremities will be thrown into disorder. If you can retire with your army and military stores, do, so as to pursue any other plan of operations that may afterwards appear eligible. It will be advisable, on this account, that you immediately effect a junction with all the other officers on the western service, and retire to that part of our territory, which (including all in your rear), as far as Nepāl, you may think yourself capable of retaining."

These are your orders. In the first place, after the immense preparations of the enemy, he will not be satisfied with these concessions; or, if he should accept of our terms, he would serve us as he did Tippoo, from whom he first accepted of an indemnification of six crones of rupees in money and territory, and afterwards wrested from him his whole country.

If we were to cede to him so much country, he would excite another disturbance at a future opportunity, and seek to wrest from us other provinces. Having lost so much territory, we should be unable to maintain our army on its present footing; and our military force being once reduced, what means should we have left to defend our eastern possessions? While we retain Bischur, Gurwhāl is secure; if the former be abandoned, the Booteans of Rewaeen will certainly betray us. The English having thus acquired the Dhoon and Rewaeen, it will be impossible for us to maintain Gurwhāl; and, being deprived of the latter, Kumaoon and Dhotee will also be lost to us. After the seizure of these provinces, Acham, Joomla, Dooloo, Duelekh, will be wrested from us in succession.

You say, "that a proclamation has been issued to the inhabitants of the eastern Kurats." If they have joined the enemy, the other Kurats will do so likewise; and then the country from Dood Koosee, on the east, to Bheree, on the west, cannot long be retained. Having lost our dominions, what is to become of our great military establishment? When our power is once reduced, we shall have another Knox's mission, under pretence of concluding a treaty of alliance and friendship, and founding commercial establishments. If we decline receiving their mission, they will insist; and if we are unable to oppose force, and desire them to come unaccompanied by troops, they will not comply. They will begin by introducing a company; a battalion will soon after follow; and at length an army will be assembled for the subjugation of Nepāl. Thus, you think, that if, for the present, the lowlands, the Dhoon, and the country to the Sutlej, were ceded to them, they would cease to entertain designs upon the other provinces of Nepāl: do not trust to them. They who counselled you to receive the mission of Knox, and to permit the establishment of a commercial factory, will usurp the government of Nepāl. With regard to the concessions now proposed, if you had, in the first instance, determined upon a pacific line of conduct, and agreed to restore the departments of Botwul and Sheoraj, as adjusted by the commissioners, the present contest might have been avoided. But you could not suppress your avarice, and your desire to retain those places; and having murdered their revenue-officer, a commotion arose, and war was waged for trifles.

At Jytock we have gained a victory over the enemy. If I succeed against Ochterlony, and Runjoor Sing, with Jespoo T,happa and his officers, prevail at Jytock, Runjee Sing* will rise against the enemy. In conjunction with the Sikhs, my army will make a descent into the plains, and our forces, crossing the Jumna from two different quarters, will recover possession of the Dhoon.

When we reach Hurdwar, the Nawaub of Lucknow may be expected to take a part in the cause; and, on his accession to the general coalition, we may consider ourselves secure as far as Khunka. Relying on your fortune, I trust that Bulbhudder Kooner and Rewant Kajee will soon reinforce the garrison of Jytock; and I hope, ere long, to send Arumber Punt Qazee with eight companies, when the force there will be very strong. The troops sent by you are arriving

* Chief of the Sikhs.

every day; and when they all come up, I hope we shall succeed, both here and at Jytock. Formerly, when the English endeavoured to penetrate to Sindoolee, they continued, for two years, in possession of Bareh-Pursa and Mohontee; but when you conquered Nepāl, they were either destroyed by your force, or fell victims to the climate, with the exception of a few only, who abandoned the place.

Orders should now be given to all your officers to defend Choundildil and Choundind, in Bijypoor, the two Kurats, and the ridge of Mahabharut. Suffer the enemy to retain the lowlands for a couple of years; measures can afterwards be taken to expel them. Lands transferred under a written agreement cannot again be resumed; but if they have been taken by force, force may be employed to recover them. Fear nothing, even though the Sikhs should not join us. Should you succeed now in bring our differences to an amicable terminatiōn by the cession of territory, the enemy, in the course of a few years, would take possession of Nepāl, as he did of the country of Tippoo. The present, therefore, is not the time for treaty and conciliation: these expedients should have been adopted before the murder of the revenue-officers; so must be postponed till victory shall crown our efforts. If they will then accede to the terms which I shall propose, it is well; if not, it will be my business, with the favour of God and your fortune and country, to preserve the integrity of my country, from K,hunka to the Sutlej. Let me intreat you, therefore, *never* to make peace. Formerly, when some individuals urged the adoption of a treaty of peace and commerce, I refused my assent to that measure; and I will not now suffer the honour of my prince to be sullied by concession and submission. If you are determined on this step, bestow the humiliating office on him who first advised it.

But, for me, call me to your presence. I am old, and only desire once more to kiss your feet. I can recollect the time when the Ghoorka army did not exceed 12,000 men. Through the favour of Heaven, and the renown of your forefathers, your territory was extended to Khunka, on the east; under the auspices of your father we subjugated Kumaoon; and through your fortune, we have pushed our conquests to the Sutlej. Four generations have been employed in the acquisition of all this dignity and dominion. At Nalapanee, Bulbhudder cut up 3 or 4000 of the enemy; at Jytock, Runjore Sing, with his officers, overthrew three battalions. In this place I am surrounded, and daily fighting with the enemy, and look forward with confidence for victory. All the inhabitants and chiefs of the country have joined the enemy. I must gain two or three victories before I can accomplish the object I have in view, of attaching Runjeet Sing to our cause. On his accession, and after the advance of the Sikhs and Ghoorkas towards Jumna, the chiefs of the Dukkeon may be expected to join the coalition; as also the Nawaub of Lucknow and the *Salik Rame Saadh*. Then will be the time for us to drive out the enemy and recover possession of the low countries of Palpeh, as far as Bijypoor. If we succeed in regaining these, we can attempt further conquests in the plains. There has been no fighting in your quarter yet. The Choudindee and Choudind of Bijypoor, as far as the ridge of Mahabharut and Silleeaneh, should be well defended. Countries acquired in four generations, under the administration of the T,happas, should not be abandoned, for the purpose of bringing matters to an amicable adjustment, without deep and serious reflection.

If we are victorious in the war, we can easily adjust our differences; and if we are defeated, death is preferable to reconciliation on humiliating terms.

When the Chinese army invaded Nepāl, we implored the mercy of Heaven, by offerings to the Brahmins, and the performance of religious rites; and through the favour of the one, and the intercession of the other, we succeeded in repulsing the enemy. Ever since you confiscated the jageers of the Brahmins, thousands have been in distress and poverty. Promises were given that they should be restored on the capture of Kangrah; and orders to this effect, under the red seal, were addressed to me, and Nyn Sing T,happa. We failed, however, in that object, and now there is an universal commotion.

You ought, therefore, to assemble all the Brahmins, and promise to restore to them all their lands and property, in the event of your conquering and expelling the English. By these means many thousand respectable Brahmins will put up their prayers for your protection, and the enemy will be driven forth. By the practice of charity, the territory acquired in four generations may be preserved, and, through the favour of God, our power and dominion may be still further extended. By the extension of lenity our military establishment may be maintained on its present footing, and even increased. The numerous countries which you propose to cede to the enemy yielded a revenue equal to the maintenance of 4000 men, and Kangrah might have been captured. By the cession of these provinces the fear of your name, and the splendor of your court, will no longer remain. By the capture of Kangrah your name would have been rendered formidable; but, though that has not happened, a powerful impression has nevertheless been made on the people of the plains, by the extension of our conquests to the Sutlej. To effect a reconciliation, by the cession of the country to the west of the Jumna, would give rise to the idea that the Ghoorkhas were unable to oppose the English; would lower the dignity of your name in the plains; and cause a reduction of your army to the extent of 4000 men.

The enemy will, therefore, acquire possession of Bischur, and, after that, the conquest of Gurwhāl will be easy. Nor will it be possible in that case for us to retain Kumaoon, and with it we must lose Dhotee, Acham, and Jomleh. He may be expected to penetrate even to Bischur. If the English once establish themselves firmly in possession of a part of the hills, we shall be unable to drive them out. The countries towards the Sutlej should be obstinately defended; the abandonment of the disputed tracts in the plains is the lesser evil. The possession of the former preserves to us a road to farther conquests. You ought, therefore, to direct Gooroo-Ungnat,h Pundit and Dulbhungun Pandee to give up the disputed lands of Bootul, Sheoraj, and the twenty-two villages in the vicinity of Bareh, and if possible bring our differences to a termination. To this step I have no objections, and shall feel no animosity to those who may perform this service. I must, however, declare a decided enmity to such as in bringing about a reconciliation with the English consult only their own interests, and forget their duty to you.

If they will not accept these terms, what have we to fear? The English attempted to take Bhurspore by storm; but the rajah Runjeet Sing destroyed an European regiment, and a battalion of sepoys. To the present day they have not ventured to meddle with Bhurspore, and one fort has sufficed to check their progress.

In the low country of Dhurma* they established their authority; but the rajah overthrew their army, and captured all their artillery and stores, and now continues in quiet possession of his dominions. Our proffers of peace and reconciliation will be interpreted as the result of fear; and it would be absurd to expect that the enemy will respect a treaty concluded under such circumstances. Therefore, let us confide in our swords; and, by boldly opposing the enemy, compel him to remain within his own territory; or, if he should continue to advance, stung with shame at the idea of retreating after his immense preparations, we can then

* Perhaps Burma.

give up the lands in dispute, and adjust our differences. Such, however, is the fame and terror of our swords, that Bulbhudder, with a nominal force of 600 men, but scarcely amounting to 500, destroyed an army of 3 or 4000 English. His force consisted of the old Goruck and Barukh companies (which were only partly composed of the inhabitants of our ancient kingdom), and of the people of the country from Bischur to Gurwhāl, and with these he destroyed, and crippled, and repulsed another. My army is similarly composed; nevertheless all descriptions are eager to meet the enemy.

In your quarter you are surrounded by the veterans of our army, and, therefore, cannot apprehend desertions among them. You have also an immense militia, and many jageerdars, who will fight for their own honour and interests. Assembling the militia of the low lands and fighting in the plains is impolitic. Call them into the hills, and cut them up by detail. (A passage occurs here, the sense of which cannot be discovered). The enemy is proud, and flushed with success, and has reduced under his subjection all the western zemindars, the rānās and rajahs of Kurnaul and the Thakoraein, and will keep a peace with no one. However, my advice is nothing.

I will direct Ram Doss to propose to General Ochterlony the abandonment on our part of the disputed lands; and will forward to you the answer which we may receive. All the rajahs, rānās, and Thakoraeen have joined the enemy, and I am surrounded. Nevertheless, we shall fight and conquer; and all my officers have taken the same resolution. The Pundits have pronounced the month of Bysack as particularly auspicious for the Ghoorkhas, and, by selecting a fortunate day, we shall surely conquer.

I am desirous of engaging the enemy slowly, and with caution, but cannot manage it, the English being always in a desperate hurry to fight. I hope, however, to be able to delay the battle till Bysack, when I will choose a favourable opportunity to fight them. When we shall have driven the enemy from hence, either Runjore Sing, or myself, according to your wishes, will repair to your person. In the present crisis, it is very advisable to write to the Emperor of China, to the Lama of Lassa, and to the other Lamas; and for this purpose I beg leave to submit the enclosed draft of a letter to their address. Any errors in it will, I trust, be forgiven by you, as I earnestly recommend that you lose no time in sending a petition to the Emperor of China, and a letter to the Lama.

---

3. *Translation of a Draft of a Petition to be addressed to the Emperor of China, by the Rajah of Nepāl, inclosed in Ummr Sing's Letter from Raj Gurh, dated 2d of March,* 1815.

" I yield obedience to the Emperor of China, and no one dare invade my dominions; or, if any power has ventured to encroach on my territory, through your favour and protection, I have been able to discomfit and expel them. Now, however, a powerful and inveterate enemy has attacked me, and, as I owe allegiance to you, I rely on obtaining your assistance and support. From Khunka to the Sutlej, for a thousand cōs, war is waging between us. Entertaining designs on Bhote (Tartary) the enemy endeavours to get possession of Nepāl; and for these objects he has fomented a quarrel, and declared war. Five or six great actions have already been fought; but, through the fortune and glory of your Imperial Majesty, I have succeeded in destroying about 20,000 of the enemy.

" But his wealth and military resources are great, and he sustains the loss without receding a step. On the contrary, numerous reinforcements continue to arrive, and my country is invaded at all points. Though I might obtain a hundred thousand soldiers from the hills and plains, yet without pay they cannot be maintained; and, though I have every desire to pay them, I have not the means.

" Without soldiers I cannot repel the enemy. Consider the Ghoorkhas as your tributaries; reflect that the English came to conquer Nepāl and Bhote; and for these reasons be graciously pleased to assist us with a sum of money, that we may levy an army, and drive forth the invaders; or if you are unwilling to assist us with subsidies, and prefer sending an army to our aid, 'tis well.

" The climate of Dhurma is temperate; and you may easily send an army of 2 or 300,000 men, by the route of Dhurma into Bengal, spreading alarm and consternation among the Europeans as far as Calcutta. The enemy has subjugated all the rajahs of the plains, and usurped the throne of the king of Dehli; and, therefore, it is to be expected that these would all unite in expelling Europeans from Hindostan. By such an event your name will be renowned throughout Jumboo Dweep; and whenever you may command, the whole of its inhabitants will be forward in your service. Should you think that the conquest of Nepāl, and the forcible separation of the Ghoorkhas from their dependence on the Emperor of China, cannot materially affect your Majesty's interests, I beseech you to reflect that, without your aid, I cannot repulse the English; that these are the people who have already subdued all India, and usurped the throne of Dehli; that, with my army and resources, I am quite unable to make head against them; and that the world will henceforth say, that the Emperor of China abandoned to their fate his tributaries and dependents. I acknowledge the supremacy of the Emperor of China above all other potentates on earth. The English, after obtaining possession of Nepāl, will advance by the routes of Buddrinauth and Mansowroar, and also by that of Diggurcheh, for the purpose of conquering Lassa. I beg, therefore, that you will write an order to the English, directing them to withdraw their forces from the territory of the Ghoorkha state, which is tributary and dependent on you, otherwise you will send an army to our aid. I beseech you, however, to lose no time in sending assistance, whether in men or money, that I may drive forth the enemy, and maintain possession of the mountains, otherwise, in a few years, he will be master of Lassa."

---

4. *Letter from Ummr Sing T,happa, and Ram Doss T,happa (his son), to Kagee Bohtawin Sing Bishnaut, dated 6th of Phagoon (2d of March,* 1815).

" Runjore Sing T,happa will have informed you of the victory gained at Jytock. There have been two trifling battles fought here: many of the English were killed. The rajahs in this country have joined the English and surrounded me. I had determined to fight the enemy with the force I had with me, notwithstanding it was putting every thing to the hazard (a game of chance); victory and defeat are in the hands of the Deity; when I was informed by the government at Nepāl, that a reinforcement of twenty-seven companies had been sent off, and Bum Sah Chowtra wrote to me that they already had arrived at Bhootana (Pintana, about half way between Almorah and Nepāl), and would speedily join me. I, therefore, waited for their arrival and junction before I attacked the enemy. The English army is posted in stockaded positions. I have received orders from government if possible to effect a peace, by sacrificing a portion of the country; but, instead of being satisfied with a part, the English aim at possessing the whole extent of the mountains to Nepāl, and have created a disturbance from the Kamuck Tishtee (near Nepāl), to the Saturrooda (probably the Sutudra, or Sutlej). Should I open any negotiation for peace, or make offers of a cession of a portion of the country, the same thing will occur as happened to Tippoo, who, during war time, gave to them three crores of Jaidad (lands held for military service), and made peace. In the end, they possessed themselves of the whole of his dominions: in a similar manner they will take a part of this country; and, extending, they will eventually seize upon Nepāl itself.

"It is not my opinion, therefore, that it would be advisable to make peace with the English, by the cession of any part of the country. I would rather advise that, if possible, it be defended by force of arms, and every means of opposition. You have done well in collecting the companies, and defending the Gurwhal country. It is your duty thus to do service to your master, who will show his approbation, and reward you. Do not be uneasy for this quarter. By the blessing of God, and the good fortune of our prince, the English shall be driven back.

"If I could but gain a victory or two over the enemy, the sikhs would come to my assistance, and with their co-operation we would drive the English from the country, and rid the land of its enemies. Be urgent with the armies that may have arrived from the eastward to join me without delay, and keep me informed from time to time of your welfare and affairs."

---

5. Letter of Gowree Sah to Kishna Oopurettee, dated Chyt, 5th day, Burwar.

The fort of Mornee, situated some miles from Blackhill, being occupied by a Ghoorka force, it was desirable to get possession of it; but it was not deemed worth the expense of men that an assault would have cost, and therefore a negotiation was set on foot to gain it. It was commanded by Gowree Sah, a brave, faithful old soldier, to whom Kishen Oopulee Soubahdar, who had deserted to us from the enemy, as well as Lall Sahee and some others, were desired to write, sounding him as to the likelihood of his being brought to give up the place. The following correspondence took place with Gowree Sah: it will be found exhibiting a fine picture of steady calm fidelity. The whole is translated almost *verbatim*.

Your note has been received and understood: to what you write about the fort I reply; I have eaten their salt, and if the debt of salt be not discharged, a man is lost hereafter. I was born of a Rajapoot woman, and carried in her arms. There is not any great good in long life. You write I have received only 2500 rupees, and now am in the fort for so small a debt. Money is nothing. I have eaten the salt, and drink the water of the Ghoorkas. If I return this I shall be happy when I die. What need is there of writing more? You are yourself wise, and understand what it is I wish to express.

A second letter was sent, which produced this answer.

6. *Letter from the same to the same, 8th Chyte.*

"You ask a reply to the letter you have sent. I have replied once, which is as good as a hundred times. I have said and still say, until Raj,gurh and Jytock fall, I will answer you with powder and ball. I have plenty of it."

---

7. *Letter from the same to Lal Sahee his nephew, and Kishna Oopurette's father, both in Colonel Ochterlony's camp; dated 6th Chyte.*

"What you write, that I am a rajah's son whose family has been destroyed by the Ghoorkhas, and that it did not become me to hold out in the fort, is answered; that I am the son of a rajpoot. I have eaten their salt, and will not disgrace my family's name nor my own name.

"If you suppose you will find me alive you are mistaken; you may find my corpse. I am born of a rajpoot: I am as such prepared to die, and thereby attain a happy regeneration."

---

8. *Letter from the same to Dhunnee Ram, of the same date.*

"Lal Sahee sent you here, and has caused you much trouble. What I first wrote to Lal Sah, I wished merely to know whether he had or had not gone over; now I know he has, and has also disgraced his house and ancestry.

"This I will not do. If I survive, I shall be fortunate; if I am slain, my state will be happy. Until Jytock and Raj,ghur fall, do not talk to me of surrender; I have eaten of Ghoorkha's salt, and have ammunition and all manner of supplies."

---

9. *Translation of a letter from Runjore Sing T,happa, Commander in Jytock, to Gouree Sah; written the 10th Chyte, or 4th April.* (Intercepted.)

"Your letter is received and understood; you write that "others are ungrateful, dastardly, and treacherous. I will support the Peeoothana* name, and prove true." In such times when you write so, I am highly gratified. By the favour of God, when this danger is past, you shall receive all honours, dress, drums, and colours, and be promoted, and the other officers under you equally rewarded. Kishna Ooperettee Soubahdar is gone to deceive and turn you aside; call him to you by any means or method, and shoot him. By so doing you will greatly please me. Uzumba Punt Qazee did not choose a happy hour, nor consulted properly. He fought and lost an action, even he is taken prisoner, but we are from that more confident and not dispirited. We will cut to pieces and drive away our foes. Be on all points at rest and confident. I send you four rupees, the present for the ensuing festival."

* The meaning of this name is unknown.

10. *Letter from Sheamul Soobahdar, his cousin, to Gouree Sah, Commander of Mornee, 4th April, 10th Chyte.*

" What you write, that Lal Sah is a traitor, and has disgraced all the rajpoots, is true: you desire me to speak to Runjore to prevent the wives and families of Dumbear Sahee, Ureemur, Dan Sahee, and Purtab Sahee, being seized, when the wife and family of Lal Sahee is put in confinement. The Qazee recollects this, and will pay attention, but he says the criminals alone shall suffer. Lal Sahee is a traitor and ungrateful, and has sent his ancestors from heaven to hell. He has lost his name and cast. The Ghoorkha empire is not to be overthrown. Be strong in your position and faithful to your trust; recollect your name and ancestry."

These letters being intercepted, and a fabricated one from Runjore put into the cover, the following answer was received from Gource Sah, dated 21st Chyte.

" Your letter has been received, stating that the enemy had approached the fort on the side of Rynka; that Punt Qazee did not consult, and went hastily to fight; that the battle was lost and himself taken prisoner; Captain Bulbhudder severely wounded, and many jummadars and soldiers killed; that the enemy had surrounded the fort on all sides, and that the garrison were starving for want of food. To this I reply, the two kingly powers are at war. You have conquered in ten or twelve battles, and are renowned. The enemy have gained one action; what of that? Do not be alarmed at having lost so many men, and being so completely surrounded. If you live and stand at present, you will gain a thousand battles more. If you feel want of confidence and despair in Jytock, the Ghoorkhas will be slain, scattered about as they are. If you stand out in Jytock, reinforcements will come from the east, and all united drive away the English if they were a thousand nations. I have consulted the shasters: until the 15th day of Bysak you will be greatly distressed; afterwards your fortune will turn. Do this; form an iron sheet and make upon it the picture of Bheem-Sing, and the hoonooman of the moon and the sun; put it, upon a Sunday, into the eastern tower of the fort: by this fortune will turn. (Bheem-Sing is one of the pandooan of the Hindoos, a very sacred character).

" Find out the name of the commander of the British army, write it upon a piece of paper, take it, and some rice, and turmerick, say the great incantation three times; having said it, send for some plum-tree wood and therewith burn it. For fighting and defence dig a ditch and fight in it. As for this fort, so long as we have water, and its four towers stand, we stand in it; when they are thrown down, we must leave it. I have grain for a period to the 15th or 20th of Bysack. I sent two * soldiers with a letter to you; send them back. What is become of the army which was coming from the east? Call it quickly."

* They were taken.

No. VI.

Official Despatches from Colonel Nicolls.

(Illustrative of the events recorded in pages 44—48.)

"Camp before Almorah, 24th April, 1815.

"SIR,—I had last night the honour to transmit a copy of a letter received from Major Patton, commanding the detachment which I ordered to march on the night of the 23d, against Hustee Dhull Chowtra.

"With the sincerest satisfaction I have the honour to transmit, for the information of his Excellency the Commander-in-Chief, a subsequent report from Major Patton; and to add, that the rout and dispersion of that chief's selected forces is fully confirmed: some have returned to Almorah, but by no means the whole force, if we can credit reports. With sentiments of regret for the death of a gallant chief, mixed with those of joy for the removal of an active and vigilant enemy, I have to announce the death of Hustee Dhul Chowtra, uncle to the reigning rajah of Nepāl. He was shot through the temple, and died on the road to Almorah.

"A sirdar, named Jeyrookah, has also been brought into Almorah, dangerously wounded through the body.

"I hope to open the eight-inch mortars upon Sillolee to-morrow; and, under the prevailing alarm and dejection, I dare say the apprehension of these formidable engines will induce the enemy to an early evacuation of the post.

"I transmit herewith a list of the killed and wounded, which is not so great as might have been expected; a circumstance on which I very heartily congratulate his Excellency the Commander-in-Chief.

"Major Patton's conduct in directing this enterprise entitles him to the warmest approbation; his decision and promptitude were only equalled by his skill and gallantry. I wish he had named the officers, European and native, who have had and embraced opportunities of distinguishing themselves, in order that I might have performed the grateful duty of bringing their achievements to the notice of his Excellency.

"This delightful task is, however, only postponed, as I feel that my pleasure at his success cannot be complete until I have held up the gallant promoters of it to the grateful admiration of their honourable employers, their country, and their sovereign.

I have, &c.

(Signed) J. NICOLLS, Colonel.

(True copy.)

(Signed) G. H. FAGAN, Adjutant-General."

To the Adjutant-General, head-quarters, Futty Ghur.

"Almorah, 25th April, 1815.

"Sir,—I have the honour to acquaint you, for the information of his Excellency the Commander-in-Chief, that I advanced at one p. m. with the 1st battalion, 4th regiment, and flank battalion, towards the enemy's principal stockade upon the north end of the Sillolee ridge. It was my intention to have established the heavy mortars in battery, within 600 or 800 yards of that work, and I had taken up the ground for that purpose, when finding that our troops were confident, and the enemy disheartened, I ordered their two stone breast-works to be carried by assault, a service cheerfully performed by the 1st battalion, 4th regiment, most gallantly led by Captain Faithful.

"The irregular infantry, under Lieutenant-Colonel Gardner's personal command, advanced by a ridge parallel to ours, and animated by the gallantry of the 1st battalion, 4th regiment, they diverged to the right when near the summit. They very easily possessed themselves of the three remaining breast-works upon the Sillolee ridge.

"Whilst this was passing, fifty men of the 4th regiment possessed themselves of a small breast-work on the left.

"The 1st battalion, 4th regiment, was halted on the ridge until the flank battalion came up. I then ordered Captain Leys to advance upon the retreating enemy, and finding five roads, the troops pursued them by each of them, until they possessed one stockade, leading to Kulmuttea, a small stone fortification and the rajah's palace.

"We have thus cut off all retreat to Kulmuttea, and perfectly divided the enemy's force, which must fall as soon as our small mortars and six-pounders come up.

"Lieutenant Wright and Captain Faithful led their men into the embrasure of the breast-work, in doing which, I regret to say the former was dangerously wounded: I saw Captain Faithful immediately cut the Ghoorkha down.

"The only other officer of that corps, or any other of whom I have received any reports as yet, of having been wounded, is Lieutenant Purvis, a very gallant officer, who led the advance in a style that will ever do him honour.

"I suppose about 40 men may be killed and wounded.

"I congratulate his Excellency the Commander-in-Chief on the glorious result of the noble exertions of the troops, whom it will be a source of pride to me, to the end of life, to have commanded.

"Major Patton's corps remained at Gungo Nath and Kātār Mull, and about 1500 of the irregulars and provincials are absent on various duties.

"It is almost superfluous to say, that the troops behaved well. It will suffice to report that they marched for nearly two hours up hill, and drove an enemy, equal in number to their own, from seven breast-works, and strong fortified houses, in less than three hours.

I have, &c.

(Signed) J. NICOLLS, Colonel.

"Lieutenant Field, 4th regiment, also conducted himself in a most admirable manner.

True copy. (Signed) G. H. FAGAN, Adjutant-general.

True copy. (Signed) J. ADAM, Secretary to Government."

"Sir, "Almorah, April 26, 1815.

"I had the honour yesterday evening to apprise you, by express, for the information of his Excellency the Commander-in-Chief, that the troops had carried the breast-works on the Sillolee ridge, and pushed their success so far as to occupy about one-third of the town, and three important positions upon the line between Kulmuttea and Salmundy.

"These advantages were quietly retained till 11 p.m., at which hour our northern post, under Lieutenant Costly, of the 1st battalion of the 4th regiment, was carried by overpowering numbers. Lieutenant Brown and Lieutenant Winfield, of the flank battalion, were instantly detached with 100 men to the assistance of the party; and Lieutenant-colonel Gardner, who happened to be with me at the moment, instantly led on one of his gholes (a ghole is a body of horse, commonly of 100 men) to the spot. By the zeal, judgment, and gallantry of these officers and troops, this valuable position was recovered and retained. The Ghoorkhas charged our troops two or three times, but were always repulsed. The loss on both sides was considerable.

"Though I believe there was no previous concert, the very sharp firing upon the hill encouraged the garrison of the fort to make a sortie: they came up to the wall of our advanced post, about six feet high or more, and threw stones over it. One Ghoorkha had the temerity to mount the wall, from which he instantly fell dead.

"Throughout the night an incessant skirmishing prevailed, occasioning many casualties. Amongst others, Lieutenant Tapley, of the 27th native infantry, received a mortal wound.

"The small mortars opened about six p. m. and one of the large ones at 12. I feel much indebted to Lieutenants Bell and Wilson for their activity in laying and bringing these mortars into use so soon.

"This morning the advanced position was pushed to within 70 yards of the fort of Almorah, and remains established there. Lieutenant Bell having thrown several eight-inch shells into the fort, the garrison was compelled to remain concealed, and Ghoorkhas and Kussias having quitted it in great numbers, it was too easily considered by our advanced parties to have been evacuated. They proceeded up the street which bounds it on the east side, in order to get to the door, by which so many had quitted it. The garrison suddenly showed themselves, and a hot fire rendered it necessary to retreat, which was accordingly done, but with a good countenance.

"At 9 a. m. a flag of truce brought me a letter from the Chowtra Bum Sah, and another from Captain Hearsay, written with the chief's concurrence, requesting that a suspension of arms might be mutually agreed to, in view to the termination of hostilities in the province, on the basis of the terms offered to the Chowtra several weeks ago by the Honourable E. Gardner. With the concurrence of Mr. Gardner, this suspension has been agreed to; and Lieutenant-colonel Gardner will meet the Chowtra and the three principal sirdars now serving, as soon as one of them, Chumoo Bundaree, can be brought in from one of their out-posts.

"The result I shall report to you this evening for his excellency's information.

I have, &c.

(Signed) J. NICOLLS, Colonel.

"5 p. m. Lieutenant-colonel Gardner has been compelled to wait till this hour for Chamoo Bundaree. I therefore shall not, by this post, be able to report as I intended.

(Signed) J. N.

To the Adjutant-general, head-quarters, Futty Ghur.

True copy. (Signed) G. H. FAGAN, Adjutant general."

To the Adjutant-general, head-quarters, Futty Ghur.

"Almorah, 27th April, 1815, 6 p. m.

"Sir,

"With sentiments of the highest satisfaction I have the honour to report to you, for the information of his Excellency the Commander-in-Chief, that I have just returned from our outpost in the town, where a convention for the surrender of the forts of Almorah yet remaining in the enemy's hands, and all other forts within the province of Kumaoon, was formally exchanged between the Honourable Edward Gardner and myself, on the part of the Honourable Company, and Jusmurdun T,happa on the part of Chowtra Bum Sāh, Unjeet Kagee, and Chamoo Bundaree, to which his own sanction and signature were also given.

"The troops, with arms and baggage, are to cross the Surdah in ten days; many have, I believe, actually taken the routes most agreeable to them personally.

I have, &c.

(Signed) J. NICOLLS, Colonel.

"Salmundi has been given up to our troops by the Chowtra's order.

True copy. (Signed) G. H. FAGAN, Adjutant-general.

True copy. (Signed) J. ADAM, Secretary to the Government."

No. VII.

(Illustrative of the events recorded in pages 44—48.)

General Orders.

By his Excellency the Governor General.

"Futty Ghur, 2d May, 1815.

"The Governor General having received official advices of the capture by assault of the fortified heights and town of Almorah, on the 25th ult. by the forces under the command of Colonel Nicolls, of the total repulse of the enemy in a night attack on our positions in the night of the same day, and of the conclusion, on the 27th ult., of a convention with the principal Ghoorkha chiefs in Kumaoon, by which, in return for permission to retire across the Surdah with their troops, they engage to evacuate all the fortified places in the province in ten days, surrendering at the moment the fortresses immediately round the capital: his Excellency is pleased to direct that a royal salute be fired at all the principal stations of the army, in honour of the signal and distinguished success of the British arms at Almorah, and the reduction to the British power of the valuable and important province of Kumaoon.

By command of his excellency
The Governor General.
(Signed) J. ADAM, Secretary to the Government.
True copy. (Signed) J. ADAM, Secretary to the Government."

From the Calcutta Gazette Extraordinary.

"Fort William, May 16, 1815.

"The Honourable the Vice President in Council has the highest satisfaction in directing the publication of the sentiments of approbation and applause of the conduct of Colonel Nicolls, and the officers and men serving under his command, in the late operations in Kumaoon, contained in the following copy of the general order issued by his Excellency the Right Honourable the Governor General, on the occasion of the brilliant success of the British arms in that province.

"*General Order by the Right Honourable the Governor General.*

"Futty Ghur, 3d May, 1815.

"The Governor General has singular satisfaction in acknowledging the important service rendered by Colonel Nicolls, in the reduction of the province of Kumaoon.

"The judgment of Colonel Nicolls in his preparatory measures, the unremitting activity with which he pursued the object entrusted to his management, and the gallant promptitude with which he seized and improved every opening that could lead to the fufilment of his instructions, not only reflect the highest credit on himself, but afford so salutary a lesson for the whole army, that his lordship cannot let slip the opportunity of recommending it to their attention.

" The success of Colonel Nicolls (and the observation will be supported by the brilliant consequences which have attended similar exertions on the part of Major-general Ochterlony), under the complicated difficulties presented by the quality of the country, the fortification by which the natural strength was assisted, and the obstinate resistance of a courageous enemy, should prove the superiority conferred by military science, and a certainty that a strenuous application of its principles must entail honourable distinction on a commander.

" Warfare in a mountainous region offers embarrassments, which when viewed at a distance appear insurmountable, but which dwindle into comparative insignificance under the grasp of vigour and genius. It is only in unusual situations, demanding readiness of resource and animated efforts, that the difference between officer and officer can be displayed. And it ought to be always present to the mind of every military man, that he who in circumstances of perplexity tries and fails, has to plead those chances from which no operation in war can be secured, his pretensions to the character of zeal and energy being in the mean time maintained; while he who contents himself with urging difficulties as an excuse for doing nothing, voluntarily registers his own inefficiency.

" The Governor General, in expressing his warm approbation of the excellent conduct of Colonel Nicolls, desires also to record the merits of those whose services in this enterprise have been indicated as possessing peculiar claim to notice.

" Colonel Nicolls has earnestly represented the admirable management of Lieutenant-Colonel Gardner at the head of his irregular corps, in forcing the enemy to abandon so many strong positions, and in finally establishing himself before Almorah; the skill and spirited decision of Major Patton (commanding the 2d battalion 5th regiment) in the attack of the detached corps which he defeated on the 23d of April; the exemplary valour manifested by Captain Faithful (commanding the 1st battalion 4th regiment) in the successive assaults of the different works of the enemy on the 25th, nobly emulated by Lieutenant Wright; and the behaviour of Captain Leys, marked equally by intrepidity and judgment, at the head of the flank battalion.

" Lieutenants Field and Purvis, of the 4th regiment, with Lieutenants Bell and Wilson of the artillery, are also mentioned in terms of strong commendation.

" To all those officers the Governor General offers his sincere applause, as likewise to all the officers (native as well as European), non-commissioned officers and men, who have so becomingly supported the character of the British army in their laborious service; and his lordship trusts that this splendid proof of what a just confidence in their own powers can achieve will satisfy our native troops of their own infinite superiority over the enemy with whom they have to cope.

By command of the right honourable

The Governor General.

(Signed) J. ADAM, Secretary to the Government.

True copy. J. ADAM, Secretary to the Government."

No. VIII.

Account of the Province of Kumaoon.

(Illustrative of the transactions related in pages 44—48.)

The province of Kumaoon is situated in the tract of hills lying between the western branch of the Gograh, known as the Kaleenuddee, and the river Ram Gunga. For some considerable time past the town of Almorah has been recognised as the capital; formerly Champawtee enjoyed that distinction.

The face of the country is similar in character to that of the neighbourhood, but it is less savage and rough than Gurwhāl. The hills are less lofty, and the valleys more susceptible of cultivation, and better cultivated. The people are said also to differ from the inhabitants of Gurwhāl and the states to the westward: they are of a softer and more effeminate nature, inclined to indolence, and are meek and enduring. It is further stated that the men are more engaged in domestic occupations, while the agricultural labours are conducted by the women;—an unnatural division of duties, which is said to have induced polygamy in a very prevailing degree, every one being anxious to secure for himself as many field labourers as possible. In general they seem to have made a much farther progress towards refinement than their neighbours in their manners and customs; even in their dress they approach more to the people of the low countries than those of the neighbouring hills. They generally wear cotton garments, and on their head a cotton cap instead of the low country turban; but those in the low parts seldom wear any of the woollen or hempen manufactures of the country.

The variations thus distinguishing them from the districts around, particularly from Gurwhāl, cannot perhaps be fully accounted for, but have their origin, partially at least, in certain political circumstances, to the operation of which they have been subjected; and among these, none perhaps contributed more than the predominance of Brahminical influence, which has subsisted from a very remote and indeed unknown period. During the time of the Rajahs of Kumaoon, we are informed that the power of the priesthood was so great that it might have been deemed absolutely a Brahminical government. The Brahmins of the Jōsi caste had so overwhelming an influence that they could do what they pleased—depose or elevate a prince. An instance of this occurred not very long ago, when a relative of the Rajah of Srenuggur was called to the government of Kumaoon by a faction of the Brahmins, and was afterwards deposed by their intrigues.

The marks, indeed, of the sacerdotal power are said to be very prevailing throughout Kumaoon, in the very ancient and comparatively magnificent temples found in different parts, which, though erected in places of far less sanctity than those removed to the recesses of the Himālā in Gurwhāl, still evince a strong degree of influence in the founders. This influence the Ghoorkhas have turned to account. When they succeeded in subjecting the country, they lost no time in gaining over many of the chief families of Brahmins, who soon proved the weakness of human nature even among the holiest seats, by yielding their assistance and exerting their influence in favour of the invaders.

The Ghoorkhas have, it is said, favoured the Kumaoonees beyond the other conquered nations: their property is more secure, and their persons are safe from violence, or from the miserable risk of being seized and sold as slaves. Many have been taken into the Ghoorkha service, to act against the countries which their ambition prompted them to attack for the aggrandisement of their power. They are, however, kept distinct from the regular troops of Nepāl, and it is said that each soldier on his return from service, or when he is disbanded, obtains a small allowance for his subsistence, generally in land.

These people are commanded most commonly by Ghoorkha soldiers, though occasionally we found natives of Kumaoon entrusted with small commands. They are armed much in the same way as the regular troops, but are far inferior to the true Ghoorkha troops of Nepāl in strength, activity, and gallantry, and indeed in every requisite of the valuable soldier. None, it is said, but those in a military capacity are permitted to go armed. A severe penalty is inflicted on those, who, without possessing this right, are found carrying offensive weapons.

The appearance of the villages in Kumaoon is said to be strikingly neat at a distance, but on a nearer approach the illusion vanishes. The houses are constructed of large blocks of stone, and are roofed with a covering of slate; they are narrow and long, some of them exhibiting a front of sixty or seventy feet. They all consist of two stories, the lower one appropriated to cattle. The upper one has usually an inclosed verandah extending the whole length of the house, and constructed of deal boards.

The roads through the villages are commonly causeways of stone, about two feet broad and three feet high, running through the centre of the streets, from which run small raised paths leading to the upper apartments, which, with the central division, separates before each house a sort of inclosure for the cattle; and these are so excessively filthy that they can only be considered as beds for the collection of manure. The effect of this disregard to cleanliness is, in all probability, one great cause of the mortality which often rages during the hot months, when multitudes are carried off by fevers. The inside of their apartments is said not to exceed in cleanliness or convenience the arrangements without.

The domestic animals found in Kumaoon appear to be the same as those met with in other parts of the hills.

The nature of their agriculture, too, seems to be very similar to that of their neighbours, but with this advantage, that the hills are so far of a shelving nature, that the cultivation can with no great difficulty be carried on to their summits. Much rice is grown in the valleys, and irrigated as in Gurwhal and Sirmore. Barley, wheat, and the other less valuable grains, are found to answer so well in the higher lands, that they can not only amply provide for the consumption of the country, but export a good deal to Bootan.

The commerce of Kumaoon is of a nature very similar to that carried on by Bischur and Gurwhāl, but considerably superior to them in extent and value.

There are two principal marts in the province for the produce of Bootan: that of Bag,heesur, which is frequented two or three times a year, in the months of Magh (January), Phagun (February), and Jyth (May); that of Chytalee, attended in the month of Cheyt (March), on the day of the full moon. This fair lasts eleven days. From these places the merchandise is conveyed to Kasheepore, Morādābād, Bareilly, and the other towns in the plains: it consists of borax, salt, gold, musk, cow-tails, zedoary, shawls, fine and coarse blankets, wool, and shawl wool.

There are two chief passes through the hills leading from Kumaoon into Bootan,—Joar to the north-west, and Darma to the south-east. They are said to be less practicable than the two great passes leading through the province of Gurwhāl, but they are more used in trade.

In every point of view Kumaoon seems to have the advantage of Gurwhāl, as a connecting district for the purpose of facilitating and encouraging trade with Bootan, and the trans-Himālāyan countries dependent on China.

Of the revenue of Kumaoon little is known: it is said that in former times it never yielded more than 1,25,000 rupees a year, and maintained an army of 4000 men. To the Ghoorkhas, with considerable oppression, it is said to have been worth 1,50,000 rupees.

The family of the late Rajah of Kumaoon originally came from Jhansee, near Allahabad. The first rajah (a Rajepoot by birth) was taken from that place and elevated to the throne at the age of sixteen or seventeen. His name was T,horchund: his son, grandson, and great-grandson succeeded, when the line became extinct. A person descended from the uncle of T,horchund, named Geanchund, was then brought from Jhansee to fill the throne. It does not appear by what authority or agency these men were called to this high and distant station.

Geanchund made several conquests and additions to the raje, and was succeeded by five consecutive descendants to Kulcānchund, who founded Almorah, the capital of the country. His son, Rooderchund, reigned in the time of the great Akber, but the line again became extinct in his grandson Bijeechund. Baz Baharchund, the son of a collateral branch, succeeded: he fought in the Dekhin in the service of Shah Jehan. Four sovereigns of his line (some of spurious race) succeeded, when Adjeetchund, the offspring of a daughter of this house by the Rajah of Beeptee, was placed on the throne, and was treacherously murdered by his relation Keeleanchund, who seized the government, and was succeeded by his son Deepchund, who was murdered by Mohun Sing, the elder brother of the ex-Rajah Lāll Sing.

This man and his brother are the great-grandchildren of the spurious issue of Baz Baharchund by a dancing woman.

Until the latter years of Kuleanchund the affairs and country of Kumaoon continued flourishing: three years before his death it was invaded by the Rohillas, under Olee Mohummud Khan, and plundered and desolated. They were expelled, however, by Buckshee Leo-Deo; but the rich possessions they held in the low country, and which constituted the best tracts of the state, were never recovered. Leo-Deo was then invested by the dying rajah with the authority of the kingdom, to be exercised in the name of his son Dheepchund, which he did for twenty-five years, when he was killed in a private quarrel, and was succeeded as prime minister by his son, Jy Kishen.

The Rānēe of Dheepchund, however, being dissatisfied with this arrangement, especially after bearing a son to the Rajah, intrigued with the Rohillas to destroy Jy Kishen, who soon after retired in disgust, and was succeeded as Bukhshee by Mohun Sing; the post of prime minister being bestowed on Kishen Sing, a bastard brother of the rajah's.

These, however, were soon after deprived of their appointments by the Ranēe, now paramount, who bestowed them on her favourite and paramour Purmanund. Mohun Sing fled to the Rohillas, and was assisted by Doundee Khan, of Bissoulee, who was jealous of the power of Hafiz Ruhmut Khan, the partisan of the Rānēe, who exercised much influence in Almorah. He defended the troops of the Rānēe, and soon after obtained possession of the persons of the Rajah and Rānēe, and established himself in the government, when one of his first acts was to put to death the Rānēe's favourite Purmamund.

Several turns of fortune befel Mohun Sing. He was deposed by an army raised by Hafiz Ruhmut-Khan to assist Kishen Sing, the rajah's brother, but was subsequently placed voluntarily at the head of the government by the advice of Jy Kishen, whom he soon after ungratefully and treacherously murdered. Some time after, Mohun Sing was again hurled from the throne by the rajahs of Gurwhāl and Dhotee, who were jealous of his rise; and they established the second son of the Gurwhāl rajah, Purdoomun Sah, in his stead. After a reign of nine years he left Kumaoon, against the wish of the people, to attempt the acquisition of the throne of Gurwhāl; and, during the troubles that ensued, Hurruk Deo, a man of good family, and one of the principal officers of state, was placed in charge of the government; and he having got possession of the person of Mohun Sing, put him to death, as a piece of retributive justice for the murder of the rajah and all his family. But soon after, Lall Sing, the brother of Mohun Sing, with the assistance of the Rohilla chief, Fyzullah Khān of Rampore, entered Kumaoon, and drove Hurruk Deo to Gurwhāl. He however did not reign long. About a year and a half afterwards (being about twenty-five years since) the Ghoorkha forces invaded the country; and, being joined by the malecontents, swept over the land, and entirely reduced it under their government.

Such are the very few, loose, and imperfect particulars I have been able to collect respecting this country, now attached to the British possessions in India. They are taken from various sources, partly from the observations of Messrs. Webb and Raper, partly from conversation with others, both natives and Europeans, who had more or less the means of making observations on the country. So imperfect an account of a province that must soon be well known had perhaps better have been omitted; but, under the belief that the facts stated are correct, it may, in the opinion of others, be thought better to say thus much, than to wait the uncertainty of a more perfect description being published.

No. IX.

(Alluded to in page 48.)

Treaty of Peace

Between the Honourable East India Company and Maha-Rajah-Bikram-Sah, rajah of Nepāl, settled between Lieutenant-Colonel Bradshaw on the part of the Honourable Company, in virtue of full powers vested in him by his Excellency the Right Honourable Francis, Earl of Moira, Knight of the Most Honourable Order of the Garter, one of his Majesty's most Honourable Privy Council, appointed by the Court of Directors of the said Honourable Company to direct and control all the affairs in the East Indies; and by Sree-Gooroo-Gujraj-Misser, and Chundee-Seekur-Opedeea, on the part of the Maha rajah, Girman-Jode-Bikram-Sah-Behauder-Shumsheer-Jung, in virtue of the powers to that effect vested in them by the said rajah of Nepāl.

Whereas war has arisen between the Honourable East India Company and the rajah of Nepāl, and whereas the parties are mutually disposed to restore the relations of peace and amity, which previously to the occurrence of the late differences had long subsisted between the states, the following terms of peace have been agreed upon.

Art. 1. There shall be perpetual peace and friendship between the Honourable East India Company and the rajah of Nepāl.

Art. 2. The rajah of Nepāl renounces all claim to the lands which were the subject of discussion between the two states before the war, and acknowledges the right of the Honourable Company to the sovereignty of these lands.

Art. 3. The rajah of Nepāl hereby cedes to the Honourable the East India Company, in perpetuity, all the undermentioned territories: namely,

First, the whole of the lowlands between the rivers Kali and Raptee.

Secondly, the whole of the lowlands (with the exception of Botwul Khass) lying between the Rapti and the Gunduck.

Thirdly, the whole of the lowlands between the Gunduck and Coosah, in which the authority of the British government has been introduced, or is in actual course of introduction.

Fourthly, all the lowlands between the river Mutchee and the Teestash.

Fifthly, all the territories within the hills eastward of the river Mutchee, including the fort and lands of Nagree, and the pass of Nagarcote, leading from Morung into the hills; together with the territory lying between that pass and Nagree. The aforesaid territory shall be evacuated by the Ghoorkha troops within forty days from this date.

Art. 4. With a view to indemnify the chiefs and barahdars of the state of Nepāl, whose interests will suffer by the alienation of the lands ceded by the foregoing article, the British government agrees to settle pensions to the aggregate amount of two lacs of rupees per annum on such chiefs as may be selected by the rajah of Nepāl, and in the proportions which the rajah may fix. As soon as the selection is made, sumruds shall be granted under the seal and signature of the governor-general for the persons respectively.

Art. 5. The rajah of Nepāl renounces for himself, his heirs, and successors, all claim to, or connexion with, the countries lying to the west of the river Kali; and engages never to have any concern with those countries, or the inhabitants thereof.

Art. 6. The rajah of Nepāl engages never to molest or disturb the rajah of Siccem in the possession of his territories; but agrees that, if any differences shall arise between the state of Nepāl and the rajah of Siccem, or the subjects of either, such difference shall be referred to the arbitration of the British government, by whose award the rajah of Nepāl engages to abide.

Art. 7. The rajah of Nepāl hereby engages never to take or retain in his service any British subject, nor the subject of any European or American state, without the consent of the British government.

Art. 8. In order to secure and improve the relations of amity and peace hereby established between the two states, it is agreed that accredited ministers from each shall reside at the court of the other.

Art. 9. This treaty, consisting of nine articles, shall be ratified by the rajah of Nepāl within fifteen days from this date; and the ratification shall be delivered to Lieutenant-Colonel Bradshaw, who engages to obtain and deliver to the rajah the ratification of the governor-general within twenty days, or sooner, if practicable.

Done at Segowley, on the 2d day of December, 1815.

Rajah of Nepal's seal.	(L. S.)	Signed PARIS BRADSHAW, Lieut.-Col.
	(L. S.)	GOOROO GUJRAJ MISSUR.
	(L. S.)	CHUNDER SEEKUR OPEDEEA.

No. X.

Account of the Assessments made by the Nepāl Government.

(Referred to in page 52.)

The list given in the text (as far as could be ascertained) is correct, as it regards the present moment; but changes occur so continually in so wild a country, and among so turbulent a people, that these distinctions may speedily alter, as they have been heretofore given to change.

The states of the Baruk Thakooraee, according to an extract from the archives of the Nepāl government, were assessed respectively at the following sums.

Keeounthul - - - -	42,000 rupees per ann.
Baghut - - - -	25,000
Coothar - - - -	4,500
Koonean - - - -	1,800
Bhuggee - - - -	7,500
Dhaminee - - - -	4,000
Bughāt - - - -	30,000
Muhlogue - - - -	3,000
Cotee - - - - -	3,000
Kearee - - - - -	1,900
Cotegooroo - - - -	9,000
T,heog - - - -	3,100
	1,34,800

The value and respective force of a few of the other small chieftain-ships are thus also ascertained from the same sources.

1. Bulsum, assessed at 6000 rupees per annum, can collect 4 or 500 men, of which about 200 may be armed with matchlocks, the rest with bows and arrows, hatchets, &c.

2. Diltee, assessed at 6000 rupees per annum, can collect from 3 to 400 men, of which not above 60 or 80 have matchlocks.

3 Khuneountee, assessed at 5000 rupees per annum, collects from 200 to 250 men, of which 30 or 40 have matchlocks.

4. Bija, a very small state, worth about 500 rupees per annum, could not turn out more than 80 men.

5. Raeen, also small, worth 2000 rupees, and can give 200 men, having 50 or 60 matchlocks.

6. Ootrock, worth 2000 rupees, cannot raise above 100 men.

7. Comharsein, worth 7500 rupees, supplies 250 men, with 100 matchlocks.

8. Mornee, worth 4300 rupees, same force in proportion.

9. Joobul, assessed at 24,000 rupees: its force and importance are detailed in the body of this work.

These, with the Baruk Thakooraee, occupy the chief part of the tract between the Jumna and Sutlej, not included under the immediate territories of either of the large states; and they form an addition of yearly revenue to the Nepālese government of 57,300 rupees, which appears from the whole country to have been nearly as follows in the aggregate.

Sirmore - - - -	80,000 rupees.
Bischur - - - -	80,000
Hundoor - - - -	15,000
Kuhloor - - - -	45,000
Baruk Thakooraee - - -	134,800
Nine states - - - -	57,300
Other small states - - -	12,000
Revenue realized from Gurwhāl, say -	200,080

We shall have 624,100 as the whole produce of the hilly tract, from the Ram Gunga river to the Sutlej inclusive.

The tributary claims on these small states are of a very complicated nature, as in several instances two or three of the primary states endeavour to substantiate their right to the homage of the same minor ones, while no rule can be traced by which to determine these rights, except that of geographical position; a criterion which must have been continually changing, as each extended his dominion or was encroached upon in turn. Thus, *Gurwhāl* claimed the allegiance of Joobul, Ootrock, Raeen, Saree, and Dodur-Coār: *Bischur* demanded that of Diltee, Kurangooloo, Khuneounter. Coteegooroo, Comharsein, Sangree, Bulsum, T,heog, Dodur-Coār, Saree, Raeen, and Seelee; while *Sirmore* exacted it from Joobul, Ootrook, Rutes, Bulsum, Raeen, Saree, and Seelee. Some of these lordships are now but nominal, having for a long time formed portions of the territory of the larger states. Thus Saree is entirely absorbed in Bischur, and the hereditary family is extinct; and the lord of Raeen has long been dispossessed by the same power. Bhuroulee has lately been seized by the chief of Bulsum; and the widow and children of the late T,hakoor, or lord, treated with great indignity, and put in confinement.

The larger states of the second class themselves, though generally owning a degree of alliance closely bordering on dependence with the greater, still claim a tributary superiority over the minor ones, in their immediate neighbourhood. Thus the small states of Koolee Mundhana and Kearee have always acknowledged such a subjection to Keeounthul; and, though our information did not extend so far to the westward, in all probability some of the small states in that quarter are similarly situated; while the larger ones, as Baghut, Bughāt, and even the smaller rajships of Hundoor and Kuhloor, enjoy a degree of independence proportioned to their own power and the weakness of their greater neighbours.

No. XI.

A List of the Purgunnahs contained in Sirmore.

(Referred to in page 73.)

1. Calsee.
2. Palwe.
3. Puchad.
4. Sein.
5. Dhurtee.
6. Mornee.
7. J,hanscor.
8. Nukaweg.
9. Roteelce Bhookee.
10. Jamtree.
11. Khoondla chandnee.
12. Barchub and Dhoar.
13. Kearda-ke-Dhoon.
14. Lowassa.
15. Rajegurh.
16. Bujgah.
17. Bagurulala.
18. Rutolee.
19. Gunjaree and Rontese.
20. Kangrah.
21. Purlejituk.
22. Habun.
23. Mandhun and Punjab.
24. Heenunghat.
25. Mornee.
26. Kansur.
27. Juggut Gurh.

No. XII.

Account of the Charges of the Wuzzeers of the State of Bischur.

(Referred to in page 270.)

THESE are stated to be as follows:

Ramdut, who seems to be the principal, lives in the village of Cōōl, purgunnah Baruhbees. His charge consists of seven purgunnahs: viz. Chowbees, Nowbees, Baruhbees, Dosowor, Gopalpoor, Nong, and, across the Sutlej river, Pundrichbees, and Raeen.

Sagurdo, uncle of Ramdut, lives in the village of Lotees. Purgunnah Must Gurh, his vuzzeereet, embraces Butaslee on the left bank of the Pabur river, Bagee, Mustgurh, which has four subdivisions.

Teckendas has in charge Tookpa of Kunnawur, which is subdivided into three parts, Nawur purgunnah, Kootlaha: these two formerly composed the state, or Thā,kooraee of Saree, conquered and added to the raj of Bischur, about forty years ago. Soopyl purgunnah, in which Bhownraguddee fort is situated. Teekurail, in the Thakooraee of Wāra, long since made an integral part of Bischur, lying chiefly in the right bank of the Pabur, and extending along its course to the snowy mountains. Jodpoor, a small purgunnah on the Seeleedan ridge, seized from Coteegooroo, about fifty years ago.

Buddree Das, who resides either at Kunchee in Chowbees purgunnah, within a mile of Serān, or at Ukha in purgunnah Sooa of Kunnawur, has under his care Sooa of Kunawur, across the Sutlej, Utharuh-bees beyond Serān on the same side, and Moonulgurh, or Sambracote, both of which districts are subdivided into several smaller parts.

Loktus vuzzeer, called Bubram, has entire sway over Seol,k,hur, the Bhotea purgunnah of Kunnawur, containing only five or six villages.

The Rānee has in Jagheer, Ryk of Kuncheon.

No. XIII.

Literal Translations of Letters from Natives.

(Referred to in page 77.)

1. *From Bagha Rawut, &c. to Toolerām (a Servant employed by the Political Agent), in correspondence with the native Chiefs.*

"We are very happy to hear an army has marched to Doon; well! if otherwise, troops ought to march by Chilkera and Kote Duvārā T,hat. There are 100 men in Lungoor, and not a soldier any where else. If the highlands are to be taken, delay is bad. The zemindars of Boongah are with us. When troops march to Lungoor, we will stop all supplies to the fort, until you march into the hills. The Ghoorkhas are our masters, and we will not trust you; we are in their hands; no aid is coming from the east to the Ghoorkhas."

---

2. *Letter of Prithee Sing of Koolee, to Tooleram.*

"We received your note, and understand its contents. You talk to us to stand up in arms, and to come to Doon, as were this the time of the year sixty, before the Ghoorkha conquest, and we, as we then were, whereas we are worse off now than our servants were then. We were even before badly off, but for the last ten years we have got over the time in want of clothes and food. I owe 500 rupees. Your note is in very pretty style, but the saying is true, 'The rajah away, his people are cut up,' and we are ill treated for keeping up any communication with you; I have not, in consequence, replied to your letters.

"The zemindars of Jounpoor, as you desired, made a stir, and are about to be punished for it; and three or four hundred men, who were in Nalapanee (Kalunga) you have not been able to drive out. If Dhoon alone was the object, why do you write to us to get us ill treated?

"If the English mean to take the hills, why have not two or three thousand men been sent to Huttoor or Chumoon? and then one third of the Gurwhal raj, all on the west of the Gunga, would have been secured. You say, 'come for one night:' I am not a bird to fly to you; if I go my family will be ruined. Seebram's defection has made us all bad in their eyes. We are here distressed; the Zazee has written from the west to seize all headmen, and send them to him; we are in constant fear of being seized. They have also put guards over our monied men (or bankers): you ought not to have written to injure us, nor unless you could have supported us with troops, which, if they quickly arrive, we shall be saved, otherwise we shall all be seized. If there is any delay, and troops do not advance, we are stamped rebels.

"Do you speak to the British officers, and obtain from them certain security, when I will join them with my family, if they will but give food and clothing, and support for the future.

"Quickly reply to this, and obtain the religious promise of the British officers. My debts also restrain me: upon this matter I trust to you, even for food on the road. What the person who carries this note says, receive as true. I have not written to the British officers, but you are there to say any thing for me; and if troops do not advance into the hills, and I come to you, I can speak what is proper. If in two or three days I have no accounts of comfort from you, they will distress us. I do not write to the British officers, for the Ghoorkhas have taken an obligation from me, that if I write to them, or hold any intercourse with them, I shall be deserving of punishment."

---

3. *Letter of the assembled Zemindars of Seekhnēanee, to Seebrām, who had come over from thence to the British.*

"Since you have joined the English you have taken no care of us; you have forsaken us. The captain (Bhulbudder), having fled from Kalunga, came to Doobra, and from Doobra came flying all night to Suckneānee. He plundered a little in his retreat. Reendeep Qaree was also encamped at Suckneānee. Both united, and went next night to Chumoon. In all they are 400 men. Rewant Qazee is also come. We are lost, if, in a day or two, troops do not reach us. We are looking out anxiously on the road. Our eyes are, day and night, towards you; if troops come we are saved, otherwise write to us, advise us what to do. We are rated rebels; they seized our people, and took them to Chumoon, but they fled. They send soldiers to seize headmen of villages. If they come to take us, write to us, advise us what to do: unless you support us we are lost to one another. When they call on us for corn, and an assemblage of the people, as they certainly will do, we will write to you for advice. We are on the look-out for troops and a ssistance. Jugdidolee has come from Sreenuggur, and taken possession of the Teree Jhoolas."*

---

4. *Letter from Runjore Sing T,happa to the Headmen of Kangrah.*

"To Goolaboo, and the other zemindars of Kangrah, health. Qazee Rewunt Coor, and Bhulbudder Coor, have arrived at Jount Gurhee in Jounpoor. Forces and commanders are arriving in all directions, and on the road from Sreenuggur and Kemaoon. You have before done well with us; do not now fear, because you have fled and left us. In eight or ten days our forces are coming thitherward; then they cross the Jumna: do you all join with Rewunt Qazee and Bhulbudder Coor. If you do, it will be well with you; otherwise all the males of your families shall be put to death, and your women carried off. Quickly do as ordered. Send immediately twenty-five maunds of lead. A letter is addressed to the headmen of Calsee; forward it."

---

5. *Letter of Runjore Sing T,happa to the Headmen of Palwe.*

"You sent Rownook,h to me, and from him I have learnt every thing. You will not allow Seeseram, Joomloo, and Ootchloo, to remain in Palwa; expel him, and come to Sein.

"Those who have them, send a son or brother; otherwise, let him come himself: forward the revenues due, and supplies. If you listen to the words of the enemy, and forget your duty, when

* Rope bridges over the Bhagiruttee at Huttoor.

my forces arrive, I will cut off every person who has given countenance to Seeseram. Whoever will seize Seeseram, and bring him to me, he shall be well rewarded. Expel him. When the brothers and sons of the headmen come in with money and supplies, they will be informed of every circumstance. When my force approaches, whoever will join it shall be well rewarded."

---

6. *Translation of a Letter from the Headmen of Palwe to the Political Agent with the British Army.*

" Your letter has been received, and your favour made known thereby. You have sent Seeseram. We, according to your orders, are attendant upon him. You ordered Seeseram to proceed to Teekree. He was departing: we stopped him. Had he gone, a Ghoorkha force was coming to this quarter; and for this reason we prevented his advance. You ordered Seeseram to retain hill soldiery. We have neither arms nor clothes, and without them how can we serve? with clubs, staves, and stones, we are at your service and pleasure: if you attend to our representation you will send troops to Sein; if you do not, all the inhabitants in that quarter will fall under the power of the Ghoorkhas. By all means send troops to Sein. We are ready to obey your orders. We forward to you the letter addressed to us by Runjore. Write to Seeseram to continue in Palwe. We sent a man to Dangee Wuzzeer, who returned a messenger, carrying back our answer. Dangee will, probably, join us; and by keeping a force in Palwe, Joobul will also be under command."

THE END.